Penguin Education

Dreams and Dreaming

Edited by S. G. M. Lee and A. R. Mayes

Penguin Modern Psychology Readings

General Editor

B. M. Foss

Advisory Board

Michael Argyle
Dalbir Bindra
P. C. Dodwell
G. A. Foulds
Max Hamilton
Marie Jahoda
Harry Kay
S. G. M. Lee
W. M. O'Neil
K. H. Pribram
R. L. Reid
Roger Russell
David Schapiro
Jane Stewart
Anne Treisman
P. E. Vernon
Peter B. Warr
George Westby

Dreams and Dreaming

Selected Readings

Edited by S. G. M. Lee and A. R. Mayes

Penguin Education

Penguin Education
A Division of Penguin Books Ltd,
Harmondsworth, Middlesex, England
Penguin Books Inc, 7110 Ambassador Road,
Baltimore, Md 21207, USA
Penguin Books Australia Ltd,
Ringwood, Victoria, Australia

First published 1973
This selection copyright © A. R. Mayes and the Estate of
S. G. M. Lee, 1973
Introduction and notes copyright © A. R. Mayes and the Estate of
S. G. M. Lee, 1973
Copyright acknowledgement for items in this volume will be found on page 479

Made and printed in Great Britain by
Hazell Watson & Viney Ltd, Aylesbury, Bucks
Set in Monotype Times Roman

This collection of Readings was the conception of Gillmore Lee. Sadly, he died without seeing the book in its final stages. I hope he would have liked the finished work.

Andrew Mayes

To the memory of
C. A. Mace

Contents

Introduction

Most people lead rather dull lives. Vivid action, drama and the absurd are relatively rare in day-to-day existence, but they are of common occurrence in the dream life of ordinary citizens. This probably accounts for the frequency of the dinner-party gambit: 'I had such an extraordinary dream last night.' This statement may, according to the belief of the dreamer, be inhibited or, indeed, encouraged by the presence of a psychologist in the party. The latter, whether an experimentalist with rats or a psychotherapist, will give the narrator his polite attention and will, rather vaguely, assume that he has been given some clues to the personality of the dreamer by the content of the dream. Everyone else is likely to be extremely bored by the narration, however bizarre its content. One's own dreams, like one's own holiday colour slides, are of great interest to oneself but not to other people. Only to the subject do both colour slides and dreams represent vivid personal experience. Without the interest aroused by this, it is doubtful whether this collection of papers would have been possible.

The great majority of our experiences we explain in common-sense terms and, for the 'ordinary' events of this world, common sense answers very well. It is only when something seems unusual to us that our curiosity as to its nature is aroused, and we begin our theory making as to the nature and ontogeny thereof. As Horton (1967) writes: 'Theory places things in a causal context wider than that provided by common sense.' And, again: 'The quest for explanatory theory is basically the quest for unity underlying apparent diversity; for simplicity underlying apparent complexity; for order underlying apparent disorder; for regularity underlying apparent anomaly.' Now dreams are, subjectively, very odd, in that they provide us with apparently purely endogenous mental stimulation which is not under our voluntary control. This, and their bizarre nature, serve to differentiate them sharply from waking mentation and, for centuries, men have asked various questions about them, typically: 'What do dreams *mean*?' 'Why do people dream?' 'How real are the contents of the dream?' 'Have dreams any usefulness to the dreamer?' All these questions differ widely, in both their form and content, one from another. Perhaps the quest has been, not so much for an inclusive theory of dreams and dreaming, but more for *ad hoc* explanations of various aspects of the phenomena. Both in the past and today, sidereal movements, lightning, the origins of mankind, madness and dreaming, all these have elicited fantastic theories of divine intervention, causation by ethereal spirits, witchcraft, etc., largely because of their apparent inexplicability in terms of common sense, and, too, because all these phenomena appear to be beyond the physical control of mankind.

It is with both dreams (in this context the content of dreams) and dreaming (in this context the formal act of having a dream, irrespective of specific content) that the present volume is concerned. The distinction is arbitrary, but it does enable us to bring some structure to a very diverse field of human inquiry. It is the first of these, 'dreams', that formed the more common concern of both the ancients and primitive man; they accepted, almost without question, the fact that dreaming occurred, but were very concerned to interpret the *meaning* of dreams, whether as a foretelling of the future, a rehearsal of elements of the past, the scenes that appeared to the soul when it left the body, evidence of bewitchment, or as messages from one or more Gods or Devils. It is only with the increase of biological knowledge of the last hundred and fifty years that we find dreaming, dreams and sleep itself beginning to be explained in more natural and mundane terms, often those of physiology.

This sequence – first, interest in the content of dreams, second, attempts to explain dreaming as part of the sleep cycle – has been re-enacted in the years of this century. First, Freud brought dreams under the category of motivated mentation and he and his followers, not content with superficial examination of the manifest (common-sense?) content of dreams, sought to uncover their *real* or latent meanings for the unconscious life of the dreamer. To this end they used methods of free-association to elements in the dream and claimed to discover within the dream, the operation of a whole system of dream work in which condensation, displacement, symbolization, etc., all served the end of keeping the real meaning of the dream from the conscious mind of the dreamer. This largely because the basis of the dream was primarily sexual, and therefore unlikely to be acceptable in the light of day. Freud's theory of dream interpretation received little credence from science at its publication and for many years a great many psychologists have hoped that a more 'rational' theory of dreams would be set up.

In the early 1950s it seemed that their wish might be granted, with the discovery by Kleitman and his associates, at the University of Chicago, of Rapid Eye Movement (REM) sleep, often associated by the sleeper, when awakened during REM periods, with the memory of recent dreaming. It did not take long before REM = Dream became the hopeful and facile equation. At last the physiological process of *dreaming*, conterminous with REM periods, was going to help to explain dreams. That this view was simplistic, and that we are still far from a full explanation of dream content, and dreaming, emerges clearly from the collection of papers in this volume.

The sequences of articles in this book is, roughly, historical. Section One deals with dreams, in the sense used above, and initially, in Part One

(Ancient Theories), we take a very brief look at the explanations of dreams attempted by our cultural and physical forefathers. Secondly, in Part Two (Depth Theories) we examine the theories of the two most influential *verstehende* psychologists of their time, Sigmund Freud and Carl Jung. As editors, our one regret here is that space reasons precluded extensive quotation from these two seminal thinkers; instead, we have had to content ourselves with authoritative synoptic accounts from two of their followers.

Part Three of Section One contains various empirical studies of dream content, ranging from survey studies to studies based on hypnotic 'dreaming' and the interests of social anthropology in dream material.

In Section Two we come to dreaming, and Part One presents a representative selection of papers concerned with the physiology of rapid eye movement sleep. The reader will find that the content of dreams is not excluded from consideration in Section Two, but merely that the emphasis changes to the formal and physiological properties of the dream state. Part Two of Section Two is concerned with the effects, on the subject, of REM deprivation – again the inevitable overlap of form and content in dreaming appears.

In Section Two we suffer from a plethora of facts rather than evidence, to use Deutsch's distinction (1960, p. 16), and this appears clearly in the papers of Section Two, which presents some modern theorizing on the nature of dreams and dreaming. Its limitations and apparent lack of connections are, at first sight, depressing. However, it is very possible that REM sleep may serve many different functions which, in phylogenesis, may have emerged at different times. Dreams themselves, if they are more than products of 'disintegrated' mental states such as drunkenness, may have acquired their adaptive function more recently than other aspects of REM sleep.

At the very least, the many non-obvious facts that have already been discovered can give the young reader some hope that an acceptable explanation of dreams and dreaming may appear within his lifetime.

References

DEUTSCH, J. A. (1960), *The Structural Basis of Behaviour*, Cambridge University Press.
HORTON, R. (1967), 'African traditional thought and Western science', *Africa*, vol. 37, pp. 50–71.

Part One
Ancient Theories of Dreams

Here we include two papers. Reading 1, by Van de Castle, is a succinct account of a variety of theories – ranging from ancient Babylon to the nineteenth century, glancing in the process at some primitive accounts of dreams and their origins. Reading 2, by Sir Thomas Browne, is a fascinating seventeenth-century account, written in his almost magical English prose, and prefiguring later scientific hypotheses, particularly those in which the dream is regarded as a motivated phenomenon, having pertinence to the personality of the dreamer.

1 R. L. Van de Castle

The Psychology of Dreaming

Excerpt from R. L. Van de Castle, *The Psychology of Dreaming*, General Learning Press, 1971, pp. 3–11.

Ancient dream theories
Babylonian and Assyrian beliefs

The Babylonians and Assyrians believed that devils and spirits of the dead caused bad influences in dreams. To defeat these evil demons, various magical practices were carried out by special temple priests to secure the help of Mamu, the Babylonian goddess of dreams. Many Babylonian and Assyrian dream books existed and a large collection of them at Nineveh dating back to about 5000 BC was found in the library of the Assyrian king Ashurnasirpal (c. 670 BC). These clay tablets contain interpretative information about various types of dreams. Most flying dreams indicated some impending disaster for the Babylonian dreamer. Differences in consequences or context altered the interpretations given to dream actions. If a man dreamed that he urinated straight ahead on a wall and it spread out into the street he would have many children, but if his urine ran into a well he would lose his property. The drinking of wine in a dream foretold a short life, while the drinking of water indicated a long one.

Egyptian beliefs

The Egyptians were less concerned than the Babylonians and Assyrians with demonology. They interpreted dreams as messages from the gods. In dreams the gods functioned in three roles: they demanded penance, warned the dreamer of forthcoming dangers, and supplied answers to questions asked by the dreamer.

Serapis was the Egyptian god of dreams and several serapeums (temples) were located throughout Egypt. The serapeum at Memphis, constructed about 3000 BC, was one of the most important. Oracles, or professional dream interpreters, known as the Learned Men of the Magic Library, resided in these temples. A professional 'shingle' found at one office door read: 'I interpret dreams, having the gods' mandate to do so; good luck; the interpreter present here is Cretan.'

Incubation, the deliberate effort to induce dreams through sleeping in these temples and engaging in such acts as praying or fasting, was widely practiced. Sometimes a 'stand-in' dreamer was sent to a temple to have a dream on behalf of someone else who could not make the journey. Should other means fail, the Egyptian was willing to resort to various magic prayers, drawings, and rites to aid in his efforts to procure dreams. In 1899 Wallis-Budge described one of these techniques. The person desiring information in a dream was to take a clean linen bag and write upon it the names of five different deities. The bag was then folded up, made into a lampwick, saturated with oil, and set afire. Before retiring, the fasting individual approached the lamp, repeated a certain formula seven times, put out the lamp, and then went to sleep to receive his sought-for answer. The dreams of royalty were given special attention because the gods were more likely to appear in them. A dream of Thutmose IV (1450 BC) is recorded on the chest of the sphinx (Brugsch-Bey, 1947).

Chinese beliefs

While Egyptians attributed dreams to an external source, the gods, Orientals believed dreams had an internal source, the dreamer's soul. The Chinese made a distinction between the material soul, which regulated body functioning and ceased with its death, and the spiritual soul, or *hun*, which left the body at death and continued to carry the appearance of the body with it. The *hun* is involved with dreams and while temporarily separated from the body can communicate with spirits or souls of the dead and return to the body with impressions from these visits. While the soul is wandering about, the dreamer is in a very vulnerable state. Since dreadful consequences would be involved if the soul failed to return quickly enough to reunite with the body, great care was taken to not suddenly arouse a sleeping subject. Similar beliefs are still held by many primitive groups.

The Chinese also recognized other sources of dreams, such as physical stimuli, and pointed out that if one slept on a belt it would induce a dream about a snake. Astrological factors, such as the position of the sun, moon, and stars as well as the time of year, were also taken into account in making dream interpretations. The earliest Chinese work on dreams is the *Meng Shu*, dating to about AD 640 (Woods, 1947).

Indian beliefs

The sacred books of wisdom in India, called the *Vedas*, were written some-time between 1500 and 1000 BC. Various lists of favorable and unfavorable dreams are recounted there, such as to ride an elephant is a lucky dream, while to ride a donkey is an unlucky one. The *Atharva Veda* indicates that images of violence and aggression were considered to lead to success and happiness if the dreamer himself were actively and assertively engaged in carrying out these activities, even though he might become mutilated in the process. Should the dreamer, however, experience any bodily defect, such as losing his hair or teeth, or should he be passively involved in receiving any injury or amputation, it was then considered to be an ill omen. The effects of bad dreams could be counteracted by rites of purification or various types of baths (de Becker, 1968).

The *Atharva Veda* also contains some provocative speculations concerning the relationship between dreams from different periods of the night and the time of their expected realization. It suggests that dreams from the first period of sleep will not come true for a year, those of the second period will not materialize for eight months, while those arising from the last part of the night are already half realized. Along somewhat similar lines, it is proposed that if several dreams succeed each other only the last one should be interpreted. This sophisticated notion implies that the temporal unfolding of dreams reflects a hierarchical arrangement of psychological motivation, which would be related to enactment of behavioral patterns. Another stimulating idea found in the *Atharva Veda* concerns an expected relationship between dream content and whether the dreamer's temperament was of a bilious, phlegmatic, or sanguine type.

Greek beliefs

The earliest Greek view of dreams was that a visit was paid to a sleeping person by a dream figure in the form of a god or a ghost. Since Greek rooms had no entry except a door, it was thought that these figures entered through the keyhole, delivered their message while standing at the head of the bed, and then exited by the same keyhole (Dodds, 1957). During the fifth century BC the idea was introduced from other cultural contacts, probably Indian, that the soul was able to leave the body and take trips or visit with the gods.

The process of incubation became a highly developed art under the Greeks. From their beginnings around the fifth century BC, incubation centers quickly spread in numbers until more than three hundred active temples were functioning throughout Greece and the Roman Empire in the second century. The temples were dedicated to Aesculapius, the god of healing or medicine, who lived during the eleventh century BC and later became deified. Within the temples were statues of the god and testimonial plaques erected by grateful previous visitors whose requests for dreams had been granted. When the god appeared to the dreamer, he would indicate what type of medicine should be administered or what action the person should follow. Later the role of the oracles, or interpreters, became more pronounced, and they would indicate on the basis of the dream recounted to them what the appropriate treatment should be. For example, someone suffering from pleurisy was told to take ashes from the temple altar, mix them with wine, and apply the mixture to his side.

The most important Greek writings about dreams came from Hippocrates, Aristotle, and Plato (Kelsey, 1968). Hippocrates placed great emphasis upon astrological features in dreams and their relationship to the physical condition of the body. Since the ancients set great store on heavenly bodies for finding directions, planting crops, and so forth, it is not surprising to find these frequently contemplated objects incorporated in their dreams. In Hippocrates' view, the body was judged to be optimally functioning if the dream depicted the heavenly bodies shining brightly and located in their usual places. If a star appeared dim and was placed above its usual position, difficulties in the head region were indicated, while a downward placement signified some disease of the bowels. Dreaming of overflowing rivers meant an excess of blood, dreams of springs indicated bladder trouble, and dreams of barren trees were associated with seminal fluid insufficiencies. Although Hippocrates placed great emphasis upon dreams as diagnostic indicators of bodily conditions, he did accept some dreams as being divine.

Aristotle argued against an astrological interpretation of dreams and rejected the notion of their divine origin since animals were also observed to dream. His theories were outlined in three brief books: *On Dreams*, *On Sleep and Waking*, and *On Prophecy in Sleep*. Aristotle accepted that dreams could be sensitive indicators of bodily conditions. Since external stimuli were reduced or absent during sleep, greater attention would be focused upon minimal internal sensations, and awareness of somatic disturbances would be more pronounced than during the waking state. Another of his contributions was to propose that dream images may serve as the starting point of waking thoughts and stimulate subsequent waking behavior similar to that of the dream. Such dreams might be erroneously viewed as prophetic in character, when in actuality they were causally linked.

Aristotle's teacher, Plato, was more interested in the emotional implications of dreams and proposed a very dynamic formulation of dreaming. In the ninth book of the *Republic*, he asserted, 'In all of us, even in good men, there is a lawless wild beast nature which peers out in sleep.' Plato pointed out that reasoning ability becomes suspended during sleep, thereby allowing the passions of desire and anger to reveal themselves with full force. Incest, murder, and sacrilege may thus become the activities pursued in dreams, although the dreamer is also capable of experiencing morally superior dreams if reason has been stimulated to heightened activity (McCurdy, 1946).

Roman beliefs

The Romans borrowed extensively from the Greeks in terms of dream theory and such practices as incubation. Dreams of many famous Romans were

recorded by Plutarch and Suetonius Tranquillus in the second century A D.
In the latter's *Lives of the Caesars*, he reported that Caesar Augustus went
about begging alms because he had been so instructed in a dream. He
placed such great reliance upon dreams because his life had once been saved
by the warning dream of a friend. A novel proposal about dreaming was
advanced by Lucretius when he suggested that dreams actually contained
separate stationary images but an illusion of motion was created because the
images replaced one another so rapidly.

Biblical, Talmudic, and Islamic beliefs

Dreams and visions are referred to in some seventy passages of the Bible. It
is often difficult to know exactly when dreams, in the modern sense of the
word, are referred to because in the Greek New Testament twelve different
words and phrases are used to convey some form of contact with reality
besides that traditionally perceived through the senses. Daniel indicated a
sophisticated knowledge of symbols when he interpreted the dream of
Nebuchadnezzar as revealing his impending mental breakdown. Another
famous interpreter was Joseph, who explained the Pharaoh's dream of the
seven fat and seven lean kine as meaning seven years of plenty would be
followed by seven years of famine. It is curious that, unlike Buddha and
Mohammed who have several of their dreams recorded, the Bible does not
refer to any dreams by Christ (Kelsey, 1968).

The Talmud, written between 600 and 200 B C, is a collection of rabbinical
literature linking the Old Testament with contemporary Judaism. There are
two Talmuds, the Palestinian and the much larger Babylonian Talmud. In
the latter are four chapters (55–8) on dreams. Probably its most widely
quoted statement regarding dreams is that of Rabbi Hisda's, 'An uninter-
preted dream is like an unread letter.' He also said that bad dreams were
preferable to good dreams because the pain they caused would be sufficient
to cause the dreamer to prevent their fulfillment, and they had, therefore, a
more transforming effect. Coupled with other rabbinical statements that
seem depreciatory toward pleasant dreams, one is struck by the masochistic
element in which suffering in dreams is to be preferred over pleasure. Perhaps, therein, lies an important clue to Jewish character. Rabbi Bizna
indicated an awareness of the multilevel meaning possible with dreams when
he reported that he once consulted twenty-four different interpreters
residing in Jerusalem and all gave a different interpretation, but all were
correct (Cohen, 1947).

The Koran is the holy book of the Mohammedans, most of which was
revealed to Mohammed through dreams. After the establishment of his new
religion had begun, Mohammed would ask his disciples every morning
about their dreams and would offer interpretations of those he thought of

value, and then he would proceed to recount his own dreams. The name of the dreamer, his age, place of origin, occupation, and rank were necessary items of information in Islamic dream interpretation. The dreams of men were also given priority, but some recognition was extended to the dreams of married women who were considered chaste and dignified. Dream interpretation was widely practiced throughout Islamic society. Its extensity can be appreciated by noting that an eleventh-century Arabian dream book, the *Tabaqat al-Mu'abbirin*, contains mention of seven thousand interpreters (de Becker, 1968). Several chapters in von Grunebaum and Caillois (1966) also document the important role played by dreams in Islamic culture.

Commentary

Although we would reject the divine origin of dreams today and would not attribute the source of dreams to nocturnal excursions of the soul, we can still derive considerable insight about dreams from the ancients. We could profit from their awareness that the dream contained important information, which they demonstrated by their willingness to go to considerable effort to secure this personal message. Although their astrological interpretations seem remote, their interpretations of many other dream symbols would certainly be acceptable to twentieth-century clinicians. It must be remembered that some of their interpretations were based upon verbal puns (for example, sun, son), which made sense in the original language but which seem far-fetched when translated. Each spoken language has its own dream language.

The possibility of prodromal dreams, indicating incipient physical disorders, was recognized by the ancients as was the possible relationship between temperament and dream content. Both ideas merit contemporary research study. The influence of the setting and atmosphere of ancient incubation centers on dream material should sensitize us to a possibly parallel role that the environment of the modern dream laboratory may play upon the dreaming behavior of the experimental subject.

Dream beliefs among primitive groups
Fusion of dreams and reality

Most 'civilized' people have difficulty in comprehending the degree to which reality was associated with dream experiences by primitive man. The view we hold was nicely summarized by John Wesley, the founder of Methodism:

A dream is a fragment of life, broken off at both ends, not connected, either with the part that goes before, or with that which follows after.... It is a kind of parenthesis inserted in life ... (Woods, 1947, p. 159).

For the primitive there is no parenthesis, no separation by commas; dream life is inextricably fused with waking thoughts. In equatorial Africa, a chief who dreamed he had traveled to Portugal and England put on European clothes in the morning and acted as it he had actually traveled to those countries. All his friends assembled around him and congratulated him (Levy-Bruhl, 1923). Among the Ashantis of Africa, dreams of adultery lead to an adultery fine (Rattray, 1927). When a Cherokee Indian dreamed of being bitten by a snake, he was treated exactly as if he had in reality been bitten (Frazer, 1936–7).

Cuna beliefs

On the islands off the Atlantic coast of Panama the Cuna Indians interpret their dreams as signifying an impending illness or disaster. Their 'dream doctors' use a variety of cures to prevent these misfortunes, and I collected several such objects in 1970 (Figure 1). The small white figure in the upper right is carved from a strong-smelling onion wood; placed in the strings of a hammock, it protects a person from seeing bad things in his dream. The other objects are used in medicine baths to cure already existing bad dreams. The long notched spear point is carved from black palm and fifty

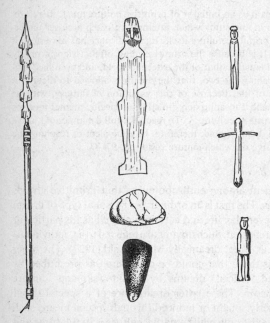

Figure 1 Cuna Indian objects used for curing bad dreams

of them are placed in a water-filled canoe in which a person bathes daily for a month. The two dark figures are rubbed on a rough stone and the powdered wood obtained is placed in water to bathe the dreamer's eyes. The tomahawk-like object is used to treat disturbing dreams of thunder and lightning. Found near riverbanks after a heavy tropical storm, these stones are old ax heads washed out from ancient burial sites located by the river's edge. If the dreamer bathes in water containing a 'sky ax', his dream spirit will be rendered invisible to the lightning.

The role of dreams in everyday life

The most extensive work on primitive dreams is *The Dream in Primitive Cultures*, published by J. S. Lincoln in 1935. He provides many examples of the important role played by dreams in primitive cultures. Among the cultural aspects influenced by dreams, he cites such activities as: murder; war; sacrificial acts; discovering 'totems'; selecting living sites; choosing careers; creating songs, dances, and religious ceremonies; discovering charms and cures; inventing new types of material objects; and naming children. This list is far from an exhaustive one.

Lincoln's conclusions about the role of dreams are noteworthy:

The importance of the dream as an initiator of primitive culture must, therefore, be given its due emphasis in any study which attempts to reach a closer understanding of the nature of primitive culture itself. Its significance has hitherto not been sufficiently grasped. It is because the primitive mind often assigns a reality value to the fantasy world equal to that of the external world, and even has difficulty at times in distinguishing the two, that the dream is allowed to dictate in large measure the course of life. Because of this valuation of fantasy, with its cultural results, we are enabled to approach directly the specific mental motives which result in specific aspects of culture. . . . To reach the full dynamics of motive and wish expressed in the dream would, therefore, be equivalent to reaching the foundation in human motive on which culture rests (pp. 97–8).

Cultural influences upon dreams

There is general agreement among anthropologists that primitive groups have two types of dreams. The first is an ordinary or personal type of dream in which the dreamer's everyday life and activities as well as his particular personality conflicts are reflected. Such dreams are referred to as 'individual' dreams by Lincoln and as 'free' dreams by Malinowski (1927). The other class of dreams includes those that could be considered as prescribed by tradition and are called 'official' dreams by Malinowski and 'culture pattern' dreams by Lincoln. These latter dreams are of a special tribal significance and are eagerly sought or induced through special means such as fasting. Such dreams exist only while a native culture is in full force and disappear when the culture breaks down and outside influences cause the dream symbols of the old culture to disappear. An example of a culture-pattern dream is the following one by a Menomini youth about the morning star:

A tall man with a big red mouth appeared from the east. The solid earth bent under his steps as though it was a marsh. He said, 'I have pity on you. . . . You shall never be in danger if you make yourself a war club such as I have and always carry it with you wherever you go. When you are in trouble, pray to me and offer me tobacco' (Skinner, 1915, p. 536).

When a Menomini youth reached fifteen years of age, he or she was eligible to seek a dream provided the youth had never experienced sexual intercourse. The person fasted for eight to ten days and prayed for a supernatural vision. It appears that all Menomini puberty dreams conformed to certain unformulated rules and the content of the dream dealt with one of the following four types of 'strong powers': the gods above such as the sun or stars; the gods below such as horned snakes or underground bears; one of the manitou animals; the Sacred Metal Cylinder.

These puberty dreams indicated what the future held in store for the dreamer. Among the Oglala Sioux, a difficult choice confronted a male youth if he were to dream of the moon as having two hands, one holding a bow and arrows and the other a burden strap of a woman. The moon would bid the dreamer to take his choice and would sometimes try to confuse him by crossing its hands. Should he become the possessor of the burden strap, he would be doomed to live the remainder of his life as a woman. He would be required to dress as a woman, marry another man, and undertake woman's work. Such a person was known as a *berdache* and suicide was his only recourse to avoid the fate meted out to him in his dream.

Commentary

Some form of conditioning process is involved in producing culture-pattern dreams. Beginning in early childhood, familiarity with, and acceptance of, mythical figures gradually develops through exposure to legend and participation in religious ceremonies that celebrate their guiding roles in the tribe's destiny. Skepticism concerning their reality is squelched by the elders, while demonstrations of acceptance are rewarded by social approval of the group. It is therefore not surprising that a Menomini dreams of the morning star as 'a tall man with a big red mouth' appearing from the east. Nor is it surprising that the Egyptians dream of Serapis, the Greeks of Aesculapuis and the Christians of angels.

By means of such dreams, cultural heritage and traditions are preserved and continued across generations. In addition to providing group acceptance, such dreams also yield the dreamer a measure of personal security since he feels that his dream contacts with the mythical figures will help insure his own welfare from the potentially harmful exigencies of life.

Another point regarding cultural conditioning of dream content should also be made. Not only can a strongly held belief system influence what will be dreamed about, it will also influence what will not be dreamed about. It is therefore understandable that although taking medicine baths may not stop certain undesirable dreams for a skeptical American, it will stop them for a believing Cuna Indian.

The dream book of Artemidorus
The content of Oneirocritica

The most famous and important dream book to come down from ancient times was compiled by a second-century Italian physician. Although born in Ephesus, he referred to himself as Artemidorus of Daldis. Artemidorus spent most of his life collecting the then available information about dreams through extensive travels, visiting incubation centers, interviewing dream interpreters, and buying old manuscripts. Among his written sources were some of the dream books collected in Ashurnasirpal's Royal Babylonian Library at Nineveh. After sifting through this vast storehouse of material, he wrote his *Oneirocritica* (the Greek word for dream is *oneiros*). This consisted of five books, three of which are devoted to a lexicon of dream interpretation, while the other two contain useful hints about how a dream interpreter should conduct himself professionally.

Artemidorus was a master of taxonomy and he proposed various classificatory systems, which were further broken down into various subclassifications. He differentiated five types of dream-related experiences: symbolic dreams such as Pharaoh's dream of the seven fat and seven lean kine; daytime visions; oracles containing divine revelations; fantasies or undisguised dreams such as a lover dreaming of his beloved; and nightmares. A further distinction, which cuts across some of the groupings above, was his differentiation between *insomnium* and *somnium* dreams. *Insomnium* dreams could be affected by bodily states or daytime concerns, generally appeared in straightforward fashion, and dealt primarily with the present. *Somnium* dreams had a deeper allegorical meaning and pertained to future events.

Before undertaking an interpretation, Artemidorus required that a full account of the dream be supplied him. There were six critical background factors that he insisted needed to be known before one could offer an interpretation. These could be framed in terms of six questions:

Natura. Were the events of the dream plausible or bizarre?

Lex. Were the dream events appropriately interconnected?

Consuetudo. Were the dream events customary for the dreamer?
Tempus. What predream events may have influenced the dream?
Ars. What was the dreamer's occupation?
Nomen. What was the dreamer's name?

After obtaining this information, Artemidorus would attempt to apply it to each separate component of the dream before moving on to a final synthesis of the complete dream. Caution against mechanically applying the interpretations he listed in his books was constantly advanced and he pointed out that the meaning of different symbols could change over time and would have different meanings between cultures. No more clear-cut illustration of Artemidorus' individualized approach could be found than that documented in Book 4 in which seven different meanings were given to seven different pregnant women, all of whom had experienced the identical dream of having given birth to a dragon (Meier, 1966). In this same book he also indicated his awareness of the possibility of verbal puns. Artemidorus claimed to have attempted to improve his interpretations by studying the dreamer's background and investigating the outcome of three thousand dreams he had obtained from these dreamers.

Commentary

Artemidorus' reputation became tarnished because of his undeserved association with the trashy dream books that were spawned in the wake of his *Oneirocritica*. He has been scornfully referred to as a mere copyist who uncritically wrote down any nonsense he heard about dreams. Remembering that Artemidorus lived in the second century, his insights into the complexities that must be considered in deducing the meaning of a particular dream are amazingly compatible with contemporary dynamic approaches. This is not to deny that many entries in his lexicon were apparently based upon the magical practices and superstitious beliefs of his time, but his dedicated concern with empirical verification and his determination to offer a flexible approach that was reflective of the individual dreamer certainly warrant him a very prominent place in the history of dream interpretation.

Pre-Freudian views of the dream
Views during the middle ages

Synesius of Cyrene, a fifth-century bishop, enthusiastically reported that dreams had greatly assisted him in the composition of his writings and had even led to the invention of various traps for hunting. He urged: 'Let us all deliver ourselves to the interpretation of dreams, men and women, young and old. . . . Sleep offers itself to all: it is an oracle always ready, to our infallible and silent counselor . . .' (Woods, 1947, p. 36). Another bishop of the same era, Saint Augustine, expressed an appreciation in his Letter IX of the close interrelationship between bodily and mental conditions. He contended that a superfluity of bile impelled us to more frequent outbursts of passionate feeling, while at the same time the superfluity of bile is an effect of our yielding to such passionate feeling. If someone became stirred by such emotions, he would find representation in his dreams. Another writer of this same era, Gregory of Nyssa, held a similar psychosomatic viewpoint and singled out the sexual passions as the fountainhead of all human passions (McCurdy, 1946). Thus, a determination could be made from one's dreams as to whether the person were lustful or chaste. The next major Christian theorist about dreams was Saint Thomas Aquinas who lived in the thirteenth century. He listed four causes of dreams: two inward ones arising from day-time preoccupations and from physical humors and two outward ones arising from physical sources (temperature or astrological forces) and from God or demons.

Demons came to play a progressively greater role in theorizing about the origin of dreams. The devil had many disguises available to him and could thus pass easily into a person's dreams. Martin Luther became so fearful that he would not be able to distinguish divine from demonic messages that he prayed to God not to speak to him in his dreams. If the devil appeared too frequently or prominently in a person's dreams, the dreamer could be suspected of being in allegiance with him and might be burned at the stake as a result. Many paintings from the Dark Ages depict leering, hideous creatures populating the dream scene of some hapless victim. A nocturnal visit by supernatural beings is illustrated in the sixteenth-century woodcut shown in Figure 2. As the Age of Reason gradually began to dawn, the concern with the demons of darkness began to disappear. Attention again became redirected toward the role of somatic factors as exemplified by the often-quoted phrase of Thomas Hobbes from the seventeenth century that dreams were caused by 'distemper of the inward parts'. The source of dreams was once more located within man and efforts to link dreams with physiological causes flourished during the next two centuries.

Views during the nineteenth century

Several theorists attempted to account for dream imagery in terms of physiological stimulation. Among the most ingenious was the contribution by K. A. Scherner (1861). He proposed that images arising from somatic sources could be represented in various symbolic ways and suggested that stimuli arising from the male sex organs might cause the dreamer to imagine a part of a clarinet or the mouthpiece of a pipe because they had the approximate shape of the male organ, while the vagina could be symbolized by a soft, slippery, narrow footpath leading across a courtyard. Not only could the form of the organ be represented but internal substances as well, so that

Figure 2 'Man Tormented by Dreams' (sixteenth-century engraving after Raphael)

muddy streets could be traceable to an intestinal stimulus or a foaming stream to a urinary stimulus.

It was recognized in the nineteenth century that the various mental activities that occurred during dreams were not available to ordinary conscious scrutiny. A book by A. T. Schofield in 1901, *The Unconscious Mind*, consisted almost entirely of quotations from the leading authorities of that time concerning their viewpoints as to how the mind functioned. The term 'unconsciousness' had actually been introduced in Germany before the beginning of the nineteenth century and the word was used in English in 1800 by Wordsworth. Frederic Myers attempted to find some unifying concept that would explain such diverse phenomena as dreams, hallucinations, hypnotism, automatic writing, and multiple personality. He collected extensive material bearing upon the manner in which these phenomena manifested themselves and evolved a theory of a subliminal self to account for them. His posthumously published book (1903) indicated that he wished to extend the meaning of the term subliminal 'so as to make it cover *all* that takes place beneath the ordinary threshold, or outside the ordinary margin of consciousness' (p. 26). In summarizing Myers' contribution, William James, the greatest American psychologist of that day, stated in 1901:

for half a century now, psychologists have fully admitted the existence of a sub-liminal mental region, under the name either of unconscious cerebration or of the involuntary life; but they have never definitely taken up the question of the extent of this region, never sought explicitly to map it out. Myers definitely attacks this problem, which, after him, it will be impossible to ignore (Murphy and Ballou, 1960, p. 218).

During the last quarter of the nineteenth century several writers indicated their conviction that a close study of dreams would be rewarded by revealing some of the unconscious components of our personality. In 1875 F. W. Hildebrandt wrote:

The dream sometimes allows us to look into the depths and folds of our very being – mainly a closed book in states of consciousness. It gives us . . . valuable insights into ourselves . . . instructive revelations of our half-hidden tendencies (p. 55).

In 1883 Ralph Waldo Emerson made the following comments on dreams:

Wise and sometimes terrible hints shall in them be thrown to the man out of a quite unknown intelligence. . . . Sleep . . . arms us with terrible freedom, so that every will rushes to a deed. A skilful man reads his dreams for his self-knowledge. . . . However monstrous and grotesque their apparitions, they have a substantial truth (pp. 7–8).

Some quotations will now be given from James Sully in 1893 to indicate in what direction the *Zeitgeist*, or spirit of the times, was headed:

The newest conception of the brain is of a hierarchy of organs, the higher and later evolved seeming to control, and in a measure to repress, the functional activities of the lower and earlier. . . . Hence in sleep we have a reversion to a more primitive type of experience. . . . We may assure, perhaps, that in each case the dream was the expansion and complete development of a vague fugitive wish of the waking mind. . . . The dream becomes a revelation. It strips the ego of its artificial wrappings and exposes it in its native nudity. It brings up from the dim depths of our sub-conscious life the primal, instinctive impulses, and discloses to us a side of ourselves which connects us with the great sentient world. . . . Some writers would regard dreaming in general as a kind of pictorial symbolism. . . .

Like some letter in cipher, the dream inscription when scrutinized closely loses its first look of balderdash and takes on the aspect of a serious, intelligible message (Woods, 1947, pp. 516–19).

Commentary

After the insightful treatment accorded dreams by Artemidorus in the second century, the dream gradually came to be linked in Christian thinking with sin, sex, and demons. The dream was something to be avoided as it allowed a portal of easy access for the devil whereby he could sway men's minds in evil directions. Under the Church Fathers, the dream fell from its previously exalted position to one of despisement, and the dream is still devaluated by many contemporary theologians.

During the nineteenth century, a scientific approach to the dream became evident. As the quotations above indicate, there was a developing conviction that dreams could provide important insights into the dreamer's personality and that the material expressed often dealt with unacceptable instincts. A subliminal, or unconscious, region was assumed to be the lodging place of these socially repressed impulses. This line of thinking was subsequently developed by Freud into an elaborate and interconnected theory of dreams and personality.

It should be recognized that many of the building blocks of Freud's theoretical structure were already available. Some of Freud's disciples, who were to address him in letters as 'Dear Master', were so extravagant in their praise of him that the impression is frequently given that Freud was the original discoverer of the unconscious, that he was the first to note that dreams dealt with repressed material, and that he alone recognized that dreams contained a meaningful and intelligent message.

References

BRUGSCH-BEY, H. (1947), 'The dream of King Thutmes IV', in R. Woods (ed.), *The World of Dreams*, Random House.

COHEN, A. (1947), 'The Babylonian Talmud', in R. Woods (ed.), *The World of Dreams*, Random House.

DE BECKER, R. (1968), *The Understanding of Dreams and their Influence on the History of Man*, Hawthorn.

DODDS, E. R. (1957), *The Greeks and the Irrational*, Beacon Press.

EMERSON, R. W. (1883), *Lectures and Biographical Sketches*, Riverside Press.

FRAZER, J. (1936–7), *The Golden Bough: A Study in Magic and Religion*, Macmillan, 3rd edn.

HILDEBRANDT, F. W. (1875), *Der Traum und seine Verwerthung fur's Leben*, Leipzig.

KELSEY, M. T. (1968), *Dreams: The Dark Speech of the Spirit*, Doubleday.

LEVY-BRUHL, L. (1923), *Primitive Mentality*, Macmillan.

LINCOLN, J. S. (1935), *The Dream in Primitive Cultures*, Cresset Press.

MALINOWSKI, B. (1927), *Sex and Repression in Savage Society*, Harcourt, Brace & World.

McCURDY, H. G. (1946), 'The history of dream theory', *Psychol. Rev.*, vol. 53, pp. 225–33.

MEIER, C. A. (1966), 'The dream in Ancient Greece and its use in temple cures (incubation)', in G. E. von Grunebaum and R. Caillois (eds.), *The Dream and Human Societies*, University of California Press.

MURPHY, G., and BALLOU, R. (eds.) (1960), *William James on Psychical Research*, Viking Press.

MYERS, F. W. H. (1903), *Human Personality and its Survival of Bodily Death*, University Press, 1961.

RATTRAY, R. S. (1927), *Religion and Art in Ashanti*, Clarendon Press.

SCHERNER, K. A. (1861), *Las Leben des Traumes*, Berlin.

SCHOFIELD, A. T. (1901), *The Unconscious Mind*, Funk & Wagnalls.

SKINNER, A. (1915), 'Social life and ceremonial bundles of the Menomini Indians', *Amer. Mus. Nat. Hist. Anthrop. Pap.*, vol. 13, pp. 532–9.

SULLY, J. (1893), 'The dream as a revelation', in R. Woods (ed.), *The World of Dreams*, Random House, 1947.

VON GRUNEBAUM, G. E., and CAILLOIS, R. (1966), *The Dream and Human Societies*, University of California Press.

WALLIS-BUDGE, E. A. (1899), *Egyptian Magic*, Trench, Trubner.

WALSH, W. (1920), *The Psychology of Dreams*, Dodd, Mead.

WOODS, R. (ed.) (1947), *The World of Dreams*, Random House.

2 Sir Thomas Browne

On Dreams (c. 1650)

Excerpt from Martin Kinder (ed.), *On Dreams*, Walpole Press, 1929, pp. 5–12.

Half our days we pass in the shadow of the earth; and the brother of death exacteth a third part of our lives. A good part of our sleep is peered out with visions and fantastical objects, wherein we are confessedly deceived. The day supplieth us with truths; the night with fictions and falsehoods, which uncomfortably divide the natural account of our beings. And, therefore, having passed the day in sober labours and rational enquiries of truth, we are fain to betake ourselves unto such a state of being, wherein the soberest heads have acted all the monstrosities of melancholy, and which unto open eyes are no better than folly and madness.

Happy are they that go to bed with grand music, like *Pythagoras*, or have ways to compose the fantastical spirit, whose unruly wanderings take off inward sleep, filling our heads with *St Anthony's* visions, and the dreams of *Lipara* in the sober chambers of rest.

Virtuous thoughts of the day lay up good treasures for the night; whereby the impressions of imaginary forms arise into sober similitudes, acceptable unto our slumbering selves and preparatory unto divine impressions. Hereby *Solomon's* sleep was happy. Thus prepared, *Jacob* might well dream of angels upon a pillow of stone. And the best sleep of Adam might be the best of any after.

That there should be divine dreams seems unreasonably doubted by *Aristotle*. That there are demoniacal dreams we have little reason to doubt. Why may there not be angelical? If there be guardian spirits, they may not be inactively about us in sleep; but may sometimes order our dreams: and many strange hints, instigations, or discourses, which are so amazing unto us, may arise from such foundations.

But the phantasms of sleep do commonly walk in the great road of natural and animal dreams, wherein the thoughts or actions of the day are acted over and echoed in the night. Who can therefore wonder that *Chrysostom* should dream of *St Paul*, who daily read his epistles; or that *Cardan*, whose head was so taken up about the stars, should dream that his soul was in the moon! Pious persons, whose thoughts are daily busied about heaven, and the blessed state thereof, can hardly escape the nightly phantasms of it, which though sometimes taken for illuminations, or divine dreams, yet rightly perpended may prove but animal visions, and natural night-scenes of their awaking contemplations.

Many dreams are made out by sagacious exposition, and from the signature of their subjects; carrying their interpretation in their fundamental sense and mystery of similitude, whereby, he that understands upon what natural fundamental every notion dependeth, may, by symbolical adaptation, hold a ready way to read the characters of *Morpheus*. In dreams of such a nature, *Artemidorus*, *Achmet* and *Astrampsichus*, from *Greek*, *Egyptian* and *Arabian* oneiro-criticism, may hint some interpretation: who, while we read of a ladder in *Jacob's* dream, will tell us that ladders and scalary ascents signify preferment; and while we consider the dream of *Pharaoh*, do teach us that rivers overflowing speak plenty, lean oxen, famine and scarcity; and therefore it was but reasonable in *Pharaoh* to demand the interpretation from his magicians, who, being *Egyptians*, should have been well versed in symbols and the hieroglyphical notions of things. The greatest tyrant in such divinations was *Nabuchodonosor*, while, besides the interpretation, he demanded the dream itself; which being probably determined by divine immission, might escape the common road of phantasms, that might have been traced by *Satan*.

When *Alexander*, going to besiege *Tyre*, dreamt of a *Satyr*, it was no hard exposition for a *Grecian* to say, '*Tyre* will be thine.' He that dreamed that he saw his father washed by *Jupiter* and anointed by the sun, had cause to fear that he might be crucified, whereby his body would be washed by the rain, and drop by the heat of the sun. The dream of *Vespasian* was of harder exposition; as also that of the emperor *Mauritius*, concerning his successor *Phocas*. And a man might have been hard put to it, to interpret the language of *Aesculapius*, when to a consumptive person he held forth his fingers; implying thereby that his cure lay in dates, from the homonomy of the *Greek*, which signifies dates and fingers.

We owe unto dreams that *Galen* was a physician, *Dion* an historian, and that the world hath seen some notable pieces of *Cardan*; yet, he that should order his affairs by dreams, or make the night a rule unto the day, might be ridiculously deluded; wherein *Cicero* is much to be pitied, who having excellently discoursed of the vanity of dreams, was yet undone by the flattery of his own, which urged him to apply himself unto *Augustus*.

However dreams may be fallacious concerning outward events, yet may they be truly significant at home; and whereby we may more sensibly understand ourselves. Men act in sleep in some conformity unto their awaked senses; and consolations or discouragements may be drawn from dreams which intimately tell us ourselves. *Luther* was not like to fear a spirit in the night, when such an apparition would not terrify him in the day. *Alexander* would hardly have run away in the sharpest combats of sleep, nor *Demos-*

thenes have stood stoutly to it, who was scarce able to do it in his prepared senses. Persons of radical integrity will not easily be perverted in their dreams, nor noble minds do pitiful things in sleep. *Crassus* would have hardly been bountiful in a dream, whose fist was so close awake. But a man might have lived all his life upon the sleeping hand of *Antonius*.

There is an art to make dreams, as well as their interpretation; and physicians will tell us that some food makes turbulent, some gives quiet, dreams. *Cato*, who doated upon cabbage, might find the crude effects thereof in his sleep; wherein the *Egyptians* might find some advantage by their superstitious abstinence from onions. *Pythagoras* might have calmer sleeps, if he totally abstained from beans. Even *Daniel*, the great interpreter of dreams, in his leguminous diet, seems to have chosen no advantageous food for quiet sleeps, according to *Grecian* physic.

To add unto the delusion of dreams, the fantastical objects seem greater than they are; and being beheld in the vaporous state of sleep, enlarge their diameters unto us; whereby it may prove more easy to dream of giants than pigmies. *Democritus* might seldom dream of atoms, who so often thought of them. He almost might dream himself a bubble extending unto the eighth sphere. A little water makes a sea; a small puff of wind a tempest. A grain of sulphur kindled in the blood may make a flame like *Aetna*; and a small spark in the bowels of *Olympias* a lightning over all the chamber.

But, beside these innocent delusions, there is a sinful state of dreams. Death alone, not sleep, is able to put an end unto sin; and there may be a night-book of our iniquities; for beside the transgressions of the day, casuists will tell us of mortal sins in dreams, arising from evil precogitations; meanwhile human law regards not noctambulos; and if a night-walker should break his neck, or kill a man, takes no notice of it.

Dionysius was absurdly tyrannical to kill a man for dreaming that he had killed him; and really to take away his life, who had but fantastically taken away his. *Lamia* was ridiculously unjust to sue a young man for a reward, who had confessed that pleasure from her in a dream which she had denied unto his awaking senses: conceiving that she had merited somewhat from his fantastical fruition and shadow of herself. If there be such debts, we owe deeply unto sympathies; but the common spirit of the world must be ready in such arrearages.

If some have swooned, they may also have died in dreams, since death is but a confirmed swooning. Whether *Plato* died in a dream, as some deliver, he must rise again to inform us. That some have never dreamed, is as improbable as that some have never laughed. That children dream not the first half-year; that men dream not in some countries, with many more, are unto me sick men's dreams; dreams out of the ivory gate, and visions before midnight.

Part Two
Modern Depth Theories of Dreams

As the dream has, within the last century, been most intensively studied by psychoanalysis (stemming from Freud), and analytic psychology (stemming from Jung), this part attempts to give an outline of the main theoretical tenets of both schools. There can be no adequate substitute, here, for the reading of Freud's classic *The Interpretation of Dreams*, or Freud's extensive coverage in Part II of *Introductory Lectures on Psychoanalysis*, but, in lieu of this, we have substituted a fair and scholarly account by one of his closest followers, Ernest Jones (Reading 3), which is a close reflection of classical Freudian dream theory.

C. G. Jung's animadversions on the dream are scattered throughout the very large corpus of his writings. Reading 4 by Jacobi brings together the main tenets of his theory concerning the importance and function of dreams.

3 Ernest Jones

Freud's Theory of Dreams

Ernest Jones, 'Freud's theory of dreams', *American Journal of Psychology*, vol. 21, 1910, pp. 283–308. Revised in Ernest Jones, *Papers on Psycho-Analysis*, Baillière, Tindall & Cox, 5th edn 1950, pp. 217–50.

Freud's theory of dreams occupies a nodal position in his psychology, constituting as it does a point of conjunction for his various conclusions on normal and abnormal mental life respectively. From it as a starting-point he has developed outlooks that call for the earnest consideration of psychologists, for it is extensively conceded that if his conclusions are true they carry with them a revolutionary change in our knowledge of the structure and functions of the mind. These broader aspects of his theory will not here be considered, the present paper being intended merely to delineate the main outlines of the dream theory proper. Owing to the richness of the subject-matter even this purpose can here of necessity be but very imperfectly attained, so that the following description can at best only serve as an introduction to the study of his *Traumdeutung*.[1] No just criticism of the theory can be made without a careful perusal of this volume, in which Freud has in detail entered into all the manifold problems relating to dreams, has presented the evidence on which his conclusions are based, and has fully discussed rival views and anticipated the possible objections that may be raised to his own. A few illustrative examples, drawn from the writer's experience, will accompany the present paper, but in order to economize space no actual dream-analyses will be detailed, it being proposed to do this in a subsequent paper.

The method Freud uses in the investigation of dreams is that termed by him psychoanalysis, and on the question of the reliability of this method rests that of the validity of his conclusions. No account of psychoanalysis itself can be given here, for that alone would exact a long exposition, but it should explicitly be stated that the technique of this method is a complex and intricate matter the acquirement of which is not, as many writers seem over-readily to assume, an easy task, but one requiring much practice, patience, and experience. In no branch of science can the testing of the

1. First edition, 1900; fifth edition, 1919. It is advantageous to read before this more difficult volume Freud's *Vorlesungen zur Einführung in die Psychoanalyse*, Zweiter Teil, 'Der Traum', 1916. (English translation, *Introductory Lectures on Psycho-Analysis*, 1922.)

results obtained by the use of an entirely new and difficult technique be satisfactorily submitted to an off-hand trial on the part of someone quite untrained in this, and it is strange that it does not occur to those who do not directly confirm Freud's conclusions as soon as they 'try psychoanalysis' that the fact may be due, not, as they hastily infer, to the erroneousness of those conclusions, but to a more humble explanation – namely, that they have not mastered the technique. Articles purporting to disprove Freud's conclusions have been published on the basis of a casual scrutiny of three or four dreams; Freud, on the other hand, published nothing on the subject until he had made a careful study of over a thousand dreams. In my opinion the *Traumdeutung* is one of the most finished pieces of elaborate work ever given to the world; it is in any event noteworthy that in the twenty years that have elapsed since it was written only one other investigator, Silberer, has been able to make any addition – and that only a very minor one – to the theory, while not one constituent element of the theory has been disproved.

It is commonly believed in scientific circles that the mental processes of which dreams are composed arise, without any direct psychical antecedent, as the result of irregular excitation of various elements in the cerebral cortex by physiological processes occurring during sleep. This, it is maintained, accounts for the confused and bizarre nature of the mental product, and any apparently logical connection and order that frequently appear to some extent in dreams are explained by the supposition that the mental processes in question are represented in cortical elements that stand in close, anatomical or physiological, relation to one another, and so are simultaneously stimulated by the peripheral stimuli. Hence any problem as to the psychical origin of the mental processes, still more as to the *meaning* of the dream as a whole, is by the nature of things excluded as being nonexistent, and any investigation along such lines is condemned as savouring of antiquated superstitions about the 'reading of dreams' unworthy of educated people. To this attitude Freud, as must every consistent psychologist, stands in sharp opposition. He contends that dream processes, like all other mental processes, have their psychical history, that in spite of their peculiar attributes they have a legitimate and comprehensible place in the sequence of mental life, and that their origins are to be traced psychologically with as much certainty and precision as those of any other mental processes. The very possibility of this is sometimes doubted on the ground that the material to be investigated is so very uncertain and indefinite in its nature. Not only has one no guarantee that the dream has been accurately observed, remembered, and reported, but in most cases one can be pretty sure that what has actually happened is just the opposite of this – that, namely, parts of the dream are forgotten altogether, other parts are falsified in the memory, and so on, the result being that the material offered for investigation is only a partial and distorted copy of the original. However, apart from the fact that at least some dreams are clear throughout and precisely remembered, one has to accept empirically this feature of indefiniteness and study it like any other; the explanation Freud offers of it will be mentioned presently.

From one point of view dreams may be grouped into the following three categories. First may be distinguished those that are throughout both sensible and intelligible; such especially are the dreams of children. The very occurrence of such dreams, in which the mental processes fully resemble those of waking life, although they are never confounded with them, is in itself a strong argument against the view that dreams result from the isolated activity of single groups of brain cells. Secondly, there are dreams which are connected and have an evident meaning, but one the content of which is curious and surprising, so that we cannot fit them into the rest of our waking life. A person dreams, for instance, that his brother has been gored to death by a bull; he cannot account for his having come by such a curious notion, nor can he at first sight relate it to any waking thought. Thirdly, there is the most frequent type of dream, where the mental processes seem disconnected, confused, and senseless. These two latter types of dreams have a peculiar quality of strangeness and unreality; they are foreign to the other mental experiences of the subject, and cannot be inserted into any place in his waking thoughts. It is as though the subject has lived through a different range of experience, in another place or in another world, which apparently has no connection with the one to which he is accustomed. Now, Freud holds that this sense of foreignness is an illusion due to very definite causes, and that the mental processes which go to form dreams are really in direct continuity with those of waking life.

In tracing the antecedents of dream processes Freud makes use, as has been said, of the psychoanalytic method, which essentially consists in the collecting and ordering of the *free* associations that occur to the subject when he attends to any given theme and abrogates the selecting control over the incoming thoughts that is instinctively exercised by the conscious mind. If this method is applied to any component part of a dream, however senseless it may appear on the surface, mental processes are reached which are of high personal significance to the subject. The mental processes thus reached Freud terms the 'dream thoughts'; they constitute the 'latent content' of the dream in contradistinction to the 'manifest content', which is the dream as related by the subject. It is essential to keep distinct these two groups of mental processes, for on the appreciation of the difference between them rests the whole explanation of the puzzling riddles of dreams. The latent content, or dream thought, is a logical and integral part of the subject's mental life, and contains none of the incongruous absurdities and other peculiar features that characterize the manifest content of most dreams. This manifest content is to be regarded as an allegorical expression of the under-lying dream thoughts, or latent content. The distortion of the dream thoughts into the dream proper takes place according to certain well-determined psychological laws, and for very precise reasons. The core of Freud's theory, and the most original part of his contribution to the subject, resides in his tracing the cause of this distortion mainly to a 'censorship', which interposes an obstruction to the becoming conscious of unconscious psychical processes. This conception he arrived at from the analysis of various abnormal psychical manifestations, psychoneurotic symptoms, which he found to be constructed on a plan fully analogous to that of dreams. It may be remarked at this point that, quite apart from any views about the cause of the distortion, the nature and functions of the dream thoughts and other problems, the fact itself of the distortion is certain, and cannot be doubted by anyone who carefully observes a few dreams. That, for instance, the vision of a strange room in a dream is a distorted presentation of several rooms that have been actually seen, from each of which various individual features have been abstracted and fused together so as to present a new and therefore strange room, is the kind of observation that can easily be verified. Before considering, therefore, the nature of the latent content it will be well shortly to describe the distorting mechanisms by means of which it becomes transformed into the manifest content.

A dream is not, as it appears to be, a confused and haphazard congeries of mental phenomena, but a distorted and disguised expression of highly significant psychical processes that have a very definite meaning, although in order to appreciate this meaning it is first necessary to translate the manifest content of the dream into its latent content, just as a hieroglyphic script yields its meaning only after it has been interpreted. The mechanisms by means of which the manifest content has been formed from the underlying dream thoughts may be grouped under four headings.

The first of these is called *Condensation* (*Verdichtung*). Every element of the manifest content represents several dream thoughts; it is, as Freud puts it, 'over-determined' (*überdeterminiert*). Thus the material obtained by analysis of a dream is far richer and more extensive than the manifest content, and may exceed this amount by ten or twenty times. Of all the mechanisms it is the easiest to observe, and to it is mainly due the sense of foreignness that dreams give us, for it is a process with which our waking thought is not familiar (see pp. 106–9 of *Papers on Psycho-Analysis*). The representation in the manifest content of the extensive material comprising the latent content is brought about by a true condensation, rarely by the mere omission of part of the latent content. The condensation is effected in several ways. A figure in a dream may be constituted by the fusion of traits belonging to more than one actual person, and is then called a 'composite person' (*Sammelperson*). This may occur either by the fusion of some traits belonging to one person with some belonging to another, or by making prominent the traits common to the two and neglecting those not common to them; the latter process produces a result analogous to Galton's composite photograph. The same process frequently occurs with names: thus Freud mentions a dream in which the person seemed to be called Norekdal, which had been formed from the names of two of Ibsen's characters, Nora and Ekdal; I have seen the name Magna formed by fusing Maggie and Edna, and similar instances are common enough. The neologism thus produced closely resembles those met with in the psychoses, particularly in dementia praecox, and like these may refer to things as well as to persons. Lastly in this connection it should be remarked that certain of the elements in the manifest content are especially rich in associations, as if they formed particular points of junction (*Knotenpunkte*); they are in other words the 'best-determined' elements. These are intimately related to the most significant elements in the underlying dream thoughts, and also frequently show the greatest sensorial vividness in the manifest content.

Condensation subserves more than one function. *In the first place* it is the mechanism by means of which similarity, agreement, or identity between two elements in the latent content is expressed in the manifest content; the two elements simply become fused into one, thus forming a new unity. If this fusion has already taken place in the latent content the process is termed *Identification*; if it takes place during the construction of the dream itself the process is termed *Composition* (*Mischbildung*): the former process rarely concerns things, chiefly persons and places. In the process of identification a person in the dream enters into situations that really are proper to some other person, or behaves in a way characteristic of this second person. In the process of composition the fusion is revealed in the manifest content in other ways; thus a given person may appear in the dream, but bearing the name of some second one, or the figure in the dream may be composed of traits taken some from the first, others from the second person. The existence of a resemblance between two persons or places may thus be expressed in the dream by the appearance of a composite person or place built up in the way just mentioned; the important feature that the two have in common, which in this case is the essential constituent in the latent content, need not be present in the manifest content, and indeed usually is not. It is clear that by this means a considerable economy in presentation is effected, for a highly complex and abstract resemblance may be expressed by simply fusing the figures of the persons concerned. Thus, if two persons both show the sentiments of envy, fear, and malice towards the subject of the dream, these sentiments may be expressed by the appearance in the manifest content of a composite figure of the two persons. In this composite figure there may be traits common to both persons, such as colour of hair or other personal characteristics, but the essential resemblance in the underlying dream thoughts is as a rule not evident in the dream. The superficial resemblance presented in the dream is frequently thus the cover for a deeper and more significant one, and gives the clue to important constituents of the dream thoughts. The process in question may also represent merely the wish that there were such a resemblance between the two persons, and therefore, the wish that they might be exchanged in their relation to the subject. When, for instance, a married lady dreams that she is breakfasting alone with some man friend, the interpretation is often a simple matter. *In the second place* condensation, like the other distorting mechanisms, subserves the function of evading the endopsychic censorship. This is a matter that will presently be further discussed, but it is plain that a repressed and unacceptable wish that two persons or places may resemble each other in an important respect, or may be interchanged, can be expressed in the manifest content of a dream by presenting an insignificant resemblance between the two.

It might be assumed from the description given above that the process of condensation takes place in one direction only, that each element in the manifest content represents a number of elements in the latent content in the same way that a delegate represents the members of his constituency. This, however, is not so, for not only is every element in the manifest content connected with several in the latent content, but every element in the latter is connected with several in the former. In addition to this, frequently associations exist between the different elements of the entire structure of the dream, so that this often has the appearance of a tangled network until the full analysis brings law and order out of the whole.

The second distorting mechanism is that termed *Displacement* (*Verschiebung*). In most dreams it is found after analysis that there is no correspondence between the psychical intensity of a given element in the manifest content and the associated elements in the latent content. An element that stands in the foreground of interest in the former, and seems to be the central feature of the dream, may represent the least significant of the underlying dream thoughts; conversely an apparently unessential and transitory feature in the dream may represent the very core of the dream thoughts. Further, the most prominent affect in the dream, hate, anxiety, and so on, as the case may be, often accompanies elements that represent the least important part of the dream thoughts, whereas the dream thoughts that are powerfully invested with this affect may be represented in the manifest content of the dream by elements of feeble affective tone. This disturbing displacement Freud describes, using Nietzsche's phrase, as a 'transvaluation of all values'. It is a phenomenon peculiarly frequent in the psychoneuroses, in which a lively interest or an intense affect may be found associated with an unimportant idea. In both cases a transposition of affect has taken place whereby a highly significant idea is replaced by a previously indifferent and unimportant one. Often the association between the primary and secondary ideas is a very superficial one, and especially common forms of this are witty plays on the speech expression for the two ideas, and other kinds of clang association. As is well known, Jung has demonstrated[2] that this superficial association is usually the cover for a deeper hidden bond of high affective value. This mechanism of displacement is the cause of the puzzling fact that most dreams contain so many different and hardly noticed impressions of the previous day; these, having on account of their unimportance formed but few associations with previous mental processes, are made use of in the dream-making to represent more significant ideas, the affect of which is transferred to them. Displacement also explains much of the bizarreness of dreams, notably the remarkable incongruity between the intensity of the affect and the intellectual content; a person may in a dream be terrified at an apparently indifferent object, and quite at ease in the presence of what should be alarming danger.

Two special forms of displacement should be separately mentioned because of their frequency. One is the representation of an object or person thought of in the latent content by the device of allowing a part only to appear in the manifest content, the process known as *pars pro toto*, which is one of the forms of synecdoche. The other is representation by means of allusion, a process known linguistically as metonymy; it has just been referred to in connection with superficial association. There are still two other ways in which a latent dream element can be converted into, or replaced by, a manifest element – namely, visual dramatization through regression, which will presently be considered, and symbolism. Symbolism, which Freud calls the most curious chapter of the dream theory, forms such a special and important topic that I have considered it at length elsewhere (see ch. 3 of *Papers on Psycho-Analysis*); at this point I will only remark that, for some as yet unknown reason, dream symbolism differs from other symbolism in being almost exclusively sexual.

Condensation and displacement are the two main mechanisms by means of which is produced the distortion during the passage from the latent to the manifest content. The extent to which a given dream appears confused, bizarre, and meaningless as a rule varies with the extent to which these two mechanisms have been operative in its formation. The following fragmentary extracts from some dream analyses will illustrate the processes in question:

1. *I was in the country in Massachusetts, and yet seemed to be in the east not of America but of England. Above a group of people was vaguely outlined the*

2. *Diagnostische Associationsstudien*, 1906, Bd. i.

word Ölve or Ölde (which may be expressed as Öl͜de). This dream affords a particularly striking illustration of displacement, for every element in it directly led in the analysis to thoughts about the Netherlands, although no indication whatever of this country appeared in the manifest content. Massachusetts brought to my mind its capital Boston, and the original Boston in Lincolnshire.[3] That reminded me of Essex,[4] these two counties being the most low-lying (Netherlandish) ones in England. In Essex lives a friend through whom I had got to know well a number of Flemish people. On the day preceding the dream I had written a letter to someone in Maldon, a town in Essex, a name the sound of which brought to my mind Moll Flanders. The costume of the people in the dream was taken from a certain picture of Rembrandt's, which brought up a number of recent and old memories. Öl͜de was a condensation of Alva, the tyrant of the Netherlands, and Van der Velde, the name of a Flemish painter of whose works I am fond, and also of a particular Flemish friend: two days previously I had seen in the hospital a Dutchman with a very similar name. In short, turn which way I would, all parts of the dream stubbornly refused to associate themselves with anything but Netherland topics, the further analysis of which resolutely led in only one direction.

Associated, therefore, with only one word in the manifest content of the dream, which at first sight appeared to be meaningless enough, are a number of mental processes that occupy a significant place in my waking life. These, and many others which for personal reasons I cannot mention, are connected with the element in the manifest content of the dream by means of exceedingly superficial associations, chiefly ridiculous plays on words of a kind I hope I should never be guilty of when awake. Anyone, however, who is interested in the psychology of wit, or familiar with the unconscious fantasies of hysterics or the flight of ideas met with in mania and other psychoses, will not find it strange that the superficial associations and preposterous plays on words so characteristic of those fields of mental activity are common enough in yet another field – namely, that of dream formation. The question whether the associations that occur during dream analysis are made only then, and take no share in the actual formation of the dream, will not here be discussed; it is one of the objections with which Freud fully deals in the *Traumdeutung*.

3. That in the dream-making I was presumptuous enough to confound an American state with an English county is an illustration of the irresponsible liberties taken by the mental processes concerned in this production, and shows how completely they differ from our waking thoughts.

4. I might add that the latter part of the word 'Massachusetts' has a sound not very dissimilar to that of 'Essex'; further, that the meaning of the first part of it, 'chu' (which in Boston is pronounced as if it were spelt 'chew'), resembles that of the other word ('ess' is the stem of the German verb 'to eat').

2. The play on words in these dreams, which may surprise those not familiar with dream analysis, is further illustrated in the following example: *A patient dreamed that he was in a village in the neighbourhood of Paris that seemed to be called Marinier. He entered a café, but could only remember of its name that it contained an* n *and an* l. As a matter of fact, he had just been planning to visit Paris, where he would meet a particular friend who lived there. The patient was fond of making anagrams, and was very given to playing with words, both consciously and still more unconsciously, so that it was not hard to divine that the invented word Marinier together with the letters *n* and *l* were derived from a transposition of the letters in Armenonville. This was confirmed by his next remark, to the effect that on his last visit to Paris he had dined enjoyably with this very friend at the Pavillon d'Armenonville.

3. A patient, a woman of thirty-seven, dreamed that *she was sitting in a grand stand as though to watch some spectacle. A military band approached, playing a gay martial air. It was at the head of a funeral, which seemed to be of a Mr X; the casket rested on a draped gun-carriage. She had a lively feeling of astonishment at the absurdity of making such an ado about the death of so insignificant a person. Behind followed the dead man's brother and one of his sisters, and behind them his two other sisters; they were all incongruously dressed in a bright grey check. The brother advanced 'like a savage', dancing and waving his arms; on his back was a yucca-tree with a number of young blossoms.* This dream is a good example of the second of the three types mentioned above, being perfectly clear and yet apparently impossible to fit into the patient's waking mental life. The true meaning of it, however, became only too clear on analysis. The figure of Mr X veiled that of her husband. Both men had promised much when they were young, but the hopes their friends had built on them had not been fulfilled; the one had ruined his health and career by his addiction to morphia, the other by his addiction to alcohol. Under the greatest stress of emotion the patient related that her husband's alcoholic habits had completely alienated her wifely feeling for him, and that in his drunken moments he even inspired her with an intense physical loathing. In her dream her repressed wish that he would die was realized by picturing the funeral of a third person whose career resembled that of her husband's, and who, like her husband, had one brother and three sisters. Further than this, her almost savage contempt for her husband, which arose from his lack of ambition and other more intimate circumstances, came to expression in the dream by her reflection of how absurd it was that anyone should make an ado over the death of such a nonentity, and by the gaiety shown at his funeral not only by all the world (the gay air of the band; her husband is, by the way, an officer in the volunteers,

while Mr X has no connection with the army), but even by his nearest relatives (the brother's dancing, the bright clothes). It is noteworthy that no wife appeared in the dream, although Mr X is married.

In real life Mr X, who is still alive, is an indifferent acquaintance, but his brother had been engaged to be married to the patient, and they were deeply attached to each other. Her parents, however, manoeuvred to bring about a misunderstanding between the two, and at their instigation, in a fit of pique, she married her present husband, to her enduring regret. Mr X's brother was furiously jealous at this, and the paean of joy he raised in the dream does not appear so incongruous when we relate it to the idea of the death of the patient's husband as it does in reference to his own brother's death. His exuberant movements and 'dancing like a savage' reminded the patient of native ceremonies she had seen, particularly marriage ceremonies. The yucca-tree (a sturdy shrub common in the Western States) proved on analysis to be a phallic symbol, and the young blossoms represented offspring. The patient bitterly regrets never having had any children, a circumstance she ascribes to her husband's vices. In the dream, therefore, her husband dies unregretted by anyone, she marries her lover and has many children.

4. The following two dreams illustrate the formation of neologisms: The patient, a woman of thirty-nine, dreamed that *she was sitting on a stage with four others, rehearsing a play they were to take part in; it seemed to be called 'The Wreck of the Kipperling'. Her title-role was called Kipper. She felt foolish and embarrassed.* This feeling she had several times recently experienced, circumstances having placed her in an awkward and compromising situation in regard to a man and woman, for both of whom she cared. Years ago, when in school in France, she had greatly suffered from feeling awkward and silly at having to read aloud in class from French plays, a language she imperfectly pronounced. Three days before the dream she had been reading a volume of satirical poems by Owen Seaman, and being a foreigner had had considerable difficulty in understanding and appreciating them. This had distressed her, for her friends thought very highly of them. Her embarrassment culminated at the reading of one of the poems, in which Rudyard Kipling is depreciated and entitled 'Kipperling'; she much admired Kipling's writings and had felt foolish when her two friends assured her he was crude and vulgar. She resented his being nicknamed Kipperling, and said, 'Fancy giving a poet the name of a silly little fish.' From the fusion of Kipling and Kipperling, and perhaps influenced by the fact that the latter name had been employed by *Seaman*, she had coined for herself in the dream the title of Kipper. Kipper (dried herring) is frequently used in London to denote foolish people ('silly kipper').

5. In another dream the same patient imagined she was called '*Hokerring*', a neologism produced by fusing the two words 'smoked herring'; this process may be represented thus:

(SM) OKE (D)
  H   ERRING

(The parentheses indicate letters omitted in the neologism.) The term smoked herring reminded her of a bloater, and of a rather vulgar word in her native language meaning nude, pronounced bloat. This brought up infantile memories, of shyness and a sense of foolishness, that were connected with nakedness.

The construction of the manifest content out of the latent content Freud terms the *Dream-work* (*Traumarbeit*). In this, two other principal mechanisms are concerned in addition to those just mentioned of condensation and displacement. The first of these may be called *Dramatization* (*Darstellung*). It is a familiar observation that the manifest content of most dreams depicts a situation, or rather an action, so that in this respect a dream may be said to resemble a theatrical representation. This fact exercises a selecting influence on the mental processes that have to be presented (*Rücksicht auf Darstellbarkeit*), for dramatization, like the arts of painting and sculpture, is necessarily subject to definite limitations, and therefore special expedients have to be employed to indicate mental processes that cannot be directly portrayed. Just as a painter has indirectly to convey abstract mental processes by adopting certain technical devices, so a dramatist has to select and modify his material in order to make it conform to the restrictions of his art, as for instance when an action extending over years has to be presented in a couple of hours. In a dream the mental processes are dramatized so that the past and future are unrolled before our eyes in a present action; an old wish, for instance, that relates to the future is seen realized in a present situation.

It is further well known that the manifest content of most dreams is predominantly, though not exclusively, of a visual nature, and the particular process of expressing in a dream various thoughts in the form of visual pictures Freud terms *Regression*, wishing to indicate by this the retrograde movement of abstract mental processes towards their primary perceptions. The network of dream thoughts is in this way resolved into its raw material. This process of regression is characteristic of dreams as contrasted with other mental constructions formed by means of similar mechanisms, such as daydreams, psychoneurotic symptoms, and so on, though it sometimes occurs in the last named in the form of hallucinatory visions. In his discussion of the nature and function of regression Freud develops a number of important theoretical considerations regarding the structure of the mind, which, however, cannot here be gone into. He traces regression, both in dreams and in visions, partly to the resistance of the censorship, and partly to the attraction for the mental processes thus represented exerted by infantile memories, which, as is known, characteristically preserve their original visual type. In the case of dreams, though not of course in the case of waking visions, it is probable that the regression is further facilitated by the cessation during sleep of the forward movement from the sensorial to the motor side.

Under the heading of dramatization may also be included the representation of various intellectual processes. We shall presently see that the intellectual operations (judgement, etc.) that are frequently met with in the manifest content of dreams originate not in the dream-making but in the underlying dream thoughts; no intellectual work is performed in the dream-making proper. In the dream thoughts there are of course all kinds of intellectual processes, judgements, arguments, conditions, proofs, objections, and so on. None of these, however, finds any special representation in the manifest content of the dream. As a rule they are entirely omitted, only the material content of the dream thoughts being represented in the dream, and not the logical relations of these. The dream-work, however, sometimes makes use of certain special devices to indicate these logical relations indirectly; the extent to which this is done greatly varies in different dreams and in different individuals. The logical relations between the constituents of the dream thoughts, just as between those of waking thoughts, are displayed by the use of such parts of speech as 'if', 'although', 'either', 'because', etc., which, as has just been said, find no direct expression in the manifest content. Instances of the devices in question are the following: logical concatenation between two thoughts is indicated by the synchronous appearance of the elements representing these in the manifest content; thus, in the third dream related above, the husband's death, the second marriage, and the subsequent children, three logically related thoughts, are represented by three groups of elements that synchronously appear in the manifest content. Casual connection between two dream thoughts is usually not indicated at all. When indicated it is done by making the one representing element follow on the other. The commonest way of doing this is by one clause being represented in an introductory dream (*Vortraum*), the other in the main dream (*Haupttraum*); it should, however, be remarked that this splitting of the manifest content does not always indicate causal connection between the corresponding dream thoughts. A less frequent device is the bringing about of a transformation of the one element into the other; the transformation must be a direct one, not a mere replacement, as when one scene passes gradually into another, not as when one scene is simply replaced by another. Evident absurdity in the manifest content signifies the existence of mockery or scorn in the dream thoughts, as was illustrated in the third dream related above. An alternative in the dream thoughts is not expressed in the manifest content; the representing elements are merely brought together in the same connection. When an alternative (either–or) appears in the manifest content it is always the translation of 'and' in the dream thoughts; thus in the second dream related above I felt that the third letter in the word outlined was either v or d, and both of these were present in the latent content.

Opposition and contradiction between dream thoughts may be indicated in two ways in the manifest content. When the contrasting thoughts can be linked with the idea of exchange, then the representing elements may be fused into a unity, a process described above under the name of identification. Other cases of opposition, which fall into the category of the converse or reverse, may be indicated in the following curious way: two parts of the already formed dream that are connected with the dream thoughts in question are inverted. Inversion of mental processes in dream-making subserves other functions than the one just mentioned: it is, for instance, a favourite method of increasing the distortion; the simplest way of disguising a mental process is to replace it by its obverse. Some subjects seem to employ this distorting mechanism to an inordinate extent, and many dreams can be interpreted merely by inverting them. The inversion may concern either space or time. An instance of the former occurred in the third dream related above, where the yucca-tree (phallus) was attached dorsally instead of ventrally. Instances of both may be seen in the following dream by the same patient:

6. *She stood at the seashore watching a small boy, who seemed to be hers, wading into the water. This he did till the water covered him and she could only see his head bobbing up and down near the surface. The scene then changed into the crowded hall of an hotel. Her husband left her, and she 'entered into conversation with' a stranger.* The second half of the dream revealed itself in the analysis as representing a flight from her husband and the entering into intimate relations with a third person, behind whom was plainly indicated Mr X's brother mentioned in the former dream. The first part of the dream was a fairly evident birth fantasy. In dreams, as in mythology, the delivery of a child *from* the uterine waters is commonly presented by distortion as the entry of the child *into* water; among many others, the births of Adonis, Osiris, Moses and Bacchus are well-known illustrations of this. The bobbing up and down of the head into the water at once recalled to the patient the sensation of quickening she had experienced in her only pregnancy. Thinking of the boy going into the water induced a reverie in which she saw herself taking him out of the water, carrying him to a nursery, washing him and dressing him, and installing him in her household.

The second half of the manifest dream therefore represented thoughts, concerning the elopement, that belonged to the first half of the underlying latent content; the first half of the dream corresponded with the second half of the latent content, the birth fantasy. Besides this inversion in order, further inversions took place in each half of the dream. In the first half the child *entered* the water, and then his head bobbed; in the underlying dream thoughts first the quickening occurred, and then the child *left* the water (a double inversion). In the second half her husband left her; in the dream thoughts she left her husband.

Last among the dream-making mechanisms is that termed *Secondary Elaboration* (*sekundäre Bearbeitung*). It fundamentally differs from the other three in that it arises from the activity, not of the underlying dream thoughts, but of the more conscious mental processes. This remark will be more comprehensible when we presently consider the forces that go to make a dream. When the dream is apprehended in consciousness it is treated in the same way as any other perceptive content – i.e. it is not accepted in its un-altered state, but is assimilated to pre-existing conceptions. It is thus to a certain extent remodelled so as to bring it, so far as is possible, into harmony with other conscious mental processes. In other words an attempt, however unsuccessful, is made to modify it so as to render it comprehensible (*Rück-sicht auf Verständlichkeit*). This secondary elaboration is closely allied to the process I have described as rationalization (see ch. 2 of 3rd edn of *Papers on Psycho-Analysis*). As is well known, there is a pronounced tendency on the part of the mind to distort foreign experiences in such a way as to assimi-late them to what is already intelligible; in hearing or seeing a sentence in a strange tongue the subject imagines analogies to familiar words in his own, a falsifying process that frequently is carried to excess, leading to curious misunderstandings. To this secondary elaboration is due whatever degree of ordering, sequence, and consistency there may be found in a dream.

In connection with the secondary elaboration may be mentioned the allied process discovered by Silberer and named by him 'threshold sym-bolism'. He has shown that the last portion of the manifest content of a dream, just before waking, can represent the idea of waking; instances are: crossing a threshold, leaving a room, starting on a journey or arriving at a destination, etc. It is further possible, though not yet demonstrated, that the same process may occur in the midst of the dream itself, portraying varia-tions in the depth of sleep, tendency to break off the dream, etc.

Reviewing now as a whole the process of dream-making, we have above all to lay stress on the fact that in the formation of a dream no intellectual operation of any sort is carried out; the dream-work is concerned solely with translating into another form various underlying dream thoughts that were previously in existence. No creative work whatever is carried out by the process of dream-making; it performs no act of decision, calculation, judgement, comparison, conclusion, or any kind of thought. Not even the elaboration of any fantasy occurs in the dream-making, though a previously existing fantasy may be bodily taken over and woven into the dream, a fact that gives the key to the explanation of highly wrought and yet momentary dreams, such as the well-known guillotine one related to Maury. Any part of a dream that appears to indicate an intellectual operation has been taken bodily from the underlying latent content, either directly or in a distorted form; the same applies to speech phrases that may occur in a dream. Even some of the waking judgements passed on a dream belong to the latent content. To repeat, there is in the dream-work nothing but transformation of previously formed mental processes.

The dream-work proper is thus a process more distant from waking mental life than even the most determined detractor of dream activities would maintain. It is not merely more careless, incorrect, incomplete, forgetful, and illogical than waking thought, but it is something that qualitatively is absolutely different from this, so that the two cannot be compared. Dream-making proceeds by methods quite foreign to our waking mental life; it ignores obvious contradictions, makes use of highly strained analogies, and brings together widely different ideas by means of the most superficial associations, for instance by such a feeble play on words as shocks the waking mind with a keen sense of ridiculousness. The mental processes characteristic of dreams would if they occurred in a conscious waking state at once arouse grave suspicion of impaired intelligence; as Jung has clearly pointed out,[5] they are in fact processes that are frequently indistinguishable from those met with in advanced stages of dementia praecox and other psychoses.

Besides the detractors of dreams there are others who adopt the opposite attitude and ascribe to dreams various useful and valuable functions. As we shall see later, Freud holds that there is but one function of dreams – namely, to protect sleep. Several members of the post-psychoanalytical school, however, notably Maeder – and in this country Nicoll – maintain that dreams serve such functions as the formation of tentative efforts at the solution of various disturbing problems or dilemmas. In my opinion, the fallacy in this conclusion lies in confusion between the latent content of the dream and the dream-work itself. Certainly in the latent dream thoughts there are to be found the processes described by Maeder, just as numerous other kinds of intellectual operations, but this in no sense proves that the dream itself is constructed for the purpose of developing them. Dream-work is nothing but a translation.

The affect in dreams has many interesting features. The incongruous manner in which it may be present when it is not to be explained by the ideas

5. *Psychologie der Dementia praecox*, 1907.

of the dream, or be absent when from these ideas it might have been expected, has already been noted above, and is quite elucidated by psychoanalysis, which reveals that in the underlying dream thoughts the affect is logically justified and is congruous enough. The apparent incongruity is solely due to the distortion of the conceptual content, whereby a given affect becomes secondarily attached to an inappropriate idea. The third dream mentioned above well illustrates this fact; the incongruity with which Mr X's death was joyfully celebrated by his brother explains itself as soon as one realizes that the figure of Mr X in the dream represented that of another man in the latent content. The affect investing the latent content is always more intense than that present in the manifest content, so that, although strongly affective dream thoughts may produce an indifferently toned dream, the reverse never occurs – that is to say, an affective manifest content never arises from an indifferently toned latent content. Freud attributes this inhibition of the affect in dream formation partly to the cessation in sleep of the forward movement from the sensory to the motor side – he regards affective processes as essentially centrifugal – and partly to the suppressing effect of the censorship, which will presently be further considered. Another important matter is that the nature of the affect as it appears is the manifest content is the same as that of the latent content, although, as has just been said, the intensity of it is always less there than here. The influence of the dream-work on the original affect is thus different from that on the rest of the dream thoughts, in that no distortion of it takes place. As Stekel puts it in a recent article,[6] '*Im Traume ist der Affect das einzig Wahre.*' ('In dreams the only true thing is the affect.') The affect appears in the same form in the latent as in the manifest content, although through the mechanisms of transference and displacement it is in the latter otherwise associated than in the former. It should, however, be remarked that a given affect in the manifest content may represent its exact opposite in the latent content, but on closer analysis it will be found that the two opposites were already present in the latent content, and were both of them appropriate to the context; as is so often the case in waking mental life, exactly contrasting mental processes in dream thoughts are intimately associated with each other. In such cases of inversion of affect, although both occur in the latent content, the one present in the manifest content always belongs to a more superficial layer of the unconscious, so that it is the inverted affect that yields the underlying meaning of the dream. Thus a repressed death wish may be masked by grief in the manifest dream, and fear in the latter is one of the commonest coverings for repressed libidinal desire.

Having mentioned some of the mechanisms that bring about the distor-

6. *Jahrbuch der Psychoanalyse*, Bd. i., S. 485.

tion of the latent content into the manifest we may next shortly consider the material and sources from which a dream is composed. Again we have sharply to distinguish between the sources of the manifest content and those of the underlying dream thoughts; the latter will presently be dealt with apart. Three peculiar features shown by the *memory* in dreams have especially struck most observers: first the preference shown for recent impressions; secondly, that the experiences are otherwise selected than in our waking memory, in that subordinate and hardly noticed incidents seem to be better remembered than essential and important ones; and thirdly, the hypermnesia for previously forgotten incidents, especially for those of early childhood life.

The first two of these features may be considered together, for they are intimately connected. In every dream without exception occur mental processes experienced by the subject in the last waking interval (*Traumtag*); other recent experiences that have not occurred on the day actually preceding the dream are treated in just the same way as more ancient memories. There must therefore be some special quality that is of significance in dream formation attaching to the mental experiences of the preceding day. Closer attention shows that the experience in question may be either physically significant or quite indifferent; in the latter case, however, it is always associated with some underlying significant experience. The dream-instigator (*Traumerreger*) may be (a) a recent significant experience that is directly represented in the manifest content, (b) a recent significant experience that is indirectly represented in the manifest content by the appearance there of an associated indifferent experience, (c) an internal significant process (memory) that regularly is represented in the manifest content by the appearance of an associated, recent, indifferent experience. In each case, therefore, a recent experience (i.e. from the preceding day) appears directly in the dream; it is one either significant in itself or else associated with another (recent or old) significant one. The selection of incidents of subordinate interest applies only to incidents of the day before the dream. Older incidents, that at first sight appear to be unimportant, can always be shown to have *already* become on the day of their occurrence psychically significant through the secondary transference on to them of the affect of significant mental processes with which they have got associated. The material from which a dream is formed may therefore be psychically significant or the opposite, and in the latter case it always arises in some experience of the preceding day.

7. An example of an incitement from the dream-day that is also of interest in connection with the subject of memory is the following: I dreamed that *I was travelling in Bavaria and came to a place called Peterwardein.* On

waking I felt quite sure I had never seen such a name and regarded it as being probably a neologism. Two days later I was reading a book on Turkish history, when I came across the name of the place, which is an ancient fortress in South Hungary. As I knew I had been reading the same book on the evening before my dream, my interest was aroused and I turned back to see if the name had occurred earlier in the book. I then found that on the evening in question I had skimmed over a page containing a number of Hungarian place-names, of which Peterwardein was one, so that without doubt my eye must have caught the name and noted it, although I had absolutely no memory of it. I then thought of the Hungarian town Gross-wardein, and eliminating the syllables common to the two names I saw that the dream must have contained an allusion to a certain Peter Gross, whom I had met in Bavaria, and whose father[7] had been born in Hungary, a fact in which I had special reason to be interested.

The explanation Freud gives of these facts is shortly as follows: The meaning of the appearance in the manifest content of indifferent mental processes is that they are employed by the dream-work to *represent* underlying processes of great psychical significance, just as in battle the colours of a regiment, themselves of no intrinsic value, stand for the honour of the army. A more accurate analogy is the frequent occurrence in the psycho-neuroses of the transposition of a given significant affect on to an indifferent idea; for instance, intense dread of a harmless object may arise as a transposition, on to the secondarily associated idea of this object, of a dread that was fully justified in relation to the primary idea. In short, the process is another form of the displacement mechanism described above. Just as in the psychoneuroses, so also in the dream the primary underlying idea is of such a nature as to be incapable of becoming conscious (*bewusstseinsunfähig*), a matter that will presently be further discussed. Freud explains the regular occurrence in the dream of a recent experience by pointing out that this has not yet had time to form many associations, and therefore is more free to become associated with unconscious psychical processes. The circumstance is of interest as indicating that during the first sleep after a mental event, and unnoticed by our consciousness, important changes go on in our memory and conceptual material; the familiar advice to sleep over an important matter before coming to a decision probably has an important basis in fact.

The third feature, namely the hypermnesia particularly for experiences of early childhood, is of cardinal importance. Early memories, which the subject had completely forgotten, but the truth of which can often be objectively confirmed, not infrequently occur with startling fidelity even in the manifest content. This fact in itself should suggest the ontogenetic antiquity of dream

7. The brilliant Otto Gross.

processes. In the latent content the appearance of such forgotten memories is far more frequent, and Freud holds it probable that the latent content of every dream is connected with ancient mental processes that extend back to early childhood. The following instance may be given of this:

8. A patient, a man aged thirty-seven, dreamed that *he was being attacked by a man who was armed with a number of sharp weapons; the assailant was swarthy, and wore a dark moustache. He struggled and succeeded somehow in inflicting a skin wound on his opponent's left hand. The name Charles seemed to be related to the man, though not so definitely as if it were his name. The man changed into a fierce dog, which the subject of the dream succeeded in vanquishing by forcibly tearing his jaws apart so as to split his head in two.* No one could have been more astonished at the dream than the patient himself, who was a singularly inoffensive person. The name Charles led to the following free associations: A number of indifferent acquaintances having this as their Christian name – a man named Dr Charles Stuart, whom he had seen at a Scottish reunion, at which he had been present on the day before (this man, however, wears a beard) – another man present at the reunion whose personal appearance had many traits in common with his assailant in the dream – the Scottish Stuart Kings Charles I and Charles II – again the acquaintance Charles Stuart – Cromwell's designation of King Charles I, 'that man Charles Stuart' – the medical practitioner of his family, whose name was Stuart Rankings, and who had died when the patient was nine years old. Then came the memory of a painful scene, previously quite forgotten, in which the doctor had roughly extracted two teeth from the terror-stricken patient after forcibly gagging his mouth open; before he could accomplish this the doctor had had his left hand badly bitten. The date of this occurrence could from extrinsic evidence be referred to the patient's fifth year. For a number of reasons that cannot be given here it became clear that the dream thoughts altogether clustered around this childhood experience. The assailant in the dream was no other than the doctor whose treatment of the patient was nearly thirty years after his death thus fearfully avenged in the latter's dream.[8] The play on his name Stuart Rankings (Rank-kings), which enabled him to become identified first with the Stuart King Charles, and then with Charles Stuart, and finally to be called in the dream plain Charles, is interesting. It should be added that the Dr Charles Stuart mentioned above is a dental surgeon, who a week previously had in the patient's presence performed a painful tooth extraction on the latter's wife; on the day before the dream he had inquired of the patient concerning

8. The deeper interpretation of the dream will be easy to those familiar with psycho-analysis, especially when I add that the dream was accompanied by appalling dread, and that the first association to 'hand' was 'neck'.

his wife's health. The identification of the man with the dog in the latter part of the dream was greatly over-determined. The doctor in question was a noted dog fancier, and had given the patient a fine collie to whom he became greatly attached; he led a very irregular life, and the patient often heard his father refer to him as a gay dog; finally he died 'like a dog', from an accidental overdose of poison, in the presence of a number of people who were from ignorance powerless to render the slight assistance that would have saved his life.

The source of some dream material is to be found in somatic stimuli during sleep, though by no means so frequently as many writers maintain. They are, however, in no case the whole cause of the dream, but are merely woven into its fabric in exactly the same way as any other physical material, and only when they fulfil certain conditions. The exaggerated claims sometimes made out for the importance of these stimuli are easily disproved by, for instance, the following considerations. A sleeper may react to a given somatic stimulation when this is of a lively nature, such as bad pain, in one of several different ways. In the first place he may altogether ignore it, as often occurs in bodily disease; secondly he may feel it during, or even throughout, sleep without dreaming at all;[9] thirdly he may be awakened by it; and fourthly he may weave it into a dream. Even in the last instance it enters into the dream only in a disguised form, and it can be shown that this disguise depends on the nature not only of the stimulus but of the rest of the dream. The same stimulus may appear in different dreams, even of the same person, under quite different forms, and analysis of the dream regularly shows that the form adopted is altogether determined by the character and motive of the dream. In short, the dream makes use of the somatic stimulus or not according to its needs, and only when this fulfils certain requirements.

9. In some, though by no means all, of the so-called 'battle dreams' that have recently been the subject of much controversy this may perhaps be the case – that is to say, that an actual memory of a terrible situation is faithfully reproduced during sleep. This occurs only in severe cases of 'shell shock' when the patient is constantly striving in waking life to obliterate the painful memory so far as he can, but is no longer able to do so when tired and in a state of lowered consciousness – e.g. light sleep. In most cases, however, two further features are to be discovered on closer examination. In the first place, it will be found that, although the dream is mainly a replica of actual experiences, there are usually some superadded elements present that do not belong to these experiences. This means that an attempt, however unsuccessful, is being made to transform the painful and sleep-disturbing memory into something more harmless –i.e. a true dream is being constructed. The prognosis of the 'shell shock' is better when this is the case. In the second place, if the anxiety battle dreams persist for a long period one may suspect that the traumatic effect of the experience is being increased by the action of unconscious complexes with which the painful memory has become associated. In both these cases the dream comes under the formula of Freud's theory as here described.

A somatic stimulus can not only furnish psychical material to be used in the dream-making, but may occasionally serve as the effective instigator of the dream. These are usually what Freud terms 'comfort dreams' (*Bequemlichkeitsträume*), where the stimulus (mostly a painful one) is transformed into a symbol of something pleasurable, and is so prevented from disturbing the dreamer. Even here, however, the occurrence of a somatic stimulus can rarely explain the whole dream, for as a rule it at most merely arouses a complex train of thought that is already present, and out of which the dream is constructed; when it cannot do this it awakes the sleeper. The following example will perhaps make the process clearer:

9. A man *saw in front of him* in a dream *a Greek altar composed of a solid mass of writhing snakes. There were nine of them, and they finally assumed the shape of a pyramid or triangle.* He woke at this point suffering from severe colicky pains in the abdomen, and, being a medical man, the resemblance at once flashed across his mind between the idea of contracting coils of intestine and that of writhing snakes. One can hardly doubt that there was here a genetic relation between the somatic stimulus and the dream, especially as the visual projection of internal sensations into a region in front of the person is known to occur frequently both in dreams and in insanity. According to the physiological view we have here an adequate explanation of the dream. The psychologist, on the other hand, notes that there are features in the dream (the altar, the number nine, the triangular form) quite unexplained by this aetiology, and which he is, or should be, disinclined to attribute to 'chance'. Freud would say that the wish to sleep, which is the real cause of every dream (see later), had attempted to transform the disturbing sensations into a more satisfactory imagery, and so to incorporate them with an agreeable train of thought in the unconscious as to deceive the sleeper and spare him the necessity of waking; in the present case the pain proved too insistent for this to be possible, except for a short time. That at all events some psychological mechanism was at work is shown by even a slight examination of the unexplained features in the dream. The thought of them at once reminded the subject that on the preceding day a young lady had asked him why the number nine was so prominent in Greek mythology; he replied that it was because nine, being composed of three times three, possessed in a high degree the properties of the sacred number three. At this point he felt embarrassed lest she should go on to inquire why three was a sacred number, for, of course, he could not tell her of the phallic significance of this, with its relation to religious worship in general and to snake-worship in particular, and he had no simple explanation ready to his mind. Fortunately, either her curiosity was satisfied by the first answer or her attention was diverted by the general flow of conversation (it was at a

dinner-party), so the dilemma did not arise. The train of thought thus aroused and brought to an abrupt stop evidently had very intimate associations, for the dream is plainly a narcissistic and exhibitionistic one; in it the subject identifies himself with the god Priapus who was adored for his masculine attributes (here represented by the typical phallic symbol of the snake). The avoidance of haste in being content with the first superficial explanation that offers itself will always show that, as here, dreams are concerned with much more significant matters than intestinal colic.

I observed many beautiful examples of the same mechanism as the result of the air raids over London, especially those taking place during deep sleep either late at night or early in the morning. Some of my patients proved extremely ingenious in converting the noisy stimulus of warning signals and barrage gunfire into reassuring dreams, so avoiding the disagreeable necessity of waking, with its unpleasant consequences of having to get up on a cold night and take shelter, of fear, anxiety, and so on. One typical feature of such dreams was that in the earlier stages of the raid, when the firing was more distant, the disturbing stimuli could be quite successfully transformed into other imagery, while as it got louder and louder the resemblance between it and the imagery became more and more evident – i.e. the disguise was less and less perfect, until the noise was so great that the person awoke. They resemble in this respect those sexual dreams in which the early part of the dream consists of quite disguised symbolism, the meaning of which becomes more and more evident as the stimulus becomes more insistent, until the person awakes with a seminal emission.

10. A patient, a woman aged forty, dreamed that *she was buying Christmas presents in a fair. Before her was a box containing, in two rows one above the other, six bull's-eye lanterns or electric torches, of which only the front glass could be seen. At this point a report of artillery was heard and she exclaimed 'Goodness! That must be a raid.' Someone close by, however, said 'Oh no, don't you know they are beating the drums in honour of the end of the war?'* (or else *'of the victory'*, the patient having the impression of both phrases). *She was again alarmed by a second report, but was once more reassured. She then recollected that she had heard about the arrangements for the celebration*, and was thinking about the details when she was awakened by someone knocking at the door. By this time the dream had so successfully dissuaded her of any possibility of a raid that she never thought of it on waking – she didn't even hear at first the loud firing that was going on – but supposed that the lady whose rooms were below had forgotten her flat-key and wanted to be let in (there being a common door-key to both sets of rooms). She was firmly persuaded of this until she opened the door below and found that there was a raid alarm. The reports in the dream were doubtless those of the

near guns, whereas she had been able to transform the more distant earlier sounds into harmless imagery.

The imagery itself was a compromise between military thoughts and pleasanter personal ones. The news had come the day before of the victorious end to the campaign in German East Africa, though, of course, there had been no celebration of it. The box was one she was just sending to the front, and was to contain, among other things, an electric torch. The appearance of the packed objects was greatly over-determined: ammunition shells in their cases, the muzzles of guns (as a child she used constantly to see these in the sides of old wooden battleships near her home), the box of eggs out of reach that Alice tries to buy in Looking-Glass World, bull's-eye lanterns and magic lanterns that fascinated her as a child, six-chambered revolvers, all played a part; in childhood she was excited by stories in which a revolver was suddenly whipped out (she had later learnt to use one herself in connection with private theatricals that took place at a happy period of a love affair which, however, ended unfortunately). The patient was at the time suffering from ungratified sexual desire, and there was reason to think that the object she was reaching towards in the dream was a symbol of a (soldier's) phallus.

11. A patient, a man of thirty-four, dreamed that *a boatload of women and children were escaping under rifle-fire, the scene taking place in India during the Mutiny. They managed to escape, after which he was concerned with the problem of how to publish the news of their terrible sufferings in the English newspapers without too greatly harrowing the feelings of the civilian population. The scene then changed and he was charged with the task of deciding how best to punish the mutineers. Some were blown from the mouth of cannons* (as happened historically), *and others were to be mown down by guns drawn up in a city square. The latter performance was in progress, and he was debating whether there was any danger to the civilian population through shell splinters* when he awoke to the booming of the barrage. The allusions to the German outrages on civilians and women by sea and through the air are evident, but a temporarily successful effort was made by the dream to convert such thoughts into a less disturbing historical story of events that took place sixty years before and thousands of miles away.

Having partly answered the question of *how* a dream is built we may take up the more difficult one of *why* it is built, or, more accurately put, the problems concerning the forces that go to make a dream. It is impossible to do this without first referring to Freud's views on psychical repression (*Verdrängung*) and unconscious mental processes; these views in themselves call for a detailed exposition which cannot here be given, so that this part of the present paper will be even more incomplete than the rest. Freud uses the term 'conscious' to denote mental processes of which we are at a given moment conscious, 'preconscious' (*vorbewusste*) to denote mental processes of which we can spontaneously and voluntarily become conscious (e.g. a memory out of one's mind for the moment, but which can readily be recalled), and 'unconscious' to denote mental processes which the subject cannot spontaneously recall to consciousness, but which can be reproduced by employing special devices (e.g. hypnosis, psychoanalysis, etc.). He infers that the force which has to be overcome in the act of making the last-named processes conscious is the same as that which had previously opposed an obstacle to their becoming conscious – i.e. had kept them repressed in the unconscious. This force or resistance is a defensive mechanism which has kept from consciousness mental processes that were either primarily or secondarily (through association and transposition) of an unacceptable nature; in other words, these processes are unassimilable in consciousness. Returning now to the subject of dreams, we have first to remark that Freud empirically found an intimate and legitimate relation between the degree of confusion and incomprehensibility present in a given dream and the difficulty the patient experienced in communicating the free associations leading to the dream thoughts. He therefore concluded that the distortion which had obviously occurred in the dream-making was related to the resistance that prevented the unconscious dream thoughts from becoming conscious; that it was in fact a result of this resistance. He speaks of the resistance that keeps certain mental processes unconscious as the 'endopsychic censorship'.[10] In the waking state the unconscious processes cannot come to external expression, except under certain abnormal conditions. In sleep, however, the activity of the censorship, like that of all other more conscious processes, is diminished, though it is never entirely abrogated. This fact permits the unconscious processes (the latent content) to reach expression in the form of a dream, but as they still have to contend with some degree of activity on the part of the censorship, they can reach expression only in an indirect way. The distortion in the dream-work is thus a means of evading the censorship, in the same way that a veiled phraseology is a means of evading a social censorship which would not permit a disagreeable truth to be openly expressed. The dream is a compromise between the dream thoughts on the one hand and the endopsychic censorship on the other, and could not arise at all were it not for the diminished activity of the latter during sleep.

10. Considerable objection has been raised – e.g. by Bleuler, Rivers, and others – to Freud's use of the word 'censorship', but so far as I can see it is rather to the word than to the conception. It is not to be imagined that Freud understands by this term anything in the nature of a specific entity; to him it is nothing more nor less than a convenient expression to denote the sum total of repressing inhibitions.

Distortion of the dream thoughts by means of the mechanisms of condensation and displacement is by no means the only way in which the censorship manifests itself, nor is this distortion the only way in which the censorship can be evaded by the dream processes. In the first place we have already noticed above one of its manifestations under the name of secondary elaboration. This process continues even in the waking state, so that the account of a dream as related directly after waking differs from that related some time after. The fact of this change in the subsequent memory of a dream is sometimes urged as an objection to the interpretation by psychoanalysis, but the change is just as rigorously determined, and the mechanism is as precisely to be defined, as that of any other process in the dream-making. For instance, if the two accounts are compared, it will be found that the altered passage concerns what might be called a weak place in the disguise of the dream thoughts; the disguise is strengthened by the subsequent elaboration by the censorship, but the fact of the change points to the need for distortion at that given spot, a point of some value in the analysis.[11] Instead of subsequently altering this weak place the censorship may act by interposing doubt in the subject's mind as to the reliability of his memory about it; he may say 'The person in the dream seemed to carry such and such an object, but I am not sure that I haven't imagined that in thinking over the dream.' In such cases one is always safe in accepting the dubiously given point as unhesitatingly as the most vivid memory; the doubt is only one of the stages in the disguise of the underlying dream thoughts.

An interesting way in which the censorship may act is by the subject receiving the assurance during the dream that 'it is only a dream'. The explanation of this is that the action of the censorship has set in too late, after the dream has already been formed; the mental processes which have, as it were unwittingly, reached consciousness are partly divested of their significance by the subject treating them lightly as being 'only a dream'. Freud wittily describes this afterthought on the part of the censorship as an *esprit d'escalier*.

The last manifestation of the censorship is more important – namely, the tendency to forget dreams or part of them; it is an extension of the doubting process mentioned above. Freud traces this tendency to forget, as also that shown in many forgetting acts of waking life [see ch. 2 of *Papers on Psycho-*

11. I have elsewhere ('Ein klares Beispiel von sekundärer Bearbeitung', *Zentralblatt für Psychoanalyse*, Jahrg. i., S. 135) narrated an instance of this in which a patient was unconsciously impelled, in the act of relating a dream that had occurred nearly twenty years before, to alter a certain feature in it. She knew that she was changing this, but had no idea why she did it; the analysis showed that it concerned a weak place which, if left in its original form, would, in the current circumstances, have at once betrayed the meaning of the dream thoughts. Though consciously she was quite unaware of the nature of these, her intuition had felt the danger.

Analysis – Eds.], to the repressing action of the censorship. As was mentioned above, the fragmentariness of the remembered dream, together with the uncertainty and actual falsification in the memory of it, are frequently urged as casting doubt on the reliability of any psychological analysis of dreams, but if a truly empiric attitude is adopted towards the material obtainable, as elsewhere in science, it will be found that these features are in a sense part of the nature of the dream itself and have to be explained just as other features have. One should always remember that it is the same mind that produces both the dream and the subsequent changes in it, whether these are additions or falsifications.

Freud's explanation can often be experimentally confirmed. When a patient informs the physician that he had a dream the night before but that he cannot recall anything of it, it frequently happens that the overcoming of a given resistance during the psychoanalytic treatment removes the barrier to the recollection of the dream, provided, of course, that the resistance concerns the same topic in the two cases; the patient then says, 'Ah, now I can recall the dream I had.' Similarly he may suddenly during the analysis of the dream, or at any time subsequent to the relation of the dream, supply a previously forgotten fragment (*Nachtrag*); this latter fragment invariably corresponds with those dream thoughts that have undergone the most intense repression, and therefore those of greatest significance. This occurrence is extremely frequent, and may be illustrated by the following examples:[12]

12. A patient, a man aged twenty-six, dreamed that *he saw a man standing in front of a hoarding with a gate-entrance on his left. He approached the man, who received him cordially and entered 'into conversation' with him.* During the analysis he suddenly recalled that the hoarding seemed to be the wall of an 'exhibition', into which the man was entering to join a number of others. The significance of this added fragment will be evident when I mention that the patient, who had frequently indulged in paedication, was a pronounced *voyeur*.

13. A patient, a woman aged thirty-six, dreamed that *she was standing in a crowd of schoolgirls. One of them said, 'Why do you wear such untidy skirts?' and turned up the patient's skirt to show how worn the under-skirt was.* During the analysis, three days after relating the dream, the patient for the first time recalled that the under-skirt in the dream seemed to be a nightdress, and analysis of this led to the evocation of several painful memories in which lifting a nightdress played an important part; the two most significant of these had for many years been forgotten.

12. A more striking instance is related in ch. 13 of the fourth edition of *Papers on Psycho-Analysis*.

As was mentioned above, the censorship can be evaded by the dream thoughts in other ways than the usual one of distortion. They may appear in the manifest content in their unaltered form, but their significance be misunderstood by the subject when he recalls the dream. For instance, a person may dream that he sees his brother dead, the actual dream thoughts being the wish that the brother may die. The subject fails to realize that the picture corresponds with a wish, even a repressed one, partly because the nature of this is so horribly unlikely that it does not occur to his consciousness, and partly because the dream is accompanied by an emotion, anxious grief, which is apparently incongruous with a wish. Such dreams are always intensely distressing (*Angstträume*), and in a sense it may be said that the dread here replaces the distorting mechanisms of condensation and displacement.

Although Freud attaches great importance to the action of the endopsychic dream censorship in causing the transformation of the latent into the manifest content of the dream, he does not attach an exclusive importance to it in this respect. He recognizes that other factors are also at work in making the dream thoughts unintelligible to the waking consciousness. One of these factors was mentioned above in connection with regression, and it is clear that ideational material that is presented to consciousness in the regressive form of the raw material of its sensorial imagery could not be understood. Another important factor leading to distortion is the process of symbolism, one that seems to be bound up with the very nature of the unconscious mind itself and undoubtedly related to its ontogenetic and phylogenetic history.[13]

We have finally to consider the most important problems of all, those relating to the latent content or dream thoughts. The first thing that strikes one about these is their intense psychical significance. A dream never proceeds from trifles, but only from the mental processes that are of the greatest moment and interest to the subject. Dreams never deal with trivialities, however much they may appear at first sight to do so. The explanation of why incidents of subordinate interest occur in the manifest content has been given above. More than this, the dream thoughts are processes of the greatest *personal* interest, and thus invariably egocentric. We never dream about matters that concern only others, however deeply, but only about matters that concern ourselves. It has already been mentioned that the underlying dream thoughts are perfectly logical and consistent, and that the affect accompanying them is entirely congruous to their nature. Freud, therefore, not only agrees with those writers who disparage the mental quality of dreams, holding as he does that the dream-making proper contains no intellectual operation and proceeds only by means of the lower

13. For a discussion of this see ch. 3 of *Papers on Psycho-Analysis*.

forms of mental activity, but he also agrees with those other writers who maintain that dreams are a logical continuance of the most important part of our waking mental life. We dream at night only about those matters that have most concerned us by day, though on account of the distortion that takes place in the dream-making this fact is not evident. Lastly it may be added that all the dreams occurring in a given night arise from the same group of latent dream thoughts, though they usually present different aspects of them.

There are certain differences between the dreams of a young child and those of an adult. In the child, at all events before the age of four, no distortion, or very little, may take place, so that the manifest content is often identical with the latent content. In correspondence with this fact we find that children's dreams are logical and coordinate, an observation that is hard to reconcile with the commonly received opinion that dream processes arise from a dissociated activity of the brain cells, for one can see no reason why dreams should be a meaningless conglomeration of disordered and lowered mental functioning in adults when they are obviously not so in the child. Further, with young children it is easy to recognize that the dream represents the imaginary fulfilment of an ungratified wish; the child is visiting a circus that the day before he had been forbidden to go to, and so on. Now, Freud maintains that the latent content of every dream represents nothing else than the imaginary fulfilment of an ungratified wish.[14] In the child the wish is an ungratified one, but it may not have undergone repression, that is to say it is not of such a nature as to be unacceptable in consciousness; in the adult the wish is not merely one that could not be gratified, but is of such a nature as to be unassimilable in consciousness, and so has

14. It seems necessary to keep calling attention to the fact that Freud's generalization about dreams representing wish-fulfilments refers to the latent content of the dream, to the dream thoughts from which the dream proceeds, and not to the manifest content, for one constantly hears the irrelevant objection that dreams do not seem always to deal with wishes, one often expressed in the question 'How can a fear dream indicate a wish, when something is happening in it that the dreamer very much doesn't want to happen?' It is only after analysis that the latent content of the dream is known, and it is only to the latent content that the wish-fulfilment theory applies.

A more serious objection is afforded by the class of dreams, of which the so-called 'battle-dreams' are a good instance, where the whole dream appears to consist of nothing but a representation of an actual experience. Here Freud considers ('Beyond the pleasure-principle', English translation, 1922) that the dream function (that of transforming thoughts in such a way as to preserve sleep) is unable to deal with the traumatic thoughts in question, probably because these have not yet been sufficiently incorporated into the mind. Indeed, we might well refuse the name of 'dreams' at all to such intense obsessive memories that break sleep, just as one would to similarly acting painful sensations in diseases or isolated painful thoughts (e.g. grief), which may pervade sleep without giving rise to a dream proper. In such cases the dream function simply fails to act.

become repressed. It frequently happens that even in the adult a wish-fulfilment appears in the manifest content, and still more frequently that a wish-fulfilment not present in the manifest content, but revealed by psychoanalysis, concerns a wish of which the subject is quite conscious; in both these cases, however, full analysis always discloses that these wishes are merely reinforcements of deeper, unconscious ones of an associated nature. No wish, therefore, is able to produce a dream unless it is either unconscious (*bewusstseinsunfähig*) or else associated with an allied unconscious one.

It has sometimes been alleged by Freud's opponents that his generalization of all dreams representing a wish-fulfilment is the outcome of observing a few dreams of children, and that his analyses merely consist in arbitrarily twisting the dream, to gratify some *a priori* notion, until a wish can be read into it. This suggestion is historically untrue, for Freud came to the analysis of the adult dreams from the analysis, not of children's dreams, but of adult psychoneuroses.[15] He found that his patients' symptoms arose as a compromise between two opposing wishes, one of which was conscious, the other unconscious, and that they allegorically represented the imaginary fulfilment of these two wishes. He further found that an essential factor in their production was a conflict between the two wish-systems, of such a kind that the unconscious one was forcibly prevented from becoming conscious; it was unconscious because it was repressed. It frequently happened that the psychoanalysis of the patients' symptoms directly led to their dreams, and on submitting these to the analysis in exactly the same way as any other mental material he discovered that the construction of them showed close resemblances to that of the neurotic symptoms.[16] In both cases the material examined proved to be an expression of deeper mental processes; in both cases these deeper processes were unconscious and had in reaching expression undergone distortion by the endopsychic censorship. The mechanism by means of which this distortion is brought about is very similar in the two cases, the chief difference being that representation by visual pictures is much more characteristic of dreams. In both cases the unconscious mental processes arise in early childhood and constitute a repressed wish, as do all unconscious processes, and the symptom or dream represents the imaginary fulfilment of that wish in a form in which is also fused the fulfilment of the opposing wish.

15. As may well be imagined, a number of Freud's individual conclusions had been anticipated by previous writers, particularly by artists. In the *Traumdeutung* he deals fully with the scientific literature on the subject. Prescott ('Poetry and dreams', *Journal of Abnormal Psychology*, vol. 7, nos. 1 and 2) has published an interesting paper on the relation of poetry to dream-production, using English poetry as an example.
16. These resemblances are expounded and illustrated in ch. 11 of *Papers on Psycho-Analysis*.

Dreams differ from psychoneurotic symptoms in that the opposing wish is always of the same kind – namely, the wish to sleep. A dream is thus the guardian of sleep, and its function is to satisfy the activity of unconscious mental processes that otherwise would disturb sleep. The fact that sometimes a horrid dream may not only disturb sleep, but may actually wake the sleeper, in no way vitiates this conclusion. In such cases the activity of the endopsychic censorship, which is diminished during sleep, is insufficient to keep from consciousness the dream thoughts, or to compel such distortion of them as to render them unrecognizable, and recourse has to be had to the accession of energy that the censorship is capable of exerting in the waking state; metaphorically expressed, the watchman guarding the sleeping household is overpowered, and has to wake it in calling for help.

Freud couples with his discussion of dream problems a penetrating inquiry into many allied topics, such as the nature of the unconscious and the function of consciousness, that cannot here be even touched upon. I would conclude this imperfect sketch of his theory of dreams by quoting a sentence of his to the effect that ' *Die Traumdeutung ist die Via Regia zur Kenntniss des Unbewussten im Seelenleben.*' ['The interpretation of dreams is the Via Regia to the knowledge of the unconscious in mental life.']

4 Jolande Jacobi

The Psychology of C. G. Jung

Excerpt from Jolande Jacobi, *The Psychology of C. G. Jung*, Routledge & Kegan Paul, 1951, pp. 88–101.

Besides discussion and the elaboration of the material in question through context and associations, which not only the patient but the physician as well supplies, the interpretation of dreams, visions, and every kind of psychic image occupies a central position in the dialectic procedure. The patient alone, however, determines the interpretation to be given the material he brings. Only his individuality is decisive here; for he must have a vital feeling of assent, not a rational consent but a true experience. 'Whoever would avoid suggestion must therefore look upon a dream interpretation as invalid until the formula is found that wins the patient's agreement.'[1] Otherwise the next dream or the next vision inevitably brings up the same problem and keeps bringing it up until the patient has taken a new attitude as a result of his 'experience'. The often heard objection that the therapist could suggestively influence the patient with his interpretation could therefore only be made by one who does not know the nature of the unconscious; for

the possibility and danger of prejudicing the patient are greatly over-estimated. The objective-psychic, the unconscious, is as experience proves, in the highest degree independent. If this were not so it could not at all exercise its characteristic function, the compensation of consciousness. Consciousness can be trained like a parrot, but not the unconscious.[2]

If physician or patient errs in his interpretation, the unconscious, working always autonomously, corrects them strictly and uncontradictably in time. The principal instrument of the therapeutic method is for Jung too the DREAM, it being that psychic phenomenon which affords the easiest access to the contents of the unconscious and which is especially suited because of its compensatory function to clarify and explain inner relations. For 'the problem of dream analysis stands and falls with the hypothesis of the unconscious; without this the dream is a senseless conglomerate of crumbled fragments from the current day.'[3] In the same way as the dream Jung

1. *Modern Man in Search of a Soul*, p. 12.
2. *Integration of the Personality*, p. 101.
3. *Modern Man in Search of a Soul*, p. 2.

utilizes the FANTASIES and VISIONS of his patients. If, therefore, in what follows we speak only of the dream for the sake of simplicity, fantasies and visions are thereby also understood.

The fundamental difference between the Jungian and the other analytical methods consists in the fact that Jung sees in these phenomena – namely dreams, etc. – not only contents of personal conflicts but in many cases also manifestations of the collective unconscious, which, going beyond the individual conflicts, sets over against these the primordial experience of universal human problems.

The theory and method of Jungian dream analysis can be sketched here only briefly.

Jung says:

The dream cannot be explained with a psychology taken from consciousness. It is a determinate functioning, independent of will and wish, of intention and conscious choice of goal. It is an unintentional happening, as everything in nature happens. . . . It is on the whole probable that we continually dream, but consciousness makes while waking such a noise that we do not hear it. If we could succeed in keeping a continuous record we should see that the whole follows a definite trend.[4]

This implies that the dream is a natural psychic phenomenon, but of a peculiar, autonomous kind, with a purposiveness unknown to our consciousness. It has its own language and its own laws, which one cannot approach with the psychology of consciousness – as subject, so to speak. For: 'One does not dream: one is dreamed. We "undergo" the dream, we are the objects.'[5] One could almost say: We are able in the dream to experience as if they were real the myths and legends that we read when waking, and that is something essentially different.

The *roots* of the dream, as far as we can tell, lie partly in the conscious contents – impressions of the day before, remnants from the current day – partly in the constellated contents of the unconscious, which in turn can come from conscious contents or from spontaneous unconscious processes. These latter processes, betraying no reference to consciousness, can be derived from anywhere. Their origins can be somatic, physical and psychological events in the environment, or events in the past and future; in the latter instance we may think, e.g., of dreams that bring a long past historical occurrence to life or prophetically anticipate a future one. There are dreams that originally had a reference to consciousness but have lost it, as if it had never existed, and now produce completely incoherent, incomprehensible fragments, then again such as represent unconscious psychic contents of the individual without being recognized as such.

4. *Seminar on Children's Dreams*, 1938–9.   5. ibid.

As already said in the first part of this treatise, Jung describes the *arrangement* of the dream images as standing outside the categories of time and space and subject to no causality. 'The dream is a mysterious message from our night-aspect.'[6] The dream is never a mere repetition of previous experiences or events – certain categories of shock-dreams excepted – not even when we believe we recognize it as such. 'It is always knit together or altered according to its end, even though often inconspicuously, but ever in a different way from that which would correspond to the ends of consciousness and causality.'[7]

The possible *significance* of dreams can be reduced to the following typical cases:

Upon a certain conscious situation a dream follows as a reaction of the unconscious, which, supplementing or compensating, refers quite clearly to the impressions of the day, so that it is evident that this dream would never have occurred without a certain impression from the day previous.

The dream follows not upon a certain conscious situation that has – more or less clearly – produced it, but as a result of a certain spontaneity of the unconscious, the latter adding to a certain conscious situation another so different from the first that a conflict arises between the two. While in the first case the fall of potential led from the stronger, conscious part to the unconscious, in the second case equilibrium exists between the two.

When, however, the contrary position, that the unconscious occupies, is stronger than the conscious position, then a fall of potential comes into being that leads from the unconscious to consciousness. Then come those significant dreams that on occasion can completely alter or even reverse a conscious attitude.

The last type, in which the whole activity and all the weight of significance lies in the unconscious, and which furnishes the most peculiar dreams, most difficult to interpret but most important in content, represents unconscious processes that no longer allow one to recognize any relation whatever to consciousness. The dreamer does not understand them and as a rule wonders greatly why he dreams thus, for not even a conditional relation is to be perceived. But just these dreams often have an overpowering character; often, too, they are oracular. Such dreams likewise appear in many cases before the outbreak of mental illnesses and severe neuroses, when a content suddenly bursts to the fore that deeply impresses the dreamer, even though he does not understand it.

In distinguishing between these different types of dreams the weight lies upon the relation in which the reactions of the unconscious stand to the

6. *Wirklichkeit der Seele*, p. 88.
7. *Seminar on Children's Dreams*, 1938–9.

conscious situation. For the most manifold transitions can be found, from a reaction of the unconscious bound to the contents of consciousness up to spontaneous manifestation of the unconscious.[8]

What is now the meaning, and what are the methods of *dream interpretation*?

Every interpretation is an hypothesis, a mere attempt at deciphering an unknown text. Seldom is an isolated, untransparent dream to be interpreted even with approximate certainty. The interpretation first reaches a relative certainty in a series of dreams, in which the subsequent dreams correct the errors in the interpretation of the preceding ones. Jung was the first to investigate whole dream series. He proceeded here from the premise that 'dreams continue like a monologue under the cover of consciousness',[9] although their chronological order does not always coincide with the actual inner order of meaning. Thus it does not unconditionally correspond to a sequence in which dream B would follow from dream A and dream C from dream B. For the real arrangement of dreams is a *radial* one; it is grouped around a 'centre of significance'. Dreams can radiate from a centre, thus:

where dream C can occur before A and dream B just as well after F as before. If this central point is revealed and elevated into consciousness it ceases to work and the dreams arise from a new centre, and so on. It is therefore extremely important that patients be directed continually to 'keep books', so to speak, upon their dreams and their interpretation, by means of which a certain continuity is assured and 'the patient learns to deal with his unconscious satisfactorily'.[10] The psychotherapeutic guidance does not then remain passive but becomes an active cooperation that takes part in the process, indicating the possible meaning of the dream and explaining to the patient what *directions* are open to him. Only after this is the interpretation to be worked up and assimilated consciously by the patient.[11]

The proper interpretation of the dream is generally an exacting task. It requires psychological empathy, ability to make combinations, intuition, familiarity with

8. ibid.
9. ibid.
10. *Modern Man in Search of a Soul*, p. 15.
11. cf. the already mentioned 'dialectical procedure'.

men and things, and above all a *specific knowledge* that depends just as much upon extensive systematic mental education as upon certain *intelligence du coeur*.[12]

Every dream content has always a manifold significance and is, as already said, conditioned by the individuality of the dreamer. To assume standard symbols, to be translated as if out of a dictionary, would be in contradiction of Jung's conception of the nature and structure of the psyche. In order to interpret a content correctly and effectively, one must go at it both with a full knowledge of the life situation and the manifest, conscious psychology of the dreamer and also with an exact reconstruction of the dream context, which is precisely the task of the analysis with its instruments of association and amplification. The psychological context of dream contents consists of that 'tissue of relations in which the dream content is naturally embedded. Theoretically one can never know this in advance and each of its parts must be postulated as unknown.'[13] Only after careful determination of the context may the attempt at an interpretation be made. A result can be reached only when the meaning determined upon the basis of the context has been correlated with the text of the dream itself and in the degree to which the meaning-reaction thus confirmed has been found to make sense. One may not, however, under any circumstances assume that the meaning thus found corresponds to a subjective expectation, for it is often something surprisingly different from what would be expected subjectively. On the contrary, a correspondence with this expectation would give every ground for mistrust. For the unconscious is as a rule amazingly 'different'. Parallel dreams whose meaning coincides with the conscious attitude are extremely rare.[14] Jung contends that one can only seldom draw conclusions from a single dream as to the entire psychic situation – at most it applies to an acute momentary problem or to one aspect of it. Only by observing, following, and interpreting a relatively long series can one gain a full picture of the cause and course of the disorder. The series replaces as it were that context which Freudian analysis seeks to disclose by means of free association. Thus with Jung 'directed association', provoked and guided by the physician on the one hand and self-determined by the chain of manifestations of the unconscious in dreams on the other, assists in revealing and regulating the psychic process. In general the standpoint of the unconscious is complementary or compensatory to consciousness.

Only from the knowledge of the conscious situation is it possible to settle what sign is to be given the unconscious contents. . . . There exists between consciousness and the dream a very finely balanced relationship. . . . In this sense one can

12. *Ueber psychische Energetik*, p. 238.
13. *Seminar on Children's Dreams*, 1938–9.
14. ibid.

declare the principle of compensation to be a fundamental rule of psychic activity in general.[15, 16]

Besides their compensatory relation to the conscious situation, which is the rule for normal persons under normal internal and external conditions, the dream contents also can exercise a reductive or prospective function, compensating either negatively, in that they 'set the individual down, as it were, on to the level of his mortal insignificance and his physiological, historic, and phylogenetic conditionedness'[17] (this material was investigated above all by Freud in an outstanding way), or positively, in that they as a kind of 'guiding conception' give the conscious, self-depreciatory attitude a 'rectified' direction. Both forms can conduce to healing. The prospective function of the dream must be distinguished from its compensatory one. The latter means in the first place that the unconscious, regarded as relative to consciousness, integrates into the conscious situation all the elements that are repressed or disregarded and are lacking to its completeness.

Compensation can be called useful in the sense of a self-regulation of the psychic organism. The prospective function on the other hand is an anticipation of future conscious performances that manifests itself in the unconscious, like a preliminary exercise or a plan sketched in advance.[18]

As is evident from the whole conception of the dream-structure, from the regard paid to the actual conscious situation, from the concept of the contextual and positional value of dream-motives, from the timelessness and spacelessness of the dream-events, the concept of causality in Jungian dream interpretation – in contrast to Freudian – can only be applied in a limited sense. 'This is not a denial of the *causae* of the dream, but a different interpretation of the associative material collected around the dream',[19] and, as we shall see later, a different method for getting to the interpretation of it. Jung does not, indeed, look in the first place for the *causae efficientes*;

15. An example of the compensatory function of the dream would be: someone dreams that it is spring, but his favourite tree in the garden bears only dry branches. This year there are no leaves and blossoms upon it. Thereby the dream means to say: Do you not see yourself in this tree? You are like this! Even though you do not want to be aware of it! The nature in you is dried up, no green grows in you, etc. These dreams are examples for persons whose consciousness has grown autonomous through over-differentiation, has gained too great an overweight. Of course a quite 'unconscious' person who lived wholly for his drives would have dreams that likewise exposed his 'other side'. Careless scoundrels often have, e.g. dreams of a moralizing content, paragons of virtue on the other hand frequently immoral dream pictures.

16. *Modern Man in Search of a Soul*, p. 20.

17. *Ueber psychische Energetik*, p. 186.

18. *Ueber psychische Energetik*, p. 142.

19. ibid., p. 157.

he finds even that 'Dreams are often anticipations that wholly lose their real meaning when regarded only causally. These anticipating dreams often give unmistakable information about the analytical situation, the correct understanding of which is of the greatest therapeutic import.'[20] This holds above all for initial dreams, i.e. those which one has at the commencement of an analysis. For 'every dream is a means of information and control'.[21]

In analysis the way leads into the 'land of childhood', i.e. to that time in which the rational consciousness of the present was not yet separated from the 'historical soul', the collective unconscious, and thus not only into that land where the complexes of childhood have their origin but into a pre-historical one that was the cradle of us all. The individual's separation from the 'land of childhood' is unavoidable, although it leads to such a removal from that twilit psyche of primordial time that a loss of the natural instincts thereby occurs.

The consequence of this is want of instinct and therefore disorientation in general human situations. The separation has, however, also the result that the 'land of childhood' remains definitely infantile and so becomes a constant source of childish inclinations and impulses. Naturally these intruders are highly unwelcome to consciousness, which therefore represses them. This repression merely increases the separation from the source and intensifies the want of instinct to the point of sterile rationalism. Consciousness therefore either is overwhelmed with infantility or must constantly defend itself against it in vain. The one-sidedly rational attitude of consciousness must, in spite of its undeniable successes, be regarded as unadapted and contrary to the demands of life. Life is dried up and longs to return to its source. The source, however, can only be found in the 'land of childhood', where one, as formerly, can receive directions from the unconscious. Not only he is childish, though, who remains a child too long but also he who parts himself from his childhood and supposes it has therewith ceased to exist. For he does not know that everything pertaining to the psyche has a double face. The one looks forward, the other back. It is ambiguous and therefore symbolic, like all living reality . . . In consciousness we stand upon a peak and childishly imagine that the road leads on to greater heights beyond the peak. That is the chimerical rainbow-bridge (see on p. 82 of *The Psychology of Jung*). In order to gain the next peak one goes nevertheless – one must go, if one will reach it – down into the land where the roads first begin to branch.'[22]

'The resistance of consciousness against the unconscious as well as the underestimation of the latter is an historical necessity in evolution, for else consciousness would never have been able to differentiate itself from the unconscious at all.'[23] The consciousness of modern man, though, has removed itself somewhat too far from its origin, the unconscious, and has even forgotten that the latter acts by no means in correspondence with our

20. *Modern Man in Search of a Soul*, p. 9.   21. ibid., p. 21.
22. *Integration of the Personality*, p. 110.   23. ibid., p. 105.

conscious intentions but autonomously. Therefore the approach to the unconscious is for civilized man, primarily because of its threatening likeness to mental disorder, usually associated with panic terror.

To 'analyse' the unconscious as a passive object has nothing hazardous about it for the intellect – on the contrary, such an activity would correspond to rational expectation; but to 'let the unconscious happen' and to 'experience' it as a reality – that exceeds the courage as well as the ability of the average Occidental. He prefers simply not to realize the existence of this problem. The experience of the unconscious is, namely, a personal secret, communicable only with difficulty and only to the very few.[24]

In consequence of the over-differentiation of consciousness in Western man the problem of the approach to the unconscious is a specifically Occidental and modern problem.[25] The establishment of contact between consciousness and the unconscious appears, for example, to be quite a different matter for the Oriental, probably too for the African, etc.

Taking the way to the collective unconscious must be *preceded*, with Jung as with Freud, by making conscious and integrating the infantile contents of the personal unconscious, although Jung draws different deductions: 'The personal unconscious must always be disposed of first, i.e. made conscious',[26] else the way to the collective unconscious is blocked. This means that every conflict must first be taken up and scrutinized in the light of one's personally acquired experiences from that aspect in which it touches the most intimate life of the individual and the acquired psychic contents pertaining to it. For example, if a child is too closely attached to one parent or feels itself oppressed by the superior strength and prowess of an older brother, these conflicts must first be resolved before the patient proceeds to grapple with the broader problems of human existence. This way, leading up to activation of the archetypes and to harmony, to proper equilibrium between consciousness and the unconscious, is the way of 'healing' and, viewed from the technical aspect, the way of dream interpretation. The technique of resolution of a dream can thus – to recapitulate once again – be divided into the following stages: description of the present conscious situation, description of the preceding events, determination of the subjective context, in case of archaic motives comparison with mythological parallels, and finally, in complicated situations, correlation with

24. ibid., p. 106.
25. At the present time one has the impression that among whole groups of peoples these two regions have fallen into complete isolation from one another (for the over-differentiation and over-emphasis of the conscious side have as their consequence the repression and cutting off of the other) and that each exists for itself alone, lacking the healthy counterbalance of the other, compensatory member.
26. ibid., p. 111.

objective information from third persons. On the other hand, the way that the contents of the unconscious take comprises something like the following seven steps:

1. The threshold of consciousness sinks in order that the contents of the unconscious may come up.

2. The contents of the unconscious ascend in dreams, visions, and fantasies.

3. These contents are perceived and held fast by consciousness.

4. The meaning of the various contents is investigated, clarified, interpreted, and comprehended.

5. This meaning is given its place in the total psychical situation of the individual.

6. The individual accepts, digests, and assimilates the meaning found.

7. The integration of the meaning, its organic assimilation into the psyche becomes so complete that it goes over, as it were, 'into the blood' and becomes a piece of instinctive knowledge.

Jung found that most dreams show a certain structural similarity. He conceives even their structure quite differently from Freud, looking upon the majority of dreams as a kind of 'whole' with a rounded-off series of happenings, dramatically structured, and therefore admitting a meaningful grouping of its elements according to the scheme of a classic drama. A dream can be divided into parts in this way as follows:

1. *Time*, *place*, *dramatis personae*, that is, the beginning of the dream which frequently indicates the place where the action of the dream occurs, and the persons acting therein.

2. *Exposition*, i.e. the statement of the dream problem. Here the content is displayed, so to speak, that forms the basis of the dream, the problem, the theme that is given form by the unconscious in the dream, to which the unconscious will now make its pronouncement.

3. *Peripety*, which forms the 'backbone' of every dream, the weaving of the plot, the intensification of events to a crisis or to a transformation, which may also consist in a catastrophe.

4. *Lysis*, i.e. the solution, the result of a dream, its meaningful conclusion, in which it points to the needful compensation. This rough scheme, according to which most dreams are built up, forms a suitable basis for the process of interpretation.[27] Dreams exhibiting no lysis allow one to infer a fatal

27. As an example we can take the following dream of a six-year-old girl from the *Seminar on Children's Dreams* of 1938–9: 'There was a beautiful rainbow that sprang up right before me. I climbed up it till I came into the sky. From there I called down to my friend Marietta to come up too. She fussed so long that the rainbow dissolved and

development in the dreamer's life. But these are quite specific dreams, and they must not be confused with those which the dreamer recalls only fragmentarily or reproduces only incompletely and which therefore end without a lysis. For naturally every phase of a dream can seldom be deciphered at once. It often requires a careful search before its structure is wholly revealed.

Jung has introduced the concept and method of CONDITIONALISM[28] into dream interpretation, i.e. 'under conditions of such and such a kind, such and such dreams can occur'.[29] The decisive factor is thus always the situation in question with its contemporary, momentary conditions. The same problem, the same cause may have, according to the total context, a correspondingly different significance; from the viewpoint of conditionalism they can have many meanings, not just always the same one without regard to the situation and the variability of their forms of appearance. Conditionalism is an expanded form of causality, it is a manifold interpretation of causal relations and constitutes thus an attempt

to conceive strict causality by means of an interplay of conditions, to enlarge the simple significance of the relation between cause and effect by means of the manifold significance of the relations between effects. Causality in the general sense is not thereby destroyed but only accommodated to the many-sided living material,[30]

i.e. broadened and supplemented. Corresponding to this, the meaning of a given dream motive will be explained not only through its causal connections, but also through its 'situational value'[31] within the total dream context. Jung utilizes no 'free association' but a procedure that he calls *Amplification*. He thinks that free association indeed leads

always to a complex, of which it is nevertheless uncertain whether it is precisely this one that constitutes the meaning of the dream. . . . We can, of course, always get to our complexes somehow, for they are the attraction that draws all to itself.[32]

---

she fell down.' The *locality* is that of a natural event: 'There was a beautiful rainbow that sprang up right before me.' The *exposition* also points to this event: the girl climbs up the rainbow till she comes into the sky. The *peripety* or turn of events occurs when she calls to her friend to come up too. The latter hesitates to come, though, and the *lysis* follows: the rainbow dissolves and she falls down to earth.

28. The physiologist and philosopher Max Verworn (Göttingen, 1863–1921), from whom the concept of 'conditionalism' comes, defines it as follows: 'A state or process is unambiguously determined by the totality of its conditions. From this follows: 1. The same states or processes are always the expression of the same conditions; different conditions are expressed in different states and processes. 2. A state or process is identical with the totality of its conditions. From this follows: A state or condition is scientifically completely known when the totality of its conditions is determined' (*Kausale und Konditionale Weltanschauung*, 3rd edn, 1928).

29. *Seminar on Children's Dreams*, 1938–9.   30. ibid.
31. Cf. also p. 75 of *The Psychology of Jung*.   32. ibid.

Perhaps, though, the dream shows exactly the opposite of the content of the complex and means thereby on the one hand to emphasize that natural functioning which would be capable of freeing one from the complex and on the other to point to the way to be followed. Amplification means, therefore, in contrast to the Freudian method of '*reductio in primam figuram*', not a causally connected chain of associations to be followed backward, but a broadening and enrichment of the dream content with all possible similar, analogous images. It is further distinguished from free association in that the associations are contributed not only by the patient or dreamer but also by the physician. Often indeed it is the latter who through his contribution of analogies determines the direction that the associations of the patient take. However various these images may be, they must nevertheless all stand in a meaningful, more or less close relation to the dream content that is to be interpreted, whereas there is no limit to how far free association may lead away from the latter. Amplification is accordingly a kind of limited, bound, and directed association that returns ever and again to the centre of significance given in a dream, revolving as it were about this very centre.

Amplification is always in place where one has to do with an obscure experience, whose scanty hints have to be filled out and broadened by psychological context in order to be made intelligible. Therefore in analytical psychology we make use of amplification in the interpretation of dreams; for the dream is a hint too scanty for comprehension, which consequently must be enriched by associative and analogous material and must be clarified into intelligibility.[33]

33. *Integration of the Personality*, p. 207.

Part Three
Empirical Studies of Dreams

In this part we have tried to gather together some of the more important 'factual' studies of dreams. Reading 5, 'Children's Dreams', by C. W. Kimmins, is virtually a summary of his classic researches which resulted in the publication of his book of the same name in 1920. Following his paper, we include the comments of Paul Kline (in *Fact and Fantasy in Freudian Theory*, Methuen, 1972) upon a paper by Lee which bears many similarities methodologically to the work of Kimmins. The original paper by Lee (1958) is not included in this collection partly for reasons of space, and partly because it has already been reprinted in the Penguin Modern Psychology Readings series (Price-Williams, 1969). Still in the general area of children's dreams, we include a modern study by Foulkes, Larson, Swanson and Rardin which aptly shows the effect of the 'REM revolution' on studies of content.

Readings 8, 9 and 10 examine the relationship between hypnotically induced dreams and nocturnal dreams in order to discover what light can be thrown on the latter. Farber and Fisher describe some of their psychoanalytically oriented research on hypnotic dreams and their paper is followed by Domhoff's review that examines critically the view that hypnotic and nocturnal dreams are essentially different. In Reading 10, Hilgard and Nowlis summarize their research in which the contents of hypnotic and nocturnal dreams are compared. Their work employs the techniques for the analysis of dream content developed by Hall and Van de Castle.

The next Reading by Berger is concerned with dream content, dealing particularly with the experimental influencing of dream content.

Finally, anthropologists, as well as psychologists, have an interest in dreams as possible reflections of cultural values (LeVine, 1966; von Grunebaum and Caillois, 1966) and the summary article by D'Andrade (Reading 12) explains this interest, while covering many of the better known references.

References

KIMMINS, C. S. (1920), *Children's Dreams*, Longman.

LEE, S. G. M. (1958), 'Social influences in Zulu dreaming', *J. soc. Psychol.*, vol. 47, pp. 265–83.

LEVINE, R. A. (1966), *Dreams and Deeds: Achievement Motivation in Nigeria*, University of Chicago Press.

PRICE-WILLIAMS, D. R. (ed.) (1969), *Cross-Cultural Studies*, Penguin.

VON GRUNEBAUM, G. E., and CAILLOIS, R. (1966), *The Dream and Human Societies*, University of California Press.

5 C. W. Kimmins

Children's Dreams

C. W. Kimmins, 'Children's dreams', in C. Murchison (ed.), *A Handbook of Child Psychology*, Clark University Press, 1931, pp. 527–54.

The universality of the dream is in itself evidence of its biological significance, but in the past the scientific study of the dream has left much to be desired.

Concentration on dreams of the neurotic

The experiences of the Great War, however, brought into special prominence the position of the dream and established its importance as a most valuable instrument in the successful diagnosis of certain forms of mental disability caused by the stress and strain and the abnormal conditions imposed by the severe struggle of long-continued warfare. The special hospitals for shell-shock and similar causes of mental disturbance were largely under the control of distinguished psychologists who could use to great advantage the evidence afforded by the dreams of their patients. In many cases such investigation pointed clearly to a distant source of trouble in early childhood by repression of painful experiences, the discovery and release of which resulted in the solution of the difficulty and the ultimate complete recovery of the sufferer.

A brief account of one of these cases, which is fairly typical, will indicate that where every other line of investigation had failed, after most careful and sympathetic study by experts, the dream provided an answer to a problem which appeared to be insoluble. A soldier, fighting in France, with an excellent record, was for a short time buried by the material thrown up by a bursting shell in his immediate neighborhood, and was in total darkness until the dirt was removed. He was sent down to the clearing station and it was found that he had suffered no physical injury but that he had developed acute claustrophobia which made it impossible for him to go into the trenches again. He was sent home and in the hospital did not give the slightest response to any recognized fear tests, but the claustrophobia persisted. Fortunately, he then had a dream which seemed to have a bearing on the case. The man's mother was sent for and, in discussion, it transpired that as a young boy he had been locked up in a dark cupboard for being naughty. He was so terrified that after this painful experience he became docile and well-behaved. On becoming naughty again, after a long interval, he was once more locked up in the cupboard and he was so overcome with terror that he fainted. This experience was so distressing that the memory of it, with its emotional setting, was effectively repressed. After years had elapsed, in the return to a similar condition – the darkness caused by being buried alive – the repressed material augmented the terror of the situation. On relieving the mind of the burden of the repressed material by appropriate means, the claustrophobia disappeared, and the soldier returned to the War and had no further difficulty. Rivers (1923) had a similar claustrophobic case in which, as a boy, his patient had by accident been shut in a dark passage in which the terror was increased by a barking dog. Here also a cure was effected through the evidence afforded by a dream.

Naturally, with the great advance of the dream in its employment in the investigation of neurotic cases, and the improvement of the technique in psychoanalysis, there has been a concentration of attention on the dream in its relation to the flotsam and jetsam of the mental hospital and the consulting room. It is, however, remarkable that so little consideration has been given to the dreams of normal, healthy children. Freud (1900) in the *Traumdeutung* gives approximately 2 per cent of his space to them.

The dreams of normal children

It would be a great mistake to apply the methods which have proved so successful in pathological cases to the dreams of healthy children, although they may occasionally be of considerable value in investigating difficult cases among school children of unstable type who do not respond to ordinary methods of instruction. The dream of the normal child may be invaluable in many directions, but it should always be borne in mind that the problem is a different one from the investigation of the dream of the neurotic. There is undoubtedly a rich field for research in connection with the dreams of normal children which may yield a harvest as abundant in educational procedure as that obtained by psychoanalysis in the realm of pathology.

In *The Common Sense of Dreams*, Watt (1929), in suggesting simpler methods of interpretation, gives examples of dreams interpreted by well-known authorities and compares them with the same dreams interpreted by himself. Two of these examples are the dreams of children. Here is one (interpreted by Dr Nicoll):

I dreamed that I was in a swimming-bath full of water. My form master stood on the edge, in a red bathing-suit, and pushed me away with a long pole whenever I tried to climb out. I swam round and round in despair (p. 186).

The other (interpreted by Dr Constance Long):

Annie and I were playing in the nursery. There was an awful rumbling and the floor split open. A big dragon came out and stole my sister and swallowed her up. I was very frightened and ran to my father, who came and killed the dragon, and my sister got out (p. 189).

The age of the schoolboy of the first dream is not given, that of the second boy was seven years. The very marked divergence of the conclusions reached by two recognized experts, in full possession of the details, is illuminating as showing that the interpretation of children's dreams by adult methods is of comparatively little value. The varying symbolism from age to age, and, moreover, the extraordinary difficulty of obtaining a sufficiently accurate description of a child's dream to use it as the subject of a meticulous analysis make such an attempt a perilous enterprise.

Investigation of children's dreams

In his investigations, the writer, as a Chief Inspector of the various types of schools in London, had access to an unlimited amount of suitable material. He also had the invaluable assistance of teachers in the schools in which the children recorded their dreams. No preliminary notice of any kind was given to the children so that no discussion or preparation was possible. That this condition was carried out effectively was evident from the extraordinary variety of dream material obtained from pupils in the same class.

The dreams of very young children were related individually to skilled observers, but all dreams of children of eight years of age and over were recorded by the dreamers themselves in response to the request: 'Write a true and full account of the last dream you can remember. State your age, and also say about how long ago you had the dream you have described.'

The numbers of dreams obtained from various sources were approximately:

150 from boys and girls, five, six, and seven years of age, in infants' schools
2000 from boys, eight to fourteen years of age, in elementary schools
2000 from girls, eight to fourteen years of age, in elementary schools
300 from boys and girls, ten to fifteen years of age, in central schools
600 from boys and girls, ten to eighteen years of age, in secondary schools
300 from boys, ten to sixteen years of age, in industrial schools
300 from girls, ten to sixteen years of age, in industrial schools
110 from boys and girls, ten to sixteen years of age, in schools for the blind
140 from boys and girls, ten to sixteen years of age, in schools for the deaf

In spite of fear dreams, children in normal health delight in dreaming, and it is an evident pleasure to them to talk about or record their dreams (Sully, 1896). It will be seen by the children's accounts of their dreams that they have an abnormal power of graphic description of events in which they are intensely interested, such as those supplied by the dream material. This power so far exceeds their ability in ordinary essay-writing on topics selected by the teacher, and is, moreover, so much in advance of their general standard of achievement, that it would appear as if some fresh mental element had come into play. The matter is worthy of further investigation.

In analysing the children's dreams, the following, among other elements, have been considered: the various types of wish-fulfilment and fear dreams; kinaesthetic dreams; references to fairy stories; compensation dreams; dreams of bravery and adventure; school activities; cinemas; exciting books and death incidents; dreams in which conversations are recorded; and the presence of other witnesses than the dreamer.

The analysis simply attempts a rough classification of the type of dream peculiar to children of different ages, showing the variation from year to year and the influence of environment. The large number of dreams investigated makes the conclusions reliable within this limited sphere and points the way to a more detailed and thorough investigation. The educational possibilities of such a fascinating line of inquiry are unlimited.

Most of the dreams were recorded in November and December 1918, but those from industrial schools were obtained in March and April 1919, and those from the schools for the blind and deaf in June 1919.

An attempt was made to analyse on a similar plan the dreams of training-college students of eighteen to twenty-two years of age, but the majority of them were so heavily camouflaged that it was impossible for anyone who was not a trained expert in psychoanalysis to deal with them satisfactorily. The writer, therefore, confined his attention entirely to the dreams of school children.

Much more recently similar investigations have been carried out among a large group of physically defective children in a residential school in England. Records of a large number of dreams written under exactly the same conditions as those of the London children have also been obtained from children in American, French, and German schools. They present so many points of interest that further investigation on a more comprehensive scale would probably yield important results as indicating the child's attitude to life, as represented by the dream, at similar ages, under varying types of environment in different countries.

The nature of the dream

There are various theories with regard to the nature and purpose of the dream, of which the most important are those associated with the names of Freud, Rivers, and Watt. Freud (1900) contends that the dream is the fulfilment of a wish and that every dream has a meaning and has psychic value. Rivers (1923) regards the purpose of the dream to be the solution of a conflict, whereas Watt (1929) maintains that the removal of a reluctance or reluctances is the chief function. From the investigation of a large number of children's dreams, it would appear that, in the majority of cases, the wish-fulfilment theory affords the most obvious solution in the explanation of the dream. On the other hand, it does not appear possible, without an extension of the normal meaning of words, to bring every dream into the wish-fulfilment category.

Freud admits that children's dreams generally contain no problem to be solved. There is no necessary division into latent and manifest content. The oft-quoted Simony Hut dream (Freud, 1900), in which a child dreamed, after seeing the Hut through a telescope, that the arduous climb was over and that the Hut had been reached, is typical. He (Freud) expresses a strong doubt whether an unfulfilled wish from the day before – as in children's dreams – would suffice to create a dream in an adult. Similarly, the effect of reading a book the day before in producing a dream, also quoted by Freud, would rarely have any influence on an adult's dream:

A boy of eight dreamt that he was being driven with Achilles in a war chariot guided by Diomedes. The day before he was assiduously reading about great heroes (Watt, 1929, p. 101).

In the writer's collection of dreams, a crippled boy of nine, who had evidently been reading about St George and the dragon, gives the following account of a vivid dream:

Last night I dreamt that I was a brave Knight. A great big monster came running after the most beautiful lady I ever saw. I drew my sword and hit the monster on his back. He roared so loud that the lady screamed. I said, 'I will soon slay this monster,' and I hit him again and then I cut off its head, and he fell dead on the ground. The lady said 'You are a hero.' Then I awoke (Kimmins, 1926, p. 43).

The dream makes a very strong appeal to the young child principally because of the close relationship which exists between it and the fairy story (Sully, 1896). The conditions of the dream, with the complete absence of anything in the nature of critical reasoning, are obviously favorable to freedom for an extended use of absurd combinations in the bringing together of a great variety of previous experiences, not in their original connections, but in a new orientation, to meet the purposes of the dream. Many of these amusing combinations found in the dream would have been impossible in the waking condition without the very rare gift of an imagination capable of freeing itself from the chains of conventional methods of grouping experiences.

Bergson (see Kimmins, 1928, p. 53), who lays great stress on the presentative nature of the origin of dreams, points out that in the dream we can analyse sense impressions received from the outside world and use those elements necessary to satisfy the mood of the dreamer and the idea that fills his imagination at the time. Thus 'a gust of wind blowing down the chimney becomes the howl of a wild beast or a tuneful melody'.

The sense of time and also that of distance are obliterated; the dreamer suddenly finds himself in a different part of the world and as suddenly finds himself at home (Sully, 1896). All this adds to the wonder and charm of the dream for the child. Normal, healthy children are very rarely seen to laugh in their dreams (Kimmins, 1928), though they frequently smile, probably as the result of the pleasure derived from wish-fulfilment rather than the appreciation of any humorous element, which is recognized as humorous, in the dream state. Any evidence to the contrary is probably due to a confusion of the hypnagogic – or half-waking – state with that of true sleep. In this connection the records of dreams are more reliable than the observation of sleepers.

There is the same absence of amusement and laughter in the dreams of American children. Here is an example of one of their ludicrous fear dreams:

Once I dreamt that I was captured by cannon balls (evidently cannibals). They all began to jump and yell. I was surprised to see myself in my own parlor. There was a fire, and a kettle was over it full of boiling water. They threw me into it and once in a while the cook used to come over and stick a fork into me to see if I was cooked. Then he took me out and gave me to the chief, who was just going to bite me when I woke up (Kimmins, 1928, p. 57).

In the dreams recorded in connection with the writer's investigation, there are numerous examples of that sudden switching off from one line of thought to another which appears to be far more characteristic of children's than of adults' dreams. For example, a girl who is swimming to save a friend from drowning meets a teacher in the water, who tells her to go back to school at once, because she has been selected to take the part of Julius Caesar in the play. In other cases, in accounts given of very dramatic incidents, some school incidents, frequently of having sums marked, is interpolated, and then the action continues as if there had been no break in the exciting narrative.

As can be seen by the results of the analyses of children's dreams, the content of the dream varies from age to age in the type of wish-fulfilment, fear, main interest, and other particulars. It varies also with the state of health of the child. Certain elements appear practically at the same age with groups of children, and others disappear in equally regular order. A comparative study of wish-fulfilments is most illuminating in showing the change of interest as age increases.

A series of dreams of the same child recorded within a short time of each other, although they contain a variety of very different material, have certain characteristics of a constant nature which enter into the constitution of each and not only afford an excellent clue to the child's chief interests, but give a certain amount of evidence as to the type of mental make-up to which it belongs.

In the records of many dreams conversations are given, but these are lacking in interest. Compared with the imagery, the grotesque and irrational grouping of incidents, the conversation, which obeys a certain logical order, appears commonplace. From the investigations it appears that boys and girls of the ages of twelve and thirteen dream far less than before or after-wards. The age of maximum dreaming is given by different observers as between twenty and twenty-five years. Generally speaking, dreams increase with the variety and activity of the intellectual life (de Manacéine, 1897).

The general impression among young children is that cheese is the source of every bad thing in dreaming, and many state that for pleasant dreams the best preparation is cocoa and bread and butter for supper. There is also an impression that lying on the right side is better than the left for good dream-ing. There is much evidence in the records that any complaint involving a high temperature has a most serious effect on the nature of the dream.

According to Stern (1914), in his *Psychology of Early Childhood*, dream-ing goes back as far as the child's first year, and, although spontaneous recitals of dreams seldom occur before the fifth year, the psychoanalysts make use of the dreams of two year olds. He is of the opinion that generally dream concepts have some connection with the child's experiences of the day before the dream. With many other observers, he considers that indigestion, an over-full bladder, or a disturbed circulation may materially affect the nature of the dream.

The nature of the dream is well summarized by Watt (1929, p. 98) in the chapter on 'Reflection' in *The Common Sense of Dreams*:

The dreaming mind, we may suppose, is working on an averagely lower level and within a narrower field. Its power of abstraction is weakened and it does not make the effort of reflection required to bring its operations into connection with their intellectual causes or occasions and so to survey their adequacy as solutions methodically and logically. In other words, dreams are reveries, not acts of hard thinking.

The day-dream

The distinction between the night-dream and the day-dream is simply one of degree. In the day-dream there is also a withdrawal of the attention, more or less complete, from external sources, and there is also a greater or less degree of mental automatism. As pointed out in 'The psychology of day-dreams' (Stanley Hall and his pupils) (1907): 'The daydream shades off by almost imperceptible gradations through hypnagogic states to the dreams of sleep.' Stanley Hall's pupils express in a variety of ways the dangers of excessive day-dreaming as, for example, 'I think it is a bad habit and I wish I could stop it. It interferes with study and makes me dissatisfied with reality.' 'In the daydreams you let your mind go where it wants to and this is bad, the more I daydream the harder it is to come back to reality.'

There is no question as to the great pleasure to be derived from the reveries of day dreaming. They afford great relaxation to the mind; but the servant may become the master, and mental imagery may control the mind. Day-dreaming is often associated with high intellectual endowment and creative ability (Walsh, 1920). Robert Louis Stevenson (1904) in his 'Chapter on dreams' in the book of essays, *Across the Plains*, fully acknowledges the enormous advantage he derived from night- and day-dreaming, as in *The Strange Case of Dr Jekyll and Mr Hyde*. A long list might be given of great artists, novelists, and scientific discoverers who have contributed similar acknowledgements. Herbert Spencer was a great day-dreamer.

Normal healthy children day-dream, and in the night-dream there is frequently an overflow from the day's experiences in which any difficulties with regard to non-fulfilment of wishes are successfully overcome (Sully, 1896). The father who refuses to buy his boy a bicycle in the day becomes more generous in the boy's dream at night, in which he gets the bicycle. Where the day-dream finds expression in action later on it is of definite value to the child, but where it becomes an end in itself, simply for the pleasure it gives, there is a positive danger that it may unfit the boy or girl to face the ordinary difficulties of life successfully (Walsh, 1920).

The lonely or neglected child or one who suffers from a fully developed inferiority complex may find great solace in the day-dream and become increasingly out of touch with the healthy mental and physical activities of childhood. In many cases of ultimate imbecility the origin of the mental weakness may be traced to excessive day-dreaming.

Some children hold up to ridicule the production of absent-mindedness as the result of the day-dream. Here is an essay of a young girl:

A girl carrying a pail of milk on her head started day dreaming. She will buy hens with the price of the milk, and then the hens will lay eggs and produce many chickens. She will then become rich and go to a ball in a fine dress. She tossed her head as she refused charming suitors, and the pail fell off, and so ended her dream (Kimmins, 1926, p. 43).

Many childish fantasies may be included in the category of day-dreaming. Mary Chadwick (1928), in *Difficulties in Child Development*, regards some of these as an extension of 'let-us-pretend' games, which are so popular with young children. There appears, however, to be a specific purpose in every well-known fantasy. The peek-a-boo fantasy is one of the first to develop. A prominent fear of the child is that parent or nurse may be lost, but this game accustoms the child to going and returning. It reassures the child with reference to vanishing and reappearance. The threat, 'If you are not good I will go away and leave you', is known by the nurse to be very effective. A child does not like shut eyes and will try to open the eyes of others. When a child's eyes are shut the parent or nurse vanishes. Peek-a-boo is a basic fantasy and has all sorts of offspring as, for example, putting in the corner with the face to the wall.

The invisible-friend fantasy is very common with children from three to six years of age. It is a great relief (Chadwick, 1928) to have an invisible friend who is made to bear the child's own shortcomings. It is a mistake to impose authority on children at too early a stage; likewise it is a mistake for them not to indulge in make-believe, for this gives them a good opportunity of getting rid of primitive tendencies in a natural way without repression. The child is more imaginative because he has a wider range of outlook. Chadwick (1928) says that 'only or lonely children will always be the greatest weavers of phantasy'. The fantasy-maker must always be found in the chief role like the dreamer. Pretending to be grown-up is generally a favorite game for the young children. In childish fantasies the king frequently represents the father and the queen the mother. Fantasies of a happy home by children who are miserable in surroundings in which practically no love exists are very common as, for example, in the Cinderella fantasy. Cases of the assumption of invalidism by children who can only in that way find love and sympathy and dominate the home are well known. The craving for sympathy and 'a place in the sun' occupies a very important place in the life of a young child and gives rise to various forms of fantasy.

Varendonck (1921), by his classical searches on his own day-dreams, has raised the subject which he has undertaken, *The Psychology of Day-Dreams*, to a very high level. His study, although in a limited field, is, and must remain, an inspiration to all workers interested in the investigation of day-dreams. His book will also prove of great value to the student of the night-dream, for many of his conclusions, and the full statement of the methods by which they were reached, apply with equal force to the allied investigation. The close relation of the day- to the night-dream has already been considered. The egocentricity of the dreamer in both departments is well known. The matter for regret is that, in the circumstances, no reference was possible by Varendonck to the dreams of children.

Many investigations of the day-dream deal almost entirely with the psychology of the subject. Green (1923), in his book on *The Day-Dream*, while not neglecting the psychological aspect, stresses the educational point of view and makes his investigation, as appears in the subtitle, *A Study in Development*. With this more ambitious objective he achieves considerable success. In the day-dream you get a view of the real child, his main interests, and an indication of the mental make-up at different phases of his development far better than can be obtained in the comparatively artificial atmosphere of the classroom. This can be shown very clearly by a statement Green makes in dealing with the 'group' or 'team' stage of development.

The occurrence of the day-dream of the 'team' at the age of ten or thereabouts and the differences which mark it off from the egoistic day-dreams of the preceding period, suggest very strongly that the age of ten marks a time of transition between, say, 'childhood' and 'boyhood' or 'girlhood', just as the age of three appears to mark a transition between 'infancy' and 'childhood'. There is the further suggestion, also, that the type of education that is suitable for children below ten is not suited to children above ten, since the day-dreams are evidence that the developments which follow the tenth year are not merely a continuation of those of the earlier years. That there is such a transition is suggested by other evidence, such as that of the curve of physical growth (1923, p. 146).

Another reference to the same period is worthy of note:

The normal child of from ten to fourteen or fifteen years of age has his 'imagination' fixed upon a series of 'we will' interests. Many of those who control him wish him to set aside these and to concentrate his 'will' upon a series of 'I must' matters. Many of these latter might be translated into the 'we will' form, and the results gained a great deal more easily (1923, p. 147).

From the day-dreaming standpoint, the normal stages of development are birth to three years of age (nutrition); three to ten years of age, the development of the self-attitude; ten to fourteen years, the development of the group-attitude; and from fourteen to the end of growth, the romance period. In the writer's investigations of the night-dream, the interests which are found to dominate the different periods give considerable support to the conclusions reached in the study of the day-dream.

The dreams of children of five, six, and seven years of age

In the infants' schools, apart from a few written records by clever children of seven years of age, the dreams were told to the head mistresses individually, and not in the presence of other children, to avoid all possibility of suggestion.

In dealing with the dreams of very young children, both in spoken and written records, there are many difficulties which must be borne in mind in estimating the value of the results. The more important of these are:

1. That young children have great difficulty in separating the dreaming from the waking element.

2. That their powers of description are naturally very limited, and that their use of words may convey to the adult mind a very different impression from that which they wish to convey.

3. That the child will inevitably fill up gaps in the dream, and will reject as absurd some items in the dream which are contrary to his own experience.

4. A dream described even a few hours after awaking is a very different record from that obtained directly the child awakes, in consequence of the fusion of the dream material with waking thoughts.

Anything, therefore, in the nature of a full analysis of a young child's dream would be valueless. All that can be done is to classify the dream elements into definite groups.

In the dream records there are to be found a considerable variety of fulfilled wishes. With the five-year-old children, due to the time of their recording, about 15 per cent were prospective dreams of Christmas with Santa Claus and his presents. The decoration of the classrooms for Christmas festivities gave a great stimulus to this type of dream. With very young children the fear dream is unduly prominent. In this investigation no less than 25 per cent were of this nature. Wild animals and old men who run after the children (the 'bogey' man) figure prominently. At seven years of age children, both boys and girls, dream more about burglars than at any other age. The fear dream of animals is, curiously enough, far more common among the boys than the girls.

School activities are rarely mentioned in the records of the dreams. In the infants' school only about 1 per cent of the dreams are of this type. At these ages fairy-story dreams are common with girls but are not so frequently experienced by boys. The effect of the cinema is felt very little in the girls' dreams, but in the boys', especially at the age of seven, it is an important factor. It is significant that infant school children dream far less about food than the children in the senior departments.

Some of the more interesting facts which emerge from the consideration of the dreams of these young children are the following:

1. The passing of the ghost and the coming of the fairy. The ghost, which was in days gone by the terror of the dreaming child, has almost entirely disappeared. The fairy dream is generally one of pure enjoyment, the only objectionable feature is the appearance of the witch, which, however, is a comparatively rare occurrence.

2. At five years of age, the child is the center of the dream and is rarely a passive observer. Family relationships are not fully realized. There are many incongruities which will be seen in the following dreams:

(a) 'A burglar came into my house and stole Mother's money. He stuck a knife into me, and I dreamt that he had shot another boy after he had killed me.'

(b) 'A tiger came to our house and ate Mummy and Daddy and my brother and me and then I woke up and cried and said, "It isn't true."'

(c) 'I dreamt that teacher was married in a church and the church had flowers all over, and the gas was alight. Teacher went into a motor car and had a nice tea party.'

(d) After a visit of the King and Queen to her neighborhood, a girl of five dreamed that 'a lady was sitting on my bed, and the King and Queen were under the bed eating bread and butter and a lot of ladies were with them.'

(e) 'I dreamt that a robber came to our house and broke all the cups.'

This dream had an interesting sequel. On investigation it was found that this boy had broken a cup and was in constant fear that his mother would find it out. If the robber broke the cups it would never be known that he had broken one; so that the boy's dream was clearly a wish-fulfilment.

3. At the age of five, the experiences of conscious life carry over into the unconscious. The child mixes up the dreaming with the waking elements.

4. At the age of seven, there is a great advance. The family relationship is fully realized, and members of the family group take part in the dream. The child is not so much the central figure. At this age, he recognizes the dream phenomenon as a thing apart. There is also less confusion between the dreaming and the waking experiences, and the record of the dream becomes much more valuable.

A few examples of the dreams of children of this age will illustrate this:

(a) 'The sun and moon were on the floor in my room, so that I could not walk about, and so I went to heaven where all the lights were up, and there were many colours.'

(b) 'I dreamt a dustman put me in a box and took me in a cart, and brought me back to the wrong bed, but when I woke up, I was in the right bed.'

(c) 'I dreamt there were burglars in the room and they lit the fire and sat in a chair, and got green curtains by the door. There were flowers in the next-door garden; the burglars took them and they gave me two stamps and a sheet of paper.'

(d) 'I went to my aunty's and she gave me some biscuits; we had a tea party and a soldier on crutches came in and he said to my aunty, "Have a waltz."'

5. The dream appears to vary with the sex, temperament, and health of the child. A careful record of the dreams of children, especially those of a neurotic type, throughout the year, would be very valuable.

6. Children in poor districts dream far more about toys than do those in the well-to-do sections.

7. There appears to be no connection of the amount of dreaming with intelligence, though this appears later. Dull children dream quite as much as bright children.

8. The dreams of young children are vivid and very real. A boy of six dreamed that someone had given him a three-penny piece, and on waking, searched the bed for it.

9. The death element comes into the dreams of delicate, neurotic children, but rarely into those of healthy, normal children.

10. The rare dreams of school activities are generally associated with the playground rather than the classroom.

11. Dreams of bravery and adventure, which are common in the senior school, rarely come into the dreams of the children in the infants' school. Here is an exception. A boy of seven dreamed:

'I was an American soldier, and I had an army of soldiers, and we went into Germany and we captured the Kaiser and Little Willie.'

12. Young children sometimes imagine that they take other forms; for example, a nervous boy of five, whose father was a baker, had two dreams of this character:

(a) 'I was in a loaf of bread, and a German cut it into little bits, and saw me; I flew away – I had wings on me.'
(b) 'I was in a kettle and I drank up all the water. Mother could not find me; I went under the gas-pipes.'

One boy of five dreamed that he was a little girl; another of the same age, that he was a horse.

13. Kinaesthetic elements are uncommon in the dreams of very young children. They appear generally at about ten years of age and become very vivid and frequent at the ages of eleven and twelve.

Young children's dreams are much simpler (Sully, 1896) than those of adults, even when full allowance has been made for the inevitable simplification produced in the course of the child's narrative by the limitation of vocabulary and descriptive accuracy. They are not so clearly marked off by an atmosphere of unreality, and, moreover, they are not infrequently reported as actual occurrences.

According to Freud (1900), as has been pointed out, the unfulfilled wishes of the day preceding are insufficient to produce a dream in adults. In young children, on the other hand, the dream is often much concerned with the events of yesterday. Retrospective dreams, however, in which the dreamer goes back to an earlier stage of his existence, are far more common in the dreams of adolescents and adults. The dreams in the infants' schools having been collected at the end of November and during December accounts for so many prospective dreams of Christmas. In their dreams the actual presents are described in detail. The doll with the inevitable doll's pram bulks largely in the young girl's dream. Even up to the age of nine years, the wish for the 'pram' is definitely mentioned with the doll in 90 per cent of the dreams of this type.

The fact that very young children dream far less about food than the older children indicates that they are the last to suffer in the case of food shortage in the home. The dream is a sure indication of the position of the child in this respect, as is clearly shown by a comparison of the proportion of food dreams among children in poor and well-to-do districts. The child who dreams frequently about food may reasonably be assumed to be an underfed child. A striking case is recorded of the value of the dream in this connection. A well-known investigator was carrying on a research on the physiological effects of a short period of starvation. He remained without food for six days, and after the first day was not conscious of any personal inconvenience, but every night he dreamed of having hearty meals, though he had never experienced this type of dream before. On resuming his normal life, the food dreams ceased.

The association of the disappearance of the ghost with the advent of the fairy story is supported by evidence of the dreams of older children. There is a tendency for the ghost to reappear when the interest in the fairy story ceases, and it is much more common in boys' than in girls' dreams. Other reasons for the disappearance are the general decline of a belief in ghosts and the decrease in the amount of ghost-story literature.

The state of health of the child has an important influence on the dream. During any complaint which involves the raising of the normal temperature, dreams become much more frequent, there being often three or four in one night. The dream alters in type, and becomes increasingly vivid, and not infrequently the death element enters. The dream now conforms more closely to the neurotic type, but becomes normal again on the child's restoration to health.

In the infants' school, the careful study of dreams may yield very valuable results in giving additional information as to the actual normal temperament of the child, its unfulfilled wishes, its state of health, and in children of the neurotic type it may give important clues to the basis of the mental instability. With monthly records extending over a year, the persistent elements in the dream could be separated from the waking elements, and this would give a valuable insight into the mental make-up of the child.

Dreams of children of eight to fourteen years of age

The large number of children in the London elementary schools available for obtaining dreams makes the results far more reliable than those of the special schools such as those for the blind and deaf where much less material could be secured for the investigation. In selecting schools for the experiment, care was taken that they should be representative of the poorer as well as the districts in which the children came from fairly well-to-do homes. Comparatively few of the children under the age of fourteen came from secondary schools. In discussing rather fully the different points which emerged from the investigation, it will be noticed that many matters require much more detailed examination than was possible in the rough analysis of such a large mass of material.

The number of clearly expressed fulfilled wishes differs considerably in boys' and girls' dreams, the percentage varying from about 28 in the case of boys to 42 in the case of girls. The nature of the wishes also varies. The girl dreams far more about the return of father and relatives from the War, about presents of various kinds, about eating, and, above all, about visits to the country, travelling, and entertainments. On the other hand, boys have six times as many dreams about bravery and adventure as the girls, and these might reasonably be included among the wish-fulfilment dreams. At the age of thirteen, there is a marked increase in this type of dream among the girls.

The eating element in dreams falls off after the age of ten, and presents, other than food, decrease after this age, whereas the dreams of visits to the country tend to increase. Dreams of presents and eating, at all ages from nine to fourteen, are much more common with children from the poorer than from those in the more well-to-do districts.

Boys have more fear dreams (19 per cent) than girls (16 per cent). The most marked difference is in the fear of burglars and robbers, which appears twice as often in boys' as in girls' dreams. Girls dream rather more of strange men and women than boys, but the difference is not marked. It is the old man who is the terror of the dreaming boy and girl. He is responsible in both cases for about half the fear dreams. The fear of animals is practically the same in both sexes and is the cause of about 20 per cent of fear dreams. The larger animals, for example, lions, tigers, and bulls, predominate in boys', and dogs, rats, mice, and snakes in girls' dreams. The ghost has practically disappeared from the child's dream, but occurs occasionally when the fairy-story dream begins to wane. It is more common in boys' than in girls' dreams. Dreams of the house being on fire affect the boy equally with the girl; rather less than 10 per cent of fear dreams are of this nature.

Among kinaesthetic dreams are included falling dreams, loss of muscular control in movement and speech, and dreams in which excessive movement is the predominating element. Dreams of this type occur only occasionally among children of eight and nine years of age, and at these ages much more frequently among boys than girls. It is at the age of ten that they form an important element in children's dreams, and from that age to fourteen they increase steadily. Boys have more kinaesthetic dreams than girls, the proportion being ten to seven. The gliding, floating, and swimming elements are more common among girls, and the falling element among boys. The unmistakable appearance of this type of dream as an important factor at the age of ten deserves full investigation. It would appear, from the analysis of dream elements, that the well-to-do child is more subject to this kind of dream than the poorer child.

Although the normal child spends nearly half the day in, or associated with, the school, it is remarkable that so few dreams have any direct reference to the school; and, where this is the case, the reference is rather to the activities of the playground and swimming-bath than to those of the classroom. The girls' dreams are more influenced by school activities than the boys', but the number is almost negligible. There is not the slightest evidence of worry or overstrain in this connection even in the classroom dream. Rehearsals and performances of plays are occasional elements in dreams, and the striking success of the dreamer in his or her part is not infrequently a source of gratification. Indirectly, the school has a great influence on the dream. The fairy story has a very marked effect. The teacher, moreover, especially in girls' dreams, figures very prominently in dreams of many out-of-school experiences.

Most of the accounts of the dreams were written six months after the last air raid was experienced in London. It is interesting to observe that, especially among the children of eight and nine years of age, the memory of the air raid has practically ceased to trouble the dreamer. Among the older children, dreams of raids, especially girls' dreams, appear to be more in evidence, but they are generally vivid dreams, not of recent date.

In references to bravery and adventure there is a very marked difference between boys' and girls' dreams. The War had a much greater effect on the boys than on the girls. Even at the age of eight, boys dream of performing heroic deeds; at nine years of age, the number of dreams containing these elements increases, and continues to increase to the end of the elementary-school period. A large proportion of the dream elements of the boy are of this nature. The dreamers are often mentioned in dispatches, win the Victoria Cross, are personally thanked by the King, and on returning home from the war, are cheered by grateful crowds. Girls' dreams of bravery and adventure do not occur before the age of ten and the number of such dreams is insignificant until the age of thirteen, when there is a decided change, and deeds of valor, generally as Red Cross nurses on the battlefield, are not infrequent. The total number of boys' dreams involving deeds of valor, compared with girls', is as six to one.

Whatever may be the indirect influence of the cinema on the dreaming child, only a relatively small number of dreams appear to be directly affected, and this occurs chiefly among the older boys. The number of girls' dreams directly influenced is insignificant. The book read just before going to bed affects the dreamer and is often referred to by an explanatory note following the record of a strange dream, in which the child takes the part of one of the leading characters. Similar explanations are also sometimes given of what are evidently cinema dreams.

The influence of fairy stories on the dreamer, especially the girl dreamer, is very marked. Greatest at eight years of age, it has a considerable effect throughout the school period. Generally, the dream of this type is of the most pleasurable nature. The number of girls' dreams influenced by fairy stories is four times as great as in the case of boys. Above the age of ten the fairy story ceases to have much effect on the boys' dreams.

Definitely recorded conversations are common in children's dreams, and they are rather more frequent in girls' than in boys' dreams. At eight years of age they are comparatively rare, and at ten reach the maximum; then, in boys' dreams they decrease in number at subsequent ages, whereas among girls the maximum is reached at the same age, but the proportion is practically retained until the end of the school period.

Dreams in which the interest centers around the death of the dreamer or of some friend are not uncommon, even among children of eight years of age. Rarely the older child dreams that he is present as a spectator at his own funeral and describes the scene.

In the dream of the very young child, the dreamer is generally the only witness of the dream; later, the mother is often present, and at eight or nine years of age, other members of the family and sometimes schoolmates take part. At ten and eleven years of age, the boy's chum and the particular friend of the girl, practically always of the same sex as the dreamer, tend to replace members of the family group; and at subsequent ages, the dreamer alone, or the dreamer and friend are generally the central figures. The proportion of dreams in which the friend or friends of the dreamer take an active part is fairly constant, both in boys' and girls' dreams, throughout the school period.

Anything in the nature of sentiment between members of the opposite sex is very rarely found in the dreams of children from eight to fourteen years of age, but it is more common in girls' than in boys' dreams.

From such a large number of dreams, it is very difficult to make a selection to illustrate even a small number of the many points which have arisen during the course of the investigation.

Two examples are given of dreams of children of eight years of age, one of a boy of imaginative type and the other of a girl whose dream is based upon an air-raid experience. The mothering attitude of young girls in looking after brothers and sisters in times of danger finds expression in this record.

(a) I cannot tell you my dream last night, but I can tell you my other dream the night before. I dreamt that I was going to be washed. After I was washed, I was wrung out in the mangle. Then I was hung on the line. I was hanging on the line when it started to rain. My mother took me in and ironed me. The iron was hot. And then I woke up.

(b) I dreamt I was married and had a little girl at school, also I had a little baby. My husband was a soldier in France. My girl had long curly hair. She wore a white frock with a blue sash and white shoes and stockings. But one night as I got into bed I heard the maroons go off. My children were fast asleep, so I got the eldest up first. I dressed them, and put their hats and coats on and then dressed myself. Then I ran down the tube. A little while after I heard it was all clear, and when I got home I had just put my children to bed, when I heard a rat-tat. I went and opened the door, and my husband walked in. He was home on leave. He was an officer. I was a school teacher. I had the first class. When I woke up, I found it was only a dream.

The following dream of bravery and adventure, of a girl of thirteen years of age who was interested in the Fulham election, is typical of the bellicose attitude at this age.

I dreamt I was elected MP for Fulham. Lloyd George decided to send me out to Germany to try and persuade the Kaiser to give up fighting. I do not know how I got to Germany. I was suddenly there. The Kaiser took a fancy to me, and I lived at his palace and was educated with his children. There were four girls and three boys, and they all were dressed in brown holland. There were two other children living with us, a small French boy and an English girl. One day the Kaiser took us for a drive in his motor, and as we were going up a very steep hill, I asked the Kaiser to give up fighting. He was so amazed that he let go of the steering-wheel, and the car slid backwards down the hill and shot us through the palace windows into the dancing hall where the dancing mistress was waiting to give a lesson. Presently the Kaiser called us and told us that he must fly to Holland and that the German fleet was going to surrender. I then escaped in a submarine, and woke up when it bumped against the shores of England.

At the period of twelve to fifteen years of age children frequently have death dreams. Here is one of a girl of thirteen which is fairly typical:

Last night I had a most peculiar dream, part of which I cannot recall. At first I saw my brother in naval uniform on a ship. I then saw my mother crying, and then I seemed to be gazing into nothingness. Previous to this period I was standing beside my teacher having my sums marked. Again I saw my brother, then slowly he faded away, and all seemed in a confusion. Gradually my mother came into sight, and then a military funeral. The coffin which I dreamt bore my brother was covered with a Union Jack and crowned with flowers. This was not all; beside me in full uniform stood my brother, who was viewing his own funeral. Then came the conclusion, I saw my mother weeping, then everything faded away, and, when I awoke, I discovered that my pillow was wet with tears.

Rivers (1923), in *Conflict and Dream*, makes special reference to the night-mare:

There is little doubt that infancy and childhood form a period of life in which the human being is liable to affective disturbances of a very intense kind with the crude explosive nature which is characteristic of the nightmare.

It appears from the writer's investigation that children of twelve to fifteen years of age when suffering from influenza, or any illness involving a high temperature, are specially liable to this pathological type of dream.

The following is a particularly interesting dream, or rather series of three dreams, which were dreamed in the same night by a girl of twelve years of age. In each part the kinaesthetic element predominates. The rapid transition from one type of experience to another is very striking and assumes rather the form of a continuous nightmare than a normal dream. For convenience, it is divided into three sections.

Section 1. At the beginning I found myself in the house next door, with a lot of horrid men running after me, and when they caught me they said they were going to kill me, so I was put out between two lions and in ten minutes a huge wave was coming up the road and it came right over me. Then I heard some clapping and I had just finished singing a song before all the school.

Section 2. I was in my own bedroom and there was a lion under my bed and in the cupboard was a terrible ghost. I heard him walking about and then he came out and ran after me and I was on a bicycle riding round the bed with the ghost after me. All at once I jumped out of the window with a great scream, then I woke up and found myself on the floor.

Section 3. I went to sleep again and dreamt that Mother and Father had turned into cabbages and I was getting them ready for dinner but just as I was putting them into the saucepan they turned into people again, and asked me if I liked the aeroplane which we were in, and then I found myself in a Handley-Page. I was driving it when all of a sudden it vanished and I was swimming in the sea. When I woke up I was sitting up in bed, and it was morning so I did not dream any more that night.

Girls of twelve and thirteen dream much about religion, and there were several interesting dreams of heaven. Even in these there is a curious, almost ludicrous, admixture of everyday experiences.

One girl, after describing the scene, adds: 'Much information was given to us (girl and friend) by a nice gentleman who, I presume, was a cherub. In appearance he strongly reminded me of our school caretaker.' Another, after describing the kindness of the angels to herself and her friend, concludes: 'We had tea with them and they afterwards kindly assisted us in the washing-up.'

At eleven years of age there are many cases of people changing into animals and vice versa. The headmistress becomes a horse, an old man becomes a mauve cow with green eyes, the brother of a girl of this age changes into a dog, goes to school as usual, and she rides home on his back. Rapid alterations in the size of objects in dreams appears to occur more frequently at the ages of thirteen and fourteen than at others.

Dreams of children in industrial schools

There is no type of school in which the compensatory function of the dream is so clearly marked as in the industrial schools. The children have practically all had terrible experiences of wrecked homes and dissolute parents. Many of them have also had extensive thieving experiences which resulted in their commitment by the magistrates to these institutions. The dreams of children in these schools are of special interest, and in some respects they have marked characteristics which separate them clearly from those of normal, elementary-school children. The dreams are frequent and vivid. The age range is ten to sixteen years. There is nothing to indicate harsh treatment at the schools, and the fact that many of the teachers play a friendly part in the dreams, coming to the rescue in perilous times, and in many other ways, shows that the children are on good terms with those in authority. The comparative monotony of institutional life, however, finds undoubted solace in the dreams of fulfilled wishes and those of bravery and adventure.

The most clearly marked differences in the dreams of these children, as compared with those of normal children, are:

1. The greater number of dreams of the clearly defined wish-fulfilment type. Nearly half the dreams are of this nature.

2. The extraordinarily close approximation of the proportion of the wish-fulfilment dreams, fear dreams, and kinaesthetic dreams of the boys to those of the girls.

3. The fulfilled wishes are of a very special type, consisting principally of dreams of home-life; of visits of parents to the school; of large parcels from home, containing many presents; of changes of fortune; of success in life; of deeds of valor and promotion to positions of great responsibility. The industrial-school child is a most ambitious and imaginative dreamer.

4. The fear dreams are very similar among boys and girls. The boy, however, especially at the age of fourteen, dreams more of ghosts, and at all ages the girl dreams more of houses on fire.

5. A very marked difference is to be observed in the kinaesthetic dreams. The proportion among boys and girls is practically the same, but they are

much less frequent than among normal children. It would appear that the regular life of the institution is not conducive to this type of dream.

6. The family group takes comparatively little part in the dreams, their place being taken by the boy's chum and the girl's particular friend. The proportion of someone other than the chief figure taking part in the dream is about the same as in the dreams of normal children.

In industrial schools many boys of thirteen and fourteen dream of joining the Air Force. There are very few neurotic dreams among the girls; they are generally very imaginative but quite healthy. Among the girls, thieving very rarely comes into the dream, and of twenty-three cases recorded in the boys' dreams there appeared to be only one case for which there was any consciousness of wrong: stealing in the industrial boy's dream is simply a normal form of adventure.

In industrial schools the conditions of life of the boy and girl approximate far more closely than those of normal children attending day schools, and it is very interesting to observe, as seen in the results of the analyses, the effect upon the dream, the remarkable similarity in many important elements, especially as regards wish-fulfilment, fear, and kinaesthetic dreams.

Another reason for the extraordinary interest of the dreams of these children is that they have been thrown so much upon their own resources and have passed through such a variety of experiences that the content of the unconscious is far richer than that of the normal child who has led an uneventful and fully protected existence. In some cases the dreams, in their richness of material and effective combinations, are years ahead of those of normal children. This becomes more striking still when it is remembered how unfavorable is the nomadic life for acquiring the educational background needed for graphic description in the recording of dreams. It would seem to indicate that there is an abnormal amount of natural ability in the children of the industrial schools.

The following dream of a boy of fourteen is typical:

My last dream was of motors, motor bicycles and aeroplanes, all of which I thought I possessed. I went into business with the idea of becoming like Selfridges and to possess everything. I first had a motor bicycle, which I bought very cheaply, but thought a motor better, so I bought one. I always carried my motor bicycle at the back of my car. One day I met a nice young lady but before long forgot about her. My business becoming great I bought an aeroplane, I had many trips in my aeroplane, the greatest being to Australia. While in Australia I set up another business and last at became a millionaire. I asked my mother to come across but she would not, so I went to her. Until this time I did not possess a house but after trouble I saw a beautiful large mansion and bought it. Having nothing to do I became a doctor and became renowned for my being able to cure the influenza (Kimmins, 1926, p. 45).

Dreams of deaf and blind children

There are very clearly marked differences in the dreams of deaf and blind children. The deaf child can draw upon a rich field of visual experiences which, in their fantastic combinations, give such a wealth of interest to the dream; whereas these experiences are wanting in the dream of the child who has been blind from birth.

The percentage of clearly defined wish-fulfilments in both types of child corresponds closely to that of normal children but the wishes are of a different nature. Concerts, parties, and domestic experience bulk largely in the dreams of the blind child, and there is not that variety which corresponds to the much fuller life of the deaf child. In the latter, visits of the town child to the country form, especially among older children, a very important item, whereas in the former, there are practically no references to such experiences. The railway journey, the change of scene, and even the seaside have no message for the blind child.

The fears of the deaf and blind are somewhat in excess of those of normal children. In both the fear of animals is greater than among ordinary children, and in the case of the deaf it is twice as great as in that of the blind. The fear of fire is far greater among the blind, particularly in young children, than in any other type of child. The air raid also had a much greater terror for the blind child than for normal children. A year after the last raid it formed an unwelcome element in a large percentage of his dreams. On the whole, blind children, especially up to the age of twelve years, dream far less than deaf children, but this was not true at the time of the air raids.

It is interesting to observe that, whilst among blind children the proportion of kinaesthetic dreams for the same age is very considerably below that of normal seeing children, this type of dream is practically non-existent among deaf children. This is of considerable importance as evidence in support of the physiological theory of the kinaesthetic dream.

Bravery and adventure figure very prominently in the dreams of deaf girls, far more so than in the dreams of girls in elementary and secondary schools. Associated with this it is interesting to note that the air raid has left practically no trace on the dream of the deaf girl. The deaf girl, in fact, in her love of bravery and adventure, approximates closely to the elementary-school boy of the same age. Bravery and adventure have no place in the dream of the blind child. The fairy story makes a much stronger appeal to the deaf than to the blind girl.

Dreams in which conversations are recorded are in about the same proportion among blind as among normal children, but in deaf children they are far more common, the relative numbers being thirteen to five.

The family group or special friends enter into the dreams of both blind and deaf children in much the same proportion as in those of ordinary children.

The bravery and adventure dreams of deaf girls generally take the form of the dreamers acting as airwomen and frequently as spies. A girl of fifteen and her friend go to the Western Front disguised as Germans, set free a number of British prisoners, kill the Kaiser, and are presented with medals by the King. Another girl kills the Kaiser and is congratulated by British officers, who give her ten medals.

Deaf girls dream much of personal adornment, which is entirely lacking in dreams of blind girls.

Many blind children claim to see in their dreams. A girl of fourteen says: 'I can always see in my dreams. I have never yet had a dream without seeing quite plainly.' But the dreams recorded are generally of an uneventful nature dealing with domestic incidents in which vision takes no part. There are many auditory dreams and a few taste dreams. In the deaf child's dream descriptions of the clothes worn by the actors frequently occur, but these are rarely to be found in the dreams of the blind; and there is scarcely ever any mention of color, although some blind children associate special colors with particular objects.

Deaf children also state that in their dreams they hear clearly, and, as has been pointed out, the accounts of their dreams contain more definite conversations than those of any other type of child. The more intelligent blind children take great interest in the books specially prepared for them. An account of *Lorna Doone,* in which the child took one of the characters in the book in her dream, was of unusual interest. Blind children form great friendships with girls at the same school, and in their dreams it is frequently the girl friend who is present rather than members of the family group.

There is no evidence whatever in the dreams analysed that a child blind from birth ever sees as a dreamer, but there is abundant evidence that those who have recently become blind see clearly. The age of becoming blind appears to be the deciding factor. Jastrow and Heermann (see de Manacéine, 1897) investigated this point fully. Their researches point to the following conclusions:

1. That a child who becomes blind before the age of five never sees in his dreams.

2. That when total blindness occurs between the ages of five and seven, much depends on the mental development of the child as to whether he sees in dreams in after-life or not. The well-developed child mentally certainly does; the evidence with regard to the others is not so clear.

3. That all dreamers becoming blind after the age of seven see in dreams

even after an interval of twenty or thirty years; and apparently with little diminution in clearness.

These conclusions are well-established. The question with regard to the partially blind seeing more clearly in dreams than in waking life is more open to doubt.

The compensatory nature of the dream and its fairy element are also well shown in the stories of physically defective children. A lame boy, who dreamed of escaping from a bull by flight, adds to the record of his dream: 'I never dreamt that I had a bad leg.' Another good example of a wish-fulfilment dream is the following, of a very poor crippled boy of fourteen. He dreamed of wealth and physical vigor:

I dreamt that I had plenty of money. I drew a thousand pounds out of the bank. I was coming along the road when two men came and tried to take it from me. The two men started fighting me to get the money and I gave both of them a knockout blow. I went to bed that night and put the money under my pillow, and when I awoke I was hunting all over the bed for it. I did not find it (Kimmins, 1926, p. 48).

Physically defective children sometimes explain the origin of their dreams. A boy had an exciting dream of a man shooting rabbits from a low-flying aeroplane, and he was running along picking up the rabbits. He explains it as follows:

Early in the day we were playing cricket and I remember seeing an aeroplane and after my dream, in the morning, I heard some of the boys in the school saying that they had heard someone shooting rabbits in the evening; so I expect my dream was due to seeing an aeroplane in the day and hearing the shots of the man shooting rabbits in the evening in my sleep (Kimmins, 1926, p. 48).

The child's conception of the dream

The terrors of the dream of the child have long puzzled the observers of very young children who, though perfectly happy in the waking state, frequently have what is known as terror dreams at night. Piaget (1926), in his chapter on dreams in *The Child's Conception of the World*, throws a flood of light on this difficult question. From his interrogation of a large number of children it appears that the child's conception of the real nature of the dream is only reached after passing through very well-marked stages. The following statement which is the result of much questioning summarizes the position very clearly:

The answers obtained can be classified as belonging to three distinct stages. During the first (approximately 5–6) the child believes the dream to come from outside and to take place within the room and he thus dreams with the eyes. Also, the dream is highly emotional: dreams often come 'to pay us out,' 'because we've done something we ought not to have done,' etc. During the second stage (average age 7–8) the child supposes the source of the dream to be in the head, in thought, in the voice, etc., but the dream is in the room, in front of him. Dreaming is with the eyes; it is looking at a picture outside. The fact that it is outside does not mean that it is true: the dream is unreal, but consists in an image existing outside, just as the image of an ogre may exist, without there being a real ogre. Finally, during the third stage (about 9–10) the dream is the product of thought, it takes place inside the head (or in the eyes) and dreaming is by means of thought or else with the eyes used internally' (Piaget, 1926, pp. 90–91 of English trans.).

It is curious that so many of the children interviewed by Piaget and his colleagues regard the dream as a punishment. The following is fairly typical: a boy of seven years of age was asked to tell one of his dreams, and he said he had dreamed of robbers. Asked where the dream came from he said, 'From God.' Questioned as to why it was that God had sent him this dream, he replied, 'To pay me out because I wasn't good.' Asked what he had done to have such a dream, he said, 'I'd been naughty. I'd made Mother cry. I'd made her run round the table' (Piaget, 1926, p. 100).

A very interesting dream was told by a boy of eight years of age who had voluntarily drawn a clever sketch to illustrate it. He said, 'I dreamt that the devil wanted to boil me.' On the left in the sketch the boy is seen in bed, in the center is the devil, and on the right is the boy standing in his nightshirt in front of the devil, who is about to boil him. The dream is beside the bed before the eyes of the dreamer who watches it. The boy being in his night-shirt suggests that the devil had pulled him out of bed. On being questioned he explained, 'When I was in bed I was really there, and then when I was in my dream I was with the devil, and I was really there as well' (Piaget, 1926, pp. 110–11). This is an excellent example of a dream in the second (7–8) division.

There is no reason to suppose that the majority of the Swiss children's dreams are not those of a happy joyous childhood. The more vivid dreams are naturally remembered much longer than those of the wish-fulfilment variety, the memory of which soon fades away. It is probable that many of the dreams recorded by Piaget occurred long before the children were questioned. With English children the memory of the 'bogey-man' dream is naturally retained longer than those with no emotional setting.

Dream control

Many experiments have, from time to time, been carried out by experienced observers in attempts to affect the nature of the dream by means of applying stimuli, such as varying lights and sounds and those associated with the presentation of olfactory and tactual material, in the immediate neighborhood of the dreamer. A certain measure of success has been achieved in various directions but the results have not been sufficiently definite and suitable for general application and for the adoption of any particular line of action.

Arnold-Forster (1921), in her *Studies in Dreams*, describes the results of careful experiments conducted for many years. The book contains a particularly interesting foreword by Morton Prince, who evidently regarded her contribution to dream literature of great value.

In the hypnagogic state there is, as pointed out by Jastrow and others, an abnormal sensitiveness to impressions, as has been proved by experiments with children, and here is presented the best possible means of gaining admission of either sensorial or psychic stimuli to the dream mind. In the auto-suggestion work of Coué full use was made of this method.

Arnold-Forster gives an interesting account of her own limited and partially successful experiments in dream control, first in eliminating a certain class of dreams (bad dreams, whether of grief, evil, or fear), and, secondly, in the cultivation of the particular type of dream which she found to be most pleasurable. The formula, which she used very effectively, was 'Remember this is a dream. You are to dream no longer.' In this way she succeeded in switching off any unpleasant dream. She also found that she could use flying dreams, in which she cultivated a very special interest, for purposes of escape from terror dreams by flying down the staircase and then adopting normal flight, using slight movements of the feet and hands to assist in carrying out the flying scheme. In gliding dreams, however, no movements of hands or feet are necessary. Flying dreams apparently can be increased by meditating on flight and frequently observing the movements of birds and aeroplanes.

The flying dreams described by Arnold-Forster are of much the same order as those described by girls of about thirteen years of age in the writer's investigations. In the description of her method of recording dreams it would appear that her plan is very like that of Rivers – working backwards and then reversing. In the process of recording, great care is taken to concentrate on the memory of the dream and not to allow any other thoughts to enter consciousness. One point mentioned is of special interest. A full record was made of a dream during the night, and in the morning – after the lapse of a few hours – her memory was a blank about the dream recorded.

In Arnold-Forster's experiments it was found that warmth and cold were the physical stimuli which had most effect upon her dreams. Warm conditions appeared to be favorable to vividness and correspondingly increased the ease of recording. The suggestion is made that temperature effects on dreams need further investigation. Just before and after sleep the sense of smell appears to be abnormally acute.

Dream control in giving power over terror, grief, and evil elements greatly increases the pleasure of dream-life. In dreams there is freedom from the cares of responsibility, and this is an important element in the joys associated with dreaming. The kind of moral attitude in waking life undoubtedly influences the dream-mind. There is clearly a great field for research on the borderland state between consciousness and the dream.

As a result of an investigation of dreams, carried out with unusual thoroughness and care, De Sanctis (see de Manacéine, 1897) came to the conclusion that dream-life is a revelation of individual character. This is especially the case with young children. The dream lets in a flood of light as to the temperament and mental make-up of the child; it may also indicate the presence of repressed material in the unconscious.

References

ARNOLD-FORSTER, M. (1921), *Studies in Dreams*, Allen & Unwin.

CHADWICK, M. (1928), *Difficulties in Child Development*, Allen & Unwin.

DE MANACÉINE, M. (1897), *Sleep: Its Physiology, Pathology, Hygiene and Psychology*, trans. E. Jaubert, Scott.

FREUD, S. (1900), *Die Traumdeutung*, Deuticke, 7th edn, 1922. *The Interpretation of Dreams*, trans. A. A. Brill from 3rd German edn, Allen & Unwin, 1913.

GREEN, G. H. (1923), *The Day-Dream: A Study in Development*, University of London Press.

KIMMINS, C. W. (1926), *The Child's Attitude Toward Life: A Study of Children's Stories*, Methuen.

KIMMINS, C. W. (1928), *The Springs of Laughter (Laughter and Dreams)*, Methuen.

PIAGET, J. (1926), *La représentation du monde chez l'enfant*, Alcan. *The Child's Conception of the World*, trans. J. and A. Tomlinson, Routledge & Kegan Paul, 1929.

RIVERS, W. H. R. (1923), *Conflict and Dream*, Routledge & Kegan Paul.

SMITH, T. L. (1907), 'The psychology of daydreams', in *Aspects of Child Life and Education*, Ginn.

STERN, W. (1914), *Psychologie der frühen Kindheit, bis zum sechsten Lebensjahre*, Quelle & Meyer, 6th edn, rev. 1930. *Psychology of Early Childhood: Up to the Sixth Year of Age*, trans. A. Barwell, from 3rd German edn, Allen & Unwin, 2nd edn, rev. 1930.

STEVENSON, R. L. (1904), *Across the Plains, with Other Memories and Essays*, Scribner.

SULLY, J. (1896), *Studies of Childhood*, Appleton-Century-Crofts, new edn, 1908.

VARENDONCK, J. (1921), *The Psychology of Day-Dreams*, Allen & Unwin.

WALSH, W. S. (1920), *The Psychology of Dreams*, Dodd, Mead.

WATT, H. J. (1929), *The Common Sense of Dreams*, Clark University Press.

6 P. Kline

Fact and Fantasy in Freudian Theory

Excerpt from P. Kline, *Fact and Fantasy in Freudian Theory*, Constable, 1972, pp. 236–7.

The work of Lee

Lee studied the dreams of 600 Zulu subjects (120 of these in great detail) and provided some powerful evidence in favour of Freudian dream theory. An interesting point about this cross-cultural study is the fact that it is not possible to argue that these subjects were influenced in reporting or remembering their dreams by Freudian or Jungian dream theory! – a common jibe at psychoanalytic clinical case studies. If influenced at all in this way it would be by the Zulu dream diviners who interpret dreams which in their culture are regarded as of great importance (Galloway, 1868, quoted by Lee, 1958).

Subjects

Six hundred rural Zulus. Of these 120 female subjects were subjected to further interview.

Method

The 600 subjects were asked how much they dreamed and the content of their dreaming. In the more intensive interviews of the sub-sample, the women were asked to describe in detail two dreams. Other information was also obtained from these subjects. Thus manifest content, in Freudian terms, was the subject of the study.

Results

Many dreams had an apparent lack of latent content – i.e. the manifest content of the dream appeared to express the wish.

Lee shows that Freudian dream theory can accommodate such a finding. Thus Freud (1935) in 'An autobiographical study' argues that young children often have such undistorted dreams because repressions are not yet fully developed. Adults too can have such infantile dreams if the need is imperative. Thus a crucial test of Lee's interpretation of these Zulu dreams is to establish to what extent the dream wishes did in fact reflect imperative needs.

To test the relationship between dream material and imperative needs, the dream content was related to the obstetric history of the subjects (more than 400 women).

1. Dreamers of 'a baby' had much the worst record of married infertility. Those who had borne children had lost more than half of them and these were the youngest group (if the eldest, the deaths of their children would not have been so surprising).

Lee shows that in Zulu society there is a powerful psychological need for a baby. Failure to produce one brings contempt. Eysenck (1953) has tried to argue that the Freudian claim that dreams represent wishes is disproved by the fact that hungry people do not produce hunger dreams. However, as Lee neatly argues, this evidence tests the hypothesis that dreams reflect all wishes, which is *not* the Freudian theory. This study by Lee shows that in the case of these young Zulu girls, dreams of a baby do indeed reflect an imperative need. This finding must be regarded, therefore, as support for the Freudian claim that dreams represent wishes.

2. Sufferers from pseudocyesis (false pregnancy), which was common in the area, also tended to have the direct baby dream which again supports the Freudian notion.

3. Nine of the twenty-one subjects who had 'baby' dreams said a baby was their main wish, and four said children were their main desire. Of the ninety-seven others only eighteen gave either baby or children as their wish. This difference is significant at the 1 per cent level. Thus further support for Freudian theory comes from this finding.

4. Lee presents further data linking dreams of still water and flooding to conflicting desires for more children (a cultural norm) among those who already have sufficient of their own. Since this interpretation is largely speculative it will not be examined in further detail. Nor indeed will his other findings relating dreams of snakes and *tokoloshe* (a kind of Priapic river god) since they suffer to some extent from the same fault as orthodox psychoanalytic dream interpretations, being speculative and essentially untestable.

Comments and conclusions

This study by Lee is powerful evidence that in a sample of Zulu women certain common dreams do reflect wishes, in accordance with psychoanalytic theory. It also supports the Freudian claim that certain imperative needs may be directly expressed in the manifest content of the dream. In this sample there can be little fear that the results were biased by the subjects' knowledge of Freudian theory.

References

EYSENCK, H. J. (1953), *Uses and Abuses of Psychology*, Penguin.

FREUD, S. (1935), 'An autobiographical study', in *New Introductory Lectures in Psychoanalysis*, vol. 20, Norton.

LEE, S. G. (1958), 'Social influences in Zulu dreaming', *J. soc. Psychol.*, vol. 47, pp. 265–83.

7 David Foulkes, James D. Larson, Ethel M. Swanson and Max Rardin

Two Studies of Childhood Dreaming

David Foulkes, James D. Larson, Ethel M. Swanson and Max Rardin, 'Two studies of childhood dreaming', *American Journal of Orthopsychiatry*, vol. 39, 1969, pp. 627–43.

The discovery of electrophysiological correlates[1] of vivid dreams has made it possible to awaken subjects while they experience such dreams. Since episodes of rapid eye movement (REM) sleep recur periodically at 60–100 min intervals, awakenings can be made several times a night. Generally, about 80–90 per cent of REM-sleep awakenings produce dream recall in young adult subjects (Dement, 1965).

Subjects in electrophysiological dream studies have usually been young adults. Several studies with limited numbers of subjects and awakenings have noted that children can also recall dreams on awakenings from REM sleep, but their authors fail to elaborate on the nature of the dreams that were collected (Kales *et al.*, 1968; Köhler, Coddington and Agnew, 1968; Roffwarg, Dement and Fisher, 1964). The most extensive electrophysiological study of childhood dream content has been that of Foulkes *et al.* (1967).

These authors studied thirty-two boys aged six to twelve for two nights each, and obtained dream recall on 72 per cent of 249 REM-sleep awakenings. Both ratings and content analyses of the boys' dreams suggested that they were generally realistic in characterization (e.g. parents, siblings, male peers), setting, and plots (e.g. everyday recreational activities) and that they were relatively free of bizarre symbolism and unpleasant affect or impulse. On the basis of subsequent case studies of four of these boys (Foulkes, 1967), it was argued that the child's dreams may become bizarre and unpleasant only to the degree that he is experiencing difficulties in his waking adjustment.

These results do not agree with much clinical lore on the nature of childhood dreaming. Calvin Hall (1966), for instance, states that 'What little knowledge we have of children's dreams suggests that their dreams are much more complex and much more dreadful than has previously been thought.' There are several possible explanations of the discrepancy of the 'latency' child they studied and this statement. The 'dreadful' properties

1. EEG sleep stage 1, rapid eye movements (REMs), suppressed neck and chin electromyograms (EMGs).

of the child's dream may be seriously overestimated from daytime recall, in which only those dreams sufficiently nightmarish to produce spontaneous arousal are well recalled, and from studies of children whose unrepresentative emotional disturbance is in fact associated with particularly vivid and frightening dreams.

It is also possible, however, that the relatively affect-free quality and the realism of the dreams collected by Foulkes *et al.* reflect peculiar aspects of the 'latency' child they studied and are not representative of younger or older children. The two studies to be reported here investigate this latter alternative: laboratory dreams were collected from preschoolers and from adolescent males to determine whether they differed markedly from those of six- to twelve-year-old boys. In addition, the adolescent study included both normal and emotionally disturbed boys in an attempt to confirm the hypothesis that personality pathology in children is correlated with more unreal and unpleasant dreams. Confirmation of the hypothesis would point to sampling biases in clinical dream studies that may lead to an overestimation of the bizarreness and affect of the normal child's dream.

Study one: dreams of the preschooler
Subjects

Six boys aged 4–1 to 5–6 (median: 4–6) and six girls aged 3–0 to 5–0 (median: 4–4) were recruited through advertisements in the campus newspaper and from acquaintances of the experimenters. Nine of the twelve children were aged between 4–0 and 5–0, inclusive. Subjects were paid for their services. Their fathers represented a wide range of occupations, but all came from the broad middle stratum of society. One subject (#13) had attended nursery school.

Method

Subjects slept for two nonconsecutive nights in the laboratory. One or both parents generally accompanied the child to the laboratory and remained until the child fell asleep, sometimes staying for the entire night. Two EEG electrode placements (generally parietal and prefrontal) were made upon all subjects, and electrodes were placed lateral to the eyes of each subject for recording EOGs (electro-oculograms). All-night recordings were taken on an Offner Type R Dynograph with four channels per subject, generally comprising a monopolar parietal EEG (with neutral reference electrodes over the mastoid process), a bipolar EEG, and two monopolar (right, left) EOGs.

Identification of episodes of REM sleep proved no more difficult for these young subjects than for young adults. Awakenings were made at variable intervals after the onset of REMs (range: 2–33 min; median: 9 min). Seven awakenings were obtained over the course of the two nights for each subject; for ten of twelve subjects, there were three awakenings on night 1 and four on night 2. Awakenings generally were made in consecutive REM periods only when it appeared that the awakening schedule could not otherwise be fulfilled. In other cases, subjects were allowed several uninterrupted REM periods throughout the night.

Nocturnal interviews were conducted at the subject's bedside (except for subject 1, who was awakened over an intercom unit) and were tape-recorded for later transcription. Upon establishing effective contact with the subject, the interviewer asked him if he could remember a dream. If the answer was yes, the interviewer asked what it was about. If the answer was no, the subject was asked to think for a moment or so to see if he could remember anything; if not, he was allowed to return to sleep. When a spontaneous report was given, the interviewer asked a minimal number of unstandardized questions to clarify characters, settings, and dream activities. Where identifications of persons or places were still unclear, parents were later questioned to elucidate dream elements. The nature of the subject population did not favor a rigidly formal interview format. Interviews were conducted (except for subject 4, who was interviewed by the senior author) by an experimental assistant without any particular theoretical interest in the nature of the reports she collected. We did allow a parent to conduct some of the later interviews of two subjects (6, 9) who had not recalled any dreams, but these parental interviews yielded no dream reports.

Following their nights in the laboratory, subjects were administered three sections of Laurendeau and Pinard's (1962) tests of precausal thinking (Dream, Life, Night) and the Blacky Test (Blum, 1950). Parents were mailed two copies of the Traditional Family Ideology Scale (Levinson and Huffman, 1955) with instructions to complete them independently. Replies were received from all twenty-four parents.

Results

Adaptation to laboratory and sleep patterns. Mean time to sleep onset after lights out was 22 min (median 14·5 min, range 0–56 min). This is identical to the figure previously reported for six- to eight-year-old boys (Foulkes *et al.*, 1967). On more than 50 per cent of sixty experimental awakenings followed by another awakening on the same night, sleep (EEG stage 2) onset was achieved in 6 min or less following termination of the dream interview; in only four instances, all on night 1, did latency to sleep onset under these circumstances exceed 60 min. These data establish that subjects experienced no great difficulty in adapting to sleeping under laboratory conditions and to the interruption of their sleep by experimental awakenings.

Since sleep was interrupted at varying times of the night and following variable durations of REM sleep, meaningful figures on the proportion of total sleep time spent in REM sleep cannot be reported. Data are available, however, on a related measure of a subject's propensity to REM sleep: latency from sleep onset to his first episode of REM sleep. In a two-night study with young adults, the mean latency has been reported as 91 min (Pivik and Foulkes, 1966), while our two-night study of six- to eight-year-old and ten- to twelve-year-old boys yielded mean latencies of 170 and 153 min, respectively (Foulkes *et al.*, 1967). In the present study, mean sleep latency to REM onset was 129 min, with a night 1 mean of 144 min and a night 2 mean of 113 min. The adaptation effect was significant ($T = 13$, $p = 0.025$, 1-tail – Wilcoxon, Katti and Wilcox, 1963).

These various figures on sleep latency to initial REM onset, including the briefer latency for the preschooler than for the older child and preadolescent, agree with data reported by Fisher (1965) on the other measure of REM propensity, the percentage of undisturbed sleep spent in REM sleep. As Fisher points out, however, present REM-per cent figures during childhood are based on limited ns. Observations in the present study suggest considerable individual differences in REM sleep phenomena during early childhood, and thus the need for cautious interpretations of presently available data. Subjects' night 1 and night 2 latencies to REM onset were fairly consistent with one another (rho $= 0.67$, $p = 0.05$, 1-tail)[2] but highly variable across subjects. Subject 5 had a mean two-night latency to REM onset of 59.5 min; the comparable figure for subject 11 was 201 min. Sex differences were negligible and not significant.

Recall. Some item of substantive content was reported on thirty-seven of the eighty-four awakenings (44 per cent). The mean substantive word count for these thirty-seven reports was 21.9. The median individual subject recall value was recall on 3.5 of seven awakenings (50 per cent). Subject variability was extensive (see Table 1). Neither age nor sex discriminated total non-recallers from subjects who recalled at least one dream, although all three subjects who reported apparent dreams on every awakening were girls.

Dream content. Table 1 presents, in highly abbreviated form, some indication of the most common kind of dream that was collected from each of our eight recallers. Subject 3's dream reports were very fragmentary (snakes; streetlights [a probable incorporation of a light that the experimenter usually turned on only after his call but that on this occasion came on before the awakening]; the tape recorder and chair next to his bed; a 'soldier man'). Subject 4's dreams were of: riding his tricycle; flying a kite; riding a horse; and driving a car. Subject 5's dreams were of: taking turns with her

2. All correlations subsequently reported for Study 1 are also Spearman rank-order coefficients.

siblings riding their horse; going to school and a postman sending postcards to people; her brother riding his horse in a pasture; her grandfather looking for her mother to give her a pair of sunglasses; playing with her siblings in the backyard; a train with white signs on it; splashing in a swimming pool with her siblings. Subject 7 dreamed of sailing a boat, of his brothers building a boat and his sailing in it, and of caterpillars crawling on his sister's leg (this was also a probable incorporation of a sleep stimulus, and is discussed further below). Subject 8, like subject 3, apparently experienced a fragmentary, static visual image (mother's desk) but she also reported dissociated static images on two awakenings (red apples and people walking; a cowboy juxtaposed with her parents talking to one another) and one dream episode (a friend pressing leaves at her babysitter's house).

Table 1 **Dream recall and dream content**

Subject	Sex	Age	Recall	Mean dream word count	Most common dream theme and incidence
1	M	4–6	14%	17·0	[Only dream was of washing his hands in the bathroom]
3	M	4–6	57%	7·0	Fragmentary, apparently static percepts ($n = 4$)
4	M	4–1	57%	17·8	Playing in realistic settings ($n = 3$)
5	F	5–0	100%	25·9	Playing with siblings or siblings playing in realistic settings ($n = 4$)
6	M	4–6	0%	—	—
7	M	5–6	43%	53·3	Playing (sailing boats) ($n = 2$)
8	F	4–0	57%	35·0	Fragmentary static and/or dissociated percepts ($n = 3$)
9	M	5–4	0%	—	—
10	F	3–0	0%	—	—
11	F	4–1	100%	15·6	Animals eating ($n = 4$)
12	F	4–9	0%	—	—
13	F	4–6	100%	14·9	Animals ($n = 7$) (with milk as dream element, $n = 3$)

Dreams of subjects 11 and 13 were different in character from those reported above in that they were almost entirely populated with animals. Subject 11 reported dreams of: a horse, a teddybear eating cereal, a lamb eating ham; a green cow eating French toast; a cow eating French fries; a horse eating; a little horse; a kangaroo walking in the grass; and a toy duck and airplane. Subject 13 reported dreaming of: a man milking a cow; a farmer milking a chicken; a lamb drinking milk; a teddybear swimming; a horse trying to get into a barn because he was cold; a lamb knocking at a locked door; and a rattlesnake 'getting' a six-year-old boy.

In general, subjects' dreams, with the exception of those of subject 11, were realistic in characterization, setting, and plot or bore some demonstrable relationship to their behavior in the period immediately preceding their laboratory service. This was particularly true of subjects 4, 5, and 8, whose reports we believed, on the basis of subjects' attitudes to laboratory service and of the style in which reports were delivered on nocturnal interviews, to be least likely to be confabulatory. Subject 5's dreams, for instance, all contained direct or indirect references to familiar persons and/or recent events. She lived on a ranch and she and her siblings often did ride horses. Her dream of going to school was probably related to the fact that the subject lived 200 miles from the laboratory, and had told her siblings with some pride as she had left home that *she* was 'going to college'. Her dream of a train came one night after her aunt had taken her to the local depot to see a passenger train, of which there were none in her hometown area.

Even subject 13's animal dreams proved partially explicable in terms of recent events in her waking life: her mother reported that the subject was extremely interested in a neighbor who was nursing her baby. The girl had asked her mother if the woman had to drink milk to give milk, and the mother had replied that you just had to eat any kind of food, as, for example a cow eats grass to give milk. Subject 13's only sibling was a six-year-old brother. She was quite definite that the rattlesnake in one of her dreams was 'getting a six-year-old boy'.

The case of subject 13 accentuates a point that may be made with respect to most of the dreams of the other subjects (again except subject 11): although generally realistic or plausible, most preschoolers' dreams are not mere memories or re-creations but are 'dreams', i.e. they are worked-over and reconstructed bits of past experience. The general conclusion still holds, however, that the preschoolers' dreams are more often realistic than bizarre, usually directly related to contemporary events in the subject's life, and neither particularly more complex nor dreadful than the relatively benign dreams of pre-adolescent boys. Play topics overshadowed any other single class of manifest content.

The authors believe that subject 11 is not a genuine exception to the trends observed above. The interviewer formed the definite impression, from the manner in which this subject's nocturnal reports were given, that she was confabulating. In addition, the subject's mother indicated that the subject had told her, *before* night 1, that she was going to dream of horses. She had two such reports on night 1. Several other mothers said that their children also anticipated the things of which they would dream in the laboratory, but those anticipations were invariably incorrect. Furthermore, the subject confabulated to the experimenters about the number of her siblings, etc. in informal conversation in the laboratory. No comparable episodes of demonstrable confabulation were observed for any other subject. This subject's score on the Dream subtest, as will be noted below, indicated a low level of dream comprehension found incompatible in other subjects with any dream recall. With the exclusion of subject 11, dream recall for the remaining subjects would drop to 39 per cent (recall on thirty of seventy-seven awakenings).

Test results. Statistical tests of psychometric data will omit subject 11 for reasons noted above.

Maternal and paternal TFI scores intercorrelated only 0·14 (ns). The fathers' TFI scores correlated -0.74 with their children's dream recall ($p = 0.02$, 2-tail). Mothers' TFI scores correlated only -0.08 with these dream scores. The significant paternal-child correlation has two interesting apects. First, it is negative. With a theory stressing the complementarity, rather than the continuity, of dream experience and waking experience, it might have been predicted that the child with an authoritarian parent would be under more strict impulse control in wakefulness and hence have more vivid and memorable displacements of these impulses to sleep. Second, the parental-child correlation is large and significant only for the father. This fact also suggests a continuity of waking and sleeping fantasy, for several studies have observed that authoritarian parents, *especially fathers*, have children with relatively undeveloped waking achievement imagery (Clausen, 1966). Similarly, Marshall (1961) found that dramatic or make-believe, but not realistic, uses of language and hostility in play with peers at preschool tended to be related to paternal, but not maternal, Parental Attitude Research Instrument scores.

The results of the Laurendeau and Pinard tests[3] suggested that adequacy of conceptual development, particularly with respect to dream phenomena,

3. The Laurendeau and Pinard (1962) tests were scored independently by two of the authors. Initial agreement of classification was present for 83·3 per cent of subjects on the Dream and Night subtests and for 75·0 per cent of subjects on the Life subtest. A single reconciliation score was easily achieved for all but one discrepant case, which was resolved by a coin toss. Composite scores (a rank of mean subtest rankings) representing the children's overall performances on the three Laurendeau and Pinard subtests and their scores for the Dream subtest alone were then correlated with their dream recall. Neither rho was significant, although both were positive. The larger value observed was between ranking on the Dream subtest and laboratory dream recall (0·36). There is some suggestion, then, that adequacy of conceptual development, particularly with respect to dream phenomena, is related to the ability to report dreams in the laboratory.

The observed relationship is obviously far from perfect as the relatively low and nonsignificant correlation indicates. However, seven of nine subjects scoring at the level of at least mitigated realism (Laurendeau and Pinard's classes 2A, 2B, and 2C; the is related to the ability to report dreams in the laboratory. A certain level of comprehension of the dream (the level of mitigated realism) would seem to be a necessary but not a sufficient condition for laboratory dream recall.

A scale was devised, following the findings of Amen's (1941) study of pre-schoolers' responses to projective stimuli, to assess subjects' general level of apperceptive response to the Blacky pictures (Descriptive Ability Scale). Amen found that static description or identification reached its peak among two year olds, description in terms of overt activity of characters among three and four year olds, and description modified with imputed psychological states or motives among four year olds. DAS scores[4] on the Blacky pictures correlated 0·61 with laboratory recall ($p = 0.05$, 1-tail). Moreover, subject 5, whose ability to report mentation from sleep was successfully tested later, ranked highest on descriptive ability, while subjects 3 and 8, whose modal dream content consisted of fragmentary or non-coherent visual percepts, had the lowest descriptive ability scores of any of the recalling subjects. This simple scale of waking descriptive ability, then, demonstrated an impressive capacity to predict (and perhaps validate) subjects' verbal performance on awakenings from REM sleep.

Stimulus incorporation trials. Subject 11's case highlights a general problem in working with young children: what degree of credibility is to be attached to their verbal reports? Although this may appear incapable of resolution in dealing with reports of something as private as the dream, there are several ways of testing whether subjects can report material immediately following sleep that actually occurred during sleep. Within REM sleep, one possibility is the correlation of preawakening eye movement patterns with the nature of postawakening reports (Roffwarg et al., 1962). Another is the correlation of the report with a stimulus applied and terminated during sleep (Dement and Wolpert, 1958).

As noted above, subject 3 had one presumably incorporative dream of a light stimulus applied before he was awakened. Subject 7's caterpillar

dream at least partly subjective in character) recalled dreams, while only one of three subjects below this level had any recall. This subject with a relatively inadequate conception of the dream, but apparently perfect dream recall, was subject 11. If we are justified in excluding her as a probable confabulator, the data suggest that a certain level of comprehension of the dream (the level of mitigated realism) is a necessary but not a sufficient condition for laboratory dream recall.

4. In analysis of the Blacky stories, one category (no response or irrelevant response) was added as the low point of this scale, and descriptions of overt activity were subdivided into simple ('Blacky is walking to the people') and compound ('One day when Blacky was watching the family, the papa was patting his hand and the mama licking his face'). This yielded a five-point (0–4) scale for the analysis of each story. Mean score values for each subject were then computed independently by each of two raters, with an interjudge reliability of 0·92. The mean subject values of the two judges were then averaged to yield a single DAS score.

dream probably falls in the same class. The experimenters were startled, 4 min after his REM onset, to hear the subject cry out loudly in apparent terror. He did not awaken, however, so an experimental awakening was initiated. The interviewer immediately noticed as she entered the room that the subject's worm-like electrode chain was lying in a strange position across the back of his neck. His dream was that he was in the family car and that a brother put crawly 'caterpillar worms' on his sister's leg as they were driving to school to pick up another brother. These two episodes suggested systematic attempts at influencing subjects' dreams through stimulus application during REM sleep. Negative results, of course, would be inconclusive: subjects' dreams, accurately reported, simply may not have incorporated the stimulus. Positive results, on the other hand, would establish that the subject could, at least on some occasions, report *sleep* mentation upon experimental awakenings from REM sleep.

Subject 11 refused to return to the laboratory for this further testing. Subjects 4, 5, 8 and 13 did return to the laboratory for one night of stimulus applications during REM sleep. Four stimuli were employed: drops of water from an ear syringe; puffs of air from the same syringe; an emeryboard rubbed across the subject's skin; and a puff of cotton lightly applied to the subject's skin.

Subjects 4, 8 and 13 had much the same kind of dreams as before. No obvious incorporations were noted. Subject 5, on the other hand, did appear to incorporate at least three of the four stimuli. The cotton puff produced a dream of her sister playing with a cuddly toy lion; the airpuff a dream of a family outing in a boat on a lake, with the wind blowing in her face; and the water a dream that she was with her siblings spraying a fire near her house with a firehose (the emeryboard was associated with a dream of playing at the town park). In none of these cases did stimulus application disrupt REM-sleep patterns by producing wakefulness; in all cases stimulus application was terminated several seconds before the subject was awakened. These three dreams give clear evidence that subject 5 could report ongoing sleep mentation on laboratory awakenings. Her reports on REM-sleep stimulus-incorporation trials were, moreover, comparable to those she gave on her first two experimental nights and representative of those collected from most subjects in her age group. These considerations do not resolve the problem of potential confabulation by young subjects, but do add some confidence to the interpretation that the reports collected in the present study are *dream* reports.

Study two: dreams of the male adolescent

This second study, as suggested above, was of interest not only in determining the generalizability of results of dream studies previously conducted with pre-adolescents (Foulkes, 1967; Foulkes *et al.*, 1967) but also as an attempt to confirm that a positive association of dream vividness and affect with personality pathology holds during childhood as well as during the young-adult years.

Foulkes and Rechtschaffen (1964) found (with their results reported here in terms of a subsequent factor analysis of their rating data by Hauri, Sawyer and Rechtschaffen, 1967) that pathological scales of the MMPI tended to correlate positively with Vivid Fantasy (i.e. word counts, imaginativeness, distortion) of dream content, inconsistently with the degree of Active Control exercised over such content, positively with dream Unpleasantness and Physical Aggression, and negatively with the amount of Verbal Aggression and Heterosexuality in dream content. It was of particular interest in the present study, then, to observe whether a group of adolescents selected for demonstrated pathology would differ from controls in a manner consistent with these earlier correlational data.

Subjects

All boys aged thirteen to fifteen then resident in an institution for emotionally disturbed adolescents were recruited for service in the study ($n = 7$). The boys were from working-class backgrounds with histories of parental abandonment or neglect. A control group of boys in the same age bracket ($n = 7$) was obtained from the community. Two boys of working-class background were approached by an experimenter and asked to serve in the study themselves and to help recruit their friends. This process of recruitment produced a control sample of working-class origin and one within which, as was also true for the institutional boys, all subjects were well acquainted with one another. Each subject was paid for his service in the experiment. Boys in the institutional group ranged in age from 13–6 to 15–9 while those in the control group ranged from 13–11 to 15–7.

Method

Each boy reported to the laboratory at an hour approximating his normal bedtime. Subjects were run in pairs, with all pairs but one homogeneous for institutionalization–noninstitutionalization. Each subject served two nonconsecutive nights in the laboratory.

Shortly after the subject's arrival at the laboratory, an experimenter affixed electrodes for EEG and EOG recording to his face and scalp. Continuous recordings (a monopolar EOG from the outer canthus of the right eye, one from the outer canthus of the left eye, a monopolar parietal EEG, and a bipolar parietal-occipital EEG) were taken throughout the night on an Offner Type-R Dynograph. Subjects slept in darkened rooms connected to the control room by intercom units.

Awakenings to retrieve dream content were scheduled 10 min following the onset of REMs during the first four REM periods of that duration occurring on each laboratory night. All awakenings were made over the intercom system by the same experimenter and were tape-recorded for later transcription. When the subject indicated that he recalled a dream, he was encouraged to give a spontaneous report and was then asked to identify characters and settings and any feelings that he might have had. On occasions when the subject did not immediately recall a dream he was asked to think 'for a moment or so to see if anything comes back to you'; if it did not, he was then allowed to return to sleep.

Test administration. Following the conclusion of his laboratory service, each subject was administered the WISC (omitting Comprehension and Coding subtests) and the California Psychological Inventory (CPI). Table 2 summarizes the median scores of each sub-group for WISC and CPI variables and evaluates differences for statistical significance. In this and all subsequent intergroup comparisons, the statistical test employed is the Wilcoxon Rank-Sum Test (Wilcoxon, Katti and Wilcox, 1963).

The institutionalized boys were predictably inferior to the controls on the verbal scales of the WISC, but equalled the controls on the performance scales. Full-scale IQs ranged from 91 to 136 in the institutional group and from 106 to 130 in the controls. Control CPI medians fell below average standard scores for sixteen of eighteen scales, but the same is true of high school norms for the CPI for the same sixteen scales (Gough, 1957). The patterning of their median scale scores was almost identical to that of the high school norms. Institutional subjects showed a median profile usually similar to, but with generally slightly lower elevations than, the controls. The scales that differentiated controls from institutionals indicated greater freedom from psychological distress (Well-Being) and greater conformity and conventionality (Responsibility, Communality, Achievement via Conformity) among the controls. The two groups did not differ significantly in Psychological-Mindedness or other more cognitive dimensions (Self-Acceptance, Self-Control, Tolerance, Flexibility, Intellectual Efficiency).

Analysis of dreams. The typescript of each REM report was pasted on a file card. The file cards contained no identification of subject or institutional status and were randomly assigned code numbers. These coded cards were then rated independently by two judges, one of whom had been present while the reports had been collected some six months earlier. The other was naïve, except for judgements of Verbal Aggression. Ratings were then performed along the following dimensions (Pearson product-moment reliabilities are reported parenthetically): Imagination (0·78); Relation to Everyday Experience (0·75); Verbal Aggression (0·92); Physical Aggression

(0·91); Heterosexuality (0·75); Unpleasantness (0·78); Active Control (0·80). The first two rating scales, along with substantive Word Counts performed by the naïve rater, defined Hauri *et al.*'s (1967) Vivid Fantasy

Table 2 Test scores of institutionalized and noninstitutionalized subjects

	Institu-tionalized median (n = 7)	Noninstitu-tionalized median (n = 7)	1-tail significance
Age	14–6	15–0	—
WISC			
Verbal IQ	104	119	0·03
Performance IQ	114	114	—
Full-Scale IQ	110	116	0·08
CPI			
Dominance (Do)	23	21	—
Status (Cs)	14	13	—
Sociability (Sy)	20	20	—
Social Presence (Sp)	30	33	—
Self-Acceptance (Sa)	20	18	—
Well-Being (Wb)	22	28	0·06
Responsibility (Re)	21	26	0·06
Socialization (So)	27	32	—
Self-Control (Sc)	17	16	—
Tolerance (To)	12	11	—
Good Impression (Gi)	9	12	—
Communality (Cm)	20	26	0·07
Achievement via Conformity (Ac)	15	20	0·08
Achievement via Independence (Ai)	13	13	—
Intellectual Efficiency (Ie)	28	31	—
Psychological-Mindedness (Py)	8	8	—
Flexibility (Fx)	10	11	—
Femininity (Fe)	14	15	—

factor. Two-rater averages were employed in all subsequent analyses of the rating variables.

Two judges, one naïve as before, performed content analyses of all dream reports in the areas of characters, settings, and plots. The form of the analyses was identical to that employed previously for six- to twelve-year-old males (Foulkes *et al.*, 1967). Although plot categories deriving from the six- to twelve-year-old sample were not always fully appropriate for adolescents, they were retained to facilitate comparison across age groupings. The two analysts discussed, dream-by-dream, whatever differences emerged from their independent analyses and agreed upon one final judgement for each dream.

Results

Sleep patterns. Male adolescent sleep latencies to the initial REM period were between previously recorded values for ten- to twelve-year-old boys and those for young adults: institutional mean latency was 128·4 min, while control mean latency was 132·0 min. The difference between the two groups was not significant. A familiar finding in sleep research has been the retardation of sleep latency to REM sleep, and consequently a reduction of the percentage of sleep spent in REM sleep, on a subject's first night in the laboratory (Agnew, Webb and Williams, 1966; Rechtschaffen and Verdone, 1964). It has been suggested that this effect is mediated by initial anxiety induced by the laboratory. Our control group showed a First Night Effect (a night 1 mean latency of 152·1 min and a night 2 mean latency of 111·9 min, $T = 3$, $p = 0.05$). Recently, however, it has been reported that clinical patients may not show a significant First Night Effect (Gulevich, Dement and Zarcone, 1967) Neither did our group of disturbed adolescents (a night 1 mean latency of 135·6 min v. a night 2 mean latency of 121·3 min). For subjects with past histories involving submission to professionals for tests and diagnoses of various kinds, the environment of the sleep laboratory is much less novel and extraordinary than it is for the normal control subject. It was evident from their waking laboratory behavior that the institutionals in our study were considerably more at ease there than were the controls, and on both night 1 and night 2 they fell asleep more quickly after lights-out. To the extent that institutionalized and noninstitutionalized subjects do perceive and react to the sleep experiment in different ways, this poses an additional interpretive difficulty in assessing the heretofore rather inconclusive data on laboratory sleep patterns as direct symptoms or causes of functional mental disturbance (Hartmann, 1967).

Recall. Some substantive recall was obtained on thirty-nine of fifty-five awakenings of institutionals (70·9 per cent) and on thirty-nine of fifty-two awakenings of controls (75·0 per cent). This difference was not significant.

Word count and ratings. All predictions were verified as to direction. Institutional dreams were longer (means of 104·1 v. 83·3 words), and rated more imaginative (mean ratings of 3·37 v. 2·63, $p = 0.09$, 1-tail) and less related to everyday experience (2·71 v. 3·17) than control dreams. They were also more unpleasant (4·22 v. 3·60, $p = 0.05$, 1-tail) than control dreams. Control dreams contained more verbal aggression (0·55 v. 0·22) and heterosexual content (1·23 v. 1·06) than institutional dreams, but less physical aggression

(0·95 v. 1·44) than institutional dreams. Mean activity ratings, for which no prediction had been made, were identical in the two groups (3·49).

Content analysis. Table 3 presents partial results of the content analysis. Data on six- to twelve-year-old boys and young-adult males are taken from a prior study (Foulkes *et al.*, 1967). It is clear from Table 3 that institutionals are like young adults in one respect: both groups, living away from parents and siblings, dream of them very seldom. The adolescent controls dream less of family characters than do the six- to twelve-year-olds, but more than do the young adults. Most strikingly, both adolescent groups show a preponderance of unfriendly social interaction dreams, something true of six- to eight-year-old boys, but reversed during later preadolescence when the ratio was 2·7 : 1, friendly to unfriendly. For male adolescent controls, the comparable ratio was 1 : 1·6 and, for the male institutional, it was 1 : 12. While the controls increased in work-study plots as compared to the six- to twelve-year-olds, the institutionals increased in the category of diffusely organized travel or movement dreams (riding 'around' in a car, etc.).

Amount of deprivation and dream variables. The institutionals were not homogeneous for parental deprivation, nor, presumably, for associated psychological disturbance. To the extent that institutionals had experienced moderately satisfactory relationships with one or both parents, there would be some overlap with the controls. Before any data were collected in the study, the authors asked the social worker from the institution at which the disturbed boys were resident to rank them on the amount and quality of their parental and other social-cultural deprivation. She did this, and, in addition, gave categorical judgements as to the severity of deprivation, placing her judgements in a sealed envelope that was not opened until all preceding data analyses were complete. It was then discovered that she had judged three of the boys 'severely deprived', two 'moderately deprived', and two 'mildly deprived'.

Comparisons were then made of the dreams of the five boys judged more than slightly deprived with the dreams of the controls. In spite of further shrinkage of sample size, it was found that institutional/control differences observed above were accentuated for each variable except Verbal Aggression when the two 'mildly deprived' boys were excluded from the analysis. The five most deprived boys differed significantly from controls (1-tail tests) in having more imaginative dreams ($\bar{X} = 3·60$, $p = 0·015$), dreams less related to everyday experience ($\bar{X} = 2·43$, $p = 0·03$), more unpleasant dreams ($\bar{X} = 4·42$, $p = 0·015$), and dreams containing more physical aggression ($\bar{X} = 1·62, p = 0·09$). The two 'mildly deprived' boys had, within the institutional subgroup, the two lowest rankings for Imagination and the two highest rankings for Relation to Everyday Experience. When allow-

Table 3 **Content analysis of male dreams at different age-levels**

Number of dreams	Young adults	13–15 year olds Institutional	Control	6–12 year olds
	72	39	39	179
Characters				
Dreamer himself	84·7%	82·1%	82·1%	83·2%
Family				
Mother	1·4	2·6	7·7	20·1
Father	4·2	2·6	7·7	17·9
Male sibs	0·0	2·6	12·8	24·0
Female sibs	1·4	2·6	10·3	12·8
Any of above	4·2	5·1	23·1	36·9
Age-mates				
Male	13·9	46·2	38·5	29·1
Female	18·1	7·7	15·4	7·3
Adults				
Male	19·5	10·3	10·3	8·4
Female	13·9	12·8	2·6	5·0
Strangers				
Age-mate M	13·9	5·1	10·3	15·1
Age-mate F	19·5	0·0	5·1	10·1
Adult M	27·8	28·2	12·8	29·6
Adult F	25·0	7·7	5·1	17·9
Settings				
Auto	13·9	10·3	2·6	5·0
Familiar buildings				
Residence	12·5	15·4	17·9	15·6
School	6·9	5·1	10·3	0·6
Out-of-doors	20·8	41·0	25·6	55·8
Indefinite	16·7	12·8	10·3	5·6
Plots				
Recreational	8·3	17·9	20·5	20·7
Work and study	9·7	2·6	17·9	2·2
Social: friendly	43·1	2·6	12·8	20·7
Social: hostile	5·6	30·8	20·5	14·0
Bodily need	2·8	5·1	2·6	6·1
Achievement	13·9	7·7	10·3	17·3
Travel/movement	9·7	25·6	10·3	13·9
Other	6·9	7·7	5·1	5·0

ances are made for the fact of some overlap between less deprived institutionals and their controls, the previously noted group differences in dream content are more readily demonstrated and more reliable statistically.

David Foulkes, James D. Larson, Ethel M. Swanson and Max Rardin 127

Correlational analysis. Another approach to the problem of within-group inhomogeneity and consequent overlap between the two subgroups was the correlation (Pearson r) of all fourteen subjects' CPI (and WISC) scores with their mean dream word counts and ratings. CPI scores, particularly those for Wb, provide an alternative definition of waking adjustment that might be sensitive to boys in one subgroup showing waking behavior more similar to that of boys in the other subgroup than to that of boys in their own.

The two rating dimensions for Vivid Fantasy (Imagination, Relation to Everyday Experience) were highly intercorrelated (-0.92). Wb correlated -0.50 with the former and 0.51 with the latter (both $p = 0.05$, 1-tail). Overall, sixteen of eighteen CPI scales correlated negatively with dream Imagination and fifteen of eighteen positively with dream Relation to Everyday Experience. Additional correlations with the realism scale indicated the most realistic dreams were reported by boys high in social dominance (Do, 0.50, $p = 0.05$, 1-tail) and intellectual flexibility (Fx, 0.45, ns) and efficiency (Ie, 0.40, ns). All these results are consistent with the pathology-dream vividness hypothesis.

Dream Unpleasantness correlated -0.48 ($p = 0.05$, 1-tail) with Wb. Fourteen of this rating dimensions' eighteen correlations with the CPI were negative, including Ai (-0.52, $p = 0.05$, 1-tail). An interesting exception to this pattern was a significant *positive* association with Fe (0.54, $p = 0.05$, 2-tail). Subjects with feminine interest patterns not only had more unpleasant dreams, they also had dreams with more physical aggression (0.43, ns). Unpleasantness ratings were highly intercorrelated with those of Physical Aggression (0.76). Other CPI correlates of the latter were To (-0.52, $p = 0.05$, 1-tail) and, as predicted, Wb (-0.59, $p = 0.025$, 1-tail).

Verbal Aggression dream ratings did not correlate significantly with any test scores. They did correlate negatively, however, with subjects' ages (-0.51, $p = 0.10$, 2-tail). Physical Aggression (0.23, ns) and especially Heterosexuality (0.64, $p = 0.02$, 2-tail), on the other hand, increased with age. These results can be interpreted as a lessening of preadolescent intellectualizations of impulses as adolescence is more fully experienced.

Finally, Dominance correlated 0.68 ($p = 0.01$, 2-tail) with the active character of the subject's role in his dreams. Apparently there is, regardless of clinical status, a direct carryover of the kind of role a person plays in wakefulness to that he plays in his own dreams. This is still further evidence of the continuity, rather than complementarity, of dreams and wakefulness (Foulkes, in press) and directly contradicts the complementarity hypothesis of Jung (1923) that the waking extravert is a sleeping introvert.

General discussion

The results of these two studies confirm two hypotheses about childhood dreaming: first, that the dreams of the child are generally realistically related to his waking life, and second, that they become relatively more bizarre and unpleasant for children with some dysfunction in waking personality.

Findings for the preschoolers in Study One are perhaps less secure than those for the adolescents in Study Two. There is the possibility, which our efforts at testing subjects' abilities for accurate dream reporting on stimulus incorporation trials and by means of correlated test data did not entirely rule out, that the preschoolers confabulated. There is also the possibility that these subjects were trying to be accurate dream reporters but lacked vocabularies and concepts with which to communicate the true nature of their dream experiences. It might be held, for instance, that their dreams only seem realistic because there were no ways for the subjects to convey the more bizarre aspects of their nocturnal thoughts. Positive correlations of recall by preschoolers with adequacy of the concept of dream on the Laurendeau–Pinard test and with Descriptive Ability Scores cast some doubt on this interpretation. In addition, we noted that subjects' stereotyped conceptions of dreams before coming to the laboratory, probably based on selective recall of their total dream production, were generally that their dreams were 'scary', often involving frightening animal figures. They *were* able to report relatively unrealistic dreams, then. That such dreams were not reported under the representative sampling conditions in the laboratory may be taken as further evidence against the hypothesis that laboratory dream reports were realistic because the preschoolers were not able to report unrealistic content. It must still be admitted, however, that both the confabulation and communication-inadequacy hypotheses have greater potential application to the preschoolers, than to other, older child subjects.

With this qualification, the authors would suggest that their results suggest a coherent interpretive framework in terms of which the dreams of children and young adolescents might best be viewed: the dream as an ego process. In the absence of disturbances introduced by personality pathology, the child's dream is characterized by generally realistic, life-related content in which impulse and affect are noticeably absent. The dream of the young adolescent is more impulse-laden, but this correlates well with the shifting dynamic interrelation of ego and impulse that accompanies the onset of adolescence. In either case, the dream is more continuous than discontinuous with waking ego functioning.

Under conditions of systematic presentation of external stimuli during sleep there is still further evidence of adaptive ego functioning. As the examples of incorporation cited above indicate, the disturbing stimulus is most often displaced or externalized in the REM-sleep dream. Subject 7's electrode chain was wrapped across his neck, but the caterpillar of which he dreamed, without affect, was crawling on his sister's leg. Freud (see 1966) noted, of course, that the dream does not 'reproduce' a disturbing stimulus, but 'deals with it' in terms of hallucinatory experience. He uses such cases to highlight the role of wishes in dreaming, but they might better be employed in exemplifying the impressive set of ego operations that can be brought to bear upon the representation of an external stimulus impinging upon the subject.

The modal dream content of the normal child appears to be in the area of play and recreational activities. It is difficult to believe that these dreams were invariably instigated by unconsummated wishes from the dream day, as the id-instinctual view of the dream proposes. Dreams of play appear mostly simply to represent extensions of the child's waking ego impulses to exploration and manipulation of his environment (White, 1963). Robert White questions whether there *needs* to be a disturbing wish to set the child's play in motion. Could it not, rather, be in large measure determined by an ego that has its own autonomous and impulse-independent functions? The present results, and those of our studies of preadolescent dreams, are entirely consistent with White's answers to these questions; what he has to say about the child's play applies equally well to the child's dreams. Both are susceptible to the intrusion of destructive id impulses, but neither is a mere passive sounding board on which such impulses create their own ego-alien dissonances. To the extent that the ego is not overwhelmed by childish emotion and impulse, it places its own constructive stamp upon the nature of both play and dream activity.

References

AGNEW, H., WEBB, W., and WILLIAMS, R. (1966), 'The first night effect: an EEG study of sleep', *Psychophysiol.*, vol. 2, pp. 263–6.

AMEN, E. (1941), 'Individual differences in apperceptive reaction: a study of responses of preschool children to pictures', *Genet. Psychol. Monogr.*, vol. 23, pp. 319–85.

BLUM, G. (1950), *The Blacky Pictures: A Technique for the Exploration of Personality Dynamics*, Psychodynamic Instruments, Ann Arbor.

CLAUSEN, J. (1966), 'Family structure, socialization and personality', in L. W. and M. L. Hoffman (eds.), *Review of Child Development Research*, vol. 2, Russell Sage Foundation, New York, pp. 1–53.

DEMENT, W. (1965), 'An essay on dreams', in T. M. Newcomb (ed.), *New Directions in Psychology*, vol. 2, Holt, Rinehart & Winston, pp. 135–257.

DEMENT, W., and WOLPERT, E. (1958), 'The relation of eye movements, body motility and external stimuli to dream content', *J. exp. Psychol.*, vol. 55, pp. 543–53.

FISHER, C. (1965), 'Psychoanalytic implications of recent research on sleep and dreaming: I. Empirical findings', *J. Amer. Psychoanal. Assn*, vol. 13, pp. 197–270.

FOULKES, D. (1967), 'Dreams of the male child: four case studies', *J. child Psychol. Psychiat.*, vol. 8, pp. 81–97.

FOULKES, D. (in press), 'Drug research and the meaning of dreams', in *Drugs and Dreams*, Lippincott.

FOULKES, D., *et al.* (1967), 'Dreams of the male child: an EEG study', *J. abnorm. Psychol.*, vol. 72, pp. 457–67.

FOULKES, D., and RECHTSCHAFFEN, A. (1964), 'Presleep determinants of dream content: effects of two films', *Percept. mot. Skills*, vol. 19, pp. 983–1005.

FREUD, S. (1966), *The Complete Introductory Lectures on Psychoanalysis*, Norton.

GOUGH, H. (1957), *Manual for the California Psychological Inventory*, Consulting Psychologists Press.

GULEVICH, G., DEMENT, W., and ZARCONE, V. (1967), 'All-night sleep recordings of chronic schizophrenics in remission', *Comprehen. Psychiat.*, vol. 8, pp. 141–9.

HALL, C. (1966), *The Meaning of Dreams*, McGraw-Hill.

HARTMANN, E. (1967), *The Biology of Dreaming*, C. C. Thomas.

HAURI, P., SAWYER, J., and RECHTSCHAFFEN, A. (1967), 'Dimensions of dreaming: a factored scale for rating dream reports', *J. abnorm. Psychol.*, vol. 72, pp. 16–22.

JUNG, C. (1923), *Psychological Types*, Harcourt, Brace & World.

KALES, J., *et al.* (1968), 'Baseline sleep and recall studies in children', *Psychophysiol.*, vol. 4, p. 391 (abstract).

KÖHLER, W., CODDINGTON, R., and AGNEW, H. (1968), 'Sleep patterns in 2-year-old children', *J. Pediat.*, vol. 72, pp. 228–33.

LAURENDEAU, M., and PINARD, A. (1962), *Causal Thinking in the Child*, International Universities Press.

LEVINSON, D., and HUFFMAN, P. (1955), 'Traditional family ideology and its relation to personality', *J. Personality*, vol. 23, pp. 251–73.

MARSHALL, H. (1961), 'Relations between home experiences and children's use of language in play interaction with peers', *Psychol. Monogr.*, vol. 75, no. 5, whole no. 509.

PIVIK, T., and FOULKES, D. (1966), '"Dream deprivation": effects on dream content', *Science*, vol. 153, pp. 1282–4.

RECHTSCHAFFEN, A., and VERDONE, P. (1964), 'Amount of dreaming: effect of incentive, adaptation to laboratory, and individual differences', *Percept. mot. Skills*, vol. 19, pp. 947–58.

ROFFWARG, H., DEMENT, W., and FISHER, C. (1964), 'Preliminary observations of the sleep-dream pattern in neonates, infants, children and adults', in E. Harms (ed.), *Problems of Sleep and Dream in Children*, Pergamon, pp. 60–72.

ROFFWARG, H., *et al.* (1962), 'Dream imagery: relation to rapid eye movements of sleep', *Arch. gen. Psychiat.*, vol. 7, pp. 235–58.

WHITE, R. (1963), 'Ego and reality in psychoanalytic theory', *Psychol. Issues*, vol. 3, no. 3.

WILCOXON, F., KATTI, S., and WILCOX, R. (1963), *Critical Values and Probability Levels for the Wilcoxon Rank Sum Test and the Wilcoxon Signed Rank Test*, Lederle Laboratories, Pearl River, New York.

ZARCONE, V., GULEVICH, G., and DEMENT, W. (1967), 'Sleep and electroconvulsive therapy', *Arch. gen. Psychiat.*, vol. 16, pp. 567–73.

8 Leslie H. Farber and Charles Fisher

An Experimental Approach to Dream Psychology through
the Use of Hypnosis

Leslie H. Farber and Charles Fisher, 'An experimental approach to dream
psychology through the use of hypnosis', *Psychoanalytic Quarterly*, vol. 12, 1943,
pp. 202–16. Reprinted in C. Scott Moss (ed.), *The Hypnotic Investigation of Dreams*,
Wiley, 1967, pp. 115–26.

Introduction

Because of the difficulty of investigating emotional processes experimentally,
the investigation of dream psychology has progressed little since the publication of Freud's *The Interpretation of Dreams*, a fact which Freud noted in
1933 when he complained that analysts 'behave as though they had nothing
more to say about the dream – as though the whole subject of dream theory
were finished and done with' (1931b, p. 16). He called attention, as an
exception, to the pioneer work of several Viennese investigators who, using
hypnosis (Schroetter) and other methods, had made a start in the experimental confirmation of the theory of dream symbolism. Unfortunately,
this research was not pursued. The last two decades have seen considerable
development of hypnotic techniques in the study of various unconscious
processes. Eisenbud (1937, 1939), Erickson (1939a, 1939b), Erickson and
Kubie (1938, 1939, 1940), Kubie (1934), Luria (1932), and others have
contributed to this literature.

To develop a method of dream study which might be more objective than
the interpretive technique used in analytic therapy, a group of average
college students were used as hypnotic subjects. With them as subjects the
following problems were investigated:

1. *The capacity of normal individuals under hypnosis to understand dream
language and the factors which might influence this understanding.* In hypnotic
and other dissociated mental states, individuals show capacity for understanding and interpreting the unconscious psychic productions of others. It
is well known that schizophrenic patients are able to interpret dreams. Some
artistic individuals manifest a special faculty for understanding the unconscious import of artistic creations. Erickson found that a hypnotized
subject in one instance was able to read and understand the automatic
writing of another person.

2. *The production of experimental dreams under hypnosis.* Earlier workers
have found that they could partially control the form and content of the
dream by suggesting under hypnosis what was to be dreamed about. Their

suggestions were restricted to a limited number of grossly sexual situations. We hoped to confirm this work and extend its scope to include a variety of dream stimuli.

3. *The nature of the relationship between hypnotist and subject.* Hypnosis fell into comparative disuse as a therapy largely because of the lack of understanding of the hypnotic relationship.

The students who participated in the project as hypnotic subjects were recruited from a Washington university by the professors, who announced to their classes that two psychiatrists were doing research with hypnosis. The volunteers were from eighteen to twenty-one years of age. Those who seemed unstable were immediately excluded, and only those who proved to be naïve about psychology, ignorant of any knowledge of the theory of dreams, were chosen. They were asked not to read about the subject for the duration of the project. Those selected were average students, with no conspicuous personal problems and no special talents, either artistic or intellectual.

Dream translation

Under hypnosis the subjects were directly presented with dreams, of which some were fantasies of the experimenters, some produced by other subjects during hypnosis, some were the dreams of friends and patients, and a few were myths and psychotic productions. For example, an eighteen-year-old girl was told under hypnosis: 'Dreams have meaning. Now that you are asleep you will be better able to understand them. A girl dreamt that she was packing her trunk when a big snake crawled into it. She was terrified and ran out of the room. What do you think the dream means?' Almost before the question was finished, the subject blushed, hesitated a second, then said, 'Well, I guess she was afraid of being seduced. The snake would be the man's sex organ and the trunk hers.'

As a control, subjects were always questioned about the dream before and after hypnosis, and in no instance did the subjects in the waking state make any comment comparable to that obtained under hypnosis. Care was taken not to ask leading questions nor to reveal the experimenters' interpretations of the dreams.

Several female subjects were given this dream: 'A boy was sitting at his desk studying when the waste basket caught on fire. He ran and got a pitcher of water and put the fire out.' Their immediate response was, 'Oh, he wet his bed', or, 'He should have gone to the bathroom'. However, a dream about a girl putting out a fire made no sense to them.

It was suggested to one subject that as a child she had wet the bed and been severely scolded by her mother. In response to this stimulus she dreamed of falling into a pond in winter and being scolded by her mother. This dream was then related to a second girl, under hypnosis, who was entirely ignorant of the genesis of the dream. Without any hesitation the second subject said, 'Oh, that girl must have wet the bed!' thus recovering the stimulus that had produced the dream.

A second example illustrating the sexual differentiation of symbols is the following dream given for translation: 'A man is sitting in a dentist's chair while the dentist tries to pull his tooth. He pulls and pulls. The dreamer is in great pain when the dream ends.' Several subjects said the dream meant that a man was having his 'vital organ' cut off. When the dental patient was a woman, the dream was translated as 'giving birth to a baby'.

An exclusive appetite for mushrooms, developed by a psychotic patient, was described to a subject under hypnosis, and she was asked what it would mean if it were a dream. She answered, 'He was very sexual. He might even be homosexual.' Since one of the authors later treated this patient, he can attest to the validity of this student's hypnotic interpretation.

During the First World War, one of the authors had the following vivid nightmare: 'I had been captured by the Kaiser and he made ready to execute me. He placed my head on a chopping block and was about to swing the axe which would end my life, when the dream ended.' Under hypnosis a student said the Kaiser was really the dreamer's father who was going to chop of his penis, not his head. She believed it was a punishment for something – probably some sexual act.

The story of Moses and the bulrushes presented as a dream to a girl subject evoked the response, 'I think somebody was going to have a baby,' adding that the bulrushes stood for pubic hair.

Because of the startling unanimity of response offered by hypnotic subjects, one might at first conclude that dreams are like puzzles which have only one answer – a sexual one. We have come to believe that these uniform sexual responses were influenced by the nature of the hypnotic relationship. Hypnosis is not only a state of consciousness, like sleep, in which dreams occur, but it is also a very striking inter-personal relationship. The most obvious characteristic of this relationship is the extreme dependence of the subjects and their feeling that the hypnotist is omnipotent. Their critical capacities, while not eliminated as Freud once thought, are certainly restricted. The hypnotist too is reacting, not only to the subject, but to the hypnotist's role of omnipotence. His reaction will in turn influence the subject. The relationship contains all the complexities of any relationship between two people, although the belief has developed, because of certain extraordinary aspects of the process, that in hypnosis one deals with something outside the bounds of normal human experience. The unique interaction at any given moment between the personality of the hypnotist and the personality of the subject will necessarily determine the experimental results.

Even under what seem to be the same experimental conditions, different hypnotists evoke totally different responses.

Many observers have compared hypnosis to sexual seduction or assault (cf. de Saussure, 1943), and it is a commonplace that a male hypnotist can hypnotize women much more easily than men. It is noteworthy that practically all the erotic dream translations cited were obtained from comparatively uninhibited women, and from one male subject who was a rather passive individual with a marked attachment for the hypnotist. Jung is said to have abandoned hypnosis when an awakening subject coyly thanked him for being so decent. 'That demonstrated to me,' he said, 'the true nature of hypnosis.' We have not found that hypnosis is very different in this respect from other transference relationships. Recognition of this factor does not detract from the method, as Jung feared, but increases its scientific validity.

The following example will illustrate how the form of the dream translation will depend on the interpersonal factors described. A shy female subject in hypnosis was told, 'Some time ago you were packing your trunk when a snake crawled into it. You became terrified and ran out of the room.' She then dreamed, 'It was night and I was lost in the jungle. It was muddy and the mud came up to my waist so that I could not move in any direction. There were little snakes on the branches of the trees above me, which kept falling on my arms and shoulders. They kept getting nearer; some of them touched me. Only the mud kept the snakes from going below my waist; they could not touch me where the mud was; they could not get in. I felt safe in the mud.' Questioned about this dream when awake, she said that the snakes were something harmful and the mud signified safety – a mere paraphrase of the dream. Hypnotized again, she was questioned by a person other than the hypnotist. Now the snakes represented something desirable, the mud a barrier to the satisfaction of her desire. First she spoke of the snakes as ideas which attracted her but which other people thought too radical; then as people whose political and social beliefs made them attractive, but who were disapproved of by others; finally, she referred to the snakes as experiences she wished to have but which convention, as represented by the mud, denied here. At this point the interlocutor left the room and the subject's hypnotist questioned her alone. There was then a general relaxation of her facial expression and quite spontaneously she said that the snakes represented a pollution which came from the phallic branches of the trees, and this was the experience she desired. Questioned by a person other than the hypnotist, her translation was on a conventional social level. The dream was perceived in sexual terms in relation to the hypnotist. Both translations are of course parts of the total dream significance.

A similar variation in translation was obtained while attempting to discover how pregnancy would be portrayed in an experimental dream. A hypnotized girl was told, 'Not long ago you discovered that a friend of yours had become pregnant; she came to you and told you how terrified she was to be caught in this way. You were shocked and did not know what to do.' She then dreamed, 'I was on an island and all around me waves were swelling; there were mountains up and down and around. There was a sudden downpour of rain. I felt that everything around me was so powerful that I was just insignificant. I did not know what to do.' Several days later the dream was recalled to her under hypnosis by a person other than the hypnotist. Although she felt the dream was about pregnancy, the small island was the social ostracism and isolation enforced by her predicament, while the rain was the gossip and insinuation which fell on her. When her own hypnotist questioned her, she said that the rain was the downpour of semen.

This difference in response raises some interesting questions. Are the sexual translations due to some direct or implied suggestive influence by the hypnotist? Although it is difficult to eliminate this factor, our impression is that neither the hypnotist nor the substitute exerted any suggestion. Or can the dominant–submissive relationship of hypnosis be a sexual experience to the subject and does this serve to determine the form of his translations? It is undoubtedly true that a number of subjects seem to regard hypnosis as a sexual experience. We believe that this specific characteristic of the relationship with the hypnotist makes for a sexual interpretation, but this cannot be stated with certainty.

Only five, or about 20 per cent of the subjects carefully studied, proved to be able translators of dreams. The explanation for the failure of the remainder of the group is not clear. It can be said, however, that these individuals were quite inhibited and rigid compared to the translators. The reasons for both the ability and inability to translate dreams will be elicited only through careful personality studies of the individual subjects.

Even among the selected group it often happened that a hypnotized subject was unable to make any statement about a dream. This type of resistance could usually be overcome by one of two opposite methods. Sometimes a subject was able to translate his own dream only when it was presented as that of another person. At other times it was necessary to transform another person's dream into his own, by suggesting that this was an actual experience which had happened to him, and then asking him to dream about it.

A pregnant woman of our acquaintance dreamt that as she lay in bed one morning she was horrified to find a number of small white worms crawling over her arm. This dream was offered to a hypnotic subject with no result. The subject was then told that she herself had recently suffered the same horrible experience. She dreamt, 'There was a white candle resting in a small dish beside my bed. The candle burned lower and lower and little wax particles kept dropping into the base of the dish.' When asked about the new dream, she said, 'The man came and that's what the dripping of the wax was.' The first dream about the worms was recalled to her and she said, 'That was the same thing.' With another subject, who was likewise unable to find any meaning in the worm dream, this same maneuver of re-dreaming elicited a dream that the subject was driving alone in a car with her arm resting on the sill of the open window. It was snowing and snowflakes kept dropping on her exposed forearm. After this dream she commented, 'Now I know what the dream about the worms meant. Some girl had had relations with a man and she was afraid of getting pregnant. They hadn't taken any precautions. The worms refer to sperm.' For some reason these two subjects translated the worm dream only after they had in effect restated the dream in their own dream language.

The production of experimental dreams

The production of experimental dreams under hypnosis was first success-fully accomplished many years ago by Karl Schroetter (1911). In 1912 this investigator reported a series of dreams containing the symbols with which psychoanalytic dream interpretation has made us familiar, and the work was offered as experimental proof for the Freudian theory of symbols. This theory received additional confirmation in the investigations of Roffen-stein (1924) and Nachmansohn (1925). As in sleep, the hypnotized subject will dream spontaneously, and he will also dream about situations that are suggested to him.

The production of such experimental dreams under hypnosis depends, however, upon the capacity of the individual subject to accept in fantasy and live through an emotionally toned situation suggested to him by the hypnotist. While the situation is being outlined, his facial expressions and bodily movements show that he is experiencing genuine emotion – often painful and sometimes very intense.

The experimental procedure we finally evolved, after considerable trial and error, is as follows: under deep hypnosis the subject is told, 'I am going to recall an experience that happened to you some time ago. You have pro-bably forgotten it, but as I describe it, you will remember it in all its details.' The experience is then described and the subject is told: 'A dream will come to you. Raise your right hand when the dream begins and lower it when the dream is finished.' After one or two minutes of dreaming, the subject will relate his dream. It should be noted that the subject is not instructed to dream about the suggested situation, but merely told that a dream will come to him. We have been more successful in eliciting dreams with this method, probably because it permits greater freedom of fantasy on the part of the subject.

The dream stimuli we have used fall into two categories: first, those which were sexual, comprising experiences of pregnancy, intercourse, bedwetting, masturbation and homosexuality; second, nonsexual stimuli, including experiences of hostility, false accusation, competition, being taken advantage of, and others. Dreams obtained by hypnosis or by posthypnotic suggestion have all the characteristics of spontaneous dreams, and the subjects do not make a distinction between them. Following the dream stimulus, the subject usually first gives us a dream which is a paraphrase of the suggested stimulus, slightly modified by the inclusion of incidents from his own life experience. As he continues dreaming his subsequent productions have more and more the bizarre and pictorial character of dreams.

Why all subjects are not able to dream under hypnosis is not clear. The reaction to a dream stimulus seems to depend upon a combination of factors which include the nature of the dream stimulus, the personality structure of the subject, and his relationship to the hypnotist. Roffenstein had great difficulty in finding a hypnotic subject who would dream, probably because he utilized dream stimuli involving highly traumatic experiences as, for instance, suggesting to a woman that she dream about a homosexual relation. We have used a more indirect method calculated to spare the moral sensibilities of the subject. To elicit a dream about pregnancy, we suggested an experience in which a friend had become pregnant. Since the dream is always personalized, we achieved the desired result in the end. Another method of bringing about the acceptance of reprehensible experiences was to place them in childhood. From one subject we were able to elicit excellent dreams by the instruction: 'I am going to recall a certain experience. This did not actually happen to you, but as I tell you about it, you will live through it as if it had.' As a final precaution, we always attempted to remove the stimulus at the end of the experiment by telling the subject that the suggested experiences had not really happened to him.

The following experimental dream involves the play on words that is so frequently encountered in dreams. A young woman was told, 'When you were a little girl you wet your bed and when you awoke in the morning your mother scolded you.' The subject then dreamed that she told a lie which made her parents so angry that they spanked her. In her first account, she omitted the bedwetting, the substance of the lie. Only after considerable questioning by us, and evasion on her part, did she state that what she had lied about was risking being 'run over in order to go to the A and P'.

We have sometimes asked subjects to draw certain objects or figures that appear in their dreams, which frequently helps to clarify their meaning. Marcinowski (1911–12) first demonstrated that landscapes in the dreams of his patients represented parts of the body, unrecognizable from the verbal descriptions. Kubie (1934) likewise reported a very instructive case, in which the meaning of a dream was revealed in a drawing representing an airplane as the male genitals.

To investigate symbolization of the female breast, a male subject was given the dream stimulus: 'One day you were walking down a street in one of the poorer sections of town and you happened to see a young woman sitting on the steps nursing an infant. Her breast was exposed and you could see the baby take the nipple in its mouth and suck at it.' His dream was: 'I came to the corner where there was an old, rundown store. I went in to look for a magazine called Famous Fantastic Mysteries. I saw some fruit – apples and oranges – and tobacco and candy. They did not have the magazine so I bought some pipe tobacco and went out. I took the Mount Pleasant street car and rode to the top of a tall hill; it was flat on top; the other side was steep. It was the end of the car line. I got off and stood on the edge and looked down.' Under hypnosis he drew a picture of the hill (Figure 1).

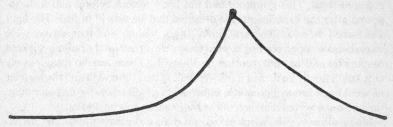

Figure 1 Mount Pleasant

The same subject was told that he had once wet his bed and had felt very much ashamed because that was the sort of thing a child did. He dreamt that he called his mother and told her about wetting the bed. The doctor came and advised an operation. He went to the hospital in a cab with his mother, was prepared for the operation, and was greatly frightened as he was taken to the operating room. Next he was walking out of the hospital and down 13th street to a hardware store in order to buy a woodworking tool. Asked under hypnosis to draw the tool, he drew the head of a hammer.

Past experiences are sometimes incorporated into the dream. A girl, given the dream stimulus of an experience in which she had been caught masturbating by her mother, dreamed: 'My sister and I, dressed in our best clothes, were making mud pies with mud which we kept in a rusty tomato can. We splattered the front of our dresses and mother scolded us, saying that it was my fault that my sister was doing it too.' She later remembered this to be an incident from her childhood, possibly a screen memory.

Another subject, told that while walking through the woods she had been frightened by seeing a snake, dreamed that she and her father climbed a steep, winding path to the top of a hill on which there was a reservoir. As they walked back she leaned on her father's arm. When awake she recalled having made such an excursion to a reservoir with her father. Shortly afterward she went home on vacation and in describing to her father her work with us, she mentioned this dream. He was startled and visibly upset but unwilling to give any explanation. The father's reaction permits the speculation that the girl's casual recollection is a screen memory for an early trauma. As an association to snake, it suggests seeing the father's penis. That experimental dreams might be used to recover forgotten experiences was proposed by Nachmansohn who made similar observations.

We gave a male subject the dream stimulus of having eaten some green apples and developing a severe diarrhea. We suggested to him in detail the nature of his symptoms and described the number, kind, changing color and consistency of his stools. All through his subsequent narration he coughed and spluttered. This symptom had not been present before, and it disappeared after the experiment. He dreamed that he was ill in bed. The light was turned on and off several times. It got 'lighter and then darker'. He started and stopped reading several times. He turned on the radio but it kept running on and on, interrupting his thoughts. There was no music – only talk – until finally he turned it off. We believe that the cough and the manner of speaking were symptomatic equivalents of diarrhea by displacement, similar to the verbal diarrhea of the radio which ran on and on.

Many subjects will, when asked, produce a dream without any dream stimulus. These spontaneous dreams often have a manifest content corresponding to the chief conscious interests of the individual. A geology major, with a marked interest in architecture, dreamed repeatedly of architectural groupings and landscapes.

On several occasions we asked a woman physician to be present during hypnotic sessions. During these sessions the subject's spontaneous dreams changed in character. With a woman present, he dreamed of climbing a staircase; of a sewer pipe running through a tunnel; of driving a car around the left side of a mountain into a tunnel.

The hypnotic subject is thus found to be not simply a passive object whose dreams can be manipulated at will by an omnipotent hypnotist. Hypnotic behavior is a meaningful, goal-directed striving, its nature determined by the dynamic unconscious. The subject's spontaneous dreams are influenced by his own unconscious needs and the interaction of these with the hypnotist and any other persons included in the hypnotic situation. Similarly, the dreams elicited in response to dream stimuli are not simple reflections of the stimulus but reveal the needs and wishes of the subject.

Manifestly nonsexual dream stimuli usually evoke dreams expressing the social situation in terms of 'body language'. A young girl was given as a stimulus a situation in which, falsely accused by a friend of cheating in an examination, she became very angry but because of circumstances was unable to deny the accusation. The subject then dreamed that a dentist was trying to pull her tooth despite her frightened protests that the nurse had taken the anaesthetic out of the wrong bottle. In her dream the humiliating accusation is portrayed as bodily assault and deprivation.

A boy was told that he had a rival in his geology class with whom he had trouble competing because he refused to defer to the teacher as the other boy did. The subject then dreamed: 'The geology class went on a field trip. We came to an outcropping of rock and I started chipping at it with my hammer. A flying fragment of rock hit the other boy in the face, cutting him. That made me feel fine.' Here academic competition becomes a bodily assault on his rival. The examples indicate how a familiar dream symbol may portray a variety of human experiences. Thus, tooth-pulling may represent not only castration and childbirth but also socially insulting predicaments; the attack with the hammer may represent not only homosexual assault but also scholastic rivalry.

Summary

A method is presented for the study of dreams and other unconscious processes by hypnosis. In hypnosis certain subjects have more awareness of the meaning of dream language than in the waking state. This awareness is influenced by the relationship between hypnotist and subject. The similarity of this relationship with other interpersonal relationships was pointed out, as well as the possibility of using this method for the study of transference. A number of experimental dreams, evoked by both sexual and nonsexual dream stimuli, are presented and their special characteristics discussed. The results obtained illustrate the great plasticity of the dream language and argue against too narrow interpretation of symbols.

Commentary by Charles Fisher

I have not done any work in hypnosis for many years and have kept up with the literature in only a casual sort of way. In regard to the paper by L. H. Farber and myself, it seems that the several attempts over the years which have been made to replicate the aspect of this study that has to do with the ability to hypnotize subjects to interpret dreams have not been successful. I am unable to understand why this has been the case. Perhaps our result was due to a combination of youthful enthusiasm and the particular subject group that we worked with. Some twelve or fifteen years ago I did do an extensive study on the nature of suggestion demonstrating that suggestions will be incorporated into dreams when given in the waking state, especially if the subject is in the relatively regressed position of the psychoanalytic situation.

There is a good deal of recent work utilizing the REM–EEG method, which confirms the finding that suggestions can be incorporated into nocturnal dreams when the suggestion is given in the hypnotic state. Many investigators, because of their absence of knowledge about the psychoanalytic formulation of the primary process or their lack of skill in detecting primary process transformations of day residues, are, as a consequence, unable to detect the incorporation of a suggestion into a dream because this may occur in a distorted manner involving condensations, displacements, and so forth. It is, of course, methodologically difficult to work out objective ways of demonstrating the connections between such transformations and the original day residue and to rule out the possibility of subjective *ad hoc* interpretations. But it is possible to do so.

References

DE SAUSSURE, R. (1943), 'Transference and animal magnetism', *Psychoanal. Q.*, vol. 12, pp. 194–201.

EISENBUD, J. (1937), 'Psychology of headache: case studied experimentally', *Psychiat. Q.*, vol. 11, pp. 592–619.

EISENBUD, J. (1939), 'Method of investigating effect of repression on somatic expression of emotions in vegetative function: preliminary report', *Psychosom. Med.*, vol. 1, pp. 376–87.

ERICKSON, M. H. (1939a), 'Experimental demonstration of the psychopathology of everyday life', *Psychoanal. Q.*, vol. 8, pp. 338–53.

ERICKSON, M. H. (1939b), 'An experimental investigation of the possible anti-social use of hypnosis', *Psychiatry*, vol. 2, pp. 391–414.

ERICKSON, M. H., and KUBIE, L. S. (1938), 'The use of automatic drawing in the interpretation and relief of a state of acute obsessional depression', *Psychoanal. Q.*, vol. 7, pp. 443–66.

ERICKSON, M. H., and KUBIE, L. S. (1939), 'The permanent relief of an obsessional phobia by means of communications with an unsuspected dual personality', *Psychoanal. Q.*, vol. 8, pp. 471–509.

ERICKSON, M. H., and KUBIE, L. S. (1940), 'The translation of the cryptic automatic writing of one hypnotic subject by another in a trance-like dissociated state', *Psychoanal. Q.*, vol. 9, pp. 51–63.

FREUD, S. (1931), 'Revision of the theory of dreams', in *New Introductory Lectures on Psychoanalysis*, Norton.

KUBIE, L. S. (1934), 'Body symbolisation and development of language', *Psychoanal. Q.*, vol. 3, pp. 430–44.

LURIA, P. A. (1932), *The Nature of Human Conflicts on Emotion, Conflict and Will: An Objective Study of Disorganization and Control of Human Behavior*, Lippincott.

MARCINOWSKI, J. (1911–12), 'Gezeichnete Träume', *Zentr. Psychiat.*, vol. 11, pp. 490–518.

NACHMANSOHN, M. (1925), 'Ueber experimentell erzeugte Traeume nebst Kirtischen Bemerkungen ueber die psychoanalytische Methodik', *Z. Neurol. Psychiat.*, vol. 98, pp. 556–86. Trans. D. Rapaport, *Organization and Pathology of Thought*, Columbia University Press, 1951, pp. 257–87.

ROFFENSTEIN, G. (1924), 'Experimentelle Symbol-Traeume: ein Beitrag zur Diskussion ueber Psychoanalyse', *Z. Neurol. Psychiat.*, vol. 87, pp. 362–72. Trans. D. Rapaport, *Organization and Pathology of Thought*, Columbia University Press, 1951, pp. 249–56.

SCHROETTER, K. (1911), 'Experimentelle Traeume', *Zentr. Psychoanal.*, vol. 2, pp. 638–48. Trans. D. Rapaport, *Organization and Pathology of Thought*, Columbia University Press, 1951, pp. 234–48.

9 Bill Domhoff

Night Dreams and Hypnotic Dreams: Is There Evidence that They Are Different?

Bill Domhoff, 'Night dreams and hypnotic dreams: is there evidence that they are different?', *International Journal of Clinical and Experimental Hypnosis*, vol. 12, 1964, pp. 159–68. Reprinted in C. Scott Moss (ed.), *The Hypnotic Investigation of Dreams*, Wiley, 1967, pp. 206–13.

The method of free association is an important technique for the scientific study of dream content, but it is not a powerful enough method to win widespread acceptance for Freud's ideas. Nor is it very successful with typical dream symbols. What is needed is an experimental technique, a method for controlling dream content and for producing and translating dream symbolism. Such a potential technique, viewed by many with great promise despite its checkered history, is hypnosis. Since 1911, when Karl Schroetter reported that he had obtained symbolic hypnotic dreams from three different *S*s, it has been hoped that hypnosis might become the experimental technique capable of spearheading a systematic study of dream content.[1]

Today, however, the hopes for the hypnotic dream as the experimental key to night dream interpretation have never been dimmer. EEG studies seem to concur in finding no physiological justification for equating sleep and hypnotic trance (e.g. Diamant, Dufek, Hoskovec, Krištof, Pekárek, Roth and Velek, 1960; Schiff, Bunney and Freedman, 1961), and the more important possibility of psychological equivalence between night and hypnotic dream is seemingly ruled out by significant content differences (e.g. Brenman, 1949; Gill and Brenman, 1959).

In the face of such evidence, it may seem unrealistic to cling to the idea that hypnosis could become an important experimental adjunct to dream research. However, it is submitted that two developments in physiological and quantitative dream research expose the weaknesses of negative evidence concerning the hypnotic dream. It is further suggested that these two developments necessitate a reconsideration of the entire question.

Sleep, hypnosis, and the EEG

It is often stated that the EEG patterns of sleep and hypnosis are two different matters. Some authors gloss over the unsettled nature of the question. For example: 'The lack of EEG changes is a usual finding in this and other

1. Cf. Moss (1961) for recent suggestions.

laboratories.' The reference which is cited as corroborating evidence by Schiff *et al.* (1961) actually contains many reports of slow alpha waves and theta waves during hypnosis (Chertok and Kramarz, 1959). Schiff *et al.* (1961) showed, in the study quoted above, that the rapid eye movements now known to be indicative of night dreams were also present in the hypnotic dreams of their only experimental *S*. But they failed to consider the possibility that methodology and/or personality variables might account for the subtle, small-frequency differences between the pattern correlated with dreaming (4–6 cps, but sometimes faster), theta rhythms (5–7 cps), and slow alpha (8–9 cps). Their judgement on the matter is accepted by Barber (1962) in his critique of the hypnotically induced dream. Barber cites the Schiff *et al.* (1961) findings on one *S* as evidence for his contention that the posthypnotically suggested night dreams of his own *S*s may have taken place after the *S*s awakened during the night.[2] Barber also refers the reader to Sirna (1945). Sirna's report will be singularly disappointing as it contains no EEG data, only the conclusion that the sleep EEG and the hypnotic EEG are different. Sirna does not state his criterion for a sleep EEG (nor did he himself even obtain such data), but he does note in passing that there were slight changes in the alpha rhythm during hypnosis.

At this point the now well-known physiological and behavioral indicators of dreaming should be discussed in more detail, for they raise a fundamental question about the 'sleep EEG' used as a criterion in previous studies comparing brain wave patterns during sleep and hypnosis. The correlation between rapid eye movements (REM) and dream reports was first published by Aserinsky and Kleitman (1953), and was spelled out more completely (with the added brain wave correlate) by Dement and Kleitman (1957a, 1957b): Dement and Kleitman noted a characteristic sleep cycle: as the *S* dropped off to sleep his EEG pattern was one of low voltage, fast frequencies, ranging from the drowsy-waking 10 cps to the 4 cps frequency.[3] No rapid eye movements were seen during this initial stage I, dreams were not reported when the *S* was awakened (the *S* often maintained he was still

2. Stoyva (1961) has recently shown that posthypnotic suggestions do in fact appear in the dream content from stage I sleep: 'The present study confirmed the findings of earlier investigators that subjects could be made to dream on the night following a hypnotic trance about topics suggested by the experimenter during the trance. Furthermore, through the use of the physiological approach first described by Aserinsky and Kleitman (1955) it was established that when instructed to do so, certain subjects will dream about the suggested topic in every dream of the night' (p. 4).

3. 'Stage I. The essential characteristic was *an absolute lack of spindle activity*. In general, a low voltage, relatively fast pattern corresponding to the "B" stage of Loomis *et al.*, the "Drowsy" stage of Gibbs, and including what the Loomis group called the "A" or interrupted alpha stage. Thus, any EEG pattern between full wakefulness and the appearance of spindles was included in stage I' (Dement and Kleitman, 1957a, p. 674).

awake), and muscular tension was apparent from eye leads. The shift to slower, higher voltage frequencies was usually signaled by the appearance of sleep spindles (14–16 cps) against a low voltage background (stage II). Following this, the S moved into the slow, high voltage frequencies classically associated with sleep (stages III and IV). About sixty minutes after falling asleep, the S reversed the sequence and returned to a low voltage, nonspindling, fast frequency sleep pattern. Although similar in brain wave characteristics to the stage I of falling asleep, there were several differences. Auditory waking thresholds were higher, discrete bursts of REMs appeared, there was no muscle tension from eye leads, and dreams were usually reported upon awakening. (These differences between initial stage I and later stage I – termed 'emergent' stage I – may be important considerations for future studies comparing sleep and hypnotic trance.) This cycle – from stage I down to stage IV and back to stage I – is repeated four to six times during the night, with less time in the classical slow wave sleep as the night progresses. The details of this general picture, as well as the necessary qualifications due to individual differences, can be found in Dement and Kleitman (1957a, 1957b), Kamiya (1961), and Kleitman (1960, 1963).[4]

Because of the time and expense involved, most EEG studies of sleep have only sampled brain wave patterns during the night. In fact, it was only after Dement decided to run the EEG all night, in order to clear up discrepancies between his data and that of Aserinsky and Kleitman, that the sleep cycle was discovered. It is therefore submitted that all pre-Dement and Kleitman studies comparing sleep and hypnosis must be reconsidered. It is suspected that most past investigators used sleep spindles and/or large, slow waves as their criteria of sleep, and thereby failed to consider the possibility that the hypnotic EEG may be similar to that of stage I, the very stage of sleep associated with dreaming.[5] It is further suggested that many early investigators ignored or played down seemingly-minor changes in the hypnotic EEG as mere 'slowing of the alpha frequency' because they were not aware of the importance of stage I sleep. These considerations, plus the

4. It is true that some investigators have reported mentation upon awakening from other stages of sleep (Foulkes, 1962; Kamiya, 1961; Rechtschaffen, Verdone and Wheaton, 1962). However, as both the Foulkes (1962) and the Rechtschaffen *et al.* (1962) studies point out, such mentation is quantitatively less and qualitatively different from that of stage I. Further, methodological controls for subject bias, as introduced by Kremen (1962), suggest that some of the mentation from other stages may be methodological artifact and/or hypnopompic imagery. Finally, the close relation between stage I content and eye movements, and the several physiological concomitants of stage I (Roffwarg, Dement, Muzio and Fisher, 1962), suggest that the verbal equation of stage I, REM, and dream should be retained, at least for the time being.

5. This is clearly the case with the classic study of Loomis, Harvey and Hobart (1936, p. 276). For those who might want to re-examine the scores of conflicting studies in the light of these comments, cf. the bibliography in Kleitman (1963).

several studies that have noted 'theta rhythms' during the hypnotic trance (Chertok and Kramarz, 1959), hint that the crucial equivalence – between the hypnotic trance and stage I sleep – may well be present.[6] That the two are not greatly different also can be seen from this account of stage I:

The stage I EEG persisting throughout the eye movement periods showed considerable variation within this classification. Generally a low voltage, irregular pattern, there were also many bursts or trains of regular 7–10 cps waves in the occipital leads, and 18–25 or 5–7 cps waves in the frontals. Although all these variations were usually seen in every subject, the occipital regular waves were more common in subjects with a prominent waking alpha rhythm and were characteristically 1–2 cps slower than the waking frequency (Dement and Kleitman, 1957a, p. 678).

An objection can be raised that the aforementioned criticisms do not apply to the study by Schiff *et al.* (1961), which actually dealt with the work of Dement and Kleitman. This objection can be met with reports from other post-Dement and Kleitman investigating teams, whose results suggest that EEG changes are obtained during the hypnotic trance with slight changes in the experimental interaction. Borlone, Dittborn and Palestini (1960) found that the alpha pattern is present when the *S* answers during the trance state, but that it largely disappears, to be replaced by theta rhythms, when the *S* is not communicating with the investigator. Similarly, Fujisawa and Obonai (1960) found that when rapport was maintained with their three *S*s the EEG resembled waking alpha, while it was closer to that of classical sleep when rapport was not maintained. While neither of these investigations was concerned with hypnotic dreams, their findings underline the importance of considering methodology in evaluating the contradictory evidence on the EEG of sleep and the hypnotic trance.

The theoretical ideas of Kleitman (1963) are also relevant at this point. Taking his cue from the discovery of the near-alpha frequency associated with dreaming, Kleitman hypothesizes that alpha frequency may be an index of consciousness, of the level of analytical functioning. Kleitman points to the slower alpha of the young, the old, the bored, the alcoholic, and the dreamer as evidence for his contention, and in a personal communication adds that the hypnotized *S* may often be added to this continuum.[7] If in fact small changes in alpha frequency are shown to be indicative of significant changes in mental functioning, this would strengthen the argu-

6. Solovey and Milechnin (1960) report spontaneous rapid eye movement after ten minutes of hypnotic trance in some *S*s: 'In fact, when we made these subjects pass into a lighter hypnotic state after they had been having eye movements for some minutes, and asked them to tell us their recent experience, the subjects gave us material of an oneiroid type, which appeared to have no difference from natural dreams' (p. 132).

7. Taking the cue from their studies of sleep learning, Simon and Emmons (1956) also suggest alpha changes as an index of change in consciousness.

ment that a hypnotic trance with an EEG similar to that of stage I would be useful in studying 'dreamwork' and symbol formation.[8]

The conclusion to be drawn, it is suggested, is not that of Schiff *et al.* (1961) or Barber (1962), but that of still another investigating team conversant with the work of Dement and Kleitman:

So far, then, the EEG findings allow us to say with certainty only that hypnosis is not deep sleep. We do not have the right to say that hypnosis is the same as the ordinary waking state: first, there is some evidence – shaky, it is true – that the EEG of hypnosis will be shown to differ from the EEG of the alert waking state; and second, an individual who seems to be asleep may show EEG patterns ordinarily associated with wakefulness (the change during stimulation of the sleeper who does not awake, and during dreaming). As far as the EEG is concerned, it is still possible to call the hypnotized subject a dreamer (Gill and Brenman, 1959, p. 226).

The content of night dreams and hypnotic dreams

Since the first studies by Schroetter (1911), it has been found that some hypnotic dreams are very prosaic, while others are very similar to the traditional stereotype of the night dream – bizarre and 'symbolic'. Further, as is shown by the work of Barber (1962) and Gill and Brenman (1959), the positive (often remarkable) results of Farber and Fisher (1943), Mazer (1951) and Schroetter (1911) have not been regularly repeatable. For those interested in hypnosis as an experimental technique, it would be important to understand these contradictory findings in terms of methodological and/or personality variables. For example, the aforementioned Borlone *et al.* study (1960) suggests the importance of the *S*'s expectations as determined by prehypnotic instructions, while the Fujisawa and Obonai study (1960) emphasizes the importance of distinguishing between hypnotic states where rapport is maintained with the hypnotist and where it is not maintained. The Solovey and Milechnin study (1960) suggests that the hypnotic dream may not occur immediately, which in turn points to the possibility of shifts in the depth of hypnotic trance. Then, too, differences could perhaps be expected between states produced by passive and active methods of induction, and between states accompanied by passive suggestions (such as deepening procedures) and active suggestions (such as dreaming). Further, many investigators have stressed the central importance of the particular psycho-dynamics underlying each hypnotist–subject relationship (e.g., Farber and Fisher, 1943; Newman, Katz and Rubenstein, 1960; Rubenstein, Katz and Newman, 1957). On the question of subject

8. Kleitman (1963) emphasizes the considerable individual differences in alpha frequency. Individual differences plus the importance of establishing even 1–2 cps changes in frequency show how important it is to have the same *S*s in both sleep and hypnotic trance conditions in future studies.

variation there is the interesting study by Hilgard (1963), which shows that 'good' Ss may do very poorly on specific tasks. For example, those who do well on 'positive hallucinations' may do poorly on 'negative hallucinations' or 'dreams'. This profile approach to subject selection should assure that future studies do not disagree because 'good' Ss were picked by criteria irrelevant to success in hypnotic dreaming.

The studies most often referred to in discounting the possibility of similarities of night and hypnotic dream content are those by Brenman (1949) and Gill and Brenman (1959). These investigators placed the hypnotic responses to the instructions 'to dream' in four categories – 'embellished reminiscence', 'static pictorial image', 'quasi-allegory', and 'quasi-dream' – and gave examples of each type. The distinction between the hypnotic dream categories and night dreams, as epitomized by the examples, may not be entirely convincing to those who have read through the dream series of normal Ss, nor perhaps to those who are familiar with quantitative studies of dream content. Gill and Brenman (1959) present no quantitative comparisons of samples of night and hypnotic dreams to buttress their claims, and a search of the literature shows that no one has made such a quantitative comparison. Until a properly controlled, quantitative study is made, preferably using the same Ss in both hypnotic and sleep conditions, the statement that there are differences between the content of night and hypnotic dreams cannot be accepted without reservation.

Actually, these investigators agree that there may be a great deal of overlap between night dreams and hypnotic dreams. Brenman (1949) quotes Freud with approval in suggesting that it is still an open question as to whether even all night dreams have precisely the same structure, formal qualities, and kinds of distortion:

A dream without condensation, distortion, dramatization, above all, without wish fulfillment, surely hardly deserves the name. You will remind me that, if so, there are other mental products in sleep to which the right to be called 'dreams' would have to be refused. Actual experiences of the day are known to be simply repeated in sleep; reproductions of traumatic scenes in 'dreams' have led us only lately to revise the theory of dreams. There are dreams which by certain special qualities are to be distinguished from the usual type, which are, properly speaking, nothing but night fantasies, not having undergone additions or alterations of any kind, and in all other ways similar to the well-known daydreams. It would be awkward, certainly, to exclude these imaginings from the realm of 'dreams'.

The 'actual experiences', 'traumatic scenes', and 'night fantasies' which Freud would find awkward to exclude from the realm of dreams are qualitatively difficult to distinguish from 'embellished reminiscences', 'static pictorial images', and 'quasi-allegories'.

A second recent development in dream research – quantitative studies of dream content – is relevant at this point. Beginning in the mid-1940s Hall (1951, 1953) started collecting dreams from normal adults, college students, children, and neurotics. With a sample of nearly 10,000 dreams, he has developed manuals for classifying and quantifying every element in the dream narrative – e.g., characters, settings, objects, activities, interpersonal relations, and emotions (Hall, 1962a, 1962b, 1962c, 1962d). Early results of this research are summarized in Hall (1956), and recent findings are now being published (Hall and Domhoff, 1963a, 1963b, 1964).

The application of Hall's content categories to samples of night and hypnotic dreams would make possible a quantitative comparison of significant content variables, a first step in the attempt to demonstrate what is the crucial equivalence from the point of view of the present paper – psychological equivalence. If it is objected that the night and hypnotic dreams might differ in latent content, it is equally possible to quantify the verbalizations by which latent content is uncovered – the free associations (Hall and Domhoff, 1962). Hall's (1963) equation of male stranger=father has demonstrated the usefulness of quantitative techniques with night dreams and their attendant free associations. Further, Moss (1961) is the most recent to comment on the fact that hypnotized Ss often do very well at interpreting their own dreams. Thus, an ideal study of latent content would compare, quantitatively, free associations (waking and/or under hypnosis) to night and hypnotic dreams. Also, the similarity of the dreamwork in night and hypnotic dreams could be demonstrated by obtaining manifest content predictable from psychoanalytic experience with the representations of specific wishes and fears (cf. Farber and Fisher, 1943). Finally, for whatever a subjective criterion may be worth, several of Klein's (1930) Ss reported that they felt there was no difference between night dreaming and hypnotic dreaming. Perhaps the combination of variables leading to such a statement would also produce hypnotic dream content similar to that of night dreams.

Conclusions

The sleep EEG pattern correlated with dream reports is very similar to that sometimes obtained during hypnosis. It is concluded that there is as yet no adequate evidence for claiming that the hypnotic EEG is different from that associated with dreaming (stage I). On the other hand, while REMs have been shown to be associated with hypnotic dreaming, it is not claimed that evidence permits identification of stage I with hypnotic trance. Suggestions are made for empirical studies of this problem.

A search of the literature on hypnotic dream content reveals that there never has been a quantitative comparison of the content of samples of night dreams and hypnotic dreams. It is concluded that until such studies are made there is not adequate evidence to accept the statement that there are significant differences between night and hypnotic dreams. Suggestions are made for quantitative comparison of both the manifest and latent content of the two types of productions.

References

ASERINSKY, E., and KLEITMAN, N. (1953), 'Regularly occurring periods of eye motility and concomitant phenomena during sleep', *Science*, vol. 118, pp. 273–4.

ASERINSKY, E., and Kleitman, N. (1955), 'Two types of ocular motility occurring in sleep', *J. appl. Psychol.*, vol. 8, pp. 1–10.

BARBER, T. X. (1962), 'Toward a theory of "hypnotic" behavior: the "hypnotically induced dream"', *J. nerv. ment. Dis.*, vol. 135, pp. 206–21.

BARBER, T. X. (unpublished), 'Experimental studies on the symbolic and non-symbolic "hypnotic dream"'.

BORLONE, M., DITTBORN, J., and PALESTINI, M. (1960), 'Correlaciones electroencefalographicas dentro de una definacion operacional de hipnosis sonambulica: communicacion preliminar', *Acta hipno. latinamer.*, vol. 2, pp. 9–19.

BRENMAN, M. (1949), 'Dreams and hypnosis', *Psychoanal. Q.*, vol. 13, pp. 455–65.

CHERTOK, L., and KRAMARZ, P. (1959), 'Hypnosis, sleep and electroencephalography', *J. nerv. ment. Dis.*, vol. 128, pp. 227–38.

DEMENT, W., and KLEITMAN, N. (1957a), 'Cyclic variations in EEG during sleep and their relation to eye movements, body motility and dreaming', *EEG clin. Neurophysiol.*, vol. 9, pp. 673–90.

DEMENT, W., and KLEITMAN, N. (1957b). 'The relation of eye movement during sleep to dream activity: an objective method for the study of dreaming', *J. exp. Psychol.*, vol. 53, pp. 339–46.

DIAMANT, J., DUFEK, M., HOSKOVEC, J., KRIŠTOF, M., PEKÁREK V., ROTH, B., and VELEK, M. (1960), 'An electroencephalographic study of the waking state and hypnosis with particular reference to subclinical manifestations of sleep activity', *J. clin. exp. Hypn.*, vol. 8, pp. 199–212.

FARBER, L. H., and FISHER, C. (1943), 'An experimental approach to dream psychology through the use of hypnosis', *Psychoanal. Q.*, vol. 12, pp. 202–16.

FOULKES, D. (1962), 'Dream reports from different stages of sleep', *J. abnorm. soc. Psychol.*, vol. 65, pp. 14–25.

FUJISAWA, K., and OBONAI, T. (1960), 'The psychophysiological studies of hypnotic sleep', *Jap. J. Psychol.*, vol. 31, pp. 94–101.

GILL, M. M., and BRENMAN, M. (1959), *Hypnosis and Related States: Psychoanalytic Studies in Regression*, International Universities Press.

HALL, C. S. (1951), 'What people dream about', *Sci. Amer.*, vol. 184, pp. 60–63.

HALL, C. S. (1953), *The Meaning of Dreams*, Harper & Row.

HALL, C. S. (1956), 'Current trends in research on dreams', in D. Brower and L. E. Abt (eds.), *Progress in Clinical Psychology*, vol. 2, Grune & Stratton, pp. 239–57.

HALL, C. S. (1962a), *A Manual for Classifying Aggressions, Misfortunes, Friendly Acts and Good Fortune in Dreams*, Institute of Dream Research, Miami, Florida.

HALL, C. S. (1962b), *A Manual for Classifying Characters in Dreams*, Institute of Dream Research, Miami, Florida.

HALL, C. S. (1962c), *A Manual for Classifying Settings and Objects in Dreams*, Institute of Dream Research, Miami, Florida.

HALL, C. S. (1962d), *A Manual for Classifying Emotions in Dreams*, Institute of Dream Research, Miami, Florida.

HALL, C. S. (1963), 'Strangers in dreams', *J. Personality*, vol. 31, pp. 336–45.

HALL, C. S., and DOMHOFF, B. (1962), 'Content analysis of reported dreams', Association for the Psychophysiological Study of Sleep.

HALL, C. S., and DOMHOFF, B. (1963a), 'Aggression in dreams', *Int. J. soc. Psychiat.*, vol. 9, pp. 259–67.

HALL, C. S., and DOMHOFF, B. (1963b), 'A ubiquitous sex difference in dreams', *J. abnorm. soc. Psychol.*, vol. 66, pp. 278–80.

HALL, C. S., and DOMHOFF, B. (1964), 'Friendliness in dreams', *J. soc. Psychol.*, vol. 62, pp. 309–14.

HILGARD, E. R. (1961), 'Profiles of hypnotizability', presented at meeting of American Social and Clinical Hypnosis, San Francisco.

KAMIYA, J. (1961), 'Behavioral, subjective and physiological aspects of drowsiness and sleep', in S. R. Maddi (ed.), *Functions of Varied Experience*, Dorsey Press, pp. 145–74.

KLEIN, D. B. (1930), 'The experimental production of dreams during hypnosis', *Univ. Texas Bull.*, no. 30009, pp. 5–71.

KLEITMAN, N. (1960), 'Patterns of dreaming', *Sci. Amer.*, vol. 203, pp. 82–8.

KLEITMAN, N. (1963), *Sleep and Wakefulness*, University of Chicago Press.

KREMEN, I. (1962), 'Subject expectations as a biasing variable in the study of dreaming', presented at meeting of American Psychological Association, St Louis, Missouri.

LOOMIS, A. L., HARVEY, E. N., and HOBART, G. A. (1936), 'Electrical potentials of the human brain', *J. exp. Psychol.*, vol. 19, pp. 249–79.

MAZER, M. (1951), 'An experimental study of the hypnotic dream', *Psychiatry*, vol. 14, pp. 265–77.

MOSS, C. S. (1961), 'Experimental paradigms for the hypnotic investigation of dream symbolism', *Int. J. clin. exp. Hypn.*, vol. 9, pp. 105–17.

NEWMAN, R., KATZ, J., and RUBENSTEIN, R. (1960), 'The experimental situation as a determinant of hypnotic dreams', *Psychiatry*, vol. 2, pp. 63–73.

RECHTSCHAFFEN, A., VERDONE, P., and WHEATON, J. (1962), 'Reports of mental activity during sleep', *Canad. Psychiat. Assn J.*, vol. 7, pp. 409–14.

ROFFWARG, H. P., DEMENT, W., MUZIO, J. N., and FISHER, C. (1962), 'Dream imagery: relationship to rapid eye movement in sleep', *Arch. gen. Psychiat.*, vol. 7, pp. 235–58.

RUBENSTEIN, R., KATZ, J., and NEWMAN, R. (1957), 'On the source and determinants of hypnotic dreams', *Canad. Psychiat. Assn J.*, vol. 2, pp. 154–61.

SCHIFF, S. K., BUNNEY, W. E., and FREEDMAN, D. X. (1961), 'A study of ocular movements in hypnotically induced dreams', *J. nerv. ment. Dis.*, vol. 133, pp. 59–68.

SCHROETTER, K. (1911), 'Experimentelle Traueme', *Zentr. Psychoanal.*, vol. 2, pp. 638–48. Trans. D. Rapaport, *Organization and Pathology of Thought*, Columbia University Press, 1951, pp. 234–48.

SIMON, C., and EMMONS, W. (1956), 'EEG, consciousness and sleep', *Science*, vol. 124, pp. 1066–9.

SIRNA, A. J. (1945), 'An electroencephalographic study of the hypnotic dream', *J. Psychol.*, vol. 20, pp. 109–13.

SOLOVEY, C., and MILECHNIN, A. (1960), 'Hypnotic phenomena, suggestion and oneiric activity', *Amer. J. clin. Hypn.*, vol. 2, pp. 122–37.

STOYVA, J. M. (1961), 'The effect of suggested dreams on the length of rapid eye movement periods', unpublished Ph.D. dissertation, University of Chicago.

10 Ernest R. Hilgard and David P. Nowlis

The Contents of Hypnotic Dreams and Night Dreams: An Exercise in Method[1]

Ernest R. Hilgard and David P. Nowlis, 'The contents of hypnotic dreams and night dreams: An exercise in method', in E. Fromm and E. Shor (eds.), *Hypnosis: Research Developments and Perspectives*, Elek, 1973.

Hypnotic dreams are not identical with night dreams, but it is also true that many night dreams do not fit the stereotype of what a true dream should be like. Some night dreams are very short, some have little dramatic quality, distortion may be absent, the dreamer may know that he is dreaming, and so on. In comparing hypnotic dreams and night dreams it is therefore unlikely that there will be some entirely clear answer to the question: is the hypnotic dream the same or different from a night dream? The answer will doubtless be that they overlap, but perhaps some important differences may be discovered.

The problem of comparing hypnotic dreams and night dreams is an old one, enhanced first by the considerable emphasis upon dreams in the work of Freud, and, second, by the new interest in sleep and dreams occasioned by new physiological methods, including EEGs and rapid eye movements (REMs). Others have reviewed the literature thoroughly. Moss's (1967) book includes not only his own discussions but reprints of the more important articles appearing up to that time. Among these is the review by Tart (1965) in which the methodological problems are thoroughly discussed. In the past there was some polarization of opinions, as by Brenman (1949), who argued for a difference between hypnotic and night dreams, and by Mazer (1951), who took the opposite view. Authors of twenty of the thirty-four studies reviewed by Tart felt it desirable to make some comparisons between hypnotic dreams and night dreams; of these twenty, only ten favoured some equation between the two kinds of dreams, four denied the similarity, and six felt that the evidence was insufficient to state firm conclusions.

The empirical material in the present study is a by-product of routine testing of subjects by hypnotic susceptibility scales in which hypnotic dreams are suggested under two conditions, one in which the suggestion included the statement that the dream will tell something about hypnosis,

1. Modified from a paper given at the meeting of the Society for Experimental and Clinical Hypnosis, Chicago, Illinois, November 1968. The continued support of the National Institute of Mental Health, Grant MH-3859, is gratefully acknowledged.

the other in which this statement was lacking. Hence there is this modest degree of differential motivation toward content.

The methodological purpose of the investigation was to see how best to use content analysis in comparing night dreams and hypnotic dreams, a suggestion deriving from Domhoff (1964), who proposed the use of some of Hall's work on content analysis of thousands of night dreams (for example, Hall and Van de Castle, 1966). Content analysis is not a simple tool; decisions have to be made regarding what kinds of 'tokens' to count, and how much effort should be made to analyse (and count) symbolic distortions. Even among those committed to psychoanalytic theory there are disagreements concerning the nature of dreaming (for example, French and Fromm, 1964). As a starting point we decided to do what we could with categories deriving from Hall and Van de Castle, in order to compare our hypnotic dream sample with their night dream sample. We did not, however, feel it necessary to confine ourselves to these comparisons, and have made use of some comparisons with Perry (1964). The main methodological purpose is served, however, by attempting to use a content analysis with hypnotic dreams that will permit comparison with the large available collection of night dreams.

Procedure

We have collected a great many dreams within hypnosis in the course of administering the Stanford Hypnotic Susceptibility Scales, Form C, and the Profile Scales (Weitzenhoffer and Hilgard, 1962, 1967). The subjects, often inexperienced in either hypnosis or dream recall, received the following instructions on Form C:

We are very much interested in finding out what hypnosis and being hypnotized means to people. One of the best ways of finding out is through the dreams that people have while they are hypnotized. Some people dream directly about the meaning of hypnosis, while others dream about this meaning in an indirect way, symbolically, by dreaming about something which does not seem outwardly to be related to hypnosis, but may very well be. Now neither you nor I know what sort of a dream you are going to have, but I am going to allow you to rest for a little while and you are going to have a dream . . . a real dream . . . just the kind you have when you are asleep at night. When I stop talking to you very shortly, you will begin to dream. You will have a dream about hypnosis. You will dream about what hypnosis means . . . Now you are falling asleep . . . Deeper and deeper asleep . . . Very much like when you sleep at night . . . Soon you will be deep asleep, soundly asleep. As soon as I stop talking you will begin to dream. When I speak to you again you will stop dreaming, if you still happen to be dreaming, and you will listen to me just as you have been doing. If you stop dreaming before I speak to you again, you will remain pleasantly and deeply relaxed . . . Now sleep and dream . . . Deep asleep!

One or two minutes of silence followed. The hypnotist then broke the silence thus:

The dream is over; if you had a dream you can remember every detail of it clearly, very clearly. You do not feel particularly sleepy or different from the way you felt before I told you to fall asleep and to dream, and you continue to remain deeply hypnotized. Whatever you dreamed you can remember quite clearly, and I want you to describe it to me from the beginning. Now tell me about your dream, right from the beginning (Weitzenhoffer and Hilgard, 1962, pp. 21–2).

Some two-fifths of our unselected university subjects reported dreams. However, just as in the case of night sleep, a subject capable of dreaming under hypnosis does not always produce a dream upon request. In one sample of subjects, thirty-four had a dream on at least one of two opportunities, but only twenty dreamed on both occasions; six subjects who dreamed on the first day failed to dream on the second, and eight who failed to dream on the first day had a dream on the second day.

Comparison of hypnotic dreams with night dreams

How real are the dreams reported under these rather artificial circumstances? Tart (1966) found that subjects, when asked about the quality of their hypnotic dreams, reported a range from thinking or daydreaming, through watching a film or TV, to being 'in' the dream as in a vivid night dream. The report of being 'in' the dream was given by 13 per cent of fifty-four subjects who reported only borderline hypnotic states; and by 26 per cent of twenty-seven subjects who felt they had really been hypnotized. Furthermore, we attempted to relate the reality of hypnotic dreaming to the depth of trance as measured by the scores obtained on this hypnotic susceptibility scale, excluding the dream item. Less than one-tenth of those in the lower third of the susceptibility distribution who reported a dream indicated that it was of dreamlike quality, while of those in the highest third of susceptibility who reported a dream about one-third reported that their hypnotic dream was 'like a night dream'.

If dreams are selected from the reports of highly susceptible subjects, a substantial proportion are likely to be very similar to night dreams. It may be instructive to study the content of such dreams. However, before undertaking a comparison of hypnotic dreams with night dreams, it should be pointed out that we did not expect them to be exactly alike, although we expected some overlap. Some of the reasons why we believed that hypnotic dreams produced should *not* correspond precisely to night dreams, no matter how much they may resemble them, included:

1. The hypnotic subject is not really asleep, so that there is a background of critical awareness, which may alter the dream. Such waking dreams –

not to be confused with ordinary daydreams – occasionally are reported outside hypnosis, but they are rare.

2. The subject knows that he is going to report his dream. Therefore some conscious censorship doubtless is active. For example, one would expect few overtly sexual dreams under these circumstances. The frame of reference was more nearly that of a TAT story, sensitive to the setting in which it was produced.

3. Time demands are placed upon the subject. He is told to 'dream now', rather than to have a spontaneous dream occasioned by his own inner needs when they arise.

4. A topical set is created. Some of the instructions read suggested that the dream be about hypnosis. When this suggestion was given, it may very well have made some difference, as we shall see later.

5. The dream report itself is made within whatever hypnotic state the subject has achieved or believes himself to have achieved, and this may also colour his report.

Thus if we failed to find *any* difference between the hypnotic dreams and night dreams we would suspect that our content analysis measures were insensitive.

Single dreams, obtained under hypnosis from 172 subjects in the upper fourth of scores on SHSS:C (scores of 8 and above) were coded (Table 1). Nearly two-thirds of these dreams resembled typical night dreams; the others were less convincing.

Table 1 **Reality of reported hypnotic dream**

Reality as judged by coder	Number	Per cent
Subject involved, as in real night dream	109	63
Like watching movie or TV, with visual imagery	56	33
Like thinking or daydreaming	7	4
Total*	172	100

* Because there was one dream per subject the number of subjects equal the number of dreams. Those subjects not dreaming were eliminated from this study.
Source: after Hall and Van de Castle (1966).

Lacking a sample of night dreams from the same subjects, we have turned to a sample of night dreams analysed by Hall and Van de Castle (1966). This is a somewhat unsatisfactory procedure. Therefore we have interpreted the comparison as a methodological exercise, testing whether or not a code developed for night dreams would be applicable to hypnotic dreams, at least as a rough indicator of similarities and differences by which to guide further research efforts. To avoid over-interpretation of our findings we present some differences between our sample and that of Hall and Van de Castle in Table 2. Apart from the differences in the manner in which the dreams were obtained and recorded, we note to begin with that the hypnotic dreams were much shorter (averaging near the lower limit of the night dreams), and they had fewer characters in them.[2]

Table 2 **Contrast between hypnotic dream and night dream samples**

	Hypnotic dreams (present study)		Night dreams (Hall and Van de Castle)	
Subjects	College students		College students	
Dream background	Hypnosis		Sleep	
Occasion for dream	Suggested		Spontaneous	
Dream topic	'About hypnosis'		Spontaneous	
Dream report recorded	By experimenter		By subject	
Source of subjects	Classes (scored 8 or higher on SHSS:C)		Classes	
Dreams per subject	1		5	
	Male	Female	Male	Female
Number of subjects	91	81	100	100
Number of dreams	91	81	500	500
Words per dream (range)	15–123	13–238	50–300	50–300
Words per dream (mean)	52·0	57·8	unknown	unknown
Characters per dream	1·3	1·3	2·4	2·8

Source: after Hall and Van de Castle (1966).

Characters in dreams

We have followed Hall and Van de Castle in counting characters. The dreamer is not counted, and a crowd of an unspecified number of persons is counted as one person. 'Characters' include nonhuman animals and creatures as well as persons.

The mean difference in number of characters per dream is accounted for by the rapid fall-off of more than two characters besides the dreamer in the hypnotic dream, and the frequent occurrence of two or more characters in the night dream (Table 3). In the hypnotic sample, the differences between

2. Recall instructions for Hall and Van de Castle subjects included the following: 'Your report should contain, whenever possible, a description of the setting of the dream, whether it was familiar to you or not, a description of the people, their sex, age, and relationship to you, and of any animals that appeared in the dream' (p. 313).

the sexes were statistically insignificant. If we interpret the night dream sample as if there were 100 subjects in each sex group, the slightly larger number of characters among the female subjects was significant by a t-test ($p = <0.05$). The night dreams contained significantly more characters than the hypnotic dreams ($t = 6.5$, $p = 0.001$).

The kinds of characters found in the two types of dreams also differed, as shown in Table 4. While the classes with most members tended to be quite similar in hypnotic and night dreams, a few differences were rather striking. First, human characters contrast more sharply than all characters (Table 3) because of the prominence of nonhuman characters in the hypnotic dreams. Second, representations of the immediate family were less frequent in the hypnotic dreams, possibly because the office setting and the suggestion to dream about hypnosis may have depressed the number of personal family associations. Uncertainty, vagueness and metamorphosis also characterized the hypnotic dreams; there would have been even more metamorphoses if the animal and insect figures in hypnotic dreams had been included in Table 4. Again, these results may be due in part to the instructions to dream about hypnosis. Thus careful experimentation would be required to determine which aspects of dreaming are influenced by instructions.

Table 3 **Number of characters per dream**

Number of characters	Hypnotic dreams (present study)		Night dreams (Hall and Van de Castle)	
	male per cent	female per cent	male per cent	female per cent
0 (dreamer only)	31	32	6	3
1	30	28	24	19
2	25	25	30	24
3	10	10	20	25
4	4	4	12	14
5	0	1	4	7
6 and more	0	0	4	8
Total	100	100	100	100
	($N = 91$)*	($N = 81$)*	($N = 500$)†	($N = 500$)†

* One dream per S. Differences between sexes not significant.

† Five dreams per person, hence 100 Ss in each group. t—test, using $N = 100$, each sex: $t = 2.00$, $df = 198$, $p = .05$.

Source: after Hall and Van de Castle (1966).

Table 4 **Human characters found in hypnotic dreams and in night dreams, and their relative frequencies**

Human characters in dreams	Hypnotic dreams (present study) per cent of characters	Night dreams (Hall and Van de Castle) per cent of characters
Immediate family	1	12
Relatives	—	4
Known others	19	35
Prominent persons	2	1
Identified by occupation	15	12
Identified by ethnic group	4	2
Strangers	16	20
Uncertain, vague	31	13
Dead persons	1	<0·5
Imaginary persons	2	<0·5
Metamorphoses	9	1
Total, per cent	100*	100†

* Total of 163 characters from 172 dreams, one per person.
† Total of 2471 characters from 1000 dreams, five per person.
Source: after Hall and Van de Castle (1966).

Prevalence of distortions

The most striking feature of the hypnotic dream was the amount of distortion. Perry (1964), working in Sutcliffe's group in Sydney, Australia, has prepared a procedure for content analysis of dream distortions. The norms that he has provided are quite limited, but they permit a preliminary comparison between the night dreams in his sleep laboratory and the hypnotic dreams in our experiment. Considering only the agreed-upon distortions among the sixty dreams of his fourteen subjects (Perry, 1964, Table 3, pp. 22–4), we note that such distortions were found in eight of the sixty dreams or 13 per cent, and distortion in *any* dream occurred in six of his fourteen subjects or 43 per cent. The gap between the two percentages – 13 per cent and 43 per cent – shows what discrepancies can arise from analysing in terms of *dreams* or in terms of *subjects* when there is more than one dream per subject. We find in our sample that, with one dream per subject, 54 per cent showed some distortion within a hypnotically suggested dream.

In any case, the distortions found in the dreams in our study were more numerous than those reported in night dreams of the only comparable sample. This difference suggests the wisdom of taking a more intense look at the kinds of distortions we found. Some events in these hypnotic dreams could best be described as 'unusual transformation', others as 'distortions'. They are summarized in Table 5.

Table 5 Unusual transformations and distortions in hypnotic dreams

Transformation or distortion	Subjects in which this transformation is prominent (per cent)
Transformations	
Self	11
Something else	16
Scene	15
Total transformations	42
Distortions	
Floating	5
Falling	4
Staircases	1
Size changes	2
Total distortions	12
No transformations or distortions	46
Total	100
	(N = 172)

Source: after Hall and Van de Castle (1966).

Note that for this purpose the dream of each subject was assigned to one category only. Thus if a distortion of the self was prominent, the dream was not also classified as a distortion of size, even though some slight size change might have been involved. Likewise, if change in body size was the most prominent characteristic, the dream was not also classified as a distortion of the self. The categories we used are best illustrated by quotations from the recorded reports of the dreams.

Transformations of self

1. 'I was anchored in a chair, and my body felt like cast iron. Then I felt like I was away from my body – looking at myself in the chair which was now on a high pinnacle in dark black in a cave. It was about two-thirds of the way up. The cave was rough black rock. And I was observing myself in the chair all the time.'

2. 'I was with a friend, talking, but I felt as though part of me was not there, that my other self was behind me. Only my face was moving in front of this person.'

3. 'I'm in a green room, looking over the shoulder of a guy in front of me, who turned out to be me!'

Duplication of the self occurred often enough to suggest the dissociative split between the observing ego and the participating ego so often reported by hypnotic subjects. Such self-duplications were not reported in the night dreams studied by Hall and Van de Castle. The transformations of the self in the foregoing statements all involved duplication of the self, but of course the transformations listed in Table 5 also included other less dramatic changes in which the self, while not duplicated, was notably different from normal.

Transformations of something else

1. 'There was a little top, striped, and it was spinning. All of a sudden it had legs and arms, and then there was a bicycle and a swell looking girl with frizzy hair.'

2. 'There was a room, with a big, black roll of cheese rolling down a ramp, then it stopped. It was huge like a big stone, and it grew, and I could see it.'

3. 'I was painting a picture of Charles de Gaulle, and he came out of the picture, and he was going to put me in the army.'

4. 'Then I saw Jerry, and her breath turned into a flashlight.'

5. 'There were some fish swimming that were purplish-blue, with yellow eyes. They were saying hello to some other fish. Then another fish came and swallowed up one of them. But his eyes became the eyes of the second fish.'

Transformations of scene

1. Then there was no well – trying to move in this sticky stuff – couldn't move very well and then I was in the middle of a pasture. All was free, I could move around. It was very beautiful there, yellow and green trees, and sunny there.'

2. 'First I saw a long black angle coming from the top with white stripes. Everything else was grey. Then I saw a corner of a house. It had scalloped shingles. The sun was shining a lot, but I couldn't see a lot. Then I saw a man floating with a paper face, like a pancake. First it was straight up, then sideways. It looked like my uncle, funny, only without a beard. Then it changed and looked like a stylized Lenin. Then a page came up – a girl. A page from the *Ladies' Home Journal*, I think.'

3. 'First I began to see a large purple area, upon which black images were superimposed. First there was a helicopter, then a plane that I was in,

and it was crashing. Next I saw two male faces, both ominous. The purple area became a sea in which I was swimming, with black trees on either side. When I came out, there were snakes all around.'

Distortions

Floating. 'I felt light, and I was floating out of the building, hanging over the campus.'

Falling. 'The chair formed into a kind of bag – warm. I curled into the bag and started to fall, not a fast fall, but I could see things as they passed by me. My hands were cold with no way to get them warm. The fall took about thirty seconds, no, must have been longer – from quite a height. The bag took the shape of a big tear drop.'

Staircases. 'I was with a friend of mine and we were by this big tower, it had a special staircase inside. It was very dark. We decided to climb to the top. It took a long time. We got very tired, but when we got up there we could see for a long way, all over.'

Size changes. I was sitting there in this chair, and you were there, sitting. The chair and I grew smaller, only I grew smaller faster. I could walk around in the seat of the chair, so I did. Your pencil got so big you had to rest it on your shoulder.'

Table 6 **Views or vistas in hypnotic dreams**

	Subjects reporting dreams with views or vistas (per cent)
View of	
Mountain, forest, sea	23
Cities or buildings	3
Planets, sun, void	4
Total views of	30
View from	
Mountains, cliffs, towers	1
As consequence of flying, ballooning, levitating	2
Total views from	3
No views or vistas	67
Total	100 $(N = 172)$

Source: after Hall and Van de Castle (1966).

We do not wish to give the impression that all of the dreams were as dramatic as these. Actually, there were no unusual transformations or distortions in half of the dreams, and many others lacked the dramatic qualities of those just described. However, the dreams often did have a psychedelic quality, shown in part by the frequency of views or vistas (Table 6).

It may be that the frequent references to floating, falling, staircases, and vistas were part of the symbolic representation of hypnosis called for in the instructions. We did, of course, look for the direct representation of hypnosis or the hypnotist; and found such references to be somewhat fewer than the instructions might have been expected to produce (Table 7).

Table 7 **Representation of the hypnotist or hypnosis in hypnotic dreams 'about hypnosis'**

Representation	Per cent of subjects reporting dreams
Direct	8
Indirect	25
None identifiable	67
Total	100
	(N = 172)

Source: after Hall and Van de Castle (1966).

The contrast between direct and indirect representation can best be illustrated by quotations from the recorded dreams.

Direct representation

1. 'I was watching a split screen, and on one side a hypnotist show with Pat Collins could be seen, and on the other half I imagined people who were hypnotized, young children. . . . They were trying to teach these children all sorts of functions in order to make supermen of them by educating them with hypnosis. They were trying to show that they could make people into anything using hypnosis.'

2. 'And then I saw Pluto hypnotizing Daisy Duck. And I saw the tack coming closer, and it was pulsating, and it seemed to be falling off into something else and there seemed to be a lot of colour! Amazing!'

Indirect representation

1. 'I am walking down a road in the country – a crossroad – I take the one to the left. A mountain is in the distance; it's snowy and there are

trees. I climb the mountain. It's steep with a beautiful lake at the top with rocks all around it. I sit on one of the rocks, lose my balance and fall head over heels down the bank into the lake. That's all.' (Later the subject reported that the crossroad was hypnotism: He could go either way.) 'The mountain was hypnosis – an accomplishment – falling down the hill was coming to the end of hypnosis.'

2. 'I dreamed of having my arm in a hole in a sphere and not being able to bend it, no matter how hard I tried.'

3. 'There was a little man inside of my head, and he was controlling my whole body.'

Table 8 **Representation of hypnosis or the hypnotist in dreams with and without suggestion that the dream will be about hypnosis (N = 24 subjects dreaming both times)**

		SPS Form II: told to dream about hypnosis		
		No representation of hypnosis or hypnotist	Direct or indirect representation of hypnosis or hypnotist	Total
SPS Form I: not told specifically to dream about hypnosis	Direct or indirect representation of hypnosis or hypnotist	1	3	4
	No representation of hypnosis or hypnotist	11	9	20
	Total	12	12	24

Chi square = 4·9, p < 0·025. (One-tailed test for score changes, with Yates correction; see McNemar, 1969, p. 263.)
Source: after Hall and Van de Castle (1966).

The effect of changed instructions

All the hypnotic dream material discussed so far had been dream under suggestion from Form C; only a single opportunity to dream had been given. Many of the subjects were brought back at a later time for two sessions of the Profile Scales. In Form I the subject is not instructed to dream specifically about hypnosis, while Form II repeats essentially the instructions of Form C. Accordingly, there was an opportunity to see whether there were changes in the dream content corresponding to the changes in instructions. This was an imperfect experiment because all subjects had been given Form C earlier, and all had had the profile scales in the same order. Therefore it should be considered as exploratory only. The results are summarized in Table 8. It was apparent that the dream did in fact represent hypnosis more frequently when subjects were instructed to dream about hypnosis than when the topic of the dream was unspecified, a difference significant at the 0·025 level. However, the representation was usually indirect, even when identifiable. Perhaps some sort of free association technique would have revealed that the nonscored dreams also contained hypnosis representation, but in even more disguised forms.

Sensory representation

The nature of sensory or perceptual representation in dreams was also of interest. Dreams are said to be primarily visual, with auditory imagery being a close second. We have found that tactual representation lagged only slightly behind vision, possibly because we have called attention to bodily feelings by instructing the subject to sit quietly with eyes closed (Table 9).

Table 9 Senses predominant in hypnotic dreams

Dominant sense	Hypnotic dreams per cent
Vision	56
Touch (including kinesthesis)	12
Audition	9
Taste	0
Smell	0
Not ascertained	23
Total	100
	$(N = 172)$

Source: after Hall and Van de Castle (1966).

Because there were often fleeting references to other senses, we scored only the predominant sense. This was vision in a large proportion of the cases, although some dreams stressed touch (or kinesthesis) and audition.

Implications for further research

This study has shown the feasibility of discovering differences between dream samples on the basis of content analyses such as those done by Hall and Van de Castle (1966) and by Perry (1964). We believe that some of our substantive findings are likely to hold up on further experimentation;

but this study is justified less on the basis of its findings than for its role as a feasibility study. Among further needed research steps are:

1. Dream samples in sleep and under hypnosis should be obtained from the same subjects, under conditions as similar as possible except for the hypnosis. Ideally this would mean having the subject sleep nights in the laboratory and be aroused to report spontaneous nocturnal dreams when they occur. On other occasions he would be hypnotized in bed at the same hour of the night and told to report the hypnotic dream. While these conditions are both artificial, the comparison of night dreams and hypnotic dreams requires that the differences that arise should be the result of sleep or hypnosis, and not of differences in setting that had nothing to do directly with either state.

2. Various kinds of instructions can be used in the production of hypnotic dreams (see Table 8), but great care needs to be exercised to prevent interactions with prior dream experiences under hypnosis. The ideal experiment would require a common background of hypnotic experience prior to being asked to dream under hypnosis, and with reference to the very first hypnotic dream, the administration of one of several alternative sets of instructions. This procedure would have the disadvantage of lack of practice in dreaming under hypnosis, but the advantage of no contamination through prior practice.

3. A series of dreams from the same subject proved to be fruitful in dream research on the dreams of patients (French and Fromm, 1964), and it is possible that a long series of dreams from the same subject in trance might also be revealing. Our observations along this line are clinical and unsystematic, but the possibility of fruitful results from the study of series of dreams of nonpatients in the laboratory is worth exploring.

Conclusions

1. Hypnotic dreams, even under the somewhat artificial laboratory conditions here described, have much in common with night dreams, although there had been many reasons to expect differences.

2. The more highly susceptible the subject, the more likely he is to dream under hypnosis, and the more likely it is that his dream will be like a night dream.

3. While comparative evidence is hard to come by, it appears that the Alice-in-Wonderland types of distortion are somewhat more frequent in hypnotic dreams than in night dreams. This deserves more careful study, using the same subjects for reports of night dreams, hypnotic dreams and projective fantasies.

4. The instruction to dream about hypnosis does not produce many direct references to hypnosis, but appears to increase the number of indirect references. This may be one reason for the frequency of dream distortion in our sample.

5. Interpretations of hypnotically induced dreams should probably consider the dreams to be projective products falling somewhere in between TAT stories and night dreams.

References

BRENMAN, M. (1949), 'Dreams and hypnosis', *Psychoanalytic Q.*, vol. 18, pp. 455–65.

DOMHOFF, B. (1964), 'Night dreams and hypnotic dreams: is there evidence that they are different?' *Int. J. clin. exp. Hypnosis*, vol. 12, pp. 159–68.

FRENCH, T. M., and FROMM, E. (1964), *Dream Interpretation: A New Approach*, Basic Books.

HALL, C. S., and VAN DE CASTLE, R. L. (1966), *The Content Analysis of Dreams*, Appleton-Century-Crofts.

MCNEMAR, Q. (1969), *Psychological Statistics*, 4th edn, Wiley.

MAZER, M. (1951), 'An experimental study of the hypnotic dream', *Psychiatry*, vol. 14, pp. 265–77.

MOSS, C. S. (1967), *The Hypnotic Investigation of Dreams*, Wiley.

PERRY, C. W. (1964), 'Content analysis of dream reports', in J. P. Sutcliffe (ed.), *The Relation of Imagery and Fantasy to Hypnosis*, University of Sydney Press, Australia.

TART, C. T. (1965), 'The hypnotic dream: methodological problems and a review of the literature', *Psychol. Bull.*, vol. 63, pp. 87–99.

TART, C. T. (1966), 'Types of hypnotic dreams and their relation to hypnotic depth', *J. abnorm. Psychol.*, vol. 71, pp. 371–82.

WEITZENHOFFER, A. M., and HILGARD, E. R. (1962), *Stanford Hypnotic Susceptibility Scale, Form C*, Consulting Psychologists Press, Palo Alto, California.

WEITZENHOFFER, A. M., and HILGARD, E. R. (1967), *Revised Stanford Profile Scales of Hypnotic Susceptibility, Forms I and II*, Consulting Psychologists Press, Palo Alto, California.

11 Ralph J. Berger

Experimental Modification of Dream Content
by Meaningful Verbal Stimuli

Ralph J. Berger, 'Experimental modification of dream content by meaningful verbal stimuli', *British Journal of Psychiatry*, vol. 109, 1963, pp. 722–40.

Introduction

Numerous recent electroencephalographic studies have revealed the cyclical alternation of two distinct types of sleep (Dement and Kleitman, 1957a), which have been termed 'fore-brain' and 'hind-brain' sleep by Jouvet (1962). The former is accompanied by slow waves and spindles in the electro-encephalogram (EEG) and the latter by a low-voltage, fairly fast EEG pattern; spasmodic, conjugate rapid eye movements (REMs); relaxation of neck and throat muscles in cat (Jouvet, 1962) and human (Berger, 1961); and recall of dreams following awakening (Dement and Kleitman, 1957b).

The hypothesis has been proposed that the REMs are fixational responses to visual dream events (Dement and Wolpert, 1958), which is supported by the association between the amount of rapid eye movement and the dream content (Berger and Oswald, 1962; Dement and Wolpert, 1958), and also by the presence or absence of REMs during the 'hind-brain' sleep periods of blind men in whom visual imagery was retained or absent, respectively (Berger, Olley and Oswald, 1962).

Previous studies of the effect of external stimuli on the manifest content of reported dreams have been reviewed by Ramsey (1953). These have been few and unsystematic. More recently, Dement and Wolpert (1958) recorded the EEG simultaneously with the introduction of stimuli during REM periods. However, in every study, the subject was aware of the nature of the experiment and judgement of whether a stimulus had been incorporated into the dream events or not was totally subjective.

During preliminary experiments (Berger, 1963), in which spoken words and personal names were presented below waking threshold to subjects during REM periods, and dream recall elicited soon afterwards, on two occasions, the stimulus appeared to have been incorporated into the dream events at a point in the dream appropriate to the time of presentation of the stimulus ('dream time' has been shown to correspond to 'real time' – Dement and Wolpert, 1958). Following awakening from a REM period during which 'Catherine', the name of a previous girl friend, had been played, a male subject recalled a dream in which his landlady, Mrs Cameron, appeared towards the end of the dream, immediately following a conversation in the dream with a friend about a previous girl friend 'who's figured in my life as a sex partner'. During an initial interview, he had described his relationship with Catherine as 'primarily sexual'. Another male subject, following presentation of the name 'Morag', his current girl friend, recalled a dream in which he was 'at the top of a wind-swept *moor*' and a village tobacconist was being questioned 'on what various road-signs meant . . . it seemed to be connected with the *war*'.

In both the above instances, the dream thoughts appeared to bear assonant connections with the stimuli. It was therefore decided to embark upon a controlled experiment in which subjective bias during analysis of dreams, and establishment of tenuous connections between the stimulus and dream events, could be eliminated.

The aim of the experiment was to determine, by an objective method, whether verbal stimuli would be incorporated into dream events and whether such incorporation would be dependent upon the significance of the stimulus to the sleeper. Further light might thus be thrown upon the extent of perception and its underlying analysing mechanisms during dreaming.

It was decided to use spoken personal names as stimuli and to present a single name during each REM period, but to vary the name with each successive REM period by random selection from four different names for each volunteer.

In consideration of the preliminary experiments and the study by Oswald, Taylor and Treisman (1960), in which cortical analysis of significant stimuli was shown to precede arousal, the initial hypothesis was proposed that during dreaming continual cortical analysis of environmental stimuli takes place, and that those stimuli which are potentially arousing (by virtue of their significance to the sleeper) are experienced as belonging to the dream, but are misperceived in such a way as to be compatible with the natural progression of the dream events.

It was predicted that the incorporation of such misperceptions into the dream would enable each subject and an independent judge to match each of the four stimulus names with the narrative of each of those dreams during which it had been presented, more often than would be expected by guessing correctly by chance alone. It was also predicted that names having emotional significance to the subject would be matched with the dream narratives correctly more frequently than names having no such special significance.

The opportunity was also taken of comparing the frequencies of galvanic skin response (GSR) to the emotional and neutral personal names; of determining the frequency of recall of colour in dreams; and of studying the relation between the amount of rapid eye movement activity during dreaming and the nature of the dream, as described elsewhere (Berger and Oswald, 1962).

Method

The subjects

The subjects were four male and four female normal volunteers. During the initial interview, a short personal history was obtained. Questions were put verbally in as relaxed and informal a manner as possible. Most of the questions were concerned with the subjects' impressions of the quality and pattern of their sleep and dreams, being included primarily to draw attention away from critical questions pertaining to the names of current and past friends of the opposite sex to the subject (all subjects being single).

A short description of each subject is given below.

Subject P.M. Male, aged twenty-three. Second eldest child with four brothers and three sisters. Fourth-year medical student.

Girl friends: no current girl friends.

Jenny – lasted two years and ended the previous year.

Elfriede – a German. Lasted eight months when subject aged eighteen.

Relationship with both 'more emotional than sexual', strongest with Elfriede.

Subject C.S. Female, aged twenty-one. An adopted child. No other children in adopted family. General Arts student.

Boy friends: Leslie – an Indian. Initially claimed to have 'none at present' but later admitted him to be her current boy friend whom she had known for about a year.

Norman – lasted six months when aged seventeen. Relationship was not strongly emotional with either; had never had a strongly emotional relationship with a boy. A certain amount of conflict was evident over having an Indian boy friend.

Subject G.M. Male, aged twenty. One elder brother. Psychology student.

Girl friends: Rosemary – current girl friend for six months. Relationship 'steady but not vital', not very strong sexually or emotionally.

Gillian – lasted two and a half years prior to commencing at University. Relationship 'serious but did not want to become involved'. Strongest sexually.

Subject P.H. Female, aged twenty-one. One sister and two brothers. Graduate chemical research assistant.

Boy friends: Andrew – current boy friend. Relationship 'jogs along' for one and a half years, not platonic but not so intense as with Mike.

Mike – lasted one month a year previously. Relationship had a 'sexual overlay'.

Subject K.F. Male, aged twenty. Two brothers and one sister. Third year General Arts student.

Girl friends: Maureen – current girl friend for one month. Relationship 'fairly casual' with 'sex predominant'.

Liz – One of a series of passing girl friends. About one year previously.

Subject R.H. Female, aged nineteen. One younger brother. Maths and Psychology student.

Boy friends: no current boy friends.

Edward – lasted six weeks two months previously.

Sandy – previous summer 'on and off for six weeks'. Relationship more emotional than with Edward but no sex involvement with either.

Subject E.S. Female, aged twenty. One brother and one sister. Third year General Arts student.

Boy friends: Kenny – subject K.J. Had known each other for three years and had been going out for two and a half years. Relationship strongly emotional 'with sex element'.

Chris – during first year at University. Had a 'crush on him' but did not go out with him.

Subject K.J. Male, aged twenty-one. Only child. Mechanical engineer.

Girl friends: Eileen – Subject E.S. (see above).

Gillian – lasted nine months five years previously. First 'big relationship'. 'Platonic on the surface.'

Instructions. The following instructions were given to the subjects:

'The aim of this experiment is to study the possible relations between dreams occurring on the same night.

'You will be required to fall asleep in the presence of "white noise" played at low varying volume through a loudspeaker beside your bed. This "white noise" is a continuous hissing noise, and its purpose is to try to mask random external noises which might occur outside the bedroom and possibly influence the dream. Several times during the night, you will be awakened in the middle of a dream, and I should like you to recall and narrate them to me as fully as you can without keeping anything back because you might find it embarrassing. Should any of the dreams be published or presented in any way to the public, you will in no way be identified personally as the originator of the dream.'

Selection of the stimuli

Galvanic skin responses were recorded from the palm of the hand while a list of neutral and emotionally charged words was read aloud to the subject, followed by a list of personal names of opposite sex to the subject which, included the names of current and past boy or girl friends obtained during the initial interview. This procedure was explained as being 'to test your emotionality'.

The two names selected as emotional stimuli were either the name of the current friend and the name of a previous friend which evoked a GSR of greatest amplitude, or the names of two past friends (if there was no current friend) which evoked GSRs of greatest amplitude.

From those names which provoked no GSR and, as far as could be known, did not belong to any friend or sibling of the subject, were chosen the two neutral names. They were selected, as far as was possible, to be equal in number of syllables and of maximum contrast in sound to each of the emotional names.

Equal lengths of magnetic tape, on one track of which had been recorded 'white noise' *varying in volume*, were cut and the ends spliced together to form four loops for each subject. Using a twin-track tape recorder, the stimulus name was recorded on the second track of each loop. Names played to female subjects were spoken by a female voice and those played to male subjects by a male voice. The names were spoken with somewhat unnatural clarity, with equal emphasis on each syllable as far as was possible. The length of the loops was such that four repetitions of the name were recorded on each loop at approximately four-second intervals and this interval maintained on playback over the joint in the tape.

Experimental procedure

The subjects reported to the laboratory each night (which were non-consecutive, in order to allow them to recover from the effects of interrupted sleep – Dement, 1960) about one hour prior to their usual bedtime.

Silver cup electrodes were affixed to the scalp with collodion, and to the surface of the facial skin with sticking plaster. The EEG was recorded from a prefrontal and an antero-posterior chain of electrodes; eye movements from the prefrontal electrode and an electrode below the outer canthus of each eye; and GSRs from electrodes placed over the palm of the hand and the dorsum of the ipsilateral forearm.

When all the electrodes had been attached, the subjects retired to bed in a bedroom separated from the experimenter's room by an empty room, and fell asleep to the accompaniment of the 'white noise' background played at a comfortable level, over a loudspeaker placed beside their bed, from the lower track of the particular loop of the magnetic tape.

Approximately five to ten minutes after the onset of each REM period, the stimulus was introduced by turning up the volume control of the amplifier whose input was fed from the top track of the tape loop on which

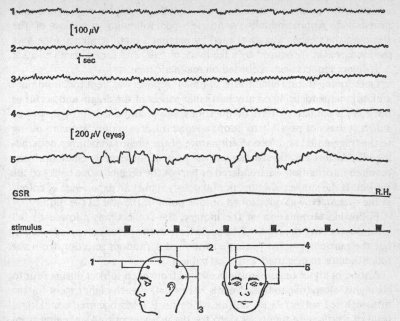

Figure 1 An example of a probable galvanic skin response (GSR) to a stimulus presentation

the stimulus name had been recorded. The outputs of both amplifiers of the twin-track tape recorder fed into the loudspeaker beside the bed so that by this method no clicks were produced which might have aroused the sleeper. As a general rule, the stimulus was played at such a level as initially to provoke a just discernible change in the EEG, usually in the form of flattening of the EEG trace or of 'humping'; or of a low voltage rhythm of high frequency continuing for one or two seconds; or on rare occasions of a brief appearance (one to two seconds) of alpha rhythm. The stimulus was allowed to continue for a dozen or so repetitions if the subject remained relatively unresponsive, but more often was introduced singly or in groups of from two to six repetitions. If marked arousal was evident, as manifested by continuous alpha rhythm for a duration of more than two seconds, sometimes accompanied by a GSR, the volume control was immediately turned down to zero and the stimulus re-introduced when the EEG had returned to a continuous B stage pattern. Owing to such moment to moment variations in the level of arousal, a constant number of repetitions and pattern of stimulation could not be maintained for all REM periods, but the number of presentations was generally of the order of a dozen, and variations in number and pattern of stimulation tended to be randomly distributed. Approximately twenty seconds following cessation of the stimulus, the sleeper was awakened by playing a high frequency tone over the loudspeaker (produced by a feedback circuit) and dream recall elicited. The dream reports were recorded on magnetic tape.

Questioning during elicitations of dream reports was kept to a minimum without undue focusing on any particular aspect of the dream and, as far as possible, a similar pattern of questions was maintained throughout the study. It was not possible to adopt a standard dream questionnaire owing to the fragmented and incoherent nature of the dream sometimes demanding elucidation and persistence on the part of the experimenter until the required information was rendered or part of the dream 'came back' to the subject. If the subject did not spontaneously report an experience of colour in the dream, he was questioned on this point at the end of the inquiry.

Following termination of the inquiry, the subject was allowed to fall asleep again until the next REM period, when the procedure was repeated, but the particular name presented followed a random selection from the four stimulus names used with that subject.

A total of about ten dreams was elicited from each subject during four to six nights' sleep (one to four dreams were recalled each night except for the fifth night of subject R.H. during which no REMs occurred), making a total of thirty-eight nights of sleep for the whole group. Awakening from REM periods was carried out on 103 occasions and dream recall occurred on eighty-nine instances, representing a frequency of recall of 86·4 per cent, which is of the same order as that found by other workers (e.g. Dement and Kleitman, 1957b). An approximately equal number of dreams were recalled following presentation of emotional and neutral stimulus names.

The subjects were only rarely awakened by a total of more than 1200 stimulus presentations. On one occasion, subjects G.M. and P.H. each reported hearing the stimulus name, and on one other occasion subject G.M. reported hearing a spoken name but was unable to remember more than the initial letter (which was not that of the stimulus name). Following each of these incidents, the subjects appeared to be convinced by an explanation that they must have misperceived noises occurring outside the bedroom or voices in the nearby corridor. At the conclusion of the series of nocturnal sessions, each subject was asked whether he or she had any further impressions or ideas to submit concerning the purpose of the experiment, other than what they had been told in the initial interview. Not one subject volunteered an explanation which bore any relation to the true nature of the experiment, including subject G.M. who had wondered whether names were being played to him in order to influence his dreams following awakening by the stimulus 'Gillian'. On other occasions, subjects reported hearing a voice repeating a name or phrase, but they clearly treated these experiences as part of their dream. All subjects appeared surprised when the nature of the experiment was finally revealed to them.

Assessment of results

When the entire series of nocturnal sessions had been completed, the subjects were called back individually, the purpose of the experiment revealed to them, and the following instructions read aloud to them:

I should like you now to listen to the tape recordings of your dream reports one at a time and after each one tell me which name you think you were stimulated by during the dream. The type of connection to look for is between the dream content and the sound of the name . . . (two examples given) . . . or any other you may think fit. Pay particular attention to things that appeared significant, striking or strange to you at the time of recall, your first words after being awakened, and the content towards the end of the dream when you were being stimulated.

If you can see no apparent connection between any of the names and the content of the dream, then make an intuitive or random guess.

The two examples of apparent assonant incorporation of the stimulus into the dream events which were given to them were, of course, obtained from other subjects. To illustrate: the dream of subject P.M., in which he was opening a safe with a jemmy which he recalled following awakening from a REM period during which the name of his girl friend, 'Jenny', had been played, might have been given as an example; or the dream of subject R.H., following presentation of the name 'Robert', in which appeared 'a rabbit in a film' which 'was slightly frightened and *distorted*'.

The four stimulus names followed by the recordings of each subject's dream reports were then played to them as they lay in the darkened bedroom where they had previously slept. The subjects then chose the one of the four stimulus names, following playback of each dream, which they considered most appropriate to the dream. They were also asked to state whether they considered their choice to be based upon a connection between the stimulus and the dream events or whether it was a guess. Those dreams with which the subjects had reported hearing the stimulus name were not included in this analysis.

It could be argued that should the subjects choose the correct stimulus name significantly more often than expected by chance (which was in fact the case – see Results), this might be due to their having heard the stimulus name during the experiment but, for various reasons, not reported it. Or, alternatively, during 'hind-brain' sleep, the stimulus names might have become associated with the dreams as a result of a complex conditioning process without directly influencing the content of the dream, and the subjects were selecting the correct stimulus by virtue of such a process. To act as a control for such an interpretation, and as an independent estimation of the effect of external stimuli on the dream, an independent judge (my colleague, Dr Ian Oswald) was presented with essentially the same task. He was thoroughly familiar with the singularities of dream thinking and of forms of incorporation which had apparently occurred during preliminary experiments, but had no prior knowledge of which stimulus was associated with each dream, not having been present during any of the nocturnal recording sessions.

The stimulus tape loops, tape recordings and typewritten transcriptions of the dreams, and a short history of each subject (as given above) were made available to him. Accompanying each dream transcription was a diagrammatic representation of the time of onset and duration of the associated rapid eye movement period; the number of repetitions, and the pattern of presentation of the stimulus; and the times and duration of spontaneous awakenings, interspersions of C stage sleep and external incidental noises (e.g. passing cars, motor cycles, etc.). The relevant parts of those transcriptions in which subjects referred to being awakened by the stimulus were covered up and the tape recording stopped prior to that point, the transcriptions alone being available for the remainder of the dream report. Knowledge of results was given following the series of matchings for each subject and performance was found to improve by adopting this method, since interest was maintained and motivation increased. The independent judge rated his choices according to three categories of decreasing confidence of being correct (I, II, III), and a fourth 'guess' category (G). He was asked to gives reasons for each choice other than when he made a guess.

Results

The results are presented in Table 1.

Table 1 **Number of correcting matchings**

	Overall score	Reduced score
Subjects	36	32
	86	78
Independent judge	34	31
	89	81
Both judges	24	
	86	

Matchings performed by the subjects

The subjects correctly matched the stimulus name which was presented during the associated R E M period with thirty-six out of the total of eighty-six dreams, performing significantly better than a chance expectancy of guessing the stimulus name correctly for one dream in four ($\chi^2 = 13\cdot04$, $p < 0\cdot001, n = 1$).

Eight of the above total of dream reports were extremely brief. In seven of these, only a fragment was recalled, such as a single object, word or phrase; for example, subject K.J. thought that he 'shouted out or heard shouted out the word "Eileen". It was rather strange', 'Eileen' being the stimulus name; and on one occasion, only a vague impression of theme was recalled. By excluding these dreams, a total of seventy-eight dream reports remained with which the subjects selected the correct stimulus name on thirty-two occasions, again performing significantly better than would be expected by chance alone ($\chi^2 = 10\cdot69, p < 0\cdot005, n = 1$).

An equal number of dream reports followed stimulation by emotional and neutral names and remained so on exclusion of the eight short dreams.

When all the dream reports were included in the analyses, their total number shall henceforth be referred to as the Overall Total and their number which were matched with the correct stimulus names shall be referred to as the Overall Score. When short dreams were excluded from the analyses, the respective terms shall be the Reduced Total and the Reduced Score.

Matchings performed by the independent judge

The independent judge was presented with a total of eighty-nine dreams, being three more than the total presented to the subjects, since the tape recordings of two dreams were not available for subject P.M., having been accidentally 'wiped clean' (the independent judge relying on the transcriptions alone); and of the three occasions on which a subject perceived the stimulus, this occurred once following a single presentation of the stimulus (this dream being rejected), and references to hearing of the stimulus in the remaining two dreams removed as described above. One of the latter two dreams which was recalled by subject G.M., from which he was awakened by and misperceived the stimulus 'Gillian' as a name beginning with the letter 'D', was included in his matching series since, at the time of the matching session which followed several months after the nocturnal sessions, he had no longer any memory of what he had heard (the tape recorder being stopped just prior to his reference to the stimulus).

Out of the Overall Total of eighty-nine dreams, the independent judge matched the correct stimulus name with thirty-four ($\chi^2 = 8\cdot27, p < 0\cdot005$, $n = 1$). When short dreams were excluded, thirty-one out of the Reduced Total of eighty-one dreams were matched with the correct stimulus name ($\chi^2 = 7\cdot61, p < 0\cdot01, n = 1$).

On four occasions, the subjects recalled a voice in the dream which repeated either the stimulus name or a word of similar sound and appeared unrelated to the main course of the dream. Subject R.H. recalled a voice repeating a word 'something like "Sinndy" . . . . I've got the feeling it was something Scottish', the name 'Sandy' having been played, being a diminutive of the Scottish name, Alexander. Subject E.S. on three occasions on separate nights recalled dreams in which a female voice repeated a word or name 'in the background of the dream, it . . . seemed to be an echo in the distance, it was quite mysterious'. On two of these occasions, the name 'John' was being repeated, that name having been played; and on the third occasion, the word 'Yes' was repeated, the name 'Chris' having been played. In all the above instances, the correct stimulus name was matched with the dreams by both judges. However, the voice seemed to the subjects to be incongruous in the dream, although they considered it to be a genuine dream experience, and since the stimulus was not incorporated into the main context of dream events as in all the other cases, it was decided to adopt the most rigid criteria for determining incorporation of the stimulus into dream events. All such dreams in which a repetitive voice was heard and all short dreams (which included one instance of an isolated repeating voice) were excluded from the analysis. On doing so, seventy-seven dreams remained, out of which twenty-seven were matched by the independent judge with the correct stimulus name, statistical significance still being reached ($\chi^2 = 4\cdot16$, $p < 0\cdot05$, $n = 1$).

Same correct matchings performed by both judges

Of the eighty-six dreams which were presented to both the subjects and the independent judge, twenty-four were matched correctly with the stimulus names by both judges. The total number of correct matchings by the subjects and the independent judge were thirty-six and thirty-three respectively.

If the correct matchings by the subjects and independent judge were entirely uncorrelated, the probability by chance alone of the same twenty-four dreams being matched with the correct stimulus name by both judges is equivalent to that of drawing twenty-four red billiard balls from a bag containing eighty-six billiard balls, of which thirty-six are coloured red and fifty white, given thirty-three draws. The probability of arriving at such a result is given by the function:

$$p = \frac{33!}{9!} \quad \frac{36!}{24!} \quad \frac{50!}{12!} \quad \frac{53!}{41!} \quad \frac{1}{86!} = 4\cdot805 \times 10^{-6}$$

Clearly, the chances of drawing more than twenty-four red balls given thirty-three draws become progressively less and one must conclude that there was a tendency for both the subjects and the independent judge to match the same dreams rather than different dreams with the correct stimulus. Such a result suggests that the external stimuli influenced a distinct number of dreams in a manner recognizable to both the subjects and the independent judge rather than a larger number of dreams recognized separately by each.

Differences of incorporation with sex of the subjects or nature of the stimulus

There were no appreciable differences in the number of correct matchings made for emotional or neutral stimuli or in relation to the sex of the subjects, or between subjects, either when the matchings were performed by the subjects or by the independent judge.

Levels of confidence

In Table 2 are presented data relating the successes of the judges with the confidence with which they matched the stimuli with the dreams.

The subjects classified their responses into two categories: 'connection' and 'guess'. Responses falling into the former were made when they thought a connection existed between the stimulus and dream events; those falling into the latter were considered to be sheer guesses.

Both for the Overall Score and the Reduced Score, the number of successes which they claimed to have arrived at by virtue of a connection between stimulus and dream events was significantly greater than those which they claimed to be guesses (for the Overall Score $\chi^2 = 4.49$, $p < 0.05$, $n = 1$, for the Reduced Score $\chi^2 = 5.11$, $p < 0.025$, $n = 1$).

The independent judge rated his matchings according to four levels of confidence (I, II, III and G). He made a significantly greater number of correct matchings at a confidence level of I than at any other confidence level (for the Overall Score $\chi^2 = 5.77$, $p < 0.025$, $n = 1$, for the Reduced Score $\chi^2 = 3.92$, $p < 0.05$, $n = 1$). For the Overall Total of eighty-nine dreams, he only rated nineteen of his matchings with a confidence level of I, of which thirteen proved to be correct, and for the Reduced Total, eleven of the seventeen matchings rated at a confidence level of I proved to be correct.

For the twenty-four same correct matchings performed by both the subjects and the independent judge, half of these were made by the independent judge at a confidence level of I although he had made less than one quarter of the common total of eighty-six matchings with this level of confidence ($\chi^2 = 10.87$, $p < 0.001$, $n = 1$).

These results clearly indicate that the judges made correct matchings consciously, with appropriate verbalization of the reasons directing their choice, rather than their performance being 'unconscious' in nature.

Table 2 Levels of confidence

The number of correct stimulus name–dream matchings made at each confidence level:

Confidence levels	Overall score	Reduced score
(a) By the subjects:		
Connection	26	24
	—	—
	47	43
Guess	10	8
	—	—
	39	35
(b) By the independent judge:		
I	13	11
	—	—
	19	17
II	8	7
	—	—
	30	28
III	12	12
	—	—
	37	34
G	1	1
	—	—
	3	2

(c) By the independent judge for the 24 correct matchings performed by both judges:

I	12
	—
	19
II	6
	—
	30
III	5
	—
	34
G	1
	—
	3

Frequency of incorporation

The frequency of correct matchings of the stimulus with the dreams varied from 38·2 per cent to 41·9 per cent, depending upon whether the judgements were performed by the subjects or by the independent judge, and whether all the dreams were considered or short dreams excluded from the series. But these figures do not represent the frequency of incorporation of the stimulus into the dream events, for these figures are in part compounded of correct matchings performed by chance alone. On the other hand, there were many dreams recalled in which appeared a number of objects, lists of names and words, or questions. On many occasions, the number of objects, names or words corresponded to, or was the same order as, the number in an uninterrupted group of repetitions of the stimulus and the time of occurrence of such events in the dream bore a close relation to the relative time at which the group of repeated stimuli was introduced during the REM period. Not all of these dreams were matched with the correct stimulus names although it is probable that incorporation was taking place. Furthermore, on two occasions the subjects dreamed of what was occurring in reality, i.e. that personal names were being played to them while they were asleep. On one of these occasions, neither judge was able to select the correct stimulus name since the subject recalled being stimulated by a variety of names but did not mention that of the stimulus. It is apparent in this instance that modification of the dream by the stimulus was taking place although correct matchings were not made.

Further, much dream material was forgotten, or claimed to have been forgotten, at the time of recall, and it is indeed surprising how frequently stimuli were matched correctly with the dreams despite the brevity of the dream material.

In order to examine the forms in which the stimuli were incorporated into the dream, one must decide which dreams were in fact modified by the stimulus. For the reasons given above, there appear to be no adequate criteria by which one can make such judgements and one must ultimately rely upon a reasonable, subjective analysis of the dream. The analysis that follows is therefore only a tentative one and it must be continually borne in mind that examples quoted may have been arrived at fortuitously.

Only those dreams in which there appeared to be a definite connection between the dream events and the stimulus were scored positive.

Out of the Overall Total of eighty-nine dreams, forty-eight were scored positive, which represents a frequency of incorporation of 54 per cent. The Reduced Score was forty-five, which represents incorporation of the stimuli into the dream events in 56 per cent of occasions.

The mode of incorporation

Of the forty-eight dreams which were considered to have been influenced by the stimulus, the mode of incorporation of the stimulus into the dream events appeared to fall into four different categories (figures in parentheses refer to the number of dreams in each category):

1. Assonance (31)
2. Association (6)
3. Direct (8)
4. Representation (3)

1. *Assonance*. In Table 3 are listed the dreams considered to bear an assonant connection with the stimulus. The majority of dreams fell into this category. That this majority was not a result of subjective bias in the form of selective 'sensitization' to similarities between sounds of words in the dream narrative and those of the stimulus names is indicated by a similar preponderance of assonant connections submitted by the independent judge; who claimed to have made twenty-three of his Overall Score of thirty-four correct matchings on the basis of assonant connections between the selected stimulus name and dream events.

Most frequently, the connection was one of a simple 'clang' between the stimulus and dream events. The examples 'Jenny – jemmy' and 'Robert – rabbit' have already been given. Further examples are: the dream of subject K.F. which he recalled following playing of the name 'Sheila' and in which reference was made to a book by Schiller; and that of subject R.H. in which a man was 'sitting on the ground digging ou*t* a *gourd* . . . a lovely, round *gourd*' when the name 'Edward' had been played. Subject K.J., following presentation of the name 'Gillian', recalled a dream, extracts of which were as follows:

I . . . was shown into a very large room . . . and a middle-aged lady was sitting up in bed . . . she rang for the maid and asked her to bring breakfast . . . it was a strange thing but I was wearing a dressing gown . . . and I was wearing pyjamas . . . and a scarf . . . and yet I had been outside . . . and I sat down beside the bed. . . . Something that seems strange – when I was sitting there, I seemed to be trying to think something about this woman . . . and I can remember remembering, as it were, that 'Oh, yes, she came – this woman came from *Chile*' . . . and I can remember her running about in her bare feet on rocky ground. . . . I remember both these things quite clearly.

This dream illustrates the frequent precedence of the description of the incorporated dream event (in this case, that the woman came from Chile, i.e. that she was a Chilean), by phrases such as 'something that seems strange . . .', 'I don't know why . . .', 'I remember suddenly thinking', or 'I had a vivid sort of picture . . .'. Sometimes, following the incorporated

Table 3 **Stimulus names and dream events bearing apparent assonant connections**

Subject	Stimulus	Dream events
P.M.	Jenny	*Jemmy.*
	Shirley	*Ster*cobi*li*n.
	Laura	*Cornwall*, *bor*der, *boulder*, *build low*, *wall*, *landlord*.
	Jenny	*Che*ques, money, 1920 (–twe*ny*), 1930 (–thir*y*).
	Elfriede	8 words – K*affa*, *fa*shion, clock-*fa*ce.
C.S.	Peter	Thr*ee ti*cks, *po*tato, *Po*rtobello.
	Norman	Lancashire dialect (*Northern*), *w*ardrobe, *dor*mitory, *li*no*leum*.
G.M.	Gillian	6 makes of motor-cycle (6 stimulus presentations).
	Diana	*D*rowsing, *d*ownwar*d*, *d*rifting, coul*dn*'t . . . , *d*own, *sand*wich.
	Shirley	*Chu*rch, *h*ymns, sai*lor*s, *kir*k.
	Diana	R*i*ce, *d*ish, R*yd*ell, Para*dise*.
	Rosemary	*Re*fectory, i m*pose*, got up (*rose* – see text).
	Shirley	Spani*sh*, de*ser*t, *shel*ter, *shelf*, gyps*y*.
P.H.	Andrew	*Land*, centrifuge, h*and*.
	Mike	*Like*.
	John	*Pon*d, Marchm*on*t, *J*im, *j*ust going *on*.
	John	*J*ag, alm*on*ds.
K.F.	Sheila	*Sl*ippers, R*eaders* (Digest), *lap*, (*sheik*, see text).
	Liz	O*li*ve *s*tones, *li*nks, shi*lli*ngs, mattres*ses*, flower*s*, log*s*.
	Sheila	*Schi*ller, bol*shie*, *phi*lo*so*phy.
	Carol	*Carel*la, cereb*ral*.
R.H.	Robert	*Rab*bit . . . was slightly frightened and distorted.
	Robert	*Lo*gic, *do*ts.
	Edward	Out a g*ourd*.
	Sandy	Sin*es and* co*ses*, p*sy*cholog*y*, math*s* deg*ree*, trigonomet*ry*, tri*angles*, formul*ae*.
	Sandy	Bi*scui*ts, boxe*s* of bi*scui*ts (see text).
E.S.	Kenny	*Co*ncert, *c*hara*c*ter, *c*omedian, ro*ck*, *crack* (Scots = canny, see text).
	Chris	Se*x*, change *is* the e*ss*ence.
	John	*Cho*ps and strawberry *jam*.
K.J.	Naomi	An *aim* to sk*i*, friend who says '*Oh*', sh*ow me*.
	Gillian	Came from *Chile* (i.e. a Chilean), *linen*.

event, the subject might add, 'It was a funny thing that . . . rather odd'. The strangeness, incongruity, or vividness of the incorporated dream event was often underlined by such phrases. The dream about the woman who came from Chile continued:

I recalled . . . that she came from Chile in her young days. I knew that in her young days she had run about barefoot on rocky ground. I don't know why I thought those things at all.

To the question, 'Those thoughts you also find strange, do you?', K.J. replied, 'Yes, only just from their almost irrelevant nature.' Subject P.M., when asked whether the dream about opening the safe had been in colour, replied:

The only thing that was in colour was the jemmy. That's right, I know, a sort of red . . . it was in colour because I knew the thing was red. And it seemed to stand out, almost, because of that.

The perception of the stimulus name, as manifested by apparent incorporation into dream events, was usually as a single assonant word, but frequently as a series of words composed of assonant vowels or consonants. Subject P.H., following the stimulus 'John', recalled a dream about driving a car accompanied by two boys:

The car was parked fairly near Blackford Pond . . . so we moved *on* and we decided we should go up to March*mon*t . . . there were people sitting . . . facing the sun . . . one of them . . . was . . . a boy I know called Jim. . . . I think it was just as I was going *on* that you woke me up.

Subject G.M., following the stimulus 'Shirley', recalled a dream of 'a Spani*sh* des*ert* . . . and a *sh*elter had been set up . . . it was constructed against . . . a sandstone *sh*elf'. Subject E.S., in response to the stimulus 'John', dreamed of '*cho*ps and strawberry *jam*'.

Occasionally, the stimulus word was perceived as a type of auditory 'gestalt' of parts of or whole words spoken in succession. For example, 'Peter' was probably perceived in a dream by subject C.S. as 'three *t*icks' against the name of a firm to whom bills had been paid. The name of the firm 'was something like "*Po*tato" or "*Por*tobello" . . .'. The first words of a dream narrative of subject K.J., following playing of the stimulus 'Naomi', were 'We're travelling up North . . . having a*n aim* to ski . . . . And I'm going up with a friend who says "*Oh*!"'. Subject R.H. experienced 'a whole lot of triangles and sine*s and c*oses' passing through her mind in a dream, the stimulus 'Sandy' having been played.

On some occasions, incorporation of the stimulus appeared to be manifested by repetition of one or more letters of the stimulus name in the dream narrative. Subject E.S. recalled a dream in which the 'K' sound of the stimulus 'Kenny' was repeated:

I was at a concert . . . some Scots character was – I think he was mainly a comedian . . . the scenery was some rock with a crack in it.

It is also possible that there was an unverbalized association between 'Scots' and 'canny'. The high frequency components of the stimulus names appeared to be incorporated more often than those of low frequency. High frequency sounds such as taps and clicks evoke K complexes very readily, although noises which appear much louder to waking consciousness fail to do so.

No consistent trends were evident in the form of response to the stimulus name the dream event took. However, the 'J' and soft 'G' sounds were on four separate occasions apparently transformed into the 'Ch' sound in the dream. 'John' became 'chops', 'Jenny' became 'cheques', and 'Gillian' was transformed into 'Chile(an)'. The masking 'white noise' would doubtless be partly instrumental in the production of such distortions.

2. *Association*. In all six instances, associations were submitted by the subject at the time of matching the stimuli with the dreams. Free association was never employed at the time of dream recall. Associations between stimulus and dream material were in all six instances rendered by the subjects, and such associations were entirely unanticipated since sufficient knowledge of the personal history of the subjects was not available for these associations to be readily apparent. Manifestations of assonant incorporation also appeared to be present, by which the independent judge was able to match four of these dreams correctly.

The following dreams are typical examples of such apparent incorporation by association:

Subject K.F. Stimulus: Maureen.
Relevant Dream Content: Being handed back his maths. book which had been marked in a peculiar manner, similar to the way his English master used to mark their books at school.
Association: The name of his English master had been More. Maureen (his current girl friend) studied maths.

Subject P.H. Stimulus: Richard.
Relevant Dream Content: Had been to a sale at a big shop in the centre of Edinburgh.
Association: Richard was the name of a shop in the centre of Edinburgh where she had been to a sale a day or so previous to the night of the dream.

3. *Direct*. This category includes all dreams in which the stimulus was apparently incorporated directly as an externalized or internalized voice.

On five of the eight occasions when this occurred, the stimulus was incorporated as a background voice repeating the stimulus name or a distorted form of it without having any apparent influence upon the main dream narrative. Once, the stimulus was experienced directly as the thought 'Eileen' (the name of his current girl friend) which the subject thought he might have shouted out in the dream. On the two other occasions, the subjects dreamed of what was taking place in reality, i.e. that a name (or names) was being played to them while they were asleep.

4. *Representation*. This category includes those dreams in which the person bearing the emotional stimulus name appeared either directly or in a disguised or transformed form.

A friend bearing an emotional stimulus name appeared in six dreams, during only two of which was that name actually played. These two were matched correctly by the independent judge, although he also matched the name of the person with one other of such dreams, believing such appearances to be incidental in the remaining three dreams.

By computing the independent probabilities of the stimulus name being played when the person bearing that name appeared in the dream ($p = 0.25$); and of selecting those two dreams during which the appropriate stimulus name was played, given three choices out of a total of six possible dreams ($p = 0.2$); the probability of arriving at the selections made by chance alone is given by:

$$p = 0.25 \times 0.2 = 0.05$$

This result suggests that the stimulus name was, in fact, incorporated into those two dreams. Both dreams differ from the others in which the person bearing an emotional stimulus name appeared in the respect that the person was cardinal to the dream. Following the stimulus 'Maureen', subject K.F. recalled a dream in which an emotion of jealousy in relation to his current girl friend, Maureen, as the object, was overtly expressed:

Ralph and myself, and Maureen, had been to a dance somewhere. . . . Ralph was telling me about some time he had been out with her before. . . . I remember feeling jealous anyway. . . . I remember him saying that they'd been there before and he'd grabbed hold of her and said, 'I want to speak to you', and she said, 'Yes?', and he'd said, 'I have terrible dreams about you', and she said, 'Oh, do you?', and he said 'Yes'. And he was completely put off by her . . . frank answer. . . . I had in my hand a round bar of soap, which was a dull green in colour, which had on it . . . 'New Cold Scent' . . . and Ralph . . . said, 'Yes, that's the stuff she had on before', and I said, 'Oh, yes, but it's not the stuff she's got on tonight'.

Subject K.J. recalled a dream in which his current girl friend, Eileen, appeared following presentation of that name, and which was remarkable for its sexual symbolism:

I remember having been with Eileen . . . having something to take in . . . having to go into town and take back a big lamp. . . . We're both away from home . . . Eileen had the lamp. . . . I was with her. . . . I don't recall saying something so much as conveying a message to Eileen . . . about arrangements for transporting this lamp . . . standing at the fireplace . . . the fireplace was cut over the corner and it was painted cream. And there was a pile of little cases beside it . . . this was where the bit about the lamp was occurring . . . Eileen . . . I don't know what she was wearing . . . .

There was no instance in which a person bearing the name of one of the neutral stimuli appeared directly in the dream.

There was only one dream in which disguised representation was apparent. Subject C.S. recalled 'an Indian woman with glasses in the dream – I can't remember why', the name 'Leslie' having been played, being the name of her Indian boy friend 'who occasionally wears glasses'. She exhibited a certain amount of conflict over her relationship with him. She spontaneously recognized the Indian woman to be a representation of Leslie at the time of the matching session.

Galvanic skin responses and presence of alpha rhythm

Figure 1 (page 173) shows an example of occasional probable galvanic skin responses (GSRs) to stimuli.

There was no significant difference between the number of fluctuations in palmar skin potential per stimulus per second (which was taken as a measure of number of GSRs) during those REM periods in which emotional stimulus names were presented and those in which neutral stimulus names were presented. There was also no significant difference between the frequency with which brief runs of alpha rhythm were provoked by neutral and emotional names.

When REM periods associated with dreams matched correctly with the stimuli by both judges were compared with those associated with dreams with which different matchings were made by the judges, similar negative results were obtained. The number of fluctuations of palmar skin potential per stimulus per second and instances of alpha rhythm per stimulus did not differ significantly during those REM periods associated with each category. Further, the number of stimuli presented per dream in each category did not differ significantly.

These results indicate that incorporation of the stimulus into the dream events was not associated with presence of alpha rhythm in the EEG (representing momentary 'wakefulness') following presentation of the stimuli.

Incidence of colour experiences

Those dream transcriptions in which distinct visual images were recalled were examined for presence of colour imagery. The results are presented in Table 4.

Table 4 **Experience of colour in dreams**

| Subject | Colour | | | Pre-experimental impression |
	Certain	Uncertain	No colour	
P.M.	1	3	4	Black-and-white
C.S.	2	3	2	Coloured
G.M.	0	3	8	Coloured
P.H.	7	3	0	Always coloured
K.F.	4	5	2	Black-and-white
R.H.	3	3	5	Usually black-and-white
E.S.	4	4	1	Coloured
K.J.	10	0	0	Coloured
Totals	31	24	22	

Dreams in which the subjects claimed to have experienced colour are divided into two categories: 'certain' and 'uncertain'. The 'certain' category includes all those reports in which the subjects claimed with conviction that colour was present, or in which a specific object was recalled as being in a colour with which such an object is not commonly associated, as when subject P.M. recalled 'the jemmy being red', or subject K.F. recalled:

The pictures . . . were like something out of *Geographical Magazine*. . . . I can remember the colours very well. There were purples and yellows and fawn colours.

Included in the 'uncertain' category are those dreams in which the subject had a vague impression of colour, a typical report being:

I think it might have been . . . it wasn't so vivid colours as some of the ones I've had . . . no, I think this was in colour.

Or those dreams in which a specific object was recalled in colour (however firm the subject's conviction), but that colour being invariably or commonly associated with that particular object; for example:

I saw the colour of the sand. I mean, I knew it was that bright, bright, terribly bright gold colour.

Fifty-five of the total of seventy-seven dreams were scored positive for presence of colour, representing a frequency of colour experience of 71 per cent. Thirty-one of those fifty-five dreams scored positive fell into the 'certain' category, representing 40 per cent of the total. The visual imagery of four of those dreams scored negative consisted entirely of printed words, such as a list of questions or a page of a book. Since words are commonly printed in black ink upon white paper, one might not expect colour to be reported. If such dreams are excluded from the analysis, the frequency of experience of colour, from a total of seventy-three dreams, was increased to 75 per cent.

Discussion

Differences between matchings by subjects and by the independent judge

Although the subjects, compared with the independent judge, had little experience of the processes involved in dream thinking, and the conditions under which they performed the stimulus matchings with the dreams were less favourable for success, since only the tape recordings were available to them with less time in which to consider their judgements, they performed equally well and even slightly better than the independent judge.

It seems likely that some of the correct judgements made by the subjects but not by the independent judge were dependent upon connections between stimulus and dream events not readily available to the independent judge owing to the particular words in which the dream description was couched. For example, subject G.M. recalled a dream in which

there was a typical story-book Nazi officer . . . and a few soldiers . . . the officer told everybody . . . that they would all obey his orders on pain of death . . . and then a bell went . . . and everyone got up to go out, and the officer told them to sit down.

G.M. correctly selected 'Rosemary' as the stimulus name, his reason being that at the end of the dream everybody '*arose*' to go out. When the tape recording was played back to him, he 're-lived' the dream and he considered the word 'arose' to be a more appropriate description of the soldiers' behaviour than 'got up'. A similar example of an unverbalized free association to an element of a dream which prompted the choice of the correct stimulus name is that of subject K.F., who recalled a dream in which a figure suddenly appeared at the end,

an oriental 'type', who had on a turban and . . . a sort of cream-coloured silk jacket with white trousers . . . with a stripe down one side. . . . I can remember . . . well, that the man was coloured . . . he was definitely Indian.

The subject correctly chose the stimulus name 'Sheila' because at the time of recall he had 'thought of the man as a *Sheik*'.

The possibility of correct matching without awareness by the subject of any reasons governing his choice should not be excluded, in the light of the study of Dixon (1958), in which subjects were able to match their responses to 'subliminal' stimuli with those same stimuli when later presented 'supraliminally' without being able to give reasons for their matchings.

The function of the dream

The experiment was not designed with a view to examining the validity of psychoanalytic interpretations of the dreaming process. However, the results appear to support the views of Freud (1911) regarding the function of dreams. Freud considered that 'the motive for dreaming lay elsewhere than in somatic sources of stimulation' and proposed that dreams were psychical in origin, the external stimulus being more frequently woven into the dream rather than provoking it. Freud suggested dreams to be 'the GUARD-IANS of sleep and not its disturbers. . . . Either the mind pays no attention at all to occasions for sensation during sleep . . . or it makes use of a dream in order to deny the stimuli; or, thirdly, if it is obliged to recognize them; it seeks for an interpretation of them . . . *in order to rob it of reality*' (italics and capitals in the original). The results of the present study are, for the most part, consistent with such an interpretation.

That external stimuli do not induce dreams, in that REM periods are not provoked by such stimuli, has been common experience (e.g. Dement and Wolpert, 1958). The proposition that the stimuli are woven into the dream to rob them of reality is appropriate to many examples of incorporation displayed in the present study. The two occasions on which the subjects dreamed that names were being played to them while they were asleep, subject P.M. even claiming to have woken up in his dream, although he in fact slept on, are similar to examples quoted by Freud.

It is more difficult, when considering the manifest content of the dream, to determine whether incorporation of the stimulus was 'into a component part of a situation which is wished for'. However, it is notable that those dream events into which the stimulus was apparently incorporated, and in which typical sexual symbols commonly attributed to Freud appeared, were frequently associated with emotional stimulus names. The dream of 'Eileen . . . a big lamp', already described, was accompanied by the name 'Eileen' who was subject K.J.'s current girl friend. Subject K.F. dreamed of

a snake of fairy lights which emerged out of one of the guitars and the snake snaked out and then snaked back again . . . and then there was a flash . . . an explosion of some kind.

The name of a previous girl friend 'Liz' had been played and it is probable that 's*lid* out of' would have been a better verbal representation of the dream imagery than 'emerged out of'. Following the stimulus name 'Edward' (being a former boy friend), subject R.H. recalled a dream of a

man ... digging out this gourd, a lovely round gourd ... with a knife ... the gourd ... it's a sort of thing like a cucumber only round, when you dry them and cut them out, you can use them for keeping – as a cup.

Subject C.S., who on her first experimental night had difficulty in dropping off to sleep owing to feelings of apprehension regarding the experiment, reported only one dream, in which she

had been tossing and turning ... you were dressed in a top hat, morning suit, and you were smoking a cigar. And someone handed me a cigarette ... which had been lit at the tipped end and at the other end. I smoked it but I wasn't burned or anything ... at the tipped end ... it was all sort of frayed and burnt. I don't know whether it was still burning at the end that I smoked it ... and I remember I inhaled. ... I don't normally inhale ... as I was smoking it ... there was an Indian woman with glasses in the dream.

and which followed the stimulus 'Leslie', the name of her current, Indian boy friend. No such classical sexual symbols were evident in the dream events into which neutral stimuli appeared to have been incorporated. Further, as has been noted above, in those dreams in which the girl friends of the subjects appeared when those particular names were played during the associated REM periods, an emotional attitude was expressed towards them. Whether this emotional expression represented an underlying 'unconscious wish' of the dreamer cannot be ascertained from the manifest content of the dream alone. However, the presence of such sexual symbolism and emotional expression is not inconsistent with Freud's interpretation.

Similarities to schizophrenic thinking

The similarities between the mechanisms of thinking in dreams and in schizophrenia have been pointed out by numerous writers.

The assonant connections observed between the external stimuli and dream events are characteristic of the flow of similar connections (among other associations) in schizophrenic speech. Jung (1906) quoted an example of such speech (taken from Pelletier):

Je suis l'*être*, l'*être* ancien, le vieil H*être*, que l'on peut écrire avec un H. Je suis universel, primordial, divin, catholique, Romain, l'eusses-tu *cru*, l'être tant cru, sup*rumu*, l'enfant Jé*sus*. Je m'appelle Paul, c'est un *nom*, ce n'est pas une néga*tion*, on en connait la significa*tion*.

Jung quoted an experiment by Stransky in which subjects talked rapidly at random under conditions of distraction for one minute. The recorded speech closely resembled that of schizophrenics, with many sound combinations; for example,

... the storks are large birds – with a long beak and live on frogs, frogs, freegs, frogs, the frogs are froogs, in the morning (Früh) in the morning they are with – breakfast (Frühstück), coffee, and with coffee they also drink cognac ....

Jung (1918) observed during his word-association experiments an increase in the number of 'clang-reactions' (e.g. dish–fish) when attention was distracted and during drowsiness; seven times as many 'clang-reactions' were observed during drowsiness compared with undistracted wakefulness, which led Jung to the speculation that 'it is known that during sleep attention is completely obliterated. Were we to succeed in producing reactions in a person sleeping (not somnambulic sleep), clang-reactions would certainly be the exclusive results.'

Jung observed many mediate associations in simple word reactions under distraction. Sometimes sound reactions were involved. To the stimulus word 'lawn', a gentleman reacted with the peculiar association 'broker'. Analysis revealed that he was completing some transaction with a loan office – 'pawnbroker'. The thought processes in the above example show a close resemblance to those by which the stimulus 'Maureen' was incorporated into the dream elicited in the present study of the mathematics master handing back subject K.F.'s mathematics book.

Freud (1911) stated that in the primary process 'we find associations based on homonyms and verbal similarities treated as equal in value to the rest'. He considered these associations to disclose the latent dream content. A typical example is that of a dream he described in which appeared references to Italy – 'gen Italien' – 'Genitalien (genitals)' (compare with 'Naomi' – 'an aim to ski').

Maury (1853) described two dreams of his own in which a similarity between the sound of words provided a link between successive dream events. In one dream, he had set out on a pilgrimage (pélérinage) to Jerusalem or Mecca, not knowing exactly whether he was a Christian or a Moslem then; after many adventures, he found himself visiting the chemist, M. *Pelle*tier, and, after conversing with him, the chemist gave him a zinc *shovel* (*pelle*) which was transformed into a great war-horse (*cheval* de bataille)[1] in a fleeting subsequent dream. In another dream, Maury was thinking of the word kilomêtre, and reading the milestones as he walked along the highway; suddenly he found himself on a big pair of grocer's

1. The association of the English word *shovel* with *cheval* is my own conjecture. There is evidence that Maury was fluent in English at least at some time in his life.

scales on which a man was putting *kilo*grammes on to one of the pans in order to weigh him; the grocer then said to him that they were not in Paris but on the island of *Gilolo*; a succession of scenes followed in which he saw a *lobel*ia flower, the General *Lo*pez, of whose death he had recently read. Finally, he woke up while he was playing a game of *loto*.

These examples from Maury are similar to the repeated sound reactions to the external stimulus which appear to occur in the dreams of the present study. It is difficult to ascertain whether these repeated sounds are individual responses to successive presentations of the stimulus, or whether an assonant response occurs to the initial stimulus, which then acts as a link between one dream scene and the next, as in Maury's examples.

Similarities to thinking in other experimental states

Oswald (1962) described misperceptions of and hallucinations to repetitive personal remarks spoken by various voices and played throughout the night to non-schizophrenic patients undergoing 'behaviour therapy'. A rubber mackintosh fetishist reported hearing the words 'rubber mackintosh' change to Brown Mackintosh, Brawn Mackintosh, and Jim Mackintosh (his name being Jim Brown); he also reported changes of 'makes him sick', hearing 'sick' as 'stick', and on the following night experienced a witch stirring his abdomen with a mixing stick. Another fetishist reported hearing the phrase, 'I tied up my brother', which was probably derived from the phrase, 'Tying up with rubber'. Other evident misperceptions observed in other patients were 'Fear and Guinness' instead of 'Beer and Guinness'; 'Miss Jick' instead of 'makes him sick'; 'He'd eight men' for 'He'd meet men'; 'Nathian ticks' and later 'Napethian tick' for 'make him sick'.

That misperception of repetitive stimuli is not dependent upon a state of drowsiness or light sleep has been shown by Warren (1961), who played tape loops, on which had been recorded various words and phrases, to normal subjects, the repetition rate generally being extremely high. Warren found that all subjects thought the stimulus to which they were listening was actually changing, many of the forms reported being quite dissimilar in sound to the stimulus; which suggests that the frequency of incorporation of external stimuli into dream events might be higher than can be estimated by the method adopted in the present study.

In Warren's study, responses to the word 'rape' revealed associations which were not present to other words with few emotional overtones. When 'rape' was played, the word 'prey' was heard more often than 'pray', although it is probably encountered less frequently; the successive changes reported by one subject included: rake, break, go ahead, leg-break, sprout, spread out. Another subject did not report hearing the word 'rape' at all, but his successive responses included: rake, break, wrench, drench, quench.

The experiences cannot be considered solely as partial perceptions of the stimulus similar to those Pritchard (1961) has described, using written words with stabilization of the image on the retina. Under Pritchard's conditions, the word 'BEER' was perceived as PEER, PEEP, BEE and BE; and the subjects were far less likely to report seeing meaningless groups of letters, such as EER. The observations of Warren, Oswald, Pritchard, and those of the present study, indicate that non-veridical perceptions are not simply fragmented or fortuitous distorted misperceptions of the stimulus, but that a microgenetic (Flavell and Draguns, 1957) dynamic process is involved, depending upon an interaction between peripheral and central processes.

The perceptual response

Oswald, Taylor and Treisman (1960) found that K complexes in the EEG during medium sleep were more likely to be provoked by the subject's own name than by other names. No difference in arousal (as measured by presence of alpha rhythm or GSRs) to neutral and emotional names was observed in the present study. However, in Oswald *et al.*'s study, the novelty of the stimuli was eliminated by playing the names to the subjects as soon as they retired to bed and continuously throughout subsequent sleep, with the result that the subjects were responding selectively to 'meaning' of the stimuli alone. On the other hand, in the present study, there were remarkably few occasions on which GSRs or alpha rhythm followed the stimuli although perceptual responses appeared to be occurring. Rechtschaffen and Shaikun (1962) observed fewer GSRs to an 80 msec auditory stimulus during REM periods compared with non-REM periods, but more frequent awakenings to the stimulus during REM periods; and other data indicate that 'hind-brain' sleep is a qualitatively different kind of sleep from the other stages of sleep (Oswald *et al.*, 1963) rather than to be considered as 'deeper' or 'lighter' sleep.

Jouvet, Michel and Mounier (1960) reported higher auditory thresholds during 'hind-brain' sleep than during 'fore-brain' sleep in cats. In the present study, those dreams in which a perceptual response to the stimulus was evident (as defined by correct matchings with the stimulus by both judges) were unaccompanied by any observable differential physiological response from those dreams in which no such perceptual response was evident. The lack of overt response to auditory stimulation during REM periods in humans may be a manifestation, not of an elevated auditory threshold, but of a perceptual response by means of which the stimulus is incorporated into the dream. Jouvet (1962), in addition to observing raised thresholds to auditory and reticular formation stimulation, as indicated by behavioural arousal and evoked potentials during 'hind-brain' sleep in cats, noted a diminution in response to auditory clicks at the level of the cochlear nucleus which was inconstant but coincided frequently with movements of the eyes and vibrissae. Jouvet has suggested that such diminution might be a manifestation of preoccupation of the cat with its dream imagery. The stimuli in the present study were frequently presented during rapid eye movement clusters, and if similar diminutions in cochlear nuclear response occur in humans during R E M periods, it is possible that those stimuli which were not incorporated into dream events were not perceived owing to blockade at the periphery.

Experience of colour in dreams

The frequency of recall of colour experience in dreams was found to be much higher than has previously been reported (Ramsey, 1953). All subjects recalled dreams in colour and two subjects, who claimed to dream in black-and-white at the time of the interview, recalled many coloured dreams. The subject's pre-experimental impression of frequency of colour dreams was generally lower than that observed during the experiment.

Many of the dreams of the present study were imageless, and of those dreams in which visual imagery was prominent, colour was not often re-called without questioning. Only those visual images which were particularly striking or significant were recalled as being in colour, or objects of which colour is an important attribute in waking life, such as clothes. Just as the dream is frequently forgotten unless the dreamer is awakened before its natural termination, so remembrance of colour fades unless a conscious effort is made to recall it at the time of awakening. Subjects frequently recalled more dreams spontaneously on awakening on mornings prior to commencement of the experiment (but following initial interview) than they were usually accustomed to do, and similarly the subjects became more aware of the presence of colour in their dreams as the experiment progressed.

Conclusions

One may conclude from the results of the present study that perception of the external world, be it impaired, does occur during the R E M periods associated with dreaming. However, the external origin of such perception is not normally recognized and external stimuli are perceived as belonging to the events of the dream. Furthermore, it seems that perceptual awareness is coincident with cortical analysis of the stimulus, but is not dependent upon the significance of the stimulus to the sleeper (as was arousal in the study of Oswald, Taylor and Treisman, 1960), although the manner in which the stimulus is perceived sometimes appears to depend upon its meaning to the sleeper.

Summary

Spoken personal names which were randomly presented during the rapid eye movement periods of dreaming were incorporated into the dream events, as manifested by the ability of the experimental subjects and an independent judge subsequently to match correctly the names presented with the associated dreams more often than would be expected by guessing correctly by chance alone. Incorporation of emotional and neutral names into the dream events occurred equally often. The manner in which the names appeared to have been incorporated into the dream events fell into four categories of decreasing frequency: (1) Assonance, (2) Direct, (3) Association, and (4) Representation. Perceptual responses to the stimulus names, as manifested by subsequent dream recall, occurred without any accompanied observable differential electroencephalographic or galvanic skin responses compared with those occasions on which no such perceptual responses were evident. The frequency of recall of colour in dreams was higher than has been previously reported.

The results are discussed in relation to the function of dreams and perception during dreaming.

References

BERGER, R. J. (1961), 'Tonus of extrinsic laryngeal muscles during sleep and dreaming', *Science*, vol. 134, p. 840.

BERGER, R. J. (1963), 'Psychophysiological studies of sleep and dreaming', Ph.D. thesis, University of Edinburgh.

BERGER, R. J., and OSWALD, I. (1962), 'Eye movements during active and passive dreams', *Science*, vol. 137, p. 601.

BERGER, R. J., OLLEY, P. C., and OSWALD, I. (1962), 'The EEG, eye movements and dreams of the blind', *Q. J. exp. Psychol.*, vol. 14, pp. 183–6.

DEMENT, W. (1960) 'The effect of dream deprivation', *Science*, vol. 131, p. 1705.

DEMENT, W., and KLEITMAN, N. (1957a), 'Cyclic variations in EEG during sleep and their relation to eye movements, body motility and dreaming', *EEG clin. Neurophysiol.*, vol. 9, pp. 673–90.

DEMENT, W., and KLEITMAN, N. (1957b), 'The relation of eye movements during sleep to dream activity, an objective method for the study of dreaming', *J. exp. Psychol.*, vol. 53, pp. 339–46.

DEMENT, W., and WOLPERT, E. A. (1958), 'The relation of eye movements, body motility and external stimuli to dream content', *J. exp. Psychol.*, vol. 55, pp. 543–53.

DIXON, N. F. (1958), 'The effect of subliminal stimulation upon autonomic and verbal behaviour', *J. abnorm. soc. Psychol.*, vol. 57, pp. 29–36.

FLAVELL, J. H., and DRAGUNS, J. (1957), 'A microgenetic approach to perception and thought', *Psychol. Bull.*, vol. 54, pp. 197–217.

FREUD, S. (1911), *Die Traumdeutung*, 3rd edn, trans. J. Strachey, 1954.

JOUVET, M. (1962), 'Recherches sur les structures nerveuses et les mécanismes responsables des differentes phases du sommeil physiologique', *Arch. Ital. Biol.*, vol. 100, pp. 125–206.

JOUVET, M., MICHEL, F., and MOUNIER, D. (1960), 'Analyse électroencéphalographique comparée du sommeil physiologique chez le chat et chez l'homme', *Rev. neurol.*, vol. 103, pp. 189–205.

JUNG, C. G. (1906), *The Psychology of Dementia Praecox*, trans. A. A. Brill, 1936.

JUNG, C. G. (1918), *Studies in Word Association*, trans. M. D. Eder.

MAURY, A. (1853), 'Nouvelle observations sur les analogies des phénomènes du rêve et de l'aliénation mentale', *Ann. méd.-psychol.*, vol. 5, pp. 404–21.

OSWALD, I. (1962), 'Induction of illusory and hallucinatory voices with considerations of behaviour therapy', *J. ment. Sci.*, vol. 108, pp. 196–212.

OSWALD, I., TAYLOR, A. M., and TREISMAN, M. (1960), 'Discriminative responses to stimulation during human sleep', *Brain*, vol. 83, pp. 440–53.

OSWALD, I., BERGER, R. J., JARAMILLO, R. A., KEDDIE, K. M. G., OLLEY, P. C., and PLUNKETT, G. B. (1963), 'Melancholia and barbiturates: a controlled EEG, body and eye movement study of sleep', *Brit. J. Psychiat.*, vol. 109, pp. 66–78.

PRITCHARD, R. M. (1961), 'Stabilized images on the retina', *Sci. Amer.*, vol. 204, pp. 72–8.

RAMSEY, G. V. (1953), 'Studies of dreaming', *Psychol. Bull.*, vol. 50, pp. 432–55.

RECHTSCHAFFEN, A., and SHAIKUN, G. (1962), 'Preliminary Report presented at Meeting of Association for the Psychophysiological Study of Sleep', Chicago, March.

WARREN, R. M. (1961), 'Illusory changes of distinct speech upon repetition – the verbal transformation effect', *Brit. J. Psychol.*, vol. 52, pp. 249–58.

12 R. G. D'Andrade

The Effect of Culture on Dreams

R. G. D'Andrade, 'The effect of culture on dreams', in F. L. K. Hsu (ed.),
Psychological Anthropology: Approaches to Culture and Personality, Dorsey Press,
1961, pp. 308–32.

Dreams, like other kinds of human behavior, can be expected to show some
degree of cultural patterning. In dreams, however, conscious self-control
and external restraints, which serve as the two great agents of conformity
with cultural norms, are almost completely absent. Cultural patterning in
dreams must come from deep within the individual rather than from conscious imitation of a cultural model, or the restrictions of cultural institutions. For this reason, cultural patterning in dreams seems especially
relevant to an understanding of which aspects of cultural norms are most
deeply internalized.

One of the simplest and most direct ways in which culture might be
expected to affect dreams is in manifest content. Certainly, peoples who have
never seen automobiles are not likely to dream of them. However, there is
evidence that dreams do not give a faithful point-by-point representation of
the sector of culture experienced and manipulated by the individual in
waking life, but instead give a selective, edited picture of the individual's
cultural world.

First, some dreams seem almost completely bare of cultural items of any
sort. Often these dreams are symbolic dreams of flying, body destruction,
landscapes, animals, and so forth. Perhaps the cultural bareness of these
dreams is due to the difficulty in translating dream images into words, and
then retranslating into the ethnographer's language. I would guess that
about one fifth of the dreams I have examined from non-Western cultures
lack any culturally distinctive materials in manifest content, although this
seems to vary by culture.

Second, certain areas of cultural life are overrepresented in the manifest
content of dreams, while other areas may be considerably underrepresented.
Within the United States, Calvin Hall finds that:

Dreams contain few ideas of a political or economic nature. They have little or
nothing to say about current events in the world of affairs. I was collecting dreams
daily from students during the last days of the war with Japan when the first
atomic bomb was exploded, yet this dramatic event did not register in a single
dream. Presidential elections, declarations of war, the diplomatic struggles of

great powers, major athletic contests, all of the happenings that appear in newspapers and become the major topics of conversation among people are pretty largely ignored in dreams.

What then is there left to dream about? There is the whole world of the personal, the intimate, the emotional and the conflictful, and it is this world of ideas out of which dreams are formed (1953, pp. 11–12).

Emotionally, the content of dreams seems to contain more negative feelings than waking life. In a content analysis of a large sample of Western dreams, Hall found that 40 per cent of the emotions displayed in dreams can be characterized as apprehension, 18 per cent as anger, and 6 per cent as sadness. Another 18 per cent of the emotions are characterized as neutral excitement and surprise, while only 18 per cent are characterized as happiness. In this same sample almost half of the dream persons were strangers to the dreamer, while about 20 per cent were family, of which 34 per cent were mother, 27 per cent father, 14 per cent brother and 12 per cent sister (Hall, 1951).

The manifest content of dreams may also reflect the sex of the dreamer. Hall finds that men in our culture dream about males twice as frequently as about females, while women dream equally about both (Hall, 1951). In Lee's study of Zulu dreams (1958), an unusual degree of difference between the manifest contents of the dreams of men and the dreams of women was found; the women dream more of babies and children, the men dream more of fighting and cattle. This difference reflects the traditional division of labor, although at the time of the study, the traditional separateness of men's and women's activities had broken down. Lee's hypothesis, that the content of dreams is laid down in the early years of life, offers an interesting avenue of exploration, which might account for the lack of political and economic activities noted by Hall.

Devereux offers a similar hypothesis about the relation between the dream content and childhood experience of a Plains Indian in psychotherapy. The items of aboriginal culture which appeared in this patient's dreams were those which 'reflected most clearly both the highest traditional values of Wolf culture (pseudonym for the patient's culture), and the least rational parts thereof: i.e., medicine bundles, magic and the like' (1951, p. 100). These aboriginal materials began to appear with greater frequency in the patient's dreams when he began to analyse his own past, and dreams with many aboriginal items were often the most significant and revealing.

Devereux speculates that the small amount of manifest content taken from the immediate present in this patient's dreams may be due to the fact that these dreams reflected life-long defense mechanisms, laid down in childhood, and also to the fact that Plains Indian children were often brought up by their grandparents, who embody the more traditional culture (1951, p. 88).

Holmberg, in his study of the Siriono, found the manifest content of dreams to be related to one of the central features of Siriono life. The Siriono are a hunting and gathering people of the interior Amazon, who are often if not always hungry and who spend much of their time in a grim search for food. Holmberg found that more than half of a sample of fifty dreams were concerned with eating food, hunting game, and collecting edible products from the forest. One of the most common dreams is that a relative out hunting has had luck and is returning with game for the dreamer (Holmberg, 1950, p. 91). He found that 'one of the striking things about food dreams is that they seem to occur just about as often when a person is not hungry as when he is hungry' (Holmberg, 1950, p. 91). This would lead one to speculate that food has come to symbolize a number of things for the Siriono besides its hunger-reducing properties.

So far some of the ways in which dreams tend to give a selective and edited picture of the dreamer's culture have been described. Schneider and Sharp, in a thorough and systematic monograph, have investigated the relation between Yir-Yoront dreams and culture. The dreams were collected by R. L. Sharp, and analysed by D. Schneider. Schneider begins with the assumption that dreams portray the dreamer's view of the world, or his 'definition of the situation', and that culture, as a system of norms, affects but is not identical with this definition of the situation.

In order to investigate the relation between Yir-Yoront dreams and culture Schneider has analysed the manifest content of 149 dreams taken from fifty-one subjects, forty-three men and eight women. Four kinds of dream situations were studied; dreams involving sex, aggression, death, and contact with white culture. Certain striking regularities in these areas were uncovered. Nineteen dreams containing explicit material on sexual intercourse were found, all from men. The partner in these dreams is in a little more than half of the cases from the approved classificatory kinship class (mother's brother's daughter), although in only one case is the sex partner actually a wife.

Perhaps the most interesting finding from a review of the dreams of sexual intercourse is that when the sex partner is of a prohibited degree of relationship, and where no adjustment to this fact has been made in waking life, the men picture (1) a specific interruption before or during the act of intercourse which occurs as (a) an organic defect of the woman's sexual organs or (b) an overt, verbal rejection of the male dreamer's advances which have little deterrent effect in the dream; (2) the magnitude of the interruption correlates with the strength of the prohibition on sexual relations. Intercourse with FaSiDa never gets started; with the SiDa, the act is completed but with difficulty; with the SiDaDa there is merely verbal rejection of the man by the woman (ch. 5, pp. 2–3).

Another interesting finding involves the expression of aggression. In

Yir-Yoront dreams both mother's brother and elder brother are frequent aggressors *against* the dreamer. This is quite different from the actual situation, in which a man gives gifts and shows respect towards his mother's brother, and treats his older brother with deference. Dreams involving death also show some surprising patterning. While there is no cultural belief in resurrection, in most of the dreams of death in which the dreamer himself dies, the dreamer then 'stands alive' or is resurrected. However, in dreams in which someone else dies, the corpse most frequently remains dead.

These findings raise some interesting questions about the relation between any fantasy product, such as dreams, and the actual experiences of the individual. Certainly most fantasy, including dreams, contains something of a 'reflection' of the individual's experiences and his 'definition of the situation'. Usually this 'reflected' material is selected and edited according to the particular interests and concerns of the person. For example, it has already been mentioned that personal and intimate materials are more likely to appear in American dreams than public and political matters.

Selection and editing of fantasy, however, results in only mild distortions of the individual's actual experience. Sometimes the distortion is more drastic, as in obvious cases of wish fulfillment. Schneider and Sharp consider the fact that the sex partner in Yir-Yoront dreams is almost always some one other than a wife to be the result of wish fulfillment, and, in a sense, still a part of the individual's definition of the situation.

Projection is a still more drastic kind of distortion. Certainly the Yir-Yoront tendency to picture mother's brother and elder brother as hostile and aggressive, when the shoe is on the other foot, would seem to fit neatly the definition of projection. Other dream materials may also involve projection, but are less discernible because the individual's actual experiences are less clearly known. For example, it may be that the dreamer's portrayal of the woman as the source of interruption of intercourse is pure projection, or this may be an accurate portrayal of what actually happens. If it is projection, this would make some sense out of such bizarre items as the woman's clitoris falling off in one of these dreams, and the other images of the woman having damaged genitals. It would then be really the man's genitals which would become injured, or which he fears would become injured if intercourse with a forbidden woman were to take place. Here the dreamer's actual 'definition of situation' is reversed, although the anxiety is still apparent as sexual in origin.

An even more elaborate kind of distortion occurs in instances of symbolization. For example, it may be that the resurrection dreams of the Yir-Yoront are symbolic dreams of repeated sexual intercourse, in which the penis dies and is then born again. The men of the Yir-Yoront 'in waking life, talk as if a single act of intercourse was more unusual than four, five, or six', but in overt sex dreams rarely have more than one act of intercourse. Perhaps the same anxiety that gives rise to this kind of bragging also motivates the 'stand alive' dreams. The following dream of a mature man may be a case in point, and gives something of the flavor of Yir-Yoront dreams in general.

I'm making a forked support for the corpse at Olwin-an. It is for Spear's sister (dead, unknown). I saw Yaltide's vagina. Her legs were far apart. A mob from the north (Yir Ma'as and others) speared me. I lay down alongside the corpse. I was full of spears. The North people cut me up. They took my bones out. They cut me up like a wallaby. They ate my liver and flesh after cooking it. I came alive again. I had healed up but had no bones, which had been smashed up and the marrow eaten. My brains, bones, etc. were all eaten. Wil (also was eaten). I rolled up belongings and left. I went along and died. I was buried. I heard people keening for me. Women were jabbing sticks in their vaginas so that blood would run out; they were sorry. Blood running down their legs, vaginas. I came alive again. Stretched arms and legs and back. I went off hunting. I killed two goannas, cooked them and woke up.

Inf.: Parkaia perhaps sent dream. My mother, who is Spear's sister (dead, unknown), was dead in the dream. Yaltelde, my sister, was simply mourning the corpse. I dreamed this last night. (dream 34.)

If this hypothesis is correct, it would help explain why 'dreams of death are noticeably lacking in intense affect', and why resurrection occurs in dreams but not as an item of cultural belief. In any case, the relation between the culture, the individual's experience, and dreams of 'standing alive' is not a simple one.

To summarize so far, it seems that there is no simple relation between culture and the manifest content of dreams. This appears to be because a dream is not exclusively a cognitive act, in which things once perceived are reshuffled and reviewed in the mind's eye. Instead, the dream is a selective, edited, and sometimes highly distorted version of the individual's experience. This selectivity and distortion is generally considered to be an effect of motivation, as well as the type of special mental process involved in dreaming. The various examples of selectivity in dream content mentioned above, such as the frequent reference to food in the dreams of the Siriono, the sex differences in the dreams of the Zulu, an acculturated Plains Indian's tendency to dream about nonrational aspects of his aboriginal culture, and Hall's finding that American dreamers dream about the personal and intimate rather than the political and economic, would, therefore, be held to be due to the particular needs of individuals in these societies. More dramatic distortions seem to be due to conflict. The Yir-Yoront projection of hostility onto the mother's brother may represent such a conflict, perhaps in this case between aggressive feelings and anxiety about retaliation.

The effect of culture on dreams may be seen more directly in the 'culture pattern dream' (Lincoln, 1935, p. 189). These dreams, which are specified and sanctioned by the culture, and which usually involve supernaturals or supernatural manifestations, are often considered visions (Lincoln, 1935, p. 189). The Crow, for example, gave great importance to culture pattern dreams, and success in life was considered to depend upon these visions. Lowie remarks that he never succeeded in securing a detailed narrative of an ordinary dream, because his informants would report only visions (1922, p. 342). Typically, culture pattern dreams of this type involve a preparatory phase of fasting, isolation and self-mutilation, followed by a hallucinatory experience, in which a spirit helper, usually in human guise, adopts the dreamer as his child, and gives him specific instructions in the use of a supernatural power.

Although it might seem likely that individuals would falsify such experiences in order to gain honor and riches, Lowie reports that this was not the case. In fact, some people were never successful in obtaining a vision, and others, who thought they had received a true revelation, later became convinced through testing their supposedly acquired powers that they had been deceived by their vision (1924, pp. 8-14).

In those cases in which an individual believes that he has had a culture pattern dream, the degree to which the content of the dream has been affected by secondary elaboration, in which the dreamer unwittingly assimilates the dream experience to a previous cultural model, remains problematic. Sometimes such a process of secondary elaboration can be seen quite clearly. Erika Bourguigon notes that in Haiti a dream may be recounted as if a particular supernatural had appeared in it, although more detailed questioning would reveal that only an ordinary person with certain characteristics which might indicate a disguised supernatural had been seen in the dream. Her conclusion, based on Haitian materials, is probably representative for other societies in which culture pattern dreaming occurs.

While it is difficult to see to what extent dreams themselves may be culturally patterned, the cultural dogma of the dreams as appearance of the gods interacts with the dream content in such a way that an interpreted version of the dream seems to be experienced by the dreamer (Bourguigon, 1954, p. 268).

The effect of acculturation on culture pattern dreaming has been discussed by Radin and King. Radin presents some evidence that as a result of acculturation, the Ottawa and Ojibwa stopped having culture pattern dreams and began to have dreams concerned only with personal problems (Radin, 1936). King documents the opposite case, in which an acculturated

Mountain Maidu Indian (whose biological father was white) had a series of culture pattern dreams which incorporated elements of Western culture (King, 1943). In this series of dreams the dreamer was able to defeat the magical attacks of malicious shamans by using both Indian and white kinds of magical power. King finds that the remarkably good adjustment of this man to Western culture is shown in these dreams, and also speculates that dreams might be fruitfully used to study psychological adjustment in acculturation.

Cultural beliefs and theories about dreams also appear to affect the content of dreams and emotional reactions to dreams. One often quoted example of the effect of dream theories is the difference between the Tikopia and the Trobriand Islanders in their emotional reactions to incest dreams (Firth, 1934). The Tikopia believe that incest dreams are inspired by malignant spirits who may impersonate relatives and seduce the dreamer. The Trobriand Islanders, on the other hand, believe more in the reality of their dreams, and react with shame and guilt to incest dreams. While the Tikopia do not react with shame and guilt, they nevertheless do not completely escape the consequences of such dreams. For the Tikopia, sexual intercourse in a dream is sexual intercourse with a spirit, and intercourse with spirits results in loss of vitality and illness. In general, Tikopia dream theory demands taboo on sexual intercourse as a goal of the dream, while Trobriand dream theory involves a taboo only on certain sexual objects, a difference which may correspond to personality features characteristic of these two societies.

A somewhat more subtle effect of dream theories on dreams has been noted by Devereux, who points out that where dreams are given certain kinds of objective reality, the dreams of individuals appear to be more egosyntonic, and in such cultures dream events tend to be more similar to real life events, and also to be more useful to the individual, who may use his dreams to plan new activities, and to attempt to integrate old and painful experiences by reworking them successfully (1951, p. 87).

Another possible effect of dream theories has been explored by Hallowell, who finds that where dreams are considered to be actual experiences of the self, as among the Ojibwa, that the self may be conceived of and experienced as capable of dream-like activities, such as physical metamorphosis, separation from the body, and the ability to shift back and forth in time. As a result of such a self-conception, and the integration of dreams with waking experiences, the 'behavioral environment' or 'habitat' of the individual may come to have radically different qualities than the 'physical environment' (1955, pp. 172–82).

The findings concerning culture pattern dreams suggest that, while it is possible for some individuals to dream as required, this is not an easy task, and for some persons even impossible. Some of the implications of this situation will be discussed below.

With respect to the ways in which cultural cognitive structures affect dreams, the findings of Firth, Devereux, and Hallowell suggest that native dream theories play a part in taming fantasy, making it more like waking life, and, reciprocally, in making waking life more like dream fantasy.

The cultural uses of dreams

In the ethnographic literature a wide range of beliefs and practices concerning dreams has been reported. These beliefs and practices enter into many different aspects of culture. One important set of culture traits relates dreams to the religious system, and includes the use of dreams to contact and gain power from supernaturals, as well as the more common beliefs that the soul wanders during dreams, meets other souls, and is responsible for its actions. Another set of traits concerns the use of dreams in the social system, in which there may be formal or informal statuses and roles involving dreams, such as dream interpreters, or shamanistic dream performances, and roles which can only be assumed if the proper dream is dreamed. An almost universal set of traits involves the use of dreams to predict the future. The last major group of traits involves emotional catharsis through ritualized methods of reacting to dream experiences, in which the effect of a bad dream may be dispelled or a good dream made to come true by a more or less elaborate ritual, such as not telling the dream, or acting out the dream commands, or making a sacrifice.

These traits are not cultural monads, but have functional relations with other phenomena, cultural, social, and individual. Two examples of such relations, concerning 'primitive dream psychotherapy' and 'unconscious role acceptance', have been discussed in the anthropological literature.

'Unconscious role acceptance' becomes a factor in a social system when culture pattern dreams are used to determine which roles an individual will assume. The dreamer may either be obligated to assume a particular role because he has had a certain type of dream, as, for example, among the Sioux, where dreams of the moon, or a hermaphroditic buffalo, require the individual to become a *berdache*, or the dreamer may be required to dream a particular culture pattern dream before he is allowed to assume a certain role, as among the Pukapuka, where qualifications for priesthood require that a man have dream contact with supernatural powers during the initiation period.

Since dreams are not under direct conscious control, the use of culture pattern dreams to determine role taking brings factors of 'unconscious choice' into consideration. A young man who is required to have a vision and obtain a spirit helper before he may have all the responsibilities and privileges of the adult role may consciously want to assume an adult role, but if on a less conscious level he feels he is not ready to become a man, dreaming the required dream would probably be an impossibility, both because of unconscious sabotage, and because typically the content of the culture pattern dream in these cases is psychologically sound, symbolizing accurately the resolution of dependency conflicts. Also, where an individual is forced into a deviant role because of his dreams, not only are unconscious factors taken into account, but a culturally legitimate excuse is given for such deviancy. Erikson, in his discussion of the Sioux, states:

A homogeneous culture such as that of the Sioux, then, deals with its deviants by finding them a secondary role, as clown, prostitute, or artist, without, however, freeing them entirely from the ridicule and horror which the vast majority must maintain in order to suppress in themselves what the deviant represents. However, the horror remains directed against the power of the spirits which have intruded themselves upon the deviant individual's dreams. It does not turn against the stricken individual himself. In this way, primitive cultures accept the power of the unconscious. As psychopathologists, we must admire the way in which these 'primitive' systems managed to maintain elastic mastery in a matter where more sophisticated systems have failed (1950, p. 137).

Another example of the use of dreams to manage psychological problems can be found in primitive psychotherapy, discussed by Devereux (1951), Kilton Stewart (1951, 1954), Toffelmier and Luomala (1936), and Wallace (1958). Generally, such therapy seems to consist of a cultural recognition that dreams reveal hidden wishes and conflicts, and a culturally prescribed method of dealing with those wishes and conflicts. The most common method of handling such wishes and conflicts seems to be to fulfill or act out the wish, once it is revealed. Anthony Wallace presents an impressive example of this method in his study of Iroquois dream theory.

Intuitively, the Iroquois had achieved a great deal of psychological sophistication. They recognized conscious and unconscious parts of the mind. They knew the great force of unconscious desires, and were aware that the frustration of these desires could cause mental and physical ('psychosomatic') illness. They understood that these desires were expressed in symbolic form by dreams, but that the individual could not always properly interpret these dreams himself. They had noted the distinction between the manifest and latent content of dreams, and employed what sounds like the technique of free association to uncover the latent meaning. And they considered that the best method for the relief of psychic and psychosomatic distress was to give the frustrated desire satisfaction, either directly or symbolically (1958, pp. 237–8).

Among the Senoi, impulses revealed in dreams are evidently handled in an unusually sociable fashion, so that if a man dreamed he was attacked by another, he would attempt to settle the differences between them through discussion and mediation (Stewart, 1951). The Navaho, on the other hand, use dreams not to reveal wishes, but to indicate proper curing rituals. Lincoln suggests that the Navaho curing ceremonies prescribed on the basis of the content of dreams have symbols similar to those of the diagnostic dreams, and that the particular curing ceremony is effective because it resolves symbolically the unconscious conflict in the dream. For example:

Dreams of death, that is, of one's own death, or the death of neighbors and relatives, also dreams that your teeth have fallen out require the Hozhonji or Chant of the Restoration of the Family.

Suggestion. Death dreams are generally death wishes, and the symbol of losing a tooth as often meaning castration anxiety because of death wishes is widespread. (Here again occurs the association of loss of a tooth, death of a relative as in the universal type dreams.) The Hozhonji is to restore the family, that is to protect it from death wishes towards the parents (Lincoln, 1935, p. 180).

It has been suggested by Stewart that a therapeutic psychological effect may be obtained if the symbolic forms which emerge in trance and dream are taken as objective dangers, and group support is given to mastering these symbolic dangers. Stewart presents a vivid if journalistic account of the psychotherapeutic methods of the Phillipine Negritos. A group of shamans cooperate in placing the patient in trance, and then encourage the patient to meet and overcome the spirit that has caused the patient's illness. This spirit, which has been attacking the patient in his dreams, is made to give the patient a song, and to become the patient's spirit helper. Stewart comments that this method seems effective in curing chronic physical ailments, such as skin irritations, headache, and recurrent fever, which probably have at least a partial psychosomatic origin. In this form of therapy, conflicts are externalized as spirits, and group support is given to overcoming their symbolic representations. Also, a spirit, once faced and overcome, is made to work for the person, and a public ritual is used to displace previous anxiety (Stewart, 1954).

A technique of dream therapy has been reported for the Diegueno Indians of southern California which seems to be similar to Western psychotherapy in its management of dreams. This technique is used to treat persons who appear to be afflicted with obsessive sexual fantasies. There are two recognized forms of this type of illness. The first, which is less serious, is characterized by symptoms of excessive dreaming, laziness, and social withdrawal. The second form of this malady is considered to be an advanced form of the first, and appears to be an actual psychosis, characterized by persistent hallucinations of a spirit lover, a supernatural bullet hawk which takes human form as a person of either sex. Persons afflicted with this hallucination are called 'spouses of that bird'.

To treat these maladies, a dream shaman is sought. The shaman attempts to get the patient to talk about his dreams and sexual life, actual and imaginary. The shaman begins by asserting that he already knows all the patient's dreams, so that there is no use in trying to conceal anything. A mild type of hypnotic trance may be used to encourage the patient's talking, except in the more severely psychotic cases, which do not respond to this kind of treatment. Along with discussion of the patient's sexual life and fantasies, the shaman also prescribes blood letting and special nourishing foods. For the unwed, marriage is recommended, apparently to help the patient shift from substitute gratification in fantasy to real life situations (Toffelmier and Luomala, 1936). The technique of therapy in this example is in many ways unusual. The technique of discussing with the patient his fantasies, including dreams, rather than permitting the patient to enact his fantasies, or to create a ritual defense against them, is particularly striking. It is not surprising that in this culture shamans are selected because of their stable (rather than unstable) personalities.

To summarize the material which has been treated so far in this section, the distinction between content, structure, function, and process in culture may provide a useful framework (Hsu, 1959). The cultural uses of dreams may be considered to be a type of culture content, having relations with the structural, functional, and procedural aspects of culture and society. Dreams may affect the structure of a society in becoming the subject matter of formal and informal roles, such as that of the dream interpreter, or in becoming a prerequisite for the ascription and achievement of roles, bringing factors of unconscious choice into the process of role allocation, as well as offering justification for the choice of deviant roles. Dreams may also function to help the individual maintain psychic equilibrium, serving as an important part of non-Western and Western psychotherapy.

Dream usages and their correlates

The next part of this section will present the results of a cross-cultural study of the conditions which affect the cultural uses of dreams. In this study I have attempted to find out why some societies have extensive uses for dreams, while other societies do not. On the basis of case history materials reported in the ethnographic literature, it seemed to me that anxiety about being alone and on one's own often gives rise to a strong preoccupation with dreams and fantasy. If this were true, then societies in which individuals frequently experience anxiety concerning isolation and self-reliance would be likely to place an especially strong cultural emphasis on dreams. I therefore attempted to specify the social conditions which would be most likely to subject individuals to this type of anxiety, so that it would be possible to predict the degree of emphasis placed on dreams in any given culture from these conditions.

Field workers interested in culture and personality have presented several examples of the effect of social isolation and the effect of cultural roles which demand independent and self-reliant action. Margaret Mead recounts the story of an orphaned Manus boy who felt isolated and unloved, and who, unlike the other Manus children, was preoccupied with fantasies about a guardian spirit which he took to be his own father (Mead, 1932, p. 183). A similar case has been reported by Dorothy Eggan, in a study of mythic materials in dreams (1955). One of her Hopi informants, who also felt isolated and abandoned, also turned inward to fantasy about a supernatural helper. Dorothy Eggan comments:

Benedict has pointed out that although the Pueblo area is surrounded by the concept of a power-giving or protecting Guardian Spirit, such a concept has not been standardized in the Pueblo groups because they are dominated by the 'necessity of the group ceremonial approach not that of individual experience' (Benedict, 1923, p. 36). But in Sam we find a man who, because of personal problems, although believing firmly in the 'group approach', was frequently made to feel less a part of the community than he needed to feel. Consequently he has elaborated the concept of *dumalaitaka* (guide or guardian spirit), which is found among the Hopi, but which is generally rather vague and unstressed, into an ever present and active spirit who comes to him in dreams, takes him to witches' meetings and on treasure hunts, gives him strength, wisdom and advice, rescues him from dangerous situations, and always assures him that he is on the right road and that his enemies are wrong (Eggan, 1955, p. 448).

Wallace, in his study of Iroquois dream theory, also concludes that anxiety about independence is related to this kind of extensive use of dreams:

. . . the typical Iroquois male, who in his daily life was a brave, generous, active, and independent spirit, nevertheless cherished some strong, if unconscious, wishes to be passive, to beg, to be cared for. This unallowable tendency, so threatening to a man's sense of self-esteem, could not appear easily even in a dream; when it did, it was either experienced as an intolerably painful episode of torture, or was put in terms of a meeting with a supernatural protector. However, the Iroquois themselves unwittingly make the translation: an active manifest dream is fulfilled by a passive receiving action. The arrangement of the dream guessing rite raises this dependency to an exquisite degree: the dreamer cannot even ask for his wish; like a baby, he must content himself with cryptic signs and symbols until someone guesses what he wants and gives it to him (1958, p. 247).

These reports indicate that anxiety about being isolated and on one's own may give rise to preoccupation with dreams and fantasy, especially fantasy about magical helpers. The content of such fantasy seems to serve as a denial of the individual's actual isolation and helplessness, thereby partially relieving these anxieties.

In order to measure the degree of cultural preoccupation with dreams, the following traits involving dreams were coded for a sample of sixty-three societies taken from the Human Relations Area Files. No society was selected unless at least a paragraph on dreams could be found in the literature, and no more than two societies have been taken from any one culture area, using Murdock's World Ethnographic Sample (1957):

(a) Supernaturals appear in dreams and give important powers, aid, ritual, and information.
(b) Religious experts (priests, shamans) expected to use their own dreams in performance of their role (e.g. curing, divination).
(c) Culture pattern dreams required before some roles may be assumed.
(d) Dreams induced by special techniques (e.g. fasting, drugs, sleeping alone, etc.).
(e) Formal or informal role of dream interpreter.
(f) Undoing ritual after some dreams (e.g. sacrifice, avoidance).
(g) Supernaturals appear in dreams and harm or foreshadow harm to the dreamer.

These particular traits were selected because they are neither universal nor extremely rare, and because they cover a wide range of types of uses of dreams. I had hoped that all of these traits would be positively correlated with each other; however, this proved not to be the case. Only four of these traits showed high significant correlations with each other: traits a, b, c, and d. The other three traits were uncorrelated with each other, and with these four.

If all seven traits had been strongly intercorrelated, it would have been reasonable to assume that there is a general factor of preoccupation with dreams. The findings seem to indicate, however, that rather than a general factor of preoccupation with dreams, there is a more limited complex centered about the use of dreams to seek and control supernatural powers. Traits a, b, and d involve this seeking and controlling of supernatural power quite directly. Trait c, involving culture pattern dreams which are required before certain roles may be assumed, is less directly related to seeking supernatural aid. However, it seems that such culture pattern dreams often consist of a visitation by a magical helper, who teaches the aspiring shaman or warrior important supernatural techniques. The other dream traits, involving dream interpretation, undoing rituals and possible supernatural harm, are unrelated to this complex, and have not been used in measuring this type of cultural preoccupation with dreams.

In view of these findings, the original hypothesis has been modified to state that anxiety about being alone and on one's own gives rise to the use of dreams to seek and control supernatural powers. The extent of this use of dreams has been measured by the number of traits a, b, c, and d reported present for each society. The median number of traits reported present for this cross-cultural sample is one. Societies with none of these four traits fall below the median, and are considered low on the use of dreams to seek and control supernatural powers. Societies with one or more traits reported present are considered high on this use of dreams.

The first condition specified as a possible cause of anxiety about isolation and independence involves residence at marriage. If, at marriage, a son or daughter moves far away from his or her parents, the loss of parental support should give rise to anxiety about being isolated and on one's own. In order to test this hypothesis, estimates of the distances that sons and daughters most usually move at marriage for each society have been taken from a cross-cultural study of residence by Whiting and D'Andrade (1959). Table 1 presents the association between the typical distances for parents and married son and the use of dreams to seek and control supernatural powers. The data in this table indicate that the further the son typically moves away from his parents, the more likely a society is to use dreams to seek and control supernatural powers. The degree of association is fairly strong, and significant at the 0·01 level. No table has been presented for the relation of distance between parents and married daughter and use of dreams because it was found that there is no association between these two measures. Apparently, anxiety suffered by women does not affect this use of dreams. Perhaps this is because religion is more frequently a man's affair, or perhaps because women may turn to their spouses in order to relieve the anxiety of loss of parental support in a way that men may not.

In order to check on these findings, Murdock's residence and family classification has been used. From the findings presented above, nonpatrilocal societies should have more uses of dreams to seek and control supernatural powers than patrilocal societies, and independent families should have more uses for dreams than extended families. Both these conditions have effects in the predicted direction and are statistically significant when considered together.

A second possible source of anxiety about being isolated and on one's own involves the subsistence economy. The relation of the subsistence economy to adult roles which demand independent and self-reliant behavior has been discussed by Barry, Child and Bacon in a study of economy and child-rearing practices (1959). They find that child-rearing practices stressing independence, self-reliance, and achievement are most typical of hunting and fishing societies, while child-rearing practices stressing obedience, responsibility, and nurturance are typical of societies with both agricultural and animal husbandry. Societies with agriculture, and without animal husbandry, fall between these extremes. The correlation between the

Table 1 Relation of most typical distance between married son and parents to use of dreams to seek and control supernatural powers

Son resides in parents' household	Son resides in same village or local group	Son resides in different village or local group
		Crow (a,b,c,d)
		Iroquois (a,b,c,d)
		Jivaro (a,b,c,d)
		Naskapi (a,b,c,d)
		Ojibwa (a,b,c,d)
		Omaha (a,b,c,d)
		Paiute (a,b,c,d)
	Comanche (a,b,c,d)	Andamans (a,b,c)
	Semang (a,b,c,d)	Copper Eskimo (a,b,c)
	Pukapuka (a,b,c)	Cuna (a,b,c)
	Chukchee (a,b)	Kaska (a,c,d)
	Rwala (b,d)	Lapps (a,b)
	Araucanians (b)	Yaruro (b,d)
	Azande (d)	Bemba (b)
Papago (a,b,c,d)	Fang (a)	Mundurucu (a)
Kapauku (a,b)	Nyakusa (b)	Trobriands (c)
Ifuago (c)	Wolof (b)	Yakut (d)
Bhil (—)	Ashanti (—)	Burmese (—)
Iban (—)	Aymara (—)	Callinago (—)
Lepcha (—)	Ifaluk (—)	Ganda (—)
Mataco (—)	Kurtatchi (—)	Karen (—)
Nama (—)	Marquesas (—)	
Samoa (—)	MinChia (—)	
Siriono (—)	Mossi (—)	
Tupinamba (—)	Riffians (—)	
	Somali (—)	
	Tallensi (—)	
	Tanala (—)	
	Thai (—)	
	Tiv (—)	
	Tubatulabal (—)	
	Yoruba (—)	

Note: the societies are grouped in colums on the basis of distance between married son and parents and in descending degree of extensiveness of use of dreams to seek and control supernatural powers. The letters in parentheses after each society designate the traits reported present. (See page 210 for definition of traits.)

form of economy and a combined child-training measure of relative 'pressure for compliance' (composed of scores for obedience, responsibility, and nurturance training) versus 'pressure for assertiveness' (composed of scores for independence, self-reliance, and achievement training) yields exceptionally strong coefficients of associations of $+0.94$ and $+0.93$ for extreme and intermediate comparisons (1959, p. 59). This very high degree of association is thought to be due to the functional adjustment of child-rearing practices to the type of adult roles necessary to maintain food production. That is, societies with both agriculture and animal husbandry can best assure future food supply by 'faithful adherence to routine' and therefore train children to be obedient and responsible, while in hunting and fishing societies individual initiative and skill is more adaptive, along with child-rearing practices stressing independence and self-reliance (1959, p. 52).

It is expected, then, that hunting and fishing societies will be likely to use dreams to seek and control supernatural powers, while societies with both agriculture and animal husbandry will be less likely to use dreams in this fashion. Societies with either agriculture or animal husbandry, but not both, should fall between these two extremes.[1] This result is predicted for two reasons. First, according to Barry and co-workers, hunting and fishing societies place greater pressure on the adult to be independent and self-reliant. Second, hunting and fishing societies also place relatively greater pressure on the child to be independent and self-reliant.

Table 2 presents the association between type of economy and the use of dreams to seek and control supernatural powers. The ratings on economy have been taken from Murdock (1957).

The results indicate that there is a strong and significant relation between the type of economy and the use of dreams. Approximately 80 per cent of the hunting and fishing societies use dreams to seek and control supernatural powers, while only 20 per cent of the societies with both agriculture and animal husbandry use dreams this way. The intermediate societies, which have either agriculture or animal husbandry, but not both, fall between the two extremes, with 60 per cent of these societies using dreams to seek and control supernatural powers.

1. Barry, Child and Bacon group together both nomadic pastoral societies and societies with a combination of animal husbandry and agriculture, evidently considering the use of animals to be the crucial determinant in accumulation of food resources. However, the combination of agriculture with animal husbandry would be more likely to produce a stable and high food output than either economy separately. For this reason the groupings of categories of economy used by Barry and his co-workers have been altered slightly in this paper, and societies with animal husbandry and no agriculture have been put in the intermediate hunting and fishing group.

Table 2 **Relation of subsistence economy to use of dreams to seek and control supernatural powers**

Agriculture plus animal husbandry	Agriculture without animal husbandry	Hunting, fishing, and animal husbandry without agriculture
		Comanche (a,b,c,d)
		Crow (a,b,c,d)
		Naskapi (a,b,c,d)
		Ojibwa (a,b,c,d)
		Omaha (a,b,c,d)
		Paiute (a,b;c,d)
		Semang (a,b,c,d)
		Andamans (a,b,c)
	Iroquois (a,b,c,d)	Copper Eskimo (a,b,c)
	Jivaro (a,b,c,d)	Kaska (a,c,d)
	Papago (a,b,c,d)	Pukapuka (a,b,c)
	Cuna (a,b,c)	*Chukchee (a,b)
	Carib (a,b)	*Lapps (a,b)
	Azande (d)	*Rwala (b,d)
Chagga (b,c)	Bemba (b)	Wishram (a,d)
Kapauku (a,b)	Fang (a)	Yaruro (b,d)
Araucanians (b)	Ifugao (c)	Caingang (d)
Nyakusa (b)	Mundurucu (a)	Tlingit (b)
Wolof (b)	Trobriands (c)	*Yakut (a)
Aymara (—)	Ashanti (—)	Callinago (—)
Bhil (—)	Ifaluk (—)	Mataco (—)
Burmese (—)	Kurtatchi (—)	*Nama (—)
Ganda (—)	Marquesas (—)	Siriono (—)
Iban (—)	Samoa (—)	*Somali (—)
Karen (—)	Subanum (—)	Tubatulabal (—)
Lepcha (—)	Tupinamba (—)	
MinChia (—)	Yoruba (—)	
Mossi (—)		
Riffians (—)		
Tallensi (—)		
Tanala (—)		
Thai (—)		
Thonga (—)		
Tiv (—)		

* Animal husbandry societies.
Note: the societies are grouped in columns on the basis of economy in descending degree of extensiveness of use of dreams to seek and control supernatural powers. The letters in parentheses after each society designate the traits reported present. (See page 210 for definition of traits.)

Unfortunately, it is not possible to decide whether this association is due to the effect of child rearing, or to the effect of role pressures on adults. A separate test, using the child-training measure of pressure for compliance versus assertiveness, results in a significant correlation of assertiveness with an extensive use of dreams. However, attempting to control the effect of economy reduces this correlation drastically, although no firm conclusion can be drawn because of the large amount of overlap between type of economy and child-rearing practices. Attempts to use other measures of child rearing involving independence training, taken from Whiting and Child (1953), and unpublished scores rated by Barry and his associates, reveal a nonsignificant tendency for early indulgence of dependency and later severe socialization of dependency to go with extensive use of dreams to seek and control supernatural powers.

Although economic conditions are related to the typical distance a son moves at marriage with the son moving further in hunting and fishing society, these two conditions seem to have clearly assessable independent effects. Within agricultural societies, the greater the distance between son and parent, the more likely a society is to use dreams to seek and control supernatural powers. The same relations hold within hunting, fishing, and pastoral societies.

In general, the findings of this cross-cultural study support the notion that anxiety about being isolated and under pressure to be self-reliant may create an involvement with a type of fantasy about magical helpers. Both the use of fantasy and dreams, rather than ritual as the means of contact with the supernatural, and the use of personal helpers, rather than impersonal forces, seem to be involved in this complex. The type of economy and the degree of isolation of the married son from his parents have been found to affect this complex strongly, with hunting and fishing societies, and societies in which the son moves far away from his parents being more likely to use dreams to seek and control supernatural powers. Based on the rather weak correlations with child-training practices, and the lack of association with the isolation of the married daughter, I suspect that this effect is mediated by what happens to adults rather than children, and what happens to men rather than women.[2]

2. There is some evidence that early childhood conditions involving the identification process, whereby a young child comes to admire and wish to be like his or her parent of the same sex, also affects the use of dreams. It is thought that strong parental same-sex identification leads to fantasy about parent-like guardian spirits, and to the use of fantasy rather than ritual or acting out to relieve anxiety. This formulation is at present still tentative, and dependent upon further research. It may be that strong early same-sex parental identification is a necessary but not sufficient cause for a strong degree of cultural emphasis on dreams, with adult role stress involving isolation and independence a later 'eliciting' factor.

As a final summary, the following general conclusions about the relations between dreams, personality, and culture are tentatively advanced.

1. There is a close association between dreams and the supernatural. This association consists of similarities between dream images and the conceptions of the supernatural, and also of the use of dreams to see and interact with the supernatural. This association does not necessarily indicate that dreams gave rise in the distant past to various conceptions of the supernatural, but would seem to indicate that similar psychological mechanisms may underlie both.

2. There are a number of small bits of evidence to support the thesis that symbolism in dreams is a universal phenomena. If true, this means that man either innately or due to experience establishes a set of identities or equivalences without cultural tuition, and without awareness, and that these equivalences are in constant use.

3. Dreams, it is assumed, can be used to reveal the dreamer's motives. Further, the relation between the dream content and these motives may be more or less indirect and disguised. The most basic (and usually the most disguised) motives involve obtaining direct physical gratification from members of the nuclear family. These motives can be found in the dreams of people from all societies. The modal ways in which these motives are represented and defended against, however, vary culturally.

4. It is also assumed that dreams have a cognitive as well as motivational component. The dreamer's waking life and, hence, his culture are represented in dreams. This representation is always distorted, however. Sometimes the distortion is mild, involving minor editing of material and bias in selection. At other times the distortion may be drastic involving complete reversal of normal experience. Such distortion is probably due in part to the press of motivation, and especially conflicts in motivation.

5. Culture may also specify the content which is appropriate to dreams under certain conditions. Where the individual is supposed to dream a certain dream, the retelling of these dreams is probably influenced by some degree of later elaboration. Acculturation may bring foreign material into such dreams, or completely break the pattern. The emotional reaction to dreams may be affected by the cultural definition of what is likely to take place in dreams, and in turn the cultural definition of the self may be affected by the kinds of events which occur in dreams.

6. Dreams have numerous cultural uses. Prediction of the future and contact with supernaturals are the most common of these uses. Dreams are also used in native psychotherapies and as a means of selecting and rejecting personnel for various roles. One special use of dreams, to seek and control super-

natural powers, seems to be caused by anxiety about being alone and needing to be able to be self-reliant. Societies in which the economy demands self-reliant behavior on the part of the men, as in hunting, and societies in which the married son must move away from his natal family into another village are more likely to use dreams to seek and control supernatural powers.

References

BARRY, H., CHILD, I. L., and BACON, M. (1959), 'Relation of child training to subsistence economy', *Amer. Anthrop.*, vol. 61, pp. 51–63.

BENEDICT, R. (1923), 'The concept of the guardian spirit in North America', *Mem. Amer. Anthrop. Assn*, no. 29.

BOURGUIGON, E. E. (1954), 'Dreams and dream interpretation in Haiti', *Amer. Anthrop.*, vol. 56, pp. 262–8.

DEVEREUX, G. (1951), *Reality and Dream*, International Universities Press.

EGGAN, D. (1955), 'The personal use of myth in dreams', *J. Amer. Folklore*, vol. 68, pp. 445–53.

ERIKSON, E. H. (1950), *Childhood and Society*, Norton.

FIRTH, R. (1934), 'The meaning of dreams in Tikopia', in E. E. Evans-Pritchard *et al.* (eds.), *Essays Presented to C. G. Seligman*, Kegan Paul, Trench, Trubner, pp. 63–74.

HALL, C. S. (1951), 'What people dream about', *Sci. Amer.*, vol. 184, pp. 60–63.

HALL, C. S. (1953), *The Meaning of Dreams*, Harper & Row.

HALLOWELL, A. I. (1955), 'The self and its behavioral environment', in *Culture and Experience*, University of Pennsylvania Press.

HOLMBERG, A. R. (1950), 'Nomads of the long bow: the Siriono of Eastern Bolivia', *Inst. Soc. Anthrop. Pubn*, no. 10.

HSU, F. K. (1959), 'Structure, function, content, and process', *Amer. Anthrop.*, vol. 61, pp. 790–805.

KING, A. R. (1943), 'The dream biography of a mountain Maidu', *Char. Personality*, vol. 11, pp. 227–34.

LEE, S. G. M. (1958), 'Social influences in Zulu dreaming', *J. soc. Psychol.*, vol. 47, pp. 265–83.

LINCOLN, J. S. (1935), *The Dream in Primitive Cultures*, Cresset Press.

LOWIE, R. H. (1922), 'The religion of the Crow Indians', *Anthrop. Pap. Amer. Mus. Nat. Hist.*, vol. 25, pp. 309–444.

LOWIE, R. H. (1924), *Primitive Religion*, Liveright, reprinted 1948.

MEAD, M. (1932), 'An investigation of the thought of primitive children with special reference to animism', *J. Roy. Anthrop. Inst.*, vol. 62, pp. 173–89.

MURDOCK, G. P. (1957), 'World ethnographic sample', *Amer. Anthrop.*, vol. 59, pp. 664–87.

RADIN, P. (1936), 'Ojibwa and Ottawa puberty dreams', in *Essays Presented to A. L. Kroeber*, University of California Press.

SCHNEIDER, D. (1941), 'Aboriginal dreams', Master's thesis, Cornell University.

SCHNEIDER, D. M., and SHARP, R. L. (no date), 'Yir-Yiront dreams', unpublished.

STEWART, K. (1951), 'Dream theory in Malaya', *Complex*, vol. 6, pp. 21–33.

STEWART, K. (1954), *Pygmies and Dream Giants*, Norton.

TOFFELMIER, G., and LUOMALA, K. (1936), 'Dreams and dream interpretation of the Diegueño Indians of Southern California', *Psychoanal. Q.*, vol. 2, pp. 195–225.

WALLACE, A. (1958), 'Dreams and wishes of the soul: a type of psychoanalytic theory among the seventeenth century Iroquois', *Amer. Anthrop.*, vol. 60, pp. 234–48.

WHITING, J. W. M., and CHILD, I. L. (1953), *Child Training and Personality: A Cross-Cultural Study*, Yale University Press.

WHITING, J. W. M., and D'ANDRADE, R. G. (1959), 'Sleeping arrangements and social structure: a cross-cultural study', presented at American Anthropological Association Annual Meeting, Mexico City, December.

Section Two Dreaming

Part One
Rapid Eye Movement Sleep and Dreams

Since the pioneering work of Aserinsky and Kleitman (1953) it has come
to be generally accepted amongst psychologists that rapid eye movement
or R E M sleep is the physiological state during which dreams occur. In
Reading 13, Berger gives a brief account of this sleep stage and
discusses, critically, its relation to dreaming. Although more detailed
reviews of R E M physiology are available (for example, see Hartmann,
1967; Snyder, 1969), Berger gives more consideration to the hypothesis
that dreams may occur in sleep states other than R E M sleep (e.g. see
Foulkes and Vogel, 1965). If R E M sleep is the dream state, and if, as has
been claimed, many dreams have sexual overtones, then one would expect
penile erections to occur in this stage of sleep. Such an association has
been found. Reading 14 is an early study of this phenomenon, our view
of which has been extended and modified by more recent work. Thus
Karacan, Hursch and Williams (1972) have found that erections and
R E M can occur independently and several experimenters have found
only weak concordance between R E M sleep and sex hormone activity
(e.g. see Branchey, Branchey and Nadler, 1971; Rubin, Kales, Alder,
Fagan and Odell, 1972). Dreams involve visual activity and the behaviour
of single neurons in the cat's visual cortex during R E M sleep is reported
by Evarts in Reading 15. Recordings have also been made from neurons
in the motor system and from those associated with motivation during
R E M sleep, and other states of consciousness (Evarts, 1964; Mink, Best
and Olds, 1967). In Reading 16, Hartmann discusses the present view of
the nightmare and the states of sleep associated with it (see also
Hadfield, 1954; Jones, 1959).

The next four Readings are investigations of the hypothesis that the
binocularly coordinated eye movements which are unique to R E M
sleep are directional responses to the dream events occurring in that state.
This hypothesis is briefly assessed by Berger in Reading 30 and is reviewed
by Kline (1972). If true, it strongly supports the view that the mental life
of R E M sleep is qualitatively different to that found in other sleep states.
Berger and Oswald (Reading 17) find a relationship between eye

movement and dream intensity in REM sleep. In the next Reading, Berger, Olley and Oswald fail to observe REMs in three men with lifelong blindness. However, Gross, Byrne and Fisher (Reading 19) find eye movements in such people when they use a mechanical method of detecting REMs in addition to the EOG method of recording used by Berger *et al.* Finally, a recent paper by Weitzenhoffer (Reading 20) shows that pursuit-like eye movements reflect dream content in hypnotic dreams.

References

ASERINSKY, E., and KLEITMAN, N. (1953), 'Regularly occurring periods of eye motility and concomitant phenomena during sleep', *Science*, vol. 118, pp. 273–4.

BRANCHEY, M., BRANCHEY, L., and NADLER, R. D. (1971), 'Effects of estrogen and progesterone on sleep patterns of female rats', *Physiol. Behav.*, vol. 6, pp. 743–6.

EVARTS, E. (1964), 'Temporal patterns of discharge of pyramidal tract neurons during sleep and waking in the monkey', *J. Neurophysiol.*, vol. 27, pp. 152–71.

FOULKES, D., and VOGEL, G. (1965), 'Mental activity at sleep onset', *J. abnorm. Psychol.*, vol. 70, pp. 231–43.

HADFIELD, J. A. (1954), *Dreams and Nightmares*, Penguin.

HARTMANN, E. (1967), *The Biology of Dreaming*, C. C. Thomas.

JONES, E. (1959), *On the Nightmare*, Grove Press.

KARACAN, I., HURSCH, C. J., and WILLIAMS, R. L. (1972), 'Some characteristics of nocturnal penile tumescence in elderly males', *J. Geront.*, vol. 27, pp. 39–45.

KLINE, P. (1972), *Fact and Fantasy in Freudian Theory*, Methuen.

MINK, W. D., BEST, J., and OLDS, J. (1967), 'Neurons in paradoxical sleep and motivated behavior', *Science*, vol. 158, pp. 1335–7.

RUBIN, R. T., KALES, A., ALDER, R., FAGAN, T., and ODELL, W. (1972), 'Gonadotrophin secretion during sleep in normal adult men', *Science*, vol. 175, pp. 196–8.

SNYDER, F. (1969), 'The physiology of dreaming', in M. Kramer (ed.), *Dream Psychology and the New Biology of Dreaming*, C. C. Thomas.

13 Ralph J. Berger

The Sleep and Dream Cycle

Ralph J. Berger, 'The sleep and dream cycle', from A. Kales (ed.), *Sleep Physiology and Pathology*, Lippincott, 1969, pp. 17–32.

The nature of sleep and dreams has been a topic of constant interest since antiquity, but has received little systematic study until recently. With the development of techniques of electrophysiology for recording from various organs throughout the body, methods for objective study of the sleep-dream process became available. The discovery of the electroencephalogram (EEG) by Berger in 1929 and its application in characterizing different levels of sleep by Loomis and associates (1937) paved the way for the discovery by Aserinsky and Kleitman (1953) that sleep consisted of two distinct phases rather than a single state that merely varied along a continuum in depth. This finding generated the vast upsurge of research on sleep and dreams that we have witnessed over the past fifteen years.

Loomis and associates (1937) classified electroencephalographic patterns that accompany the passage from wakefulness to sleep into five types, A through E. This classification was widely adopted until Aserinsky and Kleitman (1953, 1955) noted recurrent periods of sleep, roughly every ninety minutes, in which jerky, binocularly conjugate rapid eye movements (REMs) could be seen beneath the closed eyelids of the sleeper. Dement and Kleitman (1957), on the basis of a large number of subsequent all-night recordings of undisturbed sleep, defined five electroencephalographic stages of sleep: stages 1 through 4, during which REMs are absent, referred to as nonrapid eye movement (NREM) sleep stages; and a fifth stage, stage 1 REM, which is accompanied by REMs. This Dement–Kleitman system for scoring sleep stages has been the most widely used, and recently was modified (Rechtschaffen and Kales, 1968).

Figure 1 shows the electroencephalographic patterns in the EEG, eye movement in the EOG, and chin electromyographic patterns in the EMG, which accompany wakefulness and stages of sleep. During relaxed wakefulness the EEG is composed of sinusoidal alpha activity (8–12 cps) and low voltage activity of mixed frequency, accompanied by eye movements, eyelid blinks, and a high muscle tone. As the subject falls asleep, his muscles relax and his eyes begin to roll slowly from side to side, while his EEG gives way to a stage 1 pattern of relatively low voltage and mixed frequency.

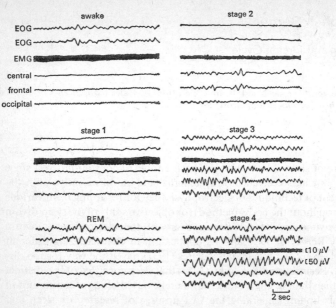

Figure 1 Stages of sleep as recorded on the electrooculogram (EOG), chin electromyogram (EMG), and electroencephalogram (central, frontal, occipital tracings). Note the high EMG and eye movements during wakefulness, compared with the low EMG and rapid eye movements (REMs) during stage REM. The EEG is similar during stage 1 and stage REM, but the EMG is high and REMs are absent in stage 1. Stages 2, 3, and 4 are characterized by slowing of frequency and increase in amplitude of the EEG. (From Kales *et al.*, 1968)

Stage 2 is characterized by 12 to 14 cps sleep spindles, similar in shape to alpha waves but higher in frequency, together with K complexes superimposed on a background of relatively low voltage and mixed frequency electroencephalographic activity. K complexes are relatively high amplitude waveforms exceeding 0·5 sec in duration, of complex shape – usually a well-delineated, negative, sharp wave immediately followed by a positive component and often, in turn, by sleep spindles. They can occur as a response to an external stimulus but also occur spontaneously (Johnson and Karpan, 1968).

Stages 3 and 4 are defined by high voltage, slow waves of 1 to 2 cps; when more than half the record consists of this slow-wave activity, it is classified as stage 4, while lesser amounts (but greater than 20 per cent) are classified as stage 3. Stage REM shows an electroencephalographic pattern similar to that of stage 1 but accompanied by episodic REMs, a low amplitude EMG

(Berger, 1961; Jacobson *et al.*, 1964), and many other physiological changes described in chapter 5.

Stage REM has been denoted by a large variety of terms including paradoxical sleep, activated sleep, deep sleep, low voltage fast sleep, emergent or ascending stage 1, and D-state. During nocturnal sleep of normal adults with regular sleep habits, stage REM follows another sleep stage and rarely occurs after an extended period of wakefulness. By contrast, the stage 1 EEG of sleep onset is unaccompanied by REMs and the muscle tone is elevated compared to that accompanying stage REM. The standard placement of electrodes for the EEG, EMG, and EOG that record these sleep stages is shown in Figure 2.

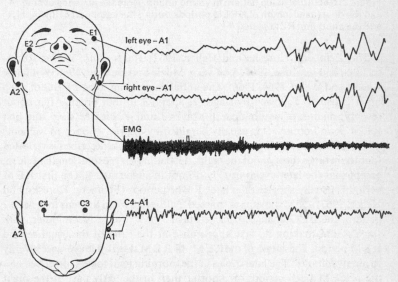

Figure 2 Electrode placement in sleep research. The top two tracings show eye movements recorded from electrodes attached laterally to the outer canthus of each eye (EOG) and referred to the ear; this produces out-of-phase deflection in the two tracings for almost all eye movements. The EMG is recorded from electrodes attached firmly beneath the chin and referred to each other. In the lower tracing, the EEG is derived from a scalp placement referred to the opposite ear. The recordings illustrate the onset of a REM sleep period. First, the EMG decreases sharply; then eye movements appear while the electroencephalographic waves change to low amplitude, mixed frequency. (From Rechtschaffen and Kales, 1968)

A typical night of sleep in young adult subjects has been defined in a number of studies in various laboratories (Figure 3) (Dement and Kleitman,

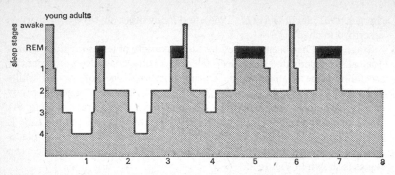

Figure 3 Nocturnal sleep pattern in young adults. Note the absence of stage 4 and the decreased length of NREM periods during the latter part of the night, and the short first REM period

1957a; Feinberg, Koresko and Heller, 1967; Kales *et al.*, 1967a; Rechtschaffen and Verdone, 1964; Roffwarg, Muzio and Dement, 1966; Williams, Agnew and Webb, 1964, 1966). The initial descending stage 1 EEG of sleep onset is usually followed by stages 2, 3, and 4 in that order. After about seventy minutes of predominantly stages 3 and 4 NREM sleep, the first REM period occurs. It is usually heralded by a series of body movements and a shift in the EEG to a stage 2 pattern. The cycle described is repeated four to six times throughout the night, depending on the total length of sleep, except that the later cycles usually do not include stage 4. The first REM period is usually shorter than later REM periods (Feinberg, Koresko and Heller, 1967) and is sometimes 'missed'; although sleep lightens to a stage 2 pattern, the EEG changes back to stage 3 or 4 after a few minutes, with stage REM making its first appearance at the time of the usual second REM period. The length of the REM–NREM sleep cycle averages seventy to ninety minutes. The later cycles in the morning tend to be shorter because the NREM sleep periods are shorter than in the early part of the night (Feinberg, Koresko and Heller, 1967; Kales *et al.*, 1967a). About 20 to 25 per cent of the total sleep time of young adults is spent in stage REM, 5 per cent in stage 1 (NREM), 50 per cent in stage 2, and 20 per cent in stages 3 and 4 combined. The pattern of sleep from night to night in a single individual remains relatively constant, except for the first night spent in the laboratory when the subject takes a longer time to fall asleep, tends to awaken more frequently, and has less REM sleep than on subsequent nights (Agnew, Webb and Williams, 1966; Dement, Kahn and Roffwarg, 1965). This disruption has been referred to as the 'first-night effect' and undoubtedly represents the effects of adaptation to sleeping in the unusual environment of a research laboratory.

Sleep in different species

Behavioral and physiological sleep has been shown to exist in reptiles, birds, and mammals (Klein, 1963; Snyder, 1966). Lower vertebrates have been insufficiently studied, but Hobson (1967) was unable to find any signs of sleep in the frog, an amphibian. Kleitman (1963) has theorized that sleep first appears with development of the cerebral cortex, upon which also depend the integrative functions that characterize waking life. However, the percentage of time spent asleep does not correlate with the degree of cortical development in various species. Thus the rabbit and cat both spend about 70 per cent of their lives asleep yet differ in relative cortical development (Berger, 1969).

REM sleep has been observed in all mammals studied so far (Klein, 1963; Snyder, 1966). A brief state of only a few seconds, which resembles REM sleep in most respects, has been seen in the bird (Klein, 1963). REM sleep with its complete constellation of physiological characteristics as seen in the mammal has not yet been observed in reptiles or amphibians (Hobson, 1967; Klein, 1963), although rapid, but nonconjugate, eye movements have been described during sleep in the chameleon (Tauber, Roffwarg and Weitzman, 1966).

Just as various species differ in how much time each spends asleep, so also do they differ in the proportion of time they spend in REM sleep. Again, the amount of REM sleep does not correlate directly with cortical development but does bear a close relation to the amount of binocularly coordinated eye movement each species displays (Berger, 1969). Figure 4 shows this relation, in which the percentage of total sleep time (TST) spent in REM sleep, normalized for the amount of time each species spends asleep (REM/TST^2), is plotted with the percentage of partial decussation at the optic chiasma for a number of different species. The amount of partial decussation serves as an index of the amount of conjugate mobility of the eyes (Walls, 1942). On the basis of these and other data, REM sleep may be functionally involved in the establishment and maintenance of binocularly coordinated eye movement, which is necessary for accurate binocular depth perception (Berger, 1969).

Not only do the amounts of time spent in the different states of sleep and wakefulness vary from one animal to another, but so do the periodicities of occurrence of the different states. Some species exhibit diurnal patterns of sleep and wakefulness; others are nocturnal; still others, such as the cat, exhibit polyphasic sleep-wakefulness patterns throughout both day and night.

The frequency of the REM–NREM cycle within a sleep period also differs among species. Man displays the longest cycle seen thus far, seventy

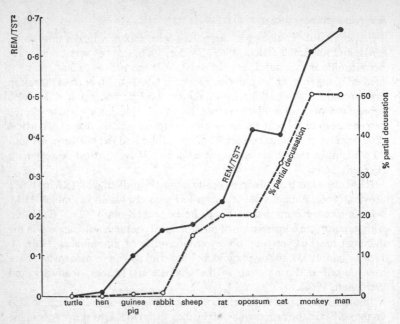

Figure 4 Percentage of total sleep time (TST), normalized for the amount of time each species spends asleep (REM/TST²), and the percentage of partial decussation at the optic chiasma for a number of different species in which sleep has been studied. (From Berger, 1969)

to ninety minutes; the mouse has the shortest, seven minutes. Weiss and Roldan (1964) compared the length of the cycle in three of the rodents, the rabbit, rat, and mouse, and found the frequency of REM sleep increased as the body weight decreased, thus suggesting that length of cycle was related to metabolic rate. This interpretation is supported by the ineffectiveness of external (Dement and Wolpert, 1958) or electrical (Kripke, Weitzman and Pollak, 1965) stimulation of the brain during NREM sleep in eliciting REM periods.

Relation between dreaming and the sleep cycle

Prior to the discovery of REM sleep, there had been a number of studies in which attempts were made to determine whether dreaming was associated with a particular stage of sleep as recorded on the EEG. Considered together, the results of these early studies indicated that dreams could be recalled following awakening from any stage of sleep (Blake, Gerard and Kleitman, 1939; Davis *et al.*, 1938; Teplitz, 1943). The cyclic recurrence of

REMs together with an activated pattern in the EEG somewhat similar to that of wakefulness caused Aserinsky and Kleitman (1955) to ponder whether this unique sleep state was the one in which dreams occurred. They found that vivid dreams were recalled 74 per cent of the time when subjects were awakened from REM periods but only 7 per cent of the time from NREM awakenings. In a later, more extensive study, Dement and Kleitman (1957b) obtained essentially the same results.

The high incidence of recall of dreams following stage REM awakenings has been confirmed in more than a score of studies. However, for NREM awakenings there has been less consistency among studies and investigators on the frequency of dream recall (Table 1), which has ranged from 0 (Wolpert and Trosman, 1958) to 74 per cent (Foulkes, 1962). This wide range is due to the differing criteria used for defining what mental experience is to be taken as a dream. If a dream is defined as a verbal report of an experience involving vivid multisensory imagery, frequently of a bizarre or unreal nature, in which the narrator himself often is actively involved, then the 7 per cent NREM recall originally obtained (Aserinsky and Kleitman, 1955) has been confirmed by most investigators. However, if a broader categorization of cognitive activities is used to define a dream, i.e. fragmentary reports of mental phenomena that may lack sensory imagery and seem closer to everyday thinking, then figures as high as 74 per cent NREM recall may be obtained (Foulkes, 1962).

Table 1 **Percentage recall of dreams following REM and NREM awakenings in sixteen studies**

	REM	NREM
Aserinsky and Kleitman (1955)	74	7
Dement (1955)	88	0
Dement and Kleitman (1957b)	79	7
Wolpert and Trosman (1958)	85	0
Goodenough et al. (1959)	69	34
Jouvet, Michel and Mounier (1960)	60	3
Snyder (1960)	62	13
Wolpert (1960)	85	24
Kremen (1961)	75	12
Foulkes (1962)	82	74
Orlinsky (1962)	86	42
Rechtschaffen, Verdone and Wheaton (1963)	86	23
Foulkes and Rechtschaffen (1964)	89	62
Goodenough et al. (1965)	76	21
Hobson, Goldfrank and Snyder (1965)	76	14
Kales et al. (1967b)	81	7

Therefore, there are distinct qualitative and quantitative differences in REM and NREM recall. Kremen (1961) found that when he asked his subjects to decide whether or not they had been dreaming, he obtained figures close to the original ones reported by Dement and Kleitman (1957b). Similar results were obtained by Kales and Jacobson (1967) when they themselves were subjects. Experienced judges not knowing from which sleep stage each report had been obtained could differentiate REM reports from NREM reports with 90 per cent success (Monroe et al., 1965). The reports were also divided into two groups: (1) reports that had the typical features of dreams and (2) reports that were more like wakeful thinking. When given these two groups of reports, the judges were still able to distinguish REM-'thinking' from NREM-'thinking' reports and REM-'dreaming' from NREM-'dreaming' reports with considerable success.

Foulkes (1964) has reported that dreams after awakenings from REM periods 9 to 24 minutes in length had more emotionality, dramatic quality, and distortion than those obtained within four to sixty seconds of REM onset. Dreams recalled from REM or NREM sleep after awakenings toward the end of the sleep period tend to become more elaborate in content compared with those obtained early in the night (Foulkes, 1966, 1967; Shapiro, Goodenough and Gryler, 1963). This increased content and vividness of dream recall is paralleled by a progressive decrease in overall depth of sleep throughout the night when 'depth' is measured by the threshold of awakening to auditory stimuli (Rechtschaffen, Hauri and Zeitlin, 1966). Between sleep stages, awakening thresholds were equal during stage REM and stage 2, increased during stage 3, and were highest in stage 4.

The considerable amounts of cognitive activity reported from NREM sleep, revealed by the later studies, led to a fervent controversy over whether dreaming is confined to REM sleep or occurs continuously throughout all stages of sleep. This debate continues to some extent today. The sharp decline in the frequency of dream reports as a function of the time of awakening after the end of an undisturbed REM period (Dement and Kleitman, 1957b; Goodenough et al., 1965; Wolpert and Trosman, 1958) supported the possibility that reports of dreaming from NREM sleep are reminiscences of experiences that occurred during a preceding REM period. However this interpretation was not supported by the finding that there is no difference in the quality of cognitive activity or frequencies with which cognitive activity is reported following awakenings from NREM periods which follow interrupted REM periods, uninterrupted REM periods, or descending stage 1 sleep (Foulkes, 1962; Foulkes, Spear and Symonds, 1966). In addition, Foulkes and associates (Foulkes and Vogel, 1965; Foulkes, Spear and Symonds, 1966), after waking subjects from stage 1 sleep-onset periods, have obtained records of extensive recall of mental activity indistinguishable from the typical report from stage REM. During these sleep-onset periods, typical REMs do not appear, although slow, rolling movements of the eyes are often present. The occurrence of complex, dreamlike, 'hypnagogic' imagery on falling asleep is frequent in some persons and is a well-known phenomenon (Oswald, 1962, p. 96).

It has also been suggested that the dreamlike experiences reported after NREM awakenings may occur while the subject is awakening to the arousing stimulus. An 'arousal' hypothesis as an explanation of NREM experiences was supported by the higher incidence of reports of 'thinking' following gradual awakenings from NREM sleep than following abrupt awakenings (Goodenough et al., 1965; Shapiro, Goodenough and Gryler, 1963; Shapiro et al., 1965). But this can be only part of the story, since there was no difference in the frequency of the reports of 'dreaming' following each type of awakening.

Additional evidence supports the temporal location of mental experiences recalled following stage-REM awakenings. Auditory, visual, or tactile stimuli presented during REM periods are frequently incorporated into subsequently reported dreams (Berger, 1963; Dement and Wolpert, 1958). The lengths of experienced time between the incorporated stimulus event and the end of the dream correlates well with the real time between the stimulus presentation and the subsequent awakening. In addition, the length of the dream report and the subject's own estimate of the length of the dream also correlate with the length of the associated REM period (Dement and Wolpert, 1958). Incorporation of external stimuli into cognitive experiences recalled following NREM awakenings has been rare (Rechtschaffen, Verdone and Wheaton, 1963), and correlations of the subjective durations of conscious experiences with the durations of the preceding NREM periods have not yet been reported.

In light of the foregoing work on the nature and extent of recall of mental activity following awakenings from different sleep stages, what can we conclude about the relation of dreaming to the sleep cycle? Most investigators now believe that mental activity does not totally cease at any time during sleep (Berger, 1967; Dement, 1967; Foulkes, 1962, 1967; Goodenough et al., 1965; Rechtschaffen, Verdone and Wheaton, 1963). It is not known whether the extent and quality of mental activity varies with the stage of sleep or whether the differences in REM and NREM reports reflect differences in ability to recall conscious experiences occurring uniformly throughout all stages of sleep. Since we cannot record the dream experiences as they occur, we have to work with only the dream reports. Thus we are presented with a logical problem of deciding which of the two interpretations of the data lies closer to reality. Rechtschaffen (1967) has suggested that we accept the most parsimonious explanation: The dream experiences of REM and NREM sleep differ, even though both interpretations are equally plausible.

However, I believe that the evidence should be most carefully weighed lest differential impairment of memory processes during REM and NREM sleep be too readily dismissed as the root of the problem. That short-term memory of dream events is a fragile process is indicated by introspective and anecdotal experience. Being sure of having had a dream but being unable to recall its specific content is a common experience in both the laboratory and everyday life. Furthermore, there are considerable individual differences in the frequency of spontaneous recall of dreams in the morning following sleep at home. Thus some people claim they have never had a dream in their lives, while others recall one or more dreams practically every night. When such subjects are awakened from REM sleep in the laboratory, differences in frequency of recall still exist, but the nondreamers do report dreams about 50 per cent of the time (Goodenough, 1967; Goodenough *et al.*, 1959). We can conclude from these studies that 'nondreamers' probably dream as often as dreamers but merely have poorer recall. The absence of elaborate recall of dreams following 90 per cent of NREM awakenings in the average subject may also be the result of poor recall, since we clearly can obtain from NREM awakenings a number of reports indistinguishable in length and content from the typical REM report.

Most NREM reports are significantly shorter than REM reports (Foulkes and Rechtschaffen, 1964; Goodenough *et al.*, 1965), as would be expected if recall from NREM sleep were impaired. But if a report is shorter, then there is less opportunity for the elaborate dramatic theme, common to REM reports, in the more limited material recalled. Thus, the typical qualitative differences between REM and NREM reports may merely reflect the differences in their lengths. Hall and Domhoff (1968) recently found that NREM reports contain significantly fewer characters, other than the dreamer himself, than REM reports. REM reports contain a significantly greater number of interactions of an emotional nature between characters (i.e. those involving sex or aggression), but there is a greater opportunity for such interactions to be recalled because there are more dream characters to interact.

Müller and Pilzecker (1900), among others (e.g. Glickman, 1961), have suggested that a short-term period of consolidation is involved in the memory process. Portnoff *et al.* (1966) reported that memory for stimulus words experienced immediately prior to onset of NREM sleep was poorer in the morning than when a few minutes of wakefulness intervened between the presentations of the stimulus words and onset of sleep. If it can be shown that memory for the same task is better when REM sleep occurs immediately following the experience, differential impairment of memory as an explanation of the differences in REM and NREM reports would receive considerable support. It might be possible to make such studies under conditions where REM sleep sometimes occurs immediately following wakefulness, as in young animals (Meier and Berger, 1965) or in narcoleptic patients (Rechtschaffen *et al.*, 1963).

Sleepwalking (Jacobson *et al.*, 1965; Kales *et al.*, 1966) occurs exclusively during NREM sleep, and sleep talking (Rechtschaffen, Goodenough and Shapiro, 1962) most frequently during this stage. Such spontaneous motor acts have traditionally been thought to represent the motor output accompanying dream experiences. When subjects are awakened from NREM sleep during or immediately after these episodic motor acts, recall of any ongoing mental activity is usually very meager or nonexistent. Speech during sleep can be relatively coherent and meaningful, and sleepwalking is sufficiently well organized for the somnambulist to steer himself around surrounding objects. Therefore, it would seem reasonable to suppose that the sleeper is experiencing conscious events related to his motor activities but that the mental experiences either are not registered in memory storage or cannot be retrieved on awakening.

Clearly, the problem of when dreaming occurs and of what mental stuff dreams are made of is presently unresolved. We do know that we dream much more, and more often each night, than had previously been thought prior to the discovery of REMs. But much work remains to be done before we can say whether we dream continuously and uniformly all night long, or whether the vividness, emotionality, and bizarreness of our mental activity ebbs and flows along with the REM peaks and NREM troughs of our nightly sleep cycles.

References

AGNEW, H. W., Jr, WEBB, W. B., and WILLIAMS, R. L. (1966), 'The first night effect: an EEG study of sleep', *Psychophysiology*, vol. 2, p. 263.

ASERINSKY, E., and KLEITMAN, N. (1953), 'Regularly occurring periods of eye motility and concomitant phenomena during sleep', *Science*, vol. 118, p. 273.

ASERINSKY, E., and KLEITMAN, N. (1955), 'Two types of ocular motility occurring in sleep', *J. appl. Physiol.*, vol. 8, p. 1.

BERGER, H. (1929), 'Über das Elektroenkephalogramm des Menschen', *Arch. Psychiat. Nervenkr.*, vol. 87, p. 527.

BERGER, R. J. (1961), 'Tonus of extrinsic laryngeal muscles during sleep and dreaming', *Science*, vol. 134, p. 840.

BERGER, R. J. (1963), 'Experimental modification of dream content by meaningful verbal stimuli', *Brit. J. Psychiat.*, vol. 109, p. 722.

BERGER, R. J. (1967), 'When is a dream is a dream is a dream?', *Exp. Neurol. Suppl.*, vol. 4, p. 15.

BERGER, R. J. (1969), 'Oculomotor control: a possible function of REM sleep', *Psychol. Rev.*, vol. 76, p. 144.

BLAKE, H., GERARD, R. W., and KLEITMAN, N. (1939), 'Factors influencing brain potentials during sleep', *J. Neurophysiol.*, vol. 2, p. 48.

DAVIS, H., *et al.* (1938), 'Human brain potentials during the onset of sleep', *J. Neurophysiol.*, vol. 1, p. 24.

DEMENT, W. C. (1955), 'Dream recall and eye movements during sleep in schizophrenics and normals', *J. nerv. ment. Dis.*, vol. 122, p. 263.

DEMENT, W. C. (1967), 'Possible physiological determinants of a possible dream-intensity cycle', *Exp. Neurol. Suppl.*, vol. 4, p. 38.

DEMENT, W. C., and KLEITMAN, N. (1957a), 'Cyclic variations in EEG during sleep and their relation to eye movements, body motility and dreaming', *EEG clin. Neurophysiol.*, vol. 9, p. 673.

DEMENT, W. C., and KLEITMAN, N. (1957b), 'The relation of eye movements during sleep to dream activity: an objective method for the study of dreaming', *J. exp. Psychol.*, vol. 53, p. 339.

DEMENT, W. C., and WOLPERT, E. A. (1958), 'The relation of eye movements, body motility and external stimuli to dream content', *J. exp. Psychol.*, vol. 55, p. 543.

DEMENT, W. C., KAHN, E., and ROFFWARG, H. P. (1965), 'The influence of the laboratory situation on the dreams of the experimental subject', *J. nerv. ment. Dis.*, vol. 140, p. 119.

FEINBERG, I., KORESKO, R. L., and HELLER, N. (1967), 'EEG sleep patterns as a function of normal and pathological aging in man', *J. psychiat. Res.*, vol. 5, p. 107.

FOULKES, W. D. (1962), 'Dream reports from different stages of sleep', *J. abnorm. Psychol.*, vol. 65, p. 14.

FOULKES, D. (1964), 'Theories of dream formation and recent studies of sleep consciousness', *Psychol. Bull.*, vol. 62, p. 236.

FOULKES, W. D. (1966), *The Psychology of Sleep*, Scribner.

FOULKES, D. (1967), 'Nonrapid eye movement mentation', *Exp. Neurol. Suppl.*, vol. 4, p. 28.

FOULKES, D., and RECHTSCHAFFEN, A. (1964), 'Presleep determinants of dream content: effects of two films', *Percept. mot. Skills*, vol. 19, p. 983.

FOULKES, D., and VOGEL, G. (1965), 'Mental activity at sleep onset', *J. abnorm. Psychol.*, vol. 70, p. 231.

FOULKES, D., SPEAR, P. S., and SYMONDS, J. D. (1966), 'Individual differences in mental activity at sleep onset', *J. abnorm. Psychol.*, vol. 71, p. 280.

GLICKMAN, S. E. (1961), 'Perseverative neural processes and consolidation of the memory trace', *Psychol. Bull.*, vol. 58, p. 218.

GOODENOUGH, D. R. (1967), 'Some recent studies of dream recall', in H. A. Witkin and H. B. Lewis (eds.), *Experimental Studies of Dreaming*, Random House, p. 128.

GOODENOUGH, D. R., *et al.* (1959), 'A comparison of "dreamers" and "nondreamers"; eye movements, electroencephalograms, and the recall of dreams', *J. abnorm. Psychol.*, vol. 59, p. 295.

GOODENOUGH, D. R., *et al.* (1965), 'Dream reporting following abrupt and gradual awakenings from different types of sleep', *J. Personality soc. Psychol.*, vol. 2, p. 170.

HALL, C. S., and DOMHOFF, G. W. (1968), Personal communication.

HOBSON, J. A. (1967), 'Electrographic correlates of behavior in the frog with special reference to sleep', *EEG clin. Neurophysiol.*, vol., 22, p. 113.

HOBSON, J. A., GOLDFRANK, F., and SNYDER, F. (1965), 'Respiration and mental activity in sleep', *J. psychiat. Res.*, vol. 3, p. 79.

JACOBSON, A., *et al.* (1964), 'Muscle tonus in human subjects during sleep and dreaming', *Exp. Neurol.*, vol. 10, p. 418.

JACOBSON, A., *et al.* (1965), 'Somnambulism: all-night electroencephalographic studies', *Science*, vol. 148, p. 975.

JOHNSON, L. C., and KARPAN, W. E. (1968), 'Autonomic correlates of the spontaneous K-complex', *Psychophysiol.*, vol. 4, p. 444.

JOUVET, M., MICHEL, F., and MOUNIER, D. (1960), 'Analyse électroencéphalographique comparée du sommeil physiologique chez le chat et chez l'homme', *Rev. Neurol.*, vol. 103, p. 189.

KALES, A., and JACOBSON, A. (1967), 'Mental activity during sleep: recall studies, somnambulism, and effects of rapid eye movement deprivation and drugs', *Exp. Neurol. Suppl.*, vol. 4, p. 81.

KALES, A., *et al.* (1966), 'Somnambulism: psychophysiological correlates: I. All-night EEG studies', *Arch. gen. Psychiat.*, vol. 14, p. 586.

KALES, A., *et al.* (1967a), 'All-night EEG sleep measurements in young adults', *Psychonom. Sci.*, vol. 7, p. 67.

KALES, A., *et al.* (1967b), 'Mentation during sleep: REM and NREM recall reports', *Percept. mot. Skills*, vol. 24, p. 555.

KALES, A., *et al.* (1968), 'Sleep and dreams: recent research on clinical aspects, UCLA Interdepartmental Conference', *Ann. int. Med.*, vol. 68, p. 1078.

KLEIN, M. (1963), 'Etude polygraphique et phylogenetique des differents états de sommeil', thèsis de médecine, BOSC edition, Lyon.

KLEITMAN, N. (1963), *Sleep and Wakefulness*, University of Chicago Press, 2nd edn.

KREMEN, I. (1961), 'Dream reports and rapid eye movements', doctoral dissertation, Harvard University.

KRIPKE, D. F., WEITZMAN, E. D., and POLLAK, C. (1965), 'Attempts to induce the rapid eye movement stage of sleep in *Macaca mulatta* by brain stem stimulation', *Psychophysiology*, vol. 2, p. 132.

LOOMIS, A. L., HARVEY, E. N., and HOBART, G. A. (1937), 'Cerebral states during sleep as studied by human brain potentials', *J. exp. Psychol.*, vol. 21, p. 127.

MEIER, G. W., and BERGER, R. J. (1965), 'Development of sleep and wakefulness patterns in the infant rhesus monkey', *Exp. Neurol.*, vol. 12, p. 257.

MONROE, L. J., *et al.* (1965), 'Discriminability of REM and NREM reports', *J. Personality soc. Psychol.*, vol. 2, p. 456.

MÜLLER, G. E., and PILZECKER, A. (1900), 'Experiementelle Beitrage zur Lehre vom Gedächtnis', *Z. Psychol. Suppl.*, vol. 1, p. 1.

ORLINSKY, D. E. (1962), 'Psychodynamic and cognitive correlates of dream recall', doctoral dissertation, University of Chicago.

OSWALD, I. (1962), *Sleeping and Waking, Physiology and Psychology*, Elsevier.

PORTNOFF, G., *et al.* (1966), 'Retention of verbal materials perceived prior to onset of non-REM sleep', *Percept. mot. Skills*, vol. 22, p. 751.

RECHTSCHAFFEN, A. (1967), 'Dream reports and dream experiences', *Exp. Neurol. Suppl.*, vol. 4, p. 4.

RECHTSCHAFFEN, A., and KALES, A. (eds.) (1968), *A Manual of Standardized Terminology, Techniques and Scoring System for Sleep Stages of Human Subjects*, Government Printing Office, Washington, DC.

RECHTSCHAFFEN, A., and VERDONE, P. (1964), 'Amount of dreaming: effect of incentive, adaptation to laboratory, and individual differences', *Percept. mot. Skills*, vol. 19, p. 947.

RECHTSCHAFFEN, A., GOODENOUGH, D. R., and SHAPIRO, A. (1962), 'Patterns of sleep talking', *Arch. gen. Psychiat.*, vol. 7, p. 418.

RECHTSCHAFFEN, A., HAURI, P., and ZEITLIN, M. (1966), 'Auditory awakening thresholds in REM and NREM sleep stages', *Percept. mot. Skills*, vol. 22, p. 927.

RECHTSCHAFFEN, A., VERDONE, P., and WHEATON, J. (1963), 'Reports of mental activity during sleep', *Canad. Psychiat. Assn J.*, vol. 8, p. 409.

RECHTSCHAFFEN, A., et al., (1963), 'Nocturnal sleep of narcoleptics', *EEG clin. Neurophysiol.*, vol. 15, p. 599.

ROFFWARG, H. P., MUZIO, J. N., and DEMENT, W. C. (1966), 'Ontogenetic development of the human sleep–dream cycle', *Science*, vol. 152, p. 604.

SHAPIRO, A., GOODENOUGH, D. R., and GRYLER, R. B. (1963), 'Dream recall as a function of method of awakening', *Psychosom. Med.*, vol. 25, p. 174.

SHAPIRO, A., et al. (1965), 'Gradual arousal from sleep: a determinant of thinking reports', *Psychosom. Med.*, vol. 27. p. 342.

SNYDER, F. (1960), 'Dream recall, respiratory variability and depth of sleep', presented to the American Psychiatric Association, Atlantic City, New Jersey, May.

SNYDER, F. (1966), 'Toward an evolutionary theory of dreaming', *Amer. J. Psychiat.*, vol. 123, p. 121.

TAUBER, E. S., ROFFWARG, H. P., and WEITZMAN, E. D. (1966), 'Eye movements and electroencephalogram activity during sleep in diurnal lizards', *Nature*, vol. 212, p. 1612.

TEPLITZ, Z. (1943), 'An electroencephalographic study of sleep and dreams', doctoral dissertation, University of Illinois.

WALLS, G. L. (1942), *The Vertebrate Eye and its Adaptive Radiation*, Cranbrook Press.

WEISS, T., and ROLDAN, E. (1964), 'Comparative study of sleep cycles in rodents', *Experientia*, vol. 20, p. 280.

WILLIAMS, R. L., AGNEW, H. W., Jr, and WEBB, W. B.. (1964), 'Sleep patterns in young adults: an EEG study', *EEG clin. Neurophysiol.*, vol. 17, p. 376.

WILLIAMS, R. L., AGNEW, H. W., Jr, and WEBB, W. B. (1966), 'Sleep patterns of the young adult female: an EEG study', *EEG clin. Neurophysiol.*, vol. 20, p. 264.

WOLPERT, E. A. (1960), 'Studies in psychophysiology of dreams: II. An electromyographic study of dreaming', *Arch. gen. Psychiat.*, vol. 2, p. 231.

WOLPERT, E. A., and TROSMAN, H. (1958), 'Studies in psychophysiology of dreams: I. Experimental evocation of sequential dream episodes', *Arch. Neurol. Psychiat.*, vol. 79, p. 603.

14 Charles Fisher, Joseph Gross and Joseph Zuch

Cycle of Penile Erection Synchronous with Dreaming
(REM) Sleep

Charles Fisher, Joseph Gross and Joseph Zuch, 'Cycle of penile erection
synchronous with dreaming (REM) sleep', *Archives of General Psychiatry*,
vol. 12, 1965, pp. 29–45.

Introduction

The discovery of the dream–sleep cycle by Aserinsky and Kleitman (1955)
and Dement and Kleitman (1957) is now well known. Briefly, it has been
found that there are regularly recurring periods of sleep which are physiologically unique, showing a characteristic EEG pattern (stage 1) together
with bursts of bilaterally synchronous, conjugate, rapid vertical and
horizontal eye movements (REMs),[1] and that this physiological pattern is
highly correlated with the sleeper's recall of detailed dream experiences.
There are generally four or five such periods in an average night's sleep,
dreaming taking up 20–25 per cent of the total sleep time. Further, the cyclic
pattern of dreaming has been found to be relatively fixed and stable and
universally present in the thousands of subjects that have by now been
investigated in numerous laboratories. Figure 1 is a schematic representation of the dream–sleep cycle of a young adult, showing five REM
dream-periods in an average seven hours and forty-eight minutes of sleep.
These periods recur about every ninety minutes, the first REMP developing
about sixty to ninety minutes after sleep onset, the average duration of the
REMPs being about twenty minutes.

About twenty years ago, there appeared two obscure articles by several
German investigators (Ohlmeyer *et al.*, 1944, 1947), describing a cycle of
penile erection during sleep. The episodes of erection were reported to recur
every 84·5 minutes and to have an average duration of 25·5 minutes. It
occurred to a number of investigators, working in the area of sleep and
dreaming with the new EEG–REM method, that the distribution, frequency, and duration of these periods of erection corresponded very closely
to those of the stage 1-REM dreaming periods, and raised the question
whether the two phenomena might not be synchronous. The first worker to
attempt to answer this question was Oswald (1962), who stated:

Preliminary studies ... on some volunteer males using an apparatus not notice-
able in use, indicated that erections only accompanied some dream periods and
could come and go briefly during a given period. ...

1. REMs stands for rapid eye movements, REMP for rapid eye movement period
and NREMP for the other stages of sleep.

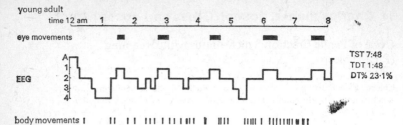

Figure 1 Graph of all-night sleep record of a young adult showing five REMPs, a tendency for them to lengthen as the night proceeds, an average REMP duration of twenty-one minutes, and their recurrence about every ninety minutes. During the first six and a half hours there were four REMPs, a distribution similar to that of the erection periods. The solid black bars represent the REMs and they coincide with the periods of stage 1 EEG. TST indicates total sleep time; TDT, total REM time, DT%, per cent TST spent in REM sleep. (From Roffwarg, Dement and Fisher, 1964)

Because of artifacts in the method he used, Oswald (personal communication) could not be sure whether erection also occurred during the non-dreaming stages of sleep.

Ohlmeyer's method involved the subject's wearing a contact ring on the penis, the breaking of an electric current during erection, and a kymographic tracing. Figure 2 shows five nights of recording with indications of the periods of erection, i.e. the indentations on the tracings between the vertical lines. The sleep periods were about six to six and a half hours in duration and there were four periods of erection one night and three in the remaining. It is to be noted that the first erection appeared about an hour to an hour and a half after sleep onset, coinciding with the time of onset of the first REMP. The cyclic distribution of the erection periods and their average lengths correspond nicely with the distribution of the REMPs and their average duration, while the 85·4 minute duration of the erection cycle shows an equally good correspondence with the ninety-minute dream cycle.

The task that we set ourselves was to make simultaneous all night recordings of REMs, brain waves, and erections, first, to attempt to confirm the findings of Ohlmeyer and his co-workers, and second, to ascertain whether the REM dream-periods and erections are, in fact, synchronous. Our problem was to develop a method of continuous all-night recording that would not only permit us to obtain a graphic tracing of on-going erection during sleep, but also to give us a quantitative estimate of the degree of erection and fluctuations in degree. This was an exploratory series of experiments in which we were attempting to perfect a method of observation and recording.

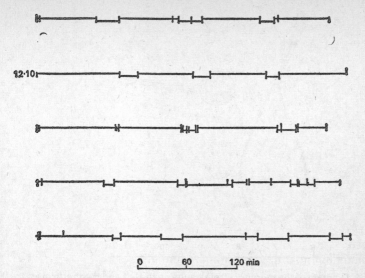

Figure 2 Tracings showing the cycle of erection during five different nights. There are three or four periods of erection each night. Indented portions of the tracing between vertical lines indicate erection periods. Observe that the first one occurs between about sixty and ninety minutes after sleep onset and that the distribution throughout the night follows closely that of the REMPs. (From Ohlmeyer, Brilmayer and Hüllstrung, 1944)

Apparatus

1. In a first attempt to record nocturnal erection, a polyvinyl tube about the size and shape of a doughnut was devised. This tube was filled with water, fitted around the base of the penis, and when pressure was exerted on its inner surface during erection a rise in the water level of a smaller tube attached to it could be observed and measured. The use of this phallo-plethysmograph is open to the criticism that because of its size and bulk any erection that occurs is caused by local stimulation. In fact, one subject inquired whether it was supposed to be 'an artificial vagina'.

2. A second method involved the measurement of changes in the skin temperature of the penis during erection. Preliminary observations indicated that with full erection the skin temperature may increase as much as 2 to 3° F, due to the increased blood flow in the cavernous tissue. Continuous, all-night recording of penile skin temperature can be carried out by attaching a small thermistor[2] to the penis (Figure 3). The small size of this attach-

2. We used the Model 43 TA Tele-Thermometer with the No. 409 probe obtained from Yellow Springs Instrument Company, Inc., Yellow Springs, Ohio.

Charles Fisher, Joseph Gross and Joseph Zuch 237

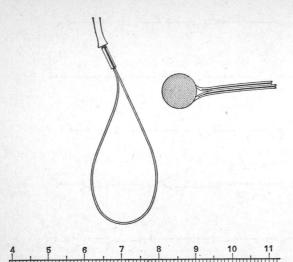

Figure 3 Diagram of the mercury strain gauge on the left and the thermistor electrode on the right. The scale is in centimeters. A cross-section of the neck of the strain gauge is shown in Figure 4

ment obviates, to a considerable degree, the possibility of local stimulation of the penis.

The thermistor consists of a thin resistance wire of a special alloy which has the property of varying its resistance as a function of temperature. It is applied directly to the surface of the penis. Variations in resistance are registered by appropriate electrical apparatus and the output is fed into the DC amplifying circuit of the Offner EEG. The temperature changes are recorded directly on the same paper on which the EEG and REM tracings are being simultaneously recorded.

3. A third method, the most sensitive, utilizes the *mercury strain gauge*.[3] The only apparatus applied to the penis consists of an elastic silicon plastic tube[4] 1 mm in diameter filled with mercury and sealed at both ends with platinum electrodes to form a loop (Figure 4).

This gauge forms one leg of a Wheatstone bridge circuit thereby enabling minute variations in resistance, as the tubing is stretched during erection, to be amplified and recorded on the DC circuit of the Offner Type T EEG. It is

3. Dr Arthur Shapiro advised and assisted in the use of this method. Dr Shapiro (1964) has independently confirmed the presence of the erection cycle.

4. This tubing (7002-020 vivosil tubing) can be obtained from Becton, Dickinson & Co., Rutherford, NJ.

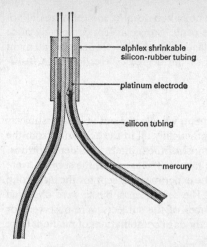

Figure 4 Cross-section of the neck of the loop shown in Figure 3, showing the sealing of the ends with platinum electrodes

thus possible to obtain a recording of the changes in circumference of the penis during erection. In order to quantify these changes the strain gauge is calibrated by measuring the amount of deflection on the graphic tracing per unit change of circumference of the gauge as it is moved down on a tapering cone-shaped testing device graduated in centimeters. The relation between the circumference change of the gauge and the rise in the tracing is roughly linear, e.g., at low gain amplification a 1 cm rise in the tracing is made equivalent to 2·5–3 cm increase in circumference.

In order to estimate the degree of erection by the strain gauge method it is necessary for each subject to take measurements of the circumference of the flaccid and erect penis since there are individual variations. Such penile measurements were not obtained in the early part of the investigation but were for the final group of eight subjects in the strain gauge-thermistor series. The average increase in circumference during erection is about 1 inch or 2·5 cm. Any increase of from 2–3 cm was found to represent full or nearly full erection. In the actual recordings two strain gauge tracings were made, one highly sensitive (gain set at 9 or 11) and the other less sensitive (gain set at 5). The former is about forty times more sensitive than the latter and is able to amplify extremely minute increases in penile circumference, measured in fractions of a millimeter.

4. Even though the attachments to the penis with the mercury strain gauge and thermistor were small in size, the possibility of local stimulation or suggestion could not be eliminated. In order to minimize this factor, we

decided to make direct observations on naked sleeping subjects who did not have any apparatus attached to the penis. Subjects slept completely nude but covered by a thin, transparent plastic sheet. They were observed all night and periodic notations were made of the degree of erection on a 0–4+ scale.

Subjects and procedure

Because of the nature of the experiment, we selected our volunteer subjects carefully. We used seventeen men, practically all in the age range from the early twenties to the early thirties, most of them interns, residents, or hospital employees. For control of the factor of suggestion, the subjects were kept in ignorance of the nature of the experiment, except for the last group of eight (strain gauge-thermistor). The seventeen subjects were observed during twenty-seven nights. A number of the subjects were observed for more than one night and several methods or combinations of methods were used on some of them.

In a preliminary interview those subjects who were not informed of the exact nature of the experiment were told that we were investigating autonomic activity, and those used for direct observation that we were studying body movement. Subjects appeared in the laboratory at their usual bed time. Several subjects worked at night and slept during the day. EEG and eye movement electrodes were attached to the head in the usual manner (Dement and Kleitman, 1957): monopolar parietal and occipital leads for EEG and two electrodes attached to the right and left outer canthi for REMs.

The strain gauge was looped firmly around the penis about an inch from the base. The thermistor, when used, was attached to the lateral aspect of the penis about an inch from the base with collodion soaked cotton. Eight subjects had a second thermistor attached to the groin. Three subjects were awakened several times on one night each in order to elicit dream content. Dream reports were also obtained from several subjects following spontaneous awakenings either at night or in the morning. With the nude subjects, direct observations were made through a small window into the sleeping room or by entering the room and observing at close quarters.

Practically all the subjects appeared to be quite unselfconscious throughout the course of the experiment and were able to sleep very well. However, it must be borne in mind that in any form of human experimentation, the very fact of observing a phenomenon may alter it. In these experiments, where electrodes are connected to the head and in addition, apparatus is attached to the penis, the subject is aware that he is under observation. The experimental situation and the relationship with the experimenter become highly charged and a great deal of unconscious fantasy and anxiety are

Table 1 Percentage erections by various methods

Method	No. REMP	% Full erection	% Partial erection	% Full and partial	% None observed	No. subjects	Night
1. Phalloplethysmograph	18	69 (13)	19 (3)	88	13 (2)	2	6
2. Direct observation	19	63 (12)	37 (7)	100	0	5	6
3. Strain gauge	19	47 (9)	47 (9)	94	5 (1)	5	7
4. Strain gauge and thermistor	30	62 (18)	38 (11)	100	0	8	8
Totals	86	60	35	95	5	20	27

aroused. With the direct observation method, even though the subjects were unaware of the nature of the experiment, they were conscious of the fact that they were naked and that their genitals were exposed. We do not pretend, therefore, that by keeping the subjects in ignorance of the nature of the experiment, which was necessary as a control procedure, that we were able to eliminate the impact of the observational procedure on the phenomenon under observation. In order to allay anxiety and maintain the subjects' cooperation, it was important to maintain an objective, matter of fact, physicianly attitude and to behave in such a way as to reduce the sexualization of the experimental situation as much as possible.

Results

Erections were found to be associated with a high percentage of REMPs by all the methods used (Table 1). Eighty-six REMPs were investigated by the four methods. The combined totals showed full erection 60 per cent, partial erection 35 per cent, and no erection 5 per cent. Thus, *full or partial erection was found in 95 per cent of the total.* Three instances of failure of erection occurred during the first REMP, which is often brief, unstable, and intermixed with stage 2. The poorest results were obtained in the initial strain gauge series (full erection, 47 per cent) when we were having technical difficulty with the apparatus. Later, with the combined strain gauge and thermistor, the results were much better and we are more confident about these recordings. Because of the failure to obtain a firm enough approximation of the thermistor to the skin of the penis, valid thermistor recordings were obtained in only two instances.

The designations full or partial erection are, in many instances, rough approximations. For one thing, as noted, we did not have measurements of the difference in circumference between the flaccid and erect states in the early part of the experiment. Increases in circumference of 2 cm or more were considered as full erection. Partial erections ranged from a minimum of 2 mm up to 2 cm. For one of the subjects in the phalloplethysmograph series, rises in the water level 5 inches or more indicated full erection and in a second subject, 3 inches or more. The most precise measurements were obtained for the strain gauge in the final strain gauge-thermistor series.

One of the most striking findings was that erections begin and end in close temporal relationship to the onset and termination of the REMPs. For each subject, we calculated the time in minutes of onset of erection and the attainment of maximum erection in relation to the onset of the REMP. Similar figures were obtained for the onset of detumescence and the attainment of full detumescence in relation to the termination of the REMPs (Table 2). In each column of Table 2 the designation 'No. REMPs' indicates the number of REMPs included in each calculation. It will be

Table 2 Time relationships of onset and termination of erections to the REMP

	Phalloplethysmograph		Visual observation		Strain gauge			Strain gauge + thermistor		
	No. REMP*	Mean	No. REMP	Mean	No. REMP	Mean	SD	No. REMP	Mean	SD
Erection onset†	14	0·2	14	2·6	18	-1·6	±2·4	21	-2·5	±3·0
Erection maximum	14	6·1	14	6·6	18	4·7	±2·2	27	5·4	±3·9
Detumescence onset	9	1·0	9	-0·6	13	0·2	±5·5	21	-0·6	±1·9
Detumescence maximum	2	10·0	11	12·1	8	9·6	±4·9	17	12·4	±2·0
	N = 6		N = 6		N = 7			N = 8		
	S = 2		S = 5		S = 5			S = 8		
	Total REMP 18		Total REMP 19		Total REMP 19			Total REMP 30		

* S D indicates standard deviation; N, number of nights; S, number of subjects; No. REMP, number of rapid eye movement periods included in calculation.

† Erection onset indicates onset of erection in minutes before (−) or after (+) start of REMP; erection maximum, first maximum erection (minutes after start of REMP); detumescence onset, onset of detumescence (minutes before (−) or after (+) end of REMP); detumescence maximum, end of detumescence (minutes after end of REMP defined by either return to baseline or unvarying level, whichever occurs first).

noticed that this figure is, in every instance, less than the total number of REMPs investigated by each method. This is because a certain amount of the data obtained had to be discarded either because of artifacts or technical difficulties with the apparatus. Also, with direct observation, notations as to the state of erection sometimes could not be made because the sleeping position of the subject prevented observation of the penis.

Figures for the four methods are quite consistent. The onset of erection occurred within a minute or so of the onset of the REMP and the onset of detumescence also occurred in very close temporal relationship to the termination of the REMP. The most accurate figures were obtained in the final strain gauge-thermistor series. Here, it can be seen that on the average, the onset of erection occurred 2·5 minutes (SD ± 3·0) before the beginning of the REMP, while detumescence began 0·6 minutes (SD ± 1·9) before the termination of the REMP. Maximum erection was attained 5·4 minutes (SD ± 3·9) after the onset of the REMP while full detumescence occurred 12·4 minutes (SD ± 2·0) after the termination of the REMP. The relatively low Standard Deviations for the figures given is a measure of the relative constancy of the observed phenomena. It is to be noted that the onsets of erection in both strain gauge series occurred on the average a minute or two before the onset of the REMP, although there were many instances when the onset took place a minute or two after the REMP began. The onset of erection before the beginning of the REMP is not revealed in the phalloplethysmograph and direct observation series because very slight degrees of erection cannot be noted by these methods. The strain gauge, on the other hand, is extremely sensitive and is able to register minute degrees of tumescence measured in fractions of a millimeter.

We are impressed by the fact that in the majority of instances, once erection is attained, it is sustained without much fluctuation throughout even very lengthy REMPs, thirty or more minutes in duration. However, there were a good many instances where there was considerable fluctuation or instances in which gradual detumescence would begin in the middle of a REMP and continue to its termination. We have not obtained variability figures which might give some indication of degrees of fluctuation. Aside from the continuation of the detumescence process, which lasted on an average from 8 to 12·4 minutes, depending upon the method used, there was no indication of erection during NREM sleep except for occasional slight episodes of tumescence in association with NREM body movements or for periods of a minute or two during stage 2 preceding the onset of the REMP.[5] This initial tumescence is generally very minor in degree and can be meas-

5. In a second series now under investigation we have recently observed a good erection during a period of stage 2 and a moderate erection in the same subject during a period of stage 1 sleep onset intermixed with alpha.

ured in a fraction of a millimeter. However, we did observe several more prolonged and greater degrees of erection during stage 2 preceding the onset of the REMP. An excellent example of this is shown in Figure 5 where an increase in penile circumference of 1 cm was registered during a ten-minute period preceding the onset of stage 1.

Preliminary observations suggest that the development of full REMP erection may be independent of the recency of sexual gratification. Thus, one subject who had intercourse five hours before the experiment, another eighteen hours, and several within twenty-four to forty-eight hours, still showed the erection cycle. One subject, an overt homosexual, who was

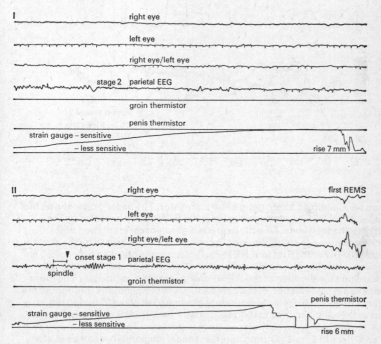

Figure 5 A ninety-second stretch of record (I and II are continuous) showing the onset of erection prior to the onset of stage 1. The less sensitive strain gauge (gain 5) in the upper graph shows a rise of 7 mm during a forty-five second period of stage 2. This is continued in the lower graph showing the onset of stage 1, with a burst of REMPs about thirty seconds after onset and a continuing rise in the strain gauge of an additional 6 mm. A gradual rise in the penis thermistor throughout the period of recording can also be noted while the groin temperature remained constant. The rapid acceleration of the sensitive strain gauge, which has to be repeatedly recentered, is to be noted

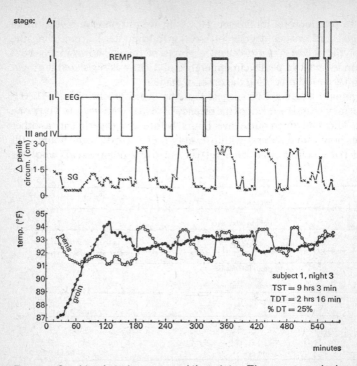

Figure 6 Combined strain gauge and thermistor. The upper graph shows the stages of the EEG plotted against time; the REMPs are indicated by the darker horizontal lines. Directly below is a graphic representation of the increases in penile circumference in centimeters as measured by the strain gauge (SG). For the first four REMPs, the increases are of an order of 2·5 cm or more indicating full erection. These increases are sustained practically throughout the duration of the REMPs with very little fluctuation. The lower graph is a representation of the penis and groin temperatures throughout the course of the night. Penis temperature gradually fell about 2° during the early part of the night and then stabilized, but with each REMP and synchronous with the increase in circumference there were rises of penile skin temperature of an order of 2·5° to 3°. During detumescence, temperature decreases at a slower rate than the circumference changes because of the time necessary for the dissipation of the heat. The groin temperature increased sharply from 87–94° in the early part of the night and thereafter remained at a relatively even level for the rest of the night. There was a slight tendency towards a fall in groin temperature of an order of 0·5° during each REMP; there is an inverse relationship between penis and groin temperatures

observed for six nights, both by direct observation and the strain gauge method, had frequent nocturnal erections in spite of the fact that he had some kind of sexual outlet at least twice a day in the approximately sixteen-hour period preceding each experimental sessions.

Figure 6 shows the extent of nocturnal erection and the results obtained on a subject with the combined thermistor-strain gauge technique. Before the experiment, it was determined that this subject has a 2·5 cm increase in penile circumference during full erection. The subject had five REMPs during an extended period of sleep of about nine hours. The first four erection periods were full and sustained, the strain gauge indicating increases in circumference of approximately 2·5 cm and the thermistor increases in temperature of 2·5–3° F. These full erections were sustained for periods of fifteen, seventeen, twenty-seven, and twenty-one minutes, respectively, approximately the full duration of each REMP. The fifth REMP was interrupted in the middle by a period of stage 2, during which the erection subsided but again resumed as the REMP continued. As an additional check on the apparatus, after the experiment, the subject self-stimulated himself to the point of nearly full erection. It was ascertained that the resulting elevation of the strain gauge recording above the baseline was of the same magnitude as that registered during the REMPs.

The strain gauge and the thermistor served as checks against one another, the graphs of the temperature and circumference changes coinciding with great exactitude. There appears to be an inverse relationship between the penis and groin temperatures. At the beginning of the night, the penis temperature gradually fell, while groin temperature rose, both approaching a baseline, which they more or less maintained for the rest of the night. With each erection, although the penis temperature rose as much as 3° F, there tended to be a dip in groin temperature of about 0·5°. These findings rule out the possibility that the temperature changes we observed during erection were influenced by ambient temperature.

Figure 7 gives a microscopic picture of the onset and termination of the first erection of the cycle just described. In this instance, three and a quarter minutes elapsed between the beginning of stage 1 and the onset of rapid tumescence, as indicated by both the strain gauge and thermistor. However, it can be seen that some slight tumescence had begun prior to this, almost simultaneously with the beginning of stage 1 as indicated by the strain gauge and the temperature change even earlier. Both the strain gauge and the thermistor show a steady state of full tumescence for a period of about fifteen minutes. Simultaneously with termination of the REMP a decrease in temperature set in. The strain gauge, on the other hand, showed a period of persistent erection for some two and a half minutes after the end of the REMP, after which rapid detumescence occurred. The temperature fall during detumescence is much slower than the decrease in circumference. The inverse relationship between penis temperature and groin temperature

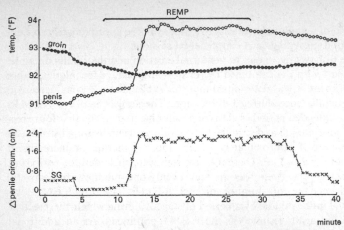

minute

Figure 7 (subject 1, night 3) Graphic representation of the first REMP (SG+ thermistors) shown in Figure 5. The duration of the REMP was twenty-one minutes. The lower tracing shows the increases in circumference (SG). A marked increase occurred three and a quarter minutes after REMP onset, was sustained with practically no fluctuation throughout the REMP, outlasted it by about two minutes when gradual detumescence set in. Full tumescence was attained after about seven minutes. The upper graph shows corresponding increase in penile skin temperature. A gradual but slow drop in skin temperature with detumescence set in simultaneously with the termination of the REMP. The inverse relationship between skin and groin temperature is indicated by the slight drop in the latter during the early part of the erection. The groin temperature is sustained at its baseline level during detumescence as the penis temperature gradually falls. Indication of the change in both the circumference and penile temperature simultaneously with the onset of the REMP can be noted. A slight rise in the strain gauge occurs simultaneously with the onset of stage 1 while penile skin temperature shows a slight increase even before the onset of stage 1

can be readily noted by the dip that occurred at the onset of the erection; the baseline was regained at the termination of the erection. A similar inverse relationship between groin and penis temperatures during erection was observed in the only other subject in whom good recordings were obtained.

Comment

We have confirmed the results of Ohlmeyer and his co-workers, demonstrating the existence of a cycle of nocturnal erection, and have shown, in addition, that the erections are coextensive with the REMPs and, therefore, presumably with dreaming. They begin and end in very close temporal relation to the onset and termination of the REMPs. We have never seen erection during NREM stages of sleep except in the few minutes preceding the onset of the REMPs and during the periods of detumescence that continue into stage 2 sleep for some minutes following termination of the REMP.[6] There is every indication that more than 90 per cent of REMPs are associated with some degree of erection, and that the misses occur almost exclusively in the first REMP of the night which is often brief and unstable. Unlike Oswald (1962), who reported that erection can come and go briefly during a given period, we have noted sustained erection throughout the duration of even lengthy REMPs in a majority of instances. Occasional failure of erection to develop, more frequent partial erections, fluctuations during a given REMP, or incidents of sudden detumescence are all in need of further investigation. Intercourse within five hours before the experiment did not appear to inhibit the appearance of the cycle of erection, but the influence of the recency of sexual gratification is also in need of further study. There did not appear to be any difference in the erection cycle in those subjects who slept during the day, confirming the finding of Ohlmeyer and his co-workers. It is our impression that the fact of being observed, if it influences the erections, does so in the direction of inhibiting them. Knowledge of the nature of the experiment did not appear to significantly alter the results.

The work of the last decade, what Snyder (1963) has called 'the new biology of dreaming', has shown that dreaming sleep constitutes a special organismic state, a third state, in some ways intermediate between the other two, namely, waking and nondreaming sleep. It cannot be placed on the ordinary sleep-waking continuum and is now considered to be a qualitatively *different* form of sleep, ontogenetically early and phylogenetically old. It is a state of very marked physiological activation, respiratory, cardiovascular, and other physiological changes approaching those of the awake organism in a state of alertness. The physiological activation is characterized, not so much by an absolute increase in level of functioning, but rather by very marked fluctuations, as compared to nondreaming sleep. In the latter, physiological functioning is quiescent and shows minor variations around a relatively steady state. It is remarkable that the stage 1 REMPs have been found by Roffwarg, Dement and Fisher (1964) to be present in the neonate, with the same characteristics as those of the adult, but accompanied by much more diffuse body movement, sucking, and smiling. Additionally, the work of Wolff (1966) indicates that neonatal REMPs are associated with frequent episodes of penile tumescence. Physiological changes that accompany dreaming sleep in the adult can thus be seen to be present in the neonate at a time when it is improbable that dreaming is taking place because psychic structure has not yet developed. The physiological activation we have described is associated with a concomitant activation of the central nervous system. The latter also has been shown to

6. See footnote 5.

be in as great a state of activity as the organism in a state of alert wakefulness with two exceptions, which long ago were stressed by Freud (1900), namely, an occlusion of sensory input and motor paralysis associated with a marked loss of muscle tone. The primary visual cortex has been shown by Evarts (1962) to be as active during dreaming as during alert wakefulness, thus confirming Freud's formulation of regressive activation of the perceptual system during dreaming. Jouvet (1961) has shown that REM sleep is regulated by a different neurophysiological mechanism than NREM sleep and is triggered off by a center in the pontile reticular formation of the brain stem. This center has important connections with the limbic system, that phylogenetically old part of the brain, the site of centers regulating those processes which constitute the physiological substrate of drives and affects. There are, for example, as shown by McLean (1963), discrete areas in the limbic system, stimulation of which produces erection. It has been suggested by Fisher and Dement (1963) that the triggering of and activation of Jouvet's pontine-limbic system is concomitant with, and forms the neurophysiological substrate of, instinctual drive discharge during dreaming sleep.

There is no doubt that in the alternating stages of REM and NREM sleep we are dealing with a highly important biological cycle and it seems probable that the physiological processes described antedate the psychological process of dreaming. Parmelee et al. (1964) have recently shown that the REMPs are present in premature infants and that 80 per cent of sleep at thirty weeks is taken up by the REMPs. By forty weeks, term, REM sleep has dropped to 50 per cent. In some as yet unexplained manner, the physiological processes become associated with visual dreaming, perhaps around the third month of life, although dreaming in nonvisual modalities may occur even earlier.

As has been noted, Wolff reported a considerable amount of erectile activity in the neonate during REMPs. In an earlier study, Halverson (1940) found a high incidence of erection in three- to twenty-week-old infants during both waking and sleeping states. From his description, erection appeared to be much more frequent during sleep states corresponding to the REMPs. It seems likely that erection during sleep persists from the neonatal period throughout life and becomes coextensive with REMP dreaming. However, before we can be certain of this, investigation of nocturnal erection at all age levels between infancy and young adulthood will have to be carried out.

It is difficult to conceptualize what the functional or adaptive value of such extensive periods of nocturnal erection can be. One's view about this matter will depend upon attitudes concerning the sexual nature of dreams and genetic considerations in regard to the beginnings of psychic structure and the time at which dreaming has its onset. Our present knowledge is insufficient to provide a definitive answer to these questions. It seems to us that the following possibilities need to be considered.

1. Neonatal REMP erection may be a physiological discharge pattern of the undifferentiated phase before the development of psychic structure, and be independent of dream content since dreaming may not be present at this time. Furthermore, neonatal erection, although it may be either a physiological discharge mechanism or a tension indicator, quite probably represents a primitive level of autoerotic organization of genital sensation and experience. The extensive REMP erections in the adult may in part involve a regression to this more primitive level of infantile genital organization, although it seems clear that higher levels of object directed genital organization may also be activated.

Spitz (1962) has shown that genital play in infant males does not begin until eight to ten months. He states that the sex drive at this stage is not implemented in terms of the genital drive, that there is drive discharge without psychological content. The penis becomes gradually libidinized in relation to affective reciprocity with the mother. Even at eight or ten months, Spitz indicates that the infant does not appear to be emotionally involved during genital play, shows an indifferent facial expression during penile manipulation, and manifests the same degree of interest in the penis as if it were a foot or other body part. Furthermore, infants who have endured maternal deprivation do not indulge in genital play at all even as late as three years of age. This failure of penile libidinization is caused by the absence of affective reciprocity with the mother, by the absence of fondling, cuddling, and body contact. In this connection, it is of interest that Harlow's (1962) mother deprived monkeys failed to show normal mating patterns when they matured. These findings of Spitz and Harlow support the idea of a primitive level of diffuse autoerotic organization of penile sensation in early infancy.

2. REMP erection may be another aspect of the *general physiological activation* that is associated with dreaming sleep, but is not necessarily *stimulated* by specific dream content. The fact that tumescence generally begins a minute or two before the onset of the REMP suggests that some physiological mechanism sets it off prior to the development of the hallucinatory dream proper. It is of considerable interest that the same limbic-midbrain centers and circuits that regulate REM sleep are involved in sexual, oral, and aggressive behavior. According to McLean (1963) there are discrete areas in the limbic system of the squirrel monkey, stimulation of which causes penile erection. He has shown that excitation of regions of the limbic system involved in oral mechanisms readily spills over into other areas less than a millimeter distant concerned with genital function and with

fearful or aggressive behavior. In the expression of dominance, the squirrel monkey develops an erection and this may represent a fusion of sexuality and aggression. There is every indication that the limbic-midbrain system is in a high state of activation during REM sleep. Penile erections may be a manifestation of the spread of activation or an overflow phenomenon within the limbic system, as the work of McLean suggests. The erections may, in part, represent an index of the rate of limbic activation, something like an indicator on a dial. This activation may involve the discharge of aggressive, genital, and oral drive energy in the physiological sense. The relationship of such physiological discharge to instinctual drive discharge in the psychoanalytic sense needs extensive investigation (see Fisher, 1965).

The erection cycle has not yet been investigated in animals. Pearson (1944) reports that the male shrew develops frequent erection accompanied by vigorous coital movements during sleep but it is not known whether this occurs during REM stages. Snyder (1964) has reported that he has observed an occasional erection in the opossum, a primitive mammal, during REM sleep but has not investigated this phenomenon systematically. Some very interesting work on the rabbit has been reported showing certain relationships between REM sleep and sexual, oral, and olfactory behavior. Sawyer *et al.* (1959) observed that the female rabbit, following either coitus or electrical stimulation of certain limbic areas or injection with placental or pituitary hormones, goes into a state of 'hyperarousal' associated with an EEG pattern which appears to be identical with that of REM sleep. This so-called PREEG (postreaction EEG) does not represent a state of hyperarousal but rather the activated state of paradoxical REM sleep. Faure, Bensch and Vincent (1962), Klein (1963) and Vincent (1964) reported that REM sleep in both the male and female rabbit is often associated with a spontaneously appearing state, described as an automatism, in which the animal manifests olfactobuccoanogenital-sexual behavior (OBAGS). During this state the animal engages in perineal licking and smelling and coprophagia. It was not stated whether the genital licking that takes place is accompanied by erection. Faure and his co-workers have shown that OBAGS is regulated by the midbrain-limbic system and that, additionally, it is under endocrine control. According to Faure, somnolence, sleep, paradoxical REM phase of sleep, and the OBAGS activity with coprophagia, appear to be a single phenomenon. During the actual OBAGS behavior, the EEG patterns of the cortex and hippocampus appear to be identical with those of paradoxical sleep. It is, of course, dangerous to extrapolate from the rabbit to man, but there may be some phylogenetic relationship between the erection cycle and the PREEG-OBAGS phenomena in the rabbit.

3. In connection with the idea that nocturnal R E M erection is a manifestation of an overflow phenomenon and spread of excitation, associated with a high state of activation of the limbic-midbrain system, there is evidence for erection as an overflow phenomenon on a psychological level. This evidence begins with Freud (1905), who, in *Three Essays on Sexuality*, pointed out that many stimuli, mechanical, intellectual, and especially comparatively intense affective processes, including even terrifying ones, trench upon sexuality. He stated:

... there are present in the organism contrivances which bring it about that in the case of a great number of internal processes sexual excitation arises as a concomitant effect, as soon as the intensity of those processes passes beyond certain quantitative limits. .... It may well be that nothing of considerable importance can occur in the organism without contributing some component to the excitation of the sexual instinct . . . .

There is other evidence that erection may be produced by apparently nonerotic stimuli and represent a channel of generalized tension release rather than a specifically erotic experience. Kinsey, Pomeroy and Martin (1948) and Ramsey (1943) have reported that many nonerotic emotionally arousing stimuli and situations can throw preadolescent boys into states of erection, anything from hearing the national anthem to seeing one's name in print. It, of course, remains a problem whether in all the instances cited by these investigators we are actually dealing with nonerotic excitation, or an overflow phenomenon, or whether the particular stimuli and the anxiety associated with them have become sexualized. Kinsey states:

Originally the pre-adolescent boy erects indiscriminately to the whole array of emotional situations, whether they be sexual or non-sexual in nature.... The picture is that of the psychosexual emerging from a much more generalized and basic physiologic capacity which becomes sexual, as an adult knows it, through experience and conditioning.

Halverson (1940) demonstrated that when infant males are disturbed in their suckling activity by removing the bottle they may develop erection. Wolff (1966) also showed that in the neonate, erection readily substitutes for other autonomic or motor discharge patterns, such as sucking or startles. In this connection, the question may be raised whether R E M erection in the neonate, infant, or preadolescent represents a 'discharge' phenomenon or is an indicator of 'tension'. For example, when the male infant, disturbed in his suckling, develops an erection, one possibility is that the inhibited oral libidinal drive tensions find substitute discharge in penile erection. Alternately, Wolff (1966) has reported that a neurologically damaged infant who had continuous priapism lost his erection only when held or fed. On the other hand, the erection that follows oral frustration may be an indicator of accumulated drive tension rather than a channel of drive discharge.

A final series of observations demonstrating the apparently nonerotic nature of some penile erections has been reported by McLean (1963), who showed that the squirrel monkey displays erection under a variety of conditions, e.g., at a distance by two strange animals presumably as a kind of greeting; when the animal looks at itself in the mirror; as a means of one animal exerting or establishing dominance over another.

4. Certain characteristics of the so-called morning or bladder erection throw some light on the nature of nocturnal R E M erection. We are in agreement with Ohlmeyer and Brilmayer (1947) that the morning erection probably has nothing to do with bladder pressure but represents the erection of the last R E M P of the night and that it is present or absent depending upon whether one awakens in the morning in R E M or N R E M sleep. These authors also found that awakening during the night with erection is as common as in the morning, in both instances, in about 50 per cent of the awakenings. The phenomenology of erection, e.g., the subjective nature of the sensation associated with it, whether or not it is connected with sexual desire, etc., is in need of further investigation. This is a matter of some importance because the subjective quality of the erection may throw some light on the nature of nocturnal and morning erections and have some bearing on the extent to which they are due to physiological activation rather than being psychologically induced. By extensive questioning of a good number of observant men, we have gained the impression that both nocturnal and morning erections are often unusually rigid, slightly uncomfortable, or even painful, frequently unassociated with sexual fantasy or desire. In fact, one may be unaware of their presence. Such nocturnal erections may occur within a few hours after sexual gratification. The apparently nonerotic nature of morning erection is indicated by the fact that it may persist, according to Kinsey, Pomeroy and Martin (1948) and Rubin (1963), in old men in their seventies and eighties for years after they have lost erectile potency, the capacity for intercourse and all erotic interest. Kinsey mentions two men of eighty-eight, impotent for fifteen years, who continued to have morning erections. These observations may have some bearing on the formulation suggested earlier that nocturnal R E M P erection may be a regression to a more primitive level of genital organization characteristic of infancy.

5. The problem of the relationship of the extensive R E M erections that have been described to dreaming and dream content raises important issues. One point of view, which we are inclined to favor, suggests that although the R E M P s associated with erection are present in the neonate, dreaming does not take place at this time because psychic structure has not yet developed. It is assumed that dreaming cannot take place until memory traces are laid down but it is not known how soon after birth this occurs. Spitz (1955)

assumes that visual imagery is not present until three months although imagery in other sensory modalities, especially touch, pressure, taste, and smell, in relation to the oral cavity may develop earlier. According to Conel (1942), the visual cortex is the last of the sensory areas to develop and does not attain maturation until about three months, and the alpha-rhythm in the occipital lobe is said not to appear until about this time. An alternative point of view by Brody (1964) assumes that dreaming can occur in the neonate. She considers the possibility that the earliest motor and autonomic discharge patterns, including erection in the neonate, may be related to dreaming and that at this early stage, memory traces are in the process of being laid down. She believes it possible that drive differentiation, or an impulse toward discharge, can occur from the moment of birth and that fragmentary memory traces, and thus fragmentary mental representations, immediately can develop with intensity sufficient for hallucinatory purposes in the first years of life. She is of the opinion that neonatal erection, as well as other autonomic and motor patterns, are measures of spontaneous discharge of autoerotic tensions of a nonspecific kind. Brody concludes that the erection cycle affords proof of the early involvement of the genital organ in all activity and of the constant biological link between sexuality and vital functions.

We are confronted with the difficulty of determining to what extent erections and dream content are influenced by physiological factors and/or psychological factors since there is a continuous interaction between the two. One way of looking at the problem is to assume that erections have a primary physiological origin and that on any given night more or less full erection will be found during every REMP providing that *inhibitory* factors are relatively in abeyance, e.g., on a psychological level severe anxiety or, on a physiological, severe fatigue which may interfere with the full development of the first or second REMPs because of the need for stage 4 sleep. Thus, the real problem would be to explain the absence of, fluctuations during, or rapid detumescence of the erection, in any particular REMP. Preliminary results from a second series of experiments now under way, and designed to investigate the relationship between erection and dream content, suggest that there may be some validity to the above assumptions. In a number of instances, we have been able to predict from the dream report that the recording of the erection would show rapid tumescence or detumescence or absence of erection. For example, with one subject, we were able in two instances to correlate rapid detumescence with two dreams which we assumed aroused severe castration anxiety, one in which the subject was being attacked by a snake and another in which he was attacked by sharks. With another dream with latent incestuous content, we correctly predicted the absence of erection. With a fourth dream, a portion of it dealing with homosexual wishes was associated with inhibition of erection and this was followed by a period of rapid tumescence associated with gratifying heterosexual content.

Overt phallic sexual activity in the manifest content of dreams is rarely seen under laboratory conditions when the subject has apparatus attached and is under observation. However, in one subject, a practicing homosexual, such dreams were rather frequent. On one occasion, he was awakened a half hour after the onset of his second R E M P when he was in a state of full erection, the awakening interrupting his dream at the moment that someone was performing fellatio on him. We have observed one nocturnal emission in a rather inhibited man whose only sexual outlet for the past year had been nocturnal emissions once or twice monthly. During a R E M P, this subject over the space of several minutes, rather quickly attained full erection and ejaculation. The emission occurred during a dream in which the subject simply held a girl's hand. However, the minimal physical contact present in the manifest dream was associated with highly charged erotic material in the latent content.

The above results have encouraged us to believe that there may be a greater correlation between dream content and the vicissitudes of the erections than we had originally believed. Little work has been done so far to attempt to correlate specific physiological variations and specific cognitive or affective elements in the associated dreams. Hobson, Goldfrank and Snyder (1964) have recently shown, however, that there is a positive correlation between the degree of physical activity, affectivity, and vividness in dream content and increased rate and variability of respiration. This was a global correlation of the R E M Ps as a whole. The only specific correlation they report is between 'respiratory content' in the dreams, e.g. speech, laughing, choking, and periods of apnea. Such content is associated with apneic periods almost twice as often as other respiratory patterns. This work also suggests that a good deal of the physiological variation associated with dreaming may be correlated with dream content. However, we have considered at some length the possibility that some erectile activity, as well as fluctuations in other physiological systems, may not be related to specific dream content but rather represent manifestations of intense physiological activation accompanying the R E M Ps. As has been noted, the R E Ms and other physiological activity are present in the neonate and in decorticate cats and humans; it is not conceivable that dreaming can take place in the latter. It is also possible that, not only may there be a partial lack of parallelism between erection as a physiological phenomenon and dream content, but sexual dreams may occur in the absence of erection. Thus, Money (1960) has reported that quadriplegics who have total spinal cord transections, do not experience sexual or genital-pelvic sensations but they, nevertheless, may continue to have dreams of seminal emission with orgasm imagery, almost as vividly as though it were the real thing. He concluded that the brain, and presumably the mind, can work independently of the genitalia in the generation of erotic experience. *It is possible that instinctual drive discharge and the psychic organization that subserves it may have a partial autonomy from the underlying physiological drive process.*

Freud (1900) considered that the majority of dreams were sexual in nature, but specifically denied that this was true of all of them, giving as exceptions, dreams of physiological need and of convenience. It needs to be considered that the extensive REMP erections may be related to sexuality in its broad psychoanalytic sense, as including genital and pregenital aspects, and as manifestations of the discharge of mobile instinctual drive energy, a discharge that also serves as the chief motivating force for dreaming. The REMP erections themselves may be taken as evidence that all dreams are sexual in nature. An alternative point of view is that it is difficult to conceive that nearly every dream would require a full or partial erection within seconds to minutes after the onset of the REMP. The fact that many of the erections have their onset several minutes before the beginning of the REMP suggests that the physiological aspect of the erection may be primary to any psychic influence, although it is not excluded that the dream work associated with NREM psychic activity during these few minutes preceding the REMP may initiate erection.

Finally, the question arises why the remarkable phenomenon of nocturnal REMP erection has not been discovered throughout the history of mankind. The most important reason is simply that when one is asleep he is not awake and cannot observe what is going on. The taboo nature of the organ and process under consideration may, in part, explain the failure to observe REMP erection in others. Additionally, people have always slept under covers while infants are swaddled or diapered. Even if the cyclic appearance of erection had been noted, the additional step of linking it with dreaming would have been difficult; this step had to await the development of objective methods of recording the presence of dreaming.

Summary

The existence of the nocturnal cycle of penile erections discovered by Ohlmeyer and his co-workers has been confirmed. Additionally, the episodes of erection have been found to be synchronous with the REMPs.

Full or partial erection has been observed in 95 per cent of eighty-six REMPs in seventeen subjects studied for twenty-seven nights. Erections begin and end in close temporal relationship to the onsets and terminations of the REMPs and in many instances begin several minutes before the onset of the dream periods.

Erection has not been observed during NREM sleep except in the few minutes prior to the onset of the REMPs and during the periods of detumescence which occur in stage 2 following the termination of the dream-periods.

The cycle of erections may be present in spite of very recent sexual gratification, occurs during daytime as well as during night-time sleep, and when the subject has knowledge of the nature of the experiment.

In an attempt to understand the functional or adaptive value of these extensive periods of nocturnal erection a number of possibilities were discussed: (a) that the erections represent a regression to the primitive level of diffuse autoerotic organization of penile sensation characteristic of early infancy; (b) that REMP erection may be another aspect of the general physiological activation associated with dreaming sleep; (c) that it may be a manifestation of an overflow phenomenon within the limbic system since the limbic-midbrain circuit appears to be in a high state of activation during REM sleep; (d) that REMP erection may represent an overflow phenomenon on a psychological level on the basis of observations that many forms of intense nonerotic stimuli are capable of producing erection in infants and preadolescent children; (e) that the so-called morning or bladder erection has nothing to do with bladder pressure but is the erection of the final REMP of the night. It was suggested that bladder erection may be nonerotic in nature and represent a regression to a more primitive level of genital organization characteristic of infancy.

The problem of the relationship of the extensive REMP erections to dreaming and dream content and the influence of physiological and/or psychological factors was discussed at length. The hypothesis has been entertained that the erection cycle has a primary physiological origin and that on any given night more or less full erection will be found during every REMP, providing that inhibitory factors are relatively in abeyance, for example, severe anxiety. Preliminary results have indicated that absence of, fluctuations during, rapid detumescences or tumescences, in any particular REMP can be correlated with dream content. Another possibility is that some of the erectile activity may not be related to specific dream content but is a manifestation of physiological activation accompanying the REMPs. It was suggested that instinctual drive discharge and the psychic organization that subserves it may have a partial autonomy from the underlying physiological 'drive' processes.

References

ASERINSKY, E., and KLEITMAN, N. (1955), 'Two types of ocular motility occurring in sleep', *J. appl. Physiol.*, vol. 8, pp. 1–11.

BRODY, S. (1964), 'Discussion of paper by C. Fisher "Cycle of penile erection synchronous with dreaming sleep"', read before the Association for Psychophysiological study of Sleep.

CONEL, J. L. (1942), *Post Natal Development of Human Cerebral Cortex*, Harvard University Press.

DEMENT, W., and KLEITMAN, N., (1957), 'Relation of eye movements during sleep to dream activity: objective method for study of dreaming', *J. exp. Psychol.*, vol. 53, pp. 339–46.

EVARTS, E. (1962), 'Activity of neurons in visual cortex of cat during sleep with low voltage fast EEG activity', *J. Neurophysiol.*, vol. 25, p. 812.

FAURE, J., BENSCH, C., and VINCENT, D. (1962), 'Au sujet des mecánismes responsables du comportement olfacto-bucco-ano-genito-sexuel du lapin: ses rapports avec le sommeil', *C R soc. biol.*, vol. 156, p. 629.

FISHER, C. (1965), 'Psychoanalytic implications of recent research on sleep and dreaming', *J. Amer. Psychoanal. Assn*, vol. 13, pp. 197–303.

FISHER, C., and DEMENT, W. (1963), 'Studies on psychopathology of sleep and dreams', *Amer. J. Psychiat.*, vol. 119, pp. 1160–68.

FREUD, S. (1900), *The Interpretation of Dreams*, vols. 4 and 5, Hogarth Press, 1953.

FREUD, S. (1905), *Three Essays on Sexuality*, Hogarth Press, 7th edn, 1953.

HALVERSON, H. M. (1940), 'Genital and sphincter behavior of male infant', *J. genet. Psychol.*, vol. 56, pp. 95–136.

HARLOW, H. F. (1962), 'Heterosexual affectional system in monkeys', *Amer. Psychol.*, vol. 17, pp. 1–9.

HOBSON, J. A., GOLDFRANK, F., and SNYDER, F. (1964), 'Respiration and mental activity in sleep', read before the Association for Psychophysiological Study of Sleep.

JOUVET, M. (1961), 'Telencephalic and rhombencephalic sleep in cat', in G. Wolstenholme and M. O'Connor (eds.), *Ciba Foundation Symposium on Nature of Sleep*, Churchill, pp. 188–206.

KINSEY, A. C., POMEROY, W. B., and MARTIN, C. E. (1948), *Sexual Behavior in Human Male*, Saunders.

KLEIN, M. (1963), 'Etude polygraphique et phylogenetique des differents états de sommeil', thése de médecine, Lyon.

MCLEAN, P. D. (1963), 'Phylogenesis', in P. H. Knapp (ed.), *Expression of Emotions in Man*, International Universities Press.

MONEY, J. (1960), 'Phantom orgasm in dreams of paraplegic men and women', *Arch. gen. Psychiat.*, vol. 3, pp. 373–83.

OHLMEYER, P., and BRILMAYER, H. (1947), 'Periodische Vorgange im Schlaf', *Pflueger arch. ges. Physiol.*, vol. 2, pp. 249–50.

OHLMEYER, P., BRILMAYER, H., and HÜLLSTRUNG, H. (1944), 'Periodische Vorgange im Schlaf', *Pflueger arch. ges. Physiol.*, vol. 248, p. 559.

OSWALD, I. (1962), *Sleeping and Waking*, Elsevier.

PARMELEE, A. H., *et al.* (1964), 'Activated sleep in premature infants', read before the Association for Psychophysiological Study of Sleep.

PEARSON, O. P. (1944), 'Reproduction in shrew (*Blarina brevicauda* Say)', *Amer. J. Anat.*, vol. 75, p. 39.

RAMSEY, G. V. (1943), 'Sexual development of boys', *Amer. J. Psychiat.*, vol. 56, pp. 217–34.

ROFFWARG, H., DEMENT, W., and FISHER, C. (1964), *Observations on Dream-Sleep Patterns in Neonates, Infants, Children and Adults*, Pergamon.

RUBIN, I. (1963), 'Sex over 65', in H. G. Beigel (ed.), *Advances in Sex Research*, Harper & Row.

SHAPIRO, A., *et al.* (1964), 'Physiological characteristics of REM periods and related kinds of sleep', read before the Association for Psychophysiological Study of Sleep.

SAWYER, C. H., *et al.* (1959), 'Physiological studies on some interactions between brain and pituitary-gonad axis in rabbit', *Endocrinology*, vol. 65, pp. 614–68.

SNYDER, F. (1963), 'New biology of dreaming', *Arch. gen. Psychiat.*, vol. 8, pp. 381–91.

SNYDER, F. (1964), 'REM state in living fossil', read before the Association for Psychophysiological Study of Sleep.

SPITZ, R. A. (1955), 'Primal cavity', *Psychoanal. Study Child*, vol. 10, p. 215.

SPITZ, R. A. (1962), 'Autoeroticism re-examined: role of early sexual behavior patterns in personality formation', *Psychoanal. Study Child*, vol. 17, pp. 283–318.

VINCENT, J. D. (1964), 'Contribution expérimentale a l'étude des mécanismes du sommeil', thése de médecine, Bordeaux.

WOLFF, P. (1966), 'The causes, controls and organization of behavior in newborn', *Psychol. Issues*, vol. 5, no. 17, pp. 1–105.

15 Edward V. Evarts

Activity of Neurons in Visual Cortex of the Cat during Sleep with Low Voltage Fast EEG Activity

Edward V. Evarts, 'Activity of neurons in visual cortex of the cat during sleep with low voltage fast EEG activity', *Journal of Neurophysiology*, vol. 25, 1962, pp. 812–16.

Introduction

Following Dement's (1958) observation that sleep in the cat is sometimes associated with low voltage fast EEG activity, a number of studies in cats with implanted electrodes have shown that the deepest stage of sleep in the cat is associated with this EEG pattern (Benoit and Bloch, 1960; Hubel, 1960a; Huttenlocher, 1960, 1961; Jouvet, 1961; Jouvet and Michel, 1960; Jouvet, Dechaume and Michel, 1960; Jouvet, Michel and Courjon, 1959; Rossi *et al.*, 1961). Observations on the activity of single neurons during sleep with low voltage fast EEG activity (S-LVF) have been carried out by Huttenlocher (1961), who found that the mean discharge rate of neurons in medial brain stem is greater during S-LVF than during either sleep with slow waves (S) or waking. The present study, carried out in the chronic cat preparation, was designed to compare the rates of discharge of neurons in the primary visual cortex during S-LVF and S. The aim was to discover whether an increase in neuronal activity during S-LVF as compared to S might occur in an area of the cerebral cortex as well as in the medial brain stem.

Methods
Data recording

Recordings were obtained from unanesthetized, unrestrained cats weighing from 2·5 to 3·5 kg. The techniques employed were, with two exceptions, the same as those described in a previous report (Evarts, 1960). The exceptions were: (a) macroelectrode recordings of nuchal electromyogram and eye movements were obtained and (b) glass-insulated platinum-iridium microelectrodes (Wolbarsht, MacNichol and Wagner, 1960) were used.

Data analysis

The criteria employed in identifying S and S-LVF were the same as those which have been described in detail by other investigators (Benoit and Bloch, 1960; Hubel, 1960a; Huttonlocher, 1960, 1961; Jouvet, 1961; Jouvet and

Michel, 1960; Jouvet, Dechaume and Michel, 1960; Jouvet, Michel and Courjon, 1959; Rossi *et al.*, 1961): S-LVF was identified by a marked reduction in the amplitude of the nuchal electromyogram, the occurrence of eye movements, and the disappearance of slow waves from the electrocorticogram. S was identified by the occurrence of slow waves and spindles in the electrocorticogram and by the posture of the cat.

Rates of discharge of seventy-nine neurons were determined during S and S-LVF. Each of the seventy-nine neurons was observed under both conditions. For thirty-eight of the units, recording during S-LVF preceded recording during S, whereas for the remaining forty-one units, recording during S preceded recording during S-LVF. Differences between unit activity during S and S-LVF were not related to the order of recording. The duration of observation of individual units varied from twenty minutes to one hour.

Results
Discharge rates during S and S-LVF

Table 1 shows the discharge rates of seventy-nine units during S and S-LVF. These rates were based on counts of discharges during approximately one minute of S and one minute of S-LVF. Of the seventy-nine units, sixty discharged more rapidly during S-LVF than during S, sixteen discharged more rapidly during S, and three discharged at the same rate during S and S-LVF. The mean rate of the seventy-nine units was 8·20/sec during S and 13·88/sec during S-LVF. The difference between these means, as determined by the t test, is statistically significant ($t = 4·98, p < 0·001$).

Relation of unit discharge to eye movements

S-LVF is associated with intermittent eye movements which often occur concurrently with movements of extremities, vibrissae, and head. In the present experiments the simultaneous recording of unit discharge and eye movements made it possible to search for relationships between them. In most units discharge rates during S-LVF were highest during the occurrence of eye movements. Figure 1 shows the tendency of a unit to discharge rapidly during eye movements and to be less active in the absence of eye movements. A similar relationship between eye movements and unit discharge during S-LVF was observed by Huttenlocher (1961) in recordings of unit activity in the superior colliculus.

Control of possible effects of retinal stimulation during S-LVF

The neurons described in this report were recorded from cats sleeping in an illuminated cage; by opening its eyes, the cat could see its environment. Throughout both S and S-LVF cats appeared to keep their eyes closed.

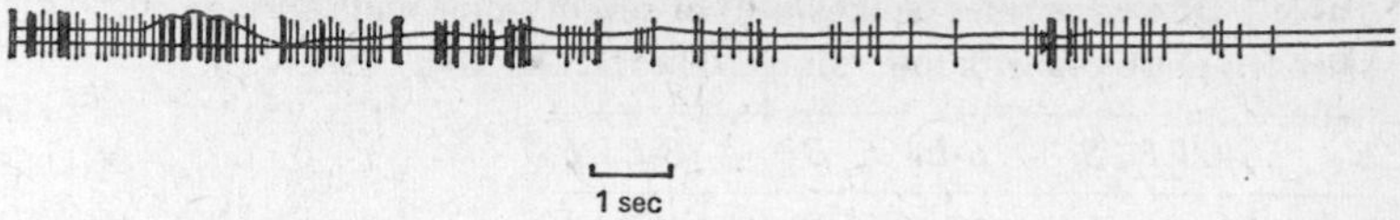

|— 1 sec

Figure 1 Relation of unit discharge and eye movements during S-LVF. Upper trace is the record of eye movements. Lower trace shows unit discharges. It may be seen that highest rates of unit discharge are associated with eye movements. This record was obtained during S-LVF.

However, it seemed possible that undetected opening of the lids might have occurred during S-LVF. Had this been the case, the high rates of neuronal discharge observed during S-LVF might have been the result of patterned retinal stimulation. In order to exclude this possibility, recordings of unit activity were obtained from cats whose eyes were covered with opaque contact occluders (Mishkin, Gunkel and Rosvold, 1959) which sufficed to eliminate visual stimulation even when the cats' eyes were fully open. Thirty-two of the units included in the present study were recorded with contact occluders in place. The difference between S and S-LVF in this group of units was similar to that in the remaining forty-seven units which were recorded from cats without contact occluders.

Discussion

S-LVF, as compared to S, has been found to be associated with an increase in the mean discharge rate of neurons in visual cortex, the majority (60/79) of the neurons in the present experiment having higher rates of discharge during S-LVF than during S. The increase in mean discharge rate observed in the present sample of neurons during S-LVF makes it clear that for neurons of visual cortex, as well as of brain stem, the deepest stage of sleep in the cat is not associated with a reduction of neuronal activity, but that, on the contrary, the rate of discharge is greater during S-LVF than during the less deep stage of sleep which is associated with EEG slow activity.

In addition to the similarity of direction of change of discharge rates of neurons in visual cortex and brain stem during S-LVF there is also considerable similarity in the quantitative effects of S-LVF on discharge rates of neurons in these loci. For twenty-eight brain-stem neurons studied by Huttenlocher (1961) during S and S-LVF the mean discharge rate was 7·48/sec during S and 14·96/sec during S-LVF. These rates are similar to those of 8·2/sec (S) and 13·88/sec (S/LVF) observed in the present study.

In contrast to the significant differences in mean rate of discharge or visual-cortex neurons during S-LVF as compared to S, significant differences in mean rate do not occur in visual-cortex neurons in S as compared to waking in the absence of retinal stimulation (Evarts, 1960). The qualifi-

Table 1 **Discharge rates (spikes/sec) of seventy-nine units during sleep (S) and sleep with low voltage fast EEG activity (S-LVF)**

S	S-LVF	S	S-LVF	S	S-LVF
0	0	2·42	28·96	9·18	42·35
0·20	0·80	2·63	6·33	9·45	9·05
0·20	1·50	2·76	2·34	10·93	39·42
0·29	1·18	3·00	8·00	11·55	5·70
0·31	0·13	3·28	5·04	11·65	5·70
0·33	0·81	3·59	9·41	12·99	7·41
0·40	1·45	3·75	10·80	13·10	51·05
0·45	1·45	3·77	7·09	14·44	21·22
0·53	0·53	4·02	4·80	14·54	16·31
0·59	0·03	4·45	7·30	14·61	5·24
0·65	5·99	4·80	5·75	15·33	22·44
0·69	1·73	4·95	19·55	16·05	18·80
0·82	2·39	5·13	11·14	16·45	20·05
0·95	2·90	5·54	4·72	16·80	21·05
1·11	3·67	5·60	9·55	16·88	6·36
1·20	0·40	5·92	17·32	19·48	37·61
1·28	2·47	6·30	3·05	19·51	26·39
1·29	1·06	6·47	18·29	19·93	15·80
1·37	1·90	6·64	7·29	20·13	25·01
1·37	5·67	7·18	7·81	24·97	33·43
1·50	2·75	7·30	17·54	25·69	28·57
1·57	17·71	7·55	8·90	25·90	20·75
1·84	4·00	8·75	7·00	28·04	50·98
2·00	5·60	8·79	20·65	28·27	73·86
2·09	5·50	9·01	31·57	29·28	45·39
2·12	7·73	9·05	33·26	32·08	49·59
2·40	3·95			$n = 79$	

Units have been ordered according to discharge rates during S. The first unit listed (with no discharges during either S or S-LVF) was observed to discharge during patterned retinal stimulation both before and after recordings of S and S-LVF.

cation of waking as occurring in the absence of retinal stimulation must be strongly emphasized. Thirty-six of the neurons included in the present sample were observed during periods when the cat was awake and looking about at its environment (Evarts, 1962). Under such conditions, most (34/36) of the neurons discharged more rapidly than they had during S; the mean rate of discharge of the thirty-six neurons during the occurrence of visual searching (15·8/sec) was significantly greater than the mean rate during S (8·2 sec).

The origin of the observed increase in discharge rates of neurons in visual cortex during S-LVF is difficult to guess. It is possible, for instance, that the increase is secondary to a change in the activity of neurons in the lateral geniculate nucleus. Hubel (1960b), in studies of spontaneous neuronal activity in this nucleus, found marked differences in firing patterns of many neurons in the lateral geniculate during sleep associated with EEG slow waves as compared to waking. No data are as yet available concerning the activity of lateral geniculate neurons during S-LVF. Likewise, data are unavailable concerning neuronal activity during S-LVF in those cortical regions which directly or indirectly project to the visual area. Moreover, in view of the limited number of cerebral regions from which activity of individual neurons has been recorded during S-LVF, it is not yet possible to estimate the extent to which S-LVF (as compared to S) is associated with a generalized increase in neuronal discharge throughout the cerebrum.

Summary

The spontaneous discharge of neurons in the primary visual cortex of the cat was recorded during sleep with low voltage fast EEG activity and during sleep with EEG slow waves. Of seventy-nine units studied, sixty had higher discharge rates during S-LVF than during S. The mean discharge rate (13·88/sec) of the sample during S-LVF was significantly greater than the mean rate (8·20/sec) during S. It is concluded that S-LVF, which is the deepest stage of sleep in the cat, is associated with increased rather than decreased activity of individual neurons in the primary visual cortex.

References

BENOIT, O., and BLOCH, V. (1960), 'Seuil d'excitabilité réticulaire et sommeil profond chez le chat', *J. physiol.* (Paris), vol. 52, pp. 17–18.

DEMENT, W. (1958), 'The occurrence of low voltage, fast, electroencephalogram patterns during behavioral sleep in the cat', *EEG clin. Neurophysiol.*, vol. 10, pp. 291–6.

EVARTS, E. V. (1960), 'Effects of sleep and waking on spontaneous and evoked discharge of single units in visual cortex', *Fed. Proc.*, vol. 19, pp. 828–37.

EVARTS, E. V. (1962), 'Activity of visual cortex neurons during waking with and without vision and during sleep', *Proceedings, XXII International Congress on Physiological Science, Leiden*, vol. 2, p. 996.

HUBEL, D. H. (1960a), 'Electrocorticograms in cats during natural sleep', *Arch. Ital. Biol.*, vol. 98, pp. 171–81.

HUBEL, D. H. (1960b), 'Single unit activity in the lateral geniculate body and optic tract of unrestrained cats', *J. Physiol.*, vol. 150, pp. 91–104.

HUTTENLOCHER, P. R. (1960), 'Effects of state of arousal on click responses in the mesencephalic reticular formation', *EEG clin. Neurophysiol.*, vol. 12, pp. 819–27.

HUTTENLOCHER, P. R. (1961), 'Evoked and spontaneous activity in single units of medial brain stem during natural sleep and waking', *J. Neurophysiol.*, vol. 24, pp. 451–68.

JOUVET, M. (1961), 'Telencephalic and rhombencephalic sleep in the cat', in G. Wolstenholm and M. O'Connor (eds.), *Ciba Foundation Symposium on the Nature of Sleep*, Churchill, pp. 188–206.

JOUVET, M., and MICHEL, F. (1960), 'Déclenchement de la "phase paradoxale" du sommeil par stimulation du tronc cérébrale chez le chat intact et mésencéphalique chronique', *C R soc. biol.*, vol. 154., pp. 636–41.

JOUVET, M., DECHAUME, J., and MICHEL, F. (1960), 'Etude des mécanismes du sommeil physiologique', *Lyon méd.*, vol. 204, pp. 479–521.

JOUVET, M., MICHEL, F., and COURJON, J. (1959), 'Sur un stade d'activité électrique cérébrale rapide au cours du sommeil physiologique', *C R soc. biol.*, vol. 153, pp. 1024–8.

MISHKIN, M., GUNKEL, R. D., and ROSVOLD, H. E. (1959), 'Contact occluders: a method for restricting vision in animals', *Science*, vol. 129, pp. 1120–21.

ROSSI, G. F., FAVALE, E., HARA, T., GIUSSANI, A., and SACCO, G. (1961), 'Researches on the nervous mechanisms underlying deep sleep in the cat', *Arch. Ital. Biol.*, vol. 99, pp. 270–92.

WOLBARSHT, M. L., MACNICHOL, E. F., and WAGNER, H. G. (1960), 'Glass insulated platinum microelectrodes', *Science*, vol. 132, pp. 1309–10.

16 Ernest Hartmann

A Note on the Nightmare

Ernest Hartmann, 'A note on the nightmare', from E. Hartmann (ed.), *Sleep and Dreaming*, International Psychiatry Clinics, vol. 7, no. 2, 1970, pp. 192–7, Little, Brown.

Nightmares, according to recent evidence, are horses of at least two very different colors: a heavy, shapeless black beast crushing the sleeper's chest as he awakens in terror, and a more ordinary reddish mare galloping off with the sleeper on a frightening and yet relatively familiar dream journey. The first is the classic incubus attack occurring early in the night during arousal from slow-wave sleep, described by Broughton and his group (Broughton, 1968; Gastaut and Broughton, 1965). The second is the frightening dream, the D-state nightmare or REM nightmare usually occurring later during the night, described by Fisher's group (1969).

This note merely documents the frequency, or rather infrequency, of these nightmares in several thousand nights of laboratory sleep study and presents a hypothesis on the conditions giving rise to the D-state nightmare.

Our laboratory has studied a total of about two thousand nights of sleep in human subjects. Some of these involved artificial awakenings, or unusual pharmacological or medical conditions, to be discussed later; but in over five hundred nights of sleep in normal adult subjects, sleeping without medication for uninterrupted nights in the laboratory, only once did a subject report a spontaneous awakening due to a nightmare. This was a 'long frightening dream' type of nightmare from a D-period awakening and occurred in a young woman just before the onset of menses. No incubus attacks were reported in this group. The subjects were on good terms with the experimenters and were very willing to report any unusual event during the night, so that we believe any nightmares recalled by the subjects would have been recorded. This is borne out by the fact that a number of nightmares were recalled under other laboratory conditions, to be discussed.

In several studies normal subjects in our laboratory were awakened five or ten minutes after the onset of a D-period at various times during the night. Such awakenings tended to result in relatively banal dream reports, and in over four hundred such awakenings there has not been a single report which could be called a nightmare. I have consulted four additional laboratories which frequently study subjects after awakenings of this kind, and there is universal agreement that a nightmare or frightening dream after such laboratory awakenings is almost never found: from approximately five thousand awakenings in these laboratories, not over ten minutes after the beginning of a D-period, I have had reports of at the very most two frightening dreams which might possibly qualify as nightmares.

Thus in relatively normal adults, in the sleep laboratory at least, it appears that nightmares are extremely rare, either as spontaneous interruptors of sleep, or as reports from the usual experimenter-induced awakenings five or ten minutes after the onset of a D-period.[1]

In our studies involving uninterrupted nights in pathological conditions or with pharmacological agents, the situation is different: there were eleven identifiable nightmares producing spontaneous awakenings in about five hundred nights. All, with one questionable exception, were of the D-state nightmare type. Three of these occurred in manic-depressive patients. One occurred twenty minutes after the onset of a D-period marked by a very high eye movement density and few body movements. One was from a night containing only two and a half hours sleep of which one-third was taken up by a long D-period ending in an awakening. A sleeping medication – Doriden – had been discontinued two days before. One episode was in a night with a great deal of awakening and interruption during which the subject changed from depression to mania; the exact onset of the nightmare was not clear. One definite nightmare occurred in a cardiac patient being studied for possible arrhythmia during the night. She had a D-state nightmare at 6 a.m., fifty minutes after the onset of an active D-period associated with many eye movements and with some ventricular extrasystoles. In drug studies, several nightmares were reported by our subjects both in and out of the laboratory one or two nights after the discontinuation of sleeping medication and antidepressant medication; this is consistent with reports by Kales *et al.* (1968, 1969).

Thus in our sleep laboratory the incubus attack is a rare or almost nonexistent phenomenon, even under unusual conditions, but the D-nightmare or REM nightmare is not quite so rare, and when it occurs my impression is that it awakens the subject out of a long active D-period, often at a time when D-pressure could be expected to be high. The only nightmare, mentioned above, reported by an apparently normal subject sleeping an uninterrupted night in the laboratory, awakened a young woman from a twenty-five-minute D-period just one day before the onset of her menstrual period,

1. It should be kept in mind that the subjects studied in sleep laboratories do not represent a cross-section of the population at large. First of all, young adults, especially male college students, are overrepresented in the sleep laboratory. More importantly, 'normal' subjects were studied, which usually meant some psychiatric or psychological test screening, varying with the laboratory and the study. In some studies a person reporting a history of nightmares might have been excluded for that reason, although I recall no such exclusions in my own studies.

at a time when our studies (Hartmann, 1966a) indicate that D-pressure may be high, and when D-pressure was certainly high in this specific case, as evidenced by her showing a 32 per cent D-time – the highest in her twenty-seven laboratory nights – and an extremely high mean eye movement density of ten eye movements per page.

The fact that children, who appear to have an unusually great need for D-time, typically report far more nightmares than adults also supports the notion that nightmares occur in situations characterized by a high D-pressure.

Interestingly, a number of adults who had never recalled nightmares under ordinary conditions reported to me that they had nightmares as they were recovering from a recent attack of Asian flu. I have heard many similar anecdotal reports of nightmares after a few days of febrile illness. Since fever and febrile illness appear to reduce D-time and to produce D-deprivation (Karacan et al., 1968), it is likely that the nights when night-mares are reported are periods of recovery from deprivation, which would be associated with high D-pressure and long D-periods.

Nightmares are frequently reported in the period of withdrawal from addiction to barbiturates, amphetamines, or alcohol (Greenberg and Pearlman, 1967; Gross and Goodenough, 1968; Oswald, 1968; Oswald and Priest, 1965), a time when high D-pressure and long D-periods are found; nightmares are seldom reported when the subject begins taking these substances. On the other hand, reserpine has often been reported to produce nightmares soon after the initiation of medication (Azima, 1958; Wilkins, 1954; Winsor, 1954). We have shown (Hartmann, 1966b) that reserpine is unique among clinically used agents in that it actually increases D-time in man. Therefore nightmares again are associated with periods when D-time and D-pressure are high – during medication with reserpine and after dis-continuation of medication with many other drugs. Poisoning by long-lasting anticholinesterase compounds has recently been shown to produce an increased D-time in man (Stoyva and Metcalf, 1968); this condition has previously been associated with frequent nightmare reports (Grob et al., 1947).

I am suggesting then that long D-periods and increased D-pressure are often associated with nightmares. However, there may be additional rele-vant factors involved in pathological or pharmacological conditions, since recovery from simple mechanically produced D-deprivation seems to result in nightmare reports less frequently than the various pathological depriva-tion conditions. The difference could be merely that in the latter conditions there is a greater tendency to awaken than in the situation of a healthy normal subject generally sleeping very soundly during recovery from mechanical D-deprivation.

Studies by Foulkes and others (Foulkes, 1966; Verdone, 1963) indicate that within a D-period there is a certain development of content so that awakenings further into the D-period produce more vivid, bizarre, and emotional content. In my experience reports from very long (> thirty minute) D-periods frequently contain at least some anxiety. I should like to suggest that every D-period as it lengthens (toward twenty, thirty, forty, or more minutes) develops an increasing possibility of producing a nightmare report upon awakening. This possibility will be strengthened when D-pressure is especially high, probably producing intensive vivid content and physiological activation, and when physical or psychological factors are present which may both stimulate stressful material in the dream and increase the possibility of awakening.

References

AZIMA, H. (1958), 'The possible dream inducing capacity of the whole root of rauwolfia serpentina', *Canad. Psychiat. Assn*, vol. 3, p. 47.

BROUGHTON, R. J. (1968), 'Sleep disorders: disorders of arousal?', *Science*, vol. 159, p. 1070.

FISHER, C., BYRNE, J. V., and EDWARDS, A. (1969), 'NREM and REM nightmares', *Psychophysiology*, vol. 6, p. 252 (abstract).

FOULKES, D. (1966), *The Psychology of Sleep*, Scribner.

GASTAUT, H., and BROUGHTON, R. J. (1965), 'A clinical and polygraphic study of episodic phenomena during sleep', *Rec. Adv. Biol. Psychiat.*, vol. 8, p. 197.

GREENBERG, R., and PEARLMAN, C. (1967), 'Delirium tremens and dreaming', *Amer. J. Psychiat.*, vol. 124, p. 37.

GROB, D., HARVEY, A., LANGWORTHY, O., and LILIENTHAL, J. (1947), 'The administration of di-isopropyl fluorophosphate (DFP) to man', *Bull. Hopkins Hosp.*, vol. 81, p. 257.

GROSS, M. M., and GOODENOUGH, D. R. (1968), 'Sleep disturbances in the acute alcoholic psychoses', in *Psychiatric Research Report 24*, American Psychiatric Association, pp. 132–47.

HARTMANN, E. (1966a), 'The D-state (dreaming sleep) and the menstrual cycle', *J. nerv. ment. Dis.*, vol. 143, p. 406.

HARTMANN, E. (1966b), 'Reserpine: its effect on the sleep-dream cycle in man', *Psychopharmacologia* (Berlin), vol. 9, p. 242.

KALES, A., LING TAN, T., SCHARF, M., KALES, J., MALMSTROM, E., ALLEN, C., and JACOBSON, A. (1968), 'Sleep patterns with sedative drugs', paper read before the Association for the Psychophysiological Study of Sleep, Denver.

KALES, A., SCHARF, M., LING TAN, T., JACOBSON, A., ALLEN, C., and MALMSTROM, E. (1969), 'Summary of short-term effects of hypnotics on sleep patterns', paper read before the Association for the Psychophysiological Study of Sleep, Boston.

KARACAN, I., WOLFF, S. M., WILLIAMS, R. L., HURSCH, C. J., and WEBB, W. B. (1968), 'The effects of fever on sleep and dream patterns', *Psychosomatics*, vol. 9, p. 331.

LEWIS, S. A., OSWALD, I., EVANS, J. I., and AKINDELE, M. O. (1969), 'Heroin and human sleep', *Psychophysiology*, vol. 6, p. 259 (abstract).

OSWALD, I., 'Drugs and sleep', *Pharmacol. Rev.*, vol. 20, p. 273.

OSWALD, I., and PRIEST, R. G. (1965), 'Five weeks to escape the sleeping pill habit', *Brit. med. J.*, vol. 4, p. 317.

STOYVA, J., and METCALF, D. (1968), 'Sleep patterns following chronic exposure to cholinesterase-inhibiting organophosphate compounds', *Psychophysiology*, vol. 5, p. 206 (abstract).

VERDONE, P. (1963), 'Variables related to the temporal reference of manifest dream content', Ph.D. dissertation, University of Chicago.

WILKINS, R. (1954), 'Clinical usage of rauwolfia alkaloids including reserpine', *Ann. N.Y. Acad. Sci.*, vol. 59, p. 36.

WINSOR, T. (1954), 'Human pharmacology of reserpine', *Ann. N.Y. Acad. Sci.*, vol. 59, p. 61.

17 Ralph J. Berger and Ian Oswald

Eye Movements during Active and Passive Dreams

Ralph J. Berger and Ian Oswald, 'Eye movements during active and passive dreams', *Science*, vol. 137, 1962, p. 601.

It is now recognized that there exist two different and alternating categories of sleep. One has been called 'hind-brain sleep' by Jouvet (1962) and is accompanied by a low-voltage and fairly fast electroencephalographic (EEG) pattern, relaxation of certain neck muscles in cat (Jouvet, 1962) and human (Berger, 1961) and, perhaps most strikingly, by bursts of conjugate, rapid eye movements with subsequent recall by the subject that he has dreamed (Dement and Kleitman, 1957). Dement and Wolpert (1958) reported evidence supporting their hypothesis that these eye movements were directional responses to the events of the dream. Yet rapid eye movements persist in cats after decortication (Jouvet, 1962). Also the fact that characteristic saw-toothed electroencephalographic waves tend to precede each burst of rapid eye movements appeared to us to cast doubt on the hypothesis; the presence or absence of these eye movements during 'hind-brain sleep' of blind men, according to the retention or absence, respectively, of visual imagery (Berger, Olley and Oswald, 1962), would support the hypothesis. One of us (Oswald, 1962) has criticized Dement and Wolpert's report but is now pleased to report confirmation of one of their findings, namely a relation between profuse eye activity and an active dream fantasy.

One of us (R.J.B.), for an entirely distinct purpose, awakened eight volunteers from periods of rapid eye movement on 103 occasions during thirty-seven nights. Dream recall occurred in eighty-nine instances and was recorded on magnetic tape. The dream reports were subsequently all presented to the other of us (I.O.), who had never been present during the nocturnal recording sessions and who had never seen the relevant electroencephalographic or eye movement records. He classified the dream reports as 'active' or 'passive' according to the nature of the events described, and especially if he felt such events would have been accompanied by many shifts of gaze, had they occurred in real life.

Subsequently R.J.B. assigned code numbers to each electroencephalographic and eye movement record and presented each to I.O., who was entirely ignorant of the dream to which each record was related and distinctly skeptical of the likelihood of the association eventually found. The eye movement periods were classified by I.O. as 'active' or 'passive' according to the frequency and size of the eye movements which occurred throughout each ten- to twenty-minute period prior to the time the subjects had been awakened, although the later in the period the movements did or did not occur, the greater the weight he attached. The whole set of records was then inspected again in a different order by I.O. and classified a second time. R.J.B. then selected the records of the twenty-two instances where divergent judgements had been made, and I.O. made a final classification of these periods of rapid eye movement.

The code was then broken. Fifty dream reports had been classified as 'active' and in forty-two instances the relevant period of rapid eye movement had been judged 'active'. Thirty-nine reports had been classified as 'passive' and in twenty-three instances the relevant period was judged 'passive'.

It is therefore confirmed that there is a significant association ($\chi^2 = 16\cdot18$; $p < 0\cdot001$) between the nature of the dream content and the amount of movement of the eyes.

References

BERGER, R. J. (1961), 'Tonus of extrinsic laryngeal muscles during sleep and dreaming', *Science*, vol. 134, p. 840.

BERGER, R. J., OLLEY, P. C., and OSWALD, I. (1962), 'The EEG, eye movements and dreams of the blind', *Q. J. exp. Psychol.*, vol. 14, pp. 183–6.

DEMENT, W., and KLEITMAN, N. (1957), 'Cyclic variations in EEG during sleep and their relation to eye movements, body motility and dreaming', *EEG clin. Neurophysiol.*, vol. 9, pp. 673–90.

DEMENT, W., and WOLPERT, E. A. (1958), 'The relation of eye movements, body motility and external stimuli to dream content', *J. exp. Psychol.*, vol. 55, pp. 543–53.

JOUVET, M. (1962), 'Recherches sur les structures nerveuses et les mécanismes responsables des différentes phases du sommeil physiologique', *Arch. Ital. Biol.*, vol. 100, pp. 125–206.

OSWALD, I. (1962), *Sleeping and Waking: Physiology and Psychology*, Elsevier.

18 Ralph J. Berger, P. Olley and Ian Oswald

The EEG, Eye Movements and Dreams of the Blind

Ralph J. Berger, P. Olley and Ian Oswald, 'The EEG, eye movements and dreams of the blind', *Quarterly Journal of Experimental Psychology*, vol. 14, 1962, pp. 183–6.

Introduction

In recent years, numerous American and French workers have described the invariable cyclical appearance, during continuous nocturnal sleep, of light sleep patterns in the electroencephalogram (EEG), accompanied by frequent and characteristic clusters of rapid conjugate eye movements (REMs) and dreaming (e.g. Dement and Kleitman, 1957a and b). The REMs have been claimed to represent scanning movements with respect to the dream visual imagery (Dement and Kleitman, 1957b). The 'REM periods with accompanying EEG picture vary in duration (twenty minutes is common) and four to six occur per night, together with characteristic muscle tonus changes' (Berger, 1961).

Schwartz and Fischgold (1960) and Jouvet, Michel and Mounier (1960) described brief appearances of 2 to 3 cps frontal EEG activity, having a characteristic 'saw-toothed' wave form associated with the REMs.

We decided to investigate the hypothesis of the American workers that the REMs represent what may be called 'looking-at-dream-picture' movements. First, by a closer examination of the time relations between the 'saw-toothed' frontal EEG activity and the onset of individual REM clusters; secondly, by studies of the EEG and eye movements during nocturnal sleep in the blind.

Jastrow (quoted by Ramsey, 1953) studied the dream reports of persons who had become blind at varying periods after birth. Those who became blind later than early childhood maintained visual imagery but there was a progressive decline of reports of visual imagery as the individual became older. A few individuals only were said still to report some visual imagery after forty years of blindness.

Method and results

The EEG 'saw-toothed' waves

In the course of other studies of all-night sleep we observed that among thirty-six normal persons, on whom suitably located electrodes had been used, were twenty-three who showed the 3 cps frontal 'saw-toothed' waves very prominently. It seemed clear to us that generally these brief bursts of EEG waves *preceded* individual REM clusters. In order to confirm this hypothesis, we recalled the first of our subjects from whom we had recorded the saw-toothed waves, and recorded one further entire night's sleep. The EEG was recorded using a left antero-posterior chain of silver cup electrodes, and eye movements by means of the most anterior EEG electrode and two other electrodes fixed just below the outer canthus of each eye. The diagonal and asymmetrical electrode placement had the advantage of economy, and allowed both horizontal and vertical REMs to be recorded on the same channels (Figure 1).

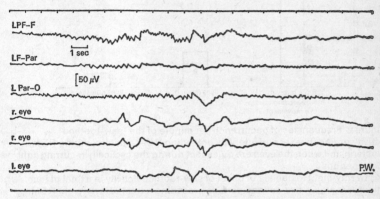

Figure 1 An example of 'saw-toothed' frontal activity preceding the appearance of a brief REM cluster by three seconds
LPF–F = left pre-frontal–frontal
LF–Par = left fronto-parietal
L Par–O = left parieto-occipital

Subsequently, with the eye movement channels and then the EEG channels of the record alternately obscured, two of us (I.O. and R.J.B. respectively) independently marked the record where it was judged that each 'saw-toothed' burst and each REM cluster began and ended. Figure 2 indicates that our hypothesis was confirmed; the onset of 'saw-toothed' frontal EEG waves is significantly ($\chi^2 = 229 \cdot 4$, $n = 2$, $p < 0 \cdot 001$) related to the five seconds preceding a REM cluster. This result was obtained by comparing the observed frequencies with those which would be expected to occur by chance, the latter being proportional to the total duration of each condition.

Ralph J. Berger, P. Olley and Ian Oswald 275

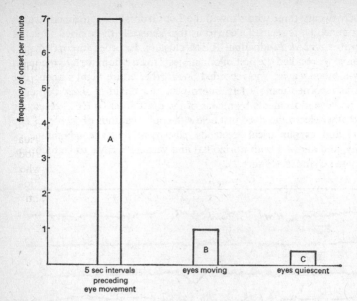

Figure 2 Frequencies of occurrence per minute of the 'saw-toothed' activity during five-second intervals preceding REM clusters, during REM clusters, and when the eyes are quiescent during the cyclically recurring light sleep periods

(A) twenty-eight instances of onset of saw-toothed activity in a total of four minutes (namely, five-second periods preceding a total of forty-eight REM clusters)

(B) twenty instances of onset of saw-toothed activity during the course of the forty-eight REM clusters of total duration twenty minutes

(C) twenty-one instances of onset of saw-toothed activity during a total of seven minutes while the eyes were quiescent during REM periods

Blind subjects

An antero-posterior chain of silver cup electrodes was used to record the EEG. A pair of electrodes was fixed at each outer canthus, to give four different electrode combinations, to enable us to recognize the occasional electrode artefact (these sometimes look like REM potentials). Eight blind male adults were studied, each having two entire nights of recording.

Three men had had life-long blindness; two, aged twenty-five and thirty, on account of severe corneal scarring (probably resulting from neonatal gonorrhoea) and one aged seventeen, on account of bilateral optic atrophy since the age of eighteen months or earlier. These men had no conception of visual imagery. A sixty-year-old man had been blind for thirty years owing to corneal scarring, and a fifty-two-year-old man for forty years owing to traumatic retinal detachment and cataracts. The latter two men both stated that they had lost the ability to picture things and claimed that no visual imagery was present in their dreams. Each was first shown to produce clear electro-oculographic potentials when the eyeballs were moved voluntarily. None of these six men had REMs in their cyclically recurring light sleep periods, during which, to judge by their subsequent reports, they nevertheless dreamed of non-visual fantasy experiences.

Three men aged twenty-three, thirty-three and forty, totally blind for ten, three and fifteen years respectively, claimed still to experience visual imagery. Each had REMs in their cyclically recurring light sleep periods differing in no way from those of normal sighted people, and each when wakened during REM periods recalled visual dreams. As an illustration, the man who had been blind for fifteen years (who had particularly active REMs) described how he dreamed he was in the swimming bath, how he did the 'crawl' rapidly to the other end where he could see his friend's wife ('her white skin and black costume, it was all very vivid') and splashed water teasingly over her. Of the eight blind men, only this last man had 'saw-toothed' waves.

Discussion

Wolpert (1960) implies a theory of peripheral control of dreaming in the statement:

Thus REMs appear to be specific to the manifest dream content, thereby confirming the suggestion put forward by Ladd as early as 1892 that during dreaming the eyeballs move gently in their sockets, taking various positions induced by the retinal phantasms as they control the dream.

A peripheral theory of this nature does not commend itself to us and we find it difficult to reconcile our observations concerning the 'saw-toothed' EEG waves with a looking-at-the-dream-pictures hypothesis. It could perhaps be argued that dreaming occurs in a series of short flashes; the frontal activity being a physiological concomitant of the commencement of each dream flash, the fantasied contents of which provoke scanning eye-movements. Dement and Wolpert (1958), however, argue strongly that dreaming is continuous. Possibly one could argue that the frontal EEG 'saw-toothed' waves are indicative of a sudden change of neurophysiological *status quo*, which itself results in more 'activity' in the dream events, so calling forth more scanning eye-movements.

A number of other theoretical objections to the looking-at-dream-pictures hypothesis have been made elsewhere (Oswald, 1962), but the presence of REMs in those blind subjects who still possessed visual imagery, and their absence in those who had either never had, or had lost visual imagery, must be considered to support the hypothesis. However, it would seem to us most economical to suppose that both the burst of EEG waves and the subsequent REM cluster are indicative of a sudden change of neurophysiological conditions, without reference to awareness of, or response to dream contents, for it is known that an artificially induced change of electro-physiological activity of the frontal cortex in the conscious human can be followed by conjugate eye-movements (Rasmussen and Penfield, 1948). It could be supposed that, owing to non-use, nervous pathways involved in the execution of conjugate eye-movements are poorly developed in those with life-long blindness, or, once established, suffer through disuse during prolonged blindness.

References

BERGER, R. J. (1961), 'Tonus of extrinsic laryngeal muscles during sleep and dreaming', *Science*, vol. 134, p. 840.

DEMENT, W., and KLEITMAN, N. (1957a), 'Cyclic variations in EEG during sleep and their relation to eye movements, body motility and dreaming', *EEG clin. Neurophysiol.*, vol. 9, pp. 673–90.

DEMENT, W., and KLEITMAN, N. (1957b), 'The relation of eye movements during sleep to dream activity: an objective method for the study of dreaming', *J. exp. Psychol.*, vol. 53, pp. 339–46.

DEMENT, W., and WOLPERT, E. A. (1958), 'The relation of eye movements, body motility and external stimuli to dream content', *J. exp. Psychol.*, vol. 55, pp. 543–53.

JOUVET, M., MICHEL, F., and MOUNIER, D. (1960), 'Analyse électroencéphalographique comparée du sommeil physiologique chez le chat et chez l'homme', *Rev. neurol.*, vol. 103, pp. 189–205.

OSWALD, I. (1962), *Sleeping and Waking: Physiology and Psychology*, Elsevier.

RAMSEY, G. V. (1953), 'Studies of dreaming', *Psychol. Bull.*, vol. 50, pp. 432–55.

RASMUSSEN, T., and PENFIELD, W. (1948), 'Movement of head and eyes from stimulation of the human frontal cortex', *Proc. Assn Res. Nerv. Ment. Dis.*, vol. 27, pp. 346–61.

SCHWARTZ, B. A., and FISCHGOLD, H. (1960), 'Introduction à l'étude polygraphique du sommeil de nuit (mouvements oculaires et cycles de sommeil)', *Vie méd.*, vol. 41, pp. 39–46.

WOLPERT, E. A. (1960), 'Studies in psychophysiology of dreams', *Arch. gen. Psychiat.*, vol. 2, pp. 231–41.

19 Joseph Gross, Joseph Byrne and Charles Fisher

Eye Movements during Emergent Stage 1 EEG in Subjects
with Lifelong Blindness

Joseph Gross, Joseph Byrne and Charles Fisher, 'Eye movements during emergent
stage I EEG in subjects with lifelong blindness', *Journal of Nervous and Mental
Disease*, vol. 141, 1965, pp. 365–70.

Since 1953, when Aserinsky and Kleitman first published their work on
recurrent rapid eye movement periods during human sleep, associated with
low voltage, fast EEG waves (now designated emergent stage 1 EEG), this
phenomenon has been confirmed and studied by a host of other researchers
(Aserinsky and Kleitman, 1953, 1955; Dement, 1955; Dement and Kleitman, 1957a). These REM periods, present in other species as well (Dement,
1958; Faure *et al.*, 1963; Klein, 1963; Weitzman, 1961), are accompanied by
changes in the functional state of the nervous system: penile erection
(Fisher, Gross and Zuch, 1965), increased presynaptic spinal inhibition
(Hodes and Dement, 1961), increase in sensory arousal threshold (Williams,
Morlock and Morlock, 1961), decreased muscle tonus (Jacobson *et al.*,
1964), bursts of coordinated fine muscle movements (Baldridge, Whitman
and Kramer, 1965), irregular respiration (Aserinsky, 1965), changes in skin
temperature (Fisher, Gross and Zuch, 1965; Snyder, 1961), increased basal
skin resistance (Hawkins *et al.*, 1962), increased discharge activity in the
visual cortex (Evarts, 1962), etc. (see Dement, 1964, for a review of the
field). In 1957, Dement and Kleitman further reported that a very high
degree of correlation was found in humans between these recurring nightly
REM phases and *dreaming*, if subjects are awakened during or shortly after
them.

Now while the REMP-dreaming cycle (also termed *paradoxical sleep* or
rhombencephalic sleep) appears to be universally present in normal humans,
there is contradictory evidence in the literature as to the presence or absence
of rapid eye movements during emergent stage 1 EEG in blind humans. In
the three reports extant, the investigators used electro-oculographic (EOG)
potentials as a means of detecting REMs. Of these, only Offenkrantz and
Wolpert (1963) found that despite EOG potentials being present during
waking in five subjects with lifelong blindness, no REMs were recorded
during sleep although periods of emergent stage 1 were present and non-
visual dreams were reported. Likewise, Berger, Olley and Oswald (1962),
found REMs only briefly present in one of eight REM periods of a blind
subject. However, Amadeo and Gomez (1966) found REMs consistently

present in seven of eight congenitally blind subjects. The remaining subject, an eight-year-old boy with retrolental fibroplasia (R L F), had no R E Ms.

Method

In an effort to clarify the question whether eye movements are actually present in blind subjects or whether their apparent absence was an artifact of the EOG method of recording, we investigated five subjects using both the EOG method of recording, and simultaneously a ceramic strain gauge,[1] placed on the eyelid according to the method described by Baldridge, Whitman and Kramer (1965). This strain gauge responds directly to mechanical movement of the eyeball. Additionally, we controlled the recordings with close direct observation. Our five subjects included a fifteen-year-old girl and a twenty-year-old boy, both with retrolental fibroplasia. The fifteen-year-old had no light perception; the twenty-year-old good light perception in one eye. The other subjects, a thirty-year-old man and two women, fifty-three and fifty-five years old, had optic atrophy of unknown etiology since early childhood. Two of them had minimal light perception. The other, fifty-five years old, had good light and minimal form perception. All subjects had almost constant, coarse nystagmus and involuntary roving movements while awake and could not direct their eyes on command. None had visual imagery; all reported having experienced nonvisual dreams.

The EEG and EOG electrodes were attached in the usual manner, as described by Dement and Kleitman (1957a): EOG electrodes were attached to the right and left outer canthi. The ceramic strain gauge was taped directly on one of the eyelids (Figure 1). This strain gauge is in essence a special resistance element bonded to a thin wafer of plastic about $\frac{1}{8}$ by $\frac{1}{2}$ inch. As the wafer is flexed, changes in the resistance of the element occur proportional to the amount of flexion and are detected by means of a bridge circuit and amplified. The moving eyeball, since it is not perfectly spherical, causes change in the contour of the eyelid as the corneal bulge shifts around and, hence, flexes the gauge. We used an Offner Type T EEG for recording.

Results

The five subjects were studied with the combined methods for a total of thirteen nights during forty-four R E M Ps. All showed sleep EEG patterns with recurrent emergent stage 1, apparently no different from normals. Rapid eye movements were present as determined by strain gauge recording or direct observation during each of the forty-four recorded emergent stage 1, EEG periods. These strain gauge recordings were confirmed by close direct visual observation in four of the five subjects. As far as the

1. Type D B-105, resistance about 1000 ohms, manufactured by Kulite-Bytrex Corp., Waltham, Mass.

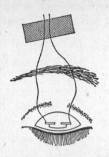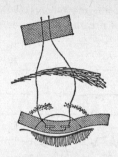

Figure 1 Schema showing placement of ceramic strain gauge on eyelid. For maximum sensitivity the center of the strain gauge should overlay the medial slope of the corneal bulge; the exposed element should face outward and be given a thin coating of petroleum jelly to prevent adherence to the overlying transparent plastic tape

EOG recording was concerned, the two younger subjects with retrolental fibroplasia had no readable deflections of EOG as recorded in the standard manner during waking or sleeping. In one of these, even with careful EOG testing at a 20 μV/cm level, no EOG deflection was present. During waking, the other three subjects had in general variable or unclearly defined EOG deflections corresponding to larger amplitude eye movements. Moreover, the EOG did not register many smaller horizontal or vertical movements which showed up on the strain gauge tracing and/or were noted by close direct observation. This was especially true during emergent stage 1, where EOG deflections were absent or diminished for all subjects, although various eye movements were being recorded by the strain gauge or observed directly (Figure 2). A normal control subject, recorded during stage 1 REM with both EOG and strain gauge, showed what amounted to virtually parallel tracings of eye movements, with the strain gauge showing more clearly very small amplitude movements (Figure 3).

The general sequential pattern of eye movements as recorded on the strain gauge tracings of our subjects during emergent stage 1 would be difficult to distinguish from that of normals, in that a similar sequence of single-eye movements or runs of multiple eye movements with interspersed periods of quiescence or occasional slow movements was common to both tracings. However, direct observation showed that in contrast to normals, the stage 1 eye movements of the blind appeared generally smaller in amplitude, often were repetitive nystagmoid jerks, tending to preponderate in one direction (which in two subjects was different from and in two subjects similar in direction to the quick component of their upright waking nystagmus), and occasionally bilaterally asynchronous. In addition, intermittent opening and closing movements of the lids were also seen in the blind. The percentage of dream-time, in our subjects, was within normal limits.

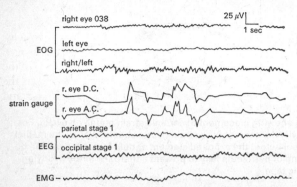

Figure 2 Emergent stage 1 EEG (REMP) in a twenty-year-old male congenitally blind subject with RLF. The EOG shows little or no deflections, while the strain gauge tracing clearly demonstrates the presence of rapid eye movements. This subject had minimal light perception in one eye

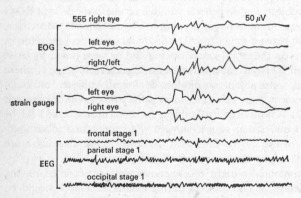

Figure 3 Emergent stage 1 EEG (REMP) in a normal male adult subject showing presence of rapid eye movement recorded simultaneously by both EOG (electrooculograph) and SG (strain gauge) methods. Experimental set-up and placement of leads identical to that of subject in Figure 2, except EOG was at higher gain in Figure 2

As far as the other EEG stages of our subjects, during sleep onset, as well as during periods of transition from 'deeper' stage 3 or 4 to stage 1 or 2 (following body movements or a noise, for example), occasional eye-jerks or rolling movements were observed. No fast or obvious rolling movements were noted in uninterrupted stages 3 or 4.

Discussion

The results reported extend the evidence for the universal presence of recurrent eye movement cycles during human sleep, even in subjects blind for as long as fifty-five years. Hitherto inferred absence of eye movements in the sleeping blind had been based on the EOG recording method, which depends on the presence of the dipolar corneofundal potential (CFP) of the eyeball. However, the EOG may be greatly diminished or absent in the blind (especially in retrolental fibroplasia or pigment degeneration)[2] and even normally may show fluctuation, e.g., during dark adaptation (Kris, 1960). It is possible that the state of consciousness itself may play a role, as in one of our subjects whose previously minimal EOG increased briefly following abrupt awakening. However, this relation would be difficult to determine without precise independent calibration of their eye movements. These factors, plus the definitely diminished amplitude of stage 1 eye movements in the blind, apparently below levels easily recordable by the EOG, may account for previously negative results. In addition, direct observation of small eye movements must be close and under conditions of good illumination, especially in subjects with loose or fleshy eyelids. Moreover, the CFP, besides being subject to functional vicissitudes, has a moot origin. While its absence or diminution in pathologic conditions of the retina would implicate that structure, recent work by Pasik, Pasik and Bender (1965) showed that, in the monkey, despite complete bilateral ablation of not only the retina but cornea and choroid as well, followed by implantation of an intrascleral plastic implant, the EOG, at first absent even during passive movement of the implant, gradually and progressively recovered and reached normal amplitude four weeks later.

Our positive results are consistent with the ablation experiments of Jouvet (1964), who found in the cat that if all cerebral structures rostral to the pons were removed spontaneous spikes still appear in the pons synchronus with lateral eye movements, during emergent stage 1. However, Reite *et al.* (1965) have shown that in the monkey, on the other hand, pontile spindling is not present during REMs – evidence that for this primate the physiologic controlling factors of emergent stage 1 REMs are displaced rostrally in favor of the limbic system. In any case it is not unexpected that mere functional loss of vision would not result in the disappearance of stage 1 eye movements when they were still present after a more radical structural ablation. Additional evidence that the stage 1 eye movements

2. See also François, Verriest and De Rouek (1957).

tend to have an autonomous persistence, independent of the ability to see, is found in recent unpublished work by Berger on monkeys raised in darkness, or with translucent eye cups depriving them of patterned vision (Berger and Meier, 1965), and Fishbein on cats reared in darkness (Fishbein, Schaumberg and Weitzman, 1965); in both species stage 1 REMs persisted.

Finally, apart from the neurophysiologic implications of these results, the question arises as to what bearing, if any, they have on the much discussed question of the relation between stage 1 eye movements and dream content. For normal subjects, Dement and Wolpert (1958) found that eye movements tend to be increased in active versus passive dreams. It would be of interest to know if a similar relation based on similar mechanisms exists for blind subjects. But as far as proving or disproving the 'looking at dream pictures' hypothesis (Berger, Olley and Oswald, 1962), i.e. that the eye movement actually scans the dream scene, as the work of Roffwarg *et al.* (1962) strongly suggests, we feel that the presence (or formerly considered absence) of eye movements during emergent stage 1 in the blind really has no direct bearing on the problem of the relation between eye movements and visual content of dreams in normal subjects. It would be just as irrelevant to deduce from the presence of mouth movements and vocalizations in unschooled congenitally deaf and dumb subjects that similar phenomena in normals can have no specific relation to meaningful verbalized content; obviously they can. In both cases the physiologic substratum is similar, but in the normal there is a superimposed level of coordination between mouth movements, vocalization and meaningful speech. Likewise, the REMs present at birth may later be taken over for scanning when visual dreaming begins.

Although evidence would indicate that in many dreams at least some REMs are specifically related to visual content, it is methodologically quite a difficult matter to demonstrate. In the normal awake subject, a great multiplicity of factors are related to eye movement. The point to point spatial pattern the normal eye traces in observing a real scene or card is not simply a function of stimulus configuration. On the one hand, other symbolic aspects of the external percept, whether it is pleasing or threatening, may modify the movement resulting in avoidance behavior or increased fixation of the eye (Luborsky, Blinder and Mackworth, 1964); on the other hand, subjective processes in the perceiver himself, whether he is alert, day dreaming, fantasying, generating or suppressing a wish, affect the eye movement both in terms of rate and direction (Antrobus, Antrobus and Singer, 1964). There is no reason, therefore, not to suppose that in the sleeping, dreaming subject an equally complex set of factors operate, influencing eye movement as a 'final common pathway'. We feel it is unlikely that the relation of eye movement to dream content will be precisely resolvable at least until some predictable correlation between mental content and eye movement in the waking subject has first been achieved.

Summary

Employing a movement transducer (ceramic strain gauge) for recording eye movements, together with direct observation, five subjects blind since birth, with no waking visual imagery, showed recurring rapid eye movement periods (REMPs) during emergent stage 1, similar to normals. At the same time, corneofundal potentials, as measured by electrooculographic recording (EOG), were absent or greatly diminished.

These results may resolve the earlier contradictory findings on REMs in subjects with lifelong blindness showing that REMs are present in such subjects as old as fifty-five and that the reported absence of REMs may be an artifact of the method (EOG) used in their detection.

References

AMADEO, M., and GOMEZ, E. (1966), 'Eye movements, attention and dreaming in subjects with lifelong blindness', *J. Canad. Psychiat. Assn*, vol. 11, pp. 501–7.

ANTROBUS, J. S., ANTROBUS, J. S., and SINGER, J. L. (1964), 'Eye movements accompanying day-dreaming, visual imagery and thought suppression', *J. abnorm. soc. Psychol.*, vol. 69, p. 244.

ASERINSKY, E. (1965), 'On respiratory parameters during sleep', *Fed. Proc.*, vol. 24, p. 339.

ASERINSKY, E., and KLEITMAN, N. (1953), 'Regularly occurring periods of eye motility and concomitant phenomena during sleep', *Science*, vol. 118, pp. 273–4.

ASERINSKY, E., and KLEITMAN, N. (1955), 'Two types of ocular motility occurring in sleep', *J. appl. Physiol.*, vol. 8, pp. 1–10.

BALDRIDGE, B., WHITMAN, R., and KRAMER, M. (1963), 'A simplified method for detecting eye movements during dreaming', *Psychosom. Med.*, vol. 25, pp. 78–82.

BALDRIDGE, B., WHITMAN, R., and KRAMER, M. (1965), 'The concurrence of fine muscle activity and REMs during sleep', *Psychosom. Med.*, vol. 27, pp. 19–26.

BERGER, R. J., and MEIER, G. W. (1965), 'Deprivation of patterned vision and the eye movements of sleep', presented to the Association for the Psychophysiological Study of Sleep.

BERGER, R. J., OLLEY, P., and OSWALD, I. (1962), 'The EEG, eye movements and dreams of the blind', *Q. J. exp. Psychol.*, vol. 14, pp. 183–6.

DEMENT, W. (1955), 'Dream recall and eye movements during sleep in schizophrenics and normals', *J. nerv. ment. Dis.*, vol. 122, pp. 263–9.

DEMENT, W. (1958), 'The occurrence of low voltage, fast, EEG patterns during behavioral sleep in the cat', *EEG clin. Neurophysiol.*, vol. 10, pp. 291–6.

DEMENT, W. (1964), 'Eye movements during sleep', in *The Oculomotor System*, Harper & Row, pp. 366–416.

DEMENT, W., and KLEITMAN, N. (1957a), 'Cyclic variations of EEG during sleep and their relation to eye movements, body motility and dreaming', *EEG clin. Neurophysiol.*, vol. 9, pp. 673–90.

DEMENT, W., and KLEITMAN, N. (1957b), 'The relation of eye movements during sleep to dream activity: an objective method for the study of dreaming', *J. exp. Psychol.*, vol. 53, pp. 339–46.

DEMENT, W., and WOLPERT, E. (1958), 'The relation of eye movements, body motility and external stimuli to dream content', *J. exp. Psychol.*, vol. 55, pp. 543–53.

EVARTS, E. (1962), 'Activity of neurons in visual cortex of cat during sleep with low voltage fast EEG activity', *J. Neurophysiol.*, vol. 25, p. 812.

FAURE, J., VINCENT, D., LeNOUËNE, J., and GEISMANN, P. (1963), 'Sommeil lent et stade paradoxal chez le lapin des deux sexes', *C R soc. biol.*, vol. 157, pp. 799–804.

FISHBEIN, W., SCHAUMBERG, N., and WEITZMAN, E. (1965), 'REMs during sleep in dark reared kittens', presented to the Association for the Psychophysiological Study of Sleep.

FISHER, C., GROSS, J., and ZUCH, J. (1965), 'Cycle of penile erection synchronous with dreaming (REM) sleep', *Arch. gen. Psychiat.*, vol. 12, pp. 29–45.

FRANÇOIS, J., VERRIEST, G., and DE ROUEK, A. (1957), 'L'électro-oculographie en tant qu'examen fonctionnel de la rétine', *Bibl. ophthal.* (Basel), vol. 49, pp. 1–67.

HAWKINS, D. R., PURYEAR, H. B., WALLACE, C. D., DEAL, W. B., and THOMAS, E. S. (1962), 'Basal skin resistance during sleep and "dreaming"', *Science*, vol. 136, pp. 321–2.

HODES, R., and DEMENT, W. (1964), 'Depression of electrically induced reflexes ("H-reflexes") in man during low voltage EEG sleep', *EEG clin. Neurophysiol.*, vol. 17, pp. 617–29.

JACOBSON, A., KALES, A., LEHMANN, D., and HOEDEMAKER, F. S. (1964), 'Muscle tonus in human subjects during sleep and dreaming', *Exp. Neurol.*, vol. 10, pp. 418–24.

JOUVET, M. (1964), 'Studies on rhombencephalic sleep', presented to the Association for the Psychophysiological Study of Sleep.

KLEIN, M. (1963), 'Etude polygraphique et phylogenetique des differents états de sommeil', thése de médecine, Lyon.

KRIS, C. (1960), *Vision: Electro-Oculography*, Year Book, Chicago, pp. 692–700.

LUBORSKY, L., BLINDER, B., and MACKWORTH, N. (1964), 'Eye fixation and the contents of recall and images as a function of heart rate', *Percept. mot. Skills*, vol. 18, pp. 421–36.

OFFENKRANTZ, W., and WOLPERT, E. (1963), 'The detection of dreaming in a congenitally blind subject', *J. nerv. ment. Dis.*, vol. 136, pp. 88–90.

PASIK, P., PASIK, T., and BENDER, M. B. (1965), 'Recovery of the electro-oculogram after total retinal ablation in monkeys', *EEG clin. Neurophysiol.*, vol. 19, pp. 291–7.

REITE, M. L., RHODES, J. M., KAVAN, E., and ADEY, W. R. (1965), 'Normal sleep patterns in the macaque monkey', *Arch. Neurol.*, vol. 12, pp. 138–44.

ROFFWARG, H. P., DEMENT, W., MUZIO, J., and FISHER, C. (1962), 'Dream imagery: relations of REMs to sleep', *Arch. gen. Psychiat.*, vol. 7, pp. 235–58.

SNYDER, F. (1961), *Report on Current Research*, Association for the Psychophysiological Study of Sleep.

WEITZMAN, E. (1961), 'A note on EEG and eye movements during behavioral sleep in monkeys', *EEG clin. Neurophysiol.*, vol. 13, pp. 790–94.

WILLIAMS, H. L., MORLOCK, H. C., MORLOCK, J. V., and LUBIN, A. (1964), 'Auditory evoked responses and EEG stages of sleep', *Ann. N.Y. Acad. Sci.*, vol. 112, pp. 172–9.

20 André M. Weitzenhoffer

A Case of Pursuit-Like Eye Movements Directly Reflecting
Dream Content during Hypnotic Dreaming

André M. Weitzenhoffer, 'A case of pursuit-like eye movements directly reflecting
dream content during hypnotic dreaming', *Perceptual and Motor Skills*, vol. 32, 1971,
pp. 701–2.

In a recent article Deckert (1964) has reported polygraphically observing
pursuit eye movements essentially indistinguishable from those seen in the
actual tracking of a swinging pendulum taking place when hypnotized and
nonhypnotized individuals were asked to imagine such a device. On the
other hand, he was *unable* to obtain comparable results when his hypnotized
*S*s were instructed to hallucinate or to dream of a swinging pendulum, even
after being exposed to an actual one. The EOG segment reproduced here is
therefore of some interest as it was obtained from a hypnotized *S* *spontaneously* dreaming of watching a watch swing at the end of a chain.[1] When
instructed on a later occasion to have this dream again, the same kind of
record resulted.

Whether this *S* really dreamed or merely imagined the pendulum is
certainly a question one can raise (Moss, 1967). If we can go by *S*'s own
evaluation, and this is all one can ever really go by in the case of dreams,
both experiences were qualitatively dream-like. Furthermore, on the
occasion of the second dream, *S* had an opportunity also to imagine a watch
swinging while not hypnotized. Although the resulting eye movements
turned out to be in no appreciable way different from the dream EOGs, *S*
felt the two kinds of experiences to have been definitely different. It should
also be noted that the dream content in the first dream incident was un-
planned by either *S* or *E* and was a surprise to both.

Leaving this issue aside, the above EOG is also of interest in that it
concurs with the point recently made by Lennox, Lange and Graham (1970)
that while one can obtain pursuit-*like* eye movements in conjunction with an
imagined, a recalled (Brown, 1968) and now a 'dreamed' swinging pendu-

1. This occurred in connection with the administration of Item 6 of the Stanford
Scale of Hypnotic Susceptibility, Form C. This *S* scored 10 on Form A and 6 on Form
C. The EOG was obtained with a standard placement of electrodes for recording
horizontal conjugate eye movements. A Beckman RS Dynograph equipped with a
Nystagmus Coupler, Type 9859, and set for a time constant of three seconds was used.
The write-out was curvilinear. The writer wishes to express his appreciation for the
loan of the Dynograph by Jay T. Shurley, M.D., Senior Medical Investigator, Okla-
homa City V.A. Hospital.

lum, the movements do not replicate by any means those one obtains with a real pendulum. Not only is it now a well demonstrated fact (Lennnox, Lange and Graham, 1970; von Noorden and Preziosi, 1966) that with a simple physical pendulum the corresponding EOG is a nearly pure sine-wave, but this was amply verified for the present S. On the other hand for all intents and purposes, this S clearly produced a *rectangular* wave[2] in the first dream. This was found to be replicated both in the second dream and in the imagination situations. The fact that the previous samples of EOGs published by Deckert, by Brown, and by Lennox *et al.* also show more rectangularity or trapezoidness than sinusoidality suggests that perhaps in the absence of essential external feedback the normal, uninterfered with mode of oscillatory traverse of the eyes is a movement with uniform velocity with a brief but definite stopping prior to reversal, at least up to amplitudes of 20 to 30°.

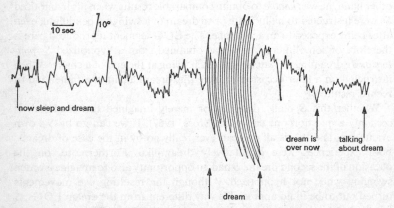

Figure 1 Eye movement excursion before, during and after the dream

As Lennox *et al.* have also reported, the amplitude of eye movements was found to be larger when S imagined with her eyes closed. The dream amplitude was of this latter order of magnitude too.

Obviously much remains to be done in this area before one can draw definite conclusions. In the meantime, the present sample of eye movements is offered in further support of the notion that the content of some imagined and dreamed visual experiences is reflected in specific ways in eye move-

2. What appears in the record as overshoots during the dream segment is primarily a distortion of the input caused by the three-second time constant which was used, as was separately verified. The input, more specifically, was actually a trapezoidal wave of considerable uniformity with a rise time of the order of 0·1 second. At the recording speed used it appeared as a near-rectangular wave.

ments. The present results also suggest there is a close relationship between nondream and dream visual and/or motor imagery.

References

BROWN, B. B. (1968), 'Visual recall ability and eye movements', *Psychophysiology*, vol. 4, pp. 300–306.

DECKERT, G. T. (1964), 'Pursuit eye movements in the absence of a moving visual stimulus', *Science*, vol. 143, pp. 1192–3.

LENNOX, J. R., LANGE, A. F., and GRAHAM, K. R. (1970), 'Eye movement amplitudes in imagined pursuit of a pendulum with eyes closed', *Psychophysiology*, vol. 6, pp. 773–7.

MOSS, C. S. (1967), *The Hypnotic Investigation of Dreams*, Wiley.

VON NOORDEN, G. K., and PREZIOSI, T. J. (1966), 'Eye movement recordings in neurological disorders', *Arch. Ophthal.*, vol. 76, pp. 162–71.

Part Two
The Effects of REM Sleep Deprivation

If REM sleep and dreams perform vital biological functions then depriving humans or animals of this kind of sleep should produce the impairments one would expect when those functions are not being performed. Even if no obvious disturbances are forthcoming, one would expect deprivation to result in a greater need for REM sleep and dreams. The Readings in this Part are a record of the progress that has been made to date in this confusing field. Although the sanguine hopes of some experimenters have not been fulfilled, many interesting phenomena have now been unearthed.

In Reading 21, Dement, who is one of the leading researchers in this field, reviews the effects of REM deprivation and describes his work which emphasizes the importance of the phasic as opposed to the tonic components of REM sleep. This distinction is discussed fully in Reading 30. Dement, Henry, Cohen and Ferguson describe a long series of experiments on animals which show that REM deprivation increases both behavioural and brain excitability (Reading 22). These findings have now been extended (see Cohen, Thomas and Dement, 1970; Morden, Conner, Mitchell, Dement and Levine, 1968). The biochemistry of REM sleep and REM deprivation is complicated and our knowledge of it is, at present, partial and confused. Some of this knowledge is displayed in the next two Readings. Hernández-Peón, Drucker, Ramírez del Angel, Chavez and Serrano (Reading 23) find an increase in brain stem dopamine in REM deprived cats, and Oswald (Reading 24) critically reviews the literature relating drugs, REM deprivation and REM sleep rebound. The chief disagreement on REM biochemistry is about the respective functions of the catecholamines and indole amines, particularly noradrenaline and serotonin (see Hartmann, 1970; Jouvet, 1967; Vogel, 1968), but acetylcholine also seems to be involved (Bowers, Hartmann and Freedman, 1966). Many theorists have related dreaming and REM sleep to one or more aspects of memory development and organization. These ideas have been tested by investigating the effects of deprivation on learning and retention.

Reading 25 is an example of such an experiment with rats. Analogous effects have been observed in humans (Greenberg, 1970; Lester, Chanes and Condit, 1969; Stern, 1970) and Hartmann and Stern (1972) have related the deprivation induced amnesia found in animals to a reversible depletion of catecholamines.

Finally, here, we include a study by Cartwright and Ratzel (Reading 26) on the effects of dream loss on waking mentation among differing subjects.

References

BOWERS, M. B., HARTMANN, E., and FREEDMAN, D. X. (1966), 'Sleep deprivation and brain acetylcholine', *Science*, vol. 153, pp. 1416–17.

COHEN, H., THOMAS, J., and DEMENT, W. C. (1970), 'Sleep stages, REM deprivation and electroconvulsive threshold in the cat', *Brain Res.*, vol. 19, pp. 317–21.

GREENBERG, R. (1970), 'Dreaming and memory', in E. Hartmann (ed.), *Sleep and Dreaming*, Little, Brown.

HARTMANN, E. (1970), 'The D-state and norepinephrine-dependent systems', in E. Hartmann (ed.), *Sleep and Dreaming*, Little, Brown.

HARTMANN, E., and STERN, W. C. (1972), 'Desynchronized sleep deprivation: learning deficit and its reversal by increased catecholamines', *Physiol. Behav.*, vol. 8, pp. 585–7.

JOUVET, M. (1967), 'Mechanisms of the states of sleep: a neuropharmacological approach', *Research Publications of the Association in Nervous and Mental Disease*, vol. 45, pp. 86–126.

LESTER, B. K., CHANES, R. E., and CONDIT, P. T. (1969), 'A clinical syndrome and EEG-sleep changes associated with amino-acid deprivation', *Amer. J. Psychiat.*, vol. 126, pp. 185–90.

MORDEN, B., CONNER, R., MITCHELL, G., DEMENT, W., and LEVINE, S. (1968), 'Effects of rapid eye movement (REM) sleep deprivation on shock-induced fighting', *Physiol. Behav.*, vol. 3, pp. 425–32.

STERN, W. C. (1970), 'The D-state, dreaming and memory', in E. Hartmann (ed.), *Sleep and Dreaming*, Little, Brown.

VOGEL, G. W. (1968), 'REM deprivation: III. Dreaming and psychosis', *Arch. gen. Psychiat.*, vol. 18, pp. 312–29.

21 William C. Dement

The Biological Role of REM Sleep (circa 1968)

William C. Dement, 'The biological role of REM sleep (circa 1968)', in A. Kales (ed.), *Sleep: Physiology and Pathology*, Lippincott, 1969, pp. 245–65.

In spite of the early and dramatic demonstration of the association of REM sleep with dreaming, Aserinsky and Kleitman's report of the discovery of REM sleep in 1953 remained virtually unnoticed by the scientific community for the rest of the decade. With the advent of the 1960s, however, REM sleep became the focus of an exceptionally intense research interest involving investigators from all scientific disciplines. None the less, we do not appear to be in any imminent danger of a final solution to what has been called 'the biological riddle of the decade' – the function or purpose of REM sleep – but some interesting new possibilities have appeared on the horizon, and several formal theoretical proposals (Berger, 1969; Roffwarg, Muzio and Dement, 1966; Snyder, 1966) have yet to be definitively tested.

Properties of REM sleep: tonic events versus phasic events

The properties of REM sleep are discussed in chapters 5 and 7 [not included here]. The descriptive aspects of REM sleep, and NREM sleep as well, have also received a detailed treatment in several books in the past year (Hartmann, 1967; Koella, 1967; Witkin and Lewis, 1967), in addition to a number of excellent reviews (Dement *et al.*, 1969; Fisher, 1965; Jouvet, 1967; Kales and Berger, 1970; Snyder and Scott, 1972; Zanchetti, 1967). Of particular relevance in the attempt to understand the function of REM sleep is the fact that the physiological concomitants of this state may be divided into two distinct classes, which have been termed *phasic events* and *tonic events* (Moruzzi, 1965). Tonic events are those long-lasting changes or characteristics that more or less define the REM period, since they are, for the most part, continuously maintained throughout its duration. EEG activation, EMG suppression, and brain temperature elevation are examples of tonic events. Phasic events refer to activities that are short-lasting and discontinuous. In addition to the rapid eye movements themselves, some of the activities that fall into this category are middle ear muscle contractions (Dewson, Dement and Simmons, 1965), cardiorespiratory irregularities (Gassel *et al.*, 1964; Snyder, Hobson and Goldfrank, 1963), muscular twitching (Dement, 1958; Luckhardt, 1915–16), and the unique bursts of monophasic sharp waves that characterize the electrical activity of the pons, oculomotor nuclei, lateral geniculate nuclei, and visual cortices (Brooks and Bizzi, 1963; Michel *et al.*, 1964) during REM periods. It seems likely that these monophasic sharp waves, hereafter referred to as PGO (pontine-geniculate-occipital) spikes, represent some sort of primary triggering process of phasic events in general, particularly eye movements. The fact that PGO spikes nearly always appear some time before the actual onset of the REM period is compatible with this notion. There are definite temporal relationships among phasic events and a marked tendency for several systems to be active at the same time.

In addition to the welcome taxonomic refinement, the distinction between tonic and phasic events must be emphasized because under certain conditions they may be dissociated. The first clear-cut demonstration of such a dissociation was accomplished by Delorme, Jeannerod and Jouvet (1965), who showed that REM periods were abolished by high doses of reserpine in the cat, but that a continuous PGO spike discharge was evident throughout the period of suppression.

An important principle is suggested by these results – namely, that at least two distinct neurological systems and/or mechanisms are involved in the REM phenomenon: (1) a system that produces REM periods, in effect, a tonic event system; and (2) a system that generates or triggers the phasic events, particularly the PGO spikes. It is possible, although by no means proved, that the phasic events rather than REM periods more specifically reflect the neurological activity underlying the experience of dreaming. Since phasic events (PGO spikes) occur in NREM sleep (although maximal discharge is during REM sleep), such a relation would be more consistent with the reported occurrence of NREM dreaming (Foulkes, 1967).

Selective REM sleep deprivation

The REM phenomenon is so ubiquitous, so complex, and so well represented in terms of brain areas allocated to its structures and mechanisms that it is not likely to have evolved solely as a caprice of nature. We must therefore assume that it does have a vital role to play – a role which we will eventually be able to describe with precision and profit. When questions have arisen concerning the function of an organ or system, the classical biological approach to the problem has been extirpation. The first systematic REM deprivation experiments were performed on human subjects in 1960 (Dement, 1960). The onset of REM periods being relatively unambiguous, it was possible to arouse sleeping subjects at the moment of transition into REM sleep and by continuing this procedure throughout entire nights, REM-sleep time could be drastically reduced without seriously curtailing the time spent in NREM sleep. The original purpose was to observe the consequences of loss of REM sleep, particularly in the realm of waking function. However, the most compelling results were found elsewhere and had to do with a dramatic shift in sleep patterns during recovery. It was noted that curtailment of REM sleep for several nights was followed on recovery nights by a marked lengthening and increased frequency of REM periods so that total REM time was elevated substantially above baseline values even if the total amount of sleep was unchanged. This REM deprivation-compensation phenomenon is by now quite well established, having been confirmed several times in human subjects (Clemes and Dement, 1967; Dement, 1965a; Dement, Greenberg and Klein, 1966; Kales et al., 1964; Sampson, 1966) as well as in experimental animals, e.g., the cat (Dement et al., 1967; Jouvet et al., 1964), rabbit (Khazan and Sawyer, 1963), monkey (Berger and Meier, 1966), rat (Morden, Mitchell and Dement, 1967), and mouse (Cohen and Dement, 1968). Although a restorative process and, by inference, a need for REM sleep is suggested, no study has shown that REM deprivation has significant functional consequences for the waking life of human subjects.

Animal experiments

The selective deprivation of REM sleep in experimental animals – in contrast to that in man – has produced clear changes in waking behavior. The reason for this seeming discrepancy is simply that, with greater experimental license, REM sleep could be eliminated for much longer periods in animal studies. The methods for accomplishing prolonged REM deprivation emphasized either (1) continuous polygraphic monitoring and around-the-clock interruption of REM periods, or (2) placing the animal in a situation where the motor inhibition associated with the REM period cannot be tolerated, for example, on a small support surrounded by water or on a treadmill moving toward a water tank. In either case the muscular atony that always accompanies REM sleep causes the cat to fall into the water and awaken. These methods have been described in detail elsewhere (Dement et al., 1967, 1969; Morden et al., 1968a). We have succeeded in REM-depriving cats for periods up to sixty-nine consecutive days. A tendency on recovery nights for the total amount of rebound to increase as REM deprivation periods were lengthened was demonstrated in cats (Dement et al., 1969) which confirmed earlier results in man (Dement, 1965). However, in most studies a plateau was reached at around twenty-five to thirty days of deprivation, after which additional loss of REM sleep elicited *no* additional compensation (see Figure 1).

The behavioral changes produced by prolonged REM sleep deprivation in cats can be characterized as an overall enhancement of motivational

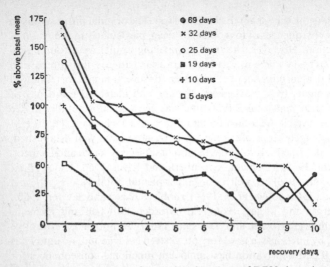

Figure 1 Recovery curves for varying durations of REM sleep deprivation. Percentage increases were computed by comparing the mean daily baseline REM time (in minutes) with the total minutes of REM sleep on each successive recovery day. All cats were maintained on a 16:8 schedule throughout (sixteen hours on treadmill to eight hours in recording cage). Note the essential identity of the thirty-two- and sixty-nine-day curves

behaviors (Clemes and Dement, 1967; Dement, 1965b, 1969; Dement *et al.*, 1967; Morden *et al.*, 1968a). The most dramatic and unequivocal behavioral change seen in the REM-deprived cat is the development of abnormal sexual behavior characterized by persistent attempts to mount other male cats (awake or anesthetized). In all positive cases, the 'hypersexuality' disappeared when the cat was allowed to recover from the deprivation. Some of the cats in this latter group were REM-deprived a second time after recovery periods ranging from two weeks to fourteen months, and in every instance the hypersexuality reappeared. We have obtained similar behavioral changes using the rat as the experimental animal (Morden *et al.*, 1968a, 1968b).

In contrast to the alteration of 'motivational' behaviors, no consistent changes were observed in the basic perceptual and motor functions, and there was no evidence of a disruption or impairment in high level processes, such as learning and memory. Finally, REM sleep deprivation, even when most prolonged, did not elicit hallucinatory behavior in cats. This was contrary to expectations, because the association of REM sleep and dream activity demonstrated in man had led us to postulate that dreaming or its feline analogue might eventually erupt into the waking state if blocked from occurring in sleep.

The early REM-deprivation studies had suggested that lost REM sleep might be made up on an exact, minute-for-minute basis, thus suggesting an obligatory quota of REM sleep, whereas the data from longer deprivation experiments in animals had revealed a sizeable discrepancy between amount of REM sleep lost during the deprivation and amount made up during the subsequent recovery. Furthermore (as mentioned earlier), when the duration of deprivation was extended beyond twenty-five to thirty days, no additional compensation was elicited.

The first major attempt to resolve the problem created by large deprivation-compensation discrepancies observed in the studies of prolonged REM suppression involved specific measurement of the frequency of *phasic events* (i.e. the number of events per minute of REM sleep). The results showed that during recovery, phasic events increase in frequency as a function of prior REM deprivation (Ferguson and Dement, 1968), thus revealing another mode of adjustment in which a change in the 'intensity' of REM sleep may also contribute to the compensatory process and obviate the need for a minute-for-minute make-up. Nearly all phasic-event systems appear to participate in this response.

If we consider, as already suggested, that the mean frequency of phasic events describes the 'intensity' of REM sleep, and if 'intensity' increases as a result of deprivation, then the notion of an obligatory REM quota becomes a little more tenable. To test this possibility, we calculated 'intensity factors' for successive REM sleep samples during deprivation and recovery by counting PGO spikes. Thus, if 100 PGO spikes occurred per minute of REM sleep in a deprived cat, as compared to an average of fifty per minute during its baseline REM periods, we would say that the post-deprivation REM sleep sample had an intensity factor of 2, or that its 'compensatory value' had doubled. However, even after correcting for intensity changes, we found that significant discrepancies remained between amount of REM sleep lost during prolonged deprivation and amount made up during recovery.

In attempting to interpret these intensity changes, we faced two possibilities: (1) that any presumed obligatory aspect of REM sleep might involve *only* the phasic events, and (2) that the REM period itself might function solely as a facilitatory state permitting maximal discharge of phasic activities without, at the same time, provoking behavioral consequences, thanks to the peripheral motor inhibition associated with REM periods. If this were true, the actual amount of REM-sleep time needed by the individual organism would be a function of the intensity of phasic discharge in REM periods plus the number of phasic events achieving alternative discharge in NREM sleep.

To test the possibility that the loss of phasic activity is at the root of the compensatory response, and also the functional equivalence of NREM and REM spikes, we decided to deprive cats of REM periods plus NREM PGO spikes by arousing them immediately after the occurrence of the first detectable PGO spike in NREM sleep. We have called this procedure 'spike deprivation' (Ferguson *et al.*, 1968). The sleep patterns of the animals were first recorded on a baseline schedule. This was followed by two days of either spike or REM sleep deprivation, after which four or five recovery days were recorded. The REM sleep rebounds following two days of spike deprivation were compared to the rebounds following an *identical* period of classical REM sleep deprivation with each cat as his own control, and the order of treatments counterbalanced. Figure 2 shows the difference between spike deprivation and REM sleep deprivation. Essentially, the spike deprivation procedure is nothing more than making the REM deprivation arousals a little sooner, which also effectively eliminates the occurrence of NREM PGO spikes. In all cats, the spike deprivation procedure resulted in a substantially larger compensatory REM rebound than the rebound following the elimination of REM sleep alone. We also found that if the standard awakenings from REM sleep deprivation were made with exceeding gentleness, each REM period could be effectively derailed, but a new buildup of NREM PGO spikes would take place almost immediately. By doing this, we were occasionally able to allow the discharge of very large numbers of PGO spikes via NREM sleep in several cats while at the same time accomplishing a total suppression of REM periods. *Two days of this latter procedure was followed by a very small or nonexistent REM sleep rebound!*

These results strongly support the suggestion that the crucial factor in the so-called REM sleep deprivation–compensation phenomenon is really the deprivation of phasic events. Postdeprivation increases in total REM time should therefore be regarded as an essentially passive response to an accumulated need to discharge phasic events, and *not* as a response to the loss of REM sleep *per se*. The marked *reduction* of the REM rebound produced by maximizing the occurrence of NREM PGO spikes during a two-day period of complete REM deprivation is direct evidence for the postulated irrelevance of the REM periods themselves.

Neuropharmacological and behavioral studies

Recent neuropharmacological evidence also points to the primacy of phasic events (PGO spike) in the REM deprivation–compensation phenomenon. Delorme *et al.* (1965) were the first to describe the complete dissociation of

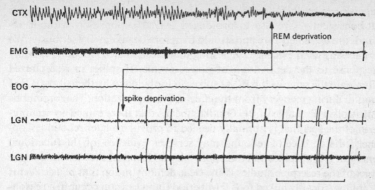

Figure 2 A comparison of 'spike' deprivation and REM deprivation. In the latter procedure, the cat would have been aroused at the exact onset of the REM period (arrow on right) signaled by EMG supression and EEG activation. If the cat had been undergoing spike deprivation, the arousal would have been made a little earlier (arrow on left), immediately after the first PGO spike. In this example, the spike deprivation arousal would have deprived the cat of ten NREM PGO spikes in addition to those that would have occurred in the subsequent REM period, and about twenty seconds of NREM sleep. Calibrations: 10 sec and 50 μV. Electroencephalograms are from surface recordings (CTX) and the lateral geniculate nucleus (LGN)

phasic events from REM periods in reserpinized cats. After administration of 0·5 mg/kg reserpine, their animals were polygraphically awake, behaviorally comatose, and showed an uninterrupted discharge of PGO spikes. Since the major effect of reserpine is a depletion of brain serotonin, dopamine, and norepinephrine, and since this depletion was associated with an absence of both REM sleep and NREM sleep, Delorme *et al.* reasoned that these amines might play important roles in the regulation of the states of sleep. Confirming this notion, they found that NREM sleep could be restored and the freely discharging PGO spikes suppressed if the reserpinized animal were given an injection of 5-hydroxytryptophan, and that the reappearance of REM sleep was facilitated by administration of dopa. Thus, serotonin appeared to be involved in the regulation of NREM sleep and norepinephrine in the regulation of REM sleep.

Professor Jouvet has reviewed his subsequent studies in chapter 7 [not included here], and his results are highly relevant to our own work. I emphasize one particular finding: that the long periods of REM sleep suppression provoked by reserpinization are *not* followed by compensatory rebounds. Other drugs have been shown to suppress REM sleep – for example, amphetamine (Oswald and Thacore, 1963; Rechtschaffen and Maron, 1964) and Parnate (Le Gassicke *et al.*, 1965). Withdrawal of these drugs is customarily followed by enormous REM rebounds. Circumstances that consistently give rise to prolonged REM suppression without rebounds are extremely rare and should therefore be taken very seriously. We have already cited evidence suggesting that a REM sleep rebound is really a response to the deprivation of phasic events. If spikes in reserpinized animals are the same as the PGO spikes, it is obvious why there is no REM rebound during recovery from the effects of reserpinization. The continuous uncontrolled discharge of PGO spikes means that there can be no accumulation of the sort that is normally needed to provoke a later rebound. Conversely, the absence of rebound may serve as evidence for the functional identity of REM spikes and reserpine spikes. However, the most important aspect of the reserpine studies is the clear demonstration that phasic events are not inextricably linked to REM periods, and can still occur in a reasonably characteristic manner even though the mechanisms producing REM periods have been totally disrupted.

What if we now assume the validity of the proposition that the primary function of REM sleep is to facilitate the discharge of phasic events? At a stroke, the problem of REM sleep is solved. But an even more perplexing problem immediately takes its place – namely, what is the purpose of the phasic activity and why should a daily discharge of these events be necessary? Since PGO spikes discharge at a maximal rate during REM periods, a rate many times that seen in NREM sleep, it is obvious that REM deprivation also results in the almost complete deprivation of spike or phasic events. It is, therefore, quite possible that the behavioral consequences of REM sleep deprivation are really due to the accumulation of undischarged phasic activities. If so, we may conclude that this accumulation leads directly to an enhancement of drive-oriented or motivational behavior.

It was mentioned earlier that the duration of REM sleep deprivation required to produce dramatic behavioral changes is quite long. The shortest duration of standard REM deprivation that elicited hypersexuality in a male cat was seven days, and the mean duration of all deprivations producing this change was eighteen days. It is of great interest, then, that only *two* days of spike deprivation was sufficient to produce the characteristic compulsive mounting behavior in four of the seven cats undergoing the procedure.

The effect of serotonin depletion

Our interest in the biological role of the phasic events of REM sleep and their possible relation to drive has led us to undertake a very intensive study of sleeping and waking behavior in cats being treated with para-chlorophenylalanine (PCPA). The studies of Koe and Weissman (1966) indicate that this compound inhibits the synthesis of serotonin in brain by blocking the hydroxylation of tryptophan. Delorme and his colleagues (1966) reported that administration of PCPA induces a profound insomnia in cats. They also reported that near-total ablation of the raphe nuclei in the brain stem is likewise followed by insomnia and a marked drop in the serotonin levels of forebrain structures (Jouvet *et al.*, 1967). The nuclei of the raphe are of great interest because they contain nearly all of the brain's complement of serotonergic neurons (Dahlstrom and Fuxe, 1964). Finally, the Lyon investigators reported that PGO spikes appear in the waking state of the PCPA-treated cats. These findings have led Jouvet to postulate that the serotonergic neurons of the raphe system and their rostrally projecting axons constitute a NREM sleep-inducing system.

Our own studies have led us to a quite different conclusion about the role of serotonin and serotonin neurons in the brain. These studies have involved continuous polygraphic and behavioral observations of cats twenty-four hours a day, seven days a week, for up to two or more months. In addition, some cats are maintained on a specifically enforced sleep–wakefulness schedule in which the recording time is less than twenty-four hours and the remainder of the time is spent on a treadmill. The treadmill completely prevents the occurrence of REM sleep and all but very brief episodes of NREM sleep. After a prolonged baseline period, we begin the administration of PCPA at some dose level, and repeat that dose each day throughout the course of the experiments. The first dose of PCPA has no observable effect, except that the REM time is generally a little higher. After the first twenty-four hours, the temporal course is subject to considerable individual variation. However, at some specific point in time, and almost literally within minutes, monophasic sharp waves bearing an exact resemblance to PGO spikes begin to appear during wakefulness in each cat. Figure 3 illustrates the development of this change.

Nearly all other important changes occur in close association with the appearance of PGO spikes in the lateral geniculate and cortical recordings of the *waking* cat. Hallucinatory behavior begins to accompany bursts of spikes. A severe insomnia develops. Finally, the animal undergoes a profound and previously undescribed behavioral change, which entails the emergence of rage behavior, hypersexuality, hyperphagia, and a sort of general personality change that may take any number of forms, to some extent depending on the cat's previous disposition. The sexual changes are more intense and dramatic than any elicited by REM deprivation alone. For example, we have seen previously indifferent male cats compulsively mount not only anesthetized male cats and passive male cats, but relentlessly stalk a raging, clawing, highly resistant tom and persevere until the quarry is finally backed into a corner where a mount can be executed.

Although the full-blown PCPA effect takes several days to develop

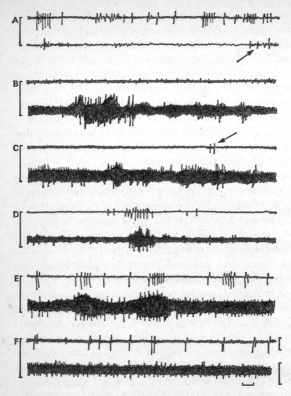

Figure 3 Development of PGO spikes in the waking state in a cat during administration of PCPA. Tracings were selected from a single four-hour time period (0400 to 0800) when the major changes occurred. The top tracing of each pair is a bipolar recording from the left lateral geniculate nucleus (LGN) and the other is the simultaneous EMG. Calibrations: 50 μV and 1 sec. A, at 1410, REM sleep with typical PGO spike activity and EMG suppression is concomitant with a flurry of muscular twitching. B, wakefulness without PGO spikes. The EMG is characteristic of the waking state, and the brief increases in discharge reflect gross body movement. C, at 0437, forty-five hours after PCPA administration, the first unequivocal PGO spike occurred during wakefulness (arrow). D, 0449, the first good burst of spike activity accompanied by searching movements of the head and eyes (note EMG upsurge). E, at 0630, the PGO spike discharge was virtually continuous, and the cat remained fully awake for several hours. F, sample illustration of the variability in discharge pattern of PGO spikes. There is a less intense, nonbursting level of PGO spike activity with a steady level in the EMG (lack of gross body movement)

(which may simply represent the time it takes to reach the critical degree of serotonin depletion), a nearly instantaneous reversal of both the electrophysiological and the behavioral changes can be accomplished by administering very small amounts of the serotonin precursor, 5-hydroxytryptophan. The first effect of PCPA appears to be a slight increase in the spike frequency within the REM periods. However, after two or three days on the drug, a slight decline is evident, and when PGO spikes appear in the waking state, the frequency *within* REM periods shows a rapid exponential fall to a substantially lower value. At first, only occasional PGO spikes are seen in the waking state, but the frequency increases very quickly to a plateau always less than the discharge rate within REM periods. PGO spikes become almost continuous in NREM sleep – that is, there are no prolonged periods of NREM without spikes. In the case of a high dose of PCPA, the frequencies in the three states appear to approach each other. It is as if all regulation had ceased, allowing the spike discharge to disperse itself more or less equally, regardless of background state.

While the initial release of PGO spikes in the waking state seems to trigger the development of a markedly accentuated drive state, the approach to a situation of complete dispersion of spike discharge seems to have the opposite effect. The animal becomes more and more lethargic and shows less and less drive-oriented behaviour. In such an animal the spikes occur less frequently in bursts and appear to lose their power to disturb the animal. Periods of NREM sleep become longer and longer, and by the seventh or eighth day of PCPA administration, the daily total of NREM sleep has returned to a maximal value, which is often very near the baseline amount. Figure 4 shows a typical result in one cat.

We have confirmed the reports of Jouvet and his colleagues that PCPA causes a severe, albeit highly transitory, insomnia. However, we have a different view about the basic cause of the insomnia. Of particular importance to this view is the fact that neither REM nor NREM sleep are significantly disturbed until PGO spikes appear in the waking state. It is our opinion that the insomnia is not primary but rather a consequence of uncontrolled PGO spike discharge. The nearly constant occurrence of spike bursts, which appear to affect the animal as if they were external stimuli, simply creates too much disturbance for him to fall asleep. Both sleep and waking repose are continuously interrupted as the animal is aroused by, and cannot help attending to, these endogenously triggered bursts of activity.

As a final test that the spikes released by PCPA into the waking state are the same as the spikes that ordinarily occur only during REM periods and the immediately prior NREM sleep periods, we have undertaken to REM-deprive a number of cats in the midst of the full-blown PCPA syndrome. At this point, daily REM time has usually equilibrated at levels 20 to 50 per cent below the nondrug baseline. Since the REM deprivation–compensation phenomenon is related to the accumulation of phasic events, we reasoned that the deprivation rebound should be low or absent in the PCPA-treated cat because PGO spikes prevented from discharging in

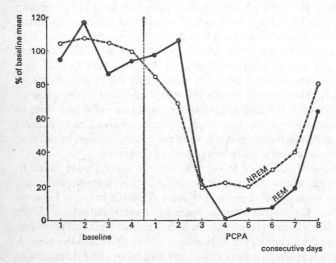

Figure 4 Changes in daily amounts of REM sleep and NREM sleep in cat receiving p-chlorophenylalanine (PCPA) and recorded twenty-four hours per day. All the recordings were carefully scored through a baseline period and eight consecutive twenty-four-hour periods on the serotonin-depleting drug. The daily values for REM and NREM sleep are expressed as per cent of the baseline mean. Note that no significant change occurs in the first two days of PCPA administration except possibly a modest rise in the total REM time. On the third PCPA day, there is a precipitous drop in both kinds of sleep. By the eighth PCPA day the sleep levels are turning toward normal (although still substantially below the baseline values). Brain serotonin is approximately zero at this point, a level suggesting that it is not a crucial agent in the production of either NREM sleep or REM sleep

REM periods would be readily discharged in wakefulness and no accumulation would take place. A fairly typical result is shown in Figure 5. Even when measured against the lower PCPA baseline REM time, there is no REM sleep rebound. This result exactly parallels our previous findings of no REM rebound after REM deprivation in schizophrenic patients (Zarcone *et al.*, 1968, 1969) and has far-reaching implications for understanding the bizarre abnormalities of behavior that accompany this illness.

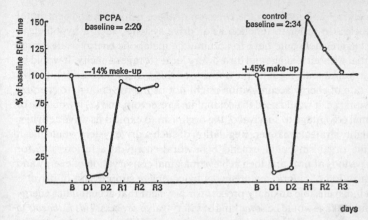

Figure 5 Rebound failure in a cat under prolonged treatment with
p-chlorophenylalanine (PCPA). The daily REM-time values in this cat
during the two deprivation periods are expressed in per cent of the baseline
REM-sleep time. Since there is usually a small reduction in the daily REM
time after an animal has been stabilized on PCPA, 100 per cent of baseline
actually represents a different value in the PCPA condition versus the control
condition. Although this cat was averaging two hours and twenty minutes of
REM sleep per day on a 12:12 schedule (twelve hours on treadmill to twelve
hours in recording cage) in the PCPA condition, two days of deprivation
resulted in no make-up at all. The REM rebound following the similar period of
deprivation prior to the administration of PCPA was of normal size. The
failure to rebound while on PCPA is to all intents an exact duplication of the
results of REM sleep deprivation in actively ill schizophrenic patients. It is
possible that the animal on long-term PCPA treatment may serve as a useful
model of the actively psychotic condition in man

REM sleep and its place in the scheme of things

All of the foregoing results have led us to postulate a functional role for
REM sleep somewhat different from our past speculations. Perhaps the
primary shift in emphasis in *current* experimentation is that it takes cog-
nizance of the almost certain fact that there are two distinct mechanisms
involved in REM sleep. One mechanism has to do with the production of
REM periods and the other mechanism has to do with elaboration and
regulation of phasic events.

Because of the effect of serotonin depletion on behavior and sleep, we
must assume that the serotonergic neurons in the brain stem are primarily
concerned with the regulation of drive. There is good evidence that the brain
stem and certain other critical loci of the CNS contain a variety of more or
less preprogramed behavioral reflexes or tendencies. It is suggested that
they also house a neural or glial system whose specific function is, in effect,

to 'energize' and maintain the emission of these behaviors and behavioral tendencies. In order to function as a 'drive system', such a hypothetical neural aggregate would have to accumulate metabolic energy as discharge potential without leakage and have a very large storage capacity. It would be highly desirable to regulate the activity of this system because (1) its own basal rate of energy accumulation might not be intense enough to energize behaviors, i.e. it would need to accumulate a reservoir, and (2) it would be of maximal advantage to survival of the organism to expend its drive activities in a highly strategic manner. Regulation of such a drive system would mean that the organism could expend behavioral energy at a furious rate for short periods of time and then achieve maximal conservation of energy and minimization of caloric requirements by complete suppression of drive.

An indispensable auxiliary process for a system that accumulates energy without leakage would be some kind of safety-valve process. *This is the role to which we believe REM sleep has been assigned.* This remarkable state, by inducing an extensive peripheral motor inhibition, can allow a great deal of neural activity to take place in the brain without any behavioral consequence. It is likely that the REM periods are to some extent triggered and maintained by the PGO spikes whose discharge they facilitate. Thus, the intensity and duration of the REM periods would be a passive reflection of the need to discharge, or of the pressure or accumulation in, the hypothetical drive reservoir. When the reservoir is depleted, as in the PCPA-treated cat, the REM-period mechanism simply produces a fairly constant, but relatively small, amount of REM sleep.

Although we have spoken of PGO spike discharge and drive discharge almost interchangeably, it is actually our assumption that these two alternatives are quite different and that the postulated drive system may discharge its energy by one of these two paths, but not both at the same time: (1) during wakefulness as it functions to energize and/or induce drive-oriented behavior, (2) during REM sleep, when its discharge is reflected by PGO-spike electrical activity. We have not seen PGO spikes either in normal animals or in PCPA-treated animals at the exact time that the animal is executing a drive-oriented response in the waking state. This and the fact that such spikes in the PCPA-treated animal are associated with hallucinations lead us to favor the notion that the discharge in REM sleep is not precisely the same as drive discharge via behavior in the waking state. In our general formulation, the suppression of drive in turn might be equated with the occurrence of NREM sleep. The overall drive state could be lowered by active suppression under the influence of serotonergic neurons or by depletion of drive energy. The eventual (in seven or eight days) lowering of drive state associated with the unrestricted PGO spike discharge produced by chronic PCPA administration is an example of the latter case. An example of the former is the fact that drive state is obviously reduced by administration of 5-hydroxytryptophan, the serotonin precursor that immediately precipitates NREM sleep in the normal animal.

In terms of a general regulation of behavior, we have postulated that the utilization of serotonin would be directly related to the need to control phasic events. This need would be greatest in the REM-deprived animal. A corollary of this notion is that the turnover or utilization of serotonin would be minimal during REM periods, REM periods being a time in which the serotonin regulatory systems are 'turned off'. Accordingly, we have assumed that REM periods occurring during the first several days of PCPA administration will buffer the fall of brain serotonin, and conversely, that the onset of the full-blown PCPA effect would occur sooner if the animal were deprived of REM periods during the first two days. This latter effect has been dramatically demonstrated in several cats.

Summary

1. The basic biological function of REM sleep continues to be a puzzle to sleep researchers although a number of theories have been propounded.

2. The physiological concomitants of REM sleep may be divided into two classes of events, *phasic* and *tonic*, which can be dissociated from each other under certain circumstances.

3. Experiments involving prolonged REM sleep deprivation have not demonstrated that this procedure is harmful to the organism. A consistent result has been enhancement of drive.

4. Both the postdeprivation REM rebound and the behavioral changes may be attributed to the accumulation of undischarged phasic activities.

5. The depletion of cerebral serotonin is followed by unrestricted discharge of PGO spikes and marked augmentation of drive-oriented behavior.

6. The rate of PGO spike discharge in the PCPA animal declines steadily, suggesting depletion of a 'reservoir'. At the same time, NREM- and REM-sleep times return to normal levels.

7. The existence of a neuronal 'drive system', which discharges either behaviorally or via REM sleep-associated phasic activities, is hypothesized. It is postulated that serotonergic neurons regulate this drive system.

8. The primary biological role of REM sleep is assumed to be that of providing a 'safety-valve' type of outlet for discharge of the drive system.

References

ASERINSKY, E., and KLEITMAN, N. (1953), 'Regularly occurring periods of eye motility, and concomitant phenomena during sleep', *Science*, vol. 118, p. 273.

BERGER, R. (1969), 'Oculomotor control: a possible function of REM sleep', *Psychol. Rev.*, vol. 76, p. 144.

BERGER, R., and MEIER, G. (1966), 'The effects of selective deprivation of states of sleep in the developing monkey', *Psychophysiology*, vol. 2, p. 354.

BROOKS, D., and BIZZI, E. (1963), 'Brain stem electrical activity during deep sleep', *Arch. Ital. Biol.*, vol. 101, p. 648.

CLEMES, S., and DEMENT, W. (1967), 'The effect of REM sleep deprivation on psychological functioning', *J. nerv. ment. Dis.*, vol. 144, p. 485.

COHEN, H., and DEMENT, W. (1968), 'Electrically induced convulsions in REM deprived mice: prolongation of the tonic phase', *Psychophysiology*, vol. 4, p. 381 (abstract).

DAHLSTROM, A., and FUXE, K. (1964), 'Evidence for the existence of monoamine neurons in the central nervous system: I. Demonstration of monoamines in the cell bodies of brain stem neurons', *Acta physiol. Scand. Suppl.*, vol. 232.

DELORME, F., FROMENT, J., and JOUVET, M. (1966), 'Suppression du sommeil par la p-chloromethamphetamine et la p-chlorophenylalanine', *C R soc. biol.*, vol. 160, p. 2347.

DELORME, F., JEANNEROD, M., and JOUVET, M. (1965). 'Effets remarquables de la réserpine sur l'activité EEG phasique ponto-géniculo-occipitale', *C R soc. biol.*, vol. 159, p. 900.

DEMENT, W. (1958), 'The occurrence of low voltage, fast, electroencephalogram patterns during behavioral sleep in the cat', *EEG clin. Neurophysiol.*, vol. 10, p. 291.

DEMENT, W. (1960), 'The effect of dream deprivation', *Science*, vol. 131, p. 1705.

DEMENT, W. (1965a), 'Studies on the function of rapid eye movement (paradoxical) sleep in human subjects', in M. Jouvet (ed.), *Aspects anatomo-fonctionnels de la physiologie du sommeil*, Centre Nationale de la Recherche Scientifique, Paris, p. 571.

DEMENT, W. (1956b), 'Recent studies on the biological role of rapid eye movement sleep', *Amer. J. Psychiat.*, vol. 122, p. 404.

DEMENT, W., GREENBERG, S., and KLEIN, R. (1966), 'The effect of partial REM sleep deprivation and delayed recovery', *J. psychiat. Res.*, vol. 4, p. 141.

DEMENT, W., et al. (1967), 'Studies on the effect of REM deprivation in humans and in animals', in S. S. Kety, E. V. Evarts and H. L. Williams (eds.), *Sleep and Altered States of Consciousness*, Williams & Wilkins, p. 456.

DEMENT, W., et al. (1969), 'Nonchemical methods and data using a biochemical model: the REM quanta', in A. Mandell (ed.), *Psychochemical Research in Man: Methods, Strategy and Theory*, Academic Press, pp. 275–325.

DEWSON, J., DEMENT, W., and SIMMONS, F. (1965), 'Middle ear muscle activity in cats during sleep', *Exp. Neurol.*, vol. 12, p. 1.

GASSEL, M., et al. (1964), 'Phasic changes in blood pressure and heart rate during the rapid eye movement episodes of desynchronized sleep in unrestrained cats', *Arch. Ital. Biol.*, vol. 102, p. 530.

FERGUSON, J., and DEMENT, W. (1968), 'Changes in the intensity of REM sleep with deprivation', *Psychophysiology*, vol. 4, p. 380 (abstract).

FERGUSON, J., et al. (1968), 'Phasic event deprivation in the cat', *Psychophysiology*, vol. 5, p. 238 (abstract).

FISHER, C. (1965), 'Psychoanalytic implications of recent research on sleep and dreaming', *J. Amer. Psychoanal. Assn*, vol. 13, p. 197.

FOULKES, D. (1967), 'Nonrapid eye movement mentation', *Exp. Neurol. Suppl.*, vol. 4, p. 28.

HARTMANN, E. (1967), *The Biology of Dreaming*, C. C. Thomas.
JOUVET, D., *et al.* (1964), 'Etude de la privation selective de la phase paradoxale du sommeil chez le chat', *C R soc. biol.*, vol. 158, p. 756.
JOUVET, M. (1967), 'Neurophysiology of the states of sleep', *Physiol. Rev.*, vol. 47, p. 117.
JOUVET, M., *et al.* (1967), 'Suppression du sommeil et diminution de la serotonine cérébrale par lesion du système du raphé chez le chat', *C R acad. sci.* (*D*), vol. 264, p. 360.
KALES, A., and BERGER, R. (1970), 'Psychopathology of sleep', in C. G. Costello (ed.), *Symptoms of Psychopathology*, Wiley, pp. 418–47.
KALES, A., *et al.* (1964), 'Dream deprivation: an experimental reappraisal', *Nature*, vol. 204, p. 1337.
KHAZAN, N., and SAWYER, C. (1963), '"Rebound" recovery from deprivation of paradoxical sleep in the rabbit', *Proc. Soc. Exp. Biol. Med.*, vol. 114, p. 536.
KOE, B., and WEISSMAN, A. (1966), 'Para-chlorophenylalanine: a specific depletor of brain serotonin', *J. Pharm. exp. Ther.*, vol. 154, p. 499.
KOELLA, W. (1967), *Sleep: Its Nature and Physiological Organization*, C. C. Thomas.
LE GASSICKE, J., *et al.* (1965), 'The clinical state, sleep and amine metabolism of a tranylcypromine ("Parnate") addict', *Brit. J. Psychol.*, vol. 3, p. 357.
LUCKHARDT, A. (1915–16), 'Contributions to the physiology of the empty stomach: XXXI. The effect of dreaming on the gastric hunger contractions', *Amer. J. Physiol.*, vol. 39, p. 330.
MICHEL, F., *et al.* (1964), 'Sur les mécanismes de l'activité de pointes au niveau du système visuel au cours de la phase paradoxale du sommeil', *C R soc. biol.*, vol. 158, p. 103.
MORDEN, B., MITCHELL, G., and DEMENT, W. (1967), 'Selective REM sleep deprivation and compensation phenomena in the rat', *Brain Res.*, vol. 5, p. 339.
MORDEN, B., *et al.* (1968a), 'Effects of rapid eye movement (REM) sleep deprivation on shock-induced fighting', *Physiol. Behav.*, vol. 3, p. 425.
MORDEN, B., *et al.* (1968b), 'Effects of REM deprivation on the mating behavior of male rats', *Psychophysiology*, vol. 5, p. 241 (abstract).
MORUZZI, G. (1965), 'General discussion', in M. Jouvet (ed.), *Aspects anatomo-fonctionnels de la physiologie du sommeil*, Centre National de la Recherche Scientifique, Paris, p. 638.
OSWALD, I., and THACORE, V. (1963), 'Amphetamine and phenmetrazine addiction', *Brit. med. J.*, vol. 2, p. 427.
RECHTSCHAFFEN, A., and MARON, L. (1964), 'The effect of amphetamine on the sleep cycle', *EEG clin. Neurophysiol.*, vol. 16, p. 438.
ROFFWARG, H., MUZIO, J., and DEMENT, W. (1966), 'The ontogenetic development of the sleep–dream cycle in the human', *Science*, vol. 152, p. 604.
SAMPSON, H. (1966), 'Psychological effects of deprivation of dreaming sleep', *J. nerv. ment. Dis.*, vol. 143, p. 305.
SNYDER, F. (1966), 'Toward an evolutionary theory of dreaming', *Amer. J. Psychiat.*, vol. 123, p. 121.
SNYDER, F., and SCOTT, J. (1972), 'Psychophysiology of sleep', in N. Greenfield and R. Sternbach (eds.), *Handbook of Psychophysiology*, Holt, Rinehart & Winston.
SNYDER, F., HOBSON, J., and GOLDFRANK, F. (1963), 'Blood pressure changes during human sleep', *Science*, vol. 142, p. 1313.

WITKIN, H., and LEWIS, H. (1967), *Experimental Studies of Dreaming*, Random House.

ZANCHETTI, A. (1967), 'Brain stem mechanisms of sleep', *Anesthesiology*, vol. 28, p. 81.

ZARCONE, V., *et al.* (1968), 'Partial REM phase deprivation and schizophrenia', *Arch. gen. Psychiat.*, vol. 18, p. 194.

ZARCONE, V., *et al.* (1969), 'REM deprivation and schizophrenia', *Biol. Psychiat.*, vol. 1, pp. 179–84.

22 William Dement, Peter Henry, Harry Cohen and James Ferguson

Studies on the Effect of REM Deprivation in Humans
and in Animals

William Dement, Peter Henry, Harry Cohen and James Ferguson, 'Studies on the
effect of REM deprivation in humans and in animals', in S. S. Kety, E. V. Evarts and
H. L. Williams (eds.), from *Sleep and Altered States of Consciousness*, Proceedings of
the Association for Research in Nervous and Mental Disease, vol. 45, Williams &
Wilkins, 1967, pp. 456–68.

It has become almost commonplace to characterize rapid eye movement
sleep as a distinct biologic state (Dement, 1965a, 1966; Jouvet, 1962;
Oswald, 1962; Snyder, 1963, 1965a and b). Granted the accuracy of this
conceptualization, it follows that the normal mammalian organism spends
its entire life alternating among three states, namely, wakefulness, sleep and
the rapid eye movement state (REMS).

The function or adaptive significance of the waking state seems self-
evident – it enables the organism to operate upon its environment in such a
way as to insure its survival. The function of sleep (slow wave sleep) also
seems self-evident, although our level of confidence is not nearly so high. At
any rate, given its properties, it seems reasonable that sleep is a state which
provides a period of rest and restoration for the organism. Standing apart
from sleep and wakefulness, however, is the REMS, and its function is by
no means self-evident. Its properties are so singular that any attempt to
predict its possible function seems quite presumptuous. None the less, it is
this very uncertainty which makes the problem unusually attractive.

Many years ago, when physiologists first began to examine gross organ
functions, the usual approach was to remove the organ under question and
observe the result. As a first approach, we have attempted the analogous
procedure – to remove REM sleep and see what happens. As mentioned
elsewhere (Dement, 1965a), the discrete nature of REM periods plus their
readily discernible physiological trademark, EEG activation coupled with
EMG suppression, makes such a procedure feasible and relatively precise.
A variety of 'REMS extirpation' experiments will be described. In general,
it appears that the selective curtailment of REMS results in a change in
the organism that is perhaps best described as the induction of a hyper-
excitable state.

Methods

We have used several techniques of REMS deprivation which range from
'optimal' to 'practical'. As a rule, curtailment of the REMS is a procedure

that continues for many days in succession, including weekends, in which all sleep must be monitored in one way or another. Thus, the requirements of the procedure in sheer man-hours have often necessitated compromise.

Optimal procedure

Perhaps the best technique for the selective deprivation of REMS is to arouse the organism at the onset of each REM period throughout the entirety of a regular, lengthy (seven to eight hours) daily sleep session. The usual signal for the arousal is the suppression of EMG potentials recorded from the neck muscles, since this event generally precedes the full-blown appearance of REMS by a few seconds or more. In the case of humans, subjects are recorded every night for about eight hours and may be accompanied by a 'watcher' during the remainder of the day to be sure that on sleep occurs outside the laboratory. Subjects may serve as their own controls at some later date, at which time the procedure is repeated in all its details, except that the arousals are made *only* during slow wave (NREM) sleep. A major problem has been that the number of REM onset interruptions mounts so rapidly that a serious reduction of total sleep time occurs. In addition, there is a marked habituation to arousing stimuli. One way of meeting this problem has been to administer a small dose of dexedrine sulfate at bedtime as an adjuvant to the awakening procedure. This drug reduces the number of arousals that are needed and allows more opportunity to accumulate slow wave sleep (Dement, 1965a).

In the case of cats, a nearly identical procedure has been used, except that during the sixteen to seventeen hours per day that are not recorded, the animals are placed on a treadmill (Figure 1) to ensure that no REMs can occur. One variation of this is to have the cat sit on a small platform in a tank of water rather than remain on the treadmill. Sometimes both water tank and treadmill are used. The awakenings during the recording period must be accomplished by hand since rapid habituation renders such things as mesencephalic stimulation useless after several days. Dexedrine does not appear to be particularly effective in the cat as a REMS suppressor.

Both cats and humans appear to tolerate this method remarkably well. The amount of behavioral slow wave sleep that can be achieved is apparently sufficient to offset the development of fatigue and debilitation.

Modified optimal procedure

Arousing the organism at the onset of each REM period requires the constant attendance of an experienced observer and perhaps two observers if multiple animals are being studied. In order to decrease the work load, we deprived some animals of REMS by keeping them in a water tank or on the treadmill (with time out for feeding, exercise, cleaning and so on) for

Figure 1 Simplified drawing of cat on treadmill. Speed of belt can be varied and is usually adjusted so that if the cat walks to the front and rides back, he will have to move within fifteen to twenty seconds to avoid falling into the water

eighteen to twenty-two hours daily. The animals were recorded each day during a single period that varied from two to four hours depending upon the condition of the animal. If the animal appeared fatigued and debilitated, he was allowed four hours recording time; if he appeared healthy and active, the minimum time was allowed.

We have found, as have Jouvet and co-workers (1964), that the cat can enter the NREM state (slow waves and spindles appear in the EEG) while sitting on the platform in the water tank. The same thing happens during short periods on the treadmill, if the animal hurries to the front and sits quietly until he is carried to the back. However, it appears to be important for maintaining the well-being of the cat, that it has an opportunity to 'rest', that is, to sleep in a recumbent position in which his muscles must no longer resist the pull of gravity. Thus, the relatively short recording period seems to provide this needed rest. Control animals are allowed two to three hours of *undisturbed* behavioral sleep daily, and also spend the remainder of the time on the treadmill. Most of the undisturbed sleep in controls is taken up by the REMS (Ferguson and Dement, 1966).

Practical procedure

In this procedure, no recording is done. Except for feeding and routine care, the animals spend all their time either in the tank or on the treadmill. Large numbers of animals can be run at the same time with this method, but the degree of fatigue and debilitation becomes quite serious. Furthermore, there is no adequate control procedure for this method.

In all these procedures, the deprivation period was preceded by a baseline period during which cats were recorded throughout seven to eight hours of undisturbed sleep per day for a varying number of consecutive days.

REM-deprived state
Changes in REMS as result of its prior deprivation

The earliest finding as a result of REMS deprivation was that its propensity to occur increased. This was seen two ways: (a) the number of arousals during each successive recording period that was required to interrupt each REM episode at its onset increased progressively; (b) the percentage of REM sleep during a subsequent period of uninterrupted sleep was strikingly increased. These findings, made originally with human subjects (Dement, 1960; 1965a; Kales *et al.*, 1964; Oswald, 1962), have been confirmed in cats by several groups of investigators (Jouvet *et al.*, 1964; Kiyono *et al.*, 1965; Siegel and Gordon, 1965).

When either the 'optimal' or the 'modified optimal' procedures were used, the number of awakenings showed considerable fluctuation from day to day, but there was an overall progressive rise and the latency for the appearance of the first REM period decreased steadily so that eventually the animals went directly from wakefulness into the REMS. An example of the latency changes is shown in Figure 2. In all cats, there was a marked rise in the percentage of REMS during the recovery period.

During recovery periods, the cats were allowed eight hours of uninterrupted sleep for two to eighteen consecutive days, the number depending on when the REMS percentage returned to the baseline level. The maximum rise was invariably on the first recovery day with a more or less exponential return to baseline thereafter. The overall increase and duration of the recovery-compensation depended upon the length of the deprivation period.

However, as previously noted by Jouvet and co-workers (1964), there seemed to be a limit to the extent of the recovery rebound of REMs. In the first place, the percentage of REMS in the first eight hours of uninterrupted recovery sleep was never more than 70. In the second place, the overall make-up of REMS appears to reach a maximum at around twenty-five to thirty days of deprivation and recovery curves for longer periods are virtually identical. This is illustrated in Figure 3 which is a plot of recovery curves for increasing durations of deprivation. Note that the curves for thirty-two and seventy days' deprivation are essentially overlapping. Also following a long period of deprivation, the duration of the first uninterrupted REMS episode is not often strikingly increased. In twenty-four instances, the first REMS period ranged from five to forty-eight minutes with a mean of

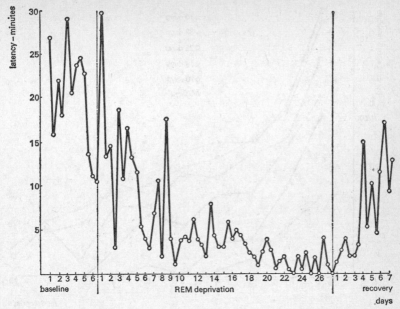

Figure 2 Plot of latency (initial onset of sleep to onset of first REMS episode) changes during baseline, REMS deprivation and recovery in one cat. In this example, the daily sleep sessions were split into two four-hour recordings that were started twelve hours apart. Thus, two latency measurements per day were recorded. By the twenty-third day of deprivation, the cat was going from wakefulness directly into the REMS. This would probably have occurred sooner except that REMS deprivation was not complete. As the number of awakenings mounted into the hundreds, the few seconds of REMS time before arousals began adding up to ten or twenty minutes per day

sixteen minutes and a mode of twelve minutes, as opposed to a mean length of ten minutes during the baseline runs. The major change accounting for increased REMS percentages was a drastic reduction in the length of the interspersed periods of slow wave sleep.

In addition to these compensatory changes in the REMS fraction, there were obvious changes in the 'intensity' of REM sleep. Some of its various manifestations were dramatically enhanced. In an early series of deprivations, we were struck by the great vigor of the muscular twitching during recovery sleep. The same thing occurred in rats. More recently, we have attempted to quantify some of these 'enhancements' and have studied four cats with electrodes implanted close to the eyes in horizontal and vertical planes, lateral geniculate electrodes, subdural thermistors and with the cats sleeping on a special 'actograph' which allowed some quantification of the

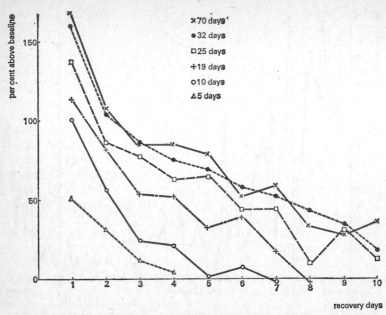

Figure 3 Recovery curves for varying durations of REMS deprivation.
Percentage increases were computed by comparing the mean daily baseline
REMS time (in minutes) with the total minutes of REMS on each successive
recovery day

twitching. The four cats were deprived by the 'practical' method for
twenty to forty-five days. Every fifth day, a single REMS episode was recorded. During REMS deprivation, the brain temperature rise was as much
as 350 per cent higher than the baseline change. However, toward the end of
the deprivation period there was a decrease until there was no change at all
in going from slow wave to REMS. Since the frequency of eye movements
and twitches continued to increase to levels of 100 to 500 per cent above
baseline, we have interpreted the temperature findings as due to some sort of
progressive change in cerebral blood flow which offsets the temperature
rise – in effect, cooling the brain faster than a possible increase in metabolic
activity heats it. The frequency of LG spikes appeared to increase, but poor
recordings prevented us from obtaining precise results.

Changes in waking state function as result of REMS deprivation

Physiological changes. Auditory recovery cycle. Dewson and co-workers
(1967) in our laboratory studied the auditory recovery cycle in three cats
who were deprived by the 'optimal' method. All measurements were made

in the waking state. The sequence of deprivation versus control arousals was reversed in one cat to control for order effects. In all cats, continuing REM deprivation was accompanied by a more rapid recovery of the potential evoked by the second of a pair of clicks. In addition, the amplitude of the second potential was well above 100 per cent at short click separations (twenty-five to seventy-five milliseconds). Baseline measurements were remarkably stable, although the cats were spending sixteen hours per day on the treadmill. The changes were progressive although not linearly related to the accruing REMS deprivation. The return to baseline level of the auditory recovery cycle generally took no longer than the return of the REM fraction. Periods of control awakenings showed no change in this measurement. Another point worth making is that successive episodes of REM deprivation separated by several weeks seemed to have a progressively larger effect on the auditory recovery cycle, suggesting that some permanent or long lasting change may have followed the initial deprivation procedure.

Seizure threshold (Cohen and Dement, 1965). We have determined the threshold of electrically induced convulsions on a large number of rats, using the water tank (practical) method and on a small number using forced arousals (optimal method). Every rat in the entire group showed a drop in seizure threshold after six days' deprivation which ranged from 5 to 50 per cent (mean, 22 per cent). No significant change occurred in the controls. Stress did not appear to be a factor in these results. Similar results were reported by Bliss in this symposium.

Heart rate. Jouvet (1965) has reported a progressive rise in heart rate in animals with lesions in the nucleus pontis caudalis which entirely suppressed REM sleep. Heart rate was measured in deprived cats during slow wave sleep and during wakefulness throughout the period of deprivation. There was a progressive rise which plateaued after thirty days of deprivation from a baseline mean of 160 beats per minute to a mean of 200 beats per minute.

Behavioral changes. Gross behavior. Up to as long as seventy days of continuous REMS deprivation, there was no impairment of motor performance. No gross abnormality was apparent. Most important, for all cats except those deprived by the 'practical' method, there was no evidence of excessive sleepiness. Rather, the animals were restless, prowled a great deal and were in general quite active.

Eating behavior. A number of tests were done on deprived cats to assess their motivation or drive to obtain food when starved, either during REMS deprivation or during a control period. In these studies, the cats were deprived by the modified optimal method and each cat served as its own control during which period it was allowed a maximum of two to three hours of uninterrupted sleep. The procedure was to starve the animal for three

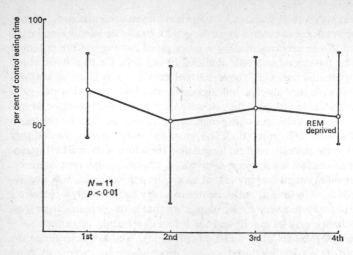

Figure 4 Change in rapidity of eating following starvation as a function of REMS deprivation. Cats were fed successive fifty-gram portions of a standard nutrient mixture until satiated. Each fifty-gram feeding was timed separately to avoid the confounding effect of slowing down and intermittency at the end of a single large *ad libitum* feeding. In general, the cats ate more when REMS-deprived. Fifth feedings were not considered since several of the portions were not finished by cats while serving as controls. Percentage reductions in eating time were computed individually for each cat which served as its own control, and the graph represents the *mean* of these values for all cats. The range is indicated by the *vertical lines*

successive days, and each day to run it through a series of tests. The tests were as follows: (a) observation of how long the cat would prowl in search of food before lying down to sleep in a free field; (b) a test in which a bowl of food was placed in the middle of a water tank to see if the cat would enter the water to get the food; (c) a test in which the cat was presented a bowl of food in which a sparkler was burning; (d) careful measurement of the rapidity of eating when finally allowed to eat following the starvation, as well as measurement of the amount.

Nearly all the cats showed a marked enhancement of their 'drive' or 'motivation' to obtain food during the REM deprived state, as opposed to the control period. For example, the speed of eating was nearly twice as fast when the cats were deprived. This is illustrated in Figure 4.

Sexual behavior. Ten male cats were deprived by the 'modified optimal' procedure for long periods of time. Each cat served as his own control and the order, deprivation–control, was reversed in five animals. All animals were observed at regular intervals in a test situation which consisted of placing them in a room for fifteen minutes with an anesthetized male cat and noting whether or not they mounted. Other casual observations were made. Four cats showed compulsive mounting behavior during REMS deprivation. This behavior disappeared during subsequent recovery and control periods. At a later date, a second period of REMS deprivation elicited the reappearance of compulsive mounting. In an earlier series of five male cats, two showed compulsive mounting behavior, but not in a structured situation. Thus, not all male cats became hypersexual, but of those who did, the change in sexual behavior occurred *only* during REMS deprivation.

A preliminary experiment was done with rats in which more quantitative observations of sexual behavior could be made. A major difference was in mounting or non-mounting in the presence of a female in heat. The control rats showed 14 per cent mounts – that is, 14 per cent of the rats mounted – whereas 80 per cent of the experimental or REMS deprived mounted (number, 29).

Psychometrics. Six human subjects have been run through six days of REM deprivation in pairs, with one subject starting on control arousals and the other being REM deprived. After a suitable recovery period, the procedure was reversed for each subject. Thus, each subject served as his own control. At the end of each run, the subjects were administered a battery of tests designed particularly to tap heightened drive and changes in impulse control. The battery was designed by Dr Stanley Clemes. Many trends in the predicted direction were apparent, but with this, as yet, small group, only the following changes were statistically significant: A modified TAT examination showed an elevation of expression of 'need' ($p < 0.001$) during REM deprivation, as opposed to control arousals and an elevated expression of feelings ($p < 0.05$). Pathognomic verbalizations were elevated on the Holtzmann Rorschach examination ($p < 0.001$).

REM sleep and convulsions

As was mentioned earlier, in deprived cats and rats, REM sleep seemed to have become a sort of convulsive state with the twitches resembling myoclonic jerks. This observation led to the speculation that REM sleep, at least in the deprived state, might have something in common with convulsive seizures. A number of experiments have been done which bear upon this point.

In the first series of experiments, four adult cats were recorded during a baseline period in which the percentage of REM sleep was assayed. Then they were recorded for an additional five days during which they received one or two electrically induced convulsions each day. The convulsions had the effect of lowering the percentage of REM sleep as well as affecting the number of eye movements and the EEG pattern. The eye movements were decreased and in some stretches of record were entirely absent. The REMS EEG showed signs of deactivation, with the frequent appearance of spindles and slow waves within a REM period. Most significant, during the subsequent recovery period, there was *no* compensatory rise in REM sleep. This suggested the possibility that the seizures in some way substituted for REM sleep. However, since the reduction of REMS was not 100 per cent, two of the cats were put through a *partial* REM deprivation procedure by the 'optimal' method, in which an equal reduction was achieved and it was noted on the recovery periods that REM sleep was indeed strikingly elevated. This is shown in Figure 5.

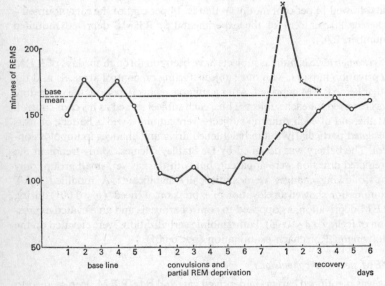

Figure 5 Changes in daily REMS time following electrically induced convulsive seizures. Each *circle* on the graph represents the mean of four cats. The *crosses* represent the average of the two cats during recovery sleep after partial REMS deprivation which reduced their daily REM time to the same level as was recorded on days when convulsions were induced

A similar study has been carried out by Gulevich, Zarcone and Cohen on nine patients who were receiving electroconvulsive therapy in a state hospital. These patients were recorded during a pretreatment baseline and then were studied intermittently during a several weeks' period when from seven to thirteen convulsions were given at the rate of three a week. There was a reduction in REM sleep. although it was not as consistent as was seen in the cats, and there was no evidence of rebound after the therapy.

Preliminary experiments were done in which deprived rats were convulsed approximately ten minutes prior to allowing them their first recovery sleep, and it was noted that the percentage of REM sleep was reduced below that seen in REMS-deprived, *nonconvulsed* rats, but the percentage was not reduced to the baseline level. A similar experiment was done in two cats and again the convulsion appeared to reduce the compensatory response of REM sleep that followed the deprivation. In addition, the deprived state seemed to protect the organism against the other changes seen in the non-deprived cat, i.e. there was no deactivation of the EEG and no marked decrease in frequency of eye movements. Finally, we have studied one epileptic patient with very definite regular seizure discharges in the EEG during sleep. The patient was deprived for four consecutive nights and it was noted that there was an increase in the number of bursts of seizure discharges in the EEG.

Discussion

There can be no question that the selective deprivation of REMS induces some sort of change in the central nervous system. The mere fact that there is recovery compensation of REMS indicates that this is so. The question is, what is the nature of this change, and what does it do? The results described herein suggest that it is a change in the direction of increased excitability and that the organism responds more vigorously to a variety of situations.

We have assumed that the changes underlying the deprived state are essentially neurochemical, although there is no direct evidence bearing upon this point. In other studies in our laboratory, we have attempted to demonstrate that CSF from a deprived cat will selectively induce an increase in REM sleep in a nondeprived recipient. The results so far have been suggestive of the pile up of a REM-inducer in the CSF, but not entirely conclusive. The work from Jouvet's laboratory certainly offers support for the involvement of monoamines in the REM mechanism, and it seems likely that deprivation might alter the concentration of one or more compounds in the catecholamine pathways.

The increase in drive-oriented behavior, we have assumed, is secondary to a more generalized hyperexcitability, although the mechanism may be more specific, particularly in view of the fact that the 'behavior' of the organism during the REM period seems to be organized on a relatively primitive level, i.e. there is a suggestion that it involves 'instinctual' behavior.

At present, we assume that something, probably a monoamine, piles up in

William Dement, Peter Henry, Harry Cohen and James Ferguson 321 the nervous system during deprivation, and that this compound is probably critical in the instigation of REM sleep in the normal animal. Of course, since two systems (phasic and tonic) are involved, it is likely that more than one compound must be implicated. If these hypothetical agents are 'used up' during REMS, the possibility arises that a grand mal convulsion may also 'use up' the same substances.

Even though we have some insight into the nature of the REM-deprived state, we are still not in a very good position to dictate its function. The REMS does not appear to be absolutely necessary to maintain life in the adult animal. In other words, prolonged deprivation is not lethal. In fact, some sort of equilibrium appears to be reached at around thirty days of deprivation. It may be that at this point, storage mechanisms are exhausted and further accumulation cannot take place. Or, there may be some suppressive effect on synthetic processes.

It seems too naïve to suggest that the REMS exists in the adult organism to prevent the nervous system from becoming overly excitable. We feel, along with Roffwarg and co-workers (1966), that a better explanation might be that this is essentially a fortuitous result of the nature of its mechanism, and that its true significance is probably developmental, i.e. that it may provide the needed activity for the developing nervous system during the fetal and neonatal periods. This may be so important that a very pre-emptive and potent biochemical regulatory mechanism is required. The nature of this mechanism may be such that an instigating substance or substances pile up when the REMS is not present, and by chance or otherwise the change in neurochemical status as a result of deprivation affects excitability and certain behavioral processes. There are, finally, a number of clinical implications with regard to these findings which have been discussed elsewhere (Dement, 1965b and c, 1966). We feel that REM deprivation in the human, however induced, might play a role in the development of the acute psychotic reaction in susceptible individuals. In others, it might affect drive or motivation. It is also obvious that ECT may involve the reversal of the REM-deprived state, and, finally, that REM deprivation might play a role in epilepsy.

References

COHEN, H., and DEMENT, W. (1965), 'Sleep: changes in threshold to electroconvulsive shock in rats after deprivation of "paradoxical" phase', *Science*, vol. 150, p. 1318.

DEMENT, W. (1960), 'The effect of dream deprivation', *Science*, vol. 131, p. 1705.

DEMENT, W. (1965a), 'Studies on the function of rapid eye movement (paradoxical) sleep in human subjects', in M. Jouvet (ed.), *Aspects anatomo-fonctionnels de la physiologie du sommeil*, Centre National de la Recherche Scientifique, Paris.

DEMENT. W. (1965b), 'Recent studies on the biological role of rapid eye movement sleep', *Amer. J. Psychiat.*, vol. 122, p. 404.

DEMENT, W. (1965c), 'REM sleep and the effects of its deprivation', Forest Hospital Lecture Series on Stress and Adaptation, Des Plaines, Illinois.

DEMENT, W. (1966), 'The psychophysiology of sleep and dreams', in S. Arieti (ed.), *American Handbook of Psychiatry*, vol. 3, Basic Books.

DEWSON, J., DEMENT, W., WAGENER, T., and NOBEL, K. (1967), 'REM sleep deprivation: a central-neural change during wakefulness', *Science*, vol. 156, pp. 403–6.

FERGUSON, J., and DEMENT, W. (1966), 'The effect of variations in total sleep time on the occurrence of rapid eye movement sleep in cats', *EEG clin. Neurophysiol.*, vol. 22, p. 109.

JOUVET, D., VIMONT, P., DELORME, F., and JOUVET, M. (1964), 'Etude de la privation selective de la phase paradoxale de sommeil chez le chat', *C R soc. biol.*, vol. 158, p. 756.

JOUVET, M. (1962), 'Recherches sur les structures nerveuses et les mécanismes responsables des différentes phases du sommeil physiologique', *Arch. Ital. Biol.*, vol. 100, p. 125.

JOUVET, M. (1965), 'Etude du sommeil chez le chat pontique chronique', in M. Jouvet (ed.), *Aspects anatomo-fonctionnels de la physiologie du sommeil*, Centre National de la Recherche Scientifique, Paris.

KALES, A., HOEDEMAKER, F., JACOBSON, A., and LICHTENSTEIN, E. (1964), 'Dream deprivation: an experimental reappraisal', *Nature*, vol. 204, p. 1337.

KIYONO, S., KAWAMOTO, T., SAKAKURA, H., and IWAMA, K. (1965), 'Effects of sleep deprivation upon the paradoxical phase of sleep in cats', *EEG clin. Neurophysiol.*, vol. 19, p. 34.

OSWALD, I. (1962), 'Sleep mechanisms: recent advances', *Proc. Roy. Soc. Med.*, vol. 55, p. 910.

ROFFWARG, H., MUZIO, J., and DEMENT, W. (1966), 'The ontogenetic development of the sleep-dream cycle in the human', *Science*, vol. 152, p. 604.

SAMPSON, H. (1965), 'Deprivation of dreaming sleep by two methods: I. Compensatory REM time', *Arch. gen. Psychiat.*, vol. 13, p. 79.

SIEGEL, J., and GORDON, T. (1965), 'Paradoxical sleep: deprivation in the cat', *Science*, vol. 148, p. 978.

SNYDER, F. (1963), 'The new biology of dreaming', *Arch. gen. Psychiat.*, vol. 8, p. 381.

SNYDER, F. (1965a), 'The organismic state associated with dreaming', in M. Greenfield and W. Lewis (eds.), *Psychoanalysis and Current Biological Thought*, University of Wisconsin Press.

SNYDER, F. (1965b), 'Progress in the new biology of dreaming', *Amer. J. Psychiat,,* vol. 122, p. 377.

23 Raúl Hernández-Peón, René Raúl Drucker, Adela Ramírez del Angel, Beatriz Chavez and Pedro Serrano

Brain Catecholamines and Serotonin in Rapid Sleep Deprivation

Raúl Hernández-Peón, René Raúl Drucker, Adela Ramírez del Angel, Beatriz Chavez and Pedro Serrano, 'Brain catecholamines and serotonin in rapid sleep deprivation', *Physiology and Behavior*, vol. 4, 1969, pp. 659-61.

At the present time it is generally accepted that central synaptic transmission is chemically mediated as that in peripheral synapses. The anatomical localization of hypnogenic and arousing structures has laid ground for approaching the problem of chemical synaptic transmission in sleep and wakefulness. Indirect evidence obtained by localized intra-cerebral chemical stimulation suggests that cholinergic excitatory synapses are present along the sleep system which seemingly has a region of convergence for its descending corticofugal and ascending spinofugal components at the bulbopontine reticular formation (Hernández-Peón, 1965c, 1967). However, the synaptic transmitter required to inhibit the mesodiencephalic arousing neurons appears to be different from acetylcholine since its local application on those neurons does not produce sleep (Hernández-Peón, 1962, 1965a). Regional neurochemistry, however, has identified a number of substances with unequal concentrations in different brain regions (Glowinski and Baldessarini, 1966; Glowinski and Iversen, 1966), but there is not enough evidence to support the contention that such substances play a physiological role in brain functioning. Since nor-adrenaline has been found in high concentrations in the hypothalamus and midbrain reticular formation of various species including man (Bertler, 1961; Bertler and Rosengren, 1959; Glowinski and Iversen, 1966), it may be that such substance acts as a synaptic transmitter in those central regions.

If one accepts that sleep results from an active inhibition of the vigilance reticular neurons located in the rostral part of the brain stem, then it is possible to suggest that the concentration of synaptic transmitters or of their chemical precursors should vary with the degree of activity of the mesodiencephalic neurons.

With this in mind determination of nor-adrenalin, dopamine, and 5-HT were made in the midbrain tegmentum and frontal cortical poles of rapid sleep deprived cats.

Method

The experiments were performed on fourteen cats of both sexes weighing between 2·5 and 3·5 kg of which eight served as controls and six were rapid sleep deprived for ten to twelve days. The animals were deprived of rapid sleep by placing them on a platform surrounded by water inside a tank. The diameter of the platform (11 cm^2) prevented total relaxation of the body musculature which is normally associated with rapid sleep. At the end of the experiment the animals were killed by decapitation, the brains were immediately removed, frozen, and pieces of 1 g of the midbrain tegmentum and frontal poles of the cortex were chemically analysed. Catecholamines were measured using a 3-hydroxy-indo-fluorimetric differential technique reported by Sourkes and Murphy (1961). Serotonin concentration was determined by the method described by Udenfriend (1962). This technique involves extraction with n-butanol from a salt saturated alkaline homogeneate, return of serotonin to an aqueous phase by the addition of heptane to n-butanol and shaking the mixed solvent with dilute acid. The acid solution was then assayed fluorimetrically and compared with an appropriate standard and blank.

Results and discussion

The results were statistically treated with the Mann–Whitney U Test. As Figure 1 shows, the concentration of noradrenalin in the midbrain tegmentum (MRF) of rapid sleep deprived cats was not significantly changed although it showed a tendency to increase. On the other hand, serotonin (5-HT) did not change significantly either, but showed a tendency to increase. Dopamine concentration in the mid-brain tegmentum, however, increased 302 per cent reaching a 0·01 level of significance. Furthermore, there was practically no overlap of dopamine concentrations between control and experimental animals. By contrast, the cortical concentrations of the three substances were not significantly altered.

The above mentioned results indicate that the state of rapid sleep deprivation is accompanied by an increase of dopamine.

The remarkable increase of dopamine in the midbrain tegmentum may be a manifestation of a compensatory mechanism of some kind that secures sufficient quantities of this precursor, in prevision of the overproduction of noradrenalin that will occur during sleep, after the prolonged activity of the mesodiencephalic arousing neurons. This interpretation agrees with the recent finding of Pujol et al. (1968) who reported a marked increase of noradrenalin synthesis in rats allowed half to five hours of sleep after ninety-one hours of rapid sleep deprivation, and is more directly supported by the fact that injections of alpha-methyl-dopa, which is known to reduce the levels

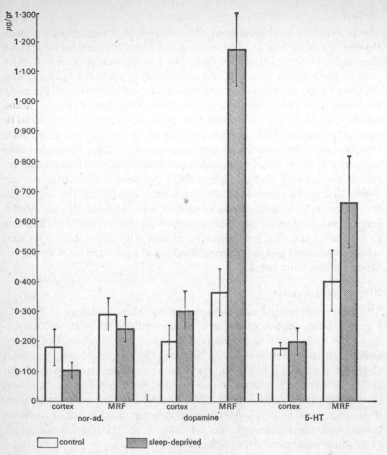

Figure 1 Mean concentrations and standard error of catechol and indolamines in cortex and MRF of sleep-deprived and control cats

of catecholamines in the brain, prevents the recovery of rapid sleep, following its deprivation (Dusan-Peyrethon, Peyrethon and Jouvet, 1968).

Since there is experimental evidence suggestive of reciprocal inhibitory influences between hypnogenic and arousing neurons (Hernández-Peón, 1956b; Hernández-Peón and Sterman, 1966), the onset of rapid sleep after a prolonged period of its deprivation could result from the abrupt dominance of the sleep system over an exhausted vigilance system. It appears as though intense inhibition of the vigilance reticular neurons during rapid sleep secures the nor-adrenalin turnover at the expense of the accumulated dopamine in the midbrain tegmentum. It may be, on the other hand, that in the case of rapid sleep deprived cats both the synthesis of nor-adrenalin from dopamine and its utilization are reduced, perhaps by the accumulation of a third substance which could be a 'sleep substance'.

As far as serotonin is concerned, nothing much can be said on the basis of the results obtained here. Serotonin has been implicated in the genesis of sleep. Serotonin neurons have been detected in the brain stem with ascending axons following the trajectory of the medial forebrain bundle up to the forebrain (Andrén, Fuxe and Larsson, 1966). Lesions in the Raphe nuclei coincidentally produce suppression of sleep and a decrease of forebrain serotonin (Jouvet, 1967). If suppression of sleep is responsible for a decrease of cerebral serotonin, sleep deprivation experimentally induced by any procedure should lead to the same chemical change. Our results disagree with this, as no decrease of 5-HT was observed.

References

ANDRÉN, N. E., FUXE, K., and LARSSON, K. (1966), 'Effect of large mesencephalic-diencephalic lesions on the nor-adrenalin, dopamine and 5-hydroxy-tryptamine neurons of the central nervous system', *Experimentia*, vol. 22, p. 842.

BERTLER, A. (1961), 'Occurrence and localization of catecholamines in the human brain', *Acta physiol. Scand.*, vol. 51, pp. 97–107.

BERTLER, A., and ROSENGREN, E. (1959), 'Occurrence and distribution of catecholamines in the brain', *Acta physiol. Scand.*, vol. 47, pp. 350–61.

DUSAN-PEYRETHON, D., PEYRETHON, J., and JOUVET, M. (1968), 'Suppression sélective du sommeil paradoxal chez le chat par alpha-methyl-Dopa', *C R soc. biol.*, vol. 162, pp. 116–18.

FRIEDE, R. L. (1966), *Topographic Brain Chemistry*, Academic Press.

GLOWINSKI, J., and BALDESSARINI, R. J. (1966), 'Metabolism of norepinephrine in the central nervous system', *Pharmacol. Rev.*, vol. 18, pp. 1201–38.

GLOWINSKI, J., and IVERSON, L. L. (1966), 'Regional studies of catecholamines in the rat brain: I. Disposition of H^2-norepinephrine, H^2-dopamine and H^2-DOPA in various regions of the brain', *J. Neurochem.*, vol. 13, pp. 655–69.

HERNÁNDEZ-PEÓN, R. (1962), 'Sleep induced by localized electrical or chemical stimulation of the forebrain', *EEG clin. Neurophysiol.*, vol. 14, pp. 423–4.

HERNÁNDEZ-PEÓN, R. (1965a), 'Central neurohumoral transmission in sleep and wakefulness', *Prog. Brain Res.*, vol. 18, pp. 96–116.

HERNÁNDEZ-PEÓN, R. (1965b), 'Die neuralen Grundlagen des Schlafes', *Arznelmittelforschung*, vol. 15, pp. 1099–118.

HERNÁNDEZ-PEÓN, R. (1965), 'A cholinergic hypnogenic forebrain–hindbrain circuit', in M. Jouvet (ed.), *Neurophysiologie des états du sommeil*, Centre National de la Recherche Scientifique, Paris, pp. 63–88.

HERNÁNDEZ-PEÓN, R. (1967), 'Neural systems in the brain stem involved in wakefulness, sleep and conscious experience', *Proc. Int. Congr. Neurol. Surg.*, Copenhagen, pp. 429–41.

HERNÁNDEZ-PEÓN, R., and STERMAN, M. B. (1966), 'Brain functions', *Ann. Rev. Psychol.*, vol. 17, pp. 363–94.

JOUVET, M. (1967), 'Mechanisms of the states of sleep: a neuro-pharmacological approach', in *Sleep and Altered States of Consciousness*, Proceedings of the Association for Research in Nervous and Mental Disease, Williams & Wilkins, pp. 86–126.

PUJOL, J. F., MOURET, J., JOUVET, M., and GLOWINSKI, J. (1968), 'Increased turnover of cerebral nor-epinephrine during rebound of paradoxical sleep in the rat', *Science*, vol. 159, pp. 112–14.

SOURKES, T. L., and MURPHY, G. E. (1961), 'Determination of catecholamine acids by differential spectrophotofluorimetry', in H. Quastel (ed.), *Methods in Medical Research*, Yearbook Medical Publications, Chicago, p. 197.

UDENFRIEND, S. (1962), 'Amino acid amines and their metabolites', in *Fluorescence Assay in Biology and Medicine*, Academic Press, pp. 125–90.

24 Ian Oswald

Human Brain Protein, Drugs and Dreams

Ian Oswald, 'Human brain protein, drugs and dreams', *Nature*, vol. 223, 1969, pp. 893–7

I intend here to draw together several remarkably long term processes affecting brain cells. Inevitably, these 'slow neurophysiological swings' (Oswald, 1967) interest the psychiatrist, for he sees, reflected in his patients' behaviour, evidence of slow brain changes over weeks, months and years. A common illness is the endogenous or autonomous depression – autonomous because, once started, it is self-perpetuating for many months. It can be treated successfully with a drug such as imipramine, yet although this reaches the human brain within hours, the mood does not begin noticeably to lift for ten days or more and many more weeks or months of treatment are needed. There can thus be responses both delayed and gradual on a slow time scale. British neurophysiology, oriented more to milliseconds than weeks, has offered disappointingly little to the psychiatrist. Recently, however, things have begun to change, chiefly through work of neuropharmacologists, and it is the action of drugs on the human brain that has been my starting point.

Addiction to a drug both develops and decays on a time scale of weeks. My first laboratory encounter with a slow human brain change came while studying the sleep of amphetamine addicts. The measurements we made were of REM (rapid eye movement, paradoxical, or 'hind-brain') sleep, the phase of sleep especially associated with dreaming. Amphetamine suppresses this kind of sleep when first administered, but repeated consumption leads to tolerance, including a return of REM sleep to the normal 20 to 25 per cent of the night. Withdrawal of drug then causes a 'rebound' increase to more than normal REM sleep (Figure 1) and especially makes REM sleep start early during the night (Oswald and Thacore, 1963). Data from six addicts suggested a return to normal in about three weeks, but a more careful look suggested that recovery was actually taking a couple of months (Figure 2).

Barbiturates also suppressed REM sleep duration and, at the same time, reduced the profusion of actual eye movements (Oswald *et al.*, 1963). If the drugs were administered for one to three weeks the effects lessened, and after they were stopped a rebound increase of REM sleep above normal

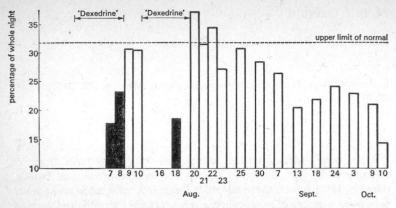

Figure 1 Effect of amphetamine ('Dexedrine') withdrawal on REM sleep, the percentage of which, in the whole night's sleep, is shown on the ordinate. The patient had been an addict for several years. An increase in the percentage of REM sleep occurs each time the drug is withdrawn. After the second withdrawal the percentage appears to decline to about the normal mean in about three weeks (but see Figure 2). (From Oswald and Thacore, 1963)

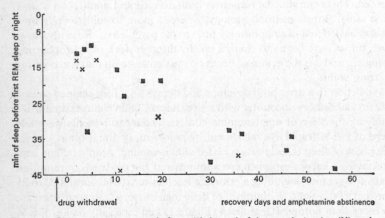

Figure 2 Slow return to normal after withdrawal of dexamphetamine (X) and 'Drinamyl' (■) from two female addicts. The scale on the ordinate is of the delay in minutes of sleep between first sleep onset and first REM sleep of the night. In the normal person, or the fully tolerant addict, this is over forty-five minutes. Drug withdrawal causes the sudden appearance of very short delays. Two months after withdrawal are needed for these to disappear. (Data from Oswald and Thacore, 1963)

occurred (Oswald and Priest, 1965) which once more lasted more than a month (Figure 3). The rebound was coupled with spontaneous complaints of vivid and unpleasant dreams and also with more than the normal amount of eye movement during REM sleep (Lewis, 1968; Oswald, 1970). These last observations have also been made by others (Allen, Kales and Berger, 1968) and indicate that REM sleep rebound has both duration and intensity factors.

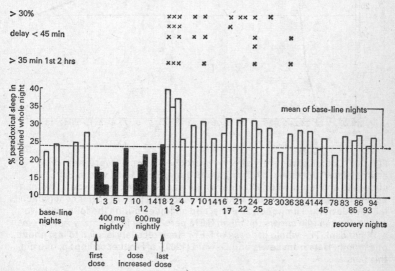

Figure 3 Effect of sodium amylobarbitone on the sleep of two men. The vertical columns indicate the percentage of REM sleep in the whole night for two men. The black columns indicate that sodium amylobarbitone reduces the percentage but that the effect lessens with repetition. The time-scale is not linear. A rebound appears after the drug is stopped and gradually, over several weeks, the REM percentages decline. There is a cross over the nights when either or both volunteers spent more than 30 per cent of the whole night in REM sleep, had a delay of less than forty-five minutes between first falling asleep and first rapid eye movements, or spent more than thirty-five minutes of the first two hours of sleep in REM sleep. These crosses, which indicate abnormality, are seen only after drug withdrawal and peter out in the sixth recovery week. (From Oswald and Priest, 1965)

Effects of anti-depressants

Recently, Lewis and I looked at REM sleep in patients who had taken overdoses of tricyclic anti-depressant drugs of the imipramine type (Lewis and Oswald, 1969). These drugs powerfully suppress REM sleep and, after overdose, a rebound, with intense dreams, again appears and recovery to normal takes a month (Figure 4).

Ian Oswald 331

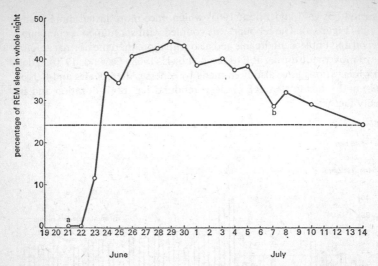

Figure 4 Course of recovery after an overdose of an anti-depressant drug amitriptyline (157 tablets, 3925 mg), on 19 June. REM sleep was initially abolished and returned on 23 June, which was also the day the young woman patient became fully alert and rational. It reached a peak of 45 per cent (which is far outside normal limits) on 29 June, and subsided during the following two weeks. Broken rule shows the mean REM percentage for normal young women at 24 per cent. The whole process of REM sleep recovery is seen to last about one month. Data from Lewis and Oswald (1969). a, First recording: b, one gin this p.m.

Suppression of REM sleep is not a property of all drugs that act on the central nervous system. Some, like fenfluramine and iprindole, have no immediate effect on REM sleep, while others, like L-trytophan or reserpine, increase REM sleep. Figure 4 reveals an obvious difference from Figures 1 and 3 in that the rebound curve does not ascend abruptly to a sharp peak but reaches its highest point ten days after overdose and seven days after REM sleep has returned. In these respects the curve resembles the sleep recovery curve after experimental administration of heroin, 7·5 mg given nightly for one week. We have recently conducted these experiments on ourselves (Lewis et al., 1970). The REM sleep rebound after heroin persisted for more than two months.

Figure 5 shows the time course of recovery after an overdose of a second type of anti-depressant treatment, namely, electro-convulsive therapy (ECT) (Callaway and Boucher, 1950). Its similarity to Figure 4 is apparent. ECT induces abnormal slow waves in the waking electroencephalogram (EEG) and it is the amount of these, crudely measured, which Figure 5

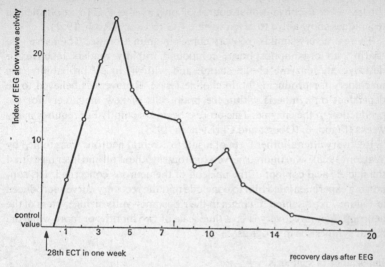

Figure 5 Course of recovery after very intensive ECT. Waking EEG slow wave activity is indicated on the vertical scale. Compare with Figure 4. (Data from Callaway and Boucher, 1950)

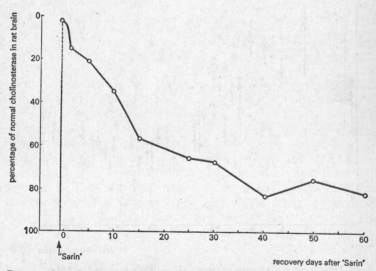

Figure 6 Course of recovery of brain cholinesterase after 'Sarin' (a 'nerve gas'). Compare especially with Figures 2 and 8. (Data from Oberst and Christensen, 1955)

shows. After a conventional course of only twelve ECTs, sophisticated techniques show a five to seven week EEG recovery (Roth, 1951).

There are very similar recovery curves in animal brains. The nerve gas, 'Sarin', an organophosphorus compound, rapidly renders inactive, or destroys, the enzyme cholinesterase and with it, in all probability, the machinery for producing brain cholinesterase. Recovery is believed to be dependent on synthesis within the brain cells of new machinery for the production of the enzyme. This process begins promptly but requires many weeks (Figure 6) (Oberst and Christensen, 1955).

Recovery after another form of insult to cerebral neurons was studied by Watson (1968), who injured nerve axons outside the skull and later measured the nucleic acid content of the nucleoli of the neurons concerned. His supporting experiments led him to conclude that the recovery curve reproduced in Figure 7 represented 'changes in the ribosome-synthesizing system of the neuron'. Again recovery is on a time scale of two months or more while the repair synthesis is in progress.

Importance of synthesis

Previous reference has been made to the drug reserpine. It depletes the brain of monoamines, including the catecholamines, which are present in certain

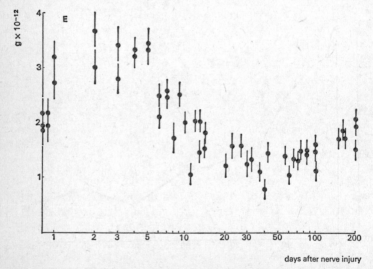

Figure 7 Time course of changes in nucleolar nucleic acid content of rat hypoglossal neurons in days after injury to the nerve outside the skull. From Watson (1968), who concluded that the changes observed were changes in the ribosome-synthesizing system of the neuron

neurons within special storage particles. Administration of 5 mg/kg of reserpine to rabbits makes brain catecholamines abruptly disappear. The reserpine itself disappears from the brain in a few hours (Hess, Shore and Brodie, 1956). The recovery curve has a now familiar appearance and is on a time scale of weeks (Figure 8) (Carlsson *et al.*, 1957). The catecholamine stores in the neurons can be stained and photographed (Dahlström and Fuxe, 1964), and the slowness of recovery led Iversen (1967, p. 239) to propose that it was dependent on the formation of new storage particles in the cell bodies – not a restocking of old cupboards, as it were, but a stocking up in new cupboards which have to be synthesized afresh during the repair process.

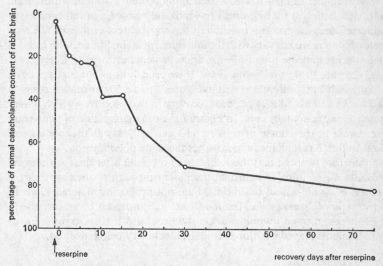

Figure 8 Course of recovery of brain catecholamines after treatment with reserpine. Compare especially with Figures 2 and 6.
(Data from Carlsson *et al.*, 1957)

I have pointed out that the peak of REM sleep rebound after the tricyclic drugs and after heroin is delayed for about ten days. Drug-accentuated EEG sleep spindles after treatment with the tricyclic drugs disappear, and so do urinary products of heroin just before the night of peak REM sleep. It takes about a day for amphetamine and sodium amylobarbitone to be eliminated from the body, and peak REM sleep rebound then seems to occur following the first day of abstinence (Figures 1 and 3). Nitrazepam, an effective and safe hypnotic, causes drug-induced fast activity in the drowsy EEG which persists for forty-eight hours. We found that the peak

REM sleep rebound after treatment with nitrazepam was delayed to the third night (Oswald and Priest, 1965). Hartmann (1966) found increased REM sleep on the first night of reserpine administration, but it was even greater on the second and third nights after a single dose.

The rate of increase of REM sleep seems to relate to the rate of disappearance of the particular drug from the brain: the peak of rebound seems to follow closely on the final disappearance of the drug, and the increase in REM sleep after reserpine may be an immediate 'rebound', consequent on the exceptional rapidity with which reserpine disappears from the brain. Thus the term 'rebound' may not always be apposite, and increased REM sleep may rather be a sign of certain types of neuronal repair.

The examples in Figures 6 to 8 each imply protein synthesis within brain cells, and I suggest that Figures 1 to 4 indicate a process of reformation of neuronal sleep-controlling machinery through protein synthesis. The time scale of synthesis must vary with the individual protein. Studies with labelled amino-acids indicate a half-life for brain proteins of three to thirty-seven days (Lajtha, 1964; McIlwain, 1966). If we crudely took fifteen days as an average half-life we should expect in Figures 1 to 8 a 50 per cent recovery in two weeks and about a 94 per cent recovery in two months – which is very close to what is actually seen. In Figure 7 there is a suggestion of temporary over-swing in the course of repair and I can only say that experience of sleep studies has long made me suspect the same phenomenon.

I therefore propose that the REM sleep rebound after drug-withdrawal indicates a reshaping of neuronal machinery through protein synthesis, a process of repair within brain cells. I am not proposing that all kinds of active repair in mammalian brain cells are accompanied by an increase in REM sleep, though I would suspect it whenever 5-hydroxytryptamine or noradrenaline played a major part in the machinery being repaired.

Dream compensation

Dement (1960) devised a technique for selective deprivation of REM sleep by behavioural means. On subsequent, undisturbed nights REM sleep was increased. The original explanation was in terms of 'compensation' for lost dreams, for which, it was supposed, there was a compelling 'need'. This explanation has fallen out of favour, but 'compensation' could be advanced as the basis of post-drug REM sleep rebound. The degree of 'compensation' seems to have been small in most experiments involving selective deprivation by Dement's method, and completed within a week.

The largest (Dement, 1965) 'compensation' seems to have been about 60 per cent. In terms of hours of REM sleep, the rebound after barbiturates, or overdose of tricyclic drug, or heroin is about 150 per cent. I have mentioned the intensity increase after drugs. It is present, too, after behavioural deprivation (Pivik and Foulkes, 1965), but there is nothing to suggest that it is greater after the latter. Dement (1965) subsequently proposed the build-up of an 'autotoxin' which could be removed by REM sleep alone. As the proposal was formulated it is hard to see the autotoxin causing a 150 per cent compensation in duration alone. The immediate increase of REM sleep caused by some drugs certainly cannot be regarded as 'compensation'.

Slow brain change is seen not only in recovery after drugs: when drugs such as morphine or barbiturates are administered repeatedly, tolerance appears in days and increases to near completeness in weeks and months (Belleville and Fraser, 1957; Martin and Fraser, 1961). The effects on REM sleep lessen (Figure 3), but the adjustment process may be complicated by short term mechanisms of the kind Dement described, and by induced adjustments of liver function which tend to inactivate the drugs before they reach the brain. Figure 9 shows some general curves of recovery. The period of drug exposure shown would be regarded as one in which not only the liver but also the brain was adjusting to the presence of the drug, paralleling the development of tolerance. During the rebound period there would be simply a slow brain change uncomplicated by the liver.

In 1960, Weiss, emphasizing the 'modifiability of the neuron' through perpetual renewal of its substance from the nuclear territory of the cell, suggested that here might be found the explanation of tolerance to drugs, a proposal since echoed by others (Goldstein and Goldstein, 1961; Sharpless, 1964; Shuster, 1961). Inhibitors of protein synthesis prevent the development of morphine tolerance during repeated administration (Cox, Ginsburg and Osman, 1968; Way, Loh and Shen, 1968). In Figure 9 the period of drug administration would be a period in which the machinery governing sleep would be modified gradually although other drugs, including reserpine, might be capable of modification through an abrupt destruction. The modifications in either case would persist after the drug had disappeared, would cause the REM sleep rebound, and would be slowly eliminated by new synthesis. But would this last synthesis be merely at a steady and inevitable pace or at a specially increased rate?

There are grounds for believing that the rate of intraneuronal synthesis which accompanies the development of tolerance to morphine is increased above normal (Way, Loh and Shen, 1968) and the same might be suspected for the reverse process of active recovery. I have, of course, already referred to increased intensity of REM sleep during recovery rebound. During the development of morphine tolerance an increased rate of synthesis of 5-hydroxytryptamine (5-HT) has been demonstrated (Way, Loh and Shen, 1968).

It can now be noted that (1) withdrawal of the morphine-type drug, heroin, would presumably leave a persisting mechanism for increased

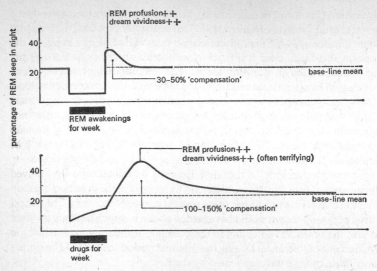

Figure 9 A representation of the two conditions in which REM sleep rebound occurs. The upper figure depicts selective deprivation of REM sleep by the techniques of Dement (1960). Most reports indicate that after this the rebound is immediately maximal and lasts only a few days and that 'compensation' is much less, in time, than the loss, though there is increase in REM sleep intensity. The lower figure depicts suppression of REM sleep by a drug, with diminishing effect as time passes. Drug withdrawal is followed by a rebound which may be maximal immediately if the drug disappears quickly from the brain, or may rise gradually to a peak if the drug leaves the brain tissue only slowly. The 'compensation' exceeds the lost REM sleep and there is increase in intensity of REM sleep. Return to normal takes several weeks. It is postulated that this rebound reflects a time of repair within brain cells

synthesis of 5-HT, which, soon unrestrained by the continuing presence of the drug, would accompany an increase of REM sleep above normal; (2) reserpine depletes stores of 5-HT but causes increased synthesis (Ashcroft et al., 1969) of 5-HT and increased REM sleep, and (3) L-tryptophan and 5-HTP can enhance REM sleep (Evans and Oswald, 1966; Oswald et al., 1966), presumably by temporarily increasing 5-HT synthesis, and comparable observations have been made by others (Hartmann, 1967; Mandell, Mandell and Jacobson, 1964).

Amines and sleep

The role of amines in sleep is currently debated. Drugs like amphetamine or imipramine are very potent in suppressing REM sleep and increasing free noradrenaline in the synaptic cleft. I have outlined evidence suggesting that 5-HT synthesis promotes REM sleep. Jouvet, by contrast, argued the same for catecholamines (Jouvet, 1967; Pujol *et al.*, 1968). I was unconvinced (Oswald, 1968) – the REM sleep of the rat is unaffected by inhibition of noradrenaline synthesis (Marantz and Rechtschaffen, 1967; Marantz *et al.*, 1968). Now Jouvet and his colleagues (Mouret *et al.*, 1968) have suggested that suppression of REM sleep by *para*-chlorophenylalanine and nialamide (in a very large dose) arises from a decrease in the concentration of metabolites of 5-HT. An alternative, however, is to point out that not only does *para*-chlorophenylalanine suppress 5-HT synthesis, but so do large doses of monoamine oxidase inhibitors (Ashcroft *et al.*, 1969) of which nialamide is one.

I said at the beginning that clinical response to imipramine was delayed for ten days or more. The same is true of clinical response to the other group of anti-depressant drugs, the monoamine oxidase inhibitors (MAOIs). Just as I believe we have got to devote more thought to slow and gradual brain processes, so we shall have more often to consider delayed processes. Again sleep research offers a tool. The administration of the MAOI, phenelzine, can sometimes seem at first to promote REM sleep at the beginning of the night, but, when used in clinical doses, it causes a moderate overall reduction in REM sleep in man. Akindele, Evans and I have, however, found that phenelzine, after a delay of up to twenty-one days of regular administration, will cause a further abrupt response, total REM sleep abolition. Far from such 'loss of dreams' causing psychological impairment, the total abolition of REM sleep, which can last many weeks, is accompanied by improvement of the mood. Again we differ from Jouvet (Mouret *et al.*, 1968) in that we observe the eventual withdrawal of MAOI to cause REM sleep rebound.

Having considered many slow brain processes, I can return to the subject of slow recovery of emotional balance. I must first add that healing of injured body tissues includes removal of clots through fibrinolysis. This process is brought about by plasmin, derived from plasminogen in the presence of plasminogen activator. The amount of this activator in blood is normally controlled by the brain (Benetato and Dumitrescu-Papahagi, 1964; Kowarzyk *et al.*, 1962). Whether this implies direct release from, say, the hypothalamus, or hypothalamic control through a target organ, is not known. The scale along the ordinate of Figure 10 is really a scale of plasminogen activator. When some Edinburgh medical students were faced with the anxiety of resitting final examinations their plasminogen activator level decreased. Recovery, despite prompt knowledge of examination success, was, for some, gradual and slow over many weeks (Cash and Allen, 1967). This could be a reflexion of another slow brain recovery following a truly final insult.

I have mentioned experiments with heroin. As others had observed, my colleagues and I found that in the healthy person heroin not merely failed to cause euphoria but was frankly unpleasant (Oswald, 1969). Why should this be? If, as Figure 10 suggests, neurons undergo active modification owing to involvement in the impact of emotional distress, whether of physical or social origin, it would not be altogether surprising if the response to heroin of the neurons of the distressed person were different from that in the normal person.

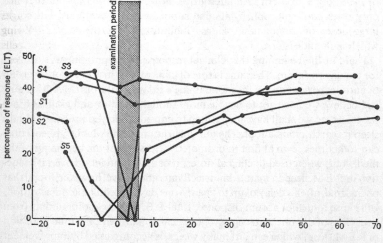

days before and after onset of examination

Figure 10 Course of recovery of a brain-governed content of blood, namely plasminogen activator (which is involved in removal of clots and tissue healing), following the severe mental stress of resitting final examinations by some medical students. ELT, euglobulin lysis test. Individual differences in response to the stress are apparent but, where abnormal responses were induced, recovery in two cases took several weeks.
(From Cash and Allen, 1967)

Synthesis within neurons

In conclusion, I suggest that REM sleep rebound betrays increased protein synthesis in the brain. I would go further and propose that REM sleep is a non-specific indication of many forms of synthesis within cerebral neurons, which would explain the 'strange' finding that streptomycin (an inhibitor of protein synthesis capable of damaging human neurons) reduces REM sleep (Dement, 1968, p. 260). The proposal is consistent with the uniquely high proportion of REM sleep in the 2 months both before and after birth in animals such as the human (Petre-Quadens et al., 1967) in which the central nervous system is not mature at birth. During these months the finer differentiation of the brain occurs. It is also consistent with the increased brain blood flow (Reivich *et al.*, 1968) and temperature (Kawamura and Sawyer, 1965) during REM sleep. NREM (non-rapid eye movement) sleep is especially enhanced after strenuous physical exercise (Baekeland and Lasky, 1966; Hobson, 1968) and, in contrast to REM sleep, is accompanied by a high concentration of growth hormone in the blood (Honda *et al.*,1969), suggesting that its chief function is for bodily restitution, while REM sleep may be chiefly for brain repair. I could also predict that conditions associated with massive learning would cause high percentages of REM sleep, for example, when an 'enriched' environment for growing rats leads to a heavier brain cortex and greater development of glial cells (Krech, 1968). Human mental retardates, it may be noted, have REM sleep reduced both in amount and intensity (Feinberg, 1968).

Finally, it seems to me that, in the study of brain and behaviour, we shall be compelled increasingly to think in terms of slow shifts of function mediated by protein synthesis. So far the latter has scarcely entered the psychiatrist's conceptual framework, but it seems as probable that it underlies personality modification through psychotherapy as that it underlies drug tolerance or REM sleep rebound. The healing of hurt minds proceeds by processes equally as slow as the healing of hurt brain cells.

References

ALLEN, C., KALES, A., and BERGER, R. J. (1968), 'An analysis of the effect of Glutethimide on REM density', *Psychophysiol.*, vol. 5, pp. 207–8.

ASHCROFT, G. W., CRAWFORD, T. B. B., DOW, R. C., and MOIR, A. T. B. (1969), 'Release of amine metabolite into ventricular perfusion fluid as an index of turnover', in G. Hooper (ed.), *Metabolism of Amines in the Brain*, Macmillan, pp. 65–9.

BAEKELAND, F., and LASKY, R. (1966), 'Exercise and sleep patterns in college athletes', *Percept. mot. Skills*, vol. 23, pp. 1203–7.

BELLEVILLE, R. E., and FRASER, H. F. (1957), 'Tolerance to some effects of barbiturates', *J. Pharmacol. exp. Ther.*, vol. 120, pp. 469–74.

BENETATO, G., and DUMITRESCU-PAPAHAGI, E. (1964), 'Efectul stimulării regiunii hipotalamice prin iradierea cu raze ultrascurte asupra activitatii fibrinolitice a plasmei sanguine în raport cu vîrsta', *Studii Cerc. Fiziol.*, vol. 9, pp. 39–45.

CALLAWAY, E., and BOUCHER, F. (1950), 'Slow wave phenomena in intensive electroshock', *EEG clin. Neurophysiol.*, vol. 2, pp. 157–62.

CARLSSON, R., ROSENGREN, E., BERTLER, A., and NILSSON, J. (1957), 'Effect of reserpine on the metabolism of catechol amines', in S. Garattini and V. Ghetti (eds.), *Psychotropic Drugs*, Elsevier, pp. 363–72.

CASH, J. D., and ALLEN, A. G. E. (1967), 'Effect of stress on the fibrinolytic reactivity to exercise', *Brit. med. J.*, vol. 2, pp. 545–8.

COX, B. M., GINSBURG, M., and OSMAN, O. H. (1968), 'Acute tolerance to narcotic analgesic drugs in rats', *Brit. J. Pharmacol.*, vol. 33, pp. 245–56.

DAHLSTRÖM, A., and FUXE, K. (1964), 'Evidence for the existence of monoamine-containing neurons in the central nervous system', *Acta Physiol. Scand.*, vol. 62, suppl. 232, pp. 1–55.

DEMENT, W. (1960), 'The effect of dream deprivation', *Science*, vol. 131, pp. 1705–7.

DEMENT, W. (1965), Studies on the function of rapid eye movement (paradoxical) sleep in human subjects', in M. Jouvet (ed.), *Neurophysiologie des états de sommeil*, Centre National de la Recherche Scientifique, Paris.

DEMENT, W. (1968), 'The psychophysiology of REM sleep, its function and possible clinical relationships', in C. Rupp (ed.), *Mind as a Tissue*, Harper & Row, pp. 214–36.

EVANS, J. I., and OSWALD, I. (1966), 'Some experiments in the chemistry of narcoleptic sleep', *Brit. J. Psychiat.*, vol. 112, pp. 401–4.

FEINBERG, I. (1968), 'Eye movement activity during sleep and intellectual function in mental retardation', *Science*, vol. 159, p. 1256.

GOLDSTEIN, D. B., and GOLDSTEIN, A. (1961), 'Possible role of enzyme inhibition and repression in drug tolerance and addiction', *Biochem. Pharmacol.*, vol. 8, p. 48.

HARTMANN, E. (1966), 'Reserpine: its effect on the sleep–dream cycle in man', *Psychopharmacologia*, vol. 9, pp. 242–7.

HARTMANN, E. (1967), 'The effect of L-tryptophan on the sleep–dream cycle in man', *Psychonom. Sci.*, vol. 8, pp. 295–6.

HESS, S. M., SHORE, P. A., and BRODIE, B. B. (1956), 'Persistence of reserpine action after disappearance of drug from brain – effect on serotonin', *J. Pharmacol. exp. Ther.*, vol. 118, pp. 84–9.

HOBSON, J. A. (1968), 'Sleep after exercise', *Science*, vol. 162, pp. 1503–5.

HONDA, Y., TAKAHASHI, K., TAKAHASHI, S., AZUMI, K., IRIE, M., TSUSHIMA, T., and SHIZUME, K. (1969), 'Growth hormone secretion during nocturnal sleep in normal subjects', *J. clin. Endocrin. Metab.*, vol. 29, pp. 20–29.

IVERSEN, L. L. (1967), *The Uptake and Storage of Noradrenalin in Sympathetic Nerves*, Cambridge University Press.

JOUVET, M. (1967), 'Mechanisms of the state of sleep: a neuropharmacological approach', *Res. Pubns Assn Nerv. Ment. Dis.*, vol. 45, pp. 86–126.

KAWAMURA, H., and SAWYER, C. H. (1965), 'Elevation in brain temperature during paradoxical sleep', *Science*, vol. 150, p. 912.

KOWARZYK, H., BACIU, I., OPRISIU, C., and KOTSCHY, M. (1962), 'Unele mecanisme de activare a fibrinolizci', *Studii Cerc. Med. Cluj.*, vol. 13, pp. 49–60.

KRECH, D. (1968), 'Brain chemistry and anatomy: implications for behavior therapy', in C. Rupp (ed.), *Mind as a Tissue*, Harper & Row, pp. 39–54.

LAJTHA, A. (1964), 'Protein metabolism of the nervous system', *Int. Rev. Neurobiol.*, vol. 6, pp. 1–98.

LEWIS, S. A. (1968), 'The quantification of rapid eye movement sleep', in A. Herxheimer (ed.), *Drugs and Sensory Functions*, Churchill.

LEWIS, S. A., and OSWALD, I. (1969), 'Overdose of tricyclic antidepressants and deductions concerning their cerebral action', *Brit. J. Psychiat.*, vol. 115, pp. 1403–10.

LEWIS, S. A., OSWALD, I., EVANS, J. I., AKINDELE, M. O., and TOMPSETT, S. L. (1970), 'Heroin and human sleep', *EEG clin. Neurophysiol.*, vol. 28, pp. 374–81.

MCILWAIN, H. (1966), *Biochemistry and the Central Nervous System*, Churchill.

MANDELL, M. P., MANDELL, A. J., and JACOBSON, A. (1964), 'Biochemical and neurophysiological studies of paradoxical sleep', *Rec. Adv. Biol. Psychiat.*, vol. 7, pp. 115–22.

MARANTZ, R., and RECHTSCHAFFEN, A. (1967), 'Effect of alpha-methyltyrosine on sleep in the rat', *Percept. mot. Skills*, vol. 25, pp. 805–8.

MARANTZ, R., RECHTSCHAFFEN, A., LOVELL, R. A., and WHITEHEAD, P. K. (1968), 'Effects of alpha-methyltyrosine on the recovery from paradoxical sleep deprivation in the rat', *Com. behav. Biol.*, vol. A2, pp. 161–4.

MARTIN, W. R., and FRASER, H. F. (1961), 'A comparative study of physiological and subjective effects of heroin and morphine administered intravenously in man', *J. Pharmacol. exp. Ther.*, vol. 133, p. 388–99.

MOURET, J., VILPPULA, A., FRANCHON, N., and JOUVET, M. (1968), 'Effets d'un inhibiteur de la monoamine oxidase sur le sommeil du rat', *CR soc. biol.*, vol. 162, pp. 914–17.

OBERST, F. W., and CHRISTENSEN, M. K. (1955) 'Regeneration of erythrocyte and brain cholinesterase activity in rats after sublethal exposures to GB vapour', *J. Pharmacol. exp. Ther.*, vol. 116, pp. 216–19.

OSWALD, I. (1967), 'Slow neurophysiological swings', *Ann. N.Y. Acad. Sci.*, vol. 138, pp. 616–22.

OSWALD, I. (1968), 'Drugs and sleep', *Pharmacol. Rev.*, vol. 20, pp. 273–303.

OSWALD, I. (1969), 'Comparisons of hypnotic drugs', *Brit. J. Psychiat.*, vol. 116, pp. 458–9.

OSWALD, I. (1970), 'Sleep, dreams and drugs', in J. H. Price (ed.), *Modern Trends in Psychological Medicine*, vol. 2, Butterworth, pp. 53–77.

OSWALD, I., and PRIEST, R. G. (1965), 'Five weeks to escape the sleeping-pill habit', *Brit. med. J.*, vol. 2, pp. 1093–9.

OSWALD, I., and THACORE, V. R. (1963), 'Amphetamine and phenmetrazine addiction', *Brit. med. J.*, vol. 2, pp. 427–31.

OSWALD, I., BERGER, R. J., JARAMILLO, R. A., KEDDIE, K. M. G., OLLEY, P. C., and PLUNKETT, G. B. (1963), 'Melancholia and barbiturates: a controlled EEG, body and eye movement study of sleep', *Brit. J. Psychiat.*, vol. 109, pp. 66–78.

OSWALD, I., ASHCROFT, G. W., BERGER, R. J., ECCLESTON, D., EVANS, J. I., and THACORE, V. R. (1966), 'Some experiments in the chemistry of normal sleep', *Brit. J. Psychiat.*, vol. 112, pp. 391–9.

PETRE-QUADENS, O., DE BARSY, A. M., DEVOS, J., and SFAELLO, Z. (1967), 'Sleep in pregnancy: evidence of foetal sleep characteristics', *J. neurol. Sci.*, vol. 4, pp. 600–605.

PIVIK, T., and FOULKES, D. (1965), '"Dream deprivation": effects on dream content', *Science*, vol. 153, pp. 1282–4.

PUJOL, J. F., MOURET, J., JOUVET, M., and GLOWINSKI, J. (1968), 'Increased turnover of cerebral norepinephrine during rebound of paradoxical sleep in the rat', *Science*, vol. 159, pp. 112–14.

REIVICH, M., ISAACS, G., EVARTS, E., and KETY, S. (1968), 'The effect of slow wave sleep and REM sleep on regional cerebral blood flow in cats', *J. Neurochem.*, vol. 15, pp. 301–6.

ROTH, M. (1951), 'Changes in the EEG under barbiturate anaesthesia produced by electro-convulsive treatment, and their significance for the theory of ECT action', *EEG clin. Neurophysiol.*, vol. 3, pp. 261–80.

SHARPLESS, S. K. (1964), 'Reorganization of function in the nervous system – use and disuse', *Ann. Rev. Physiol.*, vol. 26, pp. 357–88.

SHUSTER, L. (1961), 'Repression and de-repression of enzyme synthesis as a possible explanation of some aspects of drug action', *Nature*, vol. 189, pp. 314–15.

WATSON, W. E. (1968), 'Observations on the nucleolar and total cell body nucleic acid of injured nerve cells', *J. Physiol.*, vol. 196, pp. 655–76.

WAY, E. H., LOH, H. H., and SHEN, F. H. (1968), 'Morphine tolerance, physical dependence and synthesis of brain 5-hydroxytryptamine', *Science*, vol. 162, pp. 1290–92.

WEISS, P. (1960), 'Modifiability of the neuron', *Arch. Neurol.*, vol. 2, pp. 595–9.

WILLIAMS, R. L., AGNEW, H. W., and WEBB, W. B. (1966), 'Sleep patterns in the young adult female: an EEG study', *EEG clin. Neurophysiol.*, vol. 20, pp. 264–6.

25 Beverley E. Wolfowitz and T. L. Holdstock

Paradoxical Sleep Deprivation and Memory in Rats

Beverley E. Wolfowitz and T. L. Holdstock, 'Paradoxical sleep deprivation and memory in rats', *Communications in Behavioral Biology*, vol. 6, 1971, pp. 281–4.

Introduction

Depriving the animal of paradoxical sleep (PS) by means of the water tank method (PSD) is one of the procedures used most commonly to investigate the importance of PS in learning and memory processes of animals (Albert, Cicala and Stern, 1970; Fishbein, 1970; Fishbein, McGaugh and Swarz, 1971; Joy and Prinz, 1969; Leconte and Bloch, 1970; Lucero, 1970; Stern, 1970). Unfortunately this technique has the disadvantage that it is difficult to control for secondary effects of PSD upon learning and retention of learned tasks. Some of these secondary factors may include stress effects, such as wetness, fatigue, changes in general activity levels as well as in the wakefulness cycle. The influence of these secondary factors makes it difficult to determine whether deficits following PSD are the result of impaired memory and learning or impaired performance.

An additional problem of research in this area is that of state dependency (Overton, 1964). According to this hypothesis training subjects under one condition and testing them under another may contaminate results. For instance, Joy and Prinz (1969) reported that maximal performance during retesting for an active avoidance response in PSD rats was dependent upon the presence of the training environment.

An approach used by Fishbein *et al.* (1971) seems to contain the ingredients necessary to control for some of the inadequacies inherent in the water tank technique. Fishbein *et al.* (1971) found that electro-convulsive shock (ECS) administered to mice within one hour after removal from PSD markedly impaired retention of a passive avoidance task learned prior to PSD. On the basis of these and other findings, Fishbein *et al.* (1971) suggested that PS was necessary for long term fixation of the memory trace. If the organism was deprived of PS the memory trace was held in labile form, during which condition it was susceptible to disruption by ECS.

Unfortunately, the control subjects of Fishbein *et al.* (1971) were mice administered ECS without preceding PSD. The present study attempted to control for secondary effects of the water tank technique by using PSD animals as controls. In addition, a different species (rats) and task (active avoidance) were used to examine the proposal of Fishbein *et al.* (1971) that the memory trace, kept in labile form by PSD, can be disrupted by ECS.

Procedure

Twenty male hooded rats, all weighing in the region of 350 g, were trained in a shuttle box divided into a black and white compartment. The shuttle box measured $72 \times 30 \times 28$ cm with an 8 cm high barrier dividing the two compartments. Foot shock (1 mA) could be delivered through the grid floor of the black compartment. All animals received one training and one retention session. The training session commenced with a one-minute adaptation period in the shuttle box and was immediately followed by the first trial. At the start of each trial the animals were placed in the black compartment. The buzzer was sounded immediately and shock followed ten seconds later. The buzzer and shock continued until the rat jumped into the white compartment. Shock could be avoided by crossing the barrier before the ten-second interval elapsed. Training was continued until a criterion of three successive avoidance responses was reached. The latency of response and the number of responses to criterion were recorded.

After training, the animals were deprived of PS for seventy-two hours in the manner described by Morden, Mitchell and Dement (1967). The rats were placed on inverted flower pots with base diameters of 6·5 cm. The flower pots were kept in buckets containing 7 cm of water. Food and water were freely available to the animals during PSD.

Immediately after deprivation an ether anaesthetic was administered to all animals (see Fishbein *et al.*, 1971) and an ECS given to ten of the rats. The ECS (20 mA for 1·3 sec) was delivered by a modified LaFayette shocker, model A 615 B, in series with a Hunter timer. The shocker was connected to the ears of the animals by means of crocodile clips wrapped in cloth. The cloth was dipped in a 1 per cent saline solution before being attached to the rat's ears.

Both groups were returned to their home cages for forty-eight hours before they were tested for retention. The procedure for the retention test was the same as that for the training session with the omission of the one-minute adaptation period.

Results

A marked decrease in the number of trials to criterion was exhibited on the retention session by those animals that did not receive ECS following PSD. The animals that received ECS failed to show any savings effect, however (see Figure 1). The differential response pattern of the groups on the training and retention sessions was confirmed by a significant ECS condition × session interaction [$F(1, 18) = 18·79$, $p < 0·001$]. The failure of

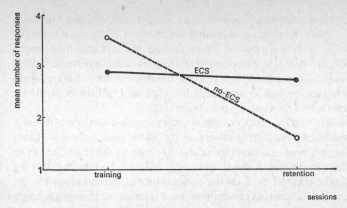

Figure 1 Mean number of responses to criterion during training and retention sessions

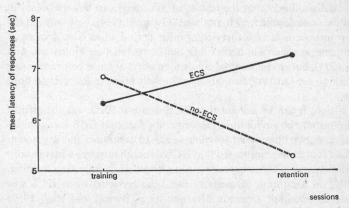

Figure 2 Mean latency of response during training and retention sessions

the animals that received ECS to show any benefit from the training they received before PSD also showed up in the latency of their avoidance responses. Although the ECS group had somewhat shorter response latencies during training than the no-ECS group, their response latencies actually increased on retention compared to the decrease exhibited by the no-ECS group (see Figure 2). The differential pattern of response of the two groups was again highly significant [$F(1, 18) = 36.88, p < 0.001$].

Discussion

The results of this study showed that seventy-two-hour PSD followed by a forty-eight-hour recovery period did not interfere with the retention of an avoidance response in rats. However, if an ECS was administered immediately after PSD the animals exhibited no memory of the task after the forty-eight-hour recovery period. These findings indicate that the memory trace is held in a labile form during PS and suggest some involvement of PS in the storage of long-term memory. Thus, the results obtained with rats on an active avoidance task complement the findings Fishbein *et al.* (1971) obtained with mice on a passive avoidance task.

It is unlikely that the results of the present experiment can be attributed to confounding by secondary effects of the water tank technique. Since control animals were also deprived of PS it is unlikely that such factors as fatigue and disturbance in the sleep cycle could have been responsible for the differential effect of ECS on the performance of the two groups in the retention test. The fact that the animals were returned to their home cages for two days prior to retention testing provides further argument against intepretation of the results in terms of performance deficits.

It is equally unlikely that the results of this study can be interpreted in terms of the state dependency hypothesis (Overton, 1964). Not only did the retention test occur after a forty-eight-hour period when considerable, if not complete, compensation of PSD had occurred (see Holdstock and Franks, 1971), but environmental conditions were the same before learning and retention sessions. All animals lived in their home cages prior to both sessions.

In addition, it can be argued that ECS and not PSD was the critical factor in memory consolidation. However, the fact that ECS was administered seventy-two hours after learning seems to contradict this argument. Numerous studies have indicated that ECS does not interfere with memory consolidation unless administered within a short while following training. Generally, no disruption of memory has been reported when ECS was administered one hour or more after learning (Barrett and Ray, 1969; Duncan, 1949; Glickman, 1961; Heriot and Coleman, 1962; McGaugh and Petrinovich, 1966; Pfingst and King, 1969; Pinel, 1969; Thompson and Dean, 1955). It is possible that PSD may have rendered the ECS a more effective amnesic agent, though. Would this be the case, it could argue against interpretation of the present data and that of Fishbein *et al.* (1971) in terms of PS involvement in processes responsible for storing long-term memory.

However, the most probable explanation of the present results seems to be in terms of a memory trace that is held in a labile form during PSD and consolidated after deprivation. Interpretation of PS involvement in memory mechanisms is in agreement with the work of several other animal laboratories (Fishbein *et al.*, 1971; Leconte and Bloch, 1970; Lucero, 1970; Stern, 1970). The issue is far from resolved, though. Negative evidence of PS involvement in memory processes has been reported (Albert *et al.*, 1970; Joy and Prinz, 1969). It remains for future research to investigate the complex interaction of variables involved in the participation of PS in learning and memory.

References

ALBERT, J., CICALA, G. A., and SIEGEL, J. (1970), 'The behavioral effects of REM sleep deprivation in rats', *Psychophysiology*, vol. 6, pp. 550–60.

BARRETT, R. J., and RAY, O. S. (1969), 'Attenuation of habituation by electroconvulsive shock', *J. comp. physiol. Psychol.*, vol. 69, pp. 133–5.

DUNCAN, C. P. (1949), 'The retroactive effect of electroshock on learning', *J. comp. physiol. Psychol.*, vol. 42, pp. 32–44.

FISHBEIN, W. (1970), 'Interferences with conversion of memory from short-term to long-term storage by partial sleep deprivation', *Commun. behav. Biol.*, vol. 5, pp. 171–5.

FISHBEIN, W., MCGAUGH, J. I., and SWARZ, J. R. (1971), 'Retrograde amnesia: electroconvulsive shock effects after termination of rapid eye movement sleep deprivation', *Science*, vol. 172, pp. 80–82.

GLICKMAN, S. E. (1961), 'Perseverative neural traces and the consolidation of the memory trace', *Psychol. Bull.*, vol. 58, pp. 218–30.

HERIOT, J. T., and COLEMAN, P. D. (1962), 'The effects of electroconvulsive shock on a modified one trial conditioned avoidance response', *J. comp. physiol. Psychol.*, vol. 55, pp. 1082–4.

HOLDSTOCK, T. L., and FRANKS, P. E. (1971), 'Some aspects of paradoxical sleep in the laboratory rat', *Psychol. Afric.*, vol. 14, pp. 38–44.

JOY, R. M., and PRINZ, P. N. (1969), 'The effect of sleep altering environments upon the acquisition and retention of a conditioned avoidance response in the rat', *Physiol. Behav.*, vol. 4, pp. 809–14.

LECONTE, P., and BLOCH, V. (1970), 'Deficit de la retention d'un conditionnement après privation de sommeil paradoxal chez le rat', *S. R. Acad. Sci. (D) Paris*, vol. 271, pp. 226–9.

LUCERO, M. A. (1970), 'Lengthening of REM sleep duration consecutive to learning in the rat', *Brain Res.*, vol. 20, pp. 319–22.

MCGAUGH, J. L., and PETRINOVICH, L. F. (1966), 'Neural consolidation and ECS re-examined', *Psychol. Rev.*, vol. 73, pp. 382–7.

MORDEN, B., MITCHELL, G., and DEMENT, W. (1967), 'Selective REM sleep deprivation and compensation phenomena in the rat', *Brain Res.*, vol. 5, pp. 339–49.

OVERTON, D. A. (1964), 'State dependent or "dissociated" learning produced with pentobarbital', *J. comp. physiol. Psychol.*, vol. 57, pp. 3–12.

PFINGST, B. E., and KING, R. A. (1969), 'Effects of posttraining electroconvulsive shock on retention test performance involving choice', *J. comp. physiol. Psychol.*, vol. 68, pp. 645–9.

PINEL, J. P. (1969), 'A short gradient of ECS-produced amnesia in a one-trial appetitive situation', *J. comp. physiol. Psychol.*, vol. 68, pp. 650–55.

STERN, W. C. (1970), 'Behavioral and biochemical aspects of rapid eye movement sleep deprivation in the rat', *Dissert. Abstr.*, vol. 31, pp. 1574–5.

THOMPSON, R., and DEAN, W. A. (1955), 'A further study of the retroactive effects of ECS', *J. comp. physiol. Psychol.*, vol. 48, pp. 488–91.

26 Rosalind Dymond Cartwright and Robert W. Ratzel

Effects of Dream Loss on Waking Behaviours

Rosalind Dymond Cartwright and Robert W. Ratzel, 'Effects of dream loss on waking behaviors', *Archives of General Psychiatry*, vol. 27, 1972, pp. 277–80.

One of the early findings from the all-night EEG-EOG monitoring of sleep was that dream experience is more regular and plentiful than had been anticipated on the basis of morning dream recall. The fact that approximately 24 per cent of the total sleep time of normal human adults is occupied by bizarre, hallucinatory fantasy occurring in four to six episodes each night (Dement, 1965) raised anew the question of dream function. One hope expressed was that this work might lead to a reconceptualization of the phenomenon of psychotic behavior. Perhaps the waking hallucinations of the insane represent a breakdown of some mechanism which in normal life keeps these behaviors confined to sleep periods (Pos, 1969; Snyder, 1963).

Dement (1960) first approached a test of this hypothesized dream function by the strategy of experimentally reducing or eliminating the sleep state associated with its occurrence, the rapid eye movement, or REM, sleep. This was the first of many studies which attempted to illuminate the role of this sleep state by looking for disruption of normal processes following its suppression.

The yield for psychology from a decade of this work has not been great: the findings are clearer for changes in sleep than in waking behavior. There are immediate effects on sleep itself while deprivation is being carried out, i.e. (1) subjects show an increase in the number of attempts to enter the REM sleep stage, both within the first night and progressively across the nights during which REM time is reduced. When normal sleep is again permitted, Ss show (2) an increase in the percentage of time occupied by the REM stage of sleep to total sleep above baseline levels, (3) an increase in the frequency of eye movement bursts within the REM periods, and (4) a decrease in the latency to the onset of the first REM cycle of the night (Dement, 1960; Kales, Hoedemaker, Jacobson and Lichtenstein, 1964; Sampson, 1965). There have not been many well-controlled studies of the effects of REM time reduction on waking behaviors of human Ss (Clemes and Dement, 1961; Greenberg et al., 1970; Lerner, 1966; Sampson, 1966). From these, there is little hard evidence to support the idea that removing the state associated with night-time hallucinatory activity leads to the intrusion of this behavior into waking life of normal Ss. The reports do suggest, though, that Ss vary widely in their tolerance levels for REM loss as measured by their response to this manipulation. Some Ss report feeling slowed down from their normal activity level, others report feeling activated. The experience of mild REM deprivation, up to approximately three nights, seems to be equivalent to a mild stress situation which mobilizes some Ss to perform better, but which disturbs the functioning of other Ss. These observations lead to the suggestion that changes in waking performance following REM deprivation may well differ in direction in different groups and, for only some, under some levels of REM loss, may there be intrusions of disruptive primary process activity.

In a previous paper (Cartwright, Monroe and Palmer, 1970), one of us reported that a group of normal young adults, REM deprived for three nights, could be typed as falling into three different response patterns. These three were labeled 'disruption', 'compensation', and 'substitution'. The disrupted pattern referred to a loss of clarity in the EEG sleep record on the first recovery night with many intrusions of stage 2 signs into stage 1 REM, making a reliable scoring very difficult. The compensation pattern was the one that has been typically reported of an increase in stage REM on the first recovery night and a decrease in latency to the first REM period of the night. The group of Ss making up the substitution pattern did not show this increase in REM per cent above base rate but did show an increase in the number of reports judges classed as dream reports from the REM onset awakenings made on the three deprivation nights. The compensator Ss had significantly fewer of these dream reports than the substitutor Ss in the content retrieved from the deprivation awakenings.

If these findings can be replicated, it would be predicted that two groups who differ in REM onset fantasy scores will also differ in REM per cent rebound and on the degree to which their daytime behavior is affected by REM time loss. Subjects with low REM onset fantasy (LOF) would be predicted to demonstrate more marked changes in waking performance than those with high onset fantasy (HOF) on the basis that, while equally REM-time deprived, their postdeprivation psychological states will differ due to their being unequal in fantasy deprivation.

The variable which seemed likely to be crucial in determining Ss' response to REM deprivation was the degree to which their dream-like activity is restricted to REM periods. Zimmerman (1970) reported that the frequency of dream reports from sleep stages other than REM is one of the characteristic differences between light and deep sleepers. He defined the depth of sleep by the decibel level of an auditory signal required to wake Ss from various sleep stages sampled throughout the night. Deep sleepers, with high auditory awakening thresholds (AAT), reported that they had been dreaming following 93 per cent of the awakenings from REM sleep periods and following 21 per cent of their awakenings from NREM sleep stages. Light sleepers reported that they had been dreaming 89 per cent of the time when wakened from a REM period and following 71 per cent of their NREM awakenings. These subjective reports were corroborated by judges' ratings of the content of these reports. The difference in the frequency of NREM dreaming found between light and deep sleepers seemed to make the AAT a reasonable variable on which to select Ss in order to investigate the effects of REM sleep loss on those whose dream experience is bound to the REM sleep state in contrast to those for whom it is not. Specifically, the following predictions were made.

1. Subjects stratified into those having high and low fantasy scores for the content retrieved from the REM onset awakenings, as measured on the Foulkes Dream-Like Fantasy Scale (1971), will be significantly different in NREM fantasy score (from stage 2 awakenings) as well. The direction of the difference is predicted to be the same: HOF Ss will have significantly higher fantasy scores from stage 2 than LOF Ss. The reasoning behind this prediction is that those who have high fantasy at REM onset, when REM time is being reduced, are more likely to be persons whose dream-like sleep fantasy is generally less restricted to REM periods, the so-called NREM dreamer.

2. HOF and LOF groups will also differ on AAT, HOF Ss being lighter sleepers than LOF Ss.

3. HOF and LOF Ss will not differ on their initial REM per cent base rate but will differ significantly in the per cent time spent in the REM state on the recovery night, HOF Ss having significantly lower recovery REM per cent than LOF Ss. This finding would confirm the previous findings of a substitutor–compensator dichotomy.

4. The Wechsler Adult Intelligence Scale (WAIS), will show little or no change for the HOF group but there will be significant change for the LOF group following deprivation. No directional prediction could be made for this hypothesis, only a between group difference in change based on the reasoning that HOF Ss are not in any significantly different psychological condition during the waking period following REM deprivation due to their substitution of REM onset fantasy for that usually experienced during the REM time experimentally eliminated. LOF Ss, in contrast, are dream, as well as REM, deprived and so will be in a psychologically different state which will be reflected in a change on their psychological test performance.

5. There will be a significant increase in Rorschach M (human movement) response for the LOF group and no significant increase in this score for the

HOF group following deprivation. This prediction is based on the findings of Lerner (1966) of an M increase for an undifferentiated group of *S*s following drug-induced REM suppression. The M is purported to be a measure of responsiveness to internal fantasy promptings (Klopfer *et al.*, 1954) and so this change is predicted to be specific to the LOF group who have not had as much fantasy expression during the preceding nights as the HOF group.

6. There will be a significant shift in the Rorschach experience balance (introversion–extroversion) as scored by the M:sum C ratio, for the LOF but not for the HOF *S*s. This prediction is based on Palmer's (1963) study which reported a balance shift following total sleep deprivation toward the introversive side of that ratio. This change in waking behavior is again predicted to be specific to the LOF group.

7. There will be some initial personality differences between those who fall into the high and low REM onset fantasy subgroups on the Minnesota Multiphasic Personality Inventory (MMPI). Work done by Pivik and Foulkes (1968) on the personality correlates of NREM dreaming lead to this expectation and the prediction that differences might be found in the K-corrected Schizophrenia (ScK) and/or Ego Strength (ES) scores of the MMPI.

Method

Twenty-four adult male student volunteers between twenty-one through twenty-six years of age were given a battery of tests including a sleep questionnaire, a Rorschach, MMPI, two verbal and two performance subtests of the WAIS. All were monitored using EEG-EOG techniques in the sleep laboratory for at least two nights to establish their auditory awakening threshold by Zimmerman's (1970) procedure. This procedure determined the 'depth' of sleep in terms of the amount of sound stimulation required to bring *S*s to full waking arousal. The stimulus was a series of 800 hertz pure-tones generated by an audio-oscillator (400 series Hewlett-Packard). Each tone sounded for one second followed by a nine-second interval of silence. The first stimulus was presented at 35 dB. The tone increased in loudness in 5 dB steps up to 110 dB. The accuracy of the high-fidelity speaker to deliver these stimuli was checked nightly at the pillow with a General Radio sound level meter. The decibel level immediately preceding the EEG indications of wakefulness was taken as the awakening threshold for that trial even though the series of tones was continued until the *S* responded 'I am awake.' The *S* was asked for a report of his mental content just prior to each awakening. These were tape recorded and transcribed for ratings on the Foulkes Dream-Like Fantasy (DF) Scale (1971). Seven awakenings were made during the night in the following order:

1. Five minutes after the onset of the first stage 4 of the night.
2. Five minutes after the onset of the next stage 2.
3. Five minutes after the onset of the first REM.
4. Five minutes after the onset of the next stage 3. A complete cycle was allowed to intervene between awakenings 4 and 5.
5. Five minutes after the onset of the next stage 2, following the end of a REM period.
6. Five minutes after the onset of the next REM period.
7. Five minutes after the onset of the next stage 2.

This procedure allowed all stages of sleep to be sampled and both REM and NREM reports to be gathered at the beginning and end of the night. Five light and five deep sleepers were selected by first computing the median threshold for each of the seven awakenings. The criterion for selecting an S as a light sleeper was that five or more of his seven awakenings be below the median threshold. Deep sleepers were selected so that five or more of his seven awakenings were above the group median. Three weeks later these ten Ss spent five additional nights in the laboratory. After a first baseline night, there were three REM-deprivation nights followed by one recovery night of uninterrupted sleep. Each S was retested on the Rorschach and WAIS just before sleeping on the fifth night. REM deprivation was carried out by voice awakenings made over the intercom at the first sign of a REM period. This might be the first rapid eye movement accompanied by a stage 1 record or an ascending stage 1 record of more than one minute duration without eye movements. Occasionally, deep sleeper Ss could not be aroused by voice alone. Under these conditions, hand awakenings were made within the first two to three minutes of REM onset.

All content reports, both those from the REM and NREM awakenings made during the AAT nights and all those obtained from the three nights of REM deprivation, were coded numerically and rated blindly by a judge naïve for the study conditions but well trained in the use of the Foulkes scale (JS). The group was dichotomized at the median on their mean DF score for the awakenings made on the three deprivation nights into five high and five low REM onset fantasy Ss (HOF and LOF). All psychological tests were scored by a different research assistant (PW) who was naïve for both subject and condition (pre- or postdeprivation).

Results

Table 1 gives the means and standard deviations for the basic scores and the t-test for differences between the HOF and LOF groups. Before any of

Table 1 Mean sleep, fantasy, and waking score differences

Variable	HOF		LOF		t	P	
	Mean	SD	Mean	SD		2-tail	1-tail
Total number of awakenings	40·40	10·14	30·4	6·45	1·863	0·10	
Mean sleep time deprivation	329·00	23·90	325·2	14·80	0·301	ns	
Mean REM time deprivation	23·20	7·66	18·4	7·60	0·990	ns	
REM onset DF	4·82	0·73	2·96	0·56	4·479	0·01	
Stage 2 DF	3·98	1·36	1·73	1·48	2·494	0·05	0·02
AAT dB	46·84	11·02	54·42	12·60	1·012	ns	
REM % base rate	20·88	3·96	22·76	4·72	0·682	ns	
REM % recovery	24·54	6·33	32·30	5·19	2·119	0·10–0·05	0·05
Predeprivation							
WAIS total	129·80	4·81	124·40	3·57	2·012	0·10–0·05	
WAIS verbal	125·80	10·08	126·80	5·49	0·195	ns	
WAIS performance	132·4	4·09	117·60	8·02	3·675	0·01	
Postdeprivation							
WAIS total	130·8	2·86	134·4	7·95	0·952	ns	
WAIS verbal	128·2	6·22	133·8	5·97	1·452	ns	
WAIS performance	130·4	10·73	131·2	15·96	0·093	ns	
Predeprivation Rorschach M+	2·4	1·52	0·6	0·54	2·496	0·05	
Postdeprivation Rorschach M+	2·2	0·83	2·0	0·70	0·408	ns	
Predeprivation M:sum C	3·2:3·1		1·4:3·1	}	$F = 9·890$		
Postdeprivation M:sum C	3·4:2·9		2·4:1·5	}		0·02	
MMPI							
ScK	64·8	15·79	51·4	4·72	1·818	0·10–0·05	
ES	56·4	4·09	51·6	3·04	2·109	0·10–0·05	
Pd	64·2	11·97	52·6	4·72	2·016	0·10–0·05	

these results can be interpreted as due to a difference in fantasy deprivation, it is important that it first be established that the groups did not differ in total amount of sleep deprivation. Table 1 shows that the groups did not differ significantly on total number of awakenings needed to accomplish the deprivation over the three nights, the mean minutes of sleep per night, nor the mean minutes of REM sleep remaining on those nights.

Table 1 shows that hypothesis 1, which predicted HOF *S*s to have higher stage 2 DF scores than LOF *S*s, is confirmed at the 0·02 level. Hypothesis 2 was not confirmed, although the direction of the difference was as predicted for HOF *S*s to be lighter sleepers than LOF *S*s.

Hypothesis 3 predicted no difference in base rate REM per cent between the two groups but a significant difference between the REM per cent on the recovery night. Both of these predictions were confirmed which replicated the original substitutor–compensator dichotomy.

Hypothesis 4 predicted more change in WAIS for LOF *S*s. Since the initial WAIS performance scores were found to be significantly different between the groups, this prediction was tested by an analysis of covariance. The $F = 5·133$ was just short of the 0·05 level although a *t*-test for matched groups showed the change in the LOF group from 124 to 134 mean IQ to be significant beyond the 0·02 level. A more detailed analysis of the post-deprivation WAIS change showed that most of the change in the LOF group could be accounted for by the Picture Arrangement score. The mean weighted predeprivation score was 11·4 for this group while the postdeprivation mean was 14·2 yielding a *t* of 2·747, a difference significant at about the 0·05 level for 4 df.

Hypothesis 5 predicted a larger increase in human movement (M) responses for the LOF than the HOF group. This was not confirmed except for M+ or good quality M responses. *S*s whose REM onset fantasy is low display more change in response to waking fantasy opportunities than those whose onset fantasy is high.

Hypothesis 6 concerning a shift in the Rorschach experience balance toward a more introversive responsiveness for the LOF group following deprivation was tested by a covariance analysis. The change from the pre-deprivation balance for the LOF group was significantly different at 0·02 from the change in the HOF group ($F = 9·890$, df 1 and 7). HOF *S*s were initially about equally balanced between responsiveness to inner and outer stimulation and did not change, whereas LOF *S*s were initially extratensive, more responsive to outer stimulation. These *S*s changed following REM deprivation to be more responsive to inner stimuli so that their postdeprivation ratio is now more normal; the normal range for the ratio being 2:1 to 1:1 (Klopfer *et al.*, 1954).

Hypothesis 7 was tested by computing the difference between HOF and

LOF groups on all clinical and validating scales of the MMPI plus the Welsh, Taylor MA (manifest anxiety), R–S (repressor–sensitizer), and ES (ego strength) special scores. Out of a total of seventeen tests, only two, the Pd (Psychopathic deviant) and ES, reached significance between the 0·10 and 0·05 level making interpretation risky. It is interesting, though, that Pivik and Foulkes' report of an r of 0·47 between MMPI ScK and NREM DF was exactly replicated. The r between stage 2 DF and ScK scores for this sample was 0·469. However, this was not significant with this small number. The between group difference for the ES score cannot be considered a confirmation of the Pivik and Foulkes findings, as the direction is reversed. It is the HOF group which has the higher ego strength score in this sample.

Comment

Normal Ss following moderate REM deprivation tend to show either no change or positive change in waking test behavior. The difference between these two response patterns appears to be related to the degree of accessibility to internal fantasy responses generally. Subjects high in REM onset fantasy differed from those low in REM onset fantasy in being usually higher in NREM fantasy scores by night and being, on the Rorschach test, more responsive to internal experience by day. These Ss show little or no postdeprivation test change following REM loss. Low REM onset fantasy Ss are generally more REM-bound for dream-like fantasy by night and on Rorschach, more responsive to external stimulation by day. These Ss do show change on tests following the reduction of REM. The changes tend to reflect an increase in accessibility to day-time fantasy; M+ responses increase, the total response balance shifts to be more internal, and even the WAIS increase is largely accounted for by an improvement on the Picture Arrangement subtest. This test, requiring the ordering of cartoon pictures of human figures into story-like sequences often humorous in nature, seems to tap much the same process as that involved in the construction of good M responses and perhaps even in dreaming. To speak quite speculatively, it appears that Ss who ordinarily do not have much interplay between their internal fantasy and their waking test responses seem to gain something from a little REM loss. Here, the change, rather than being in the nature of intrusions of uncontrolled hallucinations which disrupt reality contact, appears to involve a constructive use of fantasy which is integrated with reality responses.

Clearly, what is needed now is exploration of two types: (1) to extend the amount of deprivation to discover how far this positive effect holds, and (2) to explore the effects of mild deprivation on persons not within the normal range. It would be predicted that the positive effects of mild deprivation on the fantasy-constricted individual would be reversed either with increases in the amount of deprivation and/or with increases in the disturbance level of the *S*s.

References

CARTWRIGHT, R., MONROE, L., and PALMER, C. (1967), 'Individual differences in response to REM deprivation', *Arch. gen. Psychiat.*, vol. 16, pp. 297–303.

CLEMES, S., and DEMENT, W. (1961), 'Effect of REM sleep deprivation on psychological functioning', *J. nerv. ment. Dis.*, vol. 144, pp. 485–91.

DEMENT, W. (1960), 'Effect of dream deprivation', *Science*, vol. 131, pp. 1705–7.

DEMENT, W. (1965), 'An essay on dreams', in T. Newcomb (ed.), *New Dimensions in Psychology*, vol. 2, Holt, Rinehart & Winston, pp. 135–257.

FOULKES, D. (1971), 'Dream-like fantasy scale: a rating manual', *Psychophysiology*, vol. 7, pp. 335–6.

GREENBERG, R., *et al.* (1970), 'The effects of dream deprivation: implications for a theory of the psychological function of dreaming', *Brit. J. med. Psychol.*, vol. 43, pp. 1–11.

KALES, A., HOEDEMAKER, F. S., JACOBSON, A., and LICHTENSTEIN, E. L. (1964), 'Dream deprivation: an experimental reappraisal', *Nature*, vol. 204, pp. 1337–8.

KLOPFER, B., *et al.* (1954), *Developments in the Rorschach Technique*, World Book Co., pp. 254–5.

LERNER, B. (1966). 'Rorschach movement and dreams: a validation study using drug-induced dream deprivation', *J. abnorm. Psychol.*, vol. 71, pp. 75–86.

PALMER, J. (1963), 'Alternations in Rorschach's experience balance under conditions of food and sleep deprivation: a construct validation study', *J. proj. Tech.*, vol. 27, pp. 208–13.

PIVIK, T., and FOULKES, D. (1968), 'NREM mentation: relation to personality orientation time and time of night', *J. consult. clin. Psychol.*, vol. 32, pp. 144–51.

POS, R. (1969), 'The biology of dreaming and the informational underload (sensory deprivation) theory of psychosis', *Canad. Psychiat. Assn J.*, vol. 14, pp. 371–85.

SAMPSON, H. (1965), 'Deprivation of dreaming sleep by two methods', *Arch. gen. Psychiat.*, vol. 13, pp. 79–86.

SAMPSON, H. (1966), 'Psychological effects of deprivation of dreaming sleep', *J. nerv. ment. Dis.*, vol. 143, pp. 305–17.

SNYDER, F. (1963), 'The new biology of dreaming', *Arch. gen. Psychiat.*, vol. 8, pp. 381–91.

ZIMMERMAN, W. (1970), 'Sleep mentation and auditory awakening thresholds', *Psychophysiology*, vol. 6, pp. 540–49.

Part Three
Theories and Future Prospects

Theorizing about the function of dreams has a long history going back to classical times whereas psychologists have only begun to think about possible physiological functions for REM sleep in the past twenty years. Yet if dreams occur predominantly in REM sleep, then they may simply be a functionless epiphenomenon of this state. After all, no one has a theory of the functions of drunken thought and Kleitman (1970) has likened dreams to just this kind of thinking. Indeed, one cannot exclude the possibility that no important functions are served by REM sleep and that the environmental conditions that led to its emergence in the first mammals no longer apply. However, few psychologists believe this. A brief review of the range of theories concerning the functions of dreams and REM sleep has been written by Hartmann (1967) and examples of both kinds of theory are contained in this part of the book and in Hartmann (1970).

Reading 27 is Calvin Hall's well-known cognitive theory of dreams, which was advanced in opposition to the Freudian view which emphasizes unconscious processes (see Reading 3). Berger (1967) has recently developed a theory which combines a modified Freudian approach with information-processing concepts. This computer analogy of information processing is amplified by Evans and Newman (Reading 28) who suggest that in dreams we review and discard useless knowledge. The computer analogy has been criticized by Faraday (1972) and is difficult to test. None the less other versions of it have been proposed (for example, Dewan, 1970; Greenberg and Leidermann, 1966). Reading 29 contains Snyder's theory of the evolutionary origin of REM sleep with an assessment and criticism by Dement. This theory, which postulates a sentinel function for REM sleep, has recently been given a physiological underpinning involving pineal function by Drew and Batt (1972). In Reading 30, Berger proposes that REM sleep provides a mechanism for the establishment of the neuromuscular pathways serving the binocularly coordinated eye movements necessary for depth perception. Oswald's theory that REM sleep is a time of intense protein synthesis, serving to restore brain processes, is referred to at the end of Reading 24, but a more popular and recent account of it is available (Oswald, 1970). Much theorizing about dreaming has been dominated by the idea that there are three states of consciousness, awake, REM and non-REM sleep. This view is attacked by Grosser and Siegal (Reading 31) who describe a more sophisticated tonic–phasic model.

Finally, Hursch (Reading 32) takes a panoramic view of the whole field of dream research and concludes, *inter alia*, that the masses of data now available are going to require more vigorous organization.

References

BERGER, L. (1967), 'Function of dreams', *J. abnorm. Psychol. Monogr.*, vol. 72, pp. 1–28.

DEWAN, E. M. (1970), 'The programming (P) hypothesis for REM sleep', in E. Hartmann (ed.), *Sleep and Dreaming*, Little, Brown.

DREW, W. G., and BATT, J. (1972), 'A contribution to the evolutionary theory of dreaming: an hypothesis on the role of the pineal in species and specimen protection', *Biol. Psychiat.*, vol. 4, pp. 131–46.

FARADAY, A. (1972), *Dream Power*, Hodder & Stoughton.

GREENBERG, R., and LEIDERMANN, P. H. (1966), 'Perceptions, the dreaming process and memory: an up-to-date version of notes on a mystic writing pad', *Comp. Psychiat.*, vol. 37, pp. 517–23.

HARTMANN, E. (1967), *The Biology of Dreaming*, C. C. Thomas.

HARTMANN, E. (1970), *Sleep and Dreaming*, Little, Brown.

KLEITMAN, N. (1970), 'Does dreaming have a function?', in E. Hartmann (ed.), *Sleep and Dreaming*, Little, Brown.

OSWALD, I. (1970), 'Sleep, the great restorer', *New Scientist*, vol. 46, pp. 170–72.

27 Calvin S. Hall

A Cognitive Theory of Dreams

Calvin S. Hall, 'A cognitive theory of dreams', *Journal of General Psychology*, vol. 49, 1953, pp. 273–82.

In the final years of the nineteenth century, Freud formulated a theory of the dream which has proved exceedingly useful to the clinical practitioner and to a lesser extent to the personality theorist for verifying propositions derived from dynamic theories of personality (Harris, 1948; Polster, 1950). Freud was very proud of his first original and independent achievement in psychological theorizing, so much so that he appears to have been reluctant to alter it as he did so many other discoveries of these early years. In a singularly mistitled lecture *Revision of the Theory of Dreams* published in 1933, Freud revises his original theory to the extent of adding the italicized word to the fundamental proposition, 'the dream is an *attempted* wish-fulfillment'. In this same essay, Freud observes that 'the analysts behave as though they had nothing more to say about the dream, as though the whole subject of dream-theory was finished and done with'. Freud must have had himself in mind as well as his colleagues when he made this observation for in his valedictory (1940) he abides by his original formulation, despite the the fact that the psychoanalytic theory of the person had made great strides in the intervening forty years. Probably the most noteworthy advances made by Freud in his later years were a revised theory of anxiety, a new theory of motivation, and the development of a far reaching ego theory. Of these three, ego theory has had the greatest impact upon current psycho-analytic theorizing.

What we should like to do in this paper is to bring dream theory within the context of ego psychology by defending the proposition that dreaming is a cognitive process. Before addressing ourselves to this thesis, let us define a dream. A dream is a succession of images, predominantly visual in quality, which are experienced during sleep. A dream commonly has one or more scenes, several characters in addition to the dreamer, and a sequence of actions and interactions usually involving the dreamer. It resembles a motion picture or dramatic production in which the dreamer is a partici-pant-observer. Although a dream is an hallucination, the dreamer experi-ences it as he does any perceptual phenomenon. Scenes, people, objects, and actions are experienced as though they were impressing themselves on the senses from the external world. The world of dreams, it goes without saying, is a world of pure projection.

The principal thesis of this paper is that these images of a dream are the embodiment of thoughts. They are a medium by which a psychological process, cognition, is transformed into a form that can be perceived. Although images are the only means by which ideas find sensible expression in dreams, other media such as words, numbers, gestures and pictures are employed in waking life for making one's thoughts known. When thought is made perceptible, it is said to be communicated. Unlike the communications of waking life, which may have an audience of millions, the audience of a dream consists of only one person, the dreamer himself. A dream is a highly private showing of the dreamer's thoughts.

In order to develop the thesis of this paper, it is necessary to say a few words about thinking. Thinking is a process of conceiving. The end-product of this process is a conception (idea). A conception is an item of knowledge, a formulation of experience which has meaning for a person. It is derived ultimately from experience but is not dependent for its existence at any given moment upon the reception of sensory impressions from the external world or from one's body. In other words, conceiving is an autonomous process that requires no direct sensory data. It may be contrasted with perceiving, a process which is dependent upon direct stimulation of the senses. One *perceives* a wintry landscape when one looks out at a scene as it exists in the world and incorporates through the eyes a pattern of light waves which is the raw material for the formation of a perception.[1] One has a *conception* of winter when one thinks of it as being a time of cold weather, snow, short days, icy streets and bare trees. One can conceive of winter at any time of the year, but one can only perceive winter during the winter. Although not a great deal is known about the process of conceiving, we are fairly well acquainted with its products, i.e. conceptions or ideas, since they are rendered perceptible in a variety of forms including dreams. An artist expresses his conceptions in visual terms, while writers and speakers use words to make their ideas public. Mathematicians employ numbers and symbols for conveying their thoughts, and musicians express themselves in patterns of tone, rhythm, intensity, and quality. A dancer embodies her ideas in physical movement, a sculptor in three dimensional forms, and an architect in buildings. The formulation and communication of ideas are the essence of all creative endeavors.

We return now to dreaming and dreams. If dreaming is defined as thinking that occurs during sleep, and if thinking consists essentially of generating

1. It is doubtful whether a pure perception ever takes place. Perceptions are probably always acted upon and changed by autochthonous processes within the person, the chief of which may be conceiving.

ideas, then dreaming is also a process of conceiving and the resulting dream images may be viewed as the embodiment of conceptions. That which is invisible, namely a conception, becomes visible when it is transformed into a dream image. The images of a dream are pictures of conceptions. A dream is a work of art which requires of the dreamer no particular talent, special training, or technical competence. Dreaming is a creative enterprise in which all may and most do participate.

If dreaming consists of transforming conceptions into images, then dream interpretation reverses this process; images are translated into their referent ideas. How is this translation accomplished? It is accomplished by drawing inferences from material in the dream text, and by checking these inferences against other dreams of the person or against other information about the person. Although we cannot describe the methods of interpreting dreams within the limits of this paper,[2] some general remarks regarding dream interpretation may be made here. To interpret a dream means, according to the theory presented in this paper, to discover the conceptions or conceptual systems of the dreamer. These conceptions may be inferred from a number of lines of evidence, some of which are as follows: (a) the actions and qualities of the dreamer in the dream, i.e. the role or roles played by the dreamer, (b) the kind of characters introduced in the dream, (c) the actions and qualities assigned to them, (d) the nature of the interactions between the dreamer and these characters, and between the characters themselves, (e) the setting or dream scene, (f) transitions within the dream, and (g) the outcome of the dream. The final objective of dream interpretation is not to understand the dream but rather to understand the dreamer.

What kinds of conceptions are found in dreams? One is tempted to reply all kinds but this is not correct since many ideas seem to be excluded from dreams. Dreams are relatively silent regarding political and economic questions; they have little or nothing to say about current events in the world of affairs. I was collecting dreams daily from students during the last days of the war with Japan when the first atomic bomb was exploded, yet this catastrophe did not register in a single dream. Presidential elections, declarations of war, the diplomatic struggles of great powers, major athletic contests, local happenings that make the headlines, all are pretty largely ignored in dreams. A count of characters in a large sample of dreams reveals that the number of prominent people appearing in dreams is very small. Nor are intellectual, scientific, cultural and professional topics or the affairs of finance, business, and industry the subject matter of dreams.

What then is left? The whole world of the personal, the intimate, the emotional, and the conflictful remain. These are the ideas which register in

2. A discussion of this topic will be found in Hall (1953).

dreams. For the sake of discussion, we shall present a classification of some common conceptions found in dreams.

Conceptions of self

A dream is a mirror that reflects the self-conceptions of the dreamer. Ideas of self are revealed by the repertoire of parts taken by the dreamer in a series of dreams. The repertoire may consist of a few roles, or it may be extensive and varied. In one dream series, for example, the dreamer is pictured as a great general, a rich and influential man, and an important steel manufacturer. In each case, however, he loses his power by being disabled in vigorous combat with a superior force. Here we see that a self-conception of strength and potency cannot be maintained. A typical dream of strength turning into weakness is the following one.

I was sitting knee deep in quarters in my room. People kept rushing into my room and stealing handfuls of money. I chased after them, grasping them violently and retrieving my money. But after a while so many people kept grabbing my money at once that I couldn't chase them all so I just sat there and cried.

This young man's conceptions of himself are disjunctive; he is both strong and weak, with weakness winning out over strength.

Perhaps no other medium gives us a more candid picture of what a person thinks about himself than do dreams. It was Ralph Waldo Emerson who wrote: 'A skillful man reads his dreams for his self-knowledge.'

Conceptions of other people

Dreams reveal what the dreamer thinks about his mother and father, his brothers and sisters, his spouse and children, and diverse other classes of people. These conceptions, like those of self, are embodied in the roles played by the various characters. If the dreamer conceives of his father as a stern, demanding, autocratic person, the father is assigned a part that is in keeping with this conception. If he thinks of his mother as a nurturant person, she will perform some service in the dream to depict her nurturance. Young men commonly dream about being attacked by other men, thereby displaying a conception of enmity that exists in males for other males. Less commonly young men are friendly with other men. Women also conceive of men as attackers but their dreams reveal many other conceptions. In a single dream series, multiple conceptions of the same person or class of persons are the rule rather than the exception, which suggests that the average person has a network of conceptions regarding his mother, father, siblings, and various other individuals and classes with whom he interacts during waking life. These ideational or cognitive networks are conceptual systems, and it is one of the aims of dream analysis to delineate these conceptual systems.

Conceptions of the world

By the world is meant the totality of the environment, that which is not-self. In dreams as in poetic fancy the world may be invested with animistic qualities which reflect the dreamer's conceptions of the world. It may be viewed as benign, hostile, turbulent, sorrowful, lonely, or degraded depending upon the mood of the dreamer. These world-conceptions are often conveyed by the character of the dream setting. If the dreamer feels that the world presents a cold, bleak face, he may materialize this conception in the form of a cold climate and a bleak, rocky setting. A dreamer who feels that his world is one of turbulence and agitation, may dream of thunderstorms, raging seas, battles, milling crowds, and traffic jams. A feeling that the world is benign and peaceful can be scenically represented in dreams by serene natural settings.

Conceptions of impulses, prohibitions, and penalties

Since dreams are filled with impulse gratification, in particular those of sex and aggression, it is not surprising that Freud came to the conclusion that wish-fulfillment is the essence of dreams, and that the objective of dream analysis is the discovery of the wish which is fulfilled. It is hardly necessary, however, to consult dreams in order to learn that man seeks gratification of his urges. What dreams can tell us more profitably is how the dreamer conceives of his impulses, for it is these conceptions, not the impulses directly, that ordinarily elicit specific ways of behaving. Most people experience a sex drive, but they differ in respect to their conceptions of the sex drive. The sex impulse may be regarded variously as wicked, as unclean, as a mechanical pressure needing periodic release, as a natural force serving reproduction, as a way of expressing love and tenderness, or as a primitive and uncontrollable form of energy against which one wages a losing battle. Among our collection of nocturnal emission dreams, these and many other conceptions of this biological force appear. The following dream reveals a purely mechanical conception of sex.

I got out of bed and went into the bathroom and attempted to turn on the water faucet. I turned and turned but no water came out. I then decided to call a plumber. Soon afterwards the door opened and an individual dressed in coveralls approached me. Upon closer examination I discovered the plumber was a female. I scoffed at the idea of a lady plumber, but unruffled she went to the basin, turned the faucet, and water immediately flowed. An emission occurred.

Dreams also show the person's conceptions of the obstacles that stand in the way of the gratification of his impulses. These obstacles are often prohibitions emanating from his conscience and may be represented in dreams by such obstacles as walls, curbs, and locked doors, by acts of restraint such as putting on the brakes of a car, or by the appearance of authority figures who interrupt the dreamer's pleasure. If an impulse is gratified, the dreamer may express his conception of the punishment that will be visited upon him for his transgression. He may be punished directly by another person, or he may be the victim of misfortune. In any event, the kinds of obstacles and the kinds of penalties which appear in dreams are interpreted in order to throw light upon the nature of the conceptual system which is called the superego. This conceptual system which is assumed to be detached from the ego contains the moral ideology of the person.

Conceptions of problems and conflicts

Perhaps the most important information provided by dreams is the way in which they illuminate the basic predicaments of a person as that person sees them. Dreams give one an inside view of the person's problems, a personal formulation that is not so likely to be as distorted or as superficial as are the reports made in waking life. Since it is the way in which a person conceives of his conflicts that determines his behavior, the inside view is a prerequisite for clear understanding of human conduct. As we have shown in another place (Hall, 1947), the delineation of a person's conflicts may be made by analysing a dream series.

Of what value is it to know the conceptions of a person as expressed in his dreams? How does it help the psychologist to understand the person and thereby to predict and control his behavior? Of one thing we can be quite certain, namely that these conceptions are not dependable guides to objective reality; what one conceives to be true and what is actually true do not invariably coincide. A person may conceive of his father as a stern, autocratic, unreasonable person, when, in fact, his father does not possess these characteristics in the eyes of impartial observers. Dreams should not be read for the purpose of constructing a picture of objective reality.[3]

Our thesis is that dreams are one dependable source of information regarding subjective reality, and that knowledge of subjective reality is useful precisely because it does have effects in the conduct of a person. If a boy sees his father as an autocratic authority, he will react toward his father as though he really is that way. In other words, these personal cognitions are the real antecedents of behavior.

Parenthetically, we would like to observe that psychology may have been hampered in its development because it has tended to ignore subjective

3. The expression 'objective reality' is used in contrast to 'subjective reality'. By the former, we mean those conceptions of reality which can be publicly demonstrated and repeatedly verified. By the latter, we mean those conceptions of reality which reside in a person's mind irrespective of whether these conceptions can be demonstrated and verified. Both kinds of conceptions are 'real' inasmuch as they both have 'effects'.

cognitions in favor of objective stimulus variables. Stimulus conditions are varied and the effects in behavior are noted, often without taking into consideration that the person's conception of the stimulus may be the decisive factor. People may react differently to the same stimulus because they have different conceptions of the stimulus or they may react in the same way to different stimuli because they have similar conceptions. This is a truism whose truth is too often forgotten in psychological experiments, although there are indications that the pendulum is swinging back in the direction of cognition variables (Köhler, 1938; Snygg and Combs, 1949; Tolman, 1951).

Although this is not the place to develop fully our theory of *conceptual systems*, it is not inappropriate to mention briefly our view that the conceptions of a person are organized into interconnected networks. One network may consist of the conceptions that a person has of his family, and this network in turn may be interconnected with a network of ideas about government, or religion, or education. A recent study has demonstrated in a convincing manner how ideas about minority groups are intimately related with ideas about family, religion, government, and economics (Adorno *et al.*, 1950). It is the task of psychology, as we see it, to explore these conceptual systems or personal ideologies, to show how they are interrelated, to learn how they are developed, to demonstrate how they control and regulate conduct, and to discover how they may be changed. In order to do all of these things, it is necessary to devise methods of finding out what a person's conceptions are. Attitude-opinion questionnaire methods have reached a high level of development and are employed on a large scale to determine people's beliefs about everything under the sun. The value of such methods, although great, is none the less limited by several factors inherent in the methods. The respondent may not answer a question either because he does not want to or because he does not know the answer, or he may answer it untruthfully either intentionally or unintentionally. Moreover, the wording of the question is an important variable (Newcomb). At best, questionnaires get at the conscious and verbalizable conceptions of a person.

If one assumes, as the writer does, that the contents of personal ideologies are pretty largely unconscious or preconscious, then methods have to be used which will reveal these unconscious conceptions. Projective methods, especially of the picture-story type, lend themselves to the exploration of conceptual systems, although they have not been employed to any great extent for this purpose. Picture-story tests do have one drawback, however, and that is that the person's conceptions may not be fully laid bare by the collection of pictures used. Since the material obtained will be a function of the kind of pictures shown to the person, it is possible that those conceptions which are of greatest significance for him may not be tapped. This limitation does not apply to dreams. The dreamer makes his own pictures of those conceptions that are of greatest importance to him currently. Over a period of time, his dreams will depict the essential features of his conceptual systems. Moreover, dreams tap the unconscious and bring to the surface those prototypic conceptions around which conceptual systems are formed. It is our view that prototypic conceptions have their origin in early life and that they are more likely to express themselves in dreams than through any other medium. For these reasons, we feel that dreams constitute the best material for studying the conceptual systems of a person and that such knowledge is absolutely essential if we are to understand why people behave as they do.

We shall conclude by demonstrating how the views presented in this paper may be utilized in analysing a dream. The following dream was reported by a young man.

I was at the blackboard in a school room doing a trig problem but I was having trouble with it because I could not remember the valence of nitrogen. I was about to give up on it when a girl came up to me and asked if I would like to dance. The music was good but very erratic, being very fast one instant and very slow the next; however, we were always exactly in step. She was an excellent dancer. When the music stopped we were both in the school shower but we still had our clothes on. I wanted to take hers off and make love to her but I had never done anything like that before so we just laughed and splashed water.

Then I was outside the school. It was night and lights shone in all the windows silhouetting a wild orgy of a party. I felt very lonely. I wanted to go inside but something seemed to hold me back. I heard chimes ringing in the church.

In the opening scene, we see the dreamer hard at work on a mathematical problem with which he is having difficulty. His self-conception is that of an industrious student engaged in a purely intellectual task for which he does not have the requisite knowledge. A girl appears and invites him to dance; that is, he conceives of the girl as a temptress and of himself as her victim. At her bidding, he leaves the hardships of intellectual activity for the pleasures of sensuality. Their sensuality stops short of complete fulfillment because he cannot conceive of himself as consummating the sexual act. The scene changes in line with a new conception. The dreamer now sees himself as lonely outsider looking in on a wild orgy. He would like to go in, but he is held back by an unidentified force. The church bells, embodying as they do ideas of virtue and morality, suggest that the unknown force is his own conception of moral conduct.

This dream, then, reveals two opposing conceptual systems, one which contains the young man's conception of himself as a moral, industrious, and intellectual person, the other which contains his conception of himself as a sensual being. These disjunctive conceptions tend to inhibit one another. He cannot maintain a consistent conception of himself as being either moral or sensual. When he is doing the 'right' thing, he is lured away by sexuality; when he is doing the 'wrong' thing, he is pulled away by morality. A self-conception of inadequacy for either role is portrayed by his inability to solve the intellectual task or to fulfill his sexual wish. In this dream we see that it is not the sex drive *per se* that is of significance, but rather his conception of it as being forbidden to him.

Other dreams collected from this young man help to fill out the contents of his conceptual systems. In one dream, he does consummate the sex act, but only because the girl actively seduces him. This suggests that his conception of morality can be subordinated when he sees himself as the victim of external forces. Even in this dream, however, the dreamer feels ashamed because he is so easily excited. His personal ideology regarding women is an interesting yet not uncommon one. Women are of two types: aggressively sexual women who seduce men and pure women who are to be loved in a respectful manner but with whom sexual relations are forbidden prior to marriage.

We have spoken of the disjunctive nature of the dreamer's moral and immoral self-conceptions. In one dream he makes a partial fusion of these opposed views.

I was studying for a test with my girl. We were lying on the bed in her room reviewing our notes and asking each other questions about them. As each topic would come up, instead of discussing the text, I would demonstrate a different point in making love to her. Although each type of love making seemed different, it never got beyond the kissing stage.

Work and sex are integrated, although the sex impulse is kept within bounds. The girl in the dream is one of the 'nice' girls in the dreamer's life toward whom he would not be likely to have unrestrained sexual feelings.

Concluding statement

The argument presented in this paper consists of the following assertions:

1. Dreaming is a cognitive activity, and a dream is a pictorial representation of the dreamer's conceptions.

2. Dream interpretation consists of discovering the conceptions that lie behind the dream images.

3. Conceptions represented in dreams usually fall into one of the following classes: (a) self-conceptions, (b) conceptions of other people, (c) conceptions of the world, (d) conceptions of impulses, prohibitions and penalties, and (e) conceptions of conflicts.

4. Conceptions are organized into conceptual systems, and these systems are the antecedents of behavior.

5. Dreams provide excellent material for the analysis of conceptual systems since they portray unconscious and prototypic conceptions.

6. The theory presented in this paper represents an extension of ego psychology to include dreaming as a function of the ego.

References

ADORNO, T. W., FRENKEL-BRUNSWIK, E., LEVINSON, D. J., and SANDFORD, R. N. (1950), *The Authoritarian Personality*, Harper & Row.

FREUD, S. (1933), *New Introductory Lectures on Psycho-Analysis*, Norton.

FREUD, S. (1940), *An Outline of Psychoanalysis*, Norton, 1949.

HALL, C. S. (1947), 'Diagnosing personality by the analysis of dreams', *J. abnorm. soc. Psychol.*, vol. 42, pp. 68–79.

HALL, C. S. (1953), 'A cognitive theory of dream symbols', *J. gen. Psychol.*, vol. 48, pp. 169–86.

HARRIS, I. (1948), 'Observations concerning typical anxiety dreams', *Psychiatry*, vol. 11, pp. 301–9.

KÖHLER, W. (1938), *The Place of Value in a World of Facts*, Liveright.

NEWCOMB, T. M. (1950), *Social Psychology*, Dryden Press.

POLSTER, E. (1950), 'An investigation of ego functioning in dreams', Ph.D. thesis, Western Reserve University.

SNYGG, D., and COMBS, A. W. (1949), *Individual Behavior*, Harper & Row.

TOLMAN, E. C. (1951), *Collected Papers in Psychology*, University of California Press.

28 C. R. Evans and E. A. Newman

Dreaming: An Analogy from Computers

C. R. Evans and E. A. Newman, 'Dreaming: an analogy from computers',
New Scientist, no. 419, 1964, pp. 577–9.

The maligned expression, 'electronic brain', which seemed likely to slip into an unshakeable position in the English language, has rather surprisingly lost ground to the more accurate and less loaded word, 'computer'. Fifteen years ago, when the first major computers were coming into operation, 'electronic brain' was in common lay usage. Computer technologists themselves objected to the implication that they were simply erecting unwieldy and relatively inefficient copies of the human brain, while psychologists on the other hand thought that there was no reason to suppose that computers embodied any of the little-understood principles of the human brain.

Today we know a good deal more about computer science and fractionally more about the brain, and as a result it now seems that the computer–brain analogy has become more realistic and more meaningful. In this article we wish to take advantage of this shift in attitude, and to propose a tentative approach to a problem of classic interest to psychiatrists and psychologists – the meaning and function of dreams. At the very least, it seems that concepts originating from computer science may provoke interesting new thoughts about human brain functions.

Certain important new concepts which helped towards a partial understanding of dream processes were developed in the nineteenth century and, although they were greeted at the time with much alarm, they have remained unmatched as general theoretical foundations to the present day. The foremost, the Freudian, brought forward the startling hypothesis that dreams mirrored vital psychological factors and gave, in fact, a truer picture of the individual personality state than did his normal day-to-day utterances and general behaviour. Another classic theory, the Jungian, suggested that the human race shared a significant number of rudimentary dream patterns in the same way as the human race shared more overt physiological behaviour patterns, such as breathing and eating. These represent rather gross summaries of the theories, but it is true to say that both of them introduced what was, at the time, a revolutionary concept: that the sleeping life of the individual was a dynamic and vitally important facet of existence, and that sleep was not simply a state of regular and inevitable collapse on the part of an organism equipped with an over-complicated nervous system.

Within the past decade our attitude to the meaning and function of dreams has altered somewhat, and there has developed an increasingly critical attitude to the purely psychoanalytical view of dreaming. Recently the curious and challenging work of W. Dement in the USA has seemed, superficially at least, to support the Freudian position. Electrical records of eye movements taken during sleep reveal occasional sustained bursts of activity, persisting sometimes for minutes on end. Dement and his colleagues discovered that, if subjects were wakened during one of these periods of eye movement activity, they would, if questioned quickly, report that they had been 'having a dream'. Control subjects, woken during non-active periods, would rarely, if ever, report that they had been interrupted in the middle of a dream. In further studies it transpired that subjects whose sleep was interrupted during eye-movement (dream) periods, for more than three or four nights, showed marked psychological distress, as compared with a control group woken a comparable number of times but when eye movement activity was not taking place. As a kind of corollary to these studies it was also discovered that individuals deprived of all sleep for two or three nights spent significantly more time 'dreaming' when they were eventually allowed to sleep undisturbed.

With these remarkable experiments (which, it should be said, have not gone uncriticized) the basic significance and importance of dreaming to the psychological well-being of the individual seemed to be experimentally established. Beyond this bare statement, however, little theoretical use has been made of what seems to be very promising material.

We have attempted an extrapolation from Dement's experimental findings. It is our belief that the apparent required regularity and frequency of dream activity ('dream' periods may, according to Dement, take up 20 per cent of the sleeping period) implies a more basic, and in one sense more *physical* role for the dream than psychoanalytical theories such as the Freudian suggest.

We propose, in fact, that the dream serves primarily as a 'memory filter' – a nightly examination of the vast mass of material collected in the course of the day, with a subsequent 'rejection' of redundant or inapposite memories and responses. This is a somewhat simplified statement of our precise position, made solely in order to introduce the concept. Let us now examine it in greater detail, and, most particularly, attempt to relate it to our knowledge of computer operations.

General experience suggests very strongly that an important portion of human memory takes a form closely analogous to an interlocking set of digital computer programs. Now this is not to imply that memory traces are ever identical to computer programs, nor for that matter does it imply that they are introduced into the brain or stored in it in any way at all similar to that used in digital computers. Indeed clearly they are not. Nevertheless, there are some striking similarities, not the least of these being that much memory trace is sequential; one item calling up another, and so on. There are other similarities. Human memory traces are adaptive; they evolve, as the individual's interests and requirements change, and in this they are not so different from the computer case as might at first appear. Good computer programs also evolve and are adapted to new requirements. But in the computer case the evolution is carried out by an outside agency (human operators) rather than by built-in properties as must exist in the human brain.

Computer scientists have now gained a good deal of experience in the adaptation and evolution of computer programs – particularly in cases where these are used for office routines. In such systems what tends to occur is that the programs keep up with new needs and improve their performance on old ones, by persistent minor modifications of programs. Inevitably, however, the computers get cluttered up with more and more unneeded instructions and it turns out that the increase in material tends to be exponential – doubling and redoubling over given intervals of time. In some ways this 'junk gathering' does not matter much, but in other ways it is important for two reasons. First, computers are of finite size and speed and the unnecessary routines and instructions actually waste computer-time. Secondly, the increase in material again interferes with the process of adaptation. All this can lead to functional breakdowns because of greatly reduced effective computer speed and general inflexibility.

There is, of course, a simple solution to this problem; programs must occasionally be run through and the unnecessary instructions cleaned off. There are, however, some important requirements to this cleaning-off process. It can obviously be done only when the computer is not fully engaged in doing other work – when the computer is, to use a technical term, 'off-line' – completely isolated from other tasks, major or minor. It is not hard to understand why 'off-line periods' are required, for if cleaning-up were attempted when the computer was running, disastrous results could occur through the exploration of unusual paths and the interference with current projects. If the computer were primarily concerned with wages, for instance, gigantic or minute salaries might be indicated or, worse, if the computer were in a chemical plant, serious explosions might later occur!

A further obvious requirement is that the cleaning-up should be done at regular intervals and never unduly delayed for, the longer the delay, the more new program material will be affected (because programs in a finite system must interlace and share common paths) and the more difficult the tangle will be to unravel.

That, then, is the cleaning-up process already essential to modern computers. We will not need to stretch our imaginations too far to see that the same kind of argument should apply to the developing programs which exist in living creatures. These programs, too, should have periodic clean-ups, for brains, like computers, are of finite size and speed of operation; furthermore, for the same reasons applying to the computer case, these clean-ups would have to occur in regular, non-operating periods.

In the computer at any rate there is a simple but effective way of cleaning-off a program. Certain 'wanted' instructions, instead of leading to the newly outmoded and unnecessary computing routines, must be made to lead directly (or via a small number of extra instructions) to those parts of the program appropriate to the latest method of working. The necessary modifications can perhaps most readily be made at 'choice-points' in a program, where the computer is required to decide what to do next on the basis of its previous calculations. Here, the modification may simply be a matter of biasing the choice of different ways (see Figure 1). Once that has been done and a new route established, it is not strictly necessary to remove the unwanted instructions, for since no part of the pertinent program complex now leads to them they are for all practical purposes 'forgotten'.

There might, it is true, be some slight advantage to removing the unwanted instructions entirely by erasing them in some way, for new storage space would thus be made available. As we shall see in a moment, however, storage space *per se* is not really a problem either with computers or with the living brain, and there might indeed be some value to retaining old routines which 'may come in useful one day' as new routines under new circumstances, when new links to them could perhaps be forged. More importantly, the sub-complexes may often continue to be required in completely different programs, to which access will remain via alternative sets of instruction.

The question of storage space reminds us that any theory involving processes of memory and 'forgetting' in man himself must take into account that fact that apparently forgotten material may occasionally come to light after years, even decades, of virtual dormancy. The sudden appearance of these distant memories, many of which may be entirely trivial in content, may be precipitated by some abnormal physical or psychological situation – a blow on the head, for example, or the somewhat drastic action of ECT (electro-convulsion therapy). They may even be induced experimentally, as W. Penfield and others have shown, by direct electrical stimulation of micro-regions of the brain cortex during surgery. In the latter case patients may report detached and brief 'memories' – of sights, feelings, sounds or even smells – which, they claim, 'haven't been thought of for years'.

These facts seem to suggest (though they cannot show conclusively) that all experiences which reach the level of consciousness have their 'niche' of

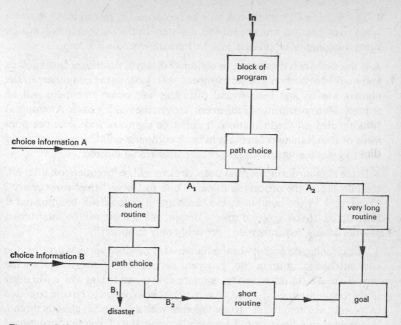

Figure 1 Schematic representation of a computer 'dream'. The normal
path from choice point A to the goal is via the long routine A_2. Previous
investigation of alternative route A_1 has suggested an unsatisfactory outcome
at choice point B when B_1 has been taken. Dreaming here allows 'safe'
exploration of alternative path B_2 which is found to lead to new shorter routine
to goal. Program examination of 'risky' pathways may be made with almost
complete safety in dreams

representation in the brain, though the trivial and redundant are sealed-off
as we have proposed. The most obvious objection to this view has always
been that the brain is of finite size. However, while estimates of the number
of nerve cells in the brain and their possible ramifications and intercon-
nections vary appreciably, all are agreed that the brain is sufficiently large
to accommodate several life-times of information sampled in day-to-day
activity. We suggest that the problem with the living brain is not one of
storage space but rather of convenience and simplicity of access.

We have indicated why, with increasing complexity in the development
and use of computers, the associated problems demand a regular examination of current programs. We have also suggested that the living brain will
require similar regular sifting periods. Assuming that this process does occur
in humans, it is possible to predict a number of likely consequences.

1. The cleaning-off activity can only be performed in special inactive states when wrong action will not lead to disaster. In the computer this will be when the complex is 'off-line'; in the human, when he is asleep.

2. If this activity is prevented, or seriously delayed, functional breakdowns and marked reduction in effective speed will occur in the computer; in the human, mental and behavioural disorders will occur and there will be appreciable impairment of judgement, etc., in the waking state. Attempts at 'waking dreams' (hallucinations?) might be vigorous. Indefinite postponment of the cleaning-off process in both computer and living brain would lead to gross malfunction and possible irreparable disorder.

3. In the human, during normal sleep, dreams will be forgotten for, after all, the purpose of the process is to cause one to 'forget' the 'unnecessary'. Conversely, in the computer, the cleaning-off process will be impaired if interrupted. If one wakes during a dream, the process will be interrupted and the dream 'remembered' – probably only temporarily.

4. The cleaning-off activity in the human will produce varying dreams, the content depending upon the 'program system' being investigated at the time. Since it is the unnecessary, uninteresting or redundant which will most likely require sealing-off, most dreams might be expected to be compounded of roughly assorted trivia, strung together with a somewhat chaotic thread. 'Nonsense' situations would frequently occur but, if lengthy 'programs' were involved, 'sensible' dream sequences might also occur.

5. The dreams with the most innocuous content would, in the normal healthy individual, be the least likely to interrupt sleep and thus be the least likely to be remembered. When the individual is in restless sleep, however, or in some feverish state, the cleaning-off even of trivia might be constantly interrupted, giving rise to repetitive obsessional dreams.

6. Dreams with violent effect, high emotional tone, or involving sudden spurts of motor activity would be more likely to interrupt sleep and would assume, on reflection, a quite disproportionate importance; their relative frequency of occurrence (as compared with 'non-significant' dreams) would be grossly over-estimated.

7. The sleep state in which the clearance system gets most effectively under way may not necessarily be identical with the deepest level of unconsciousness. The period of sleep induced by barbiturates, for instance (though there is no evidence that we know of to support this), may not be conducive to normal dreaming and may therefore be of no lasting help to the chronic insomniac.

To conclude, we recall that we have suggested that new experimental approaches to the problem of sleep and dreaming have opened up and made plausible a new view of the function of dreaming. We have linked it to our current knowledge of computer processes and proposed that the scanning and sorting of programs which becomes increasingly important as computers advance in size and complexity, should be found to have some parallel in the living brain. We suggest that this parallel process is to be found in the dynamic act of dreaming, and that the principal function of sleep, therefore, is not to provide some indefinable 'rest', but to allow the individual to dream.

We do not have to allow our imagination to run too far to envisage that, as computers continue to expand in scope and complexity, their designers might well hope to incorporate some self-scanning system which sorts and excludes programs during regular off-line periods without immediate access to external sources. In fact there already exist, in programs with what is termed a 'List-structure', processes for automatic 'junk removal'. These techniques are limited in their scope and certainly not self-regulatory. It would be picturesque and not, we believe, unreasonable to refer to automatic clearing on the part of the computer as 'dreaming'. Objections, for one reason or other, will doubtless be made, but we have tried to show that the analogy is not an unreal one.

C. R. Evans and E. A. Newman 377

29 Frederick Snyder

Toward an Evolutionary Theory of Dreaming

Frederick Snyder, 'Toward an evolutionary theory of dreaming', *American Journal of Psychiatry*, vol. 123, 1966, pp. 121–42.

In the Upanishads of ancient India it is written that existence takes three forms, the one here in this world, another in the other world, and a third in the world of dreaming. By the second half of the twentieth century scientific views of nature had nothing to say of the other world, and with the singular and therefore highly suspect exception of psychiatry, they were equally silent about the realm of dreaming. If our era will be remembered for first exploring the other world of outer space, it may be just as important that it produced the first concerted assault upon the secret workings of the brain whence comes our inner world of nightly visions.

Over scarcely more than a decade the extent of scientific effort related to this subject has come to rival previous neglect, and revelations are emerging which greatly enhance the vital significance of dreaming, even while compounding its age-old mystery. Rather than being an occasional, unpredictable and ephemeral psychic anomaly, tantalizingly glimpsed by the eye of the mind but devoid of objective correlates, it is now apparent that human dreaming is the subjective aspect of an extremely substantial, predictable, universal, and basic biological function.

The physiological characteristics of this phenomenon prove so distinctive that I consider it a third state of earthly existence, the rapid eye movement or REM state which is at least as different from sleeping and waking as each is from the other (Snyder, 1963, 1965a, 1965b), but only the briefest résumé of accumulating evidence for that contention will be presented here. The principal concerns of this discussion are the deepening mysteries with which developments of the past decade confront us.

As Whitman (1966) testifies, these experimental developments place us in a better position than ever before to learn about dreaming from the data of immediate human experience, and to make inferences about its role in the life process. Yet the fact that this third organismic state is shared by at least the entire class of mammals raises an issue not seriously encountered heretofore – that of the biological or evolutionary origin of dreaming. In part this is to question why, or how, or when, the hallucinated dramas of dreaming arose out of this unique physiological condition, but to pursue the enigma further is to ask why this third mode of existence itself arose out of the evolutionary process.

Such questions may or may not be of special pertinence to our use of dreams as mirrors of mental life, but I believe they are of compelling relevance both to understanding of dreaming as a natural phenomenon and to comprehending the significance of the biological state from which it arises. Obviously the primordial biological function of the REM state is not necessarily identical to that of human dreaming, and conjectures about that original function must be based upon and account for quite different kinds of information. Present gropings toward that end are handicapped by incomplete knowledge, inspire only tentative conviction, and may well be discredited by further research.

The essential point of this presentation is simply to emphasize that intriguing problems exist; an evolutionary theory of dreaming is called for; but regardless of that, explanation for the adaptive function of the REM state is itself a question of profound biological interest.

The common basis for all current speculation is our present estimate of what the REM state is as a physiological entity, which I shall attempt to review as briefly as possible.[1]

Descriptive résumé of the REM state

Just as it might be surmised that no one before Freud had listened so intently while persons talked about their dreams, so it must be inferred that no one prior to Eugene Aserinsky had watched so diligently while they slept. If so it would have been noted much earlier that the monotonously impassive mask of sleep is broken periodically by a strange and discreet animation, limited in adult humans to an intricate dance of vermicular movement over the surfaces of the eyelids. When these minute ripples on the calm face of sleep are transmuted through electrical signals into inked patterns of a moving graph, they become starkly tangible and unmistakably distinctive.

It then develops that these slight perturbations of the eyelids are actually due to rapid and random excursions of the globes themselves, unlike any other ocular movements during sleep, but very similar to waking changes in visual fixation. This ever varying calligraphy of rapid eye movements (or REM, as they have come to be known) occurs more or less continuously during intervals typically lasting about twenty minutes and recurring three to five times each night, but appears not at all during the rest of sleep.

Since these peculiar events were first described in 1953 (Aserinsky and

1. Since this material has been reviewed in much greater detail (Dement, 1964; Fisher, 1965; Roffwarg, Muzio and Dement, 1966; Snyder, 1965a), references will be provided only to the most recent developments.

Kleitman, 1953), their bodily reverberations have extended wherever they have been sought. During those intervals when the rapid eye movements are taking place the brain's electrical patterning is transformed from the random heaving of sleep to a flattened desynchrony, similar but not completely the same as that of attentive waking. The even breathing of sleep gives way to halting uncertainty or panting haste; the heart's rhythm now speeds or slows unaccountably and blood pressure climbs ragged heights or plunges through unpredictable descents. One organ betrays inner excitement still more than the rest, since penile engorgement almost regularly accompanies these REM intervals.

More elaborate techniques reveal that the same enlivenment takes place in vital functions throughout the body. Metabolism rises (Brebbia and Altshuler, 1965), the kidneys make less but more concentrated urine, and those chemical messengers of arousal, the corticosteroids and catecholamines, are released in special abundance (Mandell and Mandell, 1965; Mandel *et al.*, 1966).

While so much transpires within, an ingenious mechanism preserves the surface immobility of sleep. Despite twitching contractions of isolated muscle groups, the abiding tonus of muscle activity is diminished during the REM state, and the elementary reflexes of motor reactivity are no longer functional. Thus, the executors of external action are disconnected.

The very same characteristics distinguish this phenomenon wherever it has been pursued within the class of mammals, but from more drastic experimental approaches in other species a still more remarkable picture emerges. Even the fine muscles of the middle ear exhibit an 'attentive' modulation as in waking. Specific patterns of electrical activity appear in many brain regions other than the cerebral cortex, all very reminiscent of similar local patterns during alert waking. Every available means for assessing the functional level of nervous activity indicates that the REM state is a uniquely intense condition of nervous excitation. Responses of the brain evoked by peripheral stimulation take on a form like that of alert waking. Facilitation of sensory responses at thalamic way-stations is as high or higher than it is during waking. Thresholds for movement to direct stimulation of the motor cortex are as low or lower than in waking. Elegant microelectrode techniques reveal that spontaneous firing of nerve cells in many brain regions is increased beyond the level of waking.

Changes in local cerebral impedance, brain temperature, and cortical heat dissipation earlier suggested substantial increases in cerebral blood flow. Kety and his co-workers now more than confirm this by a method which provides accurate estimates of regional cerebral blood flow from patterns of autoradiographic density in brain sections after injection of a radioactive substance into the bloodstream. By this means it was found in cats that there is little change in cerebral blood flow between quiet waking and sleep, but that during the REM state circulation essentially doubles throughout the entire gray matter of the brain (Kety, 1965). This dramatic finding most probably reflects a comparable increase in local metabolism, and hence of neuronal activity level throughout the brain.

Such, then, is the present basis for assuming that the REM state is a condition of diffuse organismic excitation or activation. This is not a condition of partial arousal intermediate between sleep and waking, but now appears to be among the most extraordinarily intense activations yet discovered in the normal functioning of the central nervous system. Although similar in many respects to highly aroused waking, there are good reasons for thinking that the functional organization of central nervous activity is quite different from waking, and that the stimulus which originates this activation is intrinsic to the brain itself.

From the studies of Michel Jouvet and his colleagues we know that the necessary and sufficient mechanism for the periodic triggering of this strange excitation is located in one of the most remote and primitive portions of the brain, the pontine reticular formation, and is probably of a neuro-humoral nature (Jouvet and Mounier, 1962). The trend of recent work is the dissection of still more discrete neuroanatomical areas and neurochemical mechanisms within this pontine region which are responsible for the various components of that state. The bursts of eye movements themselves have been shown to require the nearby, vestibular nuclei, presumably stimulated in turn by the pontine mechanism (Pompeiano and Morrison, 1965).

The latest report (Jouvet, 1965) suggests that the components of the REM state are initiated by catecholamine mechanisms limited to the more lateral portions of the pontine reticular area. A tiny noradrenergic nucleus within this region, the locus coeruleus, appears to be indispensable for the muscular atonia element of the REM state in cats. During REM periods after bilateral destruction of the nucleus, animals totally unresponsive to actual visual stimuli are observed to stare fearfully at invisible objects, and even to stand on their legs and exhibit rage-like behavior. Other catecholaminergic areas just below and behind the locus coeruleus appear to be the triggering zones for these active components.

During the REM state these same areas are the site of origin for a striking and distinctive electrical pattern of particular theoretical interest. These 'monophasic spike' clusters, originating in the pons, occur simultaneously in the lateral geniculate, visual and parietal cortex, and also in the oculomotor nucleus and extrinsic eye muscles. This, then, is physical evidence of neural signals originating within the depths of the brain stem during the

REM state and being fed into both the visual afferent pathways to the cortex and the motor pathways of ocular movement.

The periodic occurrence of these dramatic episodes of intrinsically stimulated central nervous activation, far from being unusual or occasional events, now appear to be a universal and fundamental characteristic of mammalian existence. In thousands of persons studied they have been present in every one during every night of sleep. In every species studied they occur in indistinguishable form, but with special conspicuousness from the very first day of extrauterine life. They continue in decorticate persons or hydroencephalic infants, and residual elements persist even in pontine cats.

The existence of this remarkable state of intrinsically stimulated activation appearing regularly in the midst of sleep, but so different from it, does not begin to answer the question which interests us most as psychiatrists – 'how or why scripts of the dramas of our dreams are created' – but neither does dreaming explain the existence of this biological manifestation, which is undoubtedly primary. The basic mystery, then, is how the purposes of survival are served by this extraordinary condition of nervous excitation punctuating our sleep and the sleep of the entire mammalian family. Each facet of the REM state encountered tends to suggest its own speculations.

Evidence from REM deprivation

There has been just one deliberate experimental approach to this question by the researcher who has contributed more than any other to the elucidation of the REM state, William Dement. On the classical model of seeking the function of an organ by determining the effects of its removal, Dement set out to discover what might result from relentlessly depriving persons of REM state by awakening them whenever it began to occur over varying numbers of consecutive nights (Dement, 1960). The first of the incredible consequences was that the onset of REM periods became more and more frequent over successive nights, and the second, that when the subjects were at last left to sleep undisturbed, the REM state occupied half again as much of sleep. As he carried out this arduous procedure over longer and longer intervals, the extent of compensatory increases was proportional to the number of nights of deprivation, so that after sixteen nights the REM state almost seemed to fill the first recovery night of sleep (Dement, 1964).

More recent findings from REM deprivation experiments in animals over still longer periods are even more remarkable (Dement, 1967). As cats are continuously REM deprived over thirty or more days, the number of necessary awakenings climbs astronomically, and the amount of REM state during the recovery period is correspondingly extended. In addition, the active components of this condition themselves become much more intense, i.e. the muscular twitches and eye movements become so frantic as to resemble myoclonic convulsion. As one observes these phenomena the impression is inescapable that an irresistible force is steadily building and that if allowed to continue its pressure would soon become uncontainable.

There is only one current hypothesis to explain the effects of REM deprivation, and that stems from the premise that normal triggering of the REM state involves a neurochemical substance accumulating to a critical level during sleep and then being expended in some manner by the REM process. It follows that prevention of the REM state would produce an incremental propensity for these neural storms to occur. Dement has earlier suggested that the function of the REM state is to clear the nervous system of this presumably endogenous metabolite (Dement, 1964). It would seem unprecedented that such an elaborate mechanism of the central nervous system should serve a 'detoxification' function, but much about this phenomenon is unprecedented. However, when we seriously disrupt any biochemical mechanism the resulting products may have toxic properties, but this does not prove that the adaptive value of that mechanism is the destruction of those products; under natural conditions they are innocuous chemical links in the vital process.

I shall not belabor Dement further on that issue, since his work has now taken him in another direction. The most exciting implication of the REM deprivation studies has been whether the accumulation of this hypothetical neurohumor might result in drastic alterations of brain function and behavior or might ultimately result in death. Jouvet's cats permanently deprived of REM state by means of pontine lesions appeared to hallucinate, developed progressive tachycardia, and all eventually died. Over the periods that REM deprivation could be continued in man there sometimes seemed to be changes in waking behavior, but these have not been demonstrated unequivocally.

Now animal studies have shown measurable changes in neural functioning, i.e. seizure thresholds are lowered and the recovery cycles of auditory evoked responses are shortened, both indicating an abiding increase in central nervous excitability (Dement, 1965). These cats become more restless and impulsive, more rabid about eating, and many exhibit enhanced and bizarre sexual proclivities; yet, even when the deprivation is continued for as long as seventy days, they do not appear to hallucinate and they do not die. Even though nervous excitability is increased, and there appears to be specific strengthening of drive-oriented behavior, Dement's present conclusion is that the results of prolonged REM deprivation do not indicate that this state is vital to the survival of the adult organism. The changes he has observed may not be vital in the artificial setting of the laboratory, but I shall later consider the possibility that they might, indeed, be vital from an evolutionary perspective in the course of the natural struggle for survival.

The ontogenetic hypothesis

Dement now believes that the primary function of the R E M state is that of assisting the process of central nervous system development. Since this onto-genetic hypothesis has been elaborated in an excellent paper by Roffwarg, Muzio and Dement (1966) which has just appeared as a lead article in *Science*, I shall mention only a few of its salient points. The first is that the R E M state is most prominent in the earliest stage of postnatal life in all of the species in which this has been studied. In the human neonate it occupies an average of 50 per cent of sleep, and the proportion is still higher in premature infants, emerging from an undifferentiated electroencephalographic state at about thirty-one weeks of gestational age. In newborn kittens it is reported to occupy 80 per cent of sleep, while in young lambs it is three times more extensive than in sheep. Between human birth and young adulthood the total reduction in sleep involves only a 25 per cent reduction in non-R E M sleep, and a 75 per cent reduction in the R E M state.

These authors rightly insist, therefore, that any hypothesis about the function of the R E M state must explain its great prominence in the neo-natal organism. Their proposal is that the endogenous afferent stimulation of the R E M state serves to assist the processes of central nervous system maturation and differentiation while the fetus is still in utero and in the immediate postnatal period, and that this is the primary purpose of the R E M state. To support this contention they cite impressive evidence that functional stimulation does potentiate structural development of the nervous system, as well as reasons for suspecting that some sort of functional stimulation of sensory modalities does exist prior to birth, e.g., although activity usually precedes myelinization of neural structures, the primary sensory receiving areas of the brain are among the best myelinated at birth.

While it is still an assumption that the R E M state occurs in utero, and an inference that it could provide effective functional stimulation to the devel-oping brain, this argument is plausible and fraught with significant implica-tions. Unless it is simply a developmental vestige, however, these authors agree that other functional explanations are required to account for the persistence of the R E M state throughout life. It remains to be seen whether they can also encompass the ontogenetic data as well as this provocative hypothesis.

The homeostatic hypothesis

A very thoughtful effort to account for the life-long importance of the R E M state has been formulated in a still unpublished paper by Ephron and Car-rington (1965) from inferences about the contrasting physiological attributes of the R E M state and of sleep itself. Since their thinking has to do with a homeostatic interplay between the physiological effects of these two states, I shall refer to it as the 'homeostatic hypothesis'. They assume that effective brain functioning during waking depends upon the adequacy of sensory stimulation from the environment, and that the reduction of this 'exogenous afferentation' during sleep results in profound changes in cerebral cortical function, such as Bremer described as loss of cortical 'tonus' and Head characterized as loss of cortical 'vigilance'.

Although it is presumably advantageous that organisms undergo this transformation, i.e. that sleep is somehow necessary, they reason that the tendency toward loss of cortical 'tonus' inherent in sleep must be kept within adaptively appropriate limits if the capacity for waking cortical function is to be readily restored. It might be taken for granted that there are homeostatic mechanisms to achieve that end, but their nature has not been self-evident. Ephron and Carrington suggest that the REM state is just such a mechanism, serving to counteract the tendency toward lowering of cerebral 'tonus' or vigilance' during sleep by periodically providing 'endogenous afferentation', a kind of patterned sensory input somehow similar to that presented during waking perception.

In a like vein, Mandell and Mandell (1965) have suggested that the REM state is triggered by low circulating levels of required metabolites during sleep and therefore represents a mechanism for the periodic discharge of the neuroendocrine apparatus in order to maintain optimal levels of essential nutrients. Both of these views might be subsumed under a more general statement that the REM state provides periodic restoration of conditions throughout the entire organism during sleep, approximating those necessary for effective waking function.

One vexing problem in evaluating this or any other line of explanation is that regardless of how well it accords with present knowledge of the REM state, uncertain assumptions are invoked about the nature and function of sleep itself. To my knowledge it has not yet been shown, for example, that circulating nutrient levels tend to fall in the inter-REM intervals of sleep, and current understanding of what constitutes the essential physiological distinction between brain functioning of sleep and waking is still very slight. If such metaphorical concepts as cerebral 'tonus' or 'vigilance' refer to the overall intensity of nervous function, the notion that this is diminished during sleep is now challenged by contrary evidence (Evarts, 1965).

It does seem apparent that sleep represents a radically different functional organization of neuronal activity from waking and that, in some respects at least, the REM state is a condition more similar to waking. If the homeostatic hypothesis implies a periodic restoration of functional organization of nervous activity somehow similar to that of waking while the continuity of sleep is still maintained, I believe the adaptive value of such a situation can be convincingly argued.

Phylogenetic considerations

None of these hypotheses has been derived from the traditional basis of evolutionary deduction, that of phylogenetic considerations, for the excellent reason perhaps that existing knowledge is still very scant from that perspective. I shall next attempt to order the phylogenetic evidence now available, to elaborate a few speculations which it has suggested to me (Snyder, 1965c), and to highlight what I consider to be important problems for future research. This, then, is intended merely as a first and uncertain step toward an evolutionary theory of dreaming.

Often the most crucial clues as to how a biological function has served the struggle for survival are provided by information about when in evolutionary history, and under what circumstances, it first originated. The diagram (Figure 1) is a simplified view of our heritage over the past 200 million years or so, as well as a summary of present evidence concerning the phylogenetic distribution of the REM state. Slight though the latter is, I believe it permits some very solid inferences. Of the sixteen orders of surviving placental mammals, representatives of just five have been studied in this regard, but since all of these clearly exhibit the REM state, there is virtually no doubt that this phenomenon existed in our insectivore-like common ancestors at least 100 million years ago.[2] Beyond that, its unmistakable manifestation in the opossum insures that it occurred in a still more remote predecessor prior to the divergence of placental and marsupial evolution. Below the mammalian level, however, conclusions become very tentative.

Sleep is a uniquely neglected subject of comparative biological inquiry. Until the past few years it had not been examined by electrographic means in any infra-mammalians, and the range of forms investigated is still very small. Figure 1 begins with the reptiles because below that level we reach an impasse, i.e. nothing resembling sleep has been identified (Hobson, 1966). In reptiles sleep is found much as it is in mammals, but whether the REM state exists at that level is problematical. A single study of one of the more primitive surviving reptiles, the tortoise, found no evidence of it (Klein, 1963), while new observations of chameleon lizards note rapid eye movements during sleep, although brain electrical patterns remain unchanged (Tauber, Roffwarg and Weitzman, 1966). Among those specialized reptiles, the birds, hen and pigeon show clear evidence of sleep, but this is interrupted at intervals of a few minutes by abrupt drops in muscle tonus, desynchronization of the EEG, and bursts of rotatory eye movements (Klein, 1963). These episodes last no more than a few seconds, after which the bird appears to startle and to awaken briefly.

2. It might be a parallel 'homoplastic' development in each (Simpson, 1958), but this degree of convergence would be highly unlikely.

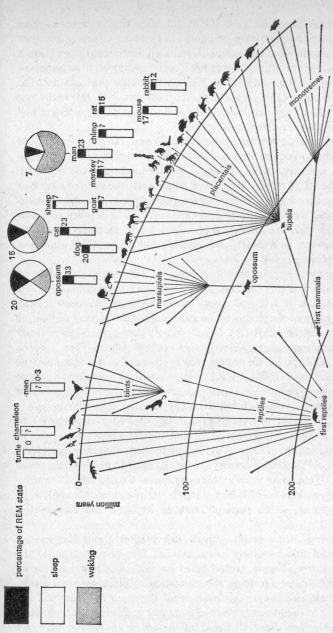

Figure 1 Available evidence concerning phylogeny of the REM state. This very simplified and stylized evolutionary schema, as well as the phylogenetic summary of REM state data, are both derived from the work of many authors. Systematic twenty-four-hour data, as indicated by the circles, have been reported only for these three species. The question marks within the bars indicate uncertainty whether REM state occurs, while the question mark beside the chimpanzee graph means that its ratio within sleep has not been estimated

Here is a puzzle, since the site of REM state triggering in the pons argues that this mechanism must have originated in nervous systems much more ancient than the mammalian or even the reptilian. But if sleep as we know it begins only with the neocortex in reptiles, it becomes difficult to imagine how we might recognize the anlage of the REM state amidst the 'non-sleep' of lower forms. Hobson (1966) reports that the most immobile state in the frog is associated with a very alert looking, desynchronized EEG pattern as well as brisk responsiveness to external stimuli.

To ponder these matters verges on science fiction, but the physiological evidence seems to require that a very old and complex neural function somehow became secondarily connected with the innovation of sleep in the creation of the REM state. If the fleeting condition in the sleep of birds is at all homologous, it may well represent a transitional phase in the transformation. Additional studies of many other species of birds, reptiles, and amphibians might hope to clarify these questions, but all we can conclude for the present is that, as a clearly recognizable entity, the REM state is a mammalian phenomenon.

Man has as much of this condition during his sleep as any placental and more than most, but this does not justify the generalization that this is a progressive feature of mammalian evolution. The degree of specialization among the orders of placentals by far outweighs their varying degrees of primitiveness, and the ratio of REM state in sleep undoubtedly reflects their divergent specializations, as it clearly does in the ungulates. Then, too, the data from various species are not necessarily comparable. For example, the small difference between ratios of REM state in man and monkeys might be meaningful only if sleep recording in man involved his being imprisoned in a restraining device like those in which monkey sleep must now be studied.

Likewise, that the cat has as large a percentage of sleep occupied by REM state as man is confounded by the fact that the cat sleeps about twice as much as man, and if cat sleep is artificially limited to eight hours over a series of days, REM state increases to levels of 25 to 35 per cent (Ferguson and Dement, 1966). With the possible exception of the ungulates, the striking thing about the ratio of REM state among placental mammals is its relative uniformity, which perhaps bespeaks its basic and conservative nature.

Few surviving forms could provide information about the relative primitiveness of this condition in mammalian life. The situation in the oriental tree shrew, Tupaia, would be of interest, since many zoologists consider it the closest surviving approximation to placental stem forms. Those mammals with the earliest roots of all, the egg-laying platypus and echidna, might or might not provide relevant information, since they themselves are highly specialized. In any event all of these animals are very rare and exceedingly difficult to maintain in captivity. Fortunately this is not the case with the animal which is considered the most primitive and at the same time the most generalized of living mammals, the opossum.

The earliest direct fossil antecedents of any living mammal, contemporaneous with the reign of the dinosaurs, are almost indistinguishable from those of the present-day opossum (Simpson, 1937), and hence zoologists bestow upon that humble animal the distinction of calling it a 'living fossil'.[3] Although the actual fossil record must be forever silent concerning the REM state, its manifestations in the opossum are therefore of unique phylogenetic significance. As I have described on other occasions (Snyder, 1965a, 1965c), the REM state in the opossum is unmistakable and in some respects more similar to that in man than the comparable condition in many other placentals.

The only feature of the opossum REM state which is apparently different from that of other mammals is the sheer extent of it, although reservations about the comparability of inter-species data apply here also. The laboratory opossum sleeps from 75 to 85 per cent of the twenty-four-hour period, day after day, and the REM state occupies an average of one-third of sleep, or about one-fifth of total time – as much or more than the daily quota of waking. Probably the best basis for comparison with the human situation is that during those intervals when sleep is most continuous it is present at least half of the time.

We can never know whether it might have been more or less conspicuous in the long history of still older mammals, or in reptiles transitional to mammals, but the opossum is our witness that this extraordinary periodic central nervous system activation in the midst of sleep came to full flower at an early stage of mammalian evolution. Since presumptively it was a much less prominent or differentiated event in the sleep of reptiles, if present at all, it is conceivable that this was one of the crucial innovations which shaped the survival and ultimately the predominance of our mammalian kind.

Before attempting to imagine how the REM function might have served such an end, let us first consider the competitive position in which the earliest mammals existed, to the extent that this can be imagined from the fragmentary fossil record. Paleontologists tell us that they appeared very soon in reptilian evolution, nearly as early as the dinosaurs, but that during the 100 million years or more that these ferocious reptiles overshadowed every corner of the earth, our predecessors were small and insignificant creatures 'crushed beneath the weight of reptilian hordes' (Romer, 1958; Simpson, 1937). They could have endured only by virtue of their unobtru-

3. Simpson (1937) states: 'One of the most remarkable facts of paleontology is the slight evolution apparently undergone by this group during the tertiary. The recent opossum is almost a living cretaceous mammal'.

siveness, and a few new biological assets – their greater speed and agility based upon slightly more complex brains and bodies. Perhaps these characteristics enabled them to forage at night for their diet of insects and worms with special haste, and then to scurry back to their hidden dens in cave or hollow tree, waiting out the eons until their time came to inherit the earth.

The REM state in mammalian survival

But in what manner might the REM state have contributed to the survival of these creatures? The greater complexity which distinguished them as mammals was made possible by longer and more protected conditions of development, as well as a higher and more stable basic metabolism. In terms of the ontogenetic hypothesis, perhaps the period of helpless development required by their cerebral advantage would have been still further prolonged without this endogenous stimulation. On the other hand, if the REM state was as prominent in primitive mammals as the opossum suggests, then perhaps the high levels found in the immediate postnatal life of placentals is an ontogenetic recapitulation of this older phylogenetic phase, like the gill arches of still earlier embryonic life. In relation to the homeostatic hypothesis, the maintenance of high and stable metabolic rate may be more pertinent.

Since without continuous activity reptiles are left helplessly inert by falling environmental temperature, a mechanism which maintained body temperature even during sustained sleep would have been a distinct survival advantage. Although metabolic changes during the sleep–REM cycle have not been studied except in man (Brebbia and Altshuler, 1965), the more striking muscular twitching of the REM state in lower animals makes it likely that the increase in metabolism is greater, and that this may be a significant or necessary contribution to mammalian temperature regulation during sustained sleep. Such a relationship to metabolism is further suggested by the fact that intervals between REM periods in various forms are directly proportional to body size and inversely proportional to metabolic rates.

Before speculating further, however, we might consider the question of sleep's own adaptive function. This is usually assumed to be one of restoration required by more intricate brains, and no doubt it is that, even though the precise nature of this restoration is still unknown. In primitive mammals there is such a disproportion between the extent of sleep and the apparent use made of cerebral energy that some additional adaptive significance seems called for. Sleep is not hibernation, which involves much more profound physiological changes, but both have the effect of minimizing metabolic requirements. The heightened metabolic rate of our primitive forebears was presumably a mixed blessing, for although it allowed them to be active at times when the reptilians could not be, it also made great caloric demands. It would have been a great advantage to spend the major portion of their furtive existence husbanding resources in this dormant state.

Such is the case in many of the most primitive surviving mammals. As mentioned earlier, the opossum spends nineteen hours a day asleep. A primitive insectivore, the European hedgehog, is said to sleep eighteen hours out of twenty-four during its 'active' season (Suomalainen, 1960), while small bats are observed to spend five-sixths of their nonhibernating existence in sleep (Matthews, 1960).[4] Matthews has pointed out that the much more restless shrew has a maximal life span of eighteen months, whereas bats of similar size have been found to survive as long as ten years (Matthews, 1960). The obvious moral is that maximal possible amount of sleep seems to be conducive to longevity, in bats at least. In addition to the metabolic factor, sleep might also be considered as an adaptive mode of behavior for creatures which probably had to spend most of the time in hiding. From the standpoint of surviving from one reproductive period to the next, and thus from one geological era to the next, a prevailing state of sleep in the relative security of the cave or hollow tree had everything to recommend it, as the opossum has so well demonstrated.[5]

Therefore, my first premise is that there is survival advantage to a maximal extent of sleep compatible with the satisfaction of nutritional needs, and that this would have been especially true in the primitive mammalian predicament.

The obvious objection to this premise is that sleep renders animals helpless to cope with certain situations of occasional danger from which none is ever entirely secure, such as invasion of the nest and attack by predators. Man and other animals have learned that under conditions of danger it is safe to sleep only if sentinels are employed to remain vigilant and to report at intervals that all is well. It would seem that a built-in physiological mechanism to bring about brief but periodic awakenings for the purpose of sampling or scanning the environment, without significantly disturbing the continuity of sleep, would make extended sleep both feasible and adaptively advantageous. It so happens that precisely such periodic arousals do occur in the sleep of the opossum, as well as all other mammals studied, since

4. Comparable data are just beginning to appear for higher mammals but are not greatly different, e.g. almost 70 per cent of laboratory existence in the domestic cat is found to be taken up by sleep (Delorme, Vimont and Jouvet, 1964).

5. That this may still be so is suggested by the fact that the opossum has not merely survived but is currently extending its range. Although arrived at entirely independently, the considerations put forward here have an almost uncanny similarity to those cited by Dement in his discussion of this paper from the thinking of the distinguished anthropologist, S. L. Washburn.

virtually every REM period is followed by some degree of arousal before sleep is resumed.

Physiological studies of the central mediator of arousal, the mesencephalic reticular activating system (RAS), suggest that this brief terminal awakening is an intrinsic feature of the sleep–REM cycle. Roldán and co-workers (1963) have shown in rats and rabbits that the responsiveness of the RAS to external stimulation gradually falls during the inter-REM intervals to its lowest level prior to and during each REM period, only to be abruptly restituted at the time of transient arousal following 80 per cent of such periods.[6] The same cycle of events is probably reflected in pulse and respiratory rates of the opossum, which gradually fall during inter-REM intervals and reach a peak once more at the point of transient arousal after most REM periods; however, they are also elevated and irregular during the REM phase (Snyder, 1965c). This is in keeping with the finding in cats that spontaneous activity of the RAS is greatly increased during REM periods (Benoit, 1964; Huttenlocher, 1961) and the unresponsiveness to external stimuli is presumably due to the 'lines being busy' with endogenous activation.

Herein lies the beauty of the REM mechanism. It is not simply a periodic restoration of responsiveness to the external world, i.e. waking, but is rather a state of heightened inward arousal, which ordinarily gives rise to only the most fleeting interruption in the continuity of sleep. Under some circumstances this post-REM arousal may be entirely lacking, and under others it may be much more extended, but under most conditions it is an inherent part of the regular sequence of events. My second premise, therefore, is that this brief but periodic arousal following REM periods serves a 'sentinel' or vigilance function.

But why should these periodic arousals be preceded by such an elaborate and extended physiological process as the REM state? Birds show such awakenings also, but they are accomplished in just a few seconds. The homeostatic hypothesis might imply that the REM state would be necessary to bring the more complex brain function of mammals from the nadir of the sleep cycle to the point of transient arousal, but perhaps another consideration is that of organismic preparedness prior to the sentinel awakenings. As the death-feigning reaction of the opossum indicates, predators tend to stand off from an inert animal, while creatures suddenly awakened from sleep are confused and especially vulnerable. Periodic awakenings during sleep would be of doubtful survival value unless the organism were already sufficiently prepared for fight or flight. It is my third premise that the REM

6. The only other quantitative data on the incidence of these awakenings consist of an 85 per cent level reported in man (Dement, 1964). I shall later mention evidence that this varies with the conditions of sleep.

state provides such preparatory activation prior to each sentinel awakening.

This, of course, is entirely compatible with the homeostatic viewpoint, and might be considered an extension of it. Their combined implications are that the REM state not only maintains the constancy of the internal environment during sleep, but at the same time helps to insure the *status quo* in relation to the external environment as well.

Like most evolutionary questions, the adaptive function of the REM state is an excellent issue for speculation and an impossible one for definitive experimental test. In terms of this 'sentinel hypothesis' the lack of REM state under laboratory conditions would have no vital consequences. The adaptive value of such a function could become apparent only among large groups of animals living in the midst of the natural struggle for survival over many, many generations. Since no such data are likely to be forthcoming, might any of the implications of this hypothesis be testable?

Implications for further investigation

The idea that the REM state provides such preparatory activation would rest upon whether increased 'critical reactivity', the capacity to respond to external demands in a differentiated and appropriate manner, could be demonstrated after REM awakenings as contrasted to sleep awakenings. This is amenable to experimental test both in animals and men and is supported by the modicum of evidence now available from human studies. Gastaut and Broughton (1965) have found that children are typically very difficult to arouse from sleep, appearing extremely confused, but that this is never the case after REM state awakenings. Similarly in adults, Fiss, Klein and Bokert (1966) report that thought content is markedly impoverished, blocked, and perseverative after sleep awakenings as contrasted with REM state awakenings.

Direct physiological evidence of 'carry-over' effects from the preceding stage of sleep after abrupt awakenings was earlier found in the cat in terms of inhibition of visual cortical reactivity and is now reported by Broughton (1966) in relation to the form and amplitude of visual evoked responses in man. Further testing of the dimensions of 'critical reactivity' and cortical responsiveness after awakening at various points in the sleep–REM state cycle would be highly relevant to this 'sentinel' hypothesis.

Another approach to evaluating this – or any adaptive hypothesis – is to study the manner in which the sleep–REM–arousal pattern is affected by naturally occurring threats to survival. This has not been extensively investigated with regard to any variable, but there are incidental observations which are indicative. When the opossum is first placed in the recording situation, which we might infer involves environmental threat, after several hours of restless exploration initial sleep is broken by a great deal of awakening, either in prolonged interludes or in short periods having approximately the intervals of REM periods. REM state itself hardly appears at all during this early phase of adaptation, but when it does begin to take place again abbreviated REM periods are almost regularly followed by longer than usual full awakenings (Snyder, 1965c).

Similarly, human subjects who are particularly anxious about the experimental situation often come to full spontaneous awakenings in the midst of their REM periods or at their very beginning. In current studies of depressed patients we are finding many individuals who do this quite consistently.

These indications suggest that the interrelation of sleep, waking, and REM state is not static but is sensitively adjusted to the degree of perceived danger. When threat is high, the REM state fails entirely to preserve the continuity of sleep, but for good biological reason. Such considerations suggest a point of confluence with the findings from experimental REM deprivation. Since REM deprivation as a natural phenomenon could be expected to result from any circumstances which seriously curtailed or disturbed the continuity of sleep, such as the presence of danger or scarcity of food supply, is it not conceivable that modest heightening of cerebral excitability or drive-oriented behavior might be adaptive in coping with these emergency situations?

This line of thinking implies that vicissitudes in REM state functioning may serve to modulate the intensity of basic drive energies, dampening them when they are less needed and stimulating them when they are called for. The consequences would extend beyond the immediate period of sleep disturbance, since REM deprivation is later compensated by more extensive and intense REM activation, perhaps providing increased organismic preparedness even while sleep is allowed to continue.

If my juxtaposition of these several hypotheses appears eclectic or even indiscriminate, that is by design, for none is sufficiently well based at this time to justify the exclusion of the rest. Beyond the fact that the proverbial analogy to the blind men examining the elephant is probably applicable to the early exploration of any complex visage of nature, there is nothing to assure us that the adaptive function of the REM state need be unitary. Within the general requirement of serving survival, the waking state certainly has multiple specific functions, and perhaps that is characteristic of each of the three modes of existence.

Still another approach to the evolutionary riddle of the REM state will depend upon much more intensive comparative study of how these three states are interrelated in a variety of animal forms of diverse life adaptations. We might expect that the kind of change seen in any one species in response to varying levels of danger would be built into the innate patterns of entire groups to varying degrees, depending upon the nature and extent of usual threats to their survival.

We might postulate, for example, that sleep would have greatest continuity and the REM state would be best developed in those forms with the highest immunity to predators, either by virtue of their own defensive strength or their use of other devices, such as inaccessibility, for protection during sleep. If we order those placentals for which REM data are available on a continuum of vulnerability, the ungulates or rabbit would rank very high; man, cat, or dog would occupy the lowest positions; while rat, mouse, or monkey would be intermediate. Thus, such a ranking would be inversely related to the ratio of REM state during sleep. This is particularly notable in the case of the ungulates, which are most exposed and defenseless at all times and exhibit a very fitful sleep pattern interspersed with much awakening and very little REM state (Ruckebusch, 1962).

At first glance it might appear paradoxical or flatly contradictory to the 'sentinel hypothesis' that the least REM state is found in the most defenseless animals, just as it is in less vulnerable forms under conditions of heightened danger. This is not so if we bear in mind the concept of a dynamic equilibrium between maximal conservation of energy via sleep and maximal protection against intercurrent danger during sleep. In threatening situations or in more vulnerable animals the former consideration is outweighed by the latter, for sustained sleep with long REM state intervals is replaced by much more frequent and extensive periods of waking and much shorter REM periods. The particular life adaptations of these animals are such that they cannot afford the survival advantage of sustained sleep, hence must spend a much larger portion of their existence satisfying nutritional requirements and in being alert to environmental danger. Klein (1963) has pointed out the great discrepancies between herbivores and carnivores in the amount of time spent feeding, and how this relates to sleep patterns. I would emphasize that all of these factors are parts of complex but integrated wholes which comprise these diverse specializations. An entirely new field of comparative zoological study will be required to make clear just how sleep and REM state fit into these patterns of adaptation, but until now zoologists themselves have been almost oblivious to this entire segment of the life process.

Speculations concerning role of dreaming consciousness

Like paleontologists who strive to reconstruct the semblance of long past life from fossil shadows or a few fragments of bone, we have little enough upon which to base our speculations about the evolutionary significance of the REM state, but still less with which to ponder its relationship to dreaming consciousness. If we define dreaming as a progression of organized and complex hallucinatory imagery (Snyder, 1965a), obviously it cannot be assumed that anything similar to that human experience occurs during the REM state of lower animals. It might be simply an amorphous riot of sensations or entirely without subjective accompaniment. But neither can we assume that something conforming to that definition does not take place wherever the REM state exists.

When we think of dreaming, ordinarily we focus upon the complex manifestations of memory and cognition which intrigue us in our own experience of it and are prone to conclude that organisms lacking those attributes, such as infants or lower animals, could not possibly 'dream'. Yet infants now appear to be capable of more complex visual perception than we might have supposed (Frantz, 1963), and even the lowly opossum has that capacity, so there is no *a priori* reason to conclude that the corresponding levels of perceptual consciousness could not be hallucinated by these creatures during sleep.

In these terms the problem of when in ontogenetic or phylogenetic history dreaming first begins would become something of a pseudo-problem. While dreaming in the human sense would be confined to humans, dreaming as a state of perceptual activation would begin in the intrauterine life of each individual, just as it presumably began with the gradual emergence of the REM state in remote ages of early mammalian life. I am suggesting that although this condition of hallucinatory consciousness in the midst of sleep might be more or less complex and organized, and more or less integrated with other of the brain's functions at various developmental or phylogenetic stages, perhaps the essence of dreaming as a biological phenomenon is simply endogenous perceptual activation. As an integral aspect of central nervous system evolution it might be assumed that this has increased in complexity together with every other aspect of neocortical functioning, but that even in its most primitive forms it might still be recognizable as an organized hallucinatory experience, if we but had access to it.

Long before similar observations were made in humans, naturalists had noted behavior during the sleep of animals which they attributed to an 'inner life' (Hediger, 1955). If we saw similar events in humans during sleep we might or might not be willing to infer the presence of dreaming, but if we observed behavior like that of cats during REM periods after release from motor inhibition by lesions of the locus coeruleus, i.e. their fearful stares at invisible objects, rage-like grimaces, and frantic thrashing about, as psychiatrists we would not hesitate to infer the presence of hallucinations. A further bit of evidence comes from the finding that after monkeys are trained to press levers whenever they are exposed to patterned visual stimuli, they do so at a very rapid rate during certain periods of apparent sleep (Vaughan, 1963). Unfortunately, physiological monitoring to distinguish REM periods was not available in that study, but it encourages the hope that some limited access to subjective aspects of the REM state in other species may be experimentally feasible in the future.

Having already escaped all pull of gravity in this flight of conjecture, I shall venture just a few additional speculations about the nature of imagery which may possibly accompany the REM state of lower animals. We might guess from the behavior of Jouvet's cats that they were reacting to a hallucinated enemy, and it would be a reasonable extension of the 'sentinel' hypothesis that preparatory cerebral activation should take the form of a hallucinated reality such as the animal might be in danger of encountering at the time of awakening. Very similar thoughts have been expressed about the function of human dreaming (Ullman, 1959).

As I watch my opossums in the laboratory, their motor activity during REM periods often seems to confirm this generalization, i.e. their breathing becomes rapid and their limbs move as in running, but there are other occasions of assiduous licking or chewing, and this does not suggest appropriate preparation for an encounter with a hungry Tyrannosaurus. The opossum has to remind me again that the 'sentinel' hypothesis arose out of two considerations. Although preparation for danger is the short-term necessity, the long-term advantage is that of maximal economy of energy. Assuming, as I have, that the extent of awakening following each REM period is somehow modulated to accord with latest estimates of expected danger, perhaps the nature of the imagery reflects the same influences. Thus, under conditions of security the hallucinations would be such as to gratify rather than frighten, thus fostering the greater continuity of sleep.

This last speculation, at least, is supported by good authority. In *The Interpretation of Dreams* Freud wrote:

I do not myself know what animals dream of. But a proverb, to which my attention was drawn by one of my students, does claim to know. 'What,' asks the proverb, 'do geese dream of?' and it replies: 'Of maize!!' The whole theory that dreams are wish fulfillments is contained in these two phrases.

In one of the most seminal insights of modern times Freud divined the integral relationship of dreaming to basic biological forces, and his spirit still provides much of the impetus for their further exploration. However laudable or naïve, all efforts thus far ventured to formulate answers to the mystery of REM state function, and much of the experimental work from which they derive, have been the products of psychiatrists. Even if the study of this intriguing biological phenomenon appears now to be only our foster child, soon to be claimed by its proper parents among the natural sciences, we can be justly proud of its nurture by our own and allied disciplines to this present point of vigorous development.

References

ASERINSKY, E., and KLEITMAN, N. (1953), 'Regularly occurring periods of eye motility, and concomitant phenomena during sleep', *Science*, vol. 118, pp. 273–4.

BENOIT, O. (1964), 'Activité unitaire du nerf optique, du genouillé latéral et de la formation réticulaire durant les différents stades de sommeil', *J. Physiologie*, vol. 56, pp. 259–62.

BREBBIA, D. R., and ALTSHULER, K. Z. (1965), 'Oxygen consumption rate and electroencephalographic stage of sleep', *Science*, vol. 150, pp. 1621–3.

BROUGHTON, R. J. (1966), 'Observations on the pathophysiology of certain paroxysmal sleep disorders', presented to Association for the Psychophysiological Study of Sleep, Gainesville, Florida.

DELORME, F., VIMONT, P., and JOUVET, D. (1964), 'Etude statistique du cycle veille–sommeil chez le chat', *C R soc. biol.*, vol. 158, pp. 2128–30.

DEMENT, W. (1960), 'The effect of dream deprivation', *Science*, vol. 131, pp. 1705–7.

DEMENT, W. (1964), 'Experimental dream studies', in J. H. Masserman (ed.), *Science and Psychoanalysis*, vol. 7, Grune & Stratton, pp. 129–84.

DEMENT, W. (1965), 'Studies on the effects of REM deprivation in humans and animals', presented to the 45th annual meeting of Association for Research in Nervous and Mental Disease, New York.

EPHRON, H., and CARRINGTON, P. (1965), 'REM sleep and cortical homeostasis: theoretical considerations', presented to Association for the Psychophysiological Study of Sleep, Washington.

EVARTS, E. V. (1965), 'Activity of individual cerebral neurons during sleep and arousal', presented to the 45th annual meeting of Association for Research in Nervous and Mental Disease, New York.

FERGUSON, J., and DEMENT, W. (1966), 'The effect of variations in total sleep time on the occurrence of rapid eye movement sleep in cats', *EEG clin. Neurophysiol.*, vol. 22, p. 109.

FISHER, C. (1965), 'Psychoanalytic implications of recent research on sleep and dreaming', *J. Amer. Psychoanal. Assn*, vol. 13, pp. 197–303.

FISS, H., KLEIN, G., and BOKERT, E. (1966), 'Waking fantasies following interruptions of two types of sleep', *Arch. gen. Psychiat.*, vol. 14, pp. 543–51.

FRANTZ, R. (1963), 'Pattern vision in new born infants', *Science*, vol. 140, p. 296.

GASTAUT, H., and BROUGHTON, R. (1965), 'A clinical and polygraphic study in episodic phenomena during sleep', in J. Wortis (ed.), *Recent Advances in Biological Psychiatry*, vol. 7, Plenum Press.

HEDIGER, H. (1955), *Studies of the Psychology and Behavior of Captive Animals in Zoos and Circuses*, Criterion Books.

HOBSON, J. A. (1966), 'Electrographic correlates of behavioral states in the frog', presented to Association for the Psychophysiological Study of Sleep, Gainesville, Florida.

HUTTENLOCHER, P. (1961), 'Evoked and spontaneous activity in single units of medial brain stem during natural sleep and waking', *J. Neurophysiol.*, vol. 24, pp. 451–68.

JOUVET, M. (1965), 'Mechanisms of the states of sleep: a neuropharmacological approach', presented to 45th annual meeting of Association for Research in Nervous and Mental Disease, New York.

JOUVET, M., and MOUNIER, J. (1962), 'Neurophysiological mechanisms of dreaming', *EEG clin. Neurophysiol.*, vol. 14, p. 424.

KETY, S. (1965), 'Relationship between energy metabolism of the brain and functional activity', presented to 45th annual meeting of Association for Research in Nervous and Mental Disease, New York.

KLEIN, M. (1963), 'Etude polygraphique et phylogénique des états de sommeil', thèse de médecine, Lyon, Bosc Frères.

MANDELL, A. J., and MANDELL, M. P. (1965), 'Biochemical aspects of rapid eye movement sleep', *Amer. J. Psychiat.*, vol. 122, pp. 391–401.

MANDELL, A. J., RUBIN, R. T., and SHEFF, R. (1966), 'Urinary excretion of 3-methoxy-4-hydroxymandelic acid during dreaming sleep in man', *Life Sci.*, vol. 5, pp. 169–74.

MATTHEWS, H. (1960), 'Comment in discussion of Suomalainen's paper on "Hibernation and sleep"', in G. E. W. Wolstenholme and M. O'Connor (eds.), *The Nature of Sleep*, Little, Brown.

POMPEIANO, O., and MORRISON, A. R. (1965), 'Vestibular influences during sleep', *Arch. Ital. Biol.*, vol. 103, pp. 569–95.

ROFFWARG, H., MUZIO, J., and DEMENT, W. (1966), 'Ontogenetic development of the human sleep–dream cycle', *Science*, vol. 152, pp. 604–19.

ROLDÁN, E., WEISS, T., and FIFKOVÁ, E. (1963), 'Excitability changes during the sleep cycle of the rat', *EEG clin. Neurophysiol.*, vol. 15, pp. 775–85.

ROMER, A. S. (1958), 'Phylogeny and behavior with special reference to vertebrate evolution', in A. Roe and G. G. Simpson (eds.), *Behavior and Evolution*, Yale University Press.

RUCKEBUSCH, Y. (1962), 'Etude comparée du sommeil physiologique chez les équidés, ruminants, porcins et carnivores adultes', *Bull. soc. sci. vet. med. comp.*, Lyon, vol. 64, pp. 374–90.

SIMPSON, E. (1937), 'The beginning of the age of mammals', *Biol. Rev.*, vol. 12, pp. 1–17.

SIMPSON, G. G. (1958), 'The study of evolution: methods and present status of theories', in A. Rose and G. G. Simpson (eds.), *Behavior and Evolution*, Yale University Press.

SNYDER, F. (1963), 'The new biology of dreaming', *Arch. gen. Psychiat.*, vol. 8, pp. 381–91.

SNYDER, F. (1965a), 'The organismic state associated with dreaming', in N. W. Greenfield and W. C. Lewis (eds.), *Psychoanalysis and Current Biological Thought*, University of Wisconsin Press.

SNYDER, F. (1965b), 'Progress in the new biology of dreaming', *Amer. J. Psychiat.*, vol. 122, pp. 377–91.

SNYDER, F. (1965c), 'Speculations about the contribution of the rapid eye movement state to mammalian survival', presented at symposium on 'Activité onirique et conscience', Lyon.

SUOMALAINEN, P. (1960), 'Hibernation and sleep', in G. E. W. Wolstenholme and M. O'Connor (eds.), *The Nature of Sleep*, Little, Brown.

TAUBER, E. S., ROFFWARG, H. P., and WEITZMAN, E. D. (1966), 'Eye movements and EEG activity during sleep in diurnal lizards', *Nature*, vol. 212, pp. 1612–13.

ULLMAN, M. (1959), 'The adaptive significance of the dream', *J. nerv. ment. Dis.*, vol. 129, pp. 144–9.

VAUGHAN, C. (1963), 'The development and use of an operant technique to provide evidence for visual imagery in the rhesus monkey under sensory deprivation', unpublished doctoral dissertation, University of Pittsburgh.

WHITMAN, R. M. (1966), 'Dreaming, dreams and dream interpretation', presented at annual meeting of the American Psychoanalytic Association, Atlantic City, New Jersey.

Discussion by William C. Dement

In addition to his other accomplishments, Dr Snyder is undoubtedly one of the most eloquent spokesmen in the area of REM research, and has proven it again. His paper represents the first explicit confrontation with what is perhaps the most basic problem posed by the existence of the REM state, and one whose solutions are likely to have far-reaching implications for all of biology.

I agree that the study of this state, and particularly its evolution and adaptive significance, might be regarded as a foster child of the psychiatric discipline. However, the thoughtful and scholarly nature of Dr Snyder's approach to what is essentially a problem of comparative zoology renders the charge of undue presumption entirely without merit. On the other hand, as an unreconstructed non-scholar, I can only justify my own attempt to contribute to the nurturance of our foster child (at the risk of seeming overly expansive) with the metaphorical contention that the greatness of Rome was in no way affected by the bemusement of the wolf that suckled Romulus.

In his presentation, Dr Snyder has done justice to the descriptive facts of the REM state. Nevertheless, its truly puzzling and unique features, the urgency of its periodic occurrence during sleep, and its apparently universal distribution throughout all units of the mammalian class, demand additional emphasis. We are dealing with a remarkable recurrent change in CNS activity which, as surveyed by the methods of modern-day electronic technology, seems to combine many of the familiar attributes of active wakefulness with features that are entirely unique, the true identity of which was concealed until recently under the cloak of a superficial and misleading resemblance to ordinary sleep.

A theory involving the function or purpose of a biological process is usually the product of inferential speculation based upon the known properties of the process under question. Although not necessarily helpful in explaining how it got there in the first place, the functional consequences or utility of a phenomenon are, as a rule, quite obvious when a detailed description is available. However, even this is not true in the case of the REM state. It may be said with little fear of contradiction that never before in the history of biological research has so much been known about something from a descriptive point of view, with so little known at the same time about its function. Yet to doubt that the REM state has a major and vital biological destiny to fulfill is to fly in the face of well-established evolutionary principles.

Here in a well-defined area of the brain stem is housed a preemptive mechanism which initiates dramatic change in every corner of the nervous system. In its task of modulating the activity of the entire brain, it has at its call widely disseminated neural networks and highly specialized biochemical and physiological processes. If such a strange and complex phenomenon evolved in mammals for no reason at all, we must doubt some of the most basic propositions of the biological sciences.

I am afraid that our only reward for past attempts to understand the primary biological role of the REM state has been an ever-increasing bafflement and curiosity. On the other hand, it is exactly this tantalizing elusiveness (the 'deepening mystery' in Dr Snyder's words) that provokes a mounting incentive to continue with what has proved an uncommonly frustrating task. The solution may, of course, turn out to be eminently simple in retrospect, and perhaps within the grasp of some advantageously unprejudiced graduate student at this very moment. However, I am inclined to believe that the greater likelihood is a long and difficult journey with an uncertain destination.

Selective deprivation of REM sleep

Before turning to a consideration of Dr Snyder's theoretical discussion, I would like to say a few words about the selective deprivation of the REM state in experimental animals (Dement, 1965a; Dement et al., 1965). In undertaking these studies, we had hoped to demonstrate (one might better say, to substantiate our faith) that the REM state must perform a vital role in the lives of adult mammals. Our intention was to deprive cats of REM sleep for whatever length of time would be required to show that they could not get along without it. We expected progressive impairment, toxic manifestations, and ultimately, death. In spite of the intended open-endedness of the experiment we were not really prepared for what actually happened, either in our thinking or in our resources. As the number of deprivation days mounted – fifteen, twenty, thirty, fifty – with no obvious impairment of the cats, our amazement increased proportionately. Finally, since the choice seemed limited to going on forever or stopping, we ceased our efforts at a maximum deprivation period of seventy days. It seemed reasonable to suppose that if the animal could endure the suppression of REM sleep for seventy consecutive days with no marked impairment of waking function, the daily occurrence of this state could not be absolutely necessary for survival.

However, this conclusion may have been premature. In the first place, we did not accomplish 100 per cent REM state deprivation with many of the cats. The basic physiological criteria of the two states of sleep are shown in Figure 1. NREM sleep is associated with high voltage, slow waves in the electroencephalogram (EEG) and continuous electromyographic (EMG) activity. REM sleep is characterized by EEG activation together with a complete suppression of EMG activity. The exact onset of REM sleep is defined as the point where EEG activation occurs in the presence of a silent EMG. As a rule, EMG suppression occurs a few seconds before EEG activation. In most of our studies, cats were deprived of REM sleep by arousing them at the onset of each REM period.

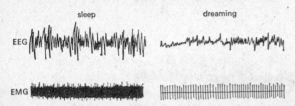

Figure 1 The basic physiological criteria of NREM sleep (often called 'sleep') and REM sleep (often called 'dreaming') in the cat. The electroencephalographic (EEG) activation and electromyographic (EMG) suppression associated with REM sleep are obvious except that a persisting EKG artifact contaminates the tracing from which EMG potentials have disappeared

Figure 2 illustrates why 100 per cent deprivation is rarely, if ever, accomplished by this method. EMG suppression served as the signal for interrupting sleep. In most instances, the awakenings were accomplished before EEG activation had taken place and therefore, by definition, before the onset of the REM state. Such an awakening is illustrated in the bottom two tracings of Figure 2. However, when the experimenter's attention strayed at a critical moment, the onset of EMG suppression would not be noticed, in which case a few seconds of REM sleep (top two tracings of Figure 2) usually slipped under the wire.

As the deprivation continued, the number of arousals required to interrupt each period at its onset mounted into the hundreds. This is illustrated in Figure 3. At this point, a few seconds now and then added up to minutes. We have made a careful tabulation of the accumulated REM sleep time in our experiments, and even with constant supervision and exhortation of the watchers, the daily REM sleep total was rarely below ten minutes.

In addition to this, we have been forced to conclude from other experiments (Ferguson and Dement, 1966a, 1966b) that REM deprivation brings about changes in the 'intensity' of REM sleep. Thus, with accruing deprivation, it is possible that ten minutes of REM sleep becomes worth twenty minutes or thirty minutes or perhaps even fulfills the daily requirement.

On the other hand, we have deprived cats by a water tank method (Dement *et al.*, 1965) which does not utilize arousals and which probably achieved 100 per cent deprivation. However, even if we assume that no REM sleep has been allowed in terms of EEG activation and EMG sup-

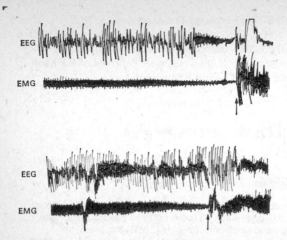

Figure 2 REM sleep deprivation arousals. In the top two tracings, an REM episode develops and is not interrupted by an awakening (arrow) for several seconds. In the bottom two tracings, the awakening occurs at the precise point of complete EMG suppression and before EEG activation. Thus no REM sleep was allowed to take place

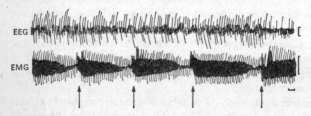

Figure 3 Frequent onset of REM episodes during terminal days of REM sleep deprivation period. If the interruptions (arrows) are not exceptionally vigorous, EEG activation and presumably full arousal do not occur, as is indicated by the almost undisturbed high amplitude activity in the EEG. Calibrations: 1 sec 50 μV

pression, it is possible that crucial manifestations of this state occur in the thirty to sixty seconds preceding the arbitrary point of onset. This possibility is illustrated in Figure 4. Lateral geniculate spiking (Michel *et al.*, 1964), a universal characteristic of REM sleep in the cat, builds up just prior to EEG activation. Other variables may change in this way. For example, Pompeiano (1965) has reported that stretch reflexes are suppressed about forty-five seconds before the onset of REM sleep, and Kanzow (1965) has made similar observations with regard to cortical blood flow changes.

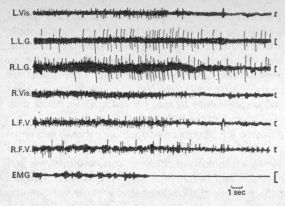

L.Vis.

L.L.G.

R.L.G.

R.Vis.

L.F.V.

R.F.V.

EMG

1 sec

Figure 4 Build-up in lateral geniculate spiking just prior to onset of a REM period. L.Vis., left visual cortex; L.L.G., left lateral geniculate nucleus; R.L.G., right lateral geniculate nucleus; R.Vis., right visual cortex; L.F.V., left frontal cortex; R.F.V., right frontal cortex; EMG, electromyogram. Calibrations: 1 sec, 50 μV

Thus, we cannot assume 100 per cent effectiveness from any technique which relies on deprivation as a function of EMG changes. I am not sure of the importance of these considerations, but it seems unlikely that we have heard the final word on the lethality of REM-state deprivation in adult animals.

Ontogenetic considerations

It has been suggested by Roffwarg, Muzio, and myself (1966) that the prime biological role of the REM state is acted out in the fetal and/or early neonatal period. This hypothesis was advanced because REM sleep did not appear necessary for the survival of the adult organism and because much larger amounts were seen in the newborn period of life (Parmelee, Wenner and Schultz, 1964; Roffwarg, Dement and Fisher, 1964). Taking the physiological nature of the REM state into account, we suggested that the massive amount of endogenous activity or 'stimulation' it engenders might be necessary for the optimal development of the CNS in the stimulus-poor intrauterine and neonatal environments.

In adult organisms, full-blown REM sleep episodes have been described only in mammals. The state does not occur in any substantial amount during the sleep of adult birds or reptiles. However, there is no compelling reason to doubt that birds and reptiles, and perhaps even more primitive vertebrates, need the REM state just as much as mammals for optimal maturation and differentiation of the CNS in early stages of development.

An assumption of the ontogenetic hypothesis is the existence of a critical time in the developmental sequence when the REM state is maximally important, at which time it should be present in peak amounts. To establish such a point of maximum occurrence in embryonic organisms is probably an impossibility at the present time, since the usual physiological indices are completely adequate only at later stages. For example, what is now called 'undifferentiated sleep' in premature infants (Petre-Quadens, 1966) may well contain the essential essence of the REM state.

If we assume, then, that the REM state is both phylogenetically and onto-genetically primitive, it should be present during the embryological stages of many organisms. However, looking at chickens, cats, and man, we find vastly different amounts at birth. In human infants, REM sleep occupies about 50 per cent of the total sleep time (Parmelee, Wenner and Schultz, 1964); in kittens, about 80 per cent (Jouvet, Valatx and Jouvet, 1961); and in newborn chicks, only about 0·6 per cent (Klein, Michel and Jouvet, 1964).

Accordingly, if we were to examine earlier stages of development in the chick, we should find higher amounts of the REM state at some time during incubation. I am aware of only one study where this has been attempted. Klein (1963) has observed chicks through a window in the eggshell during the four days prior to hatching. He noted bursts of rapid eye movements, but these occupied an even smaller fraction of time than at birth. If anything, these results suggest that the ontogenetic hypothesis should not be general-ized beyond the mammalian class.

On the other hand, it might be that the amount of the REM state at any given time depends upon the absolute degree of CNS maturation. The studies of Hamburger *et al.* (1965) suggest the possibility that the REM state may occur much earlier in the developing chicken. For example, he has detected an activity cycle in the embryo in which the activity phase reaches its maximum on the thirteenth day of incubation and declines sharply about three days prior to hatching.

It would be of great interest to study the brain stem of the developing chicken from a histochemical point of view, particularly in terms of the earliest location of monoamine oxidase activity. It has been found, for example, that monoamine oxidase activity in the fetal rat first appears at fifteen days of gestation and is localized to the area of the nucleus locus coeruleus (Shimizu and Morikawa, 1959). There is no question that the nervous system of the chicken is more mature at birth than that of cats or humans. Thus, it is no surprise to find very little REM sleep in the newborn chick if the presumed critical period is long past. The relative maturity of the cat and human nervous systems at birth cannot be stated with certainty.

Further highly specialized studies are needed to elucidate the comparative embryology of the REM state, but if it is present embryologically in birds and even in reptiles, the most pertinent question is why does it persist into adulthood *only* in mammals? An ancillary question is, since it does persist in mammals, why is the total amount so drastically reduced? This could be a consequence of cerebral cortical maturation which somehow inhibits REM sleep, but neodecortication in adult cats does not appear to increase the overall amount (Jouvet, Michel and Mounier, 1960). Or, it could be simply a decline in enzymatic activity associated with the REM mechanism to a new homeostatic level for unknown reasons.

Evolutionary theory

With regard to the main points of Dr Snyder's speculations, I must say that I am nearly in complete agreement. Indeed, a careful consideration of his arguments almost compels agreement. It is of interest that a similar formulation has been reached by a scientific colleague from another discipline – Professor Sherwood Washburn, an anthropologist at the University of California – who has transmitted his views to me in a recent communication. I might add that Professor Washburn has not been at all concerned with the problem of REM sleep in his usual endeavors. I will take the liberty of quoting his thoughts, interlaced with some of my own, which will document the fateful inevitability of Dr Snyder's line of reasoning more than extending it.

'The REM state may be thought of as a behavioral state. The theory of natural selection demands that behaviors be adaptive. If behaviors are widespread through many different kinds of mammals, they must not only be behaviorally important, but the importance must be for all kinds of animals which have the behavior.

'Taking up the question of sleep as a whole, the basic mammalian adaptation which separates mammals from reptiles is the whole system of temperature and energy control, which permits the mammal to behave with a far greater freedom from the environment than is the case of reptiles. A parallel development has taken place in birds.

'However, the success of this biological adaptation in birds and mammals is bought at a very high cost. Small mammals have very high metabolic rates and short life spans. If life is looked upon as so many heart beats, the difference between the small mammal and the large one is not so great. In general, increasing size goes with decreasing heart rate, increasing length of life, decreasing food per unit body weight per day, and increasing ability to survive short-term environmental stress. Nevertheless, compared to the turtle, a shrew buys its high activity rate and its freedom from the environment by reducing its life span from many years (perhaps over eighty in the case of the turtle) to two.

'Obviously, one way to buffer the biological cost of becoming a mammal is to time the activity so that the animal gets the maximum adaptive result from the activity. Diurnal rhythms do exactly that, and the adaptive signifi-cance of sleep as a whole may be to buffer the cost of being a mammal. This is shown particularly well in small insectivorous species of bats. The creatures are hyperactive at night and practically hibernate by day. It takes some time for the animal to awaken and get the body temperature to a level permitting flying activity.'

This might seem an ideal solution, permitting a period of great activity and a period of minimum metabolic activity, but it leaves the animal at the mercy of almost any kind of predator, except in the case of birds and bats, where, presumably, the location of their 'beds' gives them a degree of safety. The opposite extreme, however, occurs in such animals as the ante-lope, where the herd is in an extremely precarious position at night. In such a case, a mechanism ensuring periodic arousal would be highly advan-tageous.

It has been postulated by Dr Snyder that the periodic occurrence of REM sleep may be well suited to this function. His argument includes two import-ant points: first, that in many species REM periods are almost invariably terminated by arousals and that in conditions of increased danger awaken-ings from the REM state are more likely to occur early in the REM period; second, that the REM state, by virtue of its intensely activating properties, places the nervous system in a state of preparedness for immediate fight or flight.

With regard to his first point, a very short cycle length for the NREM–REM–awake sequence would be maximally advantageous. For example, it has been found that in some antelope herds, the animals sleep three minutes and awaken one, although this may or may not represent a high frequency of REM periods. However, under ordinary circumstances, where the *onset* of REM sleep is presumably not *immediately* interrupted by an arousal, its actual presence for some minutes would be a disadvantage unless the arousal threshold were *not* higher than the contiguous periods of NREM sleep, at least in terms of responding to the warning sound of a sudden attack.

Studies in the cat (Benoit and Bloch, 1960; Jouvet, 1962) have produced results which indicate that the arousal threshold during REM sleep is, in fact, very much higher than in NREM sleep. The differences have been so marked that certain groups of investigators refer to REM sleep as 'deep' sleep and NREM sleep as 'light' sleep (Moruzzi, 1963; Rossi *et al.*, 1961).

Unfortunately, the relevant studies utilized the intensity of direct, non-physiological electrical stimulation of the mesencephalic reticular formation required to elicit arousal as the measure of threshold. There is actually no good evidence that the same holds true for auditory stimulation. In addition, we know that the REM state is a state where higher nervous processes take place, such as habituation (Dement, 1965b), discrimination (Berger, 1963), and possibly even learning (Evans *et al.*, 1966). Thus, it is quite likely that with domestication, and particularly in the laboratory environment, the period of sleep is no longer dangerous and there has been a marked habituation to arousing stimuli during the REM period.

The work of Williamson (1965) in human subjects strongly suggests that if a stimulus is followed by a painful consequence, not only does discrimination take place, but the arousal threshold lightens. In our studies of REM deprivation in cats and humans, we have seen habituation to an extent where easily awakened subjects become completely impervious to arousing stimuli of enormous intensity. Yet, over the years, I have found it impossible to sneak up on any of my feline household pets during REM sleep. The slightest creak of the floor and they are awake.

As has been pointed out, REM sleep periods in many species are invariably followed by arousal, which persists for a few minutes and is followed by a new cycle of NREM–REM sleep. While such periodic arousals would certainly increase the probability of being alert to the approach of an attacker, their importance could go far beyond this in animals that sleep in groups. As suggested by Washburn, a reasonably short cycle length together with temporal dispersion would mean that at any given moment, some animals in the herd would be awake and alert to danger. Thus, in many anthropoids and ungulates, the herd would always have a sentinel.

Even in the case of humans, we have found that 85 per cent (Dement, 1962) of REM periods end with gross body movement, accompanied by at least transient EEG activation. It is perhaps only because of the artificial pressures of culture that we sleep through the night at all. In more primitive societies, this is not necessarily the case. For example, pygmy camps are described as always having someone awake.

With regard to the second point, Dr Snyder suggests that performance immediately following arousal from REM sleep ought to be better than performance immediately following arousal from NREM sleep. In addition to the modicum of available evidence supporting this position cited by Dr Snyder, I might add an anecdote from our laboratory. In testing eye movement velocity immediately after arousal, we had the impression that subjects could see better in a dimly lit room when aroused from REM sleep. We thought that this might be due to variations in dark adaptation independent of external illumination. We tested subjects with a dark adaptometer immediately after arousal from the two kinds of sleep and found no significant difference in adaptation. However, it was very apparent that in terms of manipulating the dark adaptometer, successful testing occurred much more often immediately after REM awakenings.

Dr Snyder raises the question of why periodic 'activations' of the nervous system and arousals from sleep should be preceded by such an elaborate and temporally extended physiological process as the REM state. Surely, there could be a much simpler and more economical way of accomplishing this. I think that the most parsimonious answer is that the 'sentinel' function was accorded secondarily to a state whose primary function is fulfilled at an earlier stage of development. Thus, while admirably suited to a sentinel function in those organisms where it chanced to persist into adulthood, its original development did not subserve this function, and it is not, therefore, a completely efficient design.

In addition to the inefficient complexity of the REM state, the very pronounced REM deprivation–compensation phenomenon would seem inappropriate to a sentinel function. However, to elaborate further on Dr Snyder's remarks, one can visualize at least three advantages accruing from this aspect of the REM process.

In the first place, under conditions of danger when arousals might be frequent and sleep very sparse and fitful, the accruing excitatory effect of REM deprivation might be expected to offset the fatigue and depressive effects of total sleep loss.

Secondly, if the threat is maintained and REM periods continue to be interrupted by arousals, the REM deprivation effect would lead to an even more frequent occurrence of REM periods and hence to more frequent awakenings and sampling of the environment. In the case of antelopes, we might suggest a state of chronic REM deprivation to account for the very short sleep cycle.

Finally, a slightly different advantage might be accorded to predator mammals where a vigilance function for the REM state might not be quite so important. When game is scarce, we may presume that these mammals go for long periods without food. It is possible that during these periods they sacrifice sleep time to hunting time. In such instances, REM deprivation would take place and the consequences that we see in the laboratory should occur, namely, neural hyperexcitability and drive augmentation. Presumably, these effects would favor success in the hunt, and hence, would have favored the survival of predator mammals possessing the REM mechanism as adults.

I would like to close my discussion by thanking and commending Dr Snyder for his most provocative journey through uncharted territory, and to reiterate the siren lure of the problem and its laudable resistance to easy solution. There is really nothing more gratifying than a truly difficult problem. I can only add that I hope I live long enough to see some of the solutions. Several years ago, I had a dream in which I was afflicted with cancer of the lung. The overpowering reality of this opportunity to experience future alternatives was sufficient to induce a cessation of the cigarette habit. About a year later, certain events conspired to bring about my downfall in the form of a return of the habit. I am now waiting for the REM state to perform what may be an entirely new adaptive function with unquestioned survival value – to provide me with another hallucinatory pulmonary carcinoma so that I will be impelled to quit for the second and last time.

References

BENOIT, O., and BLOCH, V. (1960), 'Seuil d'excitabilité réticulaire et sommeil profond chez le chat', *J. Physiologie*, vol. 52, pp. 17–18.

BERGER, R. (1963), 'Experimental modification of dream content in meaningful verbal stimuli', *Brit. J. Psychiat.*, vol. 109, pp. 722–40.

DEMENT, W. (1962), 'Manual for scoring EEG records for REM periods (dream time)', presented at second annual meeting of Association for the Psychophysiological Study of Sleep, Chicago.

DEMENT, W. (1965a), 'Recent studies on the biological role of rapid eye movement sleep', *Amer. J. Psychiat.*, vol. 122, pp. 404–8.

DEMENT, W. (1965b), 'Studies on the function of rapid eye movement (paradoxical) sleep in human subjects', in M. Jouvet (ed.), *Aspects anatomo-fonctionnels de la physiologie du sommeil*, Centre National de la Recherche Scientifique, Paris, pp. 571–611.

DEMENT, W., et al. (1967), 'Studies on the effect of REM deprivation in humans and animals', *Pubns Assn Res. Nerv. Ment. Dis.*, vol. 45, pp. 456–68.

EVANS, F., et al. (1966), 'Response during sleep with intervening waking amnesia', *Science*, vol. 152, pp. 666–7.

FERGUSON, J., and DEMENT, W. (1966a), 'Changes in the intensity of REM sleep with deprivation', presented at sixth annual meeting of Association for the Psychophysiological Study of Sleep, Gainesville, Florida.

FERGUSON, J., and DEMENT, W. (1966b), 'The effect of variations in total sleep time on the occurrence of rapid eye movement sleep in cats', *EEG clin. Neurophysiol.*, vol. 22, p. 109.

HAMBURGER, V., et al. (1965), 'Periodic motility of normal and spinal chick embryos between 8 and 17 days of incubation', *J. exp. Zoo.*, vol. 159, pp. 1–14.

JOUVET, D., VALATX, J., and JOUVET, M. (1961), 'Etude polygraphique du sommeil du chaton', *C R soc. biol.*, vol. 155, pp. 1660–64.

JOUVET, M. (1962), 'Recherches sur les structures nerveuses et les mécanismes résponsables des différentes phases du sommeil physiologique', *Arch. Ital. Biol.*, vol. 100, pp. 125–206.

JOUVET, M., MICHEL, F., and MOUNIER, D. (1960), 'Analyse eléctroencephalographique comparée du sommeil physiologique chez le chat et chez l'homme', *Rev. Neurol.*, vol. 108, pp. 189–205.

KANZOW, E. (1965), 'Changes in blood flow of the cerebral cortex and other vegetative changes during paradoxical sleep periods in the unrestrained cat', in M. Jouvet (ed.), *Aspects anatomo-fonctionnels de la physiologie du sommeil*, Centre National de la Recherche Scientifique, Paris, pp. 231–41.

KLEIN, M. (1963), 'Etude polygraphique et phylogénique des états de sommeil', thèse de médecine, Lyon.

KLEIN, M., MICHEL, F., and JOUVET, M. (1964), 'Etude polygraphique du sommeil chez les oiseaux', *C R soc. biol.*, vol. 1, pp. 99–102.

MICHEL, F., *et al.* (1964), 'Sur les mécanismes de l'activité des pointes au niveau du système visuel', *C R soc. biol.*, vol. 158, pp. 106–9.

MORUZZI, G. (1963), 'Active processes in the brain stem during sleep', *Harvey Lecture Series*, vol. 58, pp. 233–97.

PARMELEE, A., WENNER, W., and SCHULTZ, H. (1964), 'Infant sleep patterns from birth to 16 weeks of age', *J. Pediat.*, vol. 65, pp. 576–82.

PETRE-QUADENS, O. (1966), 'Ontogenesis of paradoxical sleep and its evolution in mental retardation', presented at sixth annual meeting of Association for the Psychophysiological Study of Sleep, Gainesville, Florida.

POMPEIANO, O. (1965), 'Ascending and descending influences of somatic afferent volleys in unrestrained cats: supraspinal inhibitory control of spinal reflexes during natural and reflexly induced sleep', in M. Jouvet (ed.), *Aspects anatomo-fonctionnels de la physiologie du sommeil*, Centre National de Recherche Scientifique, Paris, pp. 309–97.

ROFFWARG, H., DEMENT, W., and FISHER, C. (1964), 'Observations on the sleep–dream pattern in neonates, infants, children and adults', in E. Harms (ed.), *Problems of Sleep and Dream in Children*, Pergamon.

ROFFWARG, H., MUZIO, J., and DEMENT, W. (1966), 'The ontogenetic development of the sleep–dream cycle in the human', *Science*, vol. 152, pp. 604–19.

ROSSI, G., *et al.* (1961), 'Researches on the nervous mechanisms underlying deep sleep in the cat', *Arch. Ital. Biol.*, vol. 99, pp. 270–92.

SHIMIZU, N., and MORIKAWA, N. (1959), 'Histochemical study of monoamine oxidase in the developing rat brain', *Nature*, vol. 184, pp. 650–51.

WILLIAMSON, H. (1965), 'The problem of defining depth of sleep', presented at 45th annual meeting of Association for Research in Nervous and Mental Disease, New York.

30 Ralph J. Berger

Oculomotor Control: A Possible Function of REM Sleep

Ralph J. Berger, 'Oculomotor control: a possible function of REM sleep',
Psychological Review, vol. 76, 1969, pp. 144–64.

There has been a rapid expansion of research on sleep during the past decade, which was catalyzed by the discovery of Aserinsky and Kleitman (1953) that sleep is characterized by two cyclically recurring phases, rather that being a unitary state which merely exhibits a changing continuum in depth. One phase, termed rapid eye movement (REM) sleep, is accompanied by binocularly conjugate rapid eye movements; in the other phase, termed nonrapid eye movement (NREM) sleep, the eyes are either immobile or exhibit slow rolling movements. Several reviews of these developments have appeared recently (Dement, 1965a; Snyder, 1963, 1965), so only a brief description of some of the characteristics of the two sleep phases will be given.

Mammalian sleep onset normally begins with NREM sleep and is followed by the cyclical recurrence of periods of REM sleep (Dement and Kleitman, 1957a). During NREM sleep the electroencephalogram (EEG) is composed of high voltage, slow waves together with faster spindling potentials; the respiration and heart rate are regular and the blood pressure is low. The onset of each REM period is marked by striking changes, generally in the direction of a pattern of activation, so that REM sleep is sometimes called activated sleep. The appearance of the REMs themselves is accompanied by a relatively low voltage, mixed frequency, EEG pattern, with distinctive monophasic waves in the pons and visual system (Brooks and Bizzi, 1963; Mikiten, Niebyl and Hendley, 1961; Mouret, Jeannerod and Jouvet, 1963); increase in rate and irregularity of heart beat and respiration (Jouvet, Michel and Mounier, 1960; Snyder *et al.*, 1964); increase in cerebral blood flow (Kanzow, Krause and Kühnel, 1962); rise in brain temperature (Kawamura and Sawyer, 1965; Rechtschaffen *et al.*, 1965); and elevation in frequency of neuronal firing throughout sensory and motor areas of the brain (Arduini, Berlucchi and Strata, 1963; Evarts, 1962, 1964; Huttenlocher, 1961). In contrast to this pattern of activation, there is marked hypotonia of head and neck muscles (Berger, 1961; Jacobson *et al.*, 1964) and spinal reflexes are sharply attenuated (Giaquinto, Pompeiano and Somogyi, 1964a, 1964b; Hodes and Dement, 1964). In man the incidence of dream recall following awakenings from REM periods is higher than following awakenings from NREM periods (Dement and Kleitman, 1957b; Foulkes, 1962; Goodenough et al., 1959; Rechtschaffen, Verdone and Wheaton, 1963).

Hypotheses of REM sleep function

Until the discovery of the REM period, sleep had traditionally been viewed as a period of necessary organismic rest (Piéron, 1913), although little biochemical or physiological evidence has been produced to support this notion. The appearance of the activated REM phase of sleep amid a peaceful state of general quiescence immediately raised questions regarding its role in that context. Three main theories of the function of REM sleep have been proposed to date, which approach the problem from three distinct viewpoints – ontogenetic, phylogenetic, and homeostatic. Following a brief description of these theories, a new theory will be proposed which attempts to encompass a broader area of data than has been dealt with by any of these earlier theories.

The ontogenetic theory

Roffwarg, Muzio and Dement (1966) proposed that REM sleep provides endogenous afferent stimulation necessary for structural differentiation and maturation of the central nervous system during fetal and neonatal life, when brain growth is maximal. The high percentage of time spent in REM sleep in both the premature and full-term newborn mammal and its subsequent decline with increase in age was presented as the principal evidence.

The theory required the supplementary proposal for an intrinsic pre-programmed mechanism to maintain the large amounts of postnatal REM sleep, despite the massive increase in amounts of exogenous stimulation experienced following birth. Moreover, premature infants exhibit the same percentages (50 per cent) of REM sleep when they reach the equivalent conceptional age as a full-term infant, even though they have been subjected to considerably more exogenous stimulation following birth (Monod et al., 1964; Parmelee et al., 1967).

The phylogenetic theory

Snyder (1966) proposed that REM sleep first evolved in the mammal to serve a 'sentinel' or vigilance function necessary for survival from attack by other species. He suggested that REM sleep provides periodic cortical arousal throughout sleep preparatory to the brief awakenings which usually terminate REM periods, so that the animal has sufficient 'critical reactivity' to adequately 'test' the environment for dangerous elements.

A major problem which arises from this hypothesis is to explain why the most defenseless and vulnerable mammals such as the rabbit and sheep should exhibit the smallest amounts of REM sleep, while the predators such as man and cat should exhibit the highest amounts. Snyder himself pointed out this apparent contradiction to the hypothesis and attempted to overcome it by suggesting that there is a competition between the need for maximal conservation of energy obtained through sleep and the need for maximal protection from external danger during sleep. He suggested that the latter receives precedence in the small vulnerable animals so that, by contrast to the sustained sleep with long intervals between REM periods of predators, more frequent and longer wakings together with shorter REM periods are exhibited by hunted animals. However, frequent awakenings in defenseless animals such as ungulates mostly occur immediately following periods of NREM sleep (Ruckebusch, 1963). So REM sleep does not in fact seem to act in the role of providing preparatory arousal prior to awakening from REM sleep in these defenseless animals, this being the main premise of the 'sentinel' hypothesis. Snyder also failed to explain why a special state should evolve for a specific purpose, when immediate awakening from NREM sleep with behavioral immobility of the animal for a few minutes would do equally well in bringing the cortex back to a high level of activation, and allow the animal to 'regain its senses'.

The homeostatic theory

Ephron and Carrington (1966) postulated the existence of a homeostatic interplay between REM sleep and NREM sleep to account for the sequential relationship seen between these two sleep states. They proposed that the loss of cortical 'tonus' or 'vigilance' during deepening NREM sleep provides the organism with needed rest, and must be maintained within adaptively appropriate limits. In order to preserve the continuity of sleep, but maintain the level of cerebral excitation within these limits, Ephron and Carrington suggested that REM sleep serves the function of periodically increasing cortical 'tonus'.

This homeostatic hypothesis has a considerable affinity with the onto-genetic hypothesis. A need for endogenous stimulation of the central nervous system is propounded in both hypotheses: in the ontogenetic hypothesis to develop normal waking function, and in the homeostatic hypothesis to maintain normal waking function throughout later life. Together these two theories could provide an explanation of the function of REM sleep during ontogenesis and in late life. However, an explanation of the phylogenesis of REM sleep is not provided by either of these theories, since the amounts of REM sleep seen in the mammalian series do not seem to bear any simple relation with the varying degree of cortical development among different species, as is predicted by both theories. The hypothesis to be advanced in this article, although simple in view of the remarkable complexity of REM sleep, does attempt to encompass phylogenetic and ontogenetic data, as well as explain why REM sleep is maintained throughout the organism's total lifespan. It will be called the 'oculomotor innervation hypothesis'.

The oculomotor innervation hypothesis

It is proposed that REM sleep provides a mechanism for the establishment of the neuromuscular pathways involved in voluntary conjugate eye movements in both phylogenesis and ontogenesis; and that throughout mammalian life REM sleep furnishes periodic innervation of the oculomotor system during extended periods of sleep, in order to maintain facilitation of binocularly coordinated eye movement into subsequent wakefulness.

The degree of fine neuromuscular coordination necessary to execute voluntary conjugate scanning movements and disjunctive fixational movements of the eyes in the higher mammals exceeds that of any other muscle system. During NREM sleep the eyes adopt a resting position, most frequently divergent upward (Pietrusky, 1922); sometimes, occasional disconjugate rolling movements are also present. Electromyographic (EMG) activity in extraocular muscle is almost entirely absent at these times when the eyes are at rest (Breinin, 1957; Michel, Rechtschaffen and Vimont-Vicary, 1964). Because of this lack of innervation of the oculomotor system during NREM sleep and the plasticity of the central nervous system under conditions of use and disuse (Riesen, 1967), it is suggested that were it not for the intrusion of periods of REM sleep throughout extended periods of NREM sleep, the central facilitation necessary for coordination of eye movements might be temporarily lost on awakening.

In addition to providing a mechanism throughout adult life for maintaining facilitation of voluntary conjugate eye movements during sleep, it is postulated that REM sleep serves the function of establishing the neuromuscular pathways involved in conjugate eye movements in phylogenesis, and this is recapitulated during ontogenesis. Once the neural effector mechanisms for conjugate eye movement have been established by the intrinsic innervating mechanism of REM sleep, they can be regulated by the perceptual products of extrinsic visual stimulation during wakefulness, under voluntary control mediated by the cerebral cortex. The culmination of this process is seen in the highest mammals, the primates, with their ability for accurate stereoscopic depth perception.

The oculomotor innervation hypothesis and phylogenesis

Although binocular vision can be present in certain lower vertebrates, stereopsis first occurs in the mammal and is dependent upon the existence of partial decussation of optic tract fibers at the optic chiasma (Walls, 1942). Both Sherrington (1947) and Walls (1942) argue that the value of partial decussation is in giving control of all twelve ocular muscles to single cortical loci in the interests of smooth operation of conjugated eye movements. Sherrington and Walls point out the necessity for a confluence of the sensory tracts into a final common motor path if a coordinated mechanism is to result.

The appearance of partial decussation of the optic nerve fibers at the chiasma in mammalia is therefore associated with the fact that the latter is the only class of vertebrates in which the ocular movements are coordinated. Within the mammalian series the degree of spontaneous coordinated mobility of the eyes is proportional to the amount of semidecussation at the chiasma (Walls, 1962). A few uncrossed optic nerve fibers exist in the rabbit, one-third are uncrossed in the predators, such as the cat, increasing to one-half in man. One might expect that as precise coordination of eye movements becomes increasingly essential to the function of stereopsis, then if REM sleep is involved in the establishment and maintenance of such control, a correlation should be seen between the amount of partial decussation at the optic chiasma and the percentage of total sleep time (TST) spent in REM sleep (per cent REM/TST) throughout the mammalian series. Figure 1 suggests that such a rough correlation does indeed exist. Thus, hunted animals such as the rabbit, with small amounts of semidecussation, exhibit low percentages of REM sleep, while the carnivores and primates, with large amounts of semidecussation, exhibit high percentages. The REM sleep percentages were compiled from numerous studies carried out in a number of different laboratories (Delorme, Vimont and Jouvet, 1964; Jouvet and Valatx, 1962; Jouvet-Mounier and Astic, 1966; Klein, 1963; Snyder, 1966; Weiss and Roldán, 1964; Weitzmann et al., 1965; Williams, Agnew and Webb, 1964).

Although a correlation between the two measures does exist, it is far from perfect. But account should be taken of the patterning of sleep and wakefulness and the total daily amounts of time spent asleep. The proportions of time spent asleep and awake over a twenty-four-hour period for each species are also represented in Figure 1. Both the cat and the opossum spend large amounts of time sleeping in the laboratory compared with the primates and also spend a greater percentage of that time in REM sleep, even though they exhibit less partial decussation at their optic chiasmas. With less eye-movement activity present during the shorter wakeful periods in cats and opossums, compared with primates, one might expect an increased requirement for REM sleep in these animals according to the oculomotor innervation hypothesis. If the percentage of total sleep spent in REM sleep is divided by the percentage of the day spent asleep for each species, to com-

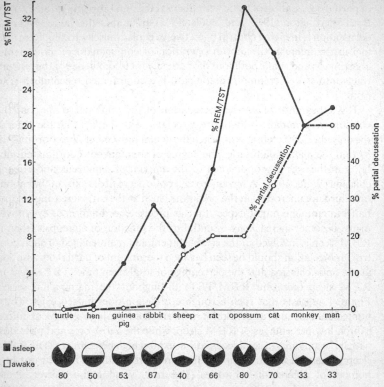

Figure 1 Percentage of total sleep time (TST) spent in rapid eye movement (REM) sleep and percentage of partial decussation at the optic chiasma plotted for various species. (At the bottom are represented the proportions of time spent asleep and awake over twenty-four hours for each species)

pensate for these differences in daily sleeping time a closer approach to a linear relationship between the degree of partial decussation and these derived values (REM/TST^2) is obtained (Figure 2). It should be pointed out that departures from an exact linear relationship, most marked in the case of the opossum, might be due to a number of factors. Thus, the function REM/TST^2 is subject to the following variations: in methods of scoring the two sleep phases among various investigators; in recording procedures and environments; in age of experimental subjects; and in colony diets and regimens.

Crucial to the oculomotor innervation hypothesis are the sleep characteristics of vertebrates whose chiasmic anatomies lie close to the transition

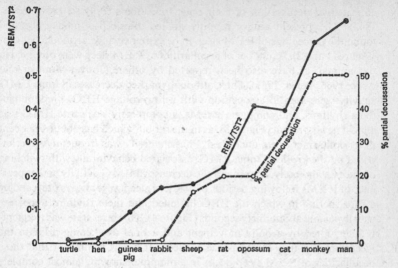

Figure 2 This figure is derived from Figure 1. (The percentage of total sleep time spent in REM sleep – % REM/TST – has been divided by the percentage of the twenty-four-hour period spent asleep for each species. The derived function REM/TST^2 and percentage of partial decussation of the optic chiasma are plotted for each species)

point from complete decussation to the inception of some uncrossed nerve fibers. A polygraphic pattern which resembles REM sleep is first seen in phylogenesis in the bird (Klein, Michel and Jouvet, 1964). Although conjugate REMs accompanied by a low voltage, desynchronized EEG pattern do occur, complete EMG hypotonia has not been observed and the periods of REM sleep are extremely brief, rarely lasting longer than a few seconds. The percentage of sleep spent in this phase is close to 0·05 per cent. Although decussation is total in the bird, it is interesting to note that some of the optic nerve fibers do recross at the suprachiasmic level (Polyak, 1957). At a lower phylogenetic level, the concomitance of EMG hypotonia, EEG desynchronization, and rapid conjugate eye movements has not been observed in reptiles or amphibia (Hobson, 1967; Klein, 1963). Although periods with rapid, but nonconjugate, eye movements have been observed during body immobility and muscular relaxation in the chameleon, concomitant EEG desynchronization and EMG hypotonia did not accompany these periods (Tauber, Roffwarg and Weitzman, 1966). It is doubtful whether the presence of nonconjugate eye movements and behavioral unresponsiveness alone are sufficient criteria for the definition of REM sleep.

The guinea pig and whale are remarkable among mammals in having almost total decussation of their optic tract fibers (Polyak, 1957; Walls, 1942). The present author recently studied the sleep of guinea pigs and found the percentage of REM sleep to be extremely low, around 5 per cent (Figures 1 and 2). A number of peculiarities of REM sleep were observed in this animal, as have also been reported by others (Jouvet-Mounier and Astic, 1966; Pellet, 1966). Thus, although marked decreases in tonic EMG activity were seen in association with a low-voltage EEG, predominant theta rhythms, and conjugate REMs, a completely isoelectric EMG was almost never present (Figure 3), as in the rabbit, which has about 1 per cent of its optic tract fibers uncrossed. Phasic activity was frequently superimposed on the low-level tonic EMG, associated behaviorally with twitching of the ears and body. Moreover, the decrease in EMG activity and appearance of REMs following periods of NREM sleep were always preceded by a short period in which the EEG flattened and theta rhythms appeared, usually lasting about thirty seconds (Figure 4). This brief state was frequently interrupted by a body movement and a brief awakening prior to the inception of a true REM phase of sleep. It seems significant that these peculiarities of REM sleep occur in a mammal showing almost complete decussation of its optic nerves, but are not seen in a mammal of the same genus which has a few ipsilateral fibers emergent from its chiasma. REM sleep in the guinea pig appears to be intermediate between the precursory REM phase in the bird and the full-blown REM phase in the rabbit, as is the anatomy of its visual pathways.

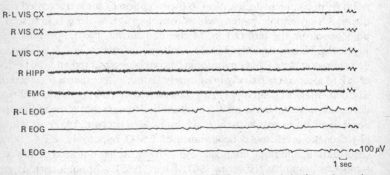

Figure 3 Example of the beginning of an REM sleep episode in the guinea pig. (Note the continuation of a small amount of tonic activity in the EMG lead, with frequent phasic activity superimposed – R, right; L, left; VIS CX, visual cortex; HIPP, hippocampus)

The oculomotor innervation hypothesis and ontogenesis

Newborn mammals spend large amounts of time in REM sleep, a phenomenon which progressively declines with maturation (Chase and Sterman, 1967;

Meier and Berger, 1965; Monod *et al.*, 1964; Parmelee *et al.*, 1967; Roffwarg, Dement and Fisher, 1964; Valatx, 1963). It is proposed that the function of REM sleep in ontogenesis is to provide intrinsic stimulation, as has been suggested by Roffwarg, Muzio and Dement (1966), but specific to the oculomotor system, rather than the entire cortex.

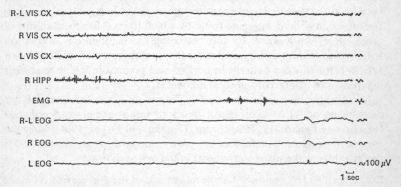

Figure 4 Example of a thirty-second period of theta rhythm in the EEG leads, characteristically preceding the onset of an REM period in the guinea pig. (The designation of channels is the same as in Figure 3)

A mechanism has not been elucidated that would explain how the neonate might be capable of learning to develop conjugate control of its eye movements given only the visual sense data provided by the environment. Such a mechanism would require perceptual recognition of the overlapping projections of the retinal images to each cortex, with adjustment of the eyes to a conjugate orientation so as to produce congruent isomorphic alignment of the images bilaterally at each visual cortex. But this would imply that perception is initially acquired under conditions of diplopia and only later followed by a recognition of the diplopia so that appropriate compensatory binocular readjustments of the eyes can then be made to eliminate the diplopia. A two-stage process in perceptual development of this nature, passing from relatively independent monocular visual perceptions to a unitary fused binocular visual perception, seems unlikely. It seems more reasonable to propose that REM sleep provides the intrinsic mechanism necessary for the development of binocular oculomotor control which, initially, is independent of peripheral visual input during wakefulness. Later, when the oculomotor neural pathways necessary for coordinated eye movement have become well-established in wakefulness and binocular visual perception has developed sufficiently, the binocular control of eye movement may be taken over by perceptual-oculomotor mechanisms for eliminating diplopia. The similar percentages of REM sleep seen in premature and full-term infants of equal conceptual age, despite their differing histories of environmental stimulation, thus becomes readily understandable. The necessity for an intrinsic brainstem mechanism to establish appropriate neuronal pathways for conjugate eye movements could not be preempted by the earlier onset of visual stimulation in premature infants, because visual stimulation at an earlier age would be incapable of providing the organism with an alternate route by which to establish mechanisms of conjugate eye movement. By this reasoning the oculomotor innervation hypothesis provides an explanation for the 'preprogrammed' maturation of REM–NREM sleep patterns in normal and premature infants and their independence from environmental influences.

Of considerable significance to this discussion is the fact that the eye movements of REM sleep in the newborn infant are always conjugate (Prechtl and Lenard, 1967; Roffwarg, Dement and Fisher, 1964), while the eye movements of wakefulness are partly uncoordinated. Worth (1903) described the wakeful eye movements in the newborn thus:

During the first few months of life the movements of the eyes are uncertain, not completely controlled by the higher centres of the brain. The eyes move more or less together, but the slightest gastric or other disturbance often causes one or other eye to deviate. But it will be noticed that this want of coordination is confined to movements in the horizontal plane. The conjugation of the two eyes for vertical movements is well developed from the earliest infancy (p. 21).

These observations are most significant to the present hypothesis, since in the human newborn vertical REMs predominate over horizontal REMs (Monod and Pajot, 1965; Roffwarg, Dement and Fisher, 1964), whereas in the adult, horizontal REMs are preponderant (Roffwarg, Dement, Muzio and Fisher, 1962). Thus, the greater amount of oculomotor innervation involved in conjugate vertical eye movement during neonatal and, probably, fetal REM sleep may lead to the earlier appearance of vertical conjugate eye movements in the waking infant. The concept of inborn anticipatory function, which is being applied here to the REMs, has been well established in the maturational patterns of other functional systems (Carmichael, 1951). Thus, functional capacities may develop in action systems of the growing organism before these functions are called into play with the environment.

Although the percentage of REM sleep is higher in the newborn than in the adult, close examination of the ontogenesis of sleep in the full-term newborn monkey has revealed an initial increase in both the total amount of sleep and the proportion of it spent in REM sleep until the seventh day of life (Meier and Berger, 1965), after which there is a progressive decline with age. It is feasible that this decline begins when a sufficiently high level of coordination of the oculomotor system has been attained that can be effectively employed during wakeful visual inspection, with subsequent sensory–motor learning of a conventional type. The need for an intrinsic innervating mechanism to develop the coordination of this system then becomes progressively less necessary, until in later life it merely serves a periodic facilitating function during sleep. It may be significant that it is on the seventh day of life that many behavioral reflexive responses first appear in the monkey, including visual fixation of small objects (Mowbray and Cadell, 1962). The notion that during ontogenesis wakefulness increasingly adopts the early functions of REM sleep is supported by the reciprocal relations between changes in wakefulness and changes in REM sleep that have been delineated during maturation in the kitten (Chase and Sterman, 1967). As the kitten matures, the amount of wakefulness increases in direct proportion to the concurrent decrease in the amount of REM sleep, and short periods of wakefulness increase in frequency while short periods of REM sleep become less frequent.

Of additional interest are the changes with age in the contingencies of REM sleep following NREM sleep and reciprocally of REM sleep following wakefulness (Meier and Berger, 1965). In the neonate, episodes of REM sleep follow periods of wakefulness more frequently than they follow periods of NREM sleep. With maturation, however, the dependence of REM sleep on the prior appearance of NREM sleep increases in all species; in adulthood this pattern becomes almost invariable, so that REM sleep is never seen immediately following extended periods of wakefulness in normal individuals (Roffwarg, Muzio and Dement, 1966). The human, owing to his unique socializing process, learns to stay awake by choice for successively longer periods each day until he finally acquires a diurnal sleep–wakefulness pattern. During extended periods of sleep he does not exhibit a constant cycling of the two phases; instead, he shows an increase in the frequency of the sleep cycle and the REM episodes early in the night are usually very short (Feinberg, Koresko and Heller, 1967; Kales *et al.*, 1967). These data seem consistent with a changeover in function of REM sleep, from an initiating mechanism for coordinated eye movement during sleep in infancy, to a periodic facilitatory function for coordinated eye movement during sleep in adulthood. Thus, if conjugate eye movements must be established in the infant by REM sleep mechanisms before they can be effectively employed in wakefulness, then REM sleep would not have to depend on the prior occurrence of NREM sleep as opposed to wakefulness. However, as this initiating role for conjugation of eye movement during REM sleep becomes less necessary with the development of perception and control of eye movement during wakefulness, there is a decrease in the amount of REM sleep, as well as in the need for episodes of REM sleep immediately following wakefulness. Thus, a steadily increasing contingency on the prior occurrence of slow wave sleep gradually develops, until eventually one only sees REM sleep following periods of NREM sleep, when REM sleep serves only the periodic function of maintaining oculomotor 'tonus' throughout extended sleep. This notion seems to be reinforced by the peculiarity of the sleep pattern of the human in whom, so to speak, 'sleep deprivation by choice' occurs each day. At the beginning of the night, the requirement for a long NREM sleep period is very great in order to perform the presumed vital recuperative functions of this stage. Later in the night the REM sleep periods occur at a more regular frequency and are of longer duration, since they have a more restrictive function that NREM sleep. This uneven distribution of sleep into its two phases continues latently throughout the day and is seen when subjects are allowed to take daytime naps (Maron, Rechtschaffen and Wolpert, 1964; Webb and Agnew, 1967; Webb, Agnew and Sternthal, 1966). Early morning naps soon after a previous night's sleep exhibit high amounts of REM sleep close to that present during the last portion of the preceding night's sleep. In naps taken progressively later in the day, the proportion of time spent in REM sleep progressively diminishes and that spent in NREM sleep increases.

Awakenings which are sustained for more than a few minutes from NREM or REM sleep are rarely followed by immediate entry or return to REM sleep. The requirement for innervation of the oculomotor system which triggers the onset of REM sleep may be partially obviated by intervening periods of wakeful eye movement. This phenomenon may also provide an explanation for the 'first night effect' (Agnew, Webb and Williams, 1966; Dement, Kahn and Roffwarg, 1965) in which human subjects show a significant depression of the percentage of time spent in REM sleep on their first night in the laboratory. They are usually apprehensive about the whole procedure, which leads to a somewhat disturbed sleep pattern, with more spontaneous awakenings throughout the night than during subsequent nights in the laboratory. It is possible that these awakenings, accompanied by rapid conjugate eye movement, may substitute for REM periods so that the amounts of REM sleep are reduced over the whole night. A similar effect may be present in people who complain of sleeping badly. Monroe (1967) has reported reduced percentages of REM sleep and more awakenings throughout the night in a group of 'poor' sleepers compared with a group of 'good' sleepers.

Not only does the percentage of REM sleep change during ontogenesis, but so also does the frequency of the REMs themselves. The frequency of REMs in infant monkeys progressively decreases after the second month of life until eighteen months of age, beyond which they were not followed

(Berger and Meier, 1965). Newborn monkeys deprived of patterned vision by insertion of translucent contact occluders over their corneas also exhibit a decrease in the frequency of REMs with maturation (Berger and Meier, 1965), but the decline is more rapid than in normal animals. The sleep of blind humans has also been studied (Berger, Olley and Oswald, 1962). Men who were either congenitally blind, or had been blind for at least thirty years and had lost the capacity for visual imagery, did not have REMs during sleep episodes otherwise characteristic of REM sleep, while men who had become blind in later life, but had been blind for less than fifteen years and still experienced visual imagery, exhibited activated sleep periods accompanied by REMs. Thus, there was a one-to-one correlation between the presence of visual imagery and the presence of REMs during activated sleep in blind men. It would seem from these data that if the visually deprived monkeys had been followed over a longer period, REMs would have eventually disappeared from their activated sleep. The amounts of activated sleep appeared normal in both the human and monkey blind subjects. From the present hypothesis, one might have predicted a decline with age in all aspects of activated sleep consequent to blindness, rather than just the REMs alone. Voluntary waking eye movements and REMs may be served by a number of common neural pathways. The inability of the blind to develop integrated voluntary eye movement might result in deterioration of these common pathways, so that REMs are not expressed during activated sleep even though their intrinsic generating mechanisms may remain intact in the brainstem. Periodic, nystagmoid eye movements, under vestibular influences, are present in most blind subjects. These involuntary eye movements may maintain sufficient 'tone' in the oculomotor apparatus to obviate a need for increasing amounts of activated sleep resulting from a lack of oculomotor innervation.

The nature of the REMs

The characteristics of the REMs have been described in some detail by Dement (1964). They are binocularly synchronous and resemble waking fixational eye movements, occurring with similar velocities in all directions. Roffwarg[1] has recently observed disjunctive eye movements during REM sleep. Michel, Rechtschaffen and Vimont-Vicary (1964) observed that during NREM sleep the EMG of extraocular muscles was at its lowest levels, becoming isoelectric in some ocular muscles while the eyes were completely at rest. During REM sleep tonic EMG activity returned in all ocular muscles to levels similar to those seen in wakefulness, although it was irregular in different muscles. During each REM, EMG activity increased

1. H. P. Roffwarg, personal communication, October 1967.

in the appropriate agonistic contracting muscles and simultaneously decreased in their antagonists. Thus, the action of the ocular muscles was organized appropriately for the execution of conjugate REMs.

Jeannerod, Mouret and Jouvet (1965) reported a remarkably constant distribution of the REMs into bursts of eye movement and into isolated movements from one REM period to another, and from one animal to another. This fixed distribution of the REMs indicates that their process of generation is not a random one but is highly organized. Other peripheral manifestations during REM sleep, although not studied as closely as the REMs, do not display equivalent degrees of independent organization. Aserinsky (1965) has, however, reported a constancy of respiratory pattern linked with REM bursts in the human. He observed a decreased amplitude of respiration and a slight increase in rate with each REM burst, compared with quiescent periods just prior to the onset of each REM burst. It therefore appears that amid a seemingly labile state, the REMs constitute a pillar of organization to which other peripheral changes may become anchored.

An experiment was recently conducted that provided evidence in strong support of the present hypothesis (Berger, 1968a). In fact the hypothesis arose serendipitously from the experiment. With the horizontal electro-oculogram as the operant, high and low rates of waking eye movement were conditioned in four monkeys, using two different schedules of positive reinforcement (Berger, 1968b). The animals were then run in counter-balanced order on each schedule for six successive sessions prior to falling asleep. The rate of REM and the total number of REMs were significantly higher during significantly longer REM sleep periods following sessions with low rates of wakeful eye movement than following sessions with high rates of wakeful eye movement. Moreover, the duration of NREM sleep preceding the onset of REM sleep (the REM sleep latency) tended to be shorter following sessions with low rates of waking eye movement than following sessions with high rates of waking eye movement. These results were contrary to processes of generalization of learning from the waking to sleeping states, or of extinction of wakeful learned responses during REM sleep. An alternative explanation had to be invoked and the present hypothesis appeared totally consistent with the results. Thus, overexercise of the oculomotor system during wakefulness may preempt the 'need' for high rates of REM and long REM periods during subsequent sleep.

The effects of sleep deprivation

If selective deprivation of REM sleep is carried out over a series of nights by repeatedly awakening experimental subjects the moment they enter each REM phase, a progressive increase in the number of awakenings necessary to prevent the onset of REM sleep occurs throughout each night and from one night to the next. When the subjects are later allowed to sleep undisturbed, there are compensatory increases in the proportion of time spent in REM sleep compared to pre-deprivation base-line levels (Dement, 1960; Kales *et al.*, 1964; Khazan and Sawyer, 1963).

If the function of REM sleep is to provide periodic facilitation of oculomotor 'tone' throughout extended periods of sleep, then the above results would be expected. The progressive increase in the frequency of entries into REM sleep phase is explained by the lack of opportunity for oculomotor innervation to occur. On successive nights throughout REM-sleep deprivation, the beginning of each night's sleep does not represent a continuation of the sleep pattern that was present at the end of the preceding night. Instead, sleep begins as usual with NREM sleep and only later is the first onset of REM sleep seen. However, REM sleep latency does become progressively shorter as REM-sleep deprivation continues over a number of nights. The frequency of entry into REM sleep also increases from night to night. The dependency of REM sleep on the prior occurrence of NREM sleep, nevertheless, still holds. Transmission of the deprivation effect across nights might be dependent upon decreases in frequency or speed of daytime eye movement subsequent to each night's REM-sleep deprivation, produced by the lack of opportunity for oculomotor innervation during sleep. A positive feedback loop might then result, such that the effects accumulate over each successive night of deprivation. The underlying physiological triggering and regulating mechanisms of REM sleep have yet to be completely defined. There is considerable evidence that they might be neurohumoral in nature (Jouvet, 1967) and that specific levels of particular neurohumours may accumulate during NREM sleep sufficient to trigger the onset of REM sleep, most likely at the locus of the pons. Dement (1965b) has suggested that these accumulations may not dissipate during the periods of intervening wakefulness between successive deprivation nights, causing the progressive changes in frequency and latency of REM onset on each successive night of REM-sleep deprivation, as well as the compensatory increases in proportion of REM sleep seen during recovery. Dement, Greenberg and Klein (1966) have recently demonstrated how the effects of REM-sleep deprivation could be 'stored' over a number of nights during which REM sleep was limited to the same amounts as had been present during base-line nights, and were evident on subsequent undisturbed nights by typical compensatory increases in amount of REM sleep.

It should be noted that the increases in frequency of onset of REM periods during REM-sleep deprivation, and the increases in proportion of time spent in this phase on recovery, are accompanied by increases in the peripheral manifestations of the phase itself, most notably the frequency of the REMs themselves (Ferguson and Dement, 1966). Such correlations between the durations and proportions of total sleep spent in the REM phase with the frequency of the REMs within REM sleep have already been described in ontogenesis and also in sleep following differing rates of eye movement during wakefulness. The profusion of the REM sleep phase is usually directly related to the profusion of the REMs within the phase itself. This is consistent with the postulated oculomotor innervation function of REM sleep. Innervation may be maximized by increases in amounts of REM sleep as well as by increases in the rate of REMs themselves.

Changes in sleep patterns following deprivation of REM sleep in new-born infant monkeys have not been observed, although compensatory effects similar to those reported in the human did result from REM-sleep deprivation in juvenile monkeys (Berger and Meier, 1966). If REM sleep is involved in the establishment of conjugate eye movement in the neonate and continues later in life only to maintain oculomotor facilitation through-out sleep, then the absence of post-REM-sleep deprivation effects in the neonate is understandable. At this early age REM sleep is probably already occurring to an optimal extent, compatible with the total economy of the organism, in order to establish the necessary oculomotor pathways for coordinated eye movement. Therefore, increases in the amount of REM sleep following REM-sleep deprivation would not be anticipated. On the other hand, an increasing resistance to forced awakenings from REM sleep might be expected, since a presumed vital function is being disrupted. A progressive increase in threshold of awakening to the arousing stimulus was, in fact, observed during REM-sleep deprivation in the infant monkey (Berger and Meier, 1966).

Selective deprivation of stage 4 NREM sleep has been shown to lead to compensatory increases in this stage on recovery at the expense of other NREM sleep stages, but without change in the amounts of REM sleep (Agnew, Webb and Williams, 1964). Deprivation of stage 4 was accomplished with very few awakenings, and the total duration of the NREM sleep stages remained constant. If the recurrence of REM periods is dependent upon the absence of oculomotor innervation throughout all stages of NREM sleep, then the amounts and periodicity of REM sleep would be expected to remain constant, as was observed.

The initial increases in amount of time spent in NREM sleep following total sleep deprivation (Berger and Oswald, 1962a; Williams *et al.*, 1964) can be explained as resulting from the increased biological demands of the organism for the restful recuperative powers which this phase of sleep is presumed to provide. The normal periodic appearance of REM phases might be usurped by this more pressing need. There may also be a concurrent decreased need for oculomotor innervation, since during their enforced wakefulness subjects would be having considerable amounts of eye movement for a more extensive time than is normal prior to eventful sleep. This might be expected to lead to decreased rates of eye movement and shorter REM periods during subsequent sleep, through a process similar to that which led to the changes in REM sleep seen in monkeys conditioned to move their eyes at different rates during wakefulness, described earlier. The secondary increases in REM sleep which follow the initial recovery of NREM sleep might be explained by the accumulation of neurohumours generated as a normal regulatory process during NREM sleep, which would be larger in amount following NREM sleep. Thus, REM-sleep deprivation is in effect produced on the first recovery night by the initial recuperation in NREM sleep and is seen in the associated decrease in the percentage of REM sleep below normal levels. This REM-sleep deprivation might then be reflected in later sleep patterns. A similar effect has already been suggested to occur in the human each day, produced by his 'sleep deprivation by choice', to explain the increasing periodicity of REM sleep throughout the night.

Partial sleep deprivation over a series of nights in the human does not result in any change in the distribution of the two sleep phases within each successive restricted sleep period (Dement and Greenberg, 1966; Webb and Agnew, 1965), although there is an increase in the amount of stage 4 within NREM sleep, mainly at the expense of stage 3. Perhaps sufficient organismic rest is provided by the limited but deeper periods of NREM sleep without disrupting the normal sequential relationship between NREM and REM sleep. Only when total sleep deprivation takes place does the need for NREM sleep encroach upon REM sleep.

Plastic changes in motor systems

Is there physiological evidence to support the notion that the oculomotor system must receive periodic innervation for effective binocular coordination to be maintained during sleep? Such evidence might relate to the possibilities that disuse of the oculomotor system leads to plastic changes in the extraocular muscles, and/or in the central neural processes serving eye movement.

Possible changes in extraocular muscles

Changes in metabolism and speed of contraction have been produced by denervation, tenotomy, and immobilization of skeletal muscle (Gutmann and Hník, 1963). Only the effects of tenotomy and immobilization may be relevant to the possible effects of spontaneous disuse of extraocular muscle, since the effects of denervation have been mainly ascribed to the interruption of a 'trophic' influence of the motoneuron on the muscle fibers, rather than to the interruption of neural impulses to the muscle fibers (Gutmann and Hník, 1962). The time course of changes produced by tenotomy and immobilization is rather long, becoming marked only after twenty to thirty days (Cole, 1960; Fischer and Ramsey, 1946; Vrbová, 1963). Experimental alteration of innervation of extraocular muscle has not been performed and it is possible that effects might appear much sooner than in skeletal muscle.

The anatomy and physiology of the ocular muscles differ in many ways from those of skeletal muscle. The ocular muscles have a richer nerve supply than any other muscles in the body, with ratios of motor nerve fibers to muscle fibers possibly being as low as 1:3 in some species (Bors, 1926; Tergast, 1873). Their speed of contraction and rate of motor unit discharge is higher than in skeletal muscles (Whitteridge, 1959). Bach-y-Rita and Ito (1966) have recently demonstrated the existence of both fast and slow fibers in cat extraocular muscle. Eye muscles contract in response to acetylcholine (Brown and Harvey, 1941) whereas skeletal muscle only contracts with close arterial injection of acetylcholine. All these differences might be indicative of differences in rates of change in extraocular and skeletal muscle resulting from changes in their innervation. The rich innervation and high speed of contraction of eye muscles suggests them to have a higher rate of metabolism than skeletal muscles which would be likely to lead to relatively rapid changes following a lack of innervation.

Possible changes in central neural processes

It has been well established that central plastic changes can result from sensory deprivation (Riesen, 1967), and that psychological processes can be influenced by very short periods of sensory restriction (Solomon, 1961). It is likely that similar rapid, plastic changes can and do occur in central processes involved in motor functions if periodic innervation of these processes does not occur.

Voluntary binocularly coordinated eye movements evolved by coming under increased control of the cerebral cortex. The electrical stimulation experiments by Penfield and Rasmussen (1950) showed that the extraocular muscles have the largest cortical representation of any of the body's muscles despite their extremely small mass. The transition from reflex to volitional action, with increased corticalization of motor function, has been described by Sherrington (1947). An increase in corticalization of motor function leads to greater plasticity in muscular control, so that new volitional acts can be learned by bringing skeletal muscles under increasing cortical control. But in order to be preserved, such learned movements must be repeatedly practiced. It seems likely, then, that coordinated eye movements are liable to plastic change. Therefore, a system might evolve to establish such movements under cortical control during ontogenesis and provide for their periodic reactivation during extended periods of sleep, to maintain their stability. However, the provision of a periodic reactivating mechanism throughout sleep would imply that central degenerative changes have a fast time course – faster than can be kept within adaptive limits by recurrent innervations of the oculomotor system during the waking periods spanning each sleeping period. Is there evidence to indicate that degenerative plastic changes can occur centrally within the course of a few hours in primates, or minutes in lower animals?

An enduring neural process appears to be needed for fixation or consolidation of learning, possibly by the action of reverberating neuronal networks (Glickman, 1961). The time for this process to occur varies from fifteen to sixty minutes from fish to man. The fixation time for centrally induced postural asymmetry in the spinal cord of the rat was demonstrated to be close to forty-five minutes (Chamberlain, Halick and Gerard, 1963).

There exist little data on the course of degenerative changes in learned motor behavior. However, Wallach and Karsh (1963) reported that monocular occlusion of each eye, alternating every two to three hours for a period of twenty-four hours, led to a marked deterioration in accuracy of depth perception. In addition, spontaneous changes in perceived depth of a binocularly viewed wire form were experienced. Monocular occlusion eliminates the binocular fixation reflex so that the occluded eye usually deviates from its position relative to the other eye, producing a mild heterophoria. It is possible that the effects were caused by a temporary lack of precise coordination of the eyes following the relatively short period of monocular occlusion. The effects were relatively short-lived, with accuracy of depth perception returning close to normal levels after twenty minutes of binocular visual experience. Perhaps it is more than coincidental that the period required for recovery was equal to the mean duration of REM periods over a night of sleep in the human.

Neurophysiological evidence

The oculomotor nuclei seem to be closely involved in the generation of the distinctive monophasic EEG waves which course their way upward from the pons throughout the visual system during REM sleep (Brooks and Bizzi, 1963; Mikiten, Niebyl and Hendley, 1961; Mouret, Jeannerod and Jouvet, 1963). These monophasic waves accompany the REMs of activated sleep and also eye movements during wakefulness in both cat (Brooks, 1966) and monkey (Berger, 1967). Each burst of EMG activity in the ocular muscles is synchronized with these monophasic waves during REM sleep (Michel, Jeannerod, Mouret, Rechtschaffen and Jouvet, 1964). That they originate in the brainstem has been shown by their elicitation in the lateral geniculate nucleus during REM sleep by electrical stimulation of the pontile reticular formation, but not vice versa (Bizzi and Brooks, 1963). They also persist in the lateral geniculate body after section of the optic nerves (Brooks, 1967a); this indicates that the dipole of negativity in the lateral geniculate body, and positivity in the terminal part of the optic tract which characterizes these waves (Brooks, 1967b), is generated by depolarization of the cell bodies of dendritic processes of lateral geniculate neurons which send centrifugal axons into the optic tract. This depolarization arises from input from the brainstem probably from the oculomotor system. Isolated monophasic waves also sometimes occur during periods of NREM sleep, increasing in frequency with the approach of an impending REM period. Jouvet (1967) has reported that the frequency of monophasic waves is relatively constant from one episode of REM sleep to another and from one cat to another, totaling 12,000–13,000 per day. Since each monophasic wave is linked with a burst of innervation to extraocular muscle (Michel *et al.*, 1964), we see again how rigidly organized oculomotor innervation is during REM sleep.

The functional significance of the monophasic waves has yet to be determined, but is obviously intricately linked with the oculomotor system. They occur synchronously in bilateral structures throughout episodes of REM sleep. It is interesting that splitting of the brainstem leads to an almost total disappearance of REM sleep (Michel and Roffwarg, 1967), but accompanied by the almost constant presence of synchronous, bilateral, isolated monophasic waves in both lateral geniculate nuclei and visual cortices. If the mechanisms of REM sleep are functionally involved with the organization of conjugate eye movement, then it is reasonable to see a disruption of these mechanisms by medial lesions of the brainstem at the level of the oculomotor nuclei, where vast numbers of fibers involved in the control of conjugate eye movement decussate. The emergence of synchronous, bilateral monophasic waves in the near-total absence of REM sleep might represent a manifestation of the disruption of the complex processes involved in the integration of the phasic conjugate REMs with the totality of the tonic REM sleep phase, in which the monophasic waves seem to play some intrinsic part. The elimination of REM sleep in the split-brain preparation has appeared somewhat puzzling since the pontile reticular nuclei, previously shown necessary for the integrity of REM sleep (Carli and Zanchetti, 1965; Jouvet, 1962), remain intact on each side of the medial lesion. The significance of the split-brain preparation might therefore lie in the interruption of decussating fibers in the brainstem. This is consistent with the present hypothesis which emphasizes the necessary integrity of such decussating fibers for the production of conjugate REMs during REM sleep. However, an alternative explanation is possible. After splitting the brainstem, in addition to the elimination of REM sleep, the amounts of

NREM sleep were drastically lowered to 8 to 10 per cent of the twenty-four-hour period. These reductions in NREM sleep may have been caused by the considerable destructions of the serotonergic Raphé nuclei, whose integrity has been demonstrated by Jouvet (1967) to be necessary for NREM sleep. Since the appearance of REM sleep is normally regulated by the prior occurrence of NREM sleep, it is possible that a large reduction in NREM sleep could lead to a secondary elimination of REM sleep; however, this has not been observed following experimental deprivation of NREM sleep by selective awakenings in the juvenile monkey (Berger and Meier, 1966). Of additional interest was the apparent blindness of the split-brain animals (Michel and Roffwarg, 1967), who also exhibited a lasting palsy of lateral ocular movements. Recovery of vertical or rotatory movements was sometimes observed, as was the reappearance of small amounts of REM sleep a week or so after the operation.

On the other hand, the presence of the REMs is not necessary for the continuation of other manifestations of activated sleep, as has already been described for congenitally blind subjects (Berger, Olley and Oswald, 1962). Morrison and Pompeiano (1966a) have reported disappearance of both the REMs and bursts of monophasic waves in the lateral geniculate nuclei following bilateral destruction of the medial and descending vestibular nuclei. The vestibular nuclei, through their ascending and descending projections, are responsible for other somatic and vegetative events which are linked in time with the REMs. Thus, phasic pyramidal discharges with associated myoclonic twitches, phasic depression of spinal reflexes, and pupillary dilations also disappear following the vestibular lesions (Morrison and Pompeiano, 1965, 1966b; Pompeiano and Morrison, 1966). It should be emphasized that the destruction of this vestibular complex has to be bilateral; unilateral lesions do not eliminate these phenomena. Jouvet and Delorme (1965) reported that bilateral destruction of the pontile nucleus locus coeruleus eliminates the tonic aspects of EEG desynchronization and EMG suppression of REM sleep. Although this result has been disputed by Carli and Zanchetti (1965), the division of REM sleep into tonic and phasic components, with their possible dependence upon separate anatomical loci, may provide an additional clue to the functional mechanisms of this peculiar state. Because the medial and descending vestibular nuclei are intimately involved in the generation of the REMs as well as in the control of the entire skeletal muscular system, it becomes apparent from the oculomotor innervation hypothesis why a mechanism for tonic suppression of nonocular musculature should necessarily be involved in the REM sleep process. The activation of the oculomotor system is possible without disturbance of sleep, since proprioception from the eye muscles is absent (Merton, 1964), and the responsiveness of the visual system to changes in retinal input is inhibited during NREM and REM sleep (Rechtschaffen and Foulkes, 1965) and during the REMs themselves (Iwama *et al.*, 1966). However, if all muscle systems were activated by the vestibular nuclei in conjunction with each REM, sleep would obviously be disturbed by the amount of afferent input thereby generated. This is strikingly apparent from the behavior of cats suffering bilateral destruction of the locus coeruleus (Jouvet and Delorme, 1965). During REM sleep these cats, while totally unresponsive to actual visual stimuli, stare at seemingly invisible objects, make pawing motions in the air, and frequently exhibit ragelike behaviour. Therefore, it is vital to the preservation of the safety and sleep of the animal that all nonocular muscles be inhibited during REM sleep. The pontile reticular formation, with its vast internuncial network, is probably the center of integration of these tonic and phasic influences during REM sleep.

The REMs and dreaming

Evaluation of data from a number of studies has led to the conclusion that dreaming is most frequently associated with the REM phase of sleep (Clemente, 1967). Dement and Kleitman (1957b) and Roffwarg *et al.* (1962) have described striking correspondences between reported visual dream imagery and the pattern of eye movements immediately prior to the awakenings from REM sleep. They proposed that the REMs might be following movements of the eyes to the visual images of the dream. Other studies are consistent with this hypothesis. Thus, high correlations were found between amounts of REM activity and reported visual dream activity (Berger and Oswald, 1962b; Dement and Wolpert, 1958) and REMs persist in subjects who have recently become blind, but are absent in the congenitally blind or those who have been blind for a long time and have lost the capacity for visual imagery (Berger, Olley and Oswald, 1962). Other data are difficult to reconcile with this hypothesis without having to introduce a number of additional postulates (Roffwarg, Muzio and Dement, 1966). Thus, REMs may be present in the absence of visual imagery as in the neonate (Chase and Sterman, 1967; Meier and Berger, 1965; Monod *et al.*, 1964; Parmelee *et al.*, 1967; Roffwarg, Dement and Fisher, 1964; Valatx, 1963) and decorticate cat (Jouvet, 1962), or human (Jouvet, Pellin and Mounier, 1961); and visual imagery may be present in the absence of REMs, as during the onset of sleep and during some NREM periods (Foulkes, 1962; Foulkes and Vogel, 1965; Foulkes, Spear and Symonds, 1966). In addition, changes in neuronal firing rate in visual (Valleala, 1967) and frontal (Bizzi, 1967) cortices which accompany the REMs commence shortly after each increase in EMG activity of the extraocular muscles rather than preceding them, contrary to what would be expected if the REMs were responses to evoked visual dream images with cortical substrata. The bearing of these and other studies on this 'scanning' problem has been discussed at greater length elsewhere (Berger, 1967). Regardless of the validity of such a scanning hypothesis, it does not have any direct bearing upon the validity of the function of the REMs proposed here. Thus, even if the REMs do bear a one-to-one relation with the visual images of dreaming, this does not necessarily imply that a direct cause and effect relationship exists between the two variables in either direction. The correlation could arise from a dependence of both the REMs and the visual imagery upon some third variable, such as a driving mechanism for each, located in the brainstem. If the REMs are the end product of periodic oculomotor innervation which ascends from the brainstem and courses its way throughout the visual system, then it may not be so surprising that the REMs could be related to contemporaneous resultant visual imagery. Electrical stimulation of discrete points in the visual cortex has revealed a topographic organization of the evoked conjugate eye movements directly related to the topographic projection of retinal points to the visual cortex (Crosby and Henderson, 1948), and it is on this relationship that an explanation of a possible relationship between the REMs and visual dream imagery may depend.

Predictions

To be of heuristic value a new theory must make certain experimental predictions; the testing of these decides whether the theory can stand as it is, be modified to accommodate an unpredicted result, or be rejected. Therefore, it is considered valuable to make some experimental predictions from the hypothesis of oculomotor innervation and REM sleep which has been proposed here.

A relationship between the amount of partial decussation in the optic chiasma, the mobility of the eyes, and the amount of REM sleep in the mammal has been suggested. It would be of interest to examine the pattern of sleep in some mammalian curiosities such as *Tarsius*, whose eyes are immobile, or in the aquatic whale who, like the guinea pig, has total decussation of its optic pathways. The present hypothesis would predict that both of these animals will show small amounts of REM sleep or that their REM sleep might exhibit certain peculiarities. Among birds, the owl has complete immobility of its eyes and one might expect that the brief episodes of rudimentary REM sleep seen in the hen will be absent in this species.

If the function of REM sleep is to provide periodic innervation of the oculomotor system in order to preserve facilitation of conjugate eye movement, possibly the most critical test of the hypothesis would be to examine the fine coordination of eye movements following awakenings at various times throughout the sleep cycle. The hypothesis would predict that coordination will be most precise following awakenings at the end of REM periods and would be least precise just prior to the onset of impending REM periods, after extended episodes of NREM sleep. The accuracy of stereoscopic depth perception, being dependent upon exact coordination of the eyes, would also be expected to show a similar relationship following awakenings throughout the sleep cycle.

Another important experiment would be to carry out REM-sleep deprivation over a series of nights, but in one series keep the subjects awake with their eyes moving rapidly for periods approximately equal to the normal length of the REM periods from which they are awakened. In another series of nights they would be requested to keep their eyes still while awake. One would predict from the present hypothesis that typical compensatory increases in REM sleep would be present on recovery following the series of nights during which the eyes were kept still, but would be absent or reduced following the series of nights during which the eyes were moved rapidly.

Naturally other predictions could be formulated, but the ones presented above are possibly the most critical to the theory.

References

AGNEW, H. W., WEBB, W. B., and WILLIAMS, R. L. (1964), 'The effects of stage four sleep deprivation', *EEG clin. Neurophysiol.*, vol. 17, pp. 68–70.

AGNEW, H. W., WEBB, W. B., and WILLIAMS, R. L. (1966), 'The first night effect: an EEG study of sleep', *Psychophysiology*, vol. 2, pp. 263–6.

ARDUINI, A., BERLUCCHI, G., and STRATA, P. (1963), 'Pyramidal activity during sleep and wakefulness', *Arch. Ital. Biol.*, vol. 101, pp. 530–44.

ASERINSKY, E. (1965), 'Periodic respiratory pattern occurring in conjunction with eye movements during sleep', *Science*, vol. 150, pp. 763–6.

ASERINSKY, E., and KLEITMAN, N. (1953), 'Regularly occurring periods of eye motility and concomitant phenomena during sleep', *Science*, vol. 118, pp. 273–4.

BACH-Y-RITA, P., and ITO, F. (1966), 'In vivo studies on fast and slow muscle fibers in cat extraocular muscles', *J. gen. Physiol.*, vol. 49, pp. 1177–98.

BERGER, R. J. (1961), 'Tonus of extrinsic laryngeal muscles during sleep and dreaming', *Science*, vol. 134, p. 840.

BERGER, R. J. (1967), 'When is a dream is a dream is a dream?', in C. D. Clemente (ed.), *Physiological Correlates of Dreaming*, *Exp. Neurol.*, suppl. 4, pp. 15–28.

BERGER, R. J. (1968a), 'Characteristics of REM sleep following different conditioned rates of waking eye movement in the monkey', *Percept. mot. Skills*, vol. 27, pp. 99–117.

BERGER, R. J. (1968b), 'Operant conditioning of eye movement in the monkey (*Macaca nemestrina*)', *J. exp. Anal. Behav.*, vol. 11, pp. 311–20.

BERGER, R. J., and MEIER, G. W. (1965), 'Deprivation of patterned vision and the eye movements of sleep', paper presented at meeting of Association for the Psychophysiological Study of Sleep.

BERGER, R. J., and MEIER, G. W. (1966), 'The effects of selective deprivation of states of sleep in the developing monkey', *Psychophysiology*, vol. 2, pp. 354–71.

BERGER, R. J., and OSWALD, I. (1962a), 'Effects of sleep deprivation on behaviour, subsequent sleep and dreaming', *J. ment. Sci.*, vol. 108, pp. 457–65.

BERGER, R. J., and OSWALD, I. (1962b), 'Eye movements during active and passive dreams', *Science*, vol. 137, p. 601.

BERGER, R. J., OLLEY, P., and OSWALD, I. (1962), 'The EEG, eye movements and dreams of the blind', *J. exp. Psychol.*, vol. 14, pp. 183–6.

BIZZI, E. (1967), 'Discharge of frontal eye field neurons during eye movements in unanesthetized monkeys', *Science*, vol. 157, pp. 1588–90.

BIZZI, E., and BROOKS, D. C. (1963), 'Functional connections between pontine reticular formation and lateral geniculate nucleus during deep sleep', *Arch. Ital. Biol.*, vol. 101, pp. 666–80.

BORS, E. (1926), 'Uber das Zahlenverthaltnis zwischen nerven-und muskelfasern', *Anatomischer Auzeiger*, vol. 60, pp. 415–16.

BREININ, G. M. (1957), 'The position of rest during anaesthesia and sleep', *Arch. Ophthal.*, vol. 57, pp. 323–6.

BROOKS, D. C. (1966), 'Visual system waves associated with eye movement in the awake and sleeping cat', *Fed. Proc.*, vol. 573, p. 25 (abstract).

BROOKS, D. C. (1967a), 'Effect of bilateral optic nerve section on visual system monophasic wave activity in the cat', *EEG clin. Neurophysiol.*, vol. 23, pp. 134–41.

BROOKS, D. C. (1967b), 'Localization of lateral geniculate nucleus monophasic waves associated with paradoxical sleep in the cat', *EEG clin. Neurophysiol.*, vol. 23, pp. 123–33.

BROOKS, D. C., and BIZZI, E. (1963), 'Brain stem electrical activity during deep sleep', *Arch. Ital. Biol.*, vol. 101, pp. 648–65.

BROWN, G. L., and HARVEY, A. M. (1941), 'Neuromuscular transmission in the extrinsic muscles of the eye', *J. Physiol.*, vol. 99, pp. 379–99.

CARLI, G., and ZANCHETTI, A. (1965), 'A study of pontine lesions suppressing deep sleep in the cat', *Arch. Ital. Biol.*, vol. 103, pp. 751–88.

CARMICHAEL, L. (1951), 'Ontogenetic development', in S. S. Stevens (ed.), *Handbook of Experimental Psychology*, Wiley.

CHAMBERLAIN, T. J., HALICK, P., and GERARD, R. W. (1963), 'Fixation of experience in the rat spinal cord', *J. Neurophysiol.*, vol. 26, pp. 662–73.

CHASE, M. H., and STERMAN, M. B. (1967), 'Maturation of patterns of sleep and wakefulness in the kitten', *Brain Res.*, vol. 5, pp. 319–29.

CLEMENTE, C. D. (ed.) (1967), 'Physiological correlates of dreaming', *Exp. Neurol.*, suppl. 4.

COLE, W. V. (1960), 'The effect of immobilization on striated muscle and the myoneural junction', *J. comp. Neurol.*, vol. 115, pp. 9–13.

CROSBY, E. C., and HENDERSON, J. W. (1948), 'The mammalian midbrain and isthmus regions: II. Fiber connections of the superior colliculus; (b) pathways concerned in automatic eye movements', *J. comp. Neurol.*, vol. 88, pp. 53–91.

DELORME, F., VIMONT, P., and JOUVET, D. (1964), 'Etude statistique du cycle veille–sommeil chez le chat', *C R soc. biol.*, vol. 158, pp. 2128–30.

DEMENT, W. (1960), 'The effect of dream deprivation', *Science*, vol. 131, pp. 1705–7.

DEMENT, W. (1964), 'Eye movements during sleep', in M. B. Bender (ed.), *The Oculomotor System*, Harper & Row.

DEMENT, W. (1965a), 'An essay on dreams', in *New Directions in Psychology*, vol 2, Holt, Rinehart & Winston.

DEMENT, W. (1965b), 'Studies on the function of rapid eye movement (paradoxical) sleep in human subjects', in *Aspects anatomo-fonctionnels de la physiologie du sommeil*, Centre National de la Recherche Scientifique, Paris.

DEMENT, W., and GREENBERG, S. (1966), 'Changes in total amount of stage four sleep as a function of partial sleep deprivation', *EEG clin. Neurophysiol.*, vol. 20, pp. 523–6.

DEMENT, W., and KLEITMAN, N. (1957a), 'Cyclic variations in EEG during sleep and their relation to eye movements, body motility and dreaming', *EEG clin. Neurophysiol.*, vol. 9, pp. 673–90.

DEMENT, W., and KLEITMAN, N. (1957b), 'The relation of eye movements during sleep to dream activity: an objective method for the study of dreaming', *J. exp. Psychol.*, vol. 53, pp. 339–46.

DEMENT, W., and WOLPERT, E. A. (1958), 'The relation of eye movements, body motility and external stimuli to dream content', *J. exp. Psychol.*, vol. 55, pp. 543–53.

DEMENT, W., GREENBERG, S., and KLEIN, R. (1966), 'The effect of partial REM sleep deprivation and delayed recovery', *J. psychiat. Res.*, vol. 4, pp. 141–52.

DEMENT, W., KAHN, E., and ROFFWARG, H. P. (1965), 'The influence of the laboratory situation on the dreams of the experimental subject', *J. nerv. ment. Dis.*, vol. 140, pp. 119–31.

EPHRON, H. S., and CARRINGTON, P. (1966), 'Rapid eye movement sleep and cortical homeostasis', *Psychol. Rev.*, vol. 73, pp. 500–526.

EVARTS, E. V. (1962), 'Activity of neurons in visual cortex of the cat during sleep with low voltage fast EEG activity', *J. Neurophysiol.*, vol. 25, pp. 812–16.

EVARTS, E. V. (1964), 'Temporal patterns of discharge of pyramidal tract neurons during sleep and waking in the monkey', *J. Neurophysiol.*, vol. 27, pp. 152–71.

FEINBERG, I., KORESKO, R. L., and HELLER, N. (1967), 'EEG sleep patterns as a function of normal and pathological aging in man', *J. psychiat. Res.*, vol. 5, pp. 107–44.

FERGUSON, J., and DEMENT, W. (1966), 'Changes in intensity of REM sleep with deprivation', paper presented to meeting of Association for the Psychophysiological Study of Sleep.

FISCHER, E., and RAMSEY, V. W. (1946), 'Changes in protein content and in some physiochemical properties of the protein during muscular atrophies of various types', *Amer. J. Physiol.*, vol. 145, pp. 571–82.

FOULKES, W. D. (1962), 'Dream reports from different stages of sleep', *J. abnorm. soc. Psychol.*, vol. 65, pp. 14–25.

FOULKES, W. D., and VOGEL, G. (1965), 'Mental activity at sleep onset', *J. abnorm. Psychol.*, vol. 70, pp. 231–43.

FOULKES, W. D., SPEAR, P. S., and SYMONDS, J. D. (1966), 'Individual differences in mental activity at sleep onset', *J. abnorm. Psychol.*, vol. 71, pp. 280–86.

GIAQUINTO, S., POMPEIANO, O., and SOMOGYI, I. (1964a), 'Supraspinal modulation of heteronymous monosynaptic and of polysynaptic reflexes during natural sleep and wakefulness', *Arch. Ital. Biol.*, vol. 102, pp. 245–81.

GIAQUINTO, S., POMPEIANO, O., and SOMOGYI, I. (1964b), 'Descending inhibitory influences on spinal reflexes during natural sleep', *Arch. Ital. Biol.*, vol. 102, pp. 282–307.

GLICKMAN, S. E. (1961), 'Perseverative neural processes and consolidation of the memory trace', *Psychol. Bull.*, vol. 58, pp. 218–33.

GOODENOUGH, D. R., *et al.* (1959), 'A comparison of "dreamers" and "non-dreamers": eye movements, electroencephalograms and the recall of dreams', *J. abnorm. soc. Psychol.*, vol. 59, pp. 295–302.

GUTMANN, E., and HNÍK, P. (1962), 'Denervation studies in research of neurotrophic relationsips', in E. Gutmann (ed.), *The Denervated Muscle*, Czechoslovak Academy of Sciences.

GUTMANN, E., and HNÍK, P. (eds.) (1963), *The Effect of Use and Disuse on Neuromuscular Functions*, Elsevier.

HOBSON, J. A. (1967), 'Electrographic correlates of behavior in the frog with special reference to sleep', *EEG clin. Neurophysiol.*, vol. 22, pp. 113–21.

HODES, R., and DEMENT, W. (1964), 'Depression of electrically induced reflexes ("H-reflexes") in man during low voltage EEG sleep', *EEG clin. Neurophysiol.*, vol. 17, pp. 617–29.

HUTTENLOCHER, P. R. (1961), 'Evoked and spontaneous activity in single units of medial brain stem during natural sleep and waking', *J. Neurophysiol.*, vol. 24, pp. 451–68.

IWAMA, K., et al. (1966), 'Responsiveness of cat lateral geniculate at pre- and postsynaptic levels during natural sleep', *Physiol. Behav.*, vol. 1, pp. 45–53.

JACOBSON, A., et al. (1964), 'Muscle tonus in human subjects during sleep and dreaming', *Exp. Neurol.*, vol. 10, pp. 418–24.

JEANNEROD, M., MOURET, J., and JOUVET, M. (1965), 'Etude de la motricité oculaire au cours de la phase paradoxale du sommeil chez le chat', *EEG clin. Neurophysiol.*, vol. 18, pp. 554–66.

JOUVET, D., and VALATX, J. L. (1956), 'Etude polygraphique du sommeil chez l'agneau', *C R soc. biol.*, vol. 156, pp. 1411–14.

JOUVET, M. (1962), 'Recherches sur les structures nerveuses et les mécanismes résponsables des différentes phases du sommeil physiologique', *Arch. Ital. Biol.*, vol. 100, pp. 125–206.

JOUVET, M. (1967), 'Mechanisms of the state of sleep: a neuropharmacological approach', in S. S. Kety, E. V. Evarts and H. L. Williams (eds.), *Sleep and Altered States of Consciousness*, Williams & Wilkins.

JOUVET, M., and DELORME, F. (1965), 'Locus coeruleus et sommeil paradoxale', *C R soc. biol.*, vol. 159, pp. 895–9.

JOUVET, M., MICHEL, F., and MOUNIER, D. (1960), 'Analyse électroencéphalographique comparée du sommeil physiologique chez le chat et chez l'homme', *Rev. Neurol.*, vol. 103, pp. 189–205.

JOUVET, M., PELLIN, B., and MOUNIER, D. (1961), 'Etude polygraphique des différentes phases du sommeil au cours des troubles de conscience chroniques (comas prolongés)', *Rev. Neurol.*, vol. 105, pp. 181–6.

JOUVET-MOUNIER, D., and ASTIC, L. (1966), 'Etude du sommeil chez le cobaye adulte et nouveau-né', *C R soc. biol.*, vol. 160, pp. 1453–7.

KALES, A., et al. (1964), 'Dream deprivation: an experimental reappraisal', *Nature*, vol. 204, pp. 1337–8.

KALES, A., et al. (1967), 'Measurements of all-night sleep in normal elderly persons: effects of aging', *J. Amer. Ger. Soc.*, vol. 15, pp. 405–14.

KANZOW, E., KRAUSE, D., and KÜHNEL, H. (1962), 'Die Vasomotorik der Hirnrinde in den Phasen desynchronisierter EEG-Activitat in naturlichen Schlaf der Katze', *Pflügers Archiv für die gesamte Physiologie des Menschen und der Tiere*, vol. 274, pp. 593–607.

KAWAMURA, H., and SAWYER, C. H. (1965), 'Elevation in brain temperature during paradoxical sleep', *Science*, vol. 150, pp. 912–13.

KHAZAN, N., and SAWYER, C. H. (1963), '"Rebound" recovery from deprivation of paradoxical sleep in the rabbit', *Proc. Soc. Exp. Biol. Med.*, vol. 114, pp. 536–9.

KLEIN, M. (1963), 'Etude polygraphique et phylogénique des différents états de sommeil', thèse de médecine, Lyon, Bosc. edn.

KLEIN, M., MICHEL, F., and JOUVET, M. (1964), 'Etude polygraphique du sommeil chez les oiseaux', *C R soc. biol.*, vol. 158, pp. 99–103.

MARON, L., RECHTSCHAFFEN, A., and WOLPERT, E. A. (1964), 'Sleep cycle during napping', *Arch. gen. Psychiat.*, vol. 11, pp. 503–8.

MEIER, G. W., and BERGER, R. J. (1965), 'Development of sleep and wakefulness patterns in the infant rhesus monkey', *Exp. Neurol.*, vol. 12, pp. 257–77.

MERTON, P. A. (1964), 'Absence of conscious position sense in the human eyes', in M. B. Bender (ed.), *The Oculomotor System*, Harper & Row.

MICHEL, F., and ROFFWARG, H. P. (1967), 'Chronic split brain stem preparation: effect on sleep–waking cycle', *Experientia*, vol. 23, pp. 126–8.

MICHEL, F., RECHTSCHAFFEN, A., and VIMONT-VICARY, P. (1964), 'Activité électrique des muscles oculaires extrinsèques au cours du cycle veille–sommeil', *C R soc. biol.*, vol. 158, pp. 106–9.

MICHEL, F., *et al.* (1964), 'Sur les mécanismes de l'activité des pointes au niveau du système visuel au cours de la phase paradoxale du sommeil', *C R soc. biol.*, vol. 158, pp. 103–6.

MIKITEN, T. H., NIEBYL, P. H., and HENDLEY, C. D. (1961), 'EEG desynchronization during behavioral sleep associated with spike discharges from the thalamus of the cat', *Fed. Proc.*, vol. 20, p. 327 (abstract).

MONOD, N., and PAJOT, N. (1965), 'Le sommeil du nouveau-né et du prematuré: I. Analyse des études polygraphiques (mouvements oculaires, respiration et EEG) chez le nouveau-né à terme', *Biol. Neonat.*, vol. 8, pp. 281–307.

MONOD, N., *et al.* (1964), 'Les premières étapes de l'organisation du sommeil chez le prematuré et le nouveau-né', *Rev. Neurol.*, vol. 110, pp. 304–5.

MONROE, L. J. (1967), 'Psychological and physiological differences between good and poor sleepers', *J. abnorm. Psychol.*, vol. 72, pp. 255–64.

MORRISON, A. R., and POMPEIANO, O. (1965), 'Vestibular influences on vegetative functions during the rapid eye movement periods of desynchronized sleep', *Experientia*, vol. 21, pp. 667–8.

MORRISON, A. R., and POMPEIANO, O. (1966a), 'Vestibular influences during sleep: IV. Functional relations between vestibular nuclei and lateral geniculate nucleus during desynchronized sleep', *Arch. Ital. Biol.*, vol. 104, pp. 425–58.

MORRISON, A. R., and POMPEIANO, O. (1966b), 'Vestibular influences during sleep: II. Effects of vestibular lesions on the pyramidal discharge during desynchronized sleep', *Arch. Ital. Biol.*, vol. 104, pp. 214–30.

MOURET, J., JEANNEROD, M., and JOUVET, M. (1963), 'L'activité électrique du système visuel au cours de la phase paradoxale du sommeil chez le chat', *J. Physiologie*, vol. 55, pp. 305–6.

MOWBREY, J. B., and CADELL, T. E. (1962), 'Early behavior patterns in rhesus monkeys', *J. comp. physiol. Psychol.*, vol. 55, pp. 350–57.

PARMELEE, A. H., *et al.* (1967), 'Sleep states in premature infants', *Devel. Med. child Neurol.*, vol. 9, pp. 70–77.

PELLET, J. (1966), 'Etude électropolygraphique et comportementale des états de veille et de sommeil chez le cobaye (*Cavia porcellus*)', *C R soc. biol.*, vol. 7, pp. 1476–82.

PENFIELD, W., and RASMUSSEN, T. (1950), *The Cerebral Cortex of Man: A Clinical Study of Localization of Function*, Macmillan.

PIÉRON, H. (1913), *Le probleme physiologique du sommeil*, Masson.

PIETRUSKY, F. (1922), 'Das Verhalten der Augen im Schlafe', *Klinische, Monatsblätter für Augenheilkunde*, vol. 68, pp. 355–60.

POLYAK, S. (1957), *The Vertebrate Visual System*, University of Chicago Press.

POMPEIANO, O., and MORRISON, A. R. (1966), 'Vestibular influences during sleep: III. Dissociation of the tonic and phasic inhibition of spinal reflexes during desynchronized sleep following vestibular lesions', *Arch. Ital. Biol.*, vol. 104, pp. 231–46.

PRECHTL, H. F. R., and LENARD, H. G. (1967), 'A study of eye movements in sleeping newborn infants', *Brain Res.*, vol. 5, pp. 477–93.

RECHTSCHAFFEN, A., and FOULKES, D. (1965), 'Effect of visual stimuli on dream content', *Percept. mot. Skills*, vol. 20, pp. 1149–60.

RECHTSCHAFFEN, A., VERDONE, P., and WHEATON, J. (1963), 'Reports of mental activity during sleep', *Canad. Psychiat. Assn J.*, vol. 8, pp. 409–14.

RECHTSCHAFFEN, A., *et al.* (1965), 'Brain temperature variations with paradoxical sleep: implications for relationships among EEG, cerebral metabolism, sleep and consciousness', *Proceedings, Symposium on Sleep and Consciousness*, Lyon.

RIESEN, A. H. (1967), 'Sensory deprivation', in E. Stellar and J. Sprague (eds.), *Progress in Physiological Psychology*, Academic Press.

ROFFWARG, H. P., DEMENT, W., and FISHER, C. (1964), 'Preliminary observations of the sleep–dream pattern of neonates, infants, children and adults', in E. Harms (ed.), *Problems of Sleep and Dream in Children*, Pergamon.

ROFFWARG, H. P., MUZIO, J. N., and DEMENT, W. (1966), 'Ontogenetic development of the human sleep–dream cycle', *Science*, vol. 152, pp. 604–19.

ROFFWARG, H. P., *et al.* (1962), 'Dream imagery: relationship to rapid eye movements of sleep', *Arch. gen. Psychiat.*, vol. 7, pp. 235–58.

RUCKEBUSCH, Y. (1963), 'Etude polygraphique et comportementale de l'évolution post-natale du sommeil physiologique chez l'agneau', *Arch. Ital. Biol.*, vol. 101, pp. 111–32.

SHERRINGTON, C. S. (1947), *The Integrative Action of the Nervous System*, Yale University Press.

SNYDER, F. (1963), 'The new biology of dreaming', *Arch. gen. Psychiat.*, vol. 8, pp. 381–91.

SNYDER, F. (1965), 'Progress in the new biology of dreaming', *Amer. J. Psychiatry*, vol. 122, pp. 377–91.

SNYDER, F. (1966), 'Toward an evolutionary theory of dreaming', *Amer. J. Psychiat.*, vol. 123, pp. 121–42.

SNYDER, F., *et al.* (1964), 'Changes in respiration, heart rate, and systolic blood pressure in human sleep', *J. appl. Physiol.*, vol. 19, pp. 417–22.

SOLOMON, P. (ed.) (1961), *Sensory Deprivation*, Harvard University Press.

TAUBER, E. S., ROFFWARG, H. P., and WEITZMAN, E. D. (1966), 'Eye movements and electroencephalogram activity during sleep in diurnal lizards', *Nature*, vol. 212, pp. 1612–13.

TERGAST, P. (1873), 'Ueber das Verhältniss von Nerve und Muskel', *Archiv für Mikroskopische Anatomie*, vol. 9, pp. 36–46.

VALATX, J. L. (1963), 'Ontogenèse des différents états de sommeil', thèse de médecine, Lyon, Beaux-Arts.

VALLEALA, P. (1967), 'The temporal relation of unit discharge in visual cortex and activity of the extraocular muscles during sleep', *Arch. Ital. Biol.*, vol. 105, pp. 1–14.

VRBOVÁ, G. (1963), 'The effect of motoneurone activity on the speed of contraction of striated muscle', *J. Physiol.*, vol. 169, pp. 513–26.

WALLACH, H., and KARSH, E. B. (1963), 'Why the modification of stereoscopic depth-perception is so rapid', *Amer. J. Psychol.*, vol. 76, pp. 413–20.

WALLS, G. L. (1942), *The Vertebrate Eye and its Adaptive Radiation*, Cranbrook Press.

WALLS, G. L. (1962), 'The evolutionary history of eye movements', *Vis. Res.*, vol. 2, pp. 69–80.

WEBB, W. B., and AGNEW, H. W. (1965), 'Sleep: effects of a restricted regime', *Science*, vol. 150, pp. 1745–7.

WEBB, W. B., and AGNEW, H. W. (1967), 'Sleep cycling within twenty-four hour periods', *J. exp. Psychol.*, vol. 74, pp. 158–60.

WEBB, W. B., AGNEW, H. W., and STERNTHAL, H. (1966), 'Sleep during the early morning', *Psychonom. Sci.*, vol. 6, pp. 277–8.

WEISS, T., and ROLDÁN, E. (1964), 'Comparative study of sleep cycles in rodents', *Experientia*, vol. 20, pp. 280–81.

WHITTERIDGE, D. (1959), 'Central control of eye movements', in J. Field, H. W. Magoun and V. E. Hall (eds.), *Handbook of Physiology*, section 1, vol. 2, American Physiological Society.

WEITZMAN, E. D., *et al.* (1965), 'Cyclic activity in sleep of *Macaca mulatta*', *Arch. Neurol.*, vol. 12, pp. 463–7.

WILLIAMS, H. L., *et al.* (1964), 'Responses to auditory stimulation, sleep loss and the EEG stages of sleep', *EEG clin. Neurophysiol.*, vol. 16, pp. 269–79.

WILLIAMS, R. L., AGNEW, H. W., and WEBB, W. B. (1964), 'Sleep patterns in young adults: an EEG study', *EEG clin. Neurophysiol.*, vol. 17, pp. 376–82.

WORTH, C. (1903), *Squint: Its Causes, Pathology and Treatment*, Blakiston's Press.

31 George S. Grosser and Andrew W. Siegal

Emergence of a Tonic-Phasic Model for Sleep and Dreaming

George S. Grosser and Andrew W. Siegal, 'Emergence of a tonic-phasic model for sleep and dreaming', *Psychological Bulletin*, vol. 75, 1971, pp. 60–72.

Recent developments in the field of sleep and dream research have been stimulated by the appearance of the new tonic-phasic model as proposed by Moruzzi (1963). In order for the investigator to gain an appreciation of the implications of this model for sleep and dream research, he must be aware of the important historical developments in this field that laid the groundwork for the emergence of the tonic-phasic model. Ernest Hartmann (1967) has completed a comprehensive survey of the literature placing emphasis on the physiological aspects of the sleep-dream cycle. Using a complementary approach, David Foulkes in *The Psychology of Sleep* (1966) has reported a number of studies which focus upon the mentation and behavioral aspects of sleep. This review refers only to those sleep and dream studies which bear directly upon the validity of the tonic-phasic model.

The evolution of the three-state model

In 1953 Aserinsky and Kleitman observed two types of ocular motility which occurred during sleep and noted that the two patterns were each associated with different electroencephalogram (EEG) tracings. Slow eye movements appeared during sleep stages 2, 3 and 4, and sleep-onset, descending stage 1. The EEG of these stages (with the exception of descending stage 1) is characterized by slow-wave, high-voltage patterns. The rapid eye movements (REMs), which are comparable to those observed in a waking subject who is actively attending an object in his visual field, occurred periodically throughout the night, first appearing after the passage of at least 100 minutes of slow-wave sleep. These REMs occurred, however, only in conjunction with fast-activity, low-voltage patterns in the EEG. This pattern has been termed 'paradoxical sleep' (Jouvet, 1961), 'ascending stage 1' (Foulkes, 1966), the 'D-State' (Hartmann, 1965), and most recently, 'stage-REM' (Rechtschaffen and Kales, 1968). The presence of REMs along with the activated EEG, which bore greater resemblance to waking than to slow-wave sleep, led the investigators to hypothesize that it was in stage-REM that dreaming occurred. Subjects who were awakened during stage-REM produced significantly greater dream recall (74 per cent) than they did when they were awakened from slow-wave sleep (7 per cent dream recall), which came to be called nonREM (NREM) sleep (Aserinsky and Kleitman, 1953). Since REMs did not occur during slow-wave sleep, several investigators confirmed the results of the original study, relating stage-REM with high dream-recall rates, NREM sleep with very low dream-recall rates, and also showing relationships between manifest dream content and eye movement patterns (Berger and Oswald, 1962; Dement and Kleitman, 1957b; Dement and Wolpert, 1958; Kleitman, 1961; Roffwarg et al., 1962).

Various investigators focused their attention on the behavior of the autonomic nervous system (ANS) during sleep (Snyder, 1967). Some of the parameters which were investigated by these researchers included heart rate (Kamiya, 1962; Rosenblatt, Zwilling and Hartmann, 1969; Snyder et al., 1964), blood pressure (Kamiya, 1962; Snyder, 1967; Snyder, Hobson and Goldfrank, 1963; Snyder et al., 1964), respiration (Aserinsky and Kleitman, 1953; Kamiya, 1962; Snyder et al. 1964), and brain oxygen consumption (Brebbia and Rechtschaffen, 1968; Kety, 1967). A penile erection cycle which appeared to be synchronous with stage-REM was also observed (Fisher, Gross and Zuch, 1965; Karacan, Goodenough and Shapiro, 1966; Korner, 1968). Changes in body temperature were observed over various sleep stages (Rechtschaffen, Cornwell and Zimmerman, 1965; Verdone, 1965). The degree of pupillary dilation was observed to change during stage-REM with the pupils of the eye becoming myotic during stage-REM, while, in NREM stages, they appear mydriatic (Bremer, 1935; Jouvet, 1961). Furthermore Scott et al. (1968) observed a decrease in salivation during stage-REM. The only measure of ANS functioning which shows an opposite trend to the above responses is the galvanic skin response (GSR), which appears to be more active during NREM sleep than in stage-REM (Kamiya, 1962; Lester, Burch and Dossett, 1967).

The trend which was inferred from these data was that, in general, vegetative functioning appeared somewhat depressed during NREM stages, and then suddenly became activated and much more variable during stage-REM (Aserinsky and Kleitman, 1953; Hartmann, 1965, 1967; Kamiya, 1962; Spreng, Johnson and Lubin, 1968).

By 1967 sufficient data had been accumulated on the physiological patterns of the sleep-dream cycle to indicate to Hartmann (1967, 1968) that this cycle clearly deserved a place among the body's other metabolism-linked cycles in any comprehensive schematic of the human organism. Several researchers have investigated the behavior of the sleep-dream cycle during various stages of the human life-cycle (Feinberg and Carlson, 1968; Foulkes et al., 1967; Globus, Gardner and Williams, 1968; Hartmann, 1968; Korner, 1968; Kripke and O'Donoghue, 1968; Roffwarg, Muzio and

Dement, 1966). Additional information on the cycle resulted from the investigation of the physiological aspects of the cycle's phylogenetic development (Hartmann, 1967, 1968). The empirical observations which were made and discussed by Hartmann, found their complement in Snyder's (1966) theoretical discussion of the phylogenetic significance of the sleep-dream cycle's evolution.

The apparent slow-wave sleep stage-REM differences in the behavior of the CNS, ANS, and the musculature (all of which are reviewed later) when viewed in the light of a series of stage-REM deprivation studies (Dement, 1960, 1965; Jouvet, 1965), all of which clearly demonstrated an organismic need for stage-REM sleep, reinforced the notion of a trichotomy of psychophysiologic stages. Combining these findings with the great differences in the rates of dream recall which were observed to exist between stage-REM and slow-wave sleep awakenings in earlier studies, the tendency to regard these states as discrete entities became explicit when Snyder stated:

The physiological characteristics of this phenomenon prove so distinctive that I consider it a third state of earthly existence, the rapid eye movement or REM state, which is at least as different from sleeping and waking as each is from the other . . . (Snyder, 1966, p. 121).

Hartmann's (1965, 1967, 1968) 'W' (waking), 'S' (NREM, slow-wave sleep) and 'D' (stage-REM) terminology is in keeping with the above three-state model, as are the neurophysiological models proposed by Jouvet (1961) and Rossi, Minobe and Candia (1963). Similarly, Jouvet (1969) presented a thoroughgoing report on the biochemical correlates of the sleep-dream cycle, as did Hartmann (1967) in his *The Biology of Dreaming*.

The origins of the tonic-phasic model

Although some of the proponents of the three-state model recognize the existence of tonic and phasic components of stage-REM (Hartmann, 1967; Jouvet, 1965), recent research indicates that the tonic-phasic *model* may account for many heretofore unexplained phenomena of sleep and dreams since the model not only emphasizes the differences between tonic and phasic phenomena to a far greater degree, but assigns greater significance to them in the total conceptualization of sleep processes.

The physiological phenomena associated with stage-REM sleep were originally dichotomized by Moruzzi (1963) into tonic components, which persist for the entire duration of stage-REM, and phasic components, which usually occur in association with periodic bursts of rapid eye movements within stage-REM. Tonic phenomena include the ascending stage I EEG, the presence of hippocampal theta-waves of five cycles per second (cps), and the tonic dropout of muscle potential in the antigravity muscles. Phasic phenomena include the occurrence of ponto-geniculate-occipital spikes (PGO), short term fluctuations of autonomic behavior, and the presence of myoclonic twitches and increased fine muscle activity. The tonic phenomena represent the background upon which phasic activation is superimposed (Hartmann, 1967; Molinari and Foulkes, 1969). The division of stage-REM into its tonic and phasic components, which is dictated by many empirical findings, creates several theoretical problems which the three-state theory is not equipped to handle (in its unmodified form). These empirical findings fall into two basic categories: (a) much of stage-REM does not resemble that highly activated phase of sleep which is more accurately referred to as phasic stage-REM; and (b) several phenomena which are clearly associated with phasic stage-REM can be observed to occur in NREM sleep stages. These phenomena include observations on both psychological and physiological dimensions. For example, high amplitude PGO spikes which occur phasically throughout stage-REM in conjunction with REM bursts (Pompeiano, 1967) have been demonstrated to occur in the lateral geniculate nucleus (LGN) during NREM stages of sleep (Thomas and Benoit, 1968). This PGO spiking (NREM LGN activation waves) becomes more and more frequent as the following stage-REM period approaches. This is an example of a phasic component of stage-REM, which is associated with stage-REM dreaming, but which can, however, occur in NREM sleep. This tends to blur the three-state theorist's distinction between REM and NREM stages. Similarly, the phasic occurrence of k-complexes, which seem to correlate with phasic electromyogram (EMG) suppressions (Pivik, Halper and Dement, 1969a), occur most frequently in stage 2 (Foulkes, 1966; Larson and Foulkes, 1969; Pivik, Halper and Dement, 1969a, 1969b). Heart-rate responses, finger vasoconstrictions, and galvanic skin responses are temporally correlated with k-complexes, but such ANS responses were not correlated with isolated sleep spindles (Johnson and Karpan, 1968). 'It is clear that some physiological model is required which recognizes both the inhomogeneity of stage-REM and the similarity of some epochs of stage-REM to much of NREM sleep' (Molinari and Foulkes, 1969, p. 28).

The evidence which dictates the employment of the tonic-phasic model in any conceptualization of sleep activity is derived from five basic lines of research: (a) the behavior of the autonomic nervous system, (b) muscular activity during sleep, (c) data on sleep mentation, (d) the functional neuroanatomy of sleep and dreaming, and (e) new findings on the result of the deprivation of phasic activation.

Autonomic nervous system

The trends noted by the majority of the earlier investigators suggested both a rise in the measures of central tendency and in the variability of autonomic responses during stage-REM, with the change in variability being the more outstanding (Foulkes, 1966; Hartmann, 1967; Kamiya, 1962; Snyder, 1966, 1967). Through the use of more sophisticated analytical techniques and more precise measurement procedures, more recent investigations (e.g., Gassel et al., 1964) have made the older data more meaningful. Gassel et al. (1964) reported bradycardia (slowing of heart rate) shortly after the onset of stage-REM. They also noted, however, tachycardia (increase of heart rate) and a rise in blood pressure shortly after the onset of the first REM burst. This tachycardia and rise in blood pressure were then followed by a reduction of blood pressure and bradycardia, thereby clarifying the variability attributed to stage-REM by earlier investigators. Although the bradycardia and fall in blood pressure which was reported by Gassel et al. (1964) appears discordant when compared with the increase in heart rate and rise in blood pressure which were reported by others (Kamiya, 1962; Snyder, 1966, 1967; Snyder et al., 1963, 1964), the increased variability of these measurements within stage-REM remains a point of agreement. In attempting to reconcile the apparently discrepant data of these researchers, one must examine their research methodologies. The use of averaged data, as employed in earlier investigations, may have been misleading since the peaks and troughs of heart rate tend to occur in clusters spaced discretely throughout stage-REM (Rosenblatt, Zwilling and Hartmann, 1969) and could not be discerned precisely since moment-to-moment changes are frequently obscured by the use of averaging techniques (Gassel et al., 1964). These findings, correlating episodes of increased autonomic variability in conjunction with bursts of REM, were confirmed by Spreng, Johnson and Lubin (1968) and Aserinsky (1967). This led Aserinsky to divide stage-REM into two sectors, which he called REM-M and REM-Q (Aserinsky, 1967). REM-M refers to segments of stage-REM sleep which contain REM bursts (periods of ocular motility), accompanied by phasic autonomic arousal, whereas REM-Q refers to tonic stage-REM which is characterized by its relative quiescence of the oculomotor musculature, and more tonic, less variable levels of ANS functioning.

Further research by Karacan, Goodenough and Shapiro (1966) illustrates a further example of phasic variability which is superimposed upon a tonic component of stage-REM. A cycle of penile erection occurring synchronously with stage-REM (erection generally lasting for the duration of the stage-REM period; Fisher, Gross and Zuch, 1965) has been demonstrated. Karacan, Goodenough and Shapiro (1966), however, showed that upon the general tonic level of erection, phasic tumescence and detumescence correspond to the anxiety content of the subject's dream. The observed phasic detumescence was associated with high anxiety content (Karacan, Goodenough and Shapiro, 1966).

The GSR observed during sleep has consistently been a 'thorn in the side' of the three-state theorist, since it is the only index of autonomic arousal to show greater activity outside of stage-REM (NREM) than during stage-REM itself (Kamiya, 1962; Lester, Burch and Dossett, 1967; McDonald, Shallenberger and Carpenter, 1968). The occurrence of spontaneous 'storms' of GSR activity outside of stage-REM suggests the presence of intense autonomic arousal existing outside of stage-REM, which is inconsistent with the three-state model's conception of slow-wave sleep as containing only depressed autonomic functioning.

The musculature

Although a wealth of studies have been conducted which describe the behavior of the musculature during sleep (see Dement, 1966; Hartmann, 1967), selection of a few critical studies illustrates the need for more inclusive explanations than can be offered by a simple three-state theory, based upon a REM–NREM dichotomy. One advantage of the tonic-phasic model is that it enables us to explain (a) both the continuities and variabilities observed within stage-REM and (b) the continuities of phasic phenomena occurring outside of stage-REM with those within stage-REM (Molinari and Foulkes, 1969). Jouvet (1965, 1967) observed a drop-out of muscle potential in the dorsal neck muscles (nucchal) of sleeping cats during stage-REM. Berger (1961) went on to observe a decrease in the tonus of the extrinsic laryngeal musculature. These two studies represent the establishment of tonic muscular phenomena which persist throughout stage-REM.

Turning to an examination of phasic muscular activity within stage-REM, we first consider a pioneer study by Kamiya (1962), in which he correlated EEG stage within the observed frequency of gross body movements (GBMs). Kamiya found the highest incidence of GBMs in stage-REM, somewhat fewer GBMs in stage 2, and so on in stages 3 and 4, respectively. Dement (Dement and Kleitman, 1957a; Dement and Wolpert, 1958) provided fine tuning on Kamiya's observation of an increase in the frequency of GBMs in stage-REM. Dement noted that GBMs occurred with significantly greater frequency immediately preceding and immediately following bursts of rapid eye movements (REM), but GBMs did not appear simultaneously with REM bursts. This effect has been referred to as the chapter-marker effect, since subjects report multiple scene, fragmented dreams following awakening from stage-REM periods in which bursts of REMs have been separated by GBMs. Dreams recalled by subjects awakening from stage-REM periods in which REM bursts were not interrupted by GBMs produce dream recall that usually consists of a 'one-act play'. Further progress was made by Baldridge, Whitman and Kramer (1965), using 'highly sensitive semiconductor strain gauges' which permitted the detection of fine muscular activity (fma) during sleep. Their research showed that integrated fine muscle activity coincided with the presence of REMs. The results of these three studies are described in Figure 1.

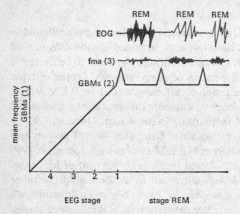

Figure 1 Sequentially diphasic behavior of the musculature within stage-REM sleep. Key: (1) The average number of gross body movements (GBMs) is linearly, and inversely, related to sleep stage (Kamiya, 1962). (2) The 'chapter marker effect' (occurrence of gross body movements between REM bursts; Dement and Wolpert, 1958). (3) Concurrence of fine muscular activity (fma) with REM bursts (Baldridge, Whitman and Kramer, 1965)

What becomes clear as one peruses Figure 1 is that the muscular activity within Stage-REM appears in a sequentially diphasic pattern, with phasic GBMs occurring immediately before and after bursts of REMs, and fma occurring concurrently with REM bursts.

Gassel, Marchiafava and Pompeiano (1964a) confirmed the previous studies using an electromyographic (EMG) technique, in which they observed both the tonic EMG suppression throughout stage-REM, upon which were superimposed phasic inhibition and myoclonic twitches.

The following studies also demonstrate the ability of the tonic-phasic model to accommodate data which illustrate the continuity of phasic events throughout the sleep cycle. Bruxism (tooth grinding), originally believed to be a phasic concomitant of REM bursts (Reding, Rubright and Rechtschaffen, 1964), was recently observed to occur in all stages of sleep, with its greatest frequency observed in stage 2, often accompanied by GBMs (Reding, Zepelin, Robinson, Smith and Zimmerman, 1968).

Similarly, Gassel et al. (1964a) observed phasic EMG suppression during stage-REM, just as Pivik, Halper and Dement (1969a) observed similar phasic EMG suppressions throughout *all* sleep stages, with the greatest frequency occurring in stages 2 and 4. Both of these sets of studies clearly demonstrate the occurrence of phasic muscular activity in NREM sleep, the kind of activity earlier attributed to stage-REM sleep exclusively.

Mentation

In the early phases of research, data on sleep mentation also contributed to the creation of what appears now to be an artificial dichotomization of REM and NREM sleep. This artificial dichotomy appears to be the result of two basic trends in the earlier stages of sleep research: (a) the extreme differences in the rate of mentation-recall experienced in REM versus NREM sleep and (b) the tendency to attribute differences of a qualitative nature to REM and NREM mentation. Dement and Kleitman (1957b) reported 79 per cent dream recall obtained from stage-REM awakenings and only 7 per cent dream recall from NREM awakenings. Jouvet, in 1960 (cited in Hartmann, 1967, p. 12), found recall in 60 per cent of his Stage-REM awakenings and only 3 per cent recall in awakenings from other sleep stages. Foulkes (1966), however, in 1960, began an investigation specifically designed to investigate the mentation of NREM sleep stages. Although he confirmed earlier reports of high frequencies of dream recall in stage-REM awakenings (87 per cent) he also found 74 per cent recall in NREM awakenings. Similarly Pivik, Halper and Dement (1969b) reported 87·5 per cent recall from REM awakenings, and 55 per cent from NREM. This discrepancy between the results of Dement and Kleitman (1957b) and Jouvet (Hartmann, 1967, p. 12), which indicated very low estimates of NREM mentation, and the results of Foulkes (1966) and Pivik, Halper and Dement (1969b), can be explained on the basis of experimental methodology (Foulkes, 1966; Hartmann, 1967) and Foulkes' findings on the nature of 'NREM mentation'. Mentation obtained from awakenings made in sleep stages other than stage-REM (NREM awakenings) were described as less well recalled, more thoughtlike, less vivid, less visual, more conceptual, and less bizarre and emotional than reports taken from stage-REM awakenings (Foulkes, 1966; Rechtschaffen, Vogel and Shaikun, 1963). The differences between the high and low NREM recall rates can now be explained. If, upon a NREM awakening, the experimenter asks a subject to report his 'dream' or asks if the subject is 'dreaming' and the subject's mental experience was of the less visual and bizarre nature of 'typical' NREM mentation, the subject may simply say that he is not dreaming. Even if he should report his less 'dreamlike' NREM mental production, the scorer, using a strict criterion of dreaming, might not count this recall at all since it is not a 'dream', and it is only dreams that the experimenter is interested in studying (Foulkes, 1966). Even the distinction drawn by Foulkes (1966) and Rechtschaffen,

Vogel and Shaikun (1963) between the qualitative differences between stage-REM and NREM stages' mentation is too clear-cut and dichotomous, and must be qualified (Foulkes, 1966, 1970a and b; Foulkes, Spear and Symonds, 1966; Pivik and Foulkes, 1968), since it has been shown that NREM reports can, at times, be almost indistinguishable from stage-REM reports (Foulkes, 1966, 1970a, 1970b; Pivik and Foulkes, 1968). The degree of 'dream-likeness' of NREM mentation has been observed to depend not only upon individual differences in personality (Pivik and Foulkes, 1968), but also upon latency of awakening (Pivik and Foulkes, 1968; Shapiro *et al.*, 1965), and time of night (Foulkes, 1966; Pivik and Foulkes, 1968). 'Dreams from the first REM period of the night have generally been found to be less vivid than those reported from later REM periods . . . Similar findings have been reported for successive periods of NREM sleep' (Foulkes, 1970b, p. 165). The dream likeness of material retrieved from sleep onset awakenings has been shown to be affected by subject variables to an even greater degree than post-sleep-onset NREM awakening reports. This suggests that 'the possibility is opened up that a psychological continuum within stage-REM may partially overlap with one in NREM sleep' (Molinari and Foulkes, 1969, p. 347). This continuity of REM and NREM mentation becomes even clearer when we consider that some degree of content interrelatedness has been observed (Offenkrantz and Rechtschaffen, 1963; Rechtschaffen, Cornwell and Zimmerman, 1963; Trosman *et al.*, 1960; Verdone, 1965). The above data on sleep mentation are clearly incongruent with the three-state theory in its unmodified form, but can be accommodated within the scope of the tonic-phasic model since they demonstrate (a) a continuation of a correlate of stage-REM (dreamlike mentation) into NREM sleep stages and (b) simultaneously exhibit extreme variability of mentation within stage-REM periods.

Further variability within single stage-REM periods has evolved out of the work of Aserinsky (1967). Aserinsky (1967) divided stage-REM into subphases using the presence of REMs as his descriptive index. Stage-REM episodes in which REMs are present were referred to as REM-motile (REM-M), while stage-REM episodes characterized by ocular quiescence were termed REM-Q. REM-M corresponds to phasic stage-REM, REM-Q to its nonphasic state. Aserinsky then suggested that these two physiologically different states might each support different 'levels of dreaming' (Aserinsky, 1967). This hypothesis was independently put forth in 1967 by Cohen *et al.* (1968). Molinari and Foulkes (1969) experimentally tested Aserinsky's hypothesis in a recent paper entitled 'Tonic and phasic events during sleep; psychological correlates and implications', in which they observed markedly different types of mentation indigenous to the REM-Q and REM-M sectors of stage-REM. REM-M was found to contain dream reports which were characterized by the predominance of 'primary visual imagery (PVE)' whereas REM-Q reports contained (a) either PVE in addition to active cognitive processes which interpret and and reflect upon the PVE, or (b) the presence of purely cognitive processes in the absence of visual imagery. Therefore, both PVE which has undergone 'secondary cognitive elaboration' and purely cognitive processes are scored 'secondary cognitive elaboration' (SCE) (Molinari and Foulkes, 1969).

Of the reports obtained from REM-M awakenings, 88 per cent were scored PVE, while REM-Q contained 20 per cent ($p < 0.005$). Reports from 80 per cent of the REM-Q awakenings were scored SCE, REM-M contained only 12 per cent. The interjudge agreement for two experimenters' scoring of SCE versus PVE mentation-reports was 95 per cent for REM-Q reports and 100 per cent for REM-M reports. The fact that reliable ratings could be made demonstrated the extreme heterogeneity of stage-REM mentation. This is congruent with the division of stage-REM into phasic and topic subdivisions.

In terms of the SCE-PVE classification REM-Q awakenings did not differ significantly from NREM ascending stage 2 (NR-A2), sleep onset stage 2 (SO-2), or sleep onset stage 1 (SO-1) awakenings. Content recalled from REM-M awakenings was qualitatively different . . . from all other awakening categories (Molinari and Foulkes, 1969, p. 353).

These findings clearly illustrate one of the areas of emphasis of the tonic-phasic model using data on its psychological dimension, intra-stage-REM variability.

The functional neuroanatomy of sleep and dreaming

Up to this point we have presented data which exemplify both tonic and phasic activities of several organ systems during sleep. Just as the central nervous system serves as the integrating mechanism for widespread physiological processes, an understanding of the tonic and phasic activities during sleep may be facilitated if one regards central neural mechanisms as a conceptual scheme which organizes and unifies various sleep phenomena – peripheral and mental.

In 1949, Moruzzi and Magoun reported that the total destruction of the midbrain reticular formation produced animals showing prolonged slow-wave sleep. This area came to be known as the ascending reticular activating system (ARAS). It was considered to be the center for wakefulness.

More recently, great progress has been made, in the laboratories of Jouvet (1961) and Moruzzi (1964), among others, in specifying the nuclei and tracts involved in arousal, NREM or slow-wave sleep, and stage-REM. A high transection of the brainstem, at the rostral midbrain, yielded the slow-wave and sleep-spindle-EEG that typifies slow-wave sleep. This effect could not be attributed to the ascending inhibitory system, the cell bodies of which are located in nuclei in the medulla. It was explained by the action of nonspecific medial thalamic nuclei (Hernández-Peón, 1965; Moruzzi 1963). These thalamic nuclei activate such a large number of cortical neurons, and have such an extensive synchronizing effect on these cells, that the ensuing cortical EEG takes on a high-voltage, low-frequency form. For evidence of regularly timed firing of cells in the medial thalamus and the ability of cortical cells to keep in step during slow-wave sleep, see Verzeano and Negishi (1961).

A negative feedback loop of inhibitory impulses from the stimulated cortex back to the stimulating nonspecific medial thalamus may participate in the synchrony by elevating thresholds across the board. As the medial thalamic neurons recover together, they simultaneously activate many cortical cells. Evidence of negative feedback loops involving the cortex and lower brain regions is to be found, for instance, in Dell, Bonvallet and Hugelin (1961). Evidence that most cortical cells fire more frequently during stage-REM sleep than they do during wakefulness has been amply provided by Evarts (1961, 1965, 1967).

With connections between thalamus and brainstem intact, however, the initiation of sleep can occur within the medulla. Stage-REM sleep was attributed by Jouvet to the activity of a particular nucleus within the pontine reticular formation (RF), the nucleus reticularis pontis caudalis (NRPC). Coagulation of this nucleus, and some nearby cell bodies, eliminated stage-REM sleep and permitted only wakefulness and slow-wave sleep to occur (Jouvet, 1961). The rostral continuation of the NRPC is the nucleus reticularis pontis oralis (NRPO; see Brodal, 1957, figure 1, pp. 10–11). After studying the effects of a series of hemisections of the pons, Rossi, Minobe and Candia (1963) altered Jouvet's 'stage-REM center' a bit, since their results suggested that the stage-REM influences originate in the rostral part of the NRPC and the caudal part of the NRPO. If lesions were made still more rostrally, slow-wave sleep predominates and stage-REM sleep does not occur. This would seem to isolate the region of the boundary of these two nuclei as the center for stage-REM sleep. The unilateral symptoms (produced by the hemisections) were cleared up after several days, a process referred to by Rossi, Minobe and Candia as 'compensation'. Since NRPC and NRPO neurons rarely have long axons with rostral terminals, Rossi, Minobe and Candia suggested that a detour around the unilateral lesion may have been established, involving the activity of short-axon neurons with collateral fibers that cross the midline.

Magnes, Moruzzi and Pompeiano (1961) have shown that the source of slow-wave sleep in the medulla is the nucleus of the tractus solitarius in the caudal medulla. Control lesions ruled out any role in slow-wave sleep for the medial lemniscus and the gracile and cuneate nuclei, which are neighboring structures. The effect occurs in cats with the brainstem separated from the spinal cord, ruling out ascending influences from the cord.

The studies described thus far were claimed to have isolated a center for wakefulness in the ARAS, a center for slow-wave sleep in the medulla, and a center for stage-REM sleep in the pons. Thus the evidence of these studies tends to support the three-state model.

Data on structure–function relationships responsible for the tonic and phasic components of stage-REM sleep highlight the need to draw a sharp distinction between these two categories. The tonic phenomena associated with stage-REM are not distinguished merely by temporal criteria. They are based on distinctly different anatomical mechanisms from those responsible for the phasic manifestations of stage-REM. Jouvet (1967) established the specific relation of the locus coeruleus (LC) to the tonic phenomena of stage-REM sleep. Bilateral coagulation of the LC, while abolishing tonic phenomena such as fast, low-voltage stage-REM EEG, permitted the emergence of a slow-wave sleep EEG concomitant with what are normally phasic components of stage REM such as rapid eye movements and muscular twitches. This result illustrates the neuroanatomical independence of tonic and phasic stage-REM mechanisms and strongly suggests that their behavior correlates should be considered independent as well.

In a series of studies, O. Pompeiano and his co-workers isolated the neural basis of several phasic aspects of stage-REM. From studies combining the methods of ablation and microelectrode recording, Marchiafava and Pompeiano (1964) found that a phasic barrage of impulses originating in the somatosensory cortex occurs during REM bursts. Bizzi, Pompeiano and Somogyi (1964), in a single-unit study of the activity of vestibular nuclei during stage-REM, established that the frequency of nerve impulses rose sharply in two of the four nuclei (namely, the medial and descending) whenever a REM burst occurred. Pompeiano (1967) followed up this finding by ablating the medial and descending vestibular nuclei (MVN and DVN). This resulted in a removal of the phasic phenomena of stage-REM. There were no REMs. The phasic PGO spikes (very high amplitude spindles recorded from pons, lateral geniculate nucleus – LGN – and occipital cortex – OC) were also removed. A somewhat lower voltage, tonic pattern of PGO waves, characterized by greater rhythmicity, remained. Thus the pons and other structures show functionally the presence of separate tonic and phasic pathways.

In a careful investigation of PGO activity, Bizzi and Brooks (1963) obtained evidence that the pontine response might cause the spiking observed in the higher visual system structures (LGN and OC), but the activity of these structures could not, in turn, trigger the pons. This unidirectional effect indicates that activity in the MVN and DVN (a) causes REMs and (b) either causes, or is closely related to the causes of, the fast, low-voltage, desynchronized activity in the higher levels of the visual nervous system. This in turn suggests that the tonic–phasic dichotomy may be more relevant to an experimental clarification of dreaming than the stage-REM–NREM dichotomy.

Two important implications of rapid eye movements can be considered. First, REMs represent an adjustment of a sensory apparatus. Second, this adjustment is a phasic activity associated with stage-REM sleep. There is no reason to doubt that the REM activity of the visual system is paralleled by phasic adjustments in other sense modalities, such as hearing. Evidence supporting this line of reasoning was provided by Dewson, Dement and Simmons (1965). Recordings from two cats with electrodes implanted in the middle ear musculature, along with EEG and neck muscle EMG electrodes, yielded the direct evidence that middle ear muscles also show phasic activation during REM bursts. When tested with pure tones, two other cats with electrodes implanted near the inner ear showed a reduction in the amplitude of electrical responses from the cochlea which were concomitant with REM bursts. This attenuation of the cochlear microphonic is partly due to the contraction of middle ear muscles; see also Williams, Tepas and Morlock (1962). It is now evident that the indirect inner ear evidence is consistent with the direct middle ear evidence. Clearly, middle ear musculature behaves much like the extra-ocular musculature during stage-REM, each phasically adjusting a specific sense receptor. Moreover, both of these reactions originate in the brainstem. The motor nuclei of the fifth and seventh cranial nerves send efferent fibers to the middle ear muscles, just as the vestibular nuclei send motor impulses to the extrinsic muscles of the eyes.

A consideration of the efferent (motor) systems yields observations which are quite analogous to the afferent system phenomena described above. Our present knowledge of the behavior of these efferent systems is largely the result of the efforts of Gassel and his colleagues. Gassel, Marchiafava and Pompeiano (1964a) analysed the myoclonic twitches that occur during stage-REM. These twitches represent a special paradox within paradoxical sleep. During the desynchronized EEG phase of sleep, there is an overall loss of tone in the antigravity muscles, including the nucchal muscles of the nape of the neck which are often used for criterion measurements of stage-REM. During a REM burst, there is a further loss of tone in these muscles, a phasic inhibition superimposed upon the tonic one. Nevertheless, paradoxically, myoclonic twitches are observed mainly during REM bursts, despite the presence of both tonic and phasic inhibition. Gassel *et al.* sought to discover a lesion that would eliminate the twitches. In their search, they established that the muscle spindle-gamma efferent reflex arcs were not involved in the twitches. Also eliminated were the vestibulospinal and pyramidal tracts. The effective lesion turned out to be in the dorsal half of the lateral funiculus of the spinal cord. It is known that reticulospinal fibers travel through that region, and it is precisely these fibers which appear to be responsible for the occurrence of REM bursts and myoclonic twitches. Specifically, these fibers originate in the descending inhibitory reticular formation of the medulla. Therefore, as is the case with afferent phasic activities, a brainstem area is the source of the nerve fibers which are responsible for the phasic activation of the musculature during sleep.

Although the afferent and efferent fibers show certain similarities in their patterns of phasic activation (for example, their dependence upon hindbrain structures as well as their temporal concurrence), it nevertheless can be shown that some differences in their patterns of phasic activation also exist. Using the reflex as a miniature unit of behavior, the afferent and efferent fiber responses to a joint electrical stimulation can be compared with one another. Studies by Gassel, Marchiafava and Pompeiano (1964b) and Hodes and Dement (1964) demonstrated that phasic inhibition of spinal reflexes occurs during REM sleep and this inhibition is attributable to brainstem structures. Electrical stimulation of peripheral nerves can be suprathreshold for afferent fibers and subthreshold for efferent fibers. This makes possible the electrical induction of reflex responses, and the method has the further advantage of providing a built-in measure of reflex thresholds. Hodes and Dement (1964) and Gassel et al. (1964a, 1964b) have shown that the thresholds of such reflexes are raised during stage-REM.

Gassel et al. (1964) observed a correlation between phasic neuromuscular phenomena and such autonomic functions as blood pressure and heart rate. The fall in blood pressure was *not* abolished by a sympathectomy of the relevant sympathetic ganglion, the cervical. This ruled out direct sympathetic stimulation as the cause of the vasomotor response. The experimenters attribute the pupillary dilation observed during REM bursts to inhibition of the parasympathetic activity of the Edinger–Westphal nucleus, which is involved in the regulation of eye movements. They reason, by analogy with this, that a similar phasic inhibition of parasympathetic vasomotor controls must cause the drop in blood pressure during REM episodes.

The autonomic phenomena parallel those of the eye muscles, inasmuch as there is an overall tonic inhibition of blood pressure during REM sleep accompanied by transient changes occurring during REM bursts. Sometimes a momentary increase of blood pressure and phasic tachycardia (heart-rate speedup) are observed at the very onset of a REM burst, but shortly after onset, the general observation is one of further blood pressure reduction and bradycardia (heart-rate slowdown) (Gassel et al., 1964).

With regard to the tonic and phasic phenomena of stage-REM, there seems to be a special nucleus for the triggering of the tonic responses, namely, the LC, while several tracts and nuclei are responsible for the several varieties of phasic responses, namely, the MVN, the DVN, the vasomotor center, the reticulospinal tract, etc. In order to do justice to the complexity of sleep phenomena, the individual mechanisms for individual sleep responses must be clarified, as well as those mechanisms that are common to all of them. As Sprague put it, 'it is not to deny the presence of functional localization to say that the integration of different attributes of a function is accomplished at many foci and levels of the central nervous system' (Sprague, 1967, p. 183). It is precisely this consideration that makes it difficult to establish definitive centers for specific sleep phenomena.

REM deprivation

What we have done thus far is to clarify and reorganize the literature on sleep and dreams which was used as support for the three-state model of psychophysiological existence, which rested upon the dichotomization of REM and NREM sleep stages. We have attempted to show how these studies, if viewed in the light of more recent and sensitive research, tend to be accommodated more easily by the tonic-phasic model. This trend can be shown perhaps most dramatically by a recent deprivation study by Ferguson et al., (1968).

It has long been known that stage-REM deprivation, caused by awakenings at the onset of stage-REM, results in marked behavioral changes and may eventually even bring about the death of the animal (Dement, 1965; Dement et al., 1967; Jouvet, 1965). The subsequent recovery of lost REM time ('REM-rebound') (Dement, 1960, 1965; Jouvet, 1965) was taken as proof of an organismic need for stage-REM sleep (Hartmann, 1967; Jouvet, 1965).

A recent study by Ferguson et al. (1968) has demonstrated that phasic events which are indigenous to all stages of sleep seem to be the crucial element in the need for stage REM sleep (Ferguson et al., 1968). Stable base-line data were taken from five cats. Each cat was used as his own control in a counterbalanced design, and selectively deprived of either stage-REM sleep or of PGO spikes which occurred both in REM and NREM sleep stages. (Six days of recovery were used between treatments.)

Those subjects who were REM deprived later showed less REM-rebound than the subjects deprived specifically of PGO spikes. In both kinds of deprivation, the rebound of REM sleep contained more than the usual number of phasic events, showing that there is a trend toward quantitative compensation for lost phasic activities. If enough PGO spikes were permitted to occur during NREM sleep, there was *no* makeup of REM sleep at all. (This may account for some of the 'exceptional' subjects who failed to show REM-rebound after REM deprivation as observed by Dement, 1960.) The results clearly demonstrate that the crucial factor in REM deprivation-compensation lies in the loss of phasic events. It may even be the case that REM time per se is irrelevant (Ferguson *et al.*, 1968).

Discussions

The tonic–phasic model accommodates data which cannot be explained easily by the three-state model. Specifically, it covers these phenomena: (a) the heightened variability of a number of mental and physiological measures within the stage-REM period, and (b) the continuity which some of these measures show throughout sleep. The new model seems to be a more productive guide for researchers in the field of sleep and dreams. The three-state model was facilitative inasmuch as it generated a great deal of research. It served as a useful 'orienting response' in the early stages of the development of an uncharted and exciting field. In the years which have passed since the original discovery of Aserinsky and Kleitman (1953), tremendous quantities of data were accumulated and impressive advances were made in recording and scoring techniques, permitting new and more effective conceptualizations to evolve. It is our belief that the emergence of the tonic–phasic model heralds a trend toward greater specificity in the focus of attention of sleep and dream researchers.

References

ASERINSKY, E. (1967), 'Physiological activity associated with segments of the rapid eye movement period', in S. Kety, E. Evarts and H. L. Williams (eds.), *Sleep and Altered States of Consciousness*, Williams & Wilkins.

ASERINSKY, E., and KLEITMAN, N. (1953), 'Regularly occurring periods of eye motility and concomitant phenomena during sleep', *Science*, vol. 118, pp. 273–4.

BALDRIDGE, B. J., WHITMAN, R. M., and KRAMER, M. (1965), 'The concurrence of fine muscle activity and REM during sleep', *Psychosom. Med.*, vol. 27, pp. 19–26.

BERGER, R. J. (1961), 'Tonus of extrinsic laryngeal muscles during sleep and dreaming', *Science*, vol. 134, p. 840.

BERGER, R. J., and OSWALD, I. (1962), 'Eye movement in active and passive dreams', *Science*, vol. 137, p. 601.

BIZZI, E., and BROOKS, D. C. (1963), 'Pontine reticular formation: relation to lateral geniculate nucleus during deep sleep', *Science*, vol. 141, pp. 270–72.

BIZZI, E., POMPEIANO, O., and SOMOGYI, I. (1964), 'Vestibular nuclei: activity of single neurons during natural sleep and wakefulness', *Science*, vol. 145, pp. 414–15.

BREBBIA, D. R., and RECHTSCHAFFEN, A., (1968), 'Oxygen consumption rate during sleep in cats', *Psychophysiology*, vol. 5, p. 245.

BREMER, F. (1935), 'Cerveau isolé et physiologie du sommeil', *C R soc. biol.*, vol. 118, pp. 1235–41.

BRODAL, A. (1957), *The Reticular Formation of the Brain Stem*, Oliver & Boyd.

COHEN, H., et al. (1968), 'Physiological characteristics of pre-REM and post-REM sleep as compared with "typical" REM and NREM patterns', Psychophysiology, vol. 4, p. 362 (abstract).

DELL, P., BONVALLET, M., and HUGELIN, A. (1961), 'Mechanisms of reticular deactivation', in G. E. W. Wolstenholme and M. O'Connor (eds.), Ciba Foundation Symposium on the Nature of Sleep, Little, Brown.

DEMENT, W. (1960), 'The effect of dream deprivation', Science, vol. 131, pp. 1705-7.

DEMENT, W. (1965), 'Recent studies on the role of rapid eye movement sleep', Amer. J. Psychiat., vol. 122, pp. 404-7.

DEMENT, W. (1966), 'Psychophysiology of sleep and dreams', in S. Arieti (ed.), American Handbook of Psychiatry, vol. 3, Basic Books.

DEMENT, W., and KLEITMAN, N. (1957a), 'Cyclic variations in EEG during sleep and their relation to eye movements, body motility and dreaming', EEG clin. Neurophysiol., vol. 9, pp. 673-90.

DEMENT, W., and KLEITMAN, N. (1957b), 'The relationship of eye movements during sleep to dream activities', J. exp, Psychol., vol. 53, pp. 339-47.

DEMENT, W., and WOLPERT, E. A. (1958), 'The relation of eye movements, bodily motility, and external stimuli to dream content', J. exp. Psychol., vol. 55, pp. 543-4.

DEMENT, W. (1967), 'Studies on the effect of REM deprivation in humans and in animals', Pubns Assn Res. Nerv. Ment. Dis., vol. 45, pp. 456-68.

DEWSON, J. H., DEMENT, W., and SIMMONS, F. B. (1965), 'Middle ear muscle activity in cats during sleep', Exp. Neurol., vol. 12, pp. 1-8.

EVARTS, E. V. (1961), 'Effects of sleep and waking on activity of single units in the unrestrained cat', in G. E. W. Wolstenholme and M. O'Connor (eds.), Ciba Foundation Symposium on the Nature of Sleep, Little, Brown.

EVARTS, E. V. (1965), 'Relation of cell size to effects of sleep in pyramidal tract neurons', Prog. Brain Res., vol. 18, pp. 81-9.

EVARTS, E. V. (1967), 'Activity of individual cerebral neurons during sleep and arousal', Pubns Assn Res. Nerv. Ment. Dis., vol. 45, pp. 319-37.

FEINBERG, I., and CARLSON, V. R. (1968), 'Sleep variables as a function of age in man', Arch. gen. Psychiat., vol. 18, pp. 239-50.

FERGUSON, J., et al. (1968), 'Phasic event deprivation in the cat', Psychophysiology, vol. 5, pp. 238-9.

FISHER, C., GROSS, J., and ZUCH, J. (1965), 'Cycle of penile erection synchronous with dreaming', Arch. gen. Psychiat., vol. 12, pp. 29-45.

FOULKES, D. (1966), The Psychology of Sleep, Scribner.

FOULKES, D. (1970a), 'Personality and dreams', Int. Psych. Clin., vol. 7, pp. 147-53.

FOULKES, D. (1970b), 'Stage REM variability and dreaming', Int. Psychiat. Clin., vol. 7, pp. 165-71.

FOULKES, D., SPEAR, P. S., and SYMONDS, J. D. (1966), 'Individual differences in mental ability at sleep onset', J. abnorm. Psychol., vol. 71, pp. 280-86.

FOULKES, D., et al. (1967), 'Dreams of the male child: an EEG study', J. abnorm. Psychol., vol. 72, pp. 457-67.

GASSEL, M. M., MARCHIAFAVA, P. L., and POMPEIANO, O. (1964a), 'Phasic changes in muscular activity during desynchronized sleep in unrestrained cats', Arch. Ital. Biol., vol. 102, pp. 449-70.

GASSEL, M. M., MARCHIAFAVA, P. L., and POMPEIANO, O. (1964b), 'Tonic and phasic inhibition of spinal reflexes during deep, desynchronized sleep in unrestrained cats', Arch. Ital. Biol., vol. 102, pp. 471-99.

GASSEL, M. M., *et al.* (1964), 'Phasic changes in blood pressure and heart rate during rapid eye movement episodes of desynchronized sleep in unrestrained cats', *Arch. Ital. Biol.*, vol. 102, pp. 530–44.

GLOBUS, G., GARDNER, R., and WILLIAMS, T. (1968), 'Relation of rapid eye movement sleep to clock time', *Psychophysiology*, vol. 5, p. 204 (abstract).

HARTMANN, E. (1965), 'The D-state: a review and discussion of studies on the physiologic state concomitant with dreaming', *New Eng. J. Med.*, vol. 273, pp. 30–35.

HARTMANN, E. (1967), *The Biology of Dreaming*, C. C. Thomas.

HARTMANN, E. (1968), 'The 90-minute sleep–dream cycle', *Arch. gen. Psychiat.*, vol. 18, pp. 280–86.

HERNÁNDEZ-PEÓN, R. (1965), 'Central neuro-humoral transmission in sleep and wakefulness', *Prog. Brain Res.*, vol. 18, pp. 96–116.

HODES, R., and DEMENT, W. (1964), 'Depression of electrically induced reflexes ("H-reflexes") in man during low voltage EEG "sleep"', *EEG clin. Neurophysiol.*, vol. 17, pp. 617–29.

JOHNSON, L. C., and KARPAN, W. E. (1968), 'Autonomic correlates of the spontaneous K-complex', *Psychophysiology*, vol. 4, p. 386 (abstract).

JOUVET, M. (1961), 'Telencephalic and rhombencephalic sleep in the cat', in G. E. W. Wolstenholme and M. O'Connor (eds.), *Ciba Foundation Symposium on the Nature of Sleep*, Little, Brown.

JOUVET, M. (1965), 'Paradoxical sleep – a study of its nature and mechanisms', *Prog. Brain Res.*, vol. 18, pp. 20–57.

JOUVET, M. (1967), 'Mechanisms of the states of sleep: a neuropharmacological approach', *Pubns Assn Res. Nerv. Ment. Dis.*, vol. 45, pp. 86–126.

JOUVET, M. (1969), 'Biogenic amines and the states of sleep', *Science*, vol. 163, pp. 32–41.

JOUVET, M., MICHEL, F., and MOUNIER, D. (1960), 'Analyse électroencephalographique comparée du sommeil physiologique chez le chat et chez l'homme', *Rev. Neurol.*, vol. 103, pp. 189–205.

KAMIYA, J. (1962), 'Behavioral and physiological concomitants of dreaming', unpublished progress report submitted to National Institute of Mental Health. Cited in D. Foulkes, *The Psychology of Sleep*, Scribner, 1966.

KARACAN, I., GOODENOUGH, D., and SHAPIRO, A. (1966), 'Erection cycle during sleep in relation to dream anxiety', *Arch. gen. Psychiat.*, vol. 15, pp. 183–9.

KETY, S. S. (1967), 'Relationship between energy metabolism of the brain and functional activity', *Pubns Assn Res. Nerv. Ment. Dis.*, vol. 45, pp. 39–45.

KLEITMAN, N. (1961), 'The nature of dreaming', in G. E. W. Wolstenholme and M. O'Connor (eds.), *Ciba Foundation Symposium on the Nature of Sleep*, Little, Brown.

KORNER, A. F. (1968), 'REM organization in neonates', *Arch. gen. Psychiat.*, vol. 19, pp. 330–40.

KRIPKE, D. F., and O'DONOGHUE, J. P. (1968), 'Perceptual deprivation, REM sleep, and an ultradian biological rhythm', *Psychophysiology*, vol. 5, pp. 231–2 (abstract).

LARSON, J. D., and FOULKES, D. (1969), 'Electromyogram suppression during sleep, dream recall, and orientation time', *Psychophysiology*, vol. 5, pp. 548–55.

LESTER, B. K., BURCH, N. R., and DOSSETT, R. C. (1967), 'Nocturnal EEG-GSR profiles: the influence of presleep states', *Psychophysiology*, vol. 3, pp. 238–48.

MAGNES, J., MORUZZI, G., and POMPEIANO, O. (1961), 'Electroencephalogram synchronizing structures in the lower brain stem', in G. E. W. Wolstenholme and M. O'Connor (eds.), *Ciba Foundation Symposium on the Nature of Sleep*, Little, Brown.

MARCHIAFAVA, P., and POMPEIANO, O. (1964), 'Pyramidal influences on spinal cord during desynchronized sleep', *Arch. Ital. Biol.*, vol. 102, pp. 500–529.

McDONALD, D. G., SHALLENBERGER, H. D., and CARPENTER, F. A. (1968), 'Spontaneous autonomic responses during sleep and wakefulness', *Psychophysiology*, vol. 4, p. 362 (abstract).

MOLINARI, S., and FOULKES, D. (1969), 'Tonic and phasic events during sleep: psychological correlates and implications', *Percept. mot. Skills*, vol. 29, pp. 343–68.

MORUZZI, G. (1963), 'Active processes in the brain stem during sleep', *Harvey Lectures Series*, vol. 58, pp. 233–97.

MORUZZI, G. (1964), 'Reticular influences on the EEG', *EEG clin. Neurophysiol.*, vol. 16, pp. 2–17.

MORUZZI, G., and MAGOUN, H. (1949), 'Brain stem reticular formation and activation of the EEG', *EEG clin. Neurophysiol.*, vol. 1, pp. 455–73.

OFFENKRANTZ, W., and RECHTSCHAFFEN, A. (1963), 'Clinical studies of sequential dreams: I. A patient in psychotherapy', *Arch. gen. Psychiat.*, vol. 8, pp. 497–508.

PIVIK, T., and FOULKES, D. (1968), 'NREM mentation: relationship to personality, orientation time, and time of night', *J. consult. Psychol.*, vol. 32, pp. 144–51.

PIVIK, T., HALPER, C., and DEMENT, W. (1969a), 'NREM phasic EMG suppression in the human', *Psychophysiology*, vol. 6, p. 217 (abstract).

PIVIK, T., HALPER, C., and DEMENT, W. (1969b), 'Phasic events and mentation during sleep', *Psychophysiology*, vol. 6, p. 215 (abstract).

POMPEIANO, O. (1967), 'The neurophysiological mechanisms of the postural and motor events during desynchronized sleep', *Pubns Assn Nerv. Ment. Dis.*, vol. 45, pp. 351–423.

RECHTSCHAFFEN, A., and KALES, A. (eds.) (1968), *A Manual of Standardized Terminology, Techniques, and Scoring System for Sleep Stages of Human Subjects*, US Government Printing Office, Washington.

RECHTSCHAFFEN, A., CORNWELL, P., and ZIMMERMAN, W. (1965), 'Brain temperature variations with paradoxical sleep in the cat', report to the Association for the Psychophysiological Study of Sleep.

RECHTSCHAFFEN, A., VOGEL, G., and SHAIKUN, G. (1963), 'Interrelatedness of mental activity during sleep', *Arch. gen. Psychiat.*, vol. 9, pp. 536–47.

REDING, G., RUBRIGHT, W., and RECHTSCHAFFEN, A. (1964), 'Sleep patterns of tooth grinding: its relationship to dreaming', *Science*, vol. 145, pp. 725–6.

REDING, G., et al. (1968), 'Sleep pattern of bruxism: a revision', *Psychophysiology*, vol. 4, p. 396 (abstract).

ROFFWARG, H. P., MUZIO, J., and DEMENT, W. (1966), 'The ontogenetic development of the human sleep–dream cycle', *Science*, vol. 152, pp. 604–18.

ROFFWARG, H. P., et al. (1962), 'Dream imagery relationship to rapid eye movements', *Arch. gen. Psychiat.*, vol. 7, pp. 235–59.

ROSENBLATT, G., ZWILLING, G., and HARTMANN, E. (1969), 'Electrocardiographic changes during sleep in patients with cardiac abnormalities', *Psychophysiology*, vol. 6, p. 233 (abstract).

Rossi, G. F., Minobe, K., and Candia, O. (1963), 'An experimental study of the hypnogenic mechanisms of the brain stem', *Arch. Ital. Biol.*, vol. 101, pp. 470–92.

Scott, J., *et al.* (1968), 'Salivation during sleep in humans', *Psychophysiology*, vol. 4, p. 363 (abstract).

Shapiro, A., *et al.* (1965), 'Gradual arousal from sleep: a determinant of thinking reports', *Psychosom. Med.*, vol. 27, pp. 342–9.

Snyder, F. (1966), 'Toward an evolutionary theory of dreaming', *J. Psychiat.*, vol. 123, pp. 121–41.

Snyder, F. (1967), 'Autonomic nervous system manifestations during sleep and dreaming', *Pubns Assn Res. Nerv. Ment. Dis.*, vol. 45, pp. 469–87.

Snyder, F., Hobson, J. A., and Goldfrank, F. (1963), 'Blood pressure changes during sleep', *Science*, vol. 142, pp. 1313–14.

Snyder, F., *et al.* (1964), 'Changes in respiration, heart rate and systolic blood pressure in human sleep', *J. appl. Psychol.*, vol. 19, pp. 417–22.

Sprague, J. M. (1967), 'The effects of chronic brain stem lesions on wakefulness, sleep and behavior', *Pubns Assn Res. Nerv. Ment. Dis.*, vol. 45, pp. 148–83.

Spreng, L. F., Johnson, L. C., and Lubin, A. (1968), 'Autonomic correlates of eye movement bursts during stage REM sleep', *Psychophysiology*, vol. 4, pp. 311–23.

Thomas, J., and Benoit, O. (1968), 'Occurrence of activation waves during slow wave sleep', *Psychophysiology*, vol. 4, pp. 384–5 (abstract).

Trosman, H., *et al.* (1960), 'Studies in psychophysiology of dreaming: relations among dreams in a sequence', *Arch. gen. Psychiat.*, vol. 3, pp. 602–7.

Verdone, P. (1965), 'Temporal reference of manifest dream content', *Percept. mot. Skills*, vol. 20, pp. 1253–68.

Verzeano, M., and Negishi, K. (1961), 'Neuronal activity in wakefulness and in sleep', in G. E. W. Wolstenholme and M. O'Connor (eds.), *Ciba Foundation Symposium on the Nature of Sleep*, Little, Brown.

Williams, H. L., Tepas, D. I., and Morlock, H. C. (1962), 'Evoked responses to clicks and electroencephalographic stages of sleep in man', *Science*, vol. 138, pp. 685–6.

32 Carolyn J. Hursch

The Scientific Study of Sleep and Dreams

Carolyn J. Hursch, 'The scientific study of sleep and dreams', in E. Hartmann (ed.), *Sleep and Dreaming*, Little, Brown, 1970, pp. 387–402.

Fortunately for the future of sleep research, it is one of the few fields of scientific investigation where the accumulation of data has preceded the expounding of theory. Doubtless this is at least partly due to the fact that sleep research represents a new field of inquiry. Its birth in the twentieth century makes it immediate heir to the technological luxury of the times. The present-day scientist, no matter what professional field issued his credentials, is much more likely to think in terms of hard data and machinery than was his counterpart in previous centuries.

Therefore sleep research emerges as a burgeoning field of inquiry, cutting across many disciplines, characterized now by a vast outpouring of fact – generated by little or no theory. True, authors of new publications in the field generally use some portion of their factual reporting space to put forth favorite ideas and guesses about some aspect of sleep. But as Webb (1968) has commented about his own theoretical remarks, 'These thoughts are launched with the fuel of only hints from current data mixed with a considerable portion of imagination.'

This state of affairs is, in many respects, a happy one. The history of science is already overloaded with accounts of infamous theories which guided believers into long, blind alleys – alleys which could have been avoided by some responsible data collecting. Some such excursions may have been due to the lack of appropriate technology. Yet one can hardly assume that the absolute zenith of technology has been reached in the present era. Doubtless by the standards of the twenty-first century, our equipment will look feeble.

The important tool which differentiates the armchair philosopher of yesterday from the laboratory scientist of today is scientific method – an instrument which cuts as incisively in one century as in the next.

And scientific method is the tool of the twentieth century. To some extent this may be because it turns out better hardware. And to some extent it may be due to the invasion of once erudite disciplines by the common man, whose heritage lies in the production of concrete objects rather than in the production of the ethereal concepts toyed with by eighteenth- and nineteenth-century philosophers. One can hardly imagine Kant's labored doctrine of a priori knowledge being produced today, nor is it likely that it would command much attention now. It seems reasonable that Fleming's contribution does.

Yet what is the role of theory? Does it have any place in today's mad rush of data collecting? Was it a useless pastime engaged in by the articulate but lethargic philosophers of past eras? Do our data tell all, or could we use a modern-day Kant, a Leibnitz or two, and a couple of Schopenhauers?

The thesis of this chapter is that at the very least, sleep research has an immediate opening for a vigorous Linnaeus. After that, a Mendeleyev would bring some welcome organization to the field, and a David Hume would contribute law and order. It would then be ready for a Von Neumann.

In the meantime, it might be well to look more closely at the common man flailing around with his scientific method. While sleep research is largely devoid of formal theory, it is doubtful that any data are ever collected without the impetus of hunches, guesses, and pet notions about the variables being investigated. The researcher is often reluctant to put forth his hunch in the form of a theory, but such hunches do direct the research, do determine what variables are examined, and do shape the ultimate direction of the field.

Therefore an area growing as fast as is the current field of sleep research could profit from having its directions shaped by meaningful theoretical guidelines rather than by the confusion of eclecticism. Such guidelines, of course, impose no obligation on the research directions of any investigator. They would, however, give greater meaning to work already done and would serve to integrate programs of research that now appear unrelated. Without a logical network of theory an important study can get overlooked or forgotten before its place in the scheme of things is realized. In fact, without the guidance of theory, there is no 'scheme of things'; there are only isolated collections of facts.

At the same time, theory must arise through the application of the same principles of scientific method that generate the data. Theories postulate networks of relationships between collections of data. Good theories do so in such a way that each of the relationships in the network has been derived empirically, or can be so derived.

Current sleep research is largely concerned with description on several different levels. What is lacking is the logic necessary to tie these levels of description together and give them cohesion and meaning. This logic would constitute the theory.

We may view the research process as the construction of building blocks which are then assembled into a scientific edifice. Each level of description provides another dimension in this construction. First-order descriptions break down the phenomenon being investigated into a static set of variables which define it. For example, sleep is now defined by certain types of brain waves on an electroencephalograph. The phenomenon is sleep, and the different types of brain waves are the variables. Second-order descriptions state the ranges of variation of these variables, i.e. the normal amounts of each type of brain wave to be found in different species, in the same species at different ages, in different segments of the sleep period, and so on. Third-order descriptions state the relationships between changes in brain waves and changes in other variables, for example, the relationship between EEG changes and changes in blood pressure, biochemistry, disease state, or experimental conditions. Fourth-order descriptions are statements of the general principles governing the relationships between sleep variables and other sets of variables. For example, if specific items in an organism's biochemistry change reliably in response to a change in one or more of the sleep variables, then a general principle might be that one of the functions of sleep is to control these biochemical processes. Whether or not the principle were correct under all conditions and across all species would be a matter for further research to confirm or deny. The collection of such fourth-order descriptions, and all that they imply, would constitute the theory.

Each level of description is dependent on all the levels below it for its accuracy. In other words, if the sleep variables are not operationally defined (first order of description) to begin with, then it would be impossible to make any meaningful statements about relationships between sleep variables and variables from other systems. Likewise, if the principles (fourth-order descriptions) are not logically stated, with the conclusions following from the premises, then it would be impossible to verify their truth or falsity.

A scientific inquiry can start with theory but, in order to generate science, it must at some time proceed down through the levels of description and establish the validity of its principles. Conversely, a science may start out with operational definitions of variables, establish parameters for these variables under different conditions, and determine their relationship to other variables. But as the volume of these data increases, there will be no logical reason to examine more relationships or more variables, unless some general laws either arise directly from the data or are postulated by a theory.

With these considerations in mind, let us evaluate where we are now in sleep research.

We know from data emerging during the past two decades that sleep is not a simple blocking out or holding state of the organism. Instead it is a complex pattern of changing neurological and biological states. Or is it?

Our EEG machine tells us that the brain engages in several different types of electrical activity during sleep, the usual number agreed upon being five: stage 1 with rapid eye movement and stages 1 through 4 without REM. One can imagine that the researcher of the twenty-first century will have a machine which will detect a dozen different types, or perhaps a hundred. For the moment, we are busy enough with these five – measuring their length, their periodicity, their percentages of total sleep, their suppression during, preceding, or following unusual conditions, their constancy, their variation across age groups, their occurrence in other species, and their responses to various chemical, biological, and psychological agents.

But what do we really have? A highly sensitive amplifier and recorder at one end. At the other, a sleeping subject with electrodes secured to the skin of his scalp and to his eye muscles, or an animal with electrodes permanently implanted in his brain. The EEG records show only the amplitude and frequency of electrical activity. This is first-order data about sleep. It describes the sleeping states in EEG language. Everything emanating from this is a product of the ingenuity of the sleep researcher. This product may be a deduction, an induction, a correlation, an inference, a coincidence, or pure fiction, depending upon how it was derived.

The five stages are the result of current agreement based on convenience, although some researchers find it more convenient to combine stages 3 and 4, while others are further subdividing stage 1-REM according to its density. The decision to use five stages is an arbitrary one. An EEG record, run at a speed of fifteen millimeters per second, for an eight-hour night of sleep is nearly 1500 feet long. One cannot classify every rise and fall of the pen. Therefore certain amplitudes and frequencies have been singled out according to how accurately they can be distinguished from other amplitudes and frequencies. All these miles of EEG recordings, then, have been reduced to five sleep stages and one waking stage.

We have merely dissected the EEG record and given different names to the parts that look different. Whether or not this is a useful classification system will depend on whether or not these names are (1) mutually exclusive and (2) exhaustive. If they are mutually exclusive, then there will be no chance of finding the same segment of EEG tracings recorded under two different stages (given, of course, an expert EEG scorer). If they are exhaustive, then everything on the EEG record can be classified as one of the five sleep stages or the waking stage.

The current practice of combining stages 3 and 4 indicates that these two stages are probably not mutually exclusive. Too often it is difficult for the scorer to determine whether a certain segment of the record belongs in stage 3 or stage 4. At the extremes, these stages are different, yet there is a gray area of uncertainty where it is impossible to differentiate them. The only solutions possible, then, are (1) to combine 3 and 4 into one stage, or (2) to separate out the gray area and call it another stage.

Also, the original stage 1 was not exhaustive. This became apparent when the observation was made that sometimes REM occurs during this stage and sometimes it does not. Therefore this was separated into two categories, stage 1 and stage 1 with REM.

Density measurements which are now being closely viewed by many researchers (Aserinsky, 1967) will gradually separate the general phenomenon of REM sleep into some number of different types of REM sleep.

Hartmann (1967) has proposed that since the REM period is 'not merely a different stage or depth of sleep, but a qualitatively different kind of sleep . . . different from ordinary sleep and from waking' that it be separated out and defined as 'the D-state: a biological state concomitant with dreaming'. He also offers a complete description of this state based on research to date.

This process of reclassification is the result of closer observation and finer measurements. Habit, practice, and one's investment in things as they are have impeded such necessary changes in science as well as many other areas of human effort, ranging from the work of Galileo to that of Rickover. In sleep research the investment in the classification of alpha, beta, gamma, and delta waves has more or less given way to the present numerical listing of stages. This listing should also give way, expand, or contract, as increasingly fine and abundant measurements are made which indicate a logical necessity for doing so.

Still in the realm of first-order description are the arbitrary groupings and summaries of the basic data, but these groupings and summaries will be affected by the rigor of our basic classification system. For example, consider the temporal sequences of the arbitrarily designated sleep stages: If there are discernible changes in defined amplitudes and frequencies of the EEG tracings, then we may state that stage 1 was followed by stage 2, and so on, and obtain frequency counts of the number of times that this happened. These changes are currently given the name *stage shifts* and require nothing but objective criteria defining each of the stages. Obviously the accuracy of the measurement of stage shifts depends on the mutually exclusive and exhaustive properties of the definitions of the stages. If these criteria have not been met, then error will be built into any measure of stage shifts.

These first-order descriptions give answers only to the question, 'What is sleep?' Answers will continue to come in for a long time because of technological improvements in measuring instruments. Methodological improvement in the definition of the variables, the reliability of the measurements, and the standardization of research procedures will also contribute answers, with or without advanced technology.

Improved methodology is also mandatory for accurate second-, third-, and fourth-order descriptions, i.e. the descriptions which answer the questions: What are the ranges of the sleep variables? To what other variables are they related? What are the role and purpose of the sleep system? It is probably safe to state that everyone in the field of sleep research has these questions, in some form, at the root of his efforts. Measuring the length of REM periods and comparing them with changes in blood pressure probably has some intrinsic interest of its own; but more likely the researcher is probing at the question of whether REM periods cause blood pressure changes, or blood pressure changes cause REM periods. This bears on other questions, such as: Is sleep a cause or an effect? Or is it sometimes one and sometimes the other, or perhaps just part of a continuing sequence of events? Does it play different roles under different conditions, or are some of its roles constant over all conditions? Is its loss to be lamented, as Macbeth lamented the sleep deprivation threat, or is its approach to be feared, as Hamlet feared his REM periods? These are higher-ordered questions, all of which depend on the answers to the lower-ordered ones. But where is the theory necessary to postulate answers to these questions which will take into account the many bits and pieces of descriptive data already available?

The sleep researcher, busy with his voluminous data, finds it more feasible to continue to examine sleep under different conditions and to keep his theoretical tendencies in check, than to close down his laboratory for a couple of years while he considers the logical implications of the data on hand. He knows, too, that every other sleep researcher is also producing data by the mile. Construction of the theoretical framework on which to hang all these data is largely left to chance.

What then does the randomly forming structure of the body of sleep research look like? What directions is it taking?

A listing of the abstracts of papers presented to the annual meeting of the Association for the Psychophysiological Study of Sleep should provide answers. This listing is shown for the years 1967 and 1968 in Table 1.

In 1967 the Association grouped the ninety-four papers presented at its annual meeting under no less than eleven topics, which includes seven papers in a category called 'Varied Topics' and twenty-five papers relegated to 'Miscellaneous'. In 1968 the number of topics jumped to fifteen for 129 papers presented, of which only ten were relegated to the miscellaneous pile. Closer examination of the lists of topics for the two years also reveals that only four of the topics used in 1967 were used again in 1968, and this includes 'Miscellaneous'. Therefore, if we exclude 'Varied Topics', we find that in the course of two successive annual meetings of the APSS, papers were presented under a total of twenty-two different topics. Quite a range of activity when one realizes that this constitutes only 223 different papers!

The above by no means indicates a criticism of the Association or its program chairmen. In fact, a perusal of the abstracts themselves indicates that without some organizational effort, these twenty-two subgroups could quite reasonably have been split into double that number.

Table 1 **Abstracts of papers presented to the 1967 and 1968 annual meetings of the Association for the Psychophysiological Study of Sleep**

1967		1968	
Topic	*Number of abstracts*	*Topic*	*Number of abstracts*
1. Environmental effects	9	1. Environmental effects	12
2. Dream content	13	2. Dream content	21
3. Neurophysiology	4	3. Neurophysiology	5
4. Autonomic functions	4	4. Phylogeny	5
5. Varied topics	7	5. Theory	6
6. Developmental, circadian	2	6. Drug effects	12
7. Symposium, EEG scoring	1	7. Neurochemistry	8
8. Biochemistry	7	8. Mental retardation	5
9. REM deprivation	13	9. Computer analysis	3
10. Sleep pathology	9	10. Biological rhythms	6
11. Miscellaneous	25	11. Physiology	6
		12. Ontogeny and pregnancy	11
		13. Psychopathology	7
		14. Deprivation	12
		15. Miscellaneous	10
Total	94	Total	129

See Society for Psychophysiological Research (1967, 1968).

The topics covered range all the way from 'Ontogeny of penile erections during sleep in infants' (Karacan *et al.*, 1968) to 'Sleep and dreaming in the elephant' (Hartmann, Bernstein and Wilson, 1968). The research was conducted on both humans and animals; investigators looked at sleep in connection with such variables as age, schizophrenia, response to drugs, aggressive behavior, pregnancy, biological rhythms, selective deprivation, neuro-humoral mechanisms, smoking, dream recall, placebo effects, wakefulness, asthmatic attacks, bruxism, hypothalamic lesions, mental retardation, noise, temperature, and oxygen availability, to list just a few of the topics within topics. Animals studied include the crocodile, cat, field frog, tree frog, monkey (*Macaca nemistrina*), monkey (*Macaca mulatta*), hedge-hog, elephant, rat, mouse, and the spiny anteater.

The above, of course, is not all of the sleep research being conducted, since only some unknown portion less than 100 per cent of ongoing sleep research is reported at such meetings. The 1969 meeting of the APSS brought forth additional topics, subtopics, and species. Clearly the above serves to illustrate the fact that sleep research is being attacked from all directions at once.

In the midst of this welter of topics, one finds a slim total of six papers under the heading of Theory. It seems that despite the diversity, or perhaps because of it, it is much easier to find out what sleep researchers are doing than it is to find out why they are doing it. Therefore the first task is obvious: a taxonomy of sleep data into meaningful categories, subdivisions, and types in order to classify data already collected. Variables being investi-gated in all species could be defined, and the changes in these variables under different conditions could be listed.

Once this classification is accomplished, it would become obvious that some areas have been neglected, some overstudied. Such classification would indicate possible relationships between categories of information already on hand. Bodies of related data would begin to emerge. For example, normative values for sleep parameters appear in many unrelated pieces of sleep research, but where is there a standard list of normative values for the amounts, percents, lengths, and periodicity of each of the five sleep stages in human beings, let alone the spiny anteater? True, there are articles in print setting forth norms for certain age groups of human subjects (Dement and Kleitman, 1957), but the groupings are broad, they are not usually separated by sex, the results are based on small numbers of subjects, and some age groups are missing. The missing groups and the sex differences may be filled in by reference to other pieces of research – research done at another time, in another place, using slightly different measures and terminology, and for another purpose.

In short, in this electronic age, the accuracy with which a capsule is sent out into space and returned to earth is considerably greater than the accuracy with which the required sleep parameters of its occupants can be stated. This is true largely because no one has set out to record, standardize, and list the necessary measurements for all relevant groupings of subjects.

Next, it is obvious from the topics listed by the APSS that current research in sleep is first-, second-, and third-order research, with perhaps the largest effort in second-order research, and the next largest in third-order research. This means that before there is a clear definition of the important variables of sleep under different conditions, investigators are attempting to relate the sleep system to other systems. There is no necessary stipulation that all research should be completed on one level before the next level is attempted. It is quite possible to clock the speed of two different automobiles at the same time, even though one knows nothing about the mechanical attributes of either automobile. But this assumes that someone *does* know the mechanical attributes in detail, and that comparing these two cars is a reasonable thing to do. If not, then the comparison could be pointless – as for instance, if one has a motor designed to pull heavy loads, and the other is built solely for speed. Trial and error comparisons will, of course, produce data: we can test for speed, then ease of handling, then endurance, power, load capacity, and so forth. But this is not an economical way to do research. A more detailed knowledge of the component parts of each of the automobiles would make it possible to find many of the answers by simple computations rather than costly test runs.

To some extent, the same is true of sleep research. In some cases it is inefficient to compare the sleep system with another set of variables when the sleep variables involved are still ill-defined and their range and variation under different conditions are unknown. For example, it would be pointless to conduct an investigation of the use of sleep-inducing drugs during the course of some pathological condition if the sleep patterns under that same condition without the drug were unknown.

Therefore a compendium of the entire range of measurements on the standardized set of sleep variables under all relevant conditions would be useful to any investigator attempting to correlate the sleep system with some other system. Obviously such correlations should not have to wait until this compendium is complete, but if the established data were systematized, then there would be empty cells waiting for all new data uncovered. The periodic table of elements did not halt research in chemistry; it did organize information already available and indicate where the gaps were. Such organization is obviously needed in sleep research at this point.

A similar development on the relationships of sleep with other body processes would likewise serve to inventory what has already been done, what still awaits investigation, and what studies should be repeated for verification of results. Correlations are performed in the absence of reasons to assume cause and effect relationships. But when strong correlations are found, it is then reasonable to test for whether or not one of the variables is actually dependent upon the other, or if a third variable is influencing both. There are enough data emanating from research on the concomitant variation of different systems during sleep for some theoretical postulations to emerge regarding such relationships. This would direct the choice of dependent variables and result in more efficient studies. Sleep research is too expensive for trial and error experiments.

In contrast to the rest of the field of sleep research, the whole matter of dreams is heavily burdened with theory, most of which could be more accurately described as folklore. Hartmann's (1967) work does bring together in one well-organized volume what is currently known about the biological concomitants of stage 1-REM. But his discussion, 'The functions of the D-state', makes it clear that current 'theories' about the phenomenon of dreaming itself, apart from the biological changes of stage 1-REM, are for the most part untested, or untestable, as they now stand.

Unlike the sleep stages, which can be recorded directly from subject to EEG paper, untouched by time lag or human interpretation, dreams can be obtained only in retrospect and in response to the experimenter's question. Enough has been written at this point about the effect of the experimenter on the subject's responses to make it clear that with properly directed questioning, one can govern the amount and content of dream reporting, whether or not one intends to. In addition there are great individual differences in recall and in ability to verbalize thoughts and feelings. There are also differences in motivation, depending upon the rapport between subject and experimenter. Literally, the experimenter is at the mercy of the subject in this situation.

Therefore adherence to rigorously standardized procedures and measurements is mandatory in order to avoid the introduction of extraneous variables – such as the subject's motivations or the experimenter's.

The amount of dream research presently being conducted and the general regression towards simplicity has a tendency to transform suggestion into fact as follows: Aserinsky and Kleitman's (1955) discovery of the correlation between REM periods and dreaming, and the corroboration of this finding by many investigators since then, has gradually led to an equating of REM with dreams. The result is that the two terms are becoming synonymous, and the REM period is often referred to as the dream period. But the findings by Aserinsky and Kleitman, and everyone since then, actually were that a correlation existed, not that REM caused dreams or dreams caused REM, or that all dreams occurred during REM, or that all REM periods contained dreams. In fact the Dement and Kleitman (1957) findings stated that 80 per cent of REM awakenings and 7 per cent of NREM awakenings resulted in dream reports. Since dreams themselves cannot be monitored, all we really know is that there is more dream reporting during REM than during NREM. This still leaves open the possibility that the increased autonomic activity of the REM period stamps more into memory than does the relative quiescence of the NREM periods. For all we know, dreams may occur uniformly throughout the night, with REM dreams being more readily recalled than NREM dreams; or perhaps the subject is more verbal immediately after REM than after the deeper stages of NREM. But the practice of awakening the subject for dream recall only during or after an

REM period is becoming built into the technology of sleep research. This can result in what may be a well-constructed fallacy, i.e. that REM equals dreaming. Even if this equation turns out to be true, the fact is being neglected that sometimes NREM equals dreaming. A theory of dreaming based entirely on REM periods will still have this fact to explain.

Lack of precise methodology in dream research is also allowing other fallacies to slip through unnoticed, such as the implication that longer dream reports indicate longer dreams, when it could easily be illustrated that one could contemplate in a second what would take several hundred words to describe; that more detailed dream reports indicate more detailed dreams, when no check of the difference in subjects' verbal ability has been made; that a night of little dreaming is followed by a night of increased dreaming, thus 'proving' a need for dreaming. (This is only true if REM equals dreams, which has not yet been proved. All we know is that REM deprivation is followed by increased REM. Since the subject can and does dream during NREM, the 'need' could just as well be attributed to some other REM-linked activity.)

In short, dream research has two urgent needs at the present time: (1) rigorous elimination or control of all extraneous variables which could in any way bias the subject's reporting of dreams, followed by careful manipulation of independent variables, one at a time, in order to determine their effects on dream reports, and (2) consistent theory which bears directly on rigorously collected data.

As in all aspects of sleep research, or any scientific endeavour, theories about dreams must be testable. An untestable theory contributes little more than a convenient repository for unexplained events. It also contributes the feeling that the matter has been 'explained', and it thereby impedes the research for a true explanation.

Consider, for example, a theory which states that dreams wipe out useless thoughts of the day. To begin with, it would be impossible to define a 'useless thought' since no one can judge, especially for someone else, what random thoughts of the day just might come in handy the next day. Even if such thoughts could be defined, how can it be determined that they have been 'wiped out'? If dreams really wiped out a 'useless thought', then the subject could never report the useless thought that was wiped out. If we were to ask the subject to list for us all useless thoughts before going to bed, this procedure in itself would probably determine that he would recall most of them the next day.

But armed with this 'theory', we can safely say that any trivia that is not remembered the next day was wiped out the night before by dreams, because it will be impossible for anyone to either confirm or deny such a statement. Therefore, the 'theory' stands – not because it has any validity, but because it is untestable. But of what use is it? Can we safely pour 'useless thoughts' into a subject, fully confident that he will have been relieved of them by the following day? How does the somnolent subject manage to make this fine discrimination between useful and useless thoughts when he is apparently incapable of doing so while he is awake? And how does the thought get 'wiped out'? We do not even know yet how memories get stamped in, much less how they are removed.

The theory does not submit to any test because the variables with which it deals are undefined and undefinable. Since it cannot be proved wrong any more than it can be proved right, it remains as a hunch to be tossed in as a solution to the mystery of why people dream. But the mystery remains unsolved.

A completely new approach to the problems of dream research is needed: one which strips away the weight of baroque theories which are patently untestable, one which operationally defines the variables it seeks to measure, and one which eliminates the contamination of other variables. It is too late in the history of science for such a well-engineered discipline as sleep research to have one of its most interesting appurtenances – the dream – supported by archaic methodology.

In general then the field of sleep research needs what any new field of science needs as the data begin to pour in – organization. This organization will bring into focus the conflicting reports of different investigators and will force standardization and operational definition of the variables. This will have a sharpening influence on research. Relationships now being sought will have a higher probability of being found – if they are there. It is difficult to state exactly when theory should enter a field of inquiry and exert its structuring influence. But the avalanche of data now pouring out of sleep laboratories leaves little doubt that for this field, formal theory is already overdue; and for dream research, conjecture has posed as theory for too long. If dreams are to emerge from the provinces of the mystic, and take their place on the EEG machine along with stages 1 through 4, then the methodology and the theory applied to them must also emerge.

In short, in only two decades, sleep research with all of its concomitants has come of age. It is time for the puberty rites of re-evaluation. The next two decades should see it attain full stature as a science.

References

ASERINSKY, E. (1967), 'Physiological activity associated with segments of the rapid eye movement period', in S. Kety, E. Evarts and H. L. Williams (eds.), *Sleep and Altered States of Consciousness*, Williams & Wilkins.

ASERINSKY, E., and KLEITMAN, N. (1955), 'Two types of ocular motility occurring in sleep', *J. appl. Physiol.*, vol. 8, p. 11.

DEMENT, W., and KLEITMAN, N. (1957), 'The relation of eye movements during sleep to dream activity: an objective method for the study of dreaming', *J. exp. Psychol.*, vol. 53, p. 339.

FEINBERG, I., and CARLSON, V. R. (1968), 'Sleep variables as a function of age in man', *Arch. gen. Psychiat.*, vol. 18, p. 239.

HARTMANN, E. (1967), *The Biology of Dreaming*, C. C. Thomas.

HARTMANN, E., BERNSTEIN, J., and WILSON, C. (1968), 'Sleep and dreaming in the elephant', *Abstracts of Papers Presented to the Seventh Annual Meeting of the Association for the Psychophysiological Study of Sleep*, vol. 4, no. 3, p. 389.

KARACAN, I., MARANS, A., BARNETT, A., and LODGE, A. (1968), 'Ontogeny of penile erection during sleep in infants', *Abstracts of Papers Presented to the Seventh Annual Meeting of the Association for the Psychophysiological Study of Sleep*, vol. 4, no. 3, p. 363.

SOCIETY FOR PSYCHOPHYSIOLOGICAL RESEARCH (1967), *Abstracts of Papers Presented to the Sixth Annual Meeting of the Association for the Psychophysiological Study of Sleep*.

SOCIETY FOR PSYCHOPHYSIOLOGICAL RESEARCH (1968), *Abstracts of Papers Presented to the Seventh Annual Meeting of the Association for the Psychophysiological Study of Sleep*.

WEBB, W. B. (1968), *Sleep: An Experimental Approach*, Macmillan.

Further Reading

General books

D. Foulkes, *The Psychology of Sleep*, Scribner, 1966.

E. Hartmann, *The Biology of Dreaming*, C. C. Thomas, 1967.

E. Hartmann, *Sleep and Dreaming*, Little, Brown, 1970.

A. Kales (ed.), *Sleep: Physiology and Pathology*, Lippincott, 1969.

N. Kleitman, *Sleep and Wakefulness*, University of Chicago Press, rev. edn, 1963.

M. Kramer (ed.), *Dream Psychology and the New Biology of Dreaming*, C. C. Thomas, 1969.

G. G. Luce, *Body Time*, Temple Smith, 1972.

G. G. Luce and J. Segal, *Sleep*, Coward-McCann, 1966.

N. Mackensie, *Dreams and Dreaming*, Aldus Books, 1965.

I. Oswald, *Sleep and Waking*, Elsevier, 1962.

I. Oswald, *Sleep*, Penguin, 1972.

Philosophy of dreams

N. Malcolm, *Dreaming*, Routledge & Kegan Paul, 1959.

History of dreams

A. J. J. Ratcliff, *A History of Dreams*, Murray Printing Co., 1923.

R. L. Van de Castle, *The Psychology of Dreaming*, General Learning Corp., 1971.

Freudian and neo-Freudian theories and their empirical examination

W. Bonime, *The Clinical Use of Dreams*, Basic Books, 1962.

A. Faraday, *Dream Power*, Hodder & Stoughton, 1972.

C. Fisher, 'Psychoanalytic implications of recent research on sleep and dreaming', *J. Amer. Psychoanal. Assn*, vol. 13, 1965, pp. 197–303.

T. French and E. Fromm, *Dream Interpretation: A New Approach*, Basic Books, 1964.

S. Freud, *New Introductory Lectures on Psychoanalysis*, 1933. Reprinted in *The Standard Edition of the Complete Psychological Works of Sigmund Freud*, vol. 22, Hogarth Press, 1966.

S. Freud, *The Interpretation of Dreams*, 1900, Allen & Unwin, 1954.

E. Fromm, *The Forgotten Language*, Gollancz, 1952.

B. S. Glick, 'Freud's dream theory and modern dream research', *Amer. J. Psychother.*, vol. 21, 1967, pp. 630–43.

C. Green, *Lucid Dreams*, Institute of Psychophysical Research, Oxford, 1968.

C. S. Hall, *The Meaning of Dreams*, McGraw-Hill, 1953, 1960.

P. Kline, *Fact and Fantasy in Freudian Theory*, Methuen, 1972.

J. H. Masserman, *Dream Dynamics*, Grune & Stratton, 1971.

C. S. Moss, *The Hypnotic Investigation of Dreams*, Wiley, 1966.

E. M. Swanson and D. Foulkes, 'Dream content and the menstrual cycle', *J. nerv. ment. Dis.*, vol. 145, 1967, pp. 358–63.

M. Ullman, 'Dreaming, life style and physiology: a comment on Adler's view of the dream', *J. indiv. Psychol.*, vol. 18, 1962, pp. 18–25.

Experimental manipulation of dream content

M. D. Austin, 'Dream recall and the bias of intellectual ability', *Nature*, vol. 231, 1971, p. 59.

L. Breger, I. Hunter and R. W. Lane, *The Effect of Stress on Dreams*, Academic Press, 1972.

R. D. Cartwright, N. Bernick and G. Borowitz, 'Effect of an erotic movie on the sleep and dreams of young men', *Arch. gen. Psychiat.*, vol. 20, 1968, pp. 262–71.

P. P. Ekeh, 'Examination dreams in Nigeria: a sociological study', *Psychiatry*, vol. 35, 1972, pp. 352–65.

D. Foulkes and A. Rechtschaffen, 'Presleep determinants of dream content: effects of two films', *Percept. mot. Skills.*, vol. 19, 1964, pp. 983–1005.

D. Foulkes, E. Belvedere and T. Brubaker, 'Televised violence and dream content', Report to the Surgeon General's Scientific Advisory Committee on Television and Social Behaviors pursuant to the Terms of Contract, H.S.M.-42-70-62.

M. Hersen, 'Nightmare behaviour: a review', *Psychol. Bull.*, vol. 78, 1972, pp. 37–48.

C. T. Tart, 'Toward the experimental control of dreaming: a review of the literature', *Psychol. Bull.*, vol. 64, 1965, pp. 81–91.

Children's dreams

D. Foulkes, T. Pivik, H. S. Steadman, P. S. Spear and J. D. Symonds, 'Dreams of the male child: an EEG study', *J. Abnorm. Psychol.*, vol. 71, 1967, pp. 457–67.

S. Freud, 'Children's dreams', in *Introductory Lectures on Psychoanalysis*, Allen & Unwin, 1922.

Some additional references on the physiology and biochemistry of dreaming

A. M. Arkin, M. F. Toth, J. Baker and J. M. Hastey, 'The degree of concordance between the content of sleep talking and mentation recalled in wakefulness', *J. nerv. ment. Dis.*, vol. 151, 1970, pp. 375–93.

R. D. Cartwright, L. J. Monroe and C. Palmer, 'Individual differences in response to REM deprivation', *Arch. gen. Psychiat.*, vol. 16, 1967, pp. 297–303.

C. D. Clemente, D. P. Purpura and F. E. Mayer, *Sleep and the Maturing Nervous System*, Academic Press, 1972.

B. R. Ekstrand, 'To sleep perchance to dream (about why we forget)', in C. P. Duncan, L. Sechrest and A. W. Melton (eds.), *Human Memory: Festschrift in Honor of Benton J. Underwood,* Meredith, 1972.

L. Goldstein, N. W. Stoltzfus and J. F. Gardocki, 'Changes in interhemispheric amplitude relationships in the EEG during sleep', *Physiol. Behav.*, vol. 8, 1972, pp. 811–16.

R. Greenberg, C. Pearlman, R. Brooks, R. Mayer and E. Hartmann, 'Dreaming and Korsakoff's psychosis', *Arch. gen. Psychiat.*, vol. 18, 1968, pp. 203–9.

R. Hernández-Peón, 'A neuropsychologic model of dreams and hallucinations', *J. nerv. ment. Dis.*, vol. 141, 1966, pp. 623–58.

M. E. Humphrey and O. L. Zangwill, 'Cessation of dreaming after brain injury', *J. Neurol. Neurosurg. Psychiat*, vol. 14, 1951, pp. 322–5.

D. J. Kupfer and F. G. Foster, 'Interval between onset of sleep and rapid-eye-movement sleep as an indicator of depression', *Lancet*, vol. 7779, 1972, pp. 684–6.

A. J. Mandell and M. P. Mandell, 'Biochemical aspects of rapid eye movement sleep', *Amer. J. Psychiat.*, vol. 122, 1965, pp. 391–401.

M. A. Pessah and H. P. Roffwarg, 'Spontaneous middle ear muscle activity in man: a rapid eye movement sleep phenomenon', *Science*, vol. 178, 1972, pp. 773–6.

C. M. Pierce, J. L. Mathis and J. T. Jabbour, 'Dream patterns in narcoleptic and hydrancephalic patients', *Amer. J. Psychiat.*, vol. 122, 1965, pp. 402–4.

H. P. Roffwarg, J. N. Muzio and W. C. Dement, 'Ontogenetic development of the human sleep–dream cycle', *Science*, vol. 152, 1966, pp. 604–19.

J. L. Singer and J. S. Antrobus, 'Eye movements during fantasies', *Arch. gen. Psychiat.*, vol. 12, 1965, pp. 71–6.

S. S. Steiner and S. J. Ellman, 'Relation between REM sleep and intracranial self-stimulation', *Science*, vol. 177, 1972, pp. 1122–4.

M. F. Toth, 'A new method for detecting eye movements in sleep', *Psychophysiology*, vol. 7, 1971, pp. 516–23.

H. L. Williams, 'The new biology of sleep', *J. psychiat. Res.*, vol. 8, 1971, pp. 445–78.

Acknowledgements

For permission to reproduce the Readings in this volume, acknowledgement is made to the following:

3 Bailliere Tindall
4 Yale University Press
5 Clark University Press
6 Methuen & Co.
7 *American Journal of Orthopsychiatry*
8 *Psychoanalytic Quarterly*
9 *International Journal of Clinical and Experimental Hypnosis*
10 Paul Elek Ltd
11 *British Journal of Psychiatry*
12 R. G. D. D'Andrade
13 J. B. Lippincott Co.
14 American Medical Association
15 American Physiological Society
16 Little, Brown & Co.
17 *Science*
18 *Quarterly Journal of Experimental Psychology*
19 Association for Research in Nervous and Mental Disease
20 *Perceptual and Motor Skills*
21 J. B. Lippincott Co.
22 Association for Research in Nervous and Mental Disease
23 Pergamon Press Ltd
24 *Nature*
25 Academic Press Inc.
26 American Medical Association
27 The Journal Press
28 *New Scientist*
29 *American Journal of Psychiatry*
30 American Psychological Association
31 American Psychological Association
32 Little, Brown & Co.

Author Index

Subject Index

AAT (auditory awakening
    thresholds) 351, 352, 354, 355
Aboriginal culture *see* Culture,
    'primitive dream psychotherapy'
Across the Plains 90
Active and passive dreams 272–3
Adam 33
Adonis 51
Aesculapius 19, 25, 34
Africa, equatorial 23
Aggression, dreams about 200–201
Air-raids
  dreams about 98
  as somatic stimuli 60
Alexander the Great 34
Amines 338–40
  see also Amphetamines;
    Catecholamines; Dopamine;
    Imipramine *and* Monoamines
Amitriptyline 332
Amphetamines 329, 330, 335, 338, 339
Amplification 78–9
Anti-depressants 331–4
Antonius 35
Anxiety
  as a need for dreams 208–17
  about marriage 211–12, 215
  about subsistence 211, 213–17
APSS (Association for the
    Psychophysiological Study of
    Sleep) 468–70
Arabian dream interpretation 34
ARAS (ascending reticular
    activating system) 452, 454
  see also RAS
Ashanti tribe 23
Ashurnasirpal, *King of Assyria* 17, 26
Association
  and incorporation of verbal
    stimuli 185, 198–90, 196
Assonance
  and incorporation of verbal stimuli
    168–9, 175, 182–5, 191–3, 196
Assyrian dream interpretation 17
Astrological factors 18, 20, 22
Atharva Veda 18–19

Auditory stimuli 194–5, 228, 229,
    351–2, 409
  see also AAT
Augustus 34
Automatic writing 29, 132
Autonomous depression 329
'Autotoxin' 337

Babylonian
  dream interpretation 17
  Library at Nineveh 17, 26
  Talmud 21
Bacchus 51
Barbiturates 329, 336, 337, 376
'Battle dreams' 58, 66
Bed-wetting, symbolism of 133–4,
    138, 139
Behavioural influence of dreams 20,
    21
Berdaches 25, 205
Beyond the Pleasure Principle 66
Biblical dream interpretation 21
Biology of Dreaming 445
Birds 225–6, 386–8, 392, 406–7,
    419, 435
Birth *see* Pregnancy and birth
Blacky Test 115, 120
Blind
  dreams of the 104–6, 168, 274–8
  eye movements in 274–8, 279–85,
    425
  visual imagery in 274, 276–7,
    284–5, 425
Bogey men 93, 97, 107
Books, effect of on dreams 87, 99
Brain
  effect of drugs on the 329–41
  protein synthesis of the 334–6, 337,
    340–41
  temperature 293, 316, 380
Bruxism *see* Tooth grinding
Buddha 21

Caesar Augustus 21
Cardan, Girolamo 33, 34
Castration 134, 141, 207, 255